WINDOWS 2000

Performance Tuning & Optimization

KENTON GARDINIER
CHRIS AMARIS

Osborne/**McGraw-Hill**

New York   Chicago   San Francisco
Lisbon   London   Madrid   Mexico City   Milan
New Delhi   San Juan Seoul   Singapore   Sydney   Toronto

Osborne/**McGraw-Hill**
2600 Tenth Street
Berkeley, California 94710
U.S.A.
To arrange bulk purchase discounts for sales promotions, premiums, or fund-raisers, please contact Osborne/**McGraw-Hill** at the above address. For information on translations or book distributors outside the U.S.A., please see the International Contact Information page immediately following the index of this book.

Windows® 2000 Performance Tuning & Optimization

1234567890 CUS CUS 01987654321

Book p/n 0-07-213363-5 and CD p/n 0-07-213362-7
parts of
ISBN 0-07-212084-3

Publisher	**Proofreader**
Brandon A. Nordin	John Schindel
Vice President & Associate Publisher	**Indexer**
Scott Rogers	David Heiret
Acquisitions Editor	**Computer Designers**
Franny Kelly	Jean Butterfield, Lauren McCarthy
Project Editor	**Illustrators**
Janet Walden	Michael Mueller, Alex Putney
Acquisitions Coordinator	**Series Design**
Alexander Corona	Peter F. Hancik
Technical Editor	**Cover Series Design**
Nick Payton	Amparo Del Rio
Copy Editor	
Judy Ziajka	

This book was composed with Corel VENTURA™ Publisher.

To my lovely wife and best friend, Amy.
You are truly a blessing in my life.
—Kenton Gardinier

This book is dedicated with love to my wife, Sophia, and my five children, Michelle, Megan, Zoe, Zachary, and Ian, for their support and for putting up with all the late hours. It is also dedicated to my parents, Jairo and Mary Jane, for buying me my first computer and thereby setting me on the path my life has taken.
—Chris Amaris

ABOUT THE AUTHORS

Kenton Gardinier is CEO and co-founder of Perpetuity Systems, a Raleigh, NC–based firm specializing in product development and consulting for customer-facing services. He has authored multiple books, print magazine articles, and online articles in areas ranging from system design to performance optimization. He serves as the President of the Triangle NT User Group and is a board member for the Worldwide Association of NT User Groups. In addition, Gardinier speaks on technology issues at conferences nationwide.

Chris Amaris is the Chief Technology Officer and co-founder of Convergent Computing, a consulting firm based in the San Francisco Bay Area. He has over 15 years experience consulting for Fortune 500 companies, leading companies in the technology selection, design, planning, implementation, and troubleshooting of complex Information Technology projects. He specializes in infrastructure migration, performance tuning, network/systems management, security, and messaging. He is a Windows 2000 MCSE, Novell CNE, Banyan CBE, and a Certified Project Manager.

CONTENTS

Part II

Tuning the Subsystems

Part III

Optimizing Connectivity and MS BackOffice

Part IV

Appendixes

Appendix D, "Windows 2000 Performance Monitor Objects and
Counters" can be found on the Web at
www.osborne.com
www.admin911.com
www.tntug.org (Triangle NT User Group)

ACKNOWLEDGMENTS

The success of a project of this magnitude is the result of team effort. The authors would like to extend their appreciation to the many people involved who helped make this book a reality. The entire Osborne staff, including Franny Kelly, Alex Corona, Janet Walden, and Judy Ziajka provided invaluable, behind-the-scenes support and we are truly thankful for their dedication. We would also like to recognize Nick Payton, from Microsoft, who kept us in check by making sure that what we wrote was technically sound.

This book wouldn't cover the range of topics that it does if it weren't for the help of our contributing authors. Rand Morimoto at Convergent Computing, you've been a true friend and have given us invaluable advice and insight. We'd also like to give special thanks to Rod Trent and Dejan Sunderic for their expertise and hard work.

There are many others that deserve to be mentioned by name, but we would specifically like to thank Shel Sigrist from IBM for his wealth of information, especially on hardware topics. We'd also like to thank BMC Software, Executive Software International, Engagent, and NetIQ for providing us with timely information and products to review.

About the Contributing Authors

Rand Morimoto, MCSE, has been in the computer industry for over 20 years and is renowned for public speaking and authoring books on networking and communication technologies. Rand is an author for Osborne/McGraw-Hill and SAMS Publishing with a number of books on information technologies, including *Designing and Deploying Exchange Server, Remote and Mobile Technologies, Windows 2000: Design and Migration,* and *Designing and Deploying Exchange 2000, Conferencing Server, and SharePoint Portal Server.* Rand travels worldwide each year and speaks at conferences and conventions on topics ranging from electronic commerce, Internet communications, network security, electronic messaging, collaborative computing, and remote and mobile technologies. Rand is also an advisor to the White House, setting domestic policy on electronic commerce and communications.

Rod Trent is the author of *Microsoft SMS Installer* (Computing/McGraw-Hill, 2000) and *Admin911: SMS* (Osborne/McGraw-Hill, 2000). He has written many technical white papers and product reviews, primarily under the theme of enterprise systems management. He is a contributing editor for SWYNK.com, and managing editor of MyCEDevice.com and MyPocketPC.com. He is the Enterprise Systems Management Expert for SearchSystemsManagement.com and SMS Forum Manager for InfoWorld.com. Rod speaks at least twice a year at different systems management conferences around the world.

Dejan Sunderic is the Principal Consultant at Trigon Blue, Inc., a consulting company based in Toronto, specializing in database and e-commerce solutions. He is the author of *SQL Server 2000 Stored Procedure Programming* (Osborne/ McGraw-Hill, 2000; for more information, visit www.TrigonBlue.com/ stored_procedure.htm) and articles in several computer and technical magazines. Contact: dejans@hotmail.com.

bout the Technical Reviewer

Nick Payton, MCSE + I, CCNA, is a Network Engineer with Microsoft Corporation, where he currently works on their global network. Prior to working at Microsoft, he was a Network Administrator for over six years while serving in the U.S. Navy.

TRODUCTION

Windows 2000, with its introduction of Active Directory (AD), its dependence on DNS, its core improvements, and more, has jumped well beyond the capabilities of its predecessor, Windows NT. It continues to prove itself to be a robust, reliable, enterprise-level network operating system. Windows 2000 is now running more large networks and mission-critical applications than ever before. As a result, the importance of Windows 2000 performance is paramount. This book is designed to be an all-inclusive, definitive resource to identifying potential performance bottlenecks and minimizing their effects on overall system performance. It is the direct result of careful analysis and the gathering of techniques proven to maximize Windows 2000's effectiveness and efficiency.

There is more to performance tuning and optimization than simply throwing financial and hardware resources at the system, or buying the latest and greatest equipment. Optimum system performance is the consummation of careful planning, empirical analysis, and proactive monitoring. These processes are certainly more challenging than they sound. Today's typical Windows 2000 systems are made up of numerous parameters and components, all of which can potentially influence system performance. Such complexity makes it all the more challenging—and all the more important—to tune your system for optimal performance. This book analyzes the most important influential components that can impact performance, and provides recommendations that will help you extract every drop of performance out of your system.

Challenges of Performance Management

Reality in today's business world is harsh, competitive, and demanding. Streamlining resources and working more efficiently have become focal points in strategic business planning. Many companies, large and small, are faced with the fact that they must strive for more, with fewer resources, in order to survive. Some companies find themselves restructuring their business strategies not necessarily to stay ahead of the game, but instead, simply to keep up with their competition.

The "more for less" approach to conducting business stems from rapid advancements in technology and the possibility that, in such a dynamic environment, anyone can come out on top. Fierce competition, combined with the availability of vast amounts of information, forces everyone to aim for a business strategy in which work quality, efficiency, and productivity can increase simultaneously. Those companies that can achieve such status are bound to succeed and satisfy the customers' needs.

The same principle of efficient, cost-effective productivity applies to system performance. If a system is not optimized for efficiency, then work cannot be accomplished effectively. The system will not perform at maximum capacity. The system may be running "just fine," but is it performing at its optimal level, or can performance be improved? When and how is it appropriate to optimize computer resources?

What Is Performance Optimization?

Performance optimization, defined in its most elementary form, is simply completing an objective or task in the shortest amount of time with minimal wasted effort or resources. It means harmonizing hardware and software resources to perform duties in a timely and efficient manner. The ultimate goal of performance optimization is to use your server's limited resources in such a way that it provides the best level of service to your internal and/or external customers.

On the surface, performance optimization may appear to be simply a matter of tweaking a few settings and expecting a performance boost. Unfortunately, however, it is often difficult to tell whether or not the system is experiencing delay due to wasted or overworked components. What guidelines do you follow to measure your server's performance? How do you establish baseline values to represent server efficiency? How do you configure your system's settings to increase capacity? When should you perform configuration changes? Will the changes uncover, or even cause, other problems within the system? All of these questions and more are answered within the context of this book. It delves into the art of performance tuning and offers concise recommendations that are guaranteed to boost performance, increase efficiency, and streamline server resources.

ɔw This Book Is Structured

If you feel unfamiliar with the theory and techniques of performance optimization, then by all means begin with Chapter 1 and proceed to the end of the book. If you are looking to solve one or more specific system problems, this outline will point you to the section you need.

Part I, "Designing Your Windows 2000 Environment for Optimal Performance," begins by examining Windows 2000 internals and feature enhancements that are specific to performance. Then we discuss the formal and informal approaches to capacity planning to help you proactively identify performance problems. Finally, we focus on designing Windows 2000 in your environment, covering everything from hardware architectures to domain design considerations.

Part II, "Tuning the Subsystems," examines Windows 2000 subsystems and components including AD, memory, disk, network, replication, security, client performance, printing, and the Registry.

Part III, "Optimizing Connectivity and MS BackOffice," analyzes ways to boost connectivity services, such as IIS and Terminal Services. It also analyzes ways to fine-tune the two most commonly used MS BackOffice products: SQL Server 2000 and Exchange 2000 Server.

Part IV, "Appendixes," contains three appendixes with a wealth of information including using the System Monitor, sources of Windows 2000 information, and a description of the products included on the book's CD. In addition, we've posted on the Web an extensive appendix that lists performance counters and related information. You can find it at the publisher's Web site (**www.osborne.com**). It's also posted at **www.admin911.com** and **www.tntug.org** (Triangle NT User Group).

TOP TEN PERFORMANCE TIPS

Although many of your performance problems cannot be solved overnight, here are the ten best tune-ups that you can make if you wish to delve immediately into the art of performance tuning. These concise recommendations are by no means "cure-alls" or guarantees for huge performance differences, but they do help alleviate burdens that may be taxing your system. The procedures listed here are examined much more thoroughly in the chapters of this book.

1. Plan and design, not once or twice, but three times. This may be a little extreme for some environments but you get the point; the more time you spend planning and designing, the higher your rate of success for properly implementing Windows 2000 with performance in mind.

2. Turn on write-back cache and zero wait states for memory within your system's BIOS.

3. Create a paging file for each physical disk. Spreading the I/O load among multiple disk drives and controllers greatly enhances performance because it allows information to be written simultaneously.

4. Set the minimum pagefile size to the highest anticipated system and user-level application requirements. Eliminating the need to increase the pagefile size for initial values speeds up application startup times and reduces disk fragmentation.

5. Turn off animated or 3-D screen savers. They typically and needlessly take away precious processor power.

6. If your budget permits, use SCSI hard disk drives and hardware RAID controllers.

7. Replace older hardware with newer, more efficient components.

8. Balance the workloads of your servers.

9. Remove unnecessary software components, such as services, device drivers, and protocols. For example, if you are not using a system for remote access services, but you have the Routing and Remote Access Service running, stop and disable it or simply remove it altogether.

10. Begin monitoring system performance and health to proactively identify problems before they affect performance.

PART I

Designing Your Windows 2000 Environment for Optimal Performance

CHAPTER 1

Understanding Your Windows 2000 Environment

Before you tune your car's engine, you have to know a variety of things about the car. You have to know what parts make up the engine and how those parts interact, the features of those parts, the tools you'll need to work on the car, and much more. Now you don't have to be an expert about all the parts or mechanics that go into building an engine (much less know all the parts that constitute a car), but the more you know about them, the better you'll understand where and how to make adjustments so that you can make your car run more smoothly, more efficiently, or even faster. The same principle applies to tuning Windows 2000. Knowing your system and the interactions among the system components helps you optimize and troubleshoot so that you can provide the best level of service and get the most out of your system.

Understanding your Windows 2000 Server environment is without a doubt one of the most important yet often overlooked aspects of performance tuning and optimization. It may seem difficult enough keeping up with daily administrative and maintenance tasks without also taking the time to understand the roles of individual server components. Nevertheless, however daunting a task this may seem, it is imperative that you have at least a basic understanding of each component and how these components interact. Understanding the environment will also help you predict future resource requirements and proactively solve problems.

This chapter provides a general overview of the Windows 2000 operating system architecture. It first examines the performance improvements built within Windows 2000. Then it explores the Windows 2000 operating system architecture, including the self-tuning mechanisms that promote efficiency. The internal components of the operating system play an integral role in every aspect of your system. This chapter then delves into the improvements made to the system to help you manage and keep up-to-date with service packs and hotfixes.

A NEW AND IMPROVED OPERATING SYSTEM

Microsoft has undoubtedly made a considerable investment in the Windows 2000 operating system. Over several years in development, Windows 2000 is the largest software development project in history, with over 30 million lines of code.

There's more than just a name change that distinguishes it from its predecessor, Windows NT. Windows 2000 is packed with new features ranging from changes in the user interface to a new directory service. The radical differentiation between it and its predecessor signifies a change in course, to an operating system that is more reliable, more robust, faster, and can scale to suit the largest of enterprises.

A Self-Sufficient Operating System

Windows 2000 is by far one of the most self-sufficient operating systems. It takes over some performance responsibilities often fulfilled by users and administrators, dynamically changing parameters as resources require them. For example, Windows 2000 dynamically increases the size of pagefile.sys as the need to swap data to disk increases. Similarly, work demands placed on Windows 2000 are constantly changing as work habits and application requirements change. It would be extremely burdensome on administrators and users if they constantly had to manually change settings in the Registry to reflect changes in requirements. To prevent such inconvenience, Microsoft has built self-tuning mechanisms into the operating system that dynamically adjust to current demands on the system.

Windows 2000 automatically controls a variety of resources, but it is also limited by what can be dynamically adjusted. Some of the more notable examples of resources that Windows 2000 manages dynamically are the amount of RAM allocated to services and applications, disk cache use, the size of the virtual memory's pagefile.sys, and several network-related parameters, such as the size of the TCP window. Windows 2000 does not and should not, however, change all configurations dynamically. For example, it will not try to increase the speed of read/write transfers to disk by moving an application to a faster drive or deplete the memory resources of one application for the benefit of another. If Windows 2000 had this much control, many changes could have disastrous consequences.

It's also important to note that even though Windows 2000 is considered a self-sufficient operating system, this doesn't necessarily mean that these self-sufficiencies will always provide you with the best solution in every single network environment. There's obviously more to tuning Windows 2000 than just letting the system adjust various settings dynamically as conditions change. On the other hand, these self-sufficiencies do provide a level of convenience and comfort.

NEW PERFORMANCE-ENHANCING FEATURES

Windows 2000 is loaded with new performance-enhancing features. Some of these features, such as its unified directory called Active Directory (AD), are visible or widely known, while others are deeply embedded within the internal architecture.

The overall goal wasn't just to provide cool new features; it was to provide a robust, reliable, scalable, manageable, and fault-tolerant operating system that can easily be tailored to the needs of organizations of all sizes. This is a pretty big feat for any organization, including Microsoft, to accomplish, but as you'll see in this chapter and throughout this book, Microsoft Windows 2000 has done quite well.

The new performance features discussed in this section aren't by any means all of the new features built into Windows 2000. However, the ones that are specifically mentioned are among the most notable, and the ones that will more than likely have the most impact on your network environment. Throughout this book, you'll learn of additional, performance-related improvements.

Manageability Improvements

Ease of use and inherent management capabilities have always been strong points for the Windows platforms. Microsoft continues to strive to improve these capabilities in Windows 2000. These improvements are designed to make administration easier and more productive.

Intellimirror

Intellimirror is not a single component or technology within Windows 2000. Instead, it is a tightly knit group of technologies that dramatically improves user and computer configuration management. The end result is a reduction in the *total cost of ownership* (TCO)—and an easier life for you and your end users.

This grouping of technologies isn't a new concept. Microsoft tried this once before, with Zero Administration for Windows (ZAW) in

Windows NT. Although ZAW went far in simplifying administration and reducing costs, Intellimirror is the true charmer. Plus, Intellimirror provides flexibility, letting you choose the features for your environment, an about-face from the ZAW implementation.

NOTE: Most of Intellimirror's features require you to employ Windows 2000 in native mode. However, you can use some features, such as Offline Files, without being in native mode.

Intellimirror offers the following core features:

▼ **Data protection and management** Thanks to the Offline Files feature, user data can be accessed from anywhere (that is, on the network or on the local machine), even when the server or network is unavailable. The Offline Files feature allows users to save data to their My Documents folder, while the system actually saves files to the network and keeps a local copy in the client's cache. Offline Files also synchronizes the data much like the Briefcase utility on Windows NT and Windows 9*x* computers. Troubles don't plague the Windows 2000 implementation as they did Briefcase, however.

■ **Roaming user support** With roaming user support, also known as folder redirection, a user's data, applications, and environment settings follow that user wherever he or she goes. One of several advantages of using this feature is that it can significantly reduce the amount of traffic on the network. For example, using standard roaming profiles like the ones you're probably used to in Windows NT can mean dragging countless megabytes worth of data across the network each time a user logs on.

▲ **Software installation and management** Remote Installation Services (RIS) is separate from Intellimirror. However, it's included here because this technology focuses on simplifying administration, reducing costs by, among other things, allowing you to install Windows 2000 and applications remotely, repair damaged installations, and remove applications with little or no intervention.

Group Policy   One of the major underlying technologies of the
Intellimirror initiative is the Group Policy Object (GPO). GPOs
essentially give you another option for managing and controlling
Intellimirror and other Windows 2000 functions.

Group Policy is Windows 2000's replacement of the System Policy
Editor in Windows NT 4.0. The System Policy Editor was used to
specify user and computer configurations, but it had many limitations.
Group Policy is designed not only to overcome the limitations
present in the System Policy Editor, but also to provide entirely
new features that facilitate Windows 2000 administration.

Group Policy is much more than an extension of the System
Policy Editor. It offers your environment a way to centrally
manage computers and users. In addition to providing centralized
management capabilities, through its ties with AD it also lets you
delegate its administrative responsibilities for tighter control over
the environment without the additional administrative burden.

Group Policy enables you to set or declare policies such as
security configuration settings, scripts (logon, logoff, startup, and
shutdown scripts), software installation, folder redirection, Registry
modification, lockdown, and much more. These policies affect users'
experience and environment configuration.

Despite the advantages of using Group Policy management, this
feature can be burdensome if you don't properly plan and design.
With its enormous functionality and flexibility come complexity and
danger. If you're not careful with Group Policies, it could wreak havoc
in your Windows 2000 environment. For instance, as extreme examples,
you could prevent all users from logging onto the domain, or you
could leave security wide open, allowing anyone to gain unauthorized
access to everything in your environment. It's also important to watch
the way Group Policy affects nested groups and containers.

System Monitor

The System Monitor (see Figure 1-1), once known as the Performance
Monitor, has evolved from its predecessor and incorporates many
important enhancements. These enhancements are not necessarily
intended to boost system performance, but rather to build levels of
productivity when monitoring your system.

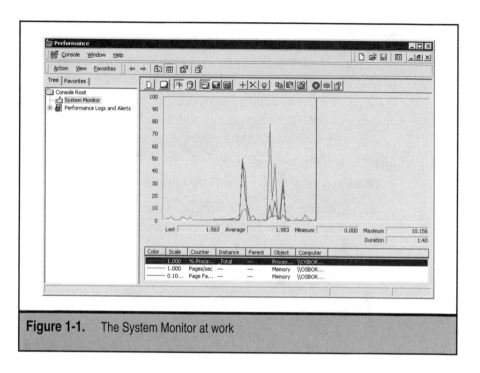

Figure 1-1.   The System Monitor at work

As mentioned earlier, the System Monitor has many new enhancements built into it, including the following:

▼   The System Monitor is now an ActiveX control, making it easier to use with other applications, such as Microsoft Office.

■   The System Monitor is a snap-in for the Microsoft Management Console (MMC), which conforms to a single, familiar interface.

■   Data can be analyzed as it is being logged.

■   You can log data or generate alerts automatically on a specified interval.

■   The System Monitor is a service so you don't have to be logged in to collect information about your system.

▲   The System Monitor incorporates a new feature called trace logging. System performance information can be traced rather than sampled for greater accuracy.

For more information on the System Monitor, consult Appendix A.

Hardware Support

Hardware device support has never been better. With the addition of true support for Plug and Play and the Windows Driver Model (WDM), Windows 2000's list of hardware devices supported meets or exceeds that of its biggest challenger, Windows 98.

Windows 2000 supports whole new classes and types of devices including, but not limited to, the following:

▼ Universal Serial Bus (USB) devices

■ An array of video-related devices, including Accelerated Graphics Port (AGP), digital cameras, multiple monitor support, and DVD

■ Firewire (IEEE 1394)

■ Human Interface Device (HID) compliance

▲ PC Card

As you can see, the list of devices supported by Windows 2000 is growing rapidly and reaching well beyond the capabilities of its predecessor. This is due largely to the underlying technologies being supported.

Windows Driver Model

The new WDM is supported in both Windows 2000 and Windows 98 systems and allows the two operating systems to use the same drivers. This translates to simplification for hardware vendors when they're developing device drivers, but it also benefits you because of the increased compatibility.

WDM also is responsible for kernel-mode streaming, which dramatically improves the performance of real-time streaming media. These functions can run faster and more efficiently in kernel mode than the previous implementations in user mode. For more information on kernel and user modes, see "Windows 2000 Internals" later in this chapter.

Plug and Play

Sometimes getting devices to work properly, or the right device drivers to install, under Windows NT was difficult at best. There was little or no way to adapt quickly to a hardware addition or change, and you often had to have detailed information regarding IRQs, DMA channels, and I/O ports. Windows NT had some support for Plug and Play, but not the true support that Windows 2000 has.

Life is definitely easier and more productive with the full support of Plug and Play. Windows 2000 can automatically recognize new devices, identify and configure resource requirements, and install the appropriate device drivers for devices supporting Plug and Play.

In addition, Windows 2000's new Device Manager now makes working with new devices much simpler. This tool, shown in Figure 1-2, is similar to the one you've probably used with Windows 9*x*. Also, for those devices that are non–Plug and Play compliant, Windows 2000 has included the Hardware Wizard (see Figure 1-3), which, as one of its many responsibilities, aids in the configuration and troubleshooting of devices.

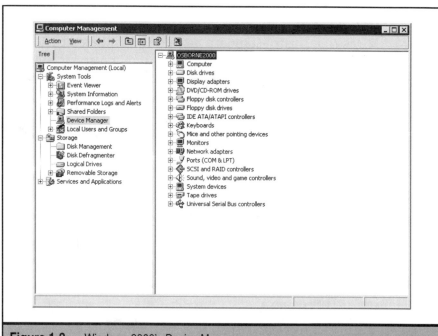

Figure 1-2. Windows 2000's Device Manager

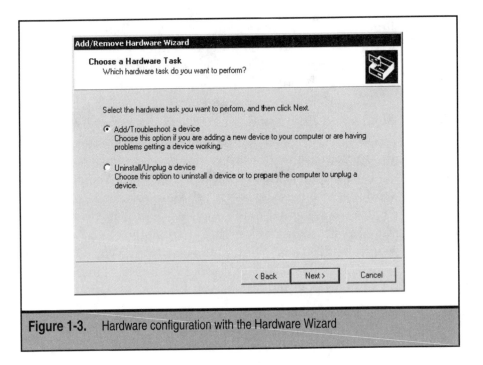

Figure 1-3. Hardware configuration with the Hardware Wizard

I2O Support

I2O is an industry-standard architecture initiated by Intel and others to optimize I/O performance by assuming responsibility from the CPU. I2O uses a dedicated processor to move interrupt-intensive tasks and processing away from the CPU so that the CPU isn't bogged down with I/O processing.

The application of I2O is growing, and the benefits are enormous. You can see this standard in storage management hardware, networked video, and more.

Network-Related Performance Improvements

Network-related performance improvements account for a large percentage of overall performance improvements in Windows 2000. These improvements significantly boost Windows 2000's ability to scale to the enterprise.

Active Directory (AD)

AD is one of the most important core services of Windows 2000. It revolutionizes the organization and management of Windows 2000 network environments, especially when compared to Windows NT.

Indeed, AD is more complex and changes the way we administer a Windows-based environment. However, from a performance point of view, it saves a considerable amount of time by centrally managing otherwise distributed directory services and logically organizes network resources such as printers, computers, users, and more. Many applications and services that use a directory to store information in Windows 2000 can use AD to consolidate directories into a single point of reference.

Limitations, ranging from domain scalability to manageability, that were present in Windows NT environments are of little or no consequence when using AD. For example, Windows NT domains were limited to 40,000 objects, whereas Windows 2000 domains can scale well into the millions of objects.

For more information on AD performance, refer to Chapter 9.

Extensible Schema   When we mention AD's extensible schema, we're really talking about metadata, which is data about data. This means that there is data, or information, on the contents of the AD (that is, objects, object attributes, and so on) that define the AD. The schema, therefore, determines which attributes are affiliated with each object.

The importance of an extensible schema from a performance point of view is that you aren't limited to the default schema provided with Windows 2000. You can modify the schema to fit the needs of your organization to enhance productivity. In most cases, however, you'll probably find that the default AD schema is more than adequate for your needs.

CAUTION: Don't attempt to modify the schema unless you are certain of how it will affect your environment. You could negatively affect system performance and reliability if you don't proceed with caution. It's always a good idea to back up your system before making such changes.

Multimaster Replication Replication of domain information has changed considerably from the Windows NT days. In Windows NT, the primary domain controller (PDC) controlled the master copy of the Security Account Manager (SAM), which contained domain-related information such as user, computer, and group accounts. Within AD, all domain controllers (DCs) are treated as equals and for the most part share in the responsibility of the domain. Therefore, all DCs have a complete read/write copy of the AD database.

Since all DCs share a copy of the AD database, it's crucial that they all have an updated copy. Multimaster replication solves this problem and strikes a balance between when updates occur and when the information is replicated. In essence, you have built-in fault tolerance of the AD database when you have more than one DC.

Equally important is the fact that only changes in the AD database are replicated to other DCs in the environment. This reduces the likelihood that replication network traffic will overwhelm the network.

For more information on replication and how to optimize the process, refer to Chapter 10.

Domain Name System (DNS)

Although DNS could be added on to Windows NT, it has never had such an important responsibility for Windows environments as it does now. DNS is now a tightly integrated component of Windows 2000 and is the primary name resolution provider.

DNS has literally stood the test of time, serving as a locator service for private networks as well as the Internet. Microsoft's decision to have Windows 2000 rely on DNS gives Windows 2000 the advantage of a robust, scalable name resolution mechanism. Embracing DNS also means embracing an industry standard. More information on maximizing DNS can be found in Chapter 8.

Dynamic DNS (DDNS) Microsoft didn't stop at just providing DNS with Windows 2000. Windows 2000 also supports RFC 2136, which is more commonly referred to as the specification defining DDNS.

DDNS dynamically updates the DNS database, allowing servers (DHCP, DC, and DNS) and clients to update resource records. One of several advantages to DDNS is that administration is greatly reduced, saving you time and effort.

TCP/IP

TCP/IP's reliability and capabilities have made it the protocol of choice not only for Windows 2000 but also for other platforms, and it is the de facto standard for Internet communication. The breadth of responsibility that it takes on in Windows 2000 is enormous. Windows 2000 heavily relies on it to support DNS, AD, and much more.

TCP/IP is continually undergoing changes and enhancements to meet ever-changing business needs and requirements. Microsoft is striving to ensure that its TCP/IP implementation meets and exceeds expectations. Windows 2000 adopts many new TCP/IP technologies; these are explained in detail in Chapter 8.

Here is a list of some of the most important improvements to the TCP/IP protocol stack from a performance point of view:

▼ **Quality of Service (QoS)** support within Windows 2000's TCP/IP extends to standards such as the Resource Reservation Protocol (RSVP), Differentiated Quality of Service, and 802.1p, to provide higher levels of service quality. Essentially, QoS is an agreement between two or more machines that guarantees a certain, expected level of throughput, traffic control, and more.

■ **NDIS 5** is a new network architecture that supports a multitude of enhancements such as multicasts, bandwidth reservation, and power management.

■ **High-speed network support**, defined in RFC 1323, is now inherent to Windows 2000. This alone is a tremendous boost to Windows 2000's performance and scalability capabilities. This standard includes support for Selective Acknowledgments (SACK), IEEE 1394, wireless networks, IP over ATM (RFC 1577), and much more.

■ **TCP-scalable window sizes** promotes dynamic adjustment to the ever-changing conditions of a network. This feature is supported by RFC 1323 and enables more efficient communication.

■ **TCP fast retransmit and recovery** supports quicker response times and recovery when packets are being dropped during the transmission. This feature was available with Windows NT Service Pack 2 and higher, but it is now an integral part of the TCP/IP protocol stack.

- **Round-Trip Time (RTT) and Retransmission Timeout (RTO)** provides calculation improvements to increase TCP/IP's efficiency by analyzing multiple samples per window of data.

- **Connection management** has been vastly improved to handle large numbers of connections.

- ▲ **Offloading mechanisms** within the protocol stack can move tasks onto another hardware device (such as an NIC) to improve performance.

DHCP Enhancements   The Dynamic Host Configuration Protocol (DHCP) is a TCP/IP-related service that provides dynamic assignment of TCP/IP information such as an IP address to clients. It saves administrators a considerable amount of time configuring client machines and resolves many issues with TCP/IP networks (such as duplicate IP address conflicts).

Several new DHCP-related features improve not only its performance but also its manageability. These features include the following:

- ▼ Integration with DNS
- ■ Enhanced monitoring and usage reporting
- ▲ Server authorization to help prevent the use of a rogue DHCP server

Kerberos Authentication

Kerberos support is an important enhancement to the Windows 2000 operating system. Windows 2000 uses the Kerberos version 5 security protocol for authentication, trust relationships, and much more. Kerberos is an open, standardized protocol that isn't just supported by Windows 2000; it's supported on a variety of other platforms, including many UNIX flavors.

Kerberos replaces Windows NT's NT LAN Manager (NTLM). The replacement gives Windows 2000 a tremendous performance boost. Kerberos is a more efficient and streamlined protocol than NTLM because it reduces the amount of communication needed for authentication. Moreover, its trust relationships are far superior to Windows NT trust relationships in regards to traffic generation and management. Kerberos is also a more secure protocol that's supported by the rest of the industry.

Internet Information Server (IIS) 5

Windows 2000's IIS version 5, shown in Figure 1-4, is loaded with a wealth of new features and improvements (refer to Chapter 15 for

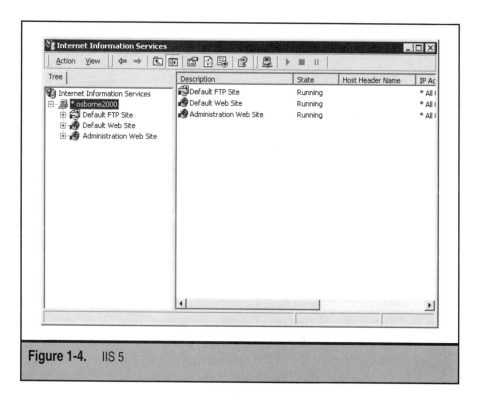

Figure 1-4.   IIS 5

more information on IIS). Performance-enhancing features include the following:

▼ **Application protection**   IIS increases reliability for your Web applications by either *pooling* processes or isolating them from other processes. Pooled processes run in a common memory space that is separate from memory areas where core IIS services are running.

■ **FTP restart**   If you've ever had to stop a download (or had a download interrupted) when using FTP and then want to resume downloading, you're probably aware that you often had to restart the download from scratch. Now you can resume the download from where you left off.

■ **HTTP compression**   HTTP compression combines compaction of Web pages with caching of static files to display Web pages more quickly. Clients and servers that are compression enabled can use this feature.

■ **New Active Server Pages (ASP) features**   ASP is a server-side scripting language supported by previous versions of IIS. Improvements have been made to streamline performance and IIS scripts.

■ **Process accounting**   When a server is hosting more than one Web site, it's often useful to know how each Web site affects the system's CPU use. Process accounting provides information on how individual Web sites use the server's CPU resources.

▲ **Process throttling**   Process throttling allows you to limit the percentage of CPU use for individual Web sites.

Core Architecture Improvements

The core of Windows 2000 is the foundation for all services and operating system functionality. It can be considered the heart as well as the brain of the system.

Many of the changes and improvements to Windows 2000's core architecture are transparent to administrators and end users, while others are quite noticeable. All, however, help to create a reliable and scalable operating system.

There's no doubt that Windows 2000 is significantly more reliable, stable, and scalable than its predecessor, Windows NT 4.0. Although many of the enhancements mentioned earlier greatly contribute to Windows 2000's overall soundness and functionality, it's the core of the operating system that supports those features.

Windows File Protection

Windows File Protection (also known as System File Protection) protects Windows 2000 from accidental and malicious file modification or deletion. If improper changes are made or a file is deleted, the service immediately retrieves the last-known good version from either the DLL cache or the installation media. This service can save you from a lot of potential downtime.

Advanced Recovery

Advanced System Recovery (ASR) is a combination of the backup, restore, repair, and recovery components within Windows 2000. It allows you to save the entire state of the system. You can then use this saved system state to quickly restore the system in case of a disaster.

Kernel-Mode-Only Dumps   If Windows 2000 experiences a system crash, it can dump the contents of memory into a file for later analysis or possible retrieval. In previous versions, your only option was to dump the entire contents of physical memory, which, depending on the amount of RAM you had installed, could take a long time. To speed up the recovery process, Windows 2000 introduces kernel-mode-only dumps. As you might expect, these dump only the portions of memory that belonged to kernel-mode operations.

Kernel-Mode Write Protection

Similar to Windows File Protection, kernel-mode write protection is vital to the stability and reliability of the system. It prevents modification of the kernel by providing read-only access. For instance, if a rogue device driver tries to access the kernel, the system won't be as susceptible to instability. If a rogue device driver actually crashes the system, it is now much easier to detect the location where the problem originated.

Job Objects

Many applications and multiuser environments, such as Terminal Services, can spawn several processes (child processes) that are dedicated to a single task. Windows NT managed these processes separately, which often used resources inefficiently. Since processes can be grouped together for a single purpose, job objects were created in Windows 2000 to use resources more efficiently and allow the operating system to manage one or more processes as a single unit.

The use of job objects also gives greater control over the processes. For example, using job objects, code can be written to restrict an application's working set.

Fewer Reboots

Another area in which Microsoft has greatly improved reliability with Windows 2000 is in the number of required system reboots. Microsoft has significantly reduced the number of required reboots in Windows 2000 to a little more than a handful. Fewer reboots means less downtime and more productivity.

64-bit Extensions

The 64-bit extensions allow Windows 2000 to scale not only today but also into the future. Also known as Enterprise Memory Architecture (EMA) or Address Windowing Extensions (AWE), the extensions allow applications to go beyond the 32-bit memory limitations and address up to 64GB of memory.

Although Windows 2000 has 64-bit extensions, this doesn't mean that Windows 2000 is a 64-bit operating system. On the contrary, it leverages these extensions to allow applications that require vast amounts of memory (large databases, ERP systems, CAD, and more) to take advantage of more memory. When 64-bit hardware becomes mainstream, these applications and Windows 2000 can more easily move to the new platform. It's important to note that the Alpha processor, which is no longer supported, is a 64-bit platform, but Windows NT could run only in 32-bit mode. In other words, it couldn't make use of the hardware.

To take advantage of the extensions, applications have to be written specifically to use the Very Large Memory (VLM) model. For more information on memory, refer to Chapter 6.

Scatter/Gather I/O

Scatter/Gather I/O is another feature in Windows 2000 designed to improve the performance of application servers on your network. It was available to Windows NT, but only through the installation of a service pack. It is now included as a feature of the operating system.

The primary advantage of this feature is that it is a more efficient technology for moving sections of physical memory to a contiguous space on the hard disk. Increased performance from this process can be gained only if applications are specifically written to take advantage of this feature.

WINDOWS 2000 OPERATING SYSTEM ARCHITECTURE

Now you have a general understanding of the vast performance improvements provided by Windows 2000. This section delves into the operating system internals and describes the interaction between the operating system and the hardware.

The goal of any operating system design is to provide an interface between the system's hardware and the applications the user executes. Windows 2000 goes one step further by supplying an intuitive interface that enables users to perform tasks with minimal technical training. Unlike UNIX variants, it shelters most users by providing an easy-to-use interface to perform daily administrative tasks, general performance tuning, and other common operations. This, too, is arguably a performance-enhancing feature, considering that administration and the like can be performed more efficiently and with greater ease. No matter how easy it is to learn the operating system and the tools used to manage and fine-tune the system, it is important to understand the basic Windows 2000 internals if you expect to successfully optimize your system.

Windows 2000 Internals

It's hard to imagine that a change in an operating system of this magnitude (more than 30 million lines of code!) didn't require a complete overhaul of Windows 2000's core services. Fortunately, Microsoft's planning the design for future enhancements has really paid off. Because Windows 2000 was built from a modular operating system (see Figure 1-5 for an illustration of the Windows NT architectural model), the development team could plug in additional components and enhance the original code as needed.

Figure 1-6 illustrates the new architectural model for Windows 2000, showing all of the internal components and the interactions

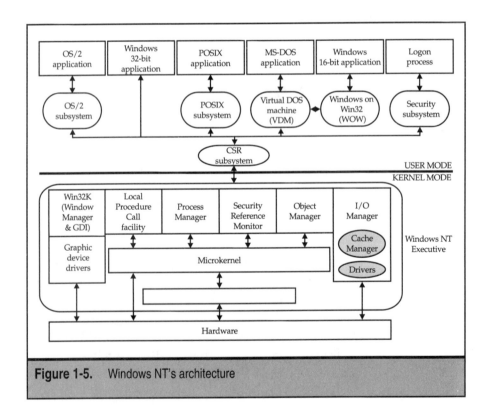

Figure 1-5. Windows NT's architecture

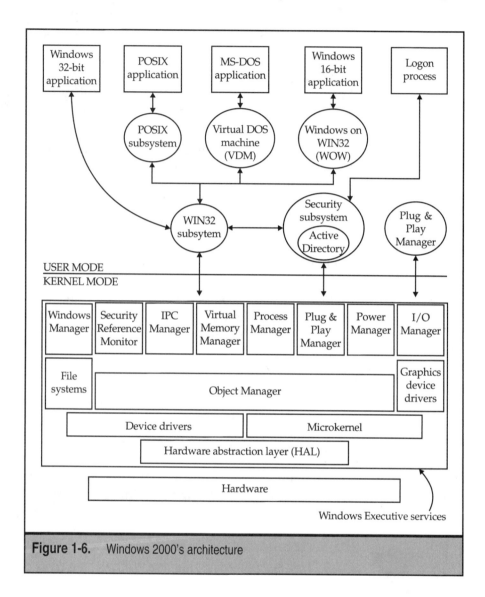

Figure 1-6.   Windows 2000's architecture

among them. As you can see, there are only a few major differences between the two operating systems. These differences and the rest of the internals are explored in the following sections.

The Windows 2000 operating system design is both modular and layered. The core of the system is divided into discrete objects according to function. Each of these objects has its own characteristics and responsibilities within the operating system and interacts with the other objects to perform tasks or instructions. These components can run in either the microprocessor's kernel mode (privileged mode) or user mode (application mode).

The Windows 2000 Executive represents the subsystems and components that run in kernel mode, including the microkernel, hardware abstraction layer (HAL), and management services. The number of components privileged enough to run in kernel mode is limited because a component must have direct access to both hardware and software resources. This restriction provides a more secure and stable environment, almost completely eliminating the possibility that an erratic program, device driver, or subsystem will disturb or crash the entire system.

All other subsystems and components, such as server subsystems and applications, execute in user mode. User mode components operate in their own address spaces and can communicate with other user mode components, as well as with the Windows 2000 Executive, through well-defined software interfaces.

Kernel Mode

The Windows 2000 Executive represents the components that run in kernel (privileged) mode. It is the underlying structure for the operating system, and it provides the basic functionality for the rest of the system. For example, when a user-mode application or process requests information, it communicates directly with the Portable Operating System Interface (POSIX) or Win32 subsystem. The subsystem then communicates with the Windows 2000 Executive.

NOTE: The OS/2 subsystem present in Windows NT is no longer supported in Windows 2000.

The Windows 2000 Executive consists of four main components:

- ▼ HAL
- ■ Microkernel
- ■ Management services
- ▲ Client-server subsystem

HAL   The hardware abstraction layer, or HAL, provides a direct link from the operating system to the hardware. It operates underneath the rest of the operating system so that applications and subsystems do not need to be aware of hardware-specific information. In previous versions of the operating system, each hardware platform (Intel, DEC Alpha, and so on) required its own unique HAL. Now Windows 2000 runs on a single platform: the Intel platform.

> **NOTE:**   HAL is also responsible for symmetrical multiprocessing (SMP) functionality (discussed in more detail in Chapter 3).

Despite the fact that Windows 2000 supports only the Intel platform, there are eight different versions of HAL, not including OEM versions. These HALs are grouped into two major classes—Advanced Configuration Power Interface (ACPI) and standard—with different versions in each class (single processor, multiprocessor, and so on), depending on your hardware configuration.

If you upgrade your system with additional processors, you should first check with your vendor and then consult Microsoft's Knowledge Base (http://www.microsoft.com/kb/) for complete information on upgrade considerations such as multiprocessor support, power features, and bus type support. You should also be aware that the Device Manager has replaced the functionality of Windows NT's UPTOMP.EXE utility, once used to upgrade an existing system to a multiprocessor system.

To identify which HAL you are using, do the following:

1. On the Control Panel, double-click the System applet.

2. On the Hardware tab, click the Device Manager button to display the Windows 2000 Device Manager.

3. Expand the Computer branch, and you'll see which version of the HAL your system is using (see Figure 1-7).

Microkernel   The microkernel is the heart of the operating system. You may wonder why this component is not called the kernel as it is in many other operating systems. The difference is that kernels in other operating systems are responsible for almost all actions and

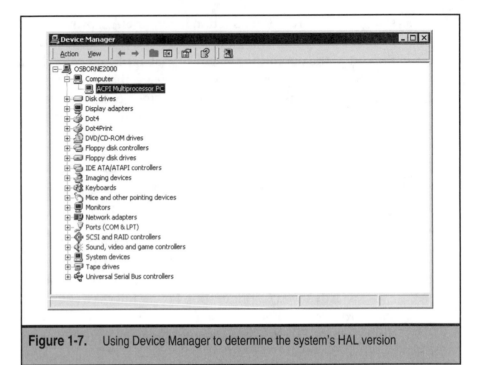

Figure 1-7.   Using Device Manager to determine the system's HAL version

functions within the system, whereas in microkernel architecture, some of those responsibilities are passed on to other components. Windows 2000's microkernel delegates some of these services, such as I/O management, to other components within the Windows 2000 Executive.

Since Windows 2000's microkernel is responsible for systemwide functionality, it is always resident in physical memory. Its duties include the following:

▼   **Thread scheduling**   *Threads* are pieces of code from a particular process that are assigned a scheduling priority (a number from 0 to 31). The microkernel allows a thread to execute for a specified time period before preempting it to allow other process threads to execute. This is the foundation of Windows 2000's ability to multitask preemptively. The microkernel itself cannot be preempted; it always has the highest priority.

■   **SMP synchronization**   A copy of the microkernel runs on
every processor present on the system. This ensures efficient
use of all processors and system resources.

▲   **Interrupts and exceptions**   Interrupts (hardware generated
delays) and exceptions (software generated delays) are
managed by the microkernel. When an interrupt occurs, the
microkernel preempts any thread currently executing so it can
service the interrupt.

Management Services   Management services interact directly with
user-mode subsystems (POSIX and Win32). These services include the
File Systems Object, Security Reference Monitor (SRM), IPC Manager,
Virtual Memory Manager, Process Manager, Plug and Play Manager,
Power Manager, I/O Manager, and Object Manager. Each service is
very important to the stability, reliability, and manageability of the
operating system and, ultimately, to user-level applications.

▼   **File Systems Object**   The File Systems Object is responsible
for operations of the installable file system (FAT, FAT32, NTFS,
CDFS, and so on) installed on the system. This object includes
the kernel-mode write protection and Windows File Protection
features. Operations are coordinated with the I/O Manager.

■   **Security Reference Monitor**   The SRM operates in
conjunction with the logon process, security subsystem, and
Object Manager to enforce system security policies. When a
user logs onto the system, he or she is assigned a security
access token. Every time a user requests a resource, the SRM
consults the object's handle and security access token to
decide whether the user has sufficient privileges to use the
requested resource.

■   **IPC Manager**   The IPC Manager enables two or more
different processes or subsystems to communicate. It is a
messaging mechanism based upon the Remote Procedure Call
(RPC) facility and conforms to the client-server model. The
clients are Windows 2000–supported applications (MS-DOS,
Win16, Win32, and POSIX), and the servers are the
environment subsystems (Win32 and POSIX).

- **Virtual Memory Manager** Many of today's applications require large amounts of memory that sometimes may not be accommodated by the limited amount of physical memory on your system. To ensure that applications have enough memory to execute, Windows 2000 uses virtual memory to compensate for limited memory resources. Virtual memory management is a combination of memory and disk management. Upon execution, each process is allocated its own address space. The address space is subdivided into pages that are used to store data. As RAM resources are depleted, pages are swapped to disk. The data that is swapped to disk can later be retrieved. The Virtual Memory Manager keeps track of which memory address space belongs to which process. It also manages the retrieval of pages from disk.

- **Process Manager** The Process Manager supervises processes and threads. This includes creation, modification, and deletion of processes and threads. Each time an application, subsystem task, or microkernel function is executed, the Process Manager is called to create a process. The Process Manager is called at least once more to create a thread, depending on how many threads are associated with the process. A process must contain at least one thread to execute. As you might expect, the Process Manager works closely with the Object Manager and the microkernel to create objects and perform scheduling, respectively. It also communicates with the SRM to ensure security for processes and process resource requests.

- **Plug and Play Manager** The Plug and Play Manager is new to Windows 2000. It is responsible for identifying a Plug and Play device's resource needs, assigning appropriate resources, such as I/O ports, IRQs, and DMAs, to the device. If another device on the system already claims those resources, the Plug and Play Manager can reconfigure resource requirements without user intervention. Finally, it determines the appropriate device drivers needed and then loads them.

- **Power Manager** The Power Manager manages power-related APIs, coordinates power events, and monitors system power activity.

- **I/O Manager**   The I/O Manager oversees the system's input and output tasks. This responsibility includes managing device, cache, and network drivers. To preserve communication and compatibility, the I/O Manager provides a uniform interface for all driver types. For example, the uniform interface allows multiple installable file systems to reside on the same system.

▲ **Object Manager**   The Object Manager has the greatest responsibility among the management services, supporting all other Windows 2000 Executive subsystems. Windows 2000 treats its physical and logical resources as objects. This includes, but is not limited to, files, disk drives, memory, and processes. The Object Manager creates, defines, modifies, and deletes these objects and makes an object's resources available for other resources to use. In addition, the Object Manager supplies each object with a handle containing access control information that is required when a process requests access to the object.

Client-Server Subsystem   In Windows 2000, the graphics device interface (GDI) and Window Manager (USER), collectively known as the client-server subsystem, remain in kernel mode as in Windows NT 4.0. Their functions have stayed in the kernel, both to improve operating system performance for graphics operations and to reduce memory requirements.

User Mode

All subsystems and applications that do not run in kernel mode run in user mode. This includes the environment subsystems (POSIX and Win32), logon process, security subsystem, and user-level applications.

The environment subsystems handle process requests for service or information. These subsystems then initiate communication with the Windows 2000 Executive to provide the service or information that the process has requested. Only the environment subsystems can issue requests to kernel-mode operations; they are the software interfaces for user-mode applications.

The environment subsystems are also the key to compatibility with other platforms, such as DOS, 16-bit Windows 3.*x*, and POSIX-compliant applications. Each subsystem emulates a particular operating system in a protected address space. Their functionality, except I/O management (keyboard, mouse, and display management) and messaging (object linking and embedding, or OLE, and dynamic data exchange, or DDE), is segregated into 16- and 32-bit operations. This ensures that a misbehaving user-level application does not disrupt the operations of the other subsystems or the operating system itself. For example, an erratic DOS application will not have any affect on the stability of a running POSIX application.

One of the most notable changes in user mode is the embedding of the AD into the security subsystem. The AD is integrated into the security subsystem instead of being its own separate subsystem because any time a request is made to access a directory object, the security subsystem must authenticate the process or user. Then the process or user must go through an authorization process (validating permissions) performed by the security subsystem and Security Reference Monitor.

Win32 Subsystem   The Win32 subsystem is Windows 2000's primary environment subsystem. This was not always the case, however. Microsoft tried to give equal responsibility to the other environment subsystems but soon realized that this caused too much duplication of operations and ultimately degraded performance. As a result, Microsoft has placed most of these redundant responsibilities on the Win32 subsystem and strengthened the Win32 set of APIs.

The Win32 subsystem provides extensive resources and functionality to other subsystems and user-level applications through a set of APIs. This structure models the client-server architecture in that Win32 acts as the server, and all other user-mode processes are clients. There are two reasons for this type of structure. First, Win32 controls all user-mode I/O, including interactions with the keyboard, mouse, and display. Second, other systems may need to communicate with each other through OLE or DDE. Both of these types of operations are accomplished through the set of APIs. When the POSIX subsystem needs either one of these services, it translates its API calls to a corresponding Win32 API call to request service.

POSIX Subsystems   In addition to the Win32 subsystem, Windows 2000 has one other protected environment subsystem: POSIX. This subsystem extends Windows 2000's application support and conforms to open systems standards. It can communicate with the rest of the system by translating its API calls to the respective Win32 API calls to be serviced by the Win32 subsystem.

The Institute of Electrical and Electronics Engineers (IEEE) developed POSIX to provide portability on UNIX systems. A set of standards has evolved ranging from POSIX.1 to POSIX.12. Windows 2000 uses the POSIX.1–compliant subsystem, meaning that it complies with the basic POSIX standards. These standards include case sensitivity and support for multiple file names. Applications conforming to this standard can execute within the POSIX subsystem in their own protected memory space.

SERVICE PACKS AND HOTFIXES

Almost everyone who has administered a Windows NT or Windows 2000 system knows the importance of keeping up-to-date with the latest bug fixes, performance upgrades, security patches, and much more. Service packs and hotfixes are intended to ensure optimal performance, reliability, and stability. Microsoft packages many of these updates into service packs and sometimes individually as hotfixes.

With Windows NT, installing service packs also meant possibly installing new operating system features or entire applications. This, more often than not, caused incompatibility issues, the deterioration of operating system reliability, and many other headaches that you'd rather not encounter, especially in production environments. Although service packs were rigorously tested by Microsoft, it is virtually impossible to test major new features with every possible system or configuration.

No More Service Pack Dilemmas

Microsoft received much criticism related to the problems surrounding service packs for Windows NT. Many of these problems stemmed from the major new features that were added. As a result, Microsoft has taken many precautions to ensure that service packs are reliable on both the Windows NT and Windows 2000 platforms.

One of the most significant improvements to service packs is that new operating system features or upgrades are no longer provided within the actual service pack installation. Only core enhancements and bug fixes are a part of the service pack installation. The result is a more reliable, more robust service pack that will most likely keep away postinstallation woes.

Microsoft also is making a concerted effort to provide service packs periodically to address customer requests and known bugs. This is key because it shows that Microsoft is standing by its commitment to provide reliable updates and enhancements in a timely fashion.

Another inconvenience with previous service packs was the separation of 56-bit and 128-bit security. Service packs from Windows 2000 Service Pack 1 (SP1) and beyond can now detect which security encryption scheme you're using and apply the appropriate level. This feature alone can save you a lot of administrative hassle.

You also had to deal with the question of whether or not to reinstall a service pack when you installed a system component or service after the service pack installation. Microsoft has now eliminated the need to reapply service packs in Windows 2000, so that system integrity is preserved. Once a service pack is installed, you don't have to worry about ensuring that components installed after the service pack are updated. It's a good idea, however, to keep the service pack media close by because if you install a Windows 2000 component or service later, Windows 2000 may ask you for the service pack files so that it can load the necessary updated files. Hence, you don't have to worry about whether or not to reapply the service pack.

Installing Service Packs

The simplest way to install a service pack is from the CD, but you can also use Web-based installation or download the service pack from http://www.microsoft.com/windows2000/downloads/default.asp when using Internet Explorer (IE). Web-based installation detects which files need updating so that you don't have to download the entire service pack. However, you're more than likely going to download a substantial amount, so you should proceed with this type of installation only if you have a high-speed Internet connection. If you don't have a high-speed connection, or you'd just rather have the service pack on CD, you can order it from the Web site mentioned earlier, or you can find it on Microsoft TechNet.

Useful information, including a FAQ, how to order the service pack CD, deployment guides, and much more, can be found at the Windows 2000 service pack Web site. You should investigate this site before proceeding with the installation. When proceeding with the actual installation, you should use the default selection to back up necessary system files before installation so that if you run into any problems, you can revert to the old installation. Remember to check the service pack's documentation to find out approximately how much disk space is required to install the service pack.

Command-Line Options

When installing a service pack, you'll have more options when you run update.exe from the command line. Table 1-1 lists the parameters you can use with update.exe.

For example, if you don't want to reboot immediately after installing the service pack, use the command **update.exe /z**.

Other CD-ROM Goodies

In addition to the service pack and documentation, Microsoft includes new features and utilities on the CD. New features and utilities are separate from the service pack installation so that you don't have to install them.

Parameter	Description
-f	Forces applications to close at shutdown.
-n	Keeps system files from being backed up so the service pack cannot be uninstalled.
-o	Automatically overwrites OEM files.
-q	Installs the service pack in quiet mode so that no user interaction is required.
-s	Allows you to integrate the service pack files in a Windows 2000 installation share. Subsequent Windows 2000 installations will automatically include the service pack update. This is also known as slipstreaming and is extremely useful when you plan to deploy the service pack to multiple machines simultaneously.
-u	Installs SP1 in unattended mode.
-z	Prevents the system from rebooting after installation.

Table 1-1.   update.exe Command-Line Parameters

New and Improved Hotfixes

Hotfixes are Microsoft's answer to quick, reliable fixes. Microsoft provides them so that you don't have to wait for the next service pack to get a problem fixed. Essentially, a hotfix is a service pack on a much smaller scale, often addressing a single problem. Prior to Windows 2000, hotfixes could become an administrative nightmare because they didn't have any built-in intelligence to check whether your current installation was more up-to-date than the hotfix.

Hotfixes now check the system to see if the update is newer or older than what already exists. If your system is older than the update, the hotfix is automatically installed. Otherwise, an error message appears, and installation is canceled. Running the hotfix from a command line using the –m or –q parameter will keep the error message from appearing; the hotfix just exits quietly. Table 1-2 lists the command-line parameters for hotfix.exe.

Parameter	Description
-f	Forces applications to close at shutdown
-l	Lists all installed hotfixes
-m	Installs the hotfix in unattended mode
-n	Keeps system files from being backed up
-q	Requires no user interaction
-y	Uninstalls the hotfix
-z	Doesn't restart the system after the hotfix is installed

Table 1-2.   hotfix.exe Command-Line Parameters

NOTE: Service packs contain prior hotfixes and service packs so that you don't have to worry about obtaining a previous service pack or hotfix before proceeding with the installation.

To keep up-to-date, periodically check the service pack or Knowledge Base Web site for the latest hotfixes.

CHAPTER 2

Capacity Planning

Have you ever found yourself in the position of having to specify a new server configuration and you either don't know where to begin or have no idea whether or not your configuration will have enough power to sustain various workloads? Have you ever wondered when you'll need to upgrade certain hardware or software resources in your infrastructure and how the upgrade may affect existing systems and applications? Do you find yourself usually in fire-fighting mode trying to solve the problem as quickly as possible so that users either do not notice the problem or feel that it was handled in a timely, efficient manner? These are just a few of the common questions you face when supporting or designing an infrastructure.

No matter how you answer these questions, you can quickly see how they affect you, your environment, and users' perceptions. So how can you change users' perceptions? How can you create or maintain a reliable, efficient Windows 2000 environment and minimize or eliminate fire fighting? These questions and many more are addressed in this chapter. By no means will this chapter be your savior for all computing problems, but it will give you a solid understanding of why you need to adhere to *capacity planning procedures,* and it will show you the benefits you can reap from doing so. The beauty of the capacity planning procedures examined in this chapter is that they can be applied to small environments and scale well into enterprise-level systems. This chapter also describes the methodologies and tools you can use to examine and proactively monitor your environment to ensure reliability, availability, and serviceability.

Keep in mind that people, processes, and technology frequently change, so if you don't know where you're going, you'll end up somewhere else.

WHAT IS CAPACITY PLANNING?

Capacity planning originated and matured in the mainframe and minicomputer environments as a way to ensure reliability, availability, and serviceability of computer resources. The capacity planning concept was also carried over quite successfully to UNIX environments. These systems often grew to support a large number of users. Engineers and administrators responsible for the systems quickly recognized the need for proactive monitoring to provide adequate support, immediately and in the future, to end users and the business structure.

History is definitely repeating itself, except that now large numbers of users and businesses are using PCs instead of mainframes or UNIX workstations to perform tasks and transactions. More and more businesses are converting their legacy systems and UNIX environments to PC-based systems because of their cost efficiency, application support, and processing power, among many other reasons. The PC industry is finally beginning to emphasize capacity planning, especially with the increasing popularity of Windows 2000 systems in the business world. The responsibilities now placed on Windows 2000 are becoming far greater than those placed on its predecessor, Windows NT, which makes capacity planning crucial to the successful management of your environment.

Capacity planning is one of the most important and most difficult responsibilities you face with both small- and large-scale Windows 2000 environments. It requires a combination of disciplines and can always be improved upon because work habits and environments continually change. Capacity planning encompasses many aspects of systems management, performance management, deductive reasoning, and forecasting. However, there is more to capacity planning than just using formulas or statistical information. You must use your subjective, creative, and intuitive insight in addition to relying on purely analytical solutions.

Capacity planning can mean many different things and can be applied to many different aspects of business. Its central concept, however, revolves around several key questions:

▼ How quickly can a task be accomplished?

■ How much work can be performed?

▲ What costs are associated with different business strategies?

Capacity planning enables you to stay one step ahead of your system and anticipate future resource requirements by evaluating existing system behavior.

Benefits of Capacity Planning

The benefits of capacity planning are astounding. It helps define the overall system by establishing baseline performance values and then, through trend and pattern analysis, provides valuable insight into where the system is heading. It is an invaluable aid for uncovering both current and potential bottlenecks. Properly implemented capacity planning procedures can reveal how specific system management activities (software and hardware upgrades, changes in network topologies, and so on) may affect performance, future resource requirements, and budgeting strategies. Capacity planning allows you to attend to performance issues proactively instead of retroactively.

DEFINING SERVICE LEVELS AND GOALS

Capacity planning seeks a balance between resources and workloads. It is extremely difficult to provide just the right amount of computing power for the tasks to be performed. If a system is powerful but underutilized, then a lot of resources are of little value and a waste of money. On the other hand, if a system cannot handle the workload, then tasks or transactions are delayed, opportunities are lost, costs increase, and the user (or customer) perceives a problem. Thus, a primary goal of capacity planning is *balance*.

Capacity planning involves working with unknown or immeasurable aspects of a system, such as the number of gigabytes or terabytes of storage the system will need in the next few months or years. Other issues may relate to user workload capacity, such as the number of system administrators that will be needed to maintain the operability of the company's Internet server. All of these questions are related to capacity planning methodologies, and their answers cannot be predicted with complete accuracy. Estimating future resource requirements is not an easy task. However, capacity planning provides a process in which you can establish benchmarks and analyze characteristics of present system resource utilization and use these to make predictions about future needs. In order to achieve a balance between capacity and workload, you must gain as much understanding and control of the environment as possible. Controlling the aspects that are within your reach greatly increases your chances of successfully maintaining the reliability, serviceability, and availability of your system.

How can you begin to proactively manage your system? First, you should establish *systemwide policies and procedures*. Policies and procedures help define service levels and shape users' expectations. Once these are defined, you can easily begin characterizing workloads, which will, in turn, help you define the *baseline performance values* needed to gauge the health of your system.

POLICIES AND PROCEDURES

You should first of all realize that whatever policies and procedures you decide to implement depend entirely on your environment. The process of defining levels of service and objectives for your system gives you a certain level of control over the system's resources. For example, you will gain a thorough understanding of how different components interact with one another and how you can expect the system to function. Without this level of control, it is difficult to understand a system's intricacies much less manage and optimize system performance. Policies and procedures also help you winnow out empirical data and transform it into information that you can use to determine current as well as future capacity requirements. In essence, policies and procedures define how the system is supposed to be used, establishing guidelines to help users understand that they can't always have total freedom to use system resources any way they see fit. In a system where policies and procedures are working successfully and where network throughput suddenly slows to a crawl, you can assume that the reason is not, for instance, that some people were playing a multiuser network game or that a few individuals were sending enormous e-mail attachments to everyone throughout the company.

Two sets of policies and procedures can be established: one set that you communicate to users, and one set that the information systems (IS) department and systems support staff use internally. For example, policies and procedures for users might include a limitation on the size of e-mail attachments and discouragement of the use of beta products (other than ones internally developed) on your network. Internal policies or procedures might include rules that all backups should be completed by 5 A.M. each workday and that routine system maintenance (server refreshes, driver updates, and so on) should be performed on Saturday mornings between 6:00 and 9:00. The following list provides additional examples of policies and procedures that might be applied to your environment:

▼ You can specify that computing resources are intended for business use only—that is, that no gaming or personal use of computers is allowed.

■ You can specify that only certain applications are supported and allowed on the network.

■ You can establish space quotas on private home directories while enforcing these policies through quota management software provided within Windows 2000.

■ You can establish replication intervals for certain databases.

▲ You can specify that users must follow a set of steps to receive technical support.

NOTE: It's equally important to understand what users' expect from the system. This can be done through interviews, questionnaires, and more.

DEFINING BASELINE VALUES

By now you may be asking, "What do I do to begin performance monitoring?" or "How do I perform capacity planning for a new Windows 2000 network or stand-alone machine?" In fact, you've already begun the process by defining policies and procedures, which cut down the amount of empirical data that you face. The next preparatory step for capacity planning is establishing baseline values so you can monitor performance. You need a starting point against which you can compare results. In determining baseline values, you deal with a lot of hard facts (statistical representations of system performance), but there are also a few variables that require your judgment and intuition. These variables are workload characterization, benchmarks, vendor-supplied information, and of course, your data collection results.

Workload Characterization

Identifying the *workloads* of a system can be an extremely challenging task, in part because resources often intertwine among different workloads and vary in processing time as well as in the amount of data being processed. Workloads are grouped, or characterized, according to the type of work being performed and the resources used. The following list shows how workloads can be characterized:

▼ Department function (research and development, manufacturing, and so on)

■ Volume of work performed

■ Batch processing

■ Real-time processing

■ Service requests needing attention within a specified time

▲ Online transactions

Once you have identified your system's workloads, you can determine the resource requirements for each and plan accordingly. This process will also help you understand the performance levels the workloads expect and demand from the system. For example, some workloads may be more memory intensive than processor intensive.

Benchmarks

Benchmarks are values that are used to measure the performance of products such as processors, video cards, hard disk drives, applications, and entire systems. They are one of the most sought-after performance indicators in the computer industry. Almost every company in the computer industry uses these values to compare itself against the competition. As you might suspect, benchmarks are used heavily in sales and marketing, but their real purpose is to indicate the levels of performance you can expect when using the product.

Most benchmarks are provided by the vendors themselves, but they can originate from a variety of other sources as well, such as magazines, benchmark organizations, and in-house testing labs. Table 2-1 lists companies and organizations that provide benchmark statistics and tools for evaluating product performance. Benchmarks can be of great value in your decision-making process, but they should not be your only source for evaluating and measuring performance. When consulting benchmark results during capacity planning, use them as guidelines only and use care in their interpretation.

Company/Organization Name	Web Address
Transaction Processing Performance Council	http://www.tpc.org
Ziff-Davis Benchmarking Operation	http://www.zdnet.com/etesting labs/filters/benchmarks/
Computer Measurement Group	http://www.cmg.org/
Windows Magazine	http://www.winmag.com/ software/wt.htm

Table 2-1. Organizations That Provide Benchmarks

CAPACITY PLANNING MODELS

Because of the diversity of components that play pivotal roles in capacity planning, the process can be approached in many different ways. Capacity planning models can be tailored and applied to virtually any planning need. Some use less formal techniques and general problem-solving strategies, while others involve systematic procedures and distinct capacity planning methodologies. The example in this chapter reflects a more formal approach to capacity planning. However, this model also has characteristics of the less formal approach because capacity planning does not rely on standardization or discrete steps to resolve planning issues.

The general problem-solving process described here stems from the many times my dad drilled into me the problem-solving skills he acquired as a Dale Carnegie instructor. Figure 2-1 shows the general problem-solving process.

As you can see in Figure 2-1, problem solving begins with the recognition that a problem exists. In capacity planning, this might be a file server's slow performance, the anticipation or effects of company growth, or the need to increase workload capacity, for example.

The next step is identifying the source of the problem. One way this is accomplished is by collecting data. Once you have identified the problem's source, you can present and then try possible solutions. Try one solution at a time and then analyze the results. Finally, ask yourself whether the problem is solved. If the problem still exists or the solution presents another problem, you return to the beginning of the problem-solving process. Otherwise, the problem is solved, and you can move on to other issues. Like capacity planning, problem solving is an ongoing process.

The more formal approach to capacity planning uses discrete stages. Each of these stages builds and relies on the other. Throughout these stages, you apply the general problem-solving principles just described. Two important preparatory stages—defining service levels

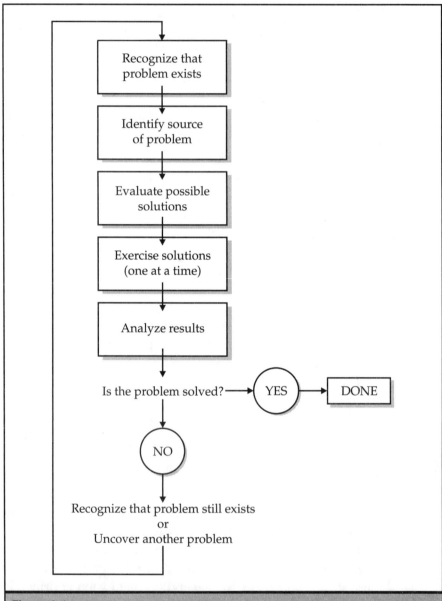

Figure 2-1.   The general problem-solving process

and determining baseline values—that are integrated into the capacity planning model have already been discussed. The following list shows the stages of capacity planning. Each one, with the exception of the two previously mentioned, is thoroughly examined later in this chapter.

- ▼ Define service levels and goals.
- ■ Determine baseline values.
- ■ Monitor system resources.
- ■ Create a measurement database.
- ■ Interpret the data.
- ▲ Report the results.

It is not essential that you follow these stages in the order they are listed here. However, each stage progresses logically from the preceding ones. For example, you cannot create a measurement database without first collecting the necessary data. The capacity planning model presented here is extremely flexible and can be tailored to any type of environment.

CAPACITY PLANNING TOOLS

A growing number of tools are available for collecting and analyzing system data and forecasting system capacity on the Windows 2000 platform. Microsoft offers some useful utilities that are either built into Windows 2000 or sold as separate products that can be used to collect and analyze data. These include Task Manager, Network Monitor, and System Monitor (also known as Performance Monitor), which are built into the operating system, and Systems Management Server (SMS), which is a stand-alone product. Data collected from these applications can be exported to other applications, such as Microsoft Excel or Access, for storage and analysis.

Built-in Utilities

The Task Manager, Network Monitor, and System Monitor come with the Windows 2000 operating system.

Task Manager

The Windows 2000 Task Manager provides multifaceted functionality. It allows you to monitor system activity in real time and to view processor, memory, application, and process status information. You can switch to other running applications or processes, and you can easily end a task or process.

To start using Task Manager, you can use any of the following four methods:

▼ Right-click the taskbar and select Task Manager.

■ Press CTRL-SHIFT-ESC.

■ Press CTRL-ALT-DELETE and then click Task Manager.

▲ Type **taskman.exe** at the command prompt.

When you execute the Task Manager, the screen that you see in Figure 2-2 will appear.

This window contains three tabs—Applications, Processes, and Performance—that you can toggle among. In addition, a status bar at the bottom of the window displays the number of running processes and the percentage of CPU and memory used, as shown in Figure 2-3.

The Task Manager presents valuable real-time performance information that can help you determine what processes or applications are problematic and give you an overall picture of the health of your system. Unfortunately, its limitations, such as its inability to store collected performance information and the breadth of its monitoring capabilities, do not make it a prime candidate for capacity planning purposes. Moreover, it can give you information pertaining to the local machine only. You must be physically at the machine to gauge performance with the Task Manager.

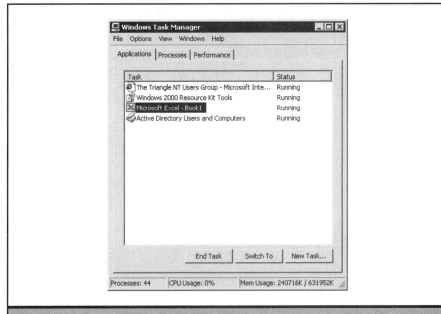

Figure 2-2.   The Task Manager window after initial startup

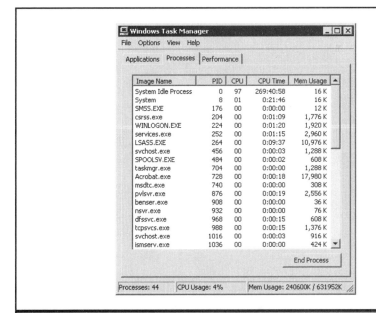

Figure 2-3.   The Task Manager displaying all processes running on the system

Network Monitor (Windows 2000 Server and SMS)

There are two flavors of Network Monitor that can be used to check network performance. One is packaged within Windows 2000, and the other is a component of SMS. Both versions have the same interface, as shown in Figure 2-4, and many functional components, but there are a few differences in what they can monitor.

The Network Monitor, built into Windows 2000, is intended to monitor only the network activity on the local machine. For security reasons, you cannot capture traffic on remote machines. The Network Monitor can, however, capture all frame types traveling into or away from the local machine:

1. In the Windows Components Wizard, select Management and Monitoring Tools and then click Details.

2. In the Management and Monitoring Tools window, select the Network Monitor check box and then click OK.

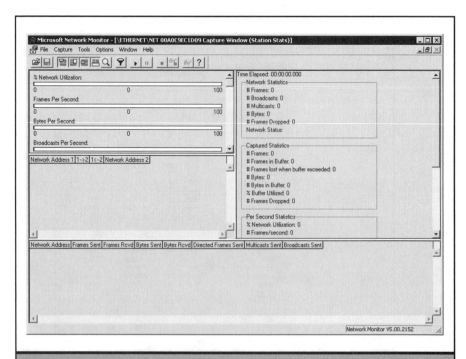

Figure 2-4.   The two versions of the Network Monitor have a similar interface

3. If you are prompted for additional files, insert your Windows 2000 Server CD or type a path to the location of the files on the network.

To use the Network Monitor, you must have the Management and Monitoring Tools installed. To install this service, follow these steps:

1. Double-click the Add/Remove Programs applet on the Control Panel.

2. In the Add/Remove Programs window, click Add/Remove Windows Components.

3. Within the Windows Components Wizard, select Management and Monitoring Tools and then click Details.

4. In the Management and Monitoring Tools window, select Network Monitor Tools and then click OK.

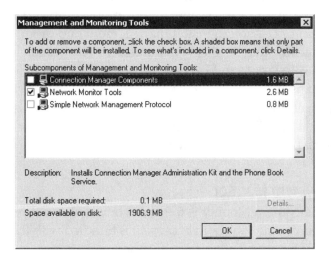

5. After the installation, locate and execute the Network Monitor from the Start | Programs | Administration Tools menu.

The SMS version of the Network Monitor is essentially an enhanced version of the one integrated into Windows 2000 Server. The primary difference between them is that the SMS version can run promiscuously throughout the network and monitor remote machines. In addition to monitoring remote machines, it can find routers present on the network, monitor the traffic circulating through the network, and resolve addresses from names.

CAUTION: The SMS version of the Network Monitor presents possible security risks because of the nature of its monitoring techniques and privileges. It can monitor network traffic traveling into and away from remote machines. Any sensitive data that the Network Monitor captures could possibly be revealed. Consequently, it is imperative that you limit the number of administrators or IS staff members who can use this version of the Network Monitor.

The SMS version of the Network Monitor coincides more with capacity planning objectives because it can monitor several machines at once from a centralized location. Using the Windows 2000 Server version limits the scope of your monitoring and data collection. It also forces you to install management and monitoring tools on every machine that needs to be monitored. This results in additional memory requirements and processing power for each machine. For capacity planning purposes, the SMS version of the Network Monitor is an excellent tool for providing real-time network analysis and establishing historical network performance statistics that can be used to examine the health of your network.

System Monitor

The System Monitor is the most commonly used performance monitoring tool, both because it is bundled with the operating system and because it allows you to monitor every system object that has measurable counters associated with it. The System Monitor is located within the Performance snap-in within the Administrative Tools group on the Start menu. Figure 2-5 shows the System Monitor startup screen.

The System Monitor is also an excellent tool because it allows you to analyze data through charts, reports, and logs that you can save for future scrutiny. This chapter assumes that you will use the System Monitor as your capacity planning tool since it is available

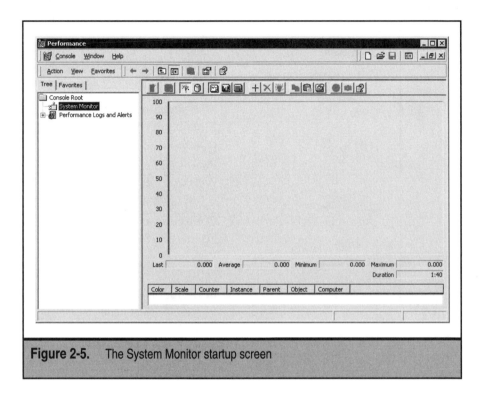

Figure 2-5.   The System Monitor startup screen

to everyone running Windows 2000 and its principles can be applied
to other utilities. Refer to Appendix A for a more complete explanation
of the System Monitor and its uses.

THIRD-PARTY UTILITIES

In addition to the Microsoft tool set, a number of third-party capacity
planning utilities are available for Windows 2000. Some of these tools
are listed in Table 2-2.

These products commonly provide a means for collecting,
analyzing, storing, and reporting statistical system information much
as Windows 2000's System Monitor does. Most, if not all, of the products
also incorporate enhancements such as scheduling or graphical
reporting capabilities. Some even integrate innovative functionality
that promises to automate many aspects of capacity planning. For

Utility Name	Company
PerformanceWorks	Landmark Systems Phone: 800-333-8666 Web site: http://www.landmark.com/ E-mail: info@landmark.com
HP Openview	Hewlett Packard Phone: 800-637-7740 Web site: http://www.openview.hp.com/
Unicenter TNG	Computer Associates Phone: 888-864-2368 Web site: http://www.cai.com/unicenter/
PerfMan	Information Systems Phone: 610-865-0300 Web site: http://www.infosysman.com/ E-mail: services@infosysman.com
RoboMon	Heroix Phone: 800-229-6500 Web site: http://www.robomon.com/ E-mail: info@heroix.com

PATROL	BMC Software
	Phone: 800-841-2031
	Web site:
	    http://www.bmc.com/products/
	    windows2000/

AppManager Suite	NetIQ Corporation
	Phone: 888-323-6768
	Web site:
	    http://www.netiq.com/products/
	    Operations/AppManager_Suite/

Luminate.NET	Luminate Phone: 650-298-7000 Web Site: http://www.luminate.com/ E-mail: info@luminate.com

Table 2-2.   Third-Party Capacity Planning Tools

example, some of the more advanced programs, such as PATROL, perform historical trend analysis and incorporate decision-support models to help you predict future system use.

Whether third-party products add enhanced storage features or GUI enhancements, most are superior in overall functionality to Windows 2000's System Monitor. However, there are advantages and disadvantages to using these utilities instead of the free, built-in utility. A couple of these products are briefly described in the following sections to give you a comparative overview that will help you decide whether to try them. As mentioned earlier, the capacity planning model used in this chapter is based on the System Monitor, but the concepts presented can be applied to the following capacity planning tools as well.

PerfMan

PerfMan, from The Information Systems Manager, is one of the easiest-to-use capacity planning utilities available (see Figure 2-6

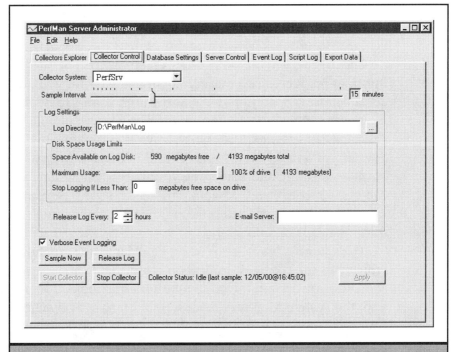

Figure 2-6.   PerfMan's Server Administrator view

for an illustration of the product). This product adequately meets requirements for monitoring and capacity planning in large or small environments. It easily scales from monitoring just a few servers and/or workstations to monitoring thousands of them. Setup and configuration take minimal effort, and the intuitive interface makes the management aspects of system monitoring a breeze.

PerfMan is similar to the System Monitor, yet it provides enhanced versions of such System Monitor functions as data storage, monitoring, and alerting. PerfMan is a component-based architecture consisting of a collector, server, script server, and Web link. The collector component is the module that handles all data collection and summarization. Collection and summarization intervals can be set in seconds, minutes, hours, days, and so on to suit your capacity planning goals. The analyst component is the module that analyzes the summarized performance data from the server module. It can be installed separately from the server module and can be used on any client machine.

PerfMan offers three distinct advantages: it automatically manages historical information, it offers extremely flexible monitoring configuration options, and its reporting functionality is highly intuitive. We will examine each of these benefits.

The first advantage is PerfMan's management of historical information. It creates a measurement database for you and manages administrative operations such as the organization associated with the storage of historical information. The amount of data that is collected can grow exponentially, leaving you with bewildering amounts of data to sift through to find relevant information. With PerfMan creating and managing your management database, you can easily retrieve any relevant data on the fly. Moreover, PerfMan saves you lots of time and removes the hassle of manually searching through heaps of data.

The second advantage of using PerfMan is the flexibility with which you can configure counter monitoring. When logging data statistics, you are not forced to monitor entire objects as you are with the System Monitor. Instead, you can selectively choose which counters to monitor from each object. You simply select the server or workstation that you want to monitor and apply the appropriate counters. PerfMan also permits you to configure default collectors, shown in Figure 2-7. A default collector is essentially a template of performance counters that you can apply to individual servers. For example, if a network has five Microsoft Exchange servers supporting the company's messaging infrastructure, you can create a default collector for a Microsoft Exchange server that has all the counters you want to monitor. You can then simply apply the default collector to the other four servers, and each one will inherit the properties of that default collector. If PerfMan did not have this functionality, you would be forced to manually configure each of the servers. This saves valuable amounts of time.

The third advantage of using PerfMan is its reporting functionality. As mentioned earlier, the analyst module is responsible for interpreting the summarized performance data. It also controls reporting. Reports

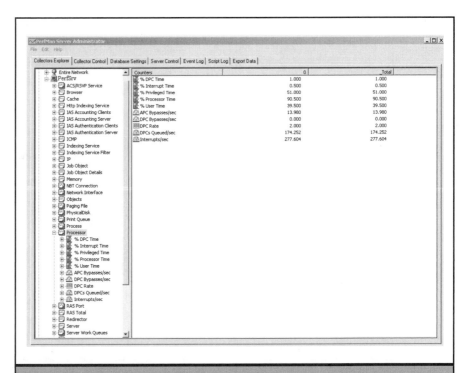

Figure 2-7.   Default collectors can be applied to individual servers in your environment

can be generated in a variety of formats such as pie, 2-D, and 3-D charts, as shown in Figure 2-8, for three types of intervals: none, peak interval, and peak planned interval. Interval designs can be configured through the server module on the Database Settings tab. Depending on the setting you select, you can view average and peak performance for every period that you specify. The peak planned interval charts are best to use when you already know what times of the day are the busiest.

In addition to PerfMan's standard reporting mechanisms, the product includes a Web Link module that allows you to publish reports in HTML for viewing from the Web. Web Link is a Java-based application that uses scripts to generate usage statistics about your environment on the fly. These analytical reports can be easily distributed to those who need the information quickly.

Selecting PerfMan as your third-party utility gives you the ability to automate many capacity planning procedures pertaining to data

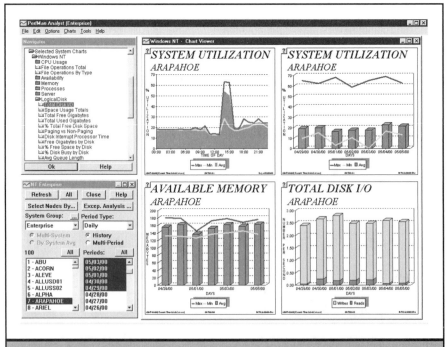

Figure 2-8.   PerfMan provides a variety of useful reporting formats to analyze summarized data

collection and storage. It is an effective yet not overly complex tool that monitors system resources, stores historical data, and can even alert you to potential problems before they arise.

PATROL

PATROL, from BMC Software, is one of the more advanced utilities for capacity planning, providing centralized administration of the monitoring, alerting, storing, and reporting of performance statistics. However, it is unique in that it not only gathers statistics from Windows 2000 (or NT), but it also provides invaluable insight into performance problems, planning, hardware consolidation management, resource balancing, and much more.

PATROL is a suite of products that can be combined to work seamlessly with one another. The base product, which collects the data from Windows 2000 counters, is PATROL for Windows 2000 The other products, listed here, can be added for a powerful combination. The following is a list of a few PATROL products for Windows 2000 solutions:

▼   PATROL for Performance Assurance

■   PATROL for Diagnostic Management

▲   PATROL for MS BackOffice Server

BMC Software also provides PATROL products for a multitude of other server products and applications that you may use in your enterprise, including firewalls, Internet services, and TCP/IP. The PATROL for Windows 2000 product, shown in Figure 2-9, is used to gather statistics of your Windows 2000 environment and monitor its health. The product captures information from all the counters that are available on a Windows 2000 system and stores them in its database. Although you may think that the collection process requires a lot of overhead considering that PATROL is collecting all available data, it actually places negligible strain on the systems being monitored.

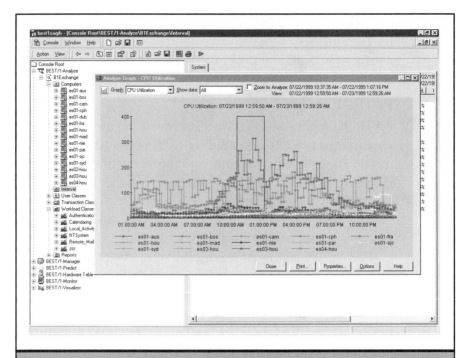

Figure 2-9.　PATROL for Windows 2000 analyzing collected data

The other products specifically mentioned here build upon what the PATROL for Windows 2000 product provides. For instance, the Performance Assurance product analyzes, models, and reports on the collected data to accurately predict how changes in applications or hardware will affect performance. It can also use hardware specifications in its modeling and analysis so that you can prototype a server consolidation or upgrade and see results without having to spend the time, effort, or expense to do so. Essentially, PATROL for Performance Assurance is your crystal ball. By unintrusively investigating different change scenarios, you can foresee how proposed solutions will affect the system, the environment, and your users. (See Figure 2-10 for an illustration of Performance Assurance.)

The information and insight that you gain from this suite of products is invaluable. You'll be surprised at how easily and how well you can stay one step ahead of the system and resolve concerns before they become problems.

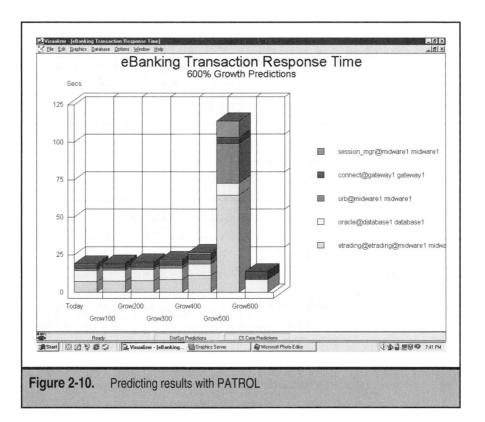

Figure 2-10.   Predicting results with PATROL

MONITORING SYSTEM RESOURCES

You can monitor numerous system resources for the purpose of
capacity planning. In fact, there are so many objects and counters that
you can monitor that you can quickly become overwhelmed with the
amount of data that you collect. If you do not carefully choose what
to monitor, you may collect so much information that the data will
be of little use. Large amounts of data can be unwieldy and can cause
you to spend most of your time organizing instead of analyzing.
Keep in mind that one of the key concepts behind capacity planning
is *efficiency*. Tailor your monitoring to the server's configuration as
accurately as possible.

There are a few important resources that you should always
monitor for every server: the memory, processor, disk subsystem,
and network subsystem. These resources are the four most common

contributors to system bottlenecks. A *bottleneck* is the slowest component of your system and can be either hardware or software. Bottlenecks limit a system's performance because your system runs only as fast as its slowest resource. For example, a file server may be equipped with a 100 MB Fast Ethernet network interface card (NIC), but if the disk subsystem is relatively antiquated, the system cannot take full advantage of the network throughput provided by the NIC. There are also residual effects of bottlenecks, such as the underconsumption of hardware resources. Resources may not be utilized because the system is trying to compensate for the bottleneck.

In addition, the way a Windows 2000 Server is configured functionally influences the resources or services that you should consider monitoring. For example, the most common Windows 2000 Server configurations enable file and print sharing, application sharing, and domain controller functions, or some combination of these. You may want to monitor the effects of replication and synchronization on domain controllers, but not for an application for file and print servers. It is important to monitor the most common contributors to system bottlenecks as well as those that pertain to the particular server configuration.

This section discusses specific counters you should monitor for each common contributor to bottlenecks. Note, however, that there are many other counters that you should consider monitoring in addition to the ones described here. This section is intended to give you a baseline or an absolute minimum number of counters to start your monitoring process. You will find more information on counters and the values you should look for in subsequent chapters.

Monitoring Memory

Of the four common contributors to bottlenecks, memory is usually the first resource to cause performance degradation. This is simply because Windows 2000 tends to devour memory. Fortunately, adding more memory is also the easiest and most economical way to upgrade performance. Figure 2-11 shows the System Monitor's screen for monitoring memory counters in real time. Refer to Chapter 6 for more information on memory and for techniques for optimizing server memory configurations.

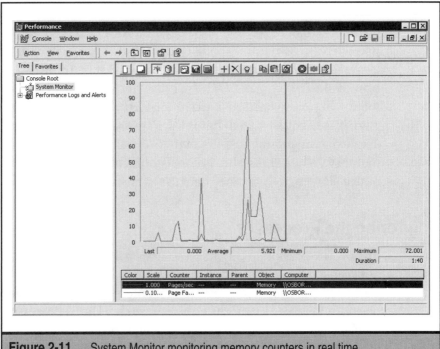

Figure 2-11. System Monitor monitoring memory counters in real time

Memory has many significant counters associated with it. However, the two counters that should always be monitored are Page Faults/sec and Pages/sec. These indicate whether the system is configured with the proper amount of RAM. For more information on memory performance, refer to Chapter 6.

A page fault occurs when a process requires code or data that is not in its *working set*. A working set is the amount of committed memory for a process or application. The Page Faults/sec counter includes both hard faults (those that require disk access) and soft faults (where the faulted page is found elsewhere in memory). Most systems can handle a large number of soft faults without sacrificing performance. However, hard faults can cause significant delays because of hard disk access times. Even the seek and transfer rates of the fastest drive available on the market are slow compared to memory speeds. The enormous latency associated with hard page faults should immediately convince you to configure the system with as much RAM as possible.

The Pages/sec counter reflects the number of pages read from or written to disk to resolve hard page faults. Hard page faults occur when a process requires code or data that is not in its working set or elsewhere in memory. The code or data must be found and retrieved from disk. This counter is the primary indicator of *thrashing* (relying too much on the hard disk drive for virtual memory) and excessive paging. Microsoft states that if the Pages/sec value is consistently above 5, you should suspect that your system may have insufficient memory. When this value is consistently above 20, you may begin to notice slower performance because of insufficient memory.

Monitoring the Processor

The processor is often the first resource analyzed when there is a noticeable decrease in system performance. For capacity planning purposes, there are two significant counters to monitor in the processor object: % Processor Time and Interrupts/sec. The % Processor Time counter indicates the percentage of overall processor utilization. If more than one processor exists on the system, an instance for each one is included along with a total (combined) value counter. If the % Processor Time counter sustains a processor use rate of 50 percent or greater for long periods of time, you should consider upgrading. When the average processor time consistently exceeds 65 percent utilization, users may notice a degradation in performance that will not be tolerable.

The Interrupts/sec counter is also a good indicator of processor utilization. It indicates the number of device interrupts that the processor is handling per second. The device interrupt can be hardware or software driven. The number of interrupts handled by the processor should not exceed 3,500 in Pentium or higher-level machines. Some ways to improve performance include off-loading some services to another less-used server, adding another processor, upgrading the existing processor, clustering, and distributing the load to an entirely new machine. For more information on processors, refer to Chapter 3.

Monitoring the Disk Subsystem

The disk subsystem consists of two main types of resources: hard disk drives and hard disk controllers. The System Monitor does not have an object directly associated with the hard disk controller because the values given in the Physical and Logical Disk objects accurately represent disk subsystem performance.

NOTE: Refer to Chapter 7 for more information on configuring and optimizing the disk subsystem as well as Chapter 3 for information on disk subsystem hardware.

In Windows NT 4.0 and earlier, both the Physical and Logical Disk objects were turned off by default because they could cause a slight performance degradation in older systems. However, in Windows 2000 the Physical Disk object is enabled automatically when Windows 2000 starts.

Today virtually every system component is more powerful than ever, and this is true for components within the disk subsystem as well. As a result, the effects of disk subsystem performance objects are becoming increasingly negligible and, depending on your system configuration, perhaps even unnoticeable. However, even though the performance degradation is minimal and possibly even unnoticeable, you should keep both the Physical and Logical Disk objects disabled unless you are using them for monitoring purposes.

Windows 2000 also gives you a little more flexibility in starting and stopping disk subsystem objects. You can use **diskperf -y** to enable disk counters, **diskperf -y \\mycomputer** to enable them on remote machines, or **diskperf -n** to disable them just as you could prior to Windows 2000. Where the flexibility comes in is in the ability to enable the Logical Disk and Physical Disk objects separately. To specify the object that you want to activate or deactivate, include a **d** for the Physical Disk object or a **v** for the Logical Disk object. For instance, to begin viewing Logical Disk statistics, you must first activate the Logical Disk performance object with the command **diskperf –yv**.

After you have finished monitoring, you should disable the disk performance counters if you don't intend to monitor again in the near future. However, one important point of capacity planning is that you need to always be watching the system and keeping abreast of trends and usage patterns so that you can spot potential problems before they actually occur. The only way to do this is to keep the disk performance counters active.

The best, but certainly not necessarily the only, disk performance counters to monitor for capacity planning are % Disk Time and Avg. Disk Queue Length. The % Disk Time counter monitors the amount of elapsed time that the selected physical or logical drive spends servicing read and write requests. Avg. Disk Queue Length indicates the number of outstanding requests (requests not yet serviced) on the physical or logical drive. This value is an instantaneous measurement rather than an average over a specified interval, but it still accurately represents the number of delays the drive is experiencing. The request delays experienced by the drive can be calculated by subtracting the number of spindles on the disk from the Avg. Disk Queue Length measurement. If the delay is frequently greater than 2, then the disks are degrading performance.

Monitoring Network Performance

Because of its many components, the network subsystem is one of the most complicated subsystems to monitor for bottlenecks. Protocols, NICs, network applications, and physical topologies all play important roles in your network. To further complicate matters, your environment may implement multiple protocol stacks. Therefore, the network performance counters you should monitor vary depending upon your system's configuration.

The important information to gain from monitoring network subsystem components is the amount of network activity and throughput. When monitoring network subsystem components, you should use other network monitoring tools in addition to the System Monitor. For example, consider using Network Monitor (either the built-in or SMS version). Using these tools together broadens the scope of monitoring and more accurately represents what is occurring within your network infrastructure. The Network Monitor displays network utilization percentages, collision rates, and other information that complements the statistics you gather with the System Monitor. Figure 2-12 shows the Network Monitor at work.

This discussion of capacity planning for the network subsystem focuses on TCP/IP. Saying that Windows 2000 relies heavily on this protocol is an understatement. The counters for TCP/IP are added to the system after the protocol is installed.

The objects available for monitoring TCP/IP are FTP Server, ICMP, IP, NIC, NetBT, TCP, UDP, and WINS Server, and there are many significant counters that you should consider monitoring. This section discusses just two for capacity planning purposes; refer to Chapter 8 for more information on what else you may want to monitor for your network configuration.

Two important counters to use for TCP/IP monitoring pertain to the NIC object. They are the Bytes Total/sec and the Output Queue Length counters. The Bytes Total/sec counter indicates the amount of inbound and outbound TCP/IP traffic experienced by your server.

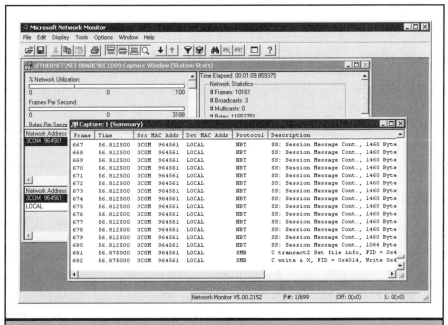

Figure 2-12. Analyzing captured network traffic with Network Monitor

The Output Queue Length counter indicates whether there are congestion or contention problems on your NIC. If the Output Queue Length value is consistently above 2, check the Bytes Total/sec counter for abnormally high values. High values for both counters suggest that there is a bottleneck in your network subsystem, and it may be time to upgrade your server network components.

There are many other counters that need to be monitored and consulted before you can accurately pinpoint the cause of abnormal counter values or network performance degradation. For example, were the abnormal Bytes Total/sec and Output Queue Length values the result of a temporary burst in network activity or unusually high collision rates? If you know that the collision rate is greater than 10 percent, then the problem may be the performance of the overall network and not just the Windows 2000 server in question.

CREATING A MEASUREMENT DATABASE

Now you should have a pretty good idea of what you need to measure for capacity planning purposes: four contributors to bottlenecks as well as the counters pertaining to the server's functionality. You are now ready to start gathering system information and creating a measurement database. Before you begin, note that there are two monitoring stages in capacity planning. The first lasts for a week or two. This is the stage where you will be collecting snapshots of system performance at frequent intervals. The second stage is a process that you will continue throughout your capacity planning implementation.

Initial data gathering intervals are more frequent than routine capacity planning intervals because you are trying to obtain a solid understanding of system statistics. During the first week, use the System Monitor to monitor the system counters you have chosen at up to one-minute intervals. Increasing the frequency of collection increases the amount of data that you gather. Create separate log files for each day to help organize the abundance of data you will collect. It is also very important that you have plenty of disk space for the log files.

Once you've begun to record your data, you can immediately start building your measurement database. The measurement database is not used only to store historical data; it serves as an organizational structure so that the data does not become unwieldy and ultimately worthless to your capacity planning efforts. Most third-party utilities provide excellent measurement databases without any intervention on your part. You just specify what to monitor, and they automatically handle measurement database creation and management. The System Monitor simply stores historical data in binary log files by default. To work around the System Monitor's limited ability to create a measurement database, you can change the binary logging format to a format more suitable for other applications to read, store, and analyze. For example, changing the file format for the System Monitor log file, as shown here, allows you to export the log files to another application such as Microsoft Access or Microsoft Excel.

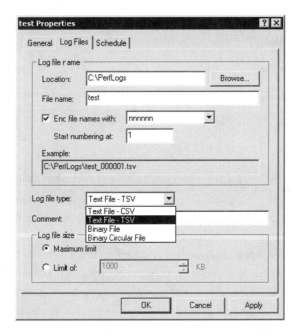

Changing the Log File Format

One of the improvements in the System Monitor is the ability to log data in formats that can automatically be exported to applications such as the ones mentioned earlier. Exporting the data to these types of applications will allow you to more efficiently organize, analyze, and report on the collected data than if you use only the System Monitor. To change the file format for the System Monitor log file so that you can export the file so it can later be analyzed by another application, use the following procedure:

1. From within the System Monitor, expand Performance Logs and Alerts.

2. Select Counter Logs and choose the log file that you have already configured.

3. Right-click the log file in the right pane and select Properties.

4. On the Log Files tab, select either the CSV or TSV file type in the Log File Type drop-down box.

It is important to note that the System Monitor allows four different log file formats:

▼ Binary file (default format)

■ Binary circular file

■ Text file–CSV

▲ Test file–TSV

The TSV file type has its columns separated by tabs, while the CSV file type has its columns separated by commas. TSV files are typically used in spreadsheet applications, and CSV files are typically suitable for databases.

With the data being logged in a format that is accessible by another application, you can easily perform queries and create graphs to help you interpret your data or even present system information in a nontechnical format. Creating and maintaining a measurement database helps you gain a fundamental understanding of the performance data by organizing your records.

Scaling Down the Data Collection

After a week of initial data collection, you should have a pretty good idea of typical system performance levels. You can now scale down the amount of data collection to a more suitable level. This will save a considerable amount of disk space plus the hassle of organizing and interpreting large amounts of data. Typically, capacity planning measurements are taken at 10-minute (600-second) and 15-minute (900-second) intervals. To scale down the amount of data collected even more, monitor the system only during peak activity. By increasing the time interval and narrowing the range of monitoring times, you can greatly reduce the size of the log files.

Another way to reduce the amount of data collected is to reduce the number of counters in the objects being monitored. It may not be necessary to monitor all counters for each object. However, you always may want to monitor the following:

- ▼ **Memory**   Page Faults/sec, Pages/sec
- ■ **Processor**   % Processor Time, Interrupts/sec
- ■ **Logical disk and physical disk**   % Disk Time, Avg. Disk Queue Length
- ▲ **Network subsystem**   Dependent on the protocols used

The counters you monitor for the network subsystem depend on the server's function and the protocols it uses. For instance, with Gateway Service for NetWare, you would monitor the Bytes Total/sec and Packets/sec counters. An important counter to monitor at all times for all Windows 2000 servers is Server: Total Bytes/sec.

Even after you reduce the amount of data you collect, you must keep an organized approach to data collection because your data still can quickly grow to an enormous size. Without organization, the data will become unwieldy, overwhelming, and ultimately useless for capacity planning purposes.

Table 2-3 shows sample performance data from the four common contributors to system bottlenecks.

NOTE: These values are simply examples and should not be consulted for target values.

Object	Counter	Minimum	Average	Maximum
Memory	Pages/sec	0	2.611	22.193
	Page Faults/sec	6.977	29.963	388.202
Processor	% Processor Time	0.496	2.693	16.854
	% Processor Time 1	0	2.67	9.184
Logical	% Disk Time	3.221	27.952	100.000
	Disk Queue Length	0	0.884	3.591
Paging File	% Usage	5.069	5.075	5.079
	% Usage Peak	27.542	27.542	27.542
Gateway Service	Bytes Total/sec	0	519.924	6323.248
	Packets/sec	0	8.039	9686

Table 2-3.   Sample Counter Statistics from the System Monitor

INTERPRETING THE DATA

You must not only understand how and when to collect data but also how to interpret the results. Interpretation requires insight to fully understand the overall health of your system. You can use the collected data to profile current resource demands, characterize workloads on each system, and uncover over- and underutilized resources. Data can also be analyzed for trends or patterns to provide historical snapshots of the system.

For example, suppose that the recent popularity of a server-based application has brought the application server's processor utilization rate to an astounding average of 80 percent. This increase may signal a need for a multiprocessor machine or simply for a processor upgrade. A capacity planning procedure can allow system management staff to predict and prepare for this event proactively. The information obtained through the capacity planning stage can yield an understanding of the general health of the system and help forecast future requirements.

REPORTING

The reporting stage is often overlooked in the capacity planning process. However, reporting directly benefits both IS staff and management.

The IS staff benefits from reports because they provide a wealth of system configuration information such as resource utilization levels, historical capacities, and forecasts in easy-to-comprehend, graphical formats. Reports can also uncover unexplored or unanticipated trends in performance or relationships among resources. The reporting stage essentially takes the technical information that you have been gathering and presents it in a format that is easier to understand. By creating reports that make the available information as clear and concise as possible, you enable the IS staff to make support decisions that benefit the system. Without a reporting process, it would be difficult, if not impossible, for staff to assess system requirements before problems arise.

Reports also provide many benefits to various management levels. System performance reports presented graphically, as shown in Figure 2-13, can be understood by almost everyone, including people without a technical background. Using charts, for example, a report can visually present a system's current performance levels and possible performance scenarios. Many business decision makers cannot afford to be bombarded with raw data and tedious details. Graphical presentations remove the unnecessary details and present clear, concise summaries of information so rational decisions can be made.

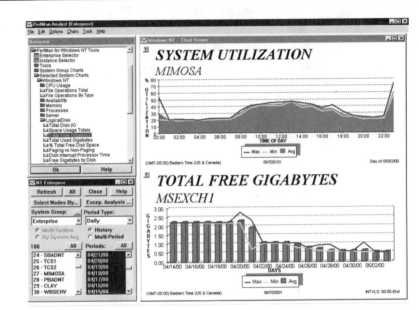

Another view of PerfMan's graphical reporting capabilities

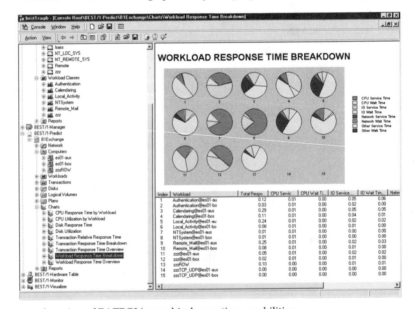

Another view of PATROL's graphical reporting capabilities

Figure 2-13.   System performance reports

CHAPTER 3

Hardware Architectures and Planning

Choosing hardware solutions for an enterprise network is no simple matter. It's imperative that the hardware solution you select today won't be too limited tomorrow. The solution that you select must not only adequately handle the current workloads in an efficient manner; it must also meet or exceed the reliability and stability requirements for your environment.

Changes in hardware technologies seem never to cease. By selecting a system architecture that can scale to meet future processing requirements, IT managers can make sure that the corporate network will have plenty of growing room to accommodate future expansion of the business.

The hardware devices that Windows 2000 supports far exceed what was supported in Windows NT; Windows 2000 provides full support for Plug and Play devices, Advanced Configuration and Power Interface (ACPI) capabilities, and much more. Unfortunately, it's impossible to cover them all in a single chapter. This chapter concentrates on the components that are most likely to affect performance today and in the near future.

SELECTING THE RIGHT HARDWARE CONFIGURATION

Selecting the right hardware configuration isn't just about buying the fastest and latest hardware; it involves a variety of other factors. In fact, many of the decisions you'll make don't involve technical considerations. However, most hardware configurations take a lot of forethought, and the decisions involved aren't trivial.

When choosing the right hardware architecture for your Windows 2000 environment, it is important to examine all of the variables (not just the hardware solutions themselves) to make the best decision regarding performance, scalability, and cost effectiveness. Although the following list is not all inclusive, it contains some of the most critical variables to consider.

▼ Vendor support

■ Budget considerations

- Foreseeable growth in user population or application use

- The types of mission-critical applications that your environment will support and how hardware solutions may affect them

▲ The capabilities of the hardware solution to support high availability, reliability, and other fault-tolerance issues

Hardware Compatibility List (HCL)

You will quickly find that Windows 2000 can cause migraines, sleepless nights, and countless other stress-related ills if it is not set up on compatible hardware. To avoid needless hassles and wasted time, make sure that you have the hardware that Windows 2000 requires. Selecting supported hardware is your first step in performance tuning and optimization.

Compatible hardware means that a Windows 2000 device driver exists for a device, such as an internal adapter, modem, or external storage device, and has successfully passed Microsoft's Windows Hardware Quality Lab's (WHQL) hardware compatibility test (HCT). The HCT is a suite of rigorous testing procedures that stress the hardware and driver beyond normal operating ranges. Original-equipment manufacturers (OEMs) usually test their products in-house first and then ship the hardware to Microsoft for the HCT. All device driver testing is performed at Microsoft to verify the interoperability of Windows 2000, the device driver, and the system or device. For more information on WHQL and the HCT, visit http://www.microsoft.com/hwtest/. Once the hardware has passed the HCT, it can be placed on the HCL.

An up-to-date HCL can be found at http://www.microsoft.com/hcl/. Here, you can search for complete systems or individual hardware components, as illustrated in Figure 3-1, that are certified to run on Windows 2000.

If a system or device is not specifically listed on the HCL, then it most likely isn't supported. Even if various models of a product are listed but the one you are using is not, you should assume that your particular model won't work. For example, if models 540, 540e, and 540ex are on the HCL, but your model, 540xl, is not, you must assume that it is not supported unless the vendor guarantees compatibility.

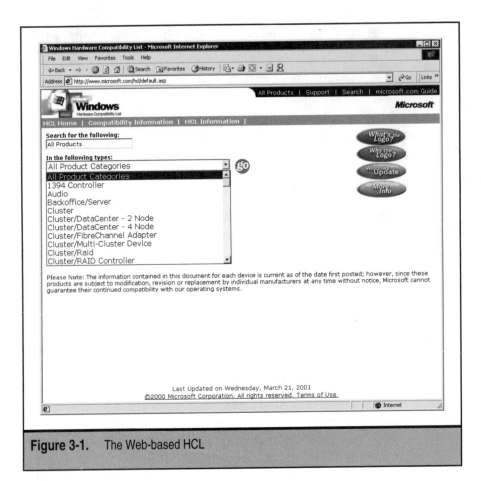

Figure 3-1. The Web-based HCL

Checking the HCL for every system or device for compatibility with Windows 2000 sounds like a hassle. However, it is well worth the effort because you will spend much more time troubleshooting an unsupported system or device than you would have verifying that it is supported.

NOTE: Windows 2000 Datacenter Server hardware compatibility guidelines are so stringent that hardware vendors must be Windows 2000 Datacenter Server certified to sell it. You can't just order Windows 2000 Datacenter Server; it's a complete hardware and software solution.

Choosing the Right Hardware Vendor

Obviously, whether you're buying a specific hardware component or entire systems for your environment, it's important that the hardware meet your needs. Equally important is that the hardware vendor meets your expectations or criteria as a suitable supplier. Meeting expectations, from the first time you talk to a representative until well after you've purchased the hardware, is an important deciding factor for your purchases.

A few of the factors that you should consider before purchasing hardware from a vendor are the following:

▼ Customer service

■ Customer support

■ Pre- and post-sales support

■ Product documentation

■ Product guarantees

■ Support packages offered

▲ Technical support

WINDOWS 2000 AND HARDWARE ARCHITECTURES

Windows 2000 is a robust, reliable, and scalable operating system and supports large enterprise networks and mission-critical applications. As a result, choosing the right server architecture for Windows 2000 is essential. Server architectures, such as symmetric multiprocessing (SMP), cellular multiprocessing (CMP), massively parallel processing (MPP), and nonuniform memory access (NUMA), are evolving to ensure scalability, reliability, and availability. The ultimate goal for these architectures is to accommodate massive growth while providing exceptional performance and promoting cost efficiency.

NOTE: SMP and CMP are well supported on the Windows 2000 platform, but NUMA architectures are just beginning to make appearances for Windows 2000. MPP isn't supported at this time, but it may be in future versions of the operating system.

Much attention has been given to the SMP architecture for its design simplicity, among its many other attributes, with its ability to scale to meet the demands of increasing workloads, but as with any architecture, SMP has its limitations. The scalability limitations of SMP have encouraged the development and/or improvement of other hardware architectures, like the ones mentioned in the preceding paragraphs.

While the ultimate goal of each of these hardware architectures is to accommodate massive growth while providing exceptional performance, each is designed to accomplish this feat in a different manner. Each, for example, offers a different approach to grouping multiple microprocessors into a single server or linking multiple servers into a cohesive cluster. While some server architectures, namely SMP and CMP, present themselves as single entities to mission-critical applications, others, namely MPP and NUMA, closely resemble a collection of independent computing nodes tied together through a high-speed interconnect technology.

Table 3-1 outlines key characteristics of each solution. The sections that follow explore each of the hardware architectures.

Architecture	Vendor Support	Number of Processors	Types of Mission-Critical Applications
SMP	Most, if not all, vendors support SMP	32	OLTP, DSS, data warehousing, data mining, messaging, Internet/intranet, and so on

Table 3-1. Key Characteristics for Hardware Architectures

Architecture	Vendor Support	Number of Processors	Types of Mission-Critical Applications
CMP	Unisys	32	OLTP, DSS, data warehousing, data mining, messaging, Internet/intranet, and so on
MPP	None for Windows 2000	Hundreds (theoretically thousands)	video-on-demand (VOD), data mining, data warehousing, OLTP
NUMA	Vendors, such as IBM, are beginning to provide NUMA solutions for Windows 2000	Thousands	OLTP, DSS, data warehousing, data mining, messaging, Internet/intranet, and so on

Table 3-1.   Key Characteristics for Hardware Architectures *(continued)*

SMP

SMP has been the de facto standard for scalability on Windows NT from the very beginning and continues to be the most common hardware architecture on Windows 2000. It is a simple design by nature, using a shared-memory model where multiple processors share the same resources such as memory space and system bus. As a result, applications running on the machine view the system as having a single processor but still can take advantage of the power of more than one processor. The hardware design coordinates the processors so that a particular piece of data is not being manipulated or modified at the same time. One of the inherent benefits of this design is that applications do not require any additional modifications to run on an SMP system.

Four- and 8-way machines are most common because scaling beyond eight processors used to present costly challenges that severely affected a server's linear scalability. However, most, if not all, of these challenges have been solved, so that 12- and 16-way machines are becoming mainstream. As more processors are added to the system, the bus architecture risks becoming saturated with the increase in communication. This is analogous to a highway system: as the number of cars traveling on the highway increases, so does the likelihood that the highway will experience traffic congestion. One possible solution is to enlarge the bus architecture. However, the minimum performance gain is not always justifiable because the cost increase for the larger buses is exorbitant.

Many vendors design 4- and 8-way processing servers and use a combination of SMP and clustering to provide a means of scaling that is cost effective, especially in terms of total cost of ownership (TCO) and performance. The popular scaling method for servers beyond eight-way machines incorporates clustering. For example, a business that is just as concerned with reliability as it is with raw performance might use a combination of SMP and clustering because it offers increased fault tolerance.

CMP

CMP, designed by Unisys, advances the standard SMP architecture by offering clustering technology within a single SMP system. It differs from the traditional clustering approach in that it can segment hardware resources within a single system rather than connecting separate machines to act as a single unit. CMP systems can be configured either as a true SMP system or as a partitioned, fault-tolerant system. In either scenario, your current applications do not require redesign to run on a CMP system. Current CMP implementations can support up to 32 Intel processors, 64GB of shared memory, and 96 PCI I/O boards. Current system configurations can also use the IA-64 (Itanium) processors once they become available from Intel.

NOTE: At the time of this writing, Unisys is the only vendor certified to support a 32-processor implementation of Windows 2000 Datacenter Server.

As mentioned earlier, a CMP system can operate as one large SMP server, but the real benefit stems from its ability to partition all system resources, including the operating system. Partitioning system resources fosters high availability and reliability because it eliminates the problem of a single point of failure. In addition, it leads to higher performance because data is not transferred through a single bus as in the SMP design. These partitions, called sub-pods, can function independently of one another or collaboratively through high-speed, shared memory paths. Each system can support up to eight sub-pods, each running its own instance of Windows 2000 and each sub-pod containing four processors and shared cache.

High availability and scalability is one of the primary advantages of the CMP architecture. It avoids the inherent limitations of SMP by incorporating directory-based cache coherency, a third level of cache, and a point-to-point, nonblocking crossbar memory interconnect. These combined features exploit Windows 2000's ability to support a large user base as well as high-end, mission-critical applications, such as Online Transaction Processing (OLTP), decision support systems (DSS), and data warehousing. The crossbar technology plays a particularly vital role in eliminating bottlenecks associated with the SMP architecture because it replaces the conventional system bus architecture. Communication between the processors, memory, and I/O devices instead uses dedicated point-to-point connections. The crossbar interconnect not only offers significantly better scaling performance with direct point-to-point communication among resources but also enhances a system's availability, because if one interconnect fails, only the resources attached to that specific interconnect are affected. The other system resources continue normal, uninterrupted operation.

For those of you needing to scale beyond 32 processors, the CMP architecture also supports clustering and other system area network (SAN) technologies that can be used to tie servers together over high-performance communication paths to function as a single system. For example, you can cluster two 32-processor CMP systems to create a 64-processor system. It is also expected that Unisys will continue to improve its Virtual Interface Architecture (VIA) piece for high-performance, low-cost clustering solutions. VIA is a specification defining the high-bandwidth communication interface among servers in a cluster. More information on VIA can be found at http://www.viarch.org/.

MPP

Although Windows 2000 doesn't natively support MPP, it's an architecture that may one day support Windows 2000 systems. MPP systems follow a distributed, shared-nothing approach to scalability. Typically, an MPP system is composed of two or more nodes each operating independently of one another. An easy way to understand the MPP architecture is to view each node as a separate system with its own instance of the operating system, one or more processors, memory, I/O, system bus, and so on. The nodes communicate and operate as a single system through interconnects.

The distributed, shared-nothing approach requires coherency among the nodes to make the nodes function as a single system. There are two approaches to providing coherency between nodes: using hardware (such as in SMP systems) or software (message passing). Since each node runs its own instance of the operating system and owns its own memory address space, MPP systems usually use software coherency due to the high cost associated with hardware coherency as well as the ease of implementation. In fact, message passing contributes to MPP's ability to scale theoretically to thousands of processors. The downside of using message passing for coherency is that latencies can be exponentially higher than hardware coherency latencies. As the number of nodes increases, the latencies incurred can degrade overall system performance.

Although MPP systems can scale to hundreds, if not thousands, of nodes with a relatively simple design, the amount of traffic generated by the operating system instances, as well as the applications among nodes, can significantly affect performance. To promote efficiency among nodes, data must be partitioned to reduce workloads and the amount of traffic being generated among nodes. This adds a level of complexity to applications running on an MPP system. The MPP design creates as many memory pools as there are nodes (each node has its own memory resource). This is in contrast to the single, shared memory pool used in SMP and CMP designs. The application must be told which memory pool contains the data that it is requesting, which is accomplished via message passing among interconnects. Usually, only static data or applications that naturally partition data benefit from this architecture. The most notable application that benefits from MPP is video-on-demand (VOD) servers. MPP is a suitable match for those businesses that need their VOD servers or Web servers (with static information) to support a large user base. Otherwise, programmers are faced with the daunting task of redesigning the application to work efficiently with MPP.

NUMA

NUMA seeks a middle ground between the simple design of SMP and the scalability of MPP. Essentially, NUMA is a hybrid of SMP and clustering. Think of the NUMA architecture as a conglomeration of small, manageable SMP nodes, each with a group of processors, memory, system bus, and so on. These nodes are attached to one another via a high-speed interconnect. At first glance, this may appear to be almost an exact replica of CMP or MPP because of the similar distributed nature. All of the nodes have small, interconnected systems, each equipped with its own processors and memory. NUMA has a few notable differences, however, which enable it to scale beyond a thousand processors on a single system. These differences are as follows:

> ▼   By keeping the number of processors within a node to a low number (usually four or less), NUMA avoids the bus bottleneck because the bus architecture within the node isn't likely to become saturated.

> ■   Although separate memory pools exist in the NUMA architecture, built-in hardware mechanisms allow the discrete memory pools to be treated as a single entity. The hardware (which has less latency than software) brings coherency to all nodes in the system, and running applications are aware of only a single memory pool.

- Similar to the MPP architecture, NUMA uses the concepts of local and remote memory. Local memory exists on the local node, and remote memory resides on other, remote nodes. From an application perspective, local and remote memory structures do not exist, because the two memory structures are managed seamlessly by the built-in hardware mechanisms. Application redesign or tweaking is not required for applications to run efficiently and effectively.

▲ To decrease the potential latencies associated with requesting memory at a remote location, NUMA uses a remote memory caching mechanism. Each node has its own remote memory cache so that it can store a portion of memory addresses from other remote nodes. Information retrieval performance is significantly improved because the process of accessing memory remotely is more efficient.

When an application issues a request to access a memory address, the request is handled either locally or remotely. Since the hardware is responsible for managing the memory pools, it first checks to see if the memory address falls within the local node's address range. If the memory address is not local, then the hardware coherency mechanisms check the node's remote memory cache before attempting to find the data in a remote node.

The NUMA architecture has several derivatives, including cache-coherent NUMA (CC-NUMA), replicated memory clusters (RMC), cache-only memory architecture (COMA), and NUMA-Q. These architectures fall into the NUMA category because their memory access times, or latencies, are not uniform. In other words, local memory access is different and faster than remote memory access.

From an architectural standpoint, the path to take for scalability today is clear; a high performance, lower cost Intel-based SMP or CMP architecture coupled with clustering technologies provides the infrastructure to scale well beyond the 32-processor barrier and into the mid-range and high-end server market. However, as more NUMA architecture solutions for Windows 2000 are developed, they will likely increasingly provide an alternative to the low-end SMP and clustering designs.

> **NOTE:** The next release of Windows 2000, called Windows XP, is expected to natively support the NUMA architecture.

PROCESSOR TECHNOLOGIES

The Intel-based PC architecture is the only platform that Windows 2000 currently supports. The other platforms are different than Intel's architecture because they are based on the *reduced instruction set computer* (RISC), while Intel uses a *complex instruction set computer* (CISC). The major difference between the two architectures is that a computer using CISC performs more tasks to process instructions than its RISC counterpart. The distinction between CISC and RISC architectures in Intel's processors is gradually diminishing. Since the introduction of the Pentium processor, the architecture has incorporated both CISC and RISC characteristics. This is not saying that Intel will eventually produce chips based on RISC, but it appears that the company is definitely working on a compromise between the two architectures.

Intel, AMD, and others have different generations or families of processors that you can choose from based on Intel's *x*86 architecture. Intel has traditionally been the PC market leader until the last few years. Now, AMD has been giving Intel a run for its money, which is ultimately better for the consumer because it increases competition.

Intel has moved away from naming its processors with *x*86 and now uses names such as Pentium, Pentium II, Pentium III, and so on to distinguish the architecture's capabilities in terms of raw performance and feature sets. Each processor is rated in terms of MHz, which basically translates into the number of instructions per second that the processor can handle.

Until the Pentium 4, Intel had built upon the *x*86 architecture. With the Pentium 4, it has moved away from the *x*86 architecture and into an all-new NetBurst microarchitecture. Like the rest of the Pentium family, the Pentium 4 uses a 32-bit architecture. However, the Pentium 4 is the first Intel processor to successfully operate with speeds in excess of 1 GHz.

NetBurst

As mentioned earlier, the NetBurst microarchitecture is a complete change from previous processor designs. Some of the most notable features that NetBurst claims to provide are the following:

▼ **400 MHz System Bus**   Actually, the system bus runs at only 100 MHz, but it pushes four times the amount of data per clock cycle, achieving the effect of 400 MHz. To efficiently support this bandwidth, Intel is using only Rambus DRAM, or RDRAM. RDRAM is detailed later in this chapter.

■ **Hyperpipelined Technology**   This technology doubles the size of the pipeline and increases branch prediction/recovery success rates.

■ **Execution Trace Cache**   The execution trace cache is a fancy name for the CPU's L1 cache. It has been reduced by 50 percent from the Pentium III architecture, to reduce latencies.

■ **Advanced Transfer Cache (ATC)**   This is the L2 cache using 128-bit cache lines. ATC offers exceptional burst rate performance.

■ **Advanced Dynamic Execution**   This feature provides a higher hit rate and more "in flight" instructions (up to 126), so the processor isn't kept waiting for data fetches.

▲ **Enhanced Floating-Point and Multimedia**   With the new Streaming SIMD Extensions 2 (SSE2), NetBurst extends MMX and SSE technologies by delivering separate 128-bit arithmetic and multimedia processing.

Future Processors

What the future of processor technology really holds is anyone's guess, and the abundance of code names, such as Foster, McKinley, Merced, and so on, makes predictions even more difficult. The easiest approach is to view the road as a forked one. One fork leads to 32-bit or IA-32 architecture development, while the other leads to 64-bit or IA-64 processing.

On the IA-32 route, Foster is garnering most of the attention. This processor will be supported by the i860 chipset, which is an upgrade from the Pentium 4's 850 chipset. It's expected to use an integrated Level 3 cache, and some even speculate that Foster will use double data rate (DDR) system memory instead of RDRAM. See "Memory Technologies" later in this chapter for more information on various types of memory.

Although it's possible for Foster to become the Pentium 4 Xeon, other IA-32 processors will also probably make their debut in the near future (in the next year or so). Each one will improve upon the last, and you'll see drastic improvements in virtually every aspect. Don't be surprised if you soon see processors that are capable of operating at blazing speeds of 2 GHz and beyond.

Intel has also been working diligently from the ground up on its 64-bit processor family. Previously code-named Merced, Itanium is now the name of choice for the IA-64 platform. The official release is just on the horizon.

The Itanium line of processors is based on the explicitly parallel instruction computing (EPIC) design philosophy, which is revolutionary when compared to the RISC and CISC processors today. Essentially, EPIC brings advanced speculation, prediction, parallelism, support for IA-64 architectures, and much more to the processor architecture. Also, you can expect Itanium to support new bus architectures such as PCI-X and InfiniBand (see "Bus Architectures" later in the chapter for more information). Initially, 733 MHz and 800 MHz versions will be available with 2 and 4MB L3 cache.

Windows 2000 doesn't support the IA-64 architecture at this time, but when the processor officially debuts, you can count on Microsoft's joining in. Microsoft isn't the only company that has to make a concerted effort to support IA-64; to take advantage of the system, operating systems as well as applications have to be rewritten to benefit from the architectural enhancements. Also, you may be able to run 32-bit operating systems and applications on IA-64 systems, but it's not worth investing in 64-bit computing when you can get the same performance from a less expensive 32-bit platform.

Already on the roadmap as the second processor in the Itanium family is the McKinley processor. You can expect, from the first rollout, that future IA-64 generations will continue to provide extraordinary performance, scalability, and availability to the high-end enterprise market.

BUS ARCHITECTURES

Communication from the CPU, RAM, and cache to other system components is off-loaded from the system bus to other data transfer buses. This releases the system bus from this responsibility and keeps it clear of slower traffic that may impede performance. There are several types of data transfer buses that communicate with other system components. Older varieties are *Industry-Standard Architecture* (ISA), *Enhanced Industry-Standard Architecture* (EISA), and *VESA Local* (VL). The *Peripheral Component Interconnect* (PCI) bus architecture is now the most common, but others are moving up.

The buses are interfaces between the system bus and the devices on your system. Their sizes are 8, 16, or 32 bits, and so on, depending on the bus used. To ensure optimum performance, you should use 32-bit or higher buses whenever possible. However, some components, such as floppy disk drives, may not be able to use 32-bit buses. In such cases, use a 16-bit bus.

The PCI expansion bus is now the industry standard, but it's quickly losing ground as newer buses are being developed. Its design overcame the limitations of the older expansion buses. Initially, PCI offered a 32-bit bus, a theoretical limit of 133 MB/s, and full support of Plug and Play technology. Plug and Play is similar to self-tuning technology in that it recognizes hardware changes and configures devices without any human intervention. Now, multiple 64-bit, 66 MHz PCI buses can be aggregated to produce bandwidths in the 400 to 500 MB/s range.

PCI-X

Despite the advancements of PCI, as standards such as Gigabit Ethernet, Fibre Channel, and so on become more commonplace, PCI buses are bottlenecking performance. As a result, the PCI-X bus was developed, not necessarily to replace the PCI bus but to extend its usefulness and compatibility.

Some of the capabilities of the PCI-X bus are as follows:

▼   Maintains compatibility with PCI standards, including 32- and 64-bit adapters

■   Supports twice as many 66 MHz, 64-bit adapters as PCI, with more efficient data transfers

■   Supports 100- and 133-MHz bus speeds

▲   Can transfer data at rates as high as 1 GB/s

Intelligent I/O (I_2O)

Another standard for Intel-based bus architectures, called *Intelligent I/O*, or *I_2O*, is quickly saturating the PC market. The goal of this industry initiative is to advance I/O systems by reducing the workload on the primary PCI bus, standardizing I/O messaging between the operating system and devices, and establishing a higher level of interoperability among different operating systems—thus increasing a system's overall efficiency and performance.

In current system designs, the processor handles most I/O interrupts. This design bottlenecks the processor's performance because the attention paid to the interrupts disrupts data processing. The I_2O standard, however, releases the processor from having to manage I/O interrupts originating from peripheral devices (such as NICs and hard drive controllers). This frees the processor to do more useful work, allowing the system to handle greater workloads and support more users.

In addition to providing performance benefits, the I_2O standard creates opportunities for developers who write device drivers. Developers can now design drivers that are independent of the operating system platform and device. This independence is achieved through a split-driver model, in which the OS services module and hardware device module are separated. Neither of the components needs to be aware of the specific implementation details of the other, such as its system structure or type of bus architecture, because communication occurs through a standard messaging interface.

InfiniBand Architecture

Envisioning the need for greater I/O bandwidth and redundancy over current industry standards, IBM co-founded and co-chairs an organization called InfiniBand Trade Association (IBTA). This organization is dedicated to designing high-speed I/O specifications. It consists of over 200 companies, including Microsoft, Dell, HP, Intel, Compaq, and Sun.

In late 2000, the team developed the InfiniBand Architecture hardware specification, which focuses on interconnect technology but redefines intercommunication among various systems into a single, integrated system. Although this specification will clearly boost expansion bus performance, its application will more than likely push many other technologies to their limits.

MEMORY TECHNOLOGIES

Deciding what kind of memory to purchase for a server is as important, if not more important, than tweaking what you already have to increase performance. There are many different flavors and configurations of memory to choose from, which can be confusing. The following list shows you some of the factors you will need to consider when purchasing memory for Windows 2000:

▼ SIMMs (single inline memory modules) for older machines, or DIMMs (dual inline memory modules) for Pentium II and higher class machines

■ Error detection and correction

■ RAM speed

■ Cache memory size

▲ Cache memory type

You should be concerned with all of these factors regardless of whether you are purchasing a new system or upgrading an existing configuration. The decisions you make may also depend on your system. For instance, some motherboards and BIOS types support only certain RAM access times, or if you have an older motherboard, it may have slots that match only the 72-pin SIMMs. Whatever you decide should be the result of well-thought-out planning, because the various memory options can significantly affect the system and system performance. Adding more memory of the wrong type or speed, for example, can severely degrade the system instead of boosting performance.

You can use the following sections as guidelines for your memory purchasing decisions. Each section highlights individual issues that you must consider and provides recommendations regarding the best possible configuration for your Windows 2000 system.

SIMMs vs. DIMMs

SIMMs and DIMMs determine how memory is packaged rather than what type of RAM it is. The most notable difference between SIMMs and DIMMs is that the metal connectors on either side of a SIMM are grouped together, whereas the metal connectors on a DIMM are independent of one another. Independent connectors mean more possible signals, which increases the number of address lines and widens the bus interface. In other words, with DIMMs, more data can travel simultaneously between main memory and the processor, which significantly boosts memory performance.

SIMMs are now obsolete. You'll be hard pressed to find even used SIMMs to upgrade the memory of your older systems. Most motherboards, Pentium II and higher, require DIMMs. Instead of using 72-pin connectors, DIMMs typically use 168 pins to connect to the rest of the system. As a result, only one DIMM is required in these architectures, whereas two SIMMs are required for older class machines. Since you can install DIMMs one at a time, you can easily mix different sizes of DIMMs together without any repercussions.

Error Detection and Correction

Older systems generally perform only rudimentary memory tests. These tests don't detect whether there are any impending memory failures. The BIOS test will probably reveal SIMMs or DIMMs that are no longer useful (damaged by static or other means), but in general, memory failures are detected only when the affected areas are accessed. Some memory failures are of little concern, but you may not know which are important until some of your data is corrupted.

What can be done to protect against performance problems due to damaged or corrupted memory? Some memory chips have error checking built directly into their designs. *Parity memory* is capable of parity checking, which determines whether the memory has any errors or failures by adding an extra bit to every byte (8 bits). *Non*parity memory, on the other hand, does not use an extra bit, and consequently does not detect memory errors. This means that parity memory can detect a problem area before data is written to it, whereas nonparity memory would let the data be written.

CAUTION: You can mix parity and nonparity memory, but it is better to use just one or the other.

If you are deciding between parity and nonparity memory, remember that it is always safer to go with parity checking. That way, you will always know when there is a physical problem with memory. Otherwise, you may never know that a problem exists until it is too late. Moreover, the extra checking routines performed with parity memory do not affect memory performance.

ECC

One of the most prominent types of parity checking for system memory is *error checking and correcting* (ECC). ECC helps intercept and correct parity errors before they cause an application, or the entire system, to halt. More specifically, it corrects all single-bit errors and detects all double-bit errors. It employs the same number of bits as traditional parity memory, but all bits serving as parity checks are grouped together instead of being spread across the 64-bit span. This requires a more organized approach to the physical structure of memory, which enables expanded error-checking capabilities.

Chipkill ECC Memory

Advances in system memory technology are drastically improving overall system reliability. One of the most notable advancements in system memory technology is chipkill memory. It protects against memory faults, including complete chip failures, which have the potential to cause significant system downtime and data loss.

Chipkill memory technology offers a level of off-the-shelf, onboard memory fault protection previously available only in the mainframe environment. Advanced failure-protection modules are especially important as the memory in systems increases to 1GB and beyond. With this significant increase in the amount of memory, systems with standard error-correction facilities are projected to have a uncorrectable error rate similar to older parity-only systems. Therefore, as the amount of memory increases, so does the potential for errors. Recent IBM studies indicate the following over a three-year period:

▼   A 32MB parity-memory-equipped server experienced 7 outages per 100 servers.

■   A 1GB ECC-memory-equipped server experienced 9 outages per 100 servers.

▲   A 4GB chipkill-equipped server experienced 6 outages per 10,000 servers.

Chipkill failure-protection DIMMS are the first to provide the self-contained ability to correct real-time, multi-bit DRAM errors, such as complete DRAM failures. Using a high-performance IBM custom controller, enhanced multi-bit error detection and correction are incorporated into the module and are transparent to the system.

The benefits of chipkill memory are enormous, and are essential especially for your Windows 2000 servers. Some of the benefits you'll see are the following:

▼   Far fewer system failures due to memory failure

■   Greater user productivity and customer access

- Better management and control of data and mission-critical transactions

- Minimized potential for data loss

▲ As many as 100 times fewer soft errors than with standard ECC memory

Mirrored Memory

Mirrored memory is yet another innovative technology that helps reduce data corruption, loss of data, and downtime associated with system memory errors. Essentially, mirrored memory employs the same concepts as RAID 1 disk subsystem technology, where data is written simultaneously to two different DIMMs. If one of the DIMMs begins to produce errors, it can set off alerts and have the system automatically switch to the mirrored DIMM. The system keeps running despite the failure, and you can plan downtime to replace the DIMM.

Hot-Swap Memory

Like other hot-swappable system components, such as fans and disk drives, hot-swap memory allows you to add memory to the system or replace memory that is failing without ever having to power off the system. As of the time of this writing, hot-swappable memory hasn't yet reached the mainstream, but this is definitely a technology to watch for in the near future.

Synchronous DRAM (SDRAM)

Over the past several years, older-style memory technologies such as EDO, BEDO RAM, and Fast Page Mode have been pushed to the wayside and have been replaced with faster, more efficient technologies. Only Pentium Pro motherboards and lower-class machines still use the older memory types. As CPU and bus speeds increased, these older memory technologies severely slowed system performance.

One of the replacements for these older technologies is SDRAM. It has proven to be an exceedingly fast and cost-effective memory technology and is used by most, if not all, system vendors. SDRAM describes a variety of different memory technologies today that have a synchronous interface, including Enhanced SDRAM (ESDRAM), Rambus DRAM (RDRAM), and others.

SDRAM adheres to standards specified by JEDEC, a standardization body of the Electronic Industries Alliance (EIA). For more information on JEDEC, visit http://www.jedec.org/. SDRAM is based on DRAM, but it incorporates three features that reduce the amount of time needed to coordinate the operations between memory and the processor: synchronous operation, cell banks, and burst mode.

▼ **Synchronous Operation**   This feature reduces the amount of time the processor spends in the wait state by using clock input that tightly integrates timing between the processor and itself.

■ **Cell Banks**   SDRAM uses two separate cell banks to allow the flow of data between the processor and memory to remain continuous. When one cell fills up or is busy, the other cell continues operation.

▲ **Burst Mode**   At times, the processor may request code or data from only a single address space. Instead of supplying just one address space, SDRAM apportions an array of consecutive address spaces in the expectation that the next instruction will be located within the block already sent out. The principle behind burst mode is similar to that behind the caching mechanisms.

SDRAM is rated in megahertz (MHz), rather than nanoseconds (ns). This makes it easier to correlate memory speed and bus speed. If you want to find out a memory chip's speed in nanoseconds, just divide 1 by the megahertz speed. For example, 1/100 MHz equals 10 ns. Table 3-2 lists some of the common speed ratings of SDRAM in terms of megahertz and nanoseconds.

Speed in MHz	Speed in ns
67	15
83	12
100	10
133	7

Table 3-2. Converting Common SDRAM Speeds

PC100 and PC133

PC100 memory and PC133 memory are certified to run reliably at 100 MHz and 133 MHz, respectively. These specifications were designed by Intel as guidelines for manufacturers, to ensure reliable high-speed operation. Coincidently, the specifications also ensured that memory would function properly on Intel's hardware, specifically Intel's motherboards and processors.

If you're using an Intel motherboard with a 100 or 133 MHz system bus, it's important that you use PC100 or PC133 memory. Using memory that conforms to the specifications guarantees that the memory will operate properly with the other hardware components at high speeds. This is analogous to ensuring that the system hardware is listed on the HCL; you may not have any problems whatsoever with hardware that's not listed, but it's better not to take the risk.

Some of Intel's specifications for memory are the following:

▼ It must comply with Intel's latest component specification.

■ Six-layer PCB boards must be used.

■ PCB boards must use power and ground planes, and the signals can't be routed.

■ The SPDs used must be compatible with the current Intel SPD Component SPEC (version 1.2).

▲ The trace length, count, placement, and topology must strictly follow Intel specification.

Enhanced SDRAM (ESDRAM)

ESDRAM is SDRAM with a little SRAM cache. This memory type reduces latency times associated with standard SDRAM and can operate in bursts of up to 200 MHz. The downside to ESDRAM is that the industry hasn't been very accepting of the new technology, and it's extremely expensive compared to other SDRAMs.

RDRAM

Rambus has developed a proprietary memory design called RDRAM that theoretically operates as fast as 800 MHz. Until recently, big names, like Intel, have also been very supportive of this type of memory.

Although this memory type is available today, many have yet to adopt this solution. There are many issues that need to be resolved. For instance, the claim that it can operate at 800 MHz has yet to be proven. In fact, the relatively small performance gain you may get from using RDRAM isn't worth the exorbitant price you'll have to pay for it. Also, some tests show that latency times are worse than with SDRAM.

Double Data Rate (DDR)

In its simplest form, DDR is a new technology that can essentially pump twice the amount of data into the same clock cycle. This memory is clocked at the same speed as other SDRAM, but operations can occur on both the rising and falling ends of the clock cycle to boost speeds in excess of 200 MHz.

Double Data Rate II (DDR II)

DDR II is the natural progression of DDR. It aims to double the amount of data over the DDR specification. This means that DDR II can pump out quadruple the amount of data that normal SDRAM can. Another advantage to this type of memory is that it reduces power consumption needs, so it could be a viable solution even for notebooks.

NOTE: DDR and DDR II aren't compatible with the standard SDRAMs because they use 184-pin DIMMs.

Mixing Memory

Is it possible to mix different types and speeds of memory? Mixing different types or speeds of memory is analogous to buying hardware that is not on the HCL for a Windows 2000 Server: It may not necessarily cause a problem, but it is not the recommended route to take. Moreover, mixing different types and speeds is not the best way to optimize system performance.

Memory speed is a key component in your decision-making process. First you must find out what speeds the motherboard and BIOS can support. Installing PC133 memory on a system that can support only PC100 access times will not increase performance; in fact, the system will access the memory only at the slower rate, providing no performance gain or other benefits. Mixing different memory speeds may present another obstacle, too. Unless the mixed speeds meet the requirements of the processor and motherboard, you will have to manually set the memory speed in the BIOS to reflect the slower speed.

Mixing memory types is another story altogether. Mixed types should be avoided wherever possible because the results are highly variable from system to system. Even mixing memory from different manufactures may be problematic. Therefore, stick to one type of memory from a single manufacturer.

NOTE: For more information on memory, refer to Chapter 6.

Caching

If you compare main memory speeds to processor speeds, you'll notice that the processor is overwhelmingly faster. In addition, hardware architectures that support parallel processing and other advanced algorithms only widen the gap in speed. The rate at which data travels from memory to the processor is critical to system performance. Unfortunately, RAM speeds are many times slower than processor speeds, so a mechanism must be in place to enable the processor to spend more time doing useful work rather than waiting on memory. One way that the system copes with the significant difference between memory and processor speeds is caching.

A *cache* is a smaller, faster type of memory that temporarily stores the most recently accessed data. It takes advantage of the likelihood that the system or application will access the same information again in the near future. If the needed data is in the cache, it can be retrieved directly from the cache without relying on the bus to push the data to the processor. This reduces the amount of time that the processor sits idle doing nothing.

The type of memory used for caching purposes is called static RAM (SRAM). Some SRAM chip sets have been clocked as fast as 4.5 ns—there is still a performance difference between processor speed and SRAM access times, but the difference is smaller.

Why not use SRAM instead of other system memory types? Although this would be a dream come true for everyone, it is not likely to happen in the near future. For starters, most hardware designs don't accommodate such an implementation. Also, in most cases, the increased speed does not justify the difference in price between other memory types and SRAM chips. When SRAM prices do fall to more reasonable levels, however, don't be surprised to see engineers scrambling to design systems to accommodate large amounts of SRAM.

There are four types of cache: internal Level 1 (L1) cache, external Level 2 (L2) cache, external Level 3 (L3) cache, and file system cache. This chapter discusses the first three cache types. For information on the file system cache, refer to Chapter 6.

Level 1 Cache

Internal, or Level 1 (L1), cache is internal to the processor itself. L1 cache is finite and usually ranges from 8 to 16K in size. A cache controller located on the processor controls the cache. The cache controller enhances the cache's performance by attempting to predict the address space that the processor will need next and then reads the addresses into the cache before the address space is requested. The fact that the cache is integrated with the processor itself makes the travel time from memory to the processor almost negligible. The chances that the processor will experience a wait state when code or data is found in the L1 cache are minimal.

NOTE: Unfortunately, the only way to optimize the performance of the L1 cache is to configure the system with as much L1 cache memory as possible.

Level 2 Cache

The external, or Level 2 (L2), cache typically is larger than the L1 cache, but it is not directly integrated with the processor. Instead, it is located on the motherboard and is controlled by a separate cache controller. In other words, if the system has both an L1 and an L2 cache, the system will also have two separate cache controllers.

The L2 cache is much larger than the L1 cache because it is responsible for mapping large amounts of system RAM. The size ranges from 64K to 2,048K (2MB), but systems are typically configured with either 256K (for systems with up to 64MB of RAM) or 512K to 1MB (for systems with more than 64MB of RAM) of L2 cache memory. Using more than the typical amount greatly increases server performance, because it helps reduce the amount of wait time experienced by the processor. The L2 cache can also serve as a buffer between the processor and memory to improve access times associated with writing to memory. If main memory is busy, the L2 cache records what the processor wants to write to memory, freeing up the processor.

Contrary to popular belief, adding more main memory to the system does not always provide the performance boost that you need. The reason for this is directly related to the amount of L2 cache in the system. Any time you add more main memory to the system, the L2 cache must map the additional address space created by the increase in main memory. As a result, the efficiency of the L2 cache slightly decreases. This is yet another reason why you should configure servers with as much L2 cache memory as possible. Windows 2000 systems with up to 128MB of RAM should have an L2 cache of at least 512K, and systems with more than 128MB of RAM should be configured with at least 1,024K.

Are there different varieties of SRAM? Which one provides the best overall performance? SRAM, used for L2 cache, comes in three distinct flavors: asynchronous SRAM (async SRAM), synchronous burst SRAM (sync SRAM), and pipelined burst SRAM (PB SRAM).

Async SRAM   Async SRAM has been used in systems dating back to the 386. Access times for this cache are typically 12 to 15 ns, which is faster than with many conventional memory types but not fast enough to keep up with modern Pentium or higher-class machines. This type of cache actually can hinder performance because it causes the processor to experience wait states. It operates much the same way as main memory in that it retrieves code or data after the processor asks for it. For this reason, it is recommended that you don't use async SRAM for your Windows 2000 systems.

Sync SRAM   Sync SRAM uses the burst method described earlier, reading in three more memory addresses than the number originally requested. In addition, its synchronous operation provides an extremely fast rate, so the processor does not experience wait states when receiving code or data. The catch, however, is that sync SRAM provides exceptional performance only when bus speeds are 66 MHz or less. Performance actually begins to decline when sync SRAM is used with higher bus speeds. However, if you are using a system with a 66 MHz or slower bus speed and it supports sync SRAM, then this type of cache will out-perform all other cache types.

PB SRAM   PB SRAM, another high-speed synchronous burst cache, employs pipelining. Pipelining uses registers to load code or data that can be used by the processor. The first cache cycle, initiated by the processor, takes three clock cycles to complete, but the speed advantage comes from the additional three sequential read operations: The next three cache cycles are each completed in one clock cycle (3-1-1-1). No matter what bus speed the system runs at, PB SRAM always operates at 3-1-1-1. It is the fastest of the three cache types for systems with bus speeds above 66 MHz.

Level 3 Cache

Research done by IBM shows that system memory accounts for 40 to 70 percent of the overall cost of a system and is gradually becoming a performance bottleneck. As a result, IBM is currently developing a Level 3, or L3, cache based on its Memory eXpansion Technology (MXT). The goal behind L3 cache is to increase memory capacity and increase overall system performance. It boasts a more efficient storage format that can help reduce costs by using less memory without sacrificing performance. Because of its enhanced data storage formatting, L3 cache would decrease reads and writes to the disk subsystem.

DISK SUBSYSTEM DEVICES

One of the most important decisions you face when configuring Windows 2000 is choosing the type of hardware components you will use for the disk subsystem. Your decision includes the drive type, disk controller type, and bus interface. As with many other components that make up a Windows 2000 system, there are plenty of choices. Thankfully, though, when it comes to performance and reliability, the choices for the disk subsystem hardware boil down to just a few.

This section focuses on the choices that you have for the type of disk drive your system will use. Other performance, reliability, and stability characteristics pertaining to disk subsystem as well as other hardware related information are discussed in Chapter 7.

In the past several years, hard drives have undergone considerable changes that not only affect how much data you can store but, more important, the speed at which you can retrieve and use stored data. There are two types of drives that are currently still in the race for high performance: drives that use IDE/EIDE and SCSI interfaces. However, newer standards, such as the Fibre Channel and FireWire technologies, which promise even greater performance enhancements, are just around the corner. This section examines the IDE/EIDE and SCSI interfaces and compares the two technologies. It also discusses some of the new technologies on the horizon.

Primary and Secondary Storage

Hard disk drives are the primary storage devices you will be most concerned with when it comes to performance. However, you should keep in mind that many forms of secondary storage devices offer storage alternatives as well as fault tolerance. These include tape drives, solid state drives (SSDs), removable drives, DVDs, and optical drives.

If you are considering SSDs, you should note that although this technology is rapidly improving and SSDs could potentially improve Windows 2000 disk subsystem performance, SSD technology is still relatively new, and some time will pass before SSDs will be recommended for use with Windows 2000 systems. It is certainly too early to count SSDs out of the performance race, however, because they are already boasting very fast access times and transfer rates. An SSD is essentially a RAM disk housed in its own casing, but instead of using the system's physical memory, SSDs commonly use Flash RAM or other high-speed chipsets. SSDs do not contain movable parts, so performance is not hindered by mechanical latencies. However, solid-state drives are not recommended at this time because Flash RAM, despite its high speed, has a finite life. It also can be written to only a finite number of times, which limits its use.

Several manufacturers have improved SSD technology over the last few years, making SSDs a viable option in some scenarios. Compaq Computer Corporation is one vendor that has made great strides in manufacturing SSDs. For more information, visit Compaq's SSD Web site, at http://www.compaq.com/products/storageworks/Hard-Disk-Storage/solidstatedisks.html.

Hard Drive Mechanics and Terminology

Before you begin considering hard disk specifications, controller cards, and so on, you should have an understanding of the physical makeup of the hard disk drive and be familiar with the terminology associated with the disk subsystem. Arming yourself with this knowledge will help you shop wisely when purchasing disk subsystem components and achieve the best level of performance for your system.

The hard disk drive consists of many moving parts that work together to read, store, and transfer data. The primary components are the platters, read/write heads, and actuator.

▼ **Platters** The platters are the actual magnetic media that store the data. The number of platters in the disk drive depends on the capacity of the drive. Each platter is attached to a central spindle and motor that spins the platters.

■ **Read/Write Heads** The heads that read and write data onto the platters are attached to a head stack assembly. The number of heads on the disk drive depends on the drive's capacity and performance characteristics. Typically, the higher the performance rating of the drive, the more heads it has. Most modern drives have heads located on either side of the disk to decrease the time it takes to read and write data. These heads (and the rest of the drive's assembly) are extremely sensitive. In fact, if dust particles were to contaminate the inside drive mechanics, the drive could be severely damaged. This is why it is so important not to open the drive chassis.

▲ **Actuator** This is the motor that rapidly moves the entire head stack assembly so the heads can read and write data.

When information is read from or written to the disk, the process proceeds in an orderly fashion. Formatting the hard drive gives the platters organization. The platter is divided into tracks, sectors, and cylinders. Figure 3-2 shows the organizational structure of each platter.

▼ **Track** Tracks are analogous to the lanes of a running track. They are narrow lanes circulating the platter. Track 0 is the innermost track, and track n (where n is the number of tracks on the platter) is the outermost track.

■ **Sector** Platters are further segmented by sectors, which are essentially containers for storing data. Typically, each sector is 512 bytes.

▲ **Cylinders** Cylinders are similar to tracks, but a cylinder is a pair of tracks on opposite sides of the platter. For example, on a disk drive with five platters, each cylinder has ten tracks.

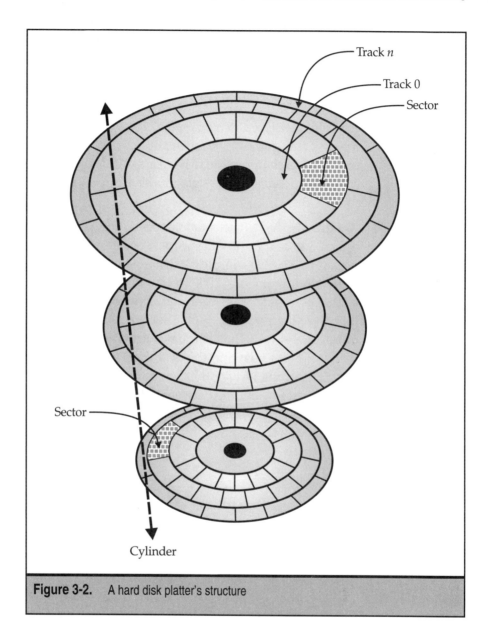

Figure 3-2.   A hard disk platter's structure

Now that you have an understanding of a hard disk drive's mechanics, you can begin thinking about performance. What factors determine a drive's performance? The most important are the data transfer rate, rotation speed, rotational latency, seek time, head switch time, cylinder switch time, and access time.

▼ **Data Transfer Rate**   The data transfer rate is the overall transfer rate of data from the hard disk to the CPU for processing and is typically measured in megabytes per second (MBps). It combines the disk transfer rate (the speed at which data is transferred to or from the platter to the drive controller) and the host transfer rate (the speed at which data travels from the drive controller to the CPU).

■ **Rotation Speed**   The rotation speed of the drive is sometimes referred to as the spindle speed. It is measured in revolutions per minute (rpm). Hard disk drives spin at a constant rate, with speeds ranging from 3,000 to 15,000 rpm. The rotation speed and data transfer rate are directly proportional, meaning that the faster the rotation, the higher the data transfer rate. It is important to note that as the rotation speed increases, so does the amount of heat that the drive produces. Thus, to keep the drive operating efficiently and to maintain the drive's life expectancy (mean time between failures), it is very important to keep the drives cool. It is always a good idea to configure the system with additional fans to keep the drives from overheating.

NOTE: The *mean time between failures*, or *MTBF*, is the average time that a disk drive will run before it fails. Manufacturers commonly boast that the MTBF is between 500,000 and 1.2 million hours—57 to 137 years!—assuming that the drive runs 24 hours a day. In truth, the drive might fail tomorrow, especially if you let it overheat, or it may last beyond your lifetime.

■ **Rotational Latency**   Rotational latency, measured in milliseconds (ms), is the amount of time it takes for the drive head to locate the requested sector after being positioned over the appropriate track. The rotational latency is inversely proportional to the rotational speed: the faster the rotation speed, the lower the rotational latency. For example, at 5,400 rpm, the latency is approximately 6 ms; at 7,200 rpm, it is approximately 4 ms; at 10,000 rpm, it is slightly under 3 ms; and at 15,000 rpm, it is 2 ms or less. Notice that the rotational latency decreases at a slightly reduced rate as the rotation speed increases.

■ **Seek Time**   This is a measurement (in ms) of the amount of time it takes the actuator arm to move from one track to the next. Obviously, the fastest seek times occur when the head reads or writes data sequentially, and the worst times occur when the actuator arm must move from the outermost to the innermost track (known as a full-stroke seek). The most relevant seek time is the average seek time because it better represents a drive's ability to find the requested data than does any single seek time. The average seek time is defined as the time it takes to locate a track during a random read. Typical average seek times for most modern drives range from 3 to 13 ms.

■ **Head Switch Time**   Head switch time is the average amount of time (in ms) required to switch to another head to read or write data. Since all heads are connected to a single actuator arm and only one head can read or write data at a time, this measurement helps define the drive's actual performance capabilities.

■ **Cylinder Switch Time**   The cylinder switch time is the average amount of time (in ms) required to move the head from one track to another located on a different cylinder.

▲ **Access Time**   The access time is a convenient combination of seek time, head switch time, and cylinder switch time.

IDE/EIDE

The IDE interface has been around since 1985 and was originally called the AT-Attachment (ATA) because of its interoperability with the IBM PC/AT computer. Its original design offered simplicity and cost efficiency—benefits it still offers today, with prices continually dropping.

However, the IDE interface provides its benefits at the cost of performance. Promises that the drives could sustain approximately 8 MBps were replaced with the reality of speeds of about 3 MBps, because the IDE architecture relies on programmed I/O (PIO), where the CPU handles all data transfers in a nonsynchronized fashion. Thus, only one transfer can take place at a time. During PIO transfers, the disk controller sends the data (ranging from 512 bytes to 64K) to memory. The CPU then moves the data to its destination. This process impedes performance and creates overhead for the CPU. In addition, because of DOS and BIOS limitations, the capacity of IDE drives is limited to 528MB. These performance inefficiencies crippled the system.

To deal with IDE's problems, Western Digital offered the Enhanced IDE (EIDE) specification. Since EIDE's introduction, transfer rates have improved considerably. EIDE still relies on PIO but achieves higher transfer rates through PIO and direct memory access (DMA) mode changes. DMA, also known as bus mastering, reduces a drive's reliance on the CPU to handle data transfers. To gain the advantages of DMA, make sure that your system is running the latest version of the BIOS and the IDE/EIDE device drivers.

In addition, extensions to the EIDE specification, such as ATA-2 and ATA-3, have introduced new PIO and DMA modes with even better transfer rates. Table 3-3 shows the various mode types and their respective transfer rates for the IDE/EIDE drive type. The ATA-3 specification, for example, uses PIO mode 5, which has a maximum transfer rate of 22.2 MBps, and DMA mode 5, which claims an astounding 33.3 MBps.

Specification	Mode	Transfer Rate (MBps)
ATA	PIO mode 0	3.3
	PIO mode 1	5.2
	PIO mode 2	8.3
	DMA mode 0	4.2

Table 3-3.   IDE/EIDE Modes and Transfer Rates

Specification	Mode	Transfer Rate (MBps)
ATA-2	PIO mode 3	11.1
	PIO mode 4	16.6
	DMA mode 1	13.3
	DMA mode 2	16.6
ATA-3/Ultra ATA	PIO mode 5	22.2
	DMA mode 3	33.3

Table 3-3.   IDE/EIDE Modes and Transfer Rates *(continued)*

EIDE has also incorporated changes to remove limitation on the drive capacity and the number of devices that can be supported on a system. It alleviates the drive capacity limitation by supporting logical block access (LBA) mode. LBA is a BIOS function that translates track, head, and sector information into logical block numbers to allow the entire disk to be recognized and used. EIDE also provides an additional channel so that an extra two drives can be attached to the system (for a total of four IDE/EIDE devices) as well as AT Application Programming Interface (ATAPI) support for nondisk peripherals such as CD-ROM drives and tape drives.

Note that to gain the best performance possible when configuring the system with more than just hard drives, the hard drives should be placed on the primary channel, and the nondisk drives should be on the secondary channel, as shown in Figure 3-3. There are two reasons for this. First, the more advanced PIO and DMA modes are generally not supported on the second channel, which would severely hamper performance if the hard drives were put on the secondary channel. Second, devices on the same channel cannot operate independently; only the channels can operate independently. Therefore, if the hard drive and nondisk drive are mixed on both channels, the hard drive will have to wait for the slower device before it can begin its next task.

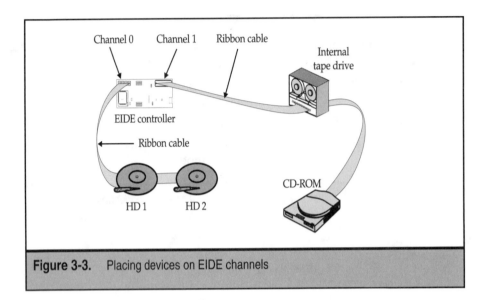

Figure 3-3. Placing devices on EIDE channels

The physical design of EIDE drives is similar to that of the original IDE drives, where the controller functions are located on the drive rather than on the disk controller itself. This keeps the price of EIDE drives comparable as well. The relatively low cost of EIDE drives and the performance enhancements achieved make the EIDE specification a viable choice for your Windows 2000 Server disk subsystem.

SCSI

SCSI is a communication standard that hosts specifications SCSI-1, SCSI-2, and SCSI-3. Each succeeding specification improves on the previous specifications, providing better performance and compatibility.

Microsoft has always touted the use of SCSI in Windows 2000 server systems for maximum disk subsystem performance. Why has Microsoft recommended SCSI over IDE/EIDE? For starters, SCSI is device independent, which means that the machine does not need to know about the SCSI controller or the devices attached to it. Its design also facilitates scalability. For example, devices (including nondisk drives) can be daisy-chained on a single controller, enabling many devices to be supported simultaneously. Some SCSI controllers allow as many as 15 additional devices to be connected! More important, however, is the performance SCSI allows. As the specifications are defined, you will clearly see why SCSI maximizes performance. The section "EIDE vs. SCSI" later in this chapter describes more reasons why Microsoft urges you to use SCSI for optimal performance.

SCSI-1

SCSI-1 was introduced in the early 1980s as the first interface specification that let a single controller manage up to seven devices in a daisy chain. It uses an 8-bit wide data path to synchronously transfer data at rates up to 5 MBps. Although the transfer rates were clearly faster than IDE rates (approximately 3 MBps) at the time, there were also other advantages to using the new specification. It is scalable (it supports up to seven SCSI devices), it uses bus-mastering techniques instead of PIO to reduce CPU processing overhead, and it multitasks I/O operations. The use of bus mastering or DMA removes much of the responsibility placed on the CPU for data transfers.

Clearly, the SCSI-1 specification started on the right foot, and it consequently rapidly gained acceptance from the industry. However, with today's demands for large disk capacity and fast transfer rates, SCSI-1 should not be considered, not even for low-end servers or workstations, much less for your Windows 2000 Server.

SCSI-2

As you might expect, SCSI-2 defines faster transfer rates and wider data paths than SCSI-1. In addition, SCSI-2 eliminated many incompatibility problems by including more device models such as CD-ROM drives, tape drives, and scanners.

SCSI-2 is blazingly fast in comparison to its predecessor. The specification offers synchronous data rates of up to 10 MBps (called Fast SCSI-2) on an 8-bit wide data path. It also incorporates a 16-bit wide data path (Fast/Wide SCSI-2) with double the transfer rate of Fast SCSI-2 (20 MBps).

SCSI-2 also supports more devices on a single controller (from 7 to 15) and offers improved cache management and parity checking compared to SCSI-1.

SCSI-3

While SCSI-2 is treated as a single specification, the SCSI-3 standard can be broken into subsets, each with its own related SCSI specification. SCSI-3 is divided into subsets because the standard is still evolving. As with the other successors to the SCSI communication standard, SCSI-3 improves on performance and maintains backward compatibility. Even though the specification is still evolving, many notable features have emerged from SCSI-3, including FAST-20, FAST-40, Fibre Channel, and FireWire. The FAST-20 specification can achieve data transfer rates of up to 20 MBps, and FAST-40 essentially can achieve data rates twice as fast (40 MBps). The Fibre Channel and FireWire specifications are discussed in detail later in this chapter.

EIDE vs. SCSI

The debate over which interface technology—EIDE or SCSI—is the best has been going on for ages, with each side claiming to offer the best solution for storage requirements. This section examines the differences between the two interfaces and the implications for Windows 2000 Server performance. More specifically, this section looks at the cost, ease of use, speed, and scalability aspects of these two interface technologies. The best choice for your Windows 2000 disk subsystem will become more apparent after you read this section.

Cost

As we know all too well, money is not an infinite resource. Most IT budgets are limited, and as a result, care must be taken when purchasing new equipment. From a price perspective, EIDE is definitely a sound choice. It offers excellent quality and relatively high performance at unbelievably low cost. A SCSI drive offers high-end drive performance and scalability—but you bear the cost; don't be surprised to pay 15 to 40 percent more for SCSI drives. Moreover, SCSI controllers are considerably more expensive than EIDE controllers.

Ease of Use

EIDE technology aims for simplicity and ease of use. When designing a system to use the EIDE interface, you have to configure at most four drives on two separate channels. Furthermore, you can set up multiple drives in a master-slave relationship without worrying about terminating electrical signals.

Ease of use is definitely one of SCSI's shortcomings. The terminology alone makes SCSI difficult to use. Design plans require you to match drive controllers types to the particular SCSI specification being used, determine the number of channels the drive controller should have, choose between single-ended or differential SCSI and active or passive electrical termination, configure SCSI IDs, and so on.

In fact, most, if not all, of the hardware problems associated with SCSI result from cabling or termination issues. It is imperative that you purchase the highest-quality cabling and terminators to avoid these unnecessary hassles. For more information on cabling and terminators, refer to "Avoiding Cabling and Termination Problems" in Chapter 7.

There is one area where SCSI does surpass EIDE in terms of ease of use. SCSI allows you to attach external devices with little additional configuration. EIDE does not let you attach external devices at all; there is no such thing as an external EIDE device that can attach to the EIDE controller. The ability to attach additional devices externally is very useful when, for instance, you need to expand hard disk drive capacity or install a device such as a scanner.

Speed

The ability to transfer large amounts of data in a small amount of time is one of the most important aspects of the disk subsystem that you should be concerned with. Both EIDE and SCSI have come a long way since their debuts, and each provides exceptional performance. The methods that these two standards use to obtain their high transfer rates have always been different. It is this difference that separates the two.

From the start, SCSI has used bus-mastering techniques for data transfers to system memory; only a few of the older SCSI drives relied on PIO for data transfers. This approach not only increases transfer rates, but it also reduces CPU use relating to data transfers. This technique uses the SCSI drive controller DMA logic rather than the system DMA controller; no CPU intervention is required to transfer data to memory. Most SCSI drive controllers are equipped with a RISC-based processor (typically from the 68000 series) that assists in processing data transfers.

SCSI also easily handles the multiple simultaneous I/O operations common in Windows 2000 and other multitasking environments. Windows 2000 uses an asynchronous I/O model that allows it to communicate with multiple devices simultaneously, and SCSI is designed to take advantage of this model. When a request for a file is issued, Windows 2000 informs the controller, and the controller passes the request over the SCSI bus. A device on the SCSI bus, called the responder, responds to the request. At this point, the device disconnects (goes offline) to find the file. Shortly thereafter, it reports to the controller that the file has been found. During the disconnection phase, another request can be initiated and sent over the SCSI bus.

The advantages of SCSI's ability to handle overlapping I/O requests can be truly appreciated only in a preemptive multitasking operating system environment such as Windows 2000. The benefits of multitasking I/O are especially salient when the system has more than one SCSI drive. This makes sense because where else would the next request go if there was only one drive and it was temporarily disconnected? When the system is configured with more than one SCSI disk drive, you can expect significant performance advantages. Multitasking and bus mastering are the two primary reasons why SCSI transfer rates can reach 20 or 40 MBps, and in some cases, more than 100 MBps.

NOTE: The SCSI-3 standard includes Fibre Channel technology, which currently claims maximum transfer rates in excess of 100 MBps.

In comparison to the SCSI standard, EIDE transfer rates are much slower. Even the new ATA-3 interface supports a maximum transfer rate of only 33.3 MBps. This may be sufficient for workstations or low-end Windows 2000 Server systems but not for high-end servers that need to support heavy transfer loads. For example, you would not want to use EIDE on SQL servers, Exchange Servers, and so on.

EIDE also has some other performance drawbacks. The ATA-2 and ATA-3 implementations do indeed enhance EIDE by providing bus mastering techniques. However, the CPU still is responsible for significantly more data transfers than is the case in systems employing SCSI. In addition, many EIDE devices still support only PIO modes of operation. You may recall that this requires the CPU to handle all data transfers, which entails CPU overhead. Performance is also hampered by the fact that EIDE can handle only one I/O operation at a time per channel, and you are limited to two channels.

Scalability

The ability to easily scale systems to meet the continually changing and challenging demands placed on the system is of utmost importance. It is critical to be able to add devices without having to go through a major system overhaul. Disk subsystems employing the EIDE standard are limited from the very beginning. As previously mentioned, EIDE can support up to 4 disk drives. What happens when the maximum disk capacity has been reached? Your only choice is to replace one or more drives. With SCSI, this is not the case even if the existing SCSI channels contain the maximum of 7 or 15 devices. To extend capacity, you simply install an additional SCSI controller adapter or add external devices. Neither of these options is available with EIDE.

SCSI also supports a wider variety of device types than EIDE. It supports both internal and external devices such as hard disk drives, CD-ROM drives, tape drives, and scanners. Although the ATAPI specification enables EIDE to support more than just hard disk drives, support is generally limited to CD-ROM drives and tape drives. External devices are presently not supported by the EIDE interface.

The Best Device for Windows 2000 Performance

SCSI defends its title as the preferred choice in a Windows 2000 environment. It provides exceptional performance and offers the most advanced solution available for configuring Windows 2000 servers with large amounts of drive capacity.

The SCSI specification continues to evolve at a more rapid pace than the IDE/EIDE specification. For instance, SCSI drives are constantly breaking speed records and now have speeds over 15,000 rpm.

The following list summarizes the reasons why you should choose SCSI over EIDE for a Windows 2000 server:

▼ True multitasking support

■ High data transfer rates, in excess of 100 MBps

■ Compatibility; SCSI supports more devices (internally and externally)

■ Bus mastering efficiency

▲ Scalability; some SCSI specifications can support up to 15 additional devices on a single channel, depending on the type of controller used

All of these performance benefits make SCSI the best choice for Windows 2000 server systems, especially in systems such as file servers that handle primarily I/O-related functions. Here is a general rule of thumb: always use SCSI, but if your budget forces you to choose less expensive EIDE, you should limit its use to low-end servers or servers primarily running memory-resident applications such as a firewall.

Fibre Channel Arbitrated Loop (FC-AL)

Based on the SCSI-3 standard and a subset of the Fibre Channel Specification Initiative, Fibre Channel Arbitrated Loop (FC-AL) is an up-and-coming architecture that promises amazing transfer speeds and device support. It uses a serial loop rather than a bus architecture, which allows data to be transferred from device to device, as shown in Figure 3-4. In a single-channel configuration, FC-AL boasts speeds of approximately 100 MBps, and in a dual-channel configuration, speeds can easily exceed 200 MBps. As you can see, FC-AL easily overcomes the bandwidth limitations of standard SCSI.

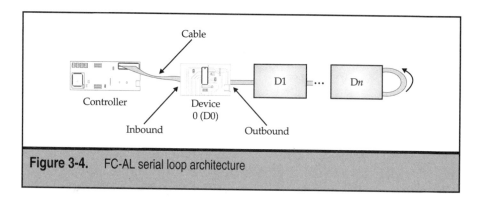

Figure 3-4. FC-AL serial loop architecture

FC-AL is actually one of three Fibre Channel topologies. The others are Fabric and Point-to-Point. FC-AL devices can be connected using either fiber optics or copper serial cables (which are commonly used in SCSI implementations). Copper cables are cheaper and work for devices in close proximity, but devices separated by a distance greater than 30 meters need fiber optics for reliable connections. The Arbitrated Loop topology attaches devices to each other in a daisy chain, which makes connecting devices a piece of cake. The last device in the chain completes the loop by connecting to a loopback connector or its own outbound connector. FC-AL currently supports up to 126 devices.

Despite the physical differences between FC-AL and standard parallel SCSI, FC-AL can incorporate parallel SCSI devices into its topology. This makes the transition from parallel SCSI to FC-AL an easier process. It is anticipated that FC-AL will eventually replace SCSI altogether.

FireWire

FireWire is another technology originating from the SCSI-3 specification. Texas Instruments and Apple developed it, and when the IEEE approved it, it also became known as the 1394 initiative. Cable versions of FireWire currently support data transfer rates of 100 (S100), 200 (S200), and 400 MBps (S400). FireWire was intended to replace standard parallel SCSI, but it will more likely replace EIDE in workstations and low-end servers.

FireWire topology is analogous to an upside-down tree, with the leaves of the tree being nodes or devices. It maps the devices through a 64-bit wide addressing model, with 10 bits for the network IDs, 6 bits for node IDs, and 48 bits for the memory address. One of the advantages of using this addressing model is that it can support an amazing number of devices (theoretically, more than 65 thousand!).

FireWire supports both asynchronous and isochronous (time-synchronized delivery) types of data transfers. Isochronous data transfers broadcast data based on channel numbers rather than a specific address and provide high bandwidth consistently. The advantage of supporting both asynchronous and isochronous formats is that both nonreal-time and real-time applications are supported. In other words, processes such as printing (nonreal time) and streaming multimedia video (real time) can coexist on the same bus.

Windows 2000 fully supports IEEE 1394 High Performance Serial Bus–compliant devices (including hard disks) connected to supported IEEE 1394 controllers. You can use IEEE 1394 hard disks for the Windows 2000 system and boot partitions, as well as for normal storage. For you to use these drives for the system or boot partition, the computer's BIOS must have IEEE 1394 boot support.

If your computer's BIOS doesn't have IEEE 1394 support enabled, you cannot install Windows 2000 on the drive during the text-mode portion of Windows 2000 Setup. The drive and partitions appear in Setup but are listed on an "unknown controller." Attempting to choose the drive or partition for installation results in the following error message:

```
Your computer's startup program cannot gain access to the disk
containing the partition or free space you chose. Setup cannot
install Windows 2000 on this hard disk.
```

This error message indicates that Setup has determined that the computer's BIOS cannot be used to access the disk that is required to start the operating system.

Windows 2000 Setup always uses the multi() syntax in the Boot.ini file when it is installed on a disk attached to an IEEE 1394 controller. If the drive or partition you selected during Setup exceeds 7.8GB in size, the IEEE 1394 controller must support and have (BIOS) INT-13 Extensions enabled.

You cannot use the scsi() syntax in the Boot.ini file to boot to a drive attached to an IEEE 1394 controller because there are no SCSI-ID jumpers associated with this type of hard disk.

Although IEEE 1394 drives are not listed as being removable devices in Disk Management, you cannot upgrade IEEE 1394 hard disks from basic to dynamic disks (described in Chapter 7) because the option is unavailable. The option is unavailable because you can easily unplug and reconnect these drives, which could cause problems with other dynamic drives in the system.

SCSI CONTROLLERS AND BUSES

At this point, it should be clear that SCSI devices have significant performance advantages over EIDE for Windows 2000. Now you need to decide what type of SCSI host adapter, system bus, and SCSI bus to choose. You have an abundance of choices, each with different specifications that yield different levels of performance. Because even a SCSI system will run only as fast as its slowest component, when it comes to disk subsystem components, faster is almost always better. More important, whatever choice you make, it is critical that you match device performance with bus performance. For example, you will reap little or no performance advantage by using slow, less expensive disk drives with a high-end 40-MBps SCSI controller unless you employ multiple disk drives that together can fully utilize the bandwidth of the controller.

From a performance standpoint, it makes no sense to discuss any system bus architecture other than PCI, PCI-X, or future bus architectures. PCI is currently the mainstream bus, so for simplicity this section will focus on that architecture.

When determining which SCSI specification to use, it is recommended that you purchase the highest performance standard that you can afford. Clearly, this will achieve the best level of performance within your reach, and it will also mean you will not need to upgrade system components as soon.

Device	Average Transfer Rate (MBps)	Specification
Host adapter	32	PCI
SCSI bus	20	Fast/Wide SCSI
SCSI disk drive 1	5.1	7,200 rpm
SCSI disk drive 2	5.1	7,200 rpm

Table 3-4.   Matching Disk Subsystem Component Bandwidth: Wasting Resources

As mentioned earlier, one of the key factors in optimizing performance is matching device performance with SCSI bus performance. In other words, if you decide to go with the Ultra Wide SCSI disk drives, make sure that you use a SCSI controller that will not hamper their high-end, 40-MBps transfer rates.

Tables 3-4 and 3-5 present examples of simplified SCSI disk subsystems to show the importance of matching the throughput capabilities of disk subsystem components to achieve optimal performance.

Device	Average Transfer Rate (MBps)	Specification
Host adapter	32	PCI
SCSI bus	10	Fast SCSI
SCSI disk drive 1	5.1	7,200 rpm
SCSI disk drive 2	5.1	7,200 rpm
SCSI disk drive 3	5.1	7,200 rpm

Table 3-5.   Matching Disk Subsystem Component Bandwidth: Overloading the Bus

As you can see in Table 3-4, the two SCSI disk drives on the system can have a combined bandwidth of approximately 10.2 MBps, and the SCSI bus itself can handle 20 MBps. This is slightly more than half of the SCSI bus's utilization capability. Is this a waste of resources? From a performance standpoint, yes. However, it does leave room to expand the capacity of the disk subsystem without having to add another SCSI host adapter or upgrade to a specification with a higher transfer rate. Figure 3-5 shows this configuration.

The three SCSI disk drives in Table 3-5 have a combined bandwidth of approximately 15.3 MBps. This is a result of SCSI's ability to multitask I/O operations even on a single channel. The system in this example has been improperly configured because the bandwidth of the SCSI bus has been exceeded. The system will never reach beyond the 10 MBps limit. To correct the problem, use a Fast/Wide SCSI or another SCSI specification that allows a transfer rate of 20 MBps or higher. It is always better to have slightly greater bandwidth capability on the SCSI host adapter than to have the adapter's capacity limit the total bandwidth of all of the devices on the SCSI chain.

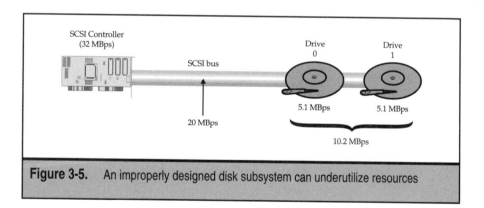

Figure 3-5.   An improperly designed disk subsystem can underutilize resources

SCSI Performance Tips

If you determine that a SCSI drive is the type of disk you will use with Windows 2000, keeping the following in mind will help you maximize its use:

▼ Bus-mastered SCSI disks, which include a processor chip on the controller, decrease the demand on the CPU.

■ To avoid disk channel congestion, use only three or four drives on each channel.

■ Choose the proper cluster size for the volume. The volume cluster size should be evenly divisible by the average file size (rounded to the nearest kilobyte). This cluster size minimizes disk I/O transaction overhead and wasted disk space. You can determine the average file size by running CHKDSK on the volume and then dividing the total kilobytes of disk usage by the number of files.

■ Add more RAM. Windows 2000 is memory hungry. If there is not enough RAM to complete operations, the operating system will use disk space.

▲ Use some form of hardware RAID (software RAID provides lower performance than hardware RAID). RAID is a series of disks configured into one volume, which provides better performance. RAID also provides redundancy and fault tolerance in some implementations.

NOTE: For more information on boosting disk subsystem performance, refer to Chapter 7.

NETWORK HARDWARE

Often there is not a lot to configure when it comes to networking hardware. Basically, you buy a machine that has certain specifications, plug it in, and let it run. This rule applies especially to "dumb" devices such as simple bridges and repeaters. However, more intelligent devices such as routers can be configured, and some configurations lend themselves to faster throughput than others. But perhaps the most important optimization you can make with networking hardware is the use of appropriate hardware in a solid network design. This section describes the basic technologies that comprise the network infrastructure necessary for proper deployment of hardware on your network.

Bridges and Repeaters

The physical size of any network is limited, because the quality of electrical signals tends to diminish as the length of the wire increases. A simple device called a *repeater* is used to amplify the electrical signals and to extend the length of a segment. Repeaters take packets from one Ethernet segment and regenerate them on an adjoining Ethernet segment. They operate only at the physical layer (layer 1) of the OSI model, and they make no decisions based on the content of the packet. They simply repeat all packets on the segment.

They also allow you to add more stations to an Ethernet segment. However, be aware of the problems associated with overloading the segment with too many stations, as discussed previously.

Bridges Block Broadcasts

Bridges operate at layer 2 of the OSI model, the data link layer. They make intelligent decisions about packet forwarding based on information in the data link header of the packet. Therefore, they do not automatically retransmit broadcasts from one segment to another. Instead they forward only frames that are destined for workstations on other segments. Bridges can join segments of a similar topology, such as Token Ring or Ethernet, or can be used for *translational bridging* of two LAN segments of different topologies, such as to connect a Token Ring segment to an Ethernet segment.

Switches

Switches operate on the same basic principles as bridges, although switches typically are faster than traditional bridges and offer more ports, to handle different topologies. We now see switches with combinations of Token Ring, Ethernet (10, 100, 1,000 Mbps), FDDI, and Asynchronous Transfer Mode (ATM), although all of these topologies are seldom incorporated in the same switch.

Switches Are Fast

Switches contain ports where you can connect either a dedicated device or a shared-media LAN. Dedicated devices often can run in full-duplex mode, because there is no other traffic on the link to contend with, effectively doubling the throughput of the topology. For example, a 10-Mbps Ethernet port can theoretically run at 20 Mbps if it is running in full-duplex mode, allowing you to connect other switches, routers, or heavily used servers as dedicated devices. Most routers, however, use software to determine the port from which the traffic will be sent and, thus, are inherently slower than switches, which perform these sorts of decisions in the hardware.

Switches allow you to logically group different switch ports to form virtual LANs (VLANs), giving network administrators some flexibility in creating workgroups or managing broadcast domains. A manager can control which LANs are directly connected to other LANs.

Switches can vary tremendously in the speed of their ports and the speed of the switching fabric. Therefore, evaluate the amount of traffic on each port in both incoming and outgoing directions before implementing a switch. The switching fabric is the internal speed of the switch, and it must be fast enough to keep up with the incoming information and send it out of the switch without delay. For example, switches often have several 100-Mbps ports and several 10-Mbps ports. You obviously would not want to place a 100-Mbps device on a 10-Mbps port, or vice versa.

Recently, some manufacturers have introduced new capabilities in their router platforms to improve the performance of packet transfers across routers.

Routers

Routers are intelligent networking components that work at the network layer, or layer 3, of the OSI model. They implement routing techniques to determine the best path between a source and destination and to forward packets between them. To do this, a router has memory to store the routing table and a processor to run the software that examines each packet as it is coming through. The router opens each packet and examines its destination address. By looking up the address on the routing table, the router determines the port on which to send out the packet. The ports are always on different segments and may use different physical protocols such as FDDI or Ethernet.

Manufacturers such as Cisco and Juniper have recently added the capability to switch across interfaces, enabling much faster performance. With this capability, router performance can rival the performance of switches for a few nodes. This is useful at the network core of structured networks, where servers and other shared devices can be directly connected to routers and still achieve high performance. However, switches are still the fastest and most cost-effective high-performance solution for large numbers of nodes. This is the case for end stations and for organizations with less-structured networks.

Routers Add Functionality

In addition to keeping broadcasts contained to a single segment, routers incorporate many other features to enhance the stability and security of the network. They often come with redundant power supplies, complete MIBs containing information about traffic patterns and errors, and access lists to control data that is put onto or taken off of the network.

Routers, unlike some of the other hardware products mentioned, have sophisticated configurations that are vendor specific and somewhat complicated. Apply these configurations with a good dose of common sense when optimizing your network infrastructure.

Here are a few recommendations you should apply to your router configurations:

▼ **Activate Only the Ports That You Are Using**   Unused ports sap CPU cycles and pose a security risk.

■ **Activate Only the Protocols That You Are Using**   Tighten security by not burdening the router's CPU with unused routing or network protocols.

▲ **Use Access Lists Only if Necessary**   Although access lists provide a useful security filter for your traffic, they are CPU and memory intensive. You might implement access lists only on the routers at the border of your network.

Starting with a good network design and using high-quality, reliable components will help ensure optimal throughput from your network infrastructure. If possible, it is an especially good idea to use equipment from the same manufacturer to ensure maximum compatibility.

Some networking hardware vendors and their contacts are listed in Table 3-6.

Device	Company	Type	Contact Information
Network Interface Cards (NICs)	3Com	Ethernet	http://www .3com.com

Table 3-6.   Network Hardware Vendors

Device	Company	Type	Contact Information
	Adaptec	Fast Ethernet	http://www .adaptec.com
	IBM	ATM, Ethernet, Fast Ethernet, Token Ring	http://www .networking .ibm.com
	Madge	Token Ring	http://www .madge.com
Hubs	3Com	Ethernet, Fast Ethernet	http://www .3com.com
	Cisco	Ethernet, Fast Ethernet, FDDI	http://www .cisco.com
	Hewlett-Packard	Ethernet, Fast Ethernet, Gigabit Ethernet	http://www .hp.com
	IBM	Ethernet, Fast Ethernet, Token Ring	http://www .networking .ibm.com
	Intel	Ethernet, Fast Ethernet	http://www .intel.com
	Enteras	Ethernet, Token Ring	http://www .enterasys.com/

Table 3-6.   Network Hardware Vendors *(continued)*

Device	Company	Type	Contact Information
	Nortel Networks	Ethernet, Token Ring	http://www .nortelnetworks .com
Switches	3Com	Ethernet, Fast Ethernet, Gigabit Ethernet	http://www .3com.com
	Cisco	Ethernet, Fast Ethernet, Gigabit Ethernet, Token Ring, FDDI, ATM	http://www .cisco.com
	Enteras	Ethernet, Fast Ethernet, Gigabit Ethernet, Token Ring	http://www .enterasys.com/
	Extreme Networks	Fast Ethernet, Gigabit Ethernet	http://www .extremenetworks .com
	Hewlett-Packard	Fast Ethernet, ATM, FDDI	http://www .hp.com
	IBM	Fast Ethernet, Token Ring, ATM, FDDI	http://www .networking.ibm .com

Table 3-6. Network Hardware Vendors *(continued)*

Device	Company	Type	Contact Information
	Nortel Networks	Ethernet, Token Ring	http://www.nortelnetworks.com
Routers	3Com	Ethernet, Fast Ethernet, T1, DS3, Token Ring, FDDI	http://www.3com.com
	Cisco	Fast Ethernet, ATM, SONET, Gigabit Ethernet, T1, DS3, FDDI, Token Ring	http://www.cisco.com
	Enteras	Fast Ethernet, ATM, SONET, Gigabit Ethernet, T1, DS3, Token Ring	http://www.enterasys.com
	Extreme Networks	Fast Ethernet, Gigabit Ethernet	http://www.extremenetworks.com
	Juniper Networks	Fast Ethernet, ATM, SONET, Gigabit Ethernet, T1, DS3	http://www.juniper.net

Table 3-6.   Network Hardware Vendors *(continued)*

NOTE: For more information on optimizing the network subsystem, refer to Chapter 8.

GRAPHICS HARDWARE CONSIDERATIONS

Because most Windows 2000 operations are based on a graphical user interface (GUI), careful planning and consideration is needed in choosing your graphics hardware components. As with many other components of a Windows 2000 system, you have many choices when deciding how to achieve the best overall performance. The two primary components you should focus on are the video adapter and the monitor; these are important in any system.

Before you can determine what kind of video adapter and monitor to configure in your Windows 2000 system, you need to look at what the video adapter will need to support. You should first consider the type of system it will be used for. For instance, will the system be used as a client machine, a server, or a machine housing high-end graphics applications and data? Just as important, you must consider the types of applications that will be used on this server. Most business applications use 2-D graphics, but applications such as CAD and computer animation tools likely use 3-D graphics or OpenGL. OpenGL is an API standard for efficiently developing advanced 3-D graphics. It is an operating-system-independent API designed from the IRIS GL specifications by Silicon Graphics (SGI).

Video Display

Many look at the process of presenting data on the screen in a readable format as black-box technology. Although it is far from a simple process, it is certainly not too difficult to understand.

Why worry about how information travels to the monitor? It is important to understand this process because it not only gives you a better understanding of the system, but it also helps you pinpoint bottlenecks in the graphics subsystem. Remember that any system or subsystem is only as fast as its slowest component. When you understand the video display process, you will know which features of the adapter provide the best performance boost.

Figure 3-6 illustrates the movement of data from the CPU to the monitor for display.

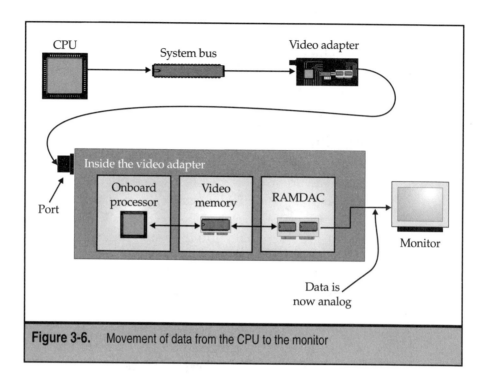

Figure 3-6.   Movement of data from the CPU to the monitor

The Video Display Process

Memory, the CPU, and the video adapter all work together to manipulate the data to produce images and text that the user can understand. The video display process begins at the CPU and ends at the monitor. Regardless of whether the graphics are 2-D or 3-D, the video display process follows these basic steps:

1. The CPU transfers digital data to the system bus, where it soon reaches the video adapter.

2. The video adapter processes the digital data and stores it in the adapter's video memory.

3. The RAM digital-to-analog converter (RAMDAC) reads the data from video adapter memory and converts the digital data to a signal (analog data) that can be read by the monitor.

4. The RAMDAC sends the analog data to the monitor for output to the screen.

The following sections examine each step to determine where potential bottlenecks may exist.

Step 1: CPU to Video Adapter   The transfer of data from the CPU to the graphics adapter involves many factors that can affect the speed at which the information travels to its destination. These factors include the CPU, the bus speed on the motherboard, and the bus speed on the graphics adapter. Since buses are relatively slow compared to the CPU, the buses are usually the cause of a bottleneck.

To ensure that data transfer occurs at the fastest speed possible, you should use PCI, rather than ISA, EISA, or VLB, for the bus that connects the graphics adapter to the motherboard. Of course, this requires a system with a spare PCI slot for the graphics adapter. Another possibility is the AGP specification, described in the section "Choosing a Graphics Adapter" later in this chapter.

NOTE: For performance reasons, some PCI devices take precedence over the graphics adapter. For example, if the system has only two PCI slots, you should use these slots for the NIC and hard disk controller instead of the graphics adapter. You are more likely to face this situation with servers than workstations.

The important point in this step is that you should use the best-performing bus possible to achieve the highest possible data transfer rate.

Step 2: Video Adapter to Video Memory   There are two potential bottlenecks in the second stage of the video display process. The first involves the graphics adapter's onboard processor because it is the component that is responsible for processing the data that comes in from the CPU. To keep performance from slowing down, make sure that the graphics processor operates at a speed of at least 200 MHz. Some of the more advanced onboard processors that support 128-bit processing have speeds in excess of 220 MHz.

The other potential bottleneck is the video memory. The key is to configure the graphics adapter with dual-port video memory with VRAM, WRAM, and so on to ensure that performance is at its highest. You must use dual-port memory because the video memory must perform more than one operation at a time to successfully keep pace with the rest of the graphics subsystem. Dual-port video memory can be read from and written to at the same time. The different types of video memory and their characteristics are examined in the section "Choosing a Graphics Adapter" later in this chapter.

The video memory is situated between the onboard processor and the RAMDAC, and it must communicate with both of these simultaneously to be effective. This is why it is important to use dual-port video memory whenever possible. The two devices that the video memory sits between are busy constantly, and the video memory must be fast enough to keep up with them both.

Step 3: Video Memory to RAMDAC   As data comes in from the onboard processor, it's temporarily stored in video memory until the RAMDAC is ready to use the data. The data is stored in video memory's frame buffer as a bitmap image. Then the data is transferred to the RAMDAC for more processing. Actually, the RAMDAC continuously reads data from video memory to maintain the display. Every time a new window is displayed, the mouse is moved, or the cursor changes, the display must be updated. Every update puts more pressure on the RAMDAC to read in more data.

When the RAMDAC receives data, it transforms the data to analog signals that the monitor can recognize. As you may have already guessed, this transformation occurs continuously; the RAMDAC is always reading in data from memory and manipulating it for display on the monitor. If you increase the resolution or refresh rate, the amount of data that the RAMDAC must read and transform also increases.

Step 4: RAMDAC to the Monitor   This final step in the video display process, in which the RAMDAC passes the analog signal to the monitor, is the least likely place for a bottleneck in the graphics subsystem. Your concern here is with the monitor itself rather than the transfer of data. The monitor must be able to handle the workload given to it by the graphics adapter. Check the monitor's characteristics to be sure that the monitor supports the resolution, refresh rate, and color depth that the graphics adapter supports. Matching the two components' characteristics reduces the possibility of a performance bottleneck and decreases the likelihood that any incompatibility may be encountered.

Choosing a Graphics Adapter

Once you have a general idea of the functions that the system will be used for, you can begin to match these functions with the functions that different video adapters support. The attributes that you need to consider when choosing a video adapter include the type of onboard processor or chipset that the adapter uses, the amount and type of video memory, the bus type and width, whether the adapter supports 2-D or 3-D graphics (or both), the resolution and refresh rate, and Windows 2000 driver support.

Onboard Processor

Speeds in information technology are constantly increasing, and onboard processor technology for graphics adapters is no exception. Of course, the faster the onboard processor, the faster the graphics adapter and the less likely that the graphics subsystem will be a bottleneck. The onboard processor takes over much of the responsibility for processing video data from the CPU, which lets the CPU tend to other tasks. Typical onboard processors can process data 32, 64, or even 128 bits at a time. To realize the full potential of the onboard processor, it is imperative that you configure the card with the proper amount of video RAM. For example, a 64-bit card with only 1MB (1×8) of video RAM will not achieve its full processing power because only 32 bits of data will be addressed at a time. If the graphics adapter had 2MB (1×8) of video memory, then video memory could potentially be read or written to 64 bits (2×32) at a time.

Video Memory

Video adapters use several types of memory, most of which are specifically designed for use with video. These include EDO, VRAM, WRAM, and SDRAM. As you can see, the various types of video memory can differ significantly in the amount of data traffic they can handle. Is it really necessary to configure the graphics adapter to use video memory with the highest possible bandwidth? Although this question may appear to have a relatively easy answer, it really depends on the type of graphics adapter you are using, how much money you are willing to spend, and the type of functionality that the graphics adapter will support (2-D or 3-D graphics or both). From a performance standpoint, faster is usually better, but there is a point beyond which the fastest available video memory may be overkill. The goal is to supply enough bandwidth so that performance is not hindered and you will not have to upgrade relatively soon. Because of the heavy demands placed on the graphics subsystem, video memory must be considerably faster than normal system RAM.

The older-style DRAM that may be used on the main system was once considered the memory type of choice for graphics adapters. Now, usually only low-end graphics adapters use this type of video memory because of its many limitations, such as its reliance on the system clock to reset it before each screen refresh operation. Other memory types, by contrast, have undergone significant changes to meet the needs of today's graphics adapters. Also, the increasing popularity of graphics-based operating systems, such as Windows 2000, and the increasing demands for higher resolution, more frequent screen refresh operations, and greater color depth necessitate the use of high-performance video memory. Video memory enhancements not found in standard DRAM include dual-port memory, masked writes to memory, clock speed synchronization—and much more.

The following paragraphs describe the types of video memory that should be considered for the system's graphics adapter.

VRAM   VRAM, otherwise known as video RAM, uses a totally different approach than that of conventional RAM. It can be accessed through two ports instead of just one, which means that it can be accessed by two different devices simultaneously, as illustrated in Figure 3-7. As discussed earlier in this chapter, video memory communicates with both the onboard processor and the RAMDAC simultaneously, which makes this dual-port feature extremely useful for providing high performance. VRAM allows the onboard processor and RAMDAC to access it simultaneously; as new information is rushing in, it is also being pumped out to the RAMDAC. As a result, VRAM yields substantially better performance than conventional RAM. The downside, however, is that VRAM is extremely expensive compared to other forms of video memory.

WRAM   Window RAM (WRAM) is another type of memory that supports two ports, like VRAM. Although WRAM uses the same dual-port technique as VRAM, it provides a performance increase of up to 50 percent over VRAM. In addition, WRAM is cheaper (by as much as 20 percent). Clearly, WRAM is a better memory choice than VRAM.

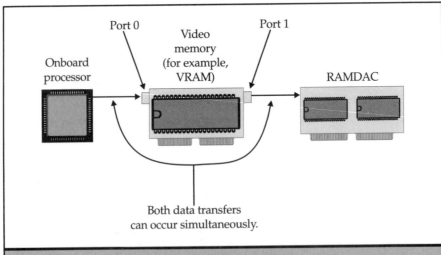

Figure 3-7.   Dual-port video memory enables two devices to access it simultaneously

RDRAM   RDRAM offers blazingly fast performance, but this technology is still only gradually seeping into the market because of relatively high costs. Consider this type of video memory, especially if your system will be used for CAD, rendering, computer animation, or other high-end graphics applications.

A new version of RDRAM, called nDRAM, is currently under development. It is expected to enable data transfer rates as high as 1,600 MHz!

SGRAM   Synchronous graphic RAM (SGRAM) is a single-port version of video memory. Although it is true that two ports are more efficient than one, SGRAM relies on other techniques to achieve high data transfer rates. SGRAM can synchronize operations with the CPU bus clock at speeds reaching 100 MHz, and it also uses various write techniques to increase total bandwidth. Moreover, SGRAM can open two memory pages instead of just one, simulating the dual-port technology of VRAM and WRAM.

Calculating the Amount of Video Memory Needed   How much video memory does the graphics adapter need? Two factors determine how much video memory is needed: the number of colors to be displayed and the screen resolution. Table 3-7 summarizes the minimum amount of video memory required to display various resolutions and color depths in 2-D. It is important to note that these are the minimum amounts required and that some of the video memory is also used to store font metrics and other graphical information. Calculating the minimum amount, however, will help you understand how to configure the right amount of video memory on the graphics adapter. It is always a good idea to configure the graphics adapter with a little more video memory than the minimum required, to account for the other graphical information that may be stored. For example, for a screen display with a resolution of 640×480 pixels and 256 colors, the minimum amount of video memory required is 1MB, but you would be wise to purchase a card with at least 2MB of video memory.

Resolution (Horizontal× Vertical)	Approximate Number of Colors Supported	Color Depth (in Bits)	Minimum Memory Required (in MB)
640×480	256	8	1
	65,000	16	1
	16.7 million	24	2
800×600	256	8	1
	65,000	16	1
	16.7 million	24	2
1,024×768	256	8	1
	65,000	16	2
	16.7 million	24	3
1,280×1,024	256	8	2
	65,000	16	3
	16.7 million	24	4
1,600×1,200	256	8	2
	65,000	16	4
	16.7 million	24	6

Table 3-7.   Video Memory Requirements at Various 2-D Resolutions and Color Depths

To calculate the minimum video memory requirements for the resolution and color depth that you plan to display, use the following formula:

Resolution × (Color depth / 8) =
Minimum video memory required (in bytes)

For example, suppose you want a resolution of 800×600 and 256 colors. You know that 256 colors is equivalent to 8-bit color ($2^8 = 256$), so your calculation is as follows: 800×600 (8 / 8) = 480,000 bytes, or approximately half a megabyte. Always round the result up to the nearest megabyte. It is unusual today to find a graphics adapter configured with less than 1MB of video memory. Therefore, in this example, the graphics adapter would need to have a minimum of 1MB of memory installed.

   You are also strongly urged to take into account future requirements. You should purchase enough video memory so that if you do decide to run at a higher resolution, the amount of memory on the graphics adapter is sufficient. The alternative is adding video memory to the graphics adapter (if it supports additional memory). In the preceding example, for instance, 2MB would be needed to run at the next higher resolution. This may seem like overkill, but the extra memory can save you time and money in the future.

2-D and 3-D Memory Requirements   Generally, 3-D graphics require much more memory than 2-D graphics running at the same resolution; 3-D graphics adapters need more video memory because an extra buffer is needed to store the third-dimension depth value. That is, 3-D graphics adapters need a total of three buffers—front, back, and Z buffers—to display the images and text on the screen. A 2-D environment does not need a Z buffer; the front and back buffers are sufficient to support just two dimensions.

   How much more memory do 3-D graphics require? To calculate the video memory requirements for 3-D graphics displays, you can use the following formula:

   Resolution × (Color depth / 8) × 3 buffers =
   Minimum video memory required

   For example, suppose you want a resolution of 800×600 and approximately 65,000 colors. You know that 65,000 colors is equivalent to 16-bit color (2^{16} = 65,536), so the calculation is (800×600) (2×3) = 2,880,000, or approximately 3MB.

   Table 3-8 shows other minimum video memory requirements at different resolutions and color depths.

Resolution (Horizontal×Vertical)	Approximate Number of Colors Supported	Minimum Memory Required (in MB)
640×480	256	1
	65,000	2
	16.7 million	3
800×600	256	2
	65,000	3
	16.7 million	5
1,024×768	256	3
	65,000	5
	16.7 million	8
1,280×1,024	256	4
	65,000	8
	16.7 million	12
1,600×1,200	256	6
	65,000	12
	16.7 million	18

Table 3-8.   Video Requirements at Various 3-D Resolutions and Color Depths

Bus Architecture

The subject of bus architectures for graphics adapters can be confusing because there are two bus architectures that are related to the graphics adapter. First, there is one bus that coincides with the system's bus architecture, such as ISA, VLB, EISA, or PCI, which is the actual connection point where the graphics adapter meets the rest of the system. The second bus is internal to the graphics adapter. The two buses are separate, but they are not completely independent of one another.

External Bus Architectures   PCI is definitely commonplace, and its performance level is more than adequate. If the server can give up a PCI slot, then it is highly recommended that you choose PCI over some other low-end bus architecture. Otherwise, you are limiting the amount of bandwidth from the graphics adapter to the rest of the system.

AGP   The accelerated graphics port (AGP) acts like a bus, but it is, in fact, a port. For this reason, only one device (the graphics adapter) can use AGP. It is designed specifically to increase the bandwidth of graphics adapters. This new technology has saturated the mainstream market and is fully supported by Windows 2000.

AGP is a logical extension to the PCI 2.1 specification. For this reason, AGP graphics adapters can use the PCI slot and sometimes even the same PCI driver, though this practice is not supported or recommended. Unlike PCI, AGP is not shared with other devices, such as SCSI and network devices. It is dedicated solely to the graphics adapter. Figure 3-8 illustrates this distinction. AGP also boasts double the performance of PCI. It operates at a minimum of 66 MHz (a bandwidth of approximately 266 MBps), while PCI operates at 33 MHz (a bandwidth of 133 Mbps), though significant improvements from AGP are generally noticeable only when moving large amounts of graphics data at high resolution. AGP also incorporates features, such as pipelined read and write operations, demultiplexed graphics data and addresses on the bus, and Direct Memory Execute (DIME), designed to minimize latencies and increase bandwidth. DIME exploits system memory for *texture mapping* (applying surface characteristics, such as color, brightness, reflection, and more to 3-D objects) operations used in 3-D graphics, which can significantly reduce the movement of texture-mapped data and reduce the overhead associated with 3-D graphics.

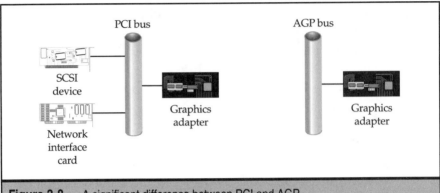

Figure 3-8. A significant difference between PCI and AGP

Internal Bus Architectures The graphics adapter's internal bus fosters communication among the onboard processor, video memory, and RAMDAC. The width of the bus is typically 32, 64, or 128 bits. This means that 4 to 16 bytes of data can be transferred from one component to another at once. Generally, the wider the bus, the better the overall performance of the card.

To take advantage of a wider bus, such as the 64-bit bus, however, you must have sufficient memory. For instance, a card with a 64-bit data bus that is configured with 1MB of video memory would not be able to take advantage of the larger bus because the memory chip itself is only 32 bits wide, as illustrated in Figure 3-9. In this case, 2MB (1×8) of video memory is needed to use the 64-bit bus. Recall from Table 3-7 that a resolution of 1,024×768 with a color depth of 256 colors requires only 1MB of video memory. However, to provide the most efficient use of the internal bus architecture (64 bits and higher), the amount of addressable memory must match the internal bus width. Therefore, without taking into account the resolution and color depth, the minimum amount of memory needed to sustain performance in a 64-bit graphics adapter is 2MB, and a 128-bit card requires 4MB.

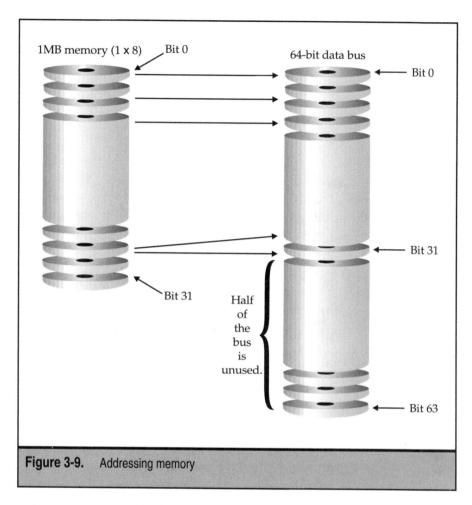

Figure 3-9.   Addressing memory

2-D and 3-D Video Adapters

Most of the work you do on a Windows 2000 server will use 2-D
graphics. Most business applications support only 2-D graphics, as
do most administrative tools using the MMC. When you consider
2-D performance, you are concerned mainly with such factors as the
speed of screen refresh operations and how smoothly you can scroll
through text and graphics; you are not concerned with such factors as
texture mapping and rendering.

Much of what can be done to improve 2-D graphics has already been accomplished. Consequently, the 2-D graphics adapters available for the Windows 2000 platform do not have extreme variations in performance. Nevertheless, you still need to choose a good-quality 2-D graphics adapter that can adequately handle large graphical workloads, especially since Windows 2000 relies on a graphical user interface.

It's getting rare to find a graphics adapters that uses purely 2-D technology. This trend is reflected in Windows 2000's support for OpenGL, DirectX, and so on. Depending on your server's function and the applications that run on the server, you may need support for 3-D graphics. 3-D performance is now becoming the distinguishing factor among graphics adapters.

What is the best choice for your Windows 2000 environment? The answer depends largely on what you will be using the system for. If the system handles CAD, rendering, or other graphics-intensive applications, then a 3-D graphics adapter is your optimal choice. For Windows 2000 machines that rely heavily on 2-D graphics but that may require 3-D graphics in the future, you have the option of incorporating both 2-D and 3-D graphics capabilities in one graphics adapter. The best overall performance will come from a graphics adapter that provides exceptional quality and has both 2-D and 3-D graphics capabilities.

Resolution and Refresh Rate

The screen resolution and refresh rate are closely related in terms of a graphics adapter's performance and should be the first things you consider when choosing a graphics adapter. These features define the quality and detail of images that are presented on the display. As the resolution increases, so does the number of pixels that make up the images on the screen. The more pixels on the screen, the finer the detail can be. However, to maintain the fine detail from the resolution, the graphics adapter must also provide an adequate refresh rate so there's no distortion or flicker.

Typical resolutions are 640×480, 800×600, 1,024×768, and 1,600×1,200, but Windows 2000 also supports resolutions of 1,152×882 and 1,280×1,024, among others. The first number in the resolution specification represents the horizontal resolution, and the second number represents the vertical resolution. Combining these values gives you the total resolution for the entire display.

Some graphics adapters support all resolutions, while others can handle only a few. In addition, the quality at which graphics adapters support different resolutions varies significantly, because graphics adapters support certain refresh rates at higher resolutions than others. It is more difficult to maintain high refresh rates as you increase the resolution because the amount of data passing through the graphics adapter increases greatly at each higher resolution. In addition, increases in the number of colors (the color depth) are also harder to support at higher resolutions, and this too can affect graphics performance.

When the resolution is increased, more resources, namely video memory and onboard processing power, are needed to achieve a particular color depth and refresh rate. The more memory and processing power the graphics adapter has to support higher resolutions, the better, because otherwise you will encounter severe performance degradation if you try to run your system in these modes. Higher resolution means that more data must be handled by the graphics adapter, and increases in the refresh rate and color depth add even more resource requirements.

In conclusion, if you plan to use the higher resolution modes, be sure that the graphics adapter can adequately support the refresh rate needed for those resolutions. The minimum refresh rate for any resolution should be 60 Hz. Also be sure to follow the recommendations outlined in Table 3-7 and 3-8 for the minimum video memory requirements. If the refresh rate and memory requirements are not met while running at higher resolutions, the graphics subsystem performance will suffer, and this will affect overall system performance.

Monitors

Working in conjunction with the graphics adapter is the monitor, which, as you well know, is the component that you use to view the information passed from the graphics adapter. It is far too common for machines to be configured with just any type of monitor. Most people just make sure it is big enough and the manufacturer has a good reputation. However, you should be sure to choose not only a good-quality monitor, but also one that matches your graphics adapter's abilities. Otherwise, you will be wasting the capabilities of the monitor or the graphics adapter or both.

As with graphics adapters, there are numerous factors to consider when choosing a monitor, including bandwidth, refresh rate, interlacing, dot pitch, resolution, size, and brand reputation. Although there is no one best choice for some of these attributes, it is important that you consider all of them to make sure that your graphics adapter and monitor capabilities match. All of these attributes are discussed in the following paragraphs.

NOTE: Windows 2000 supports the use of up to nine graphics adapters and monitors. These monitors can be synchronized and combined to form a single screen.

Bandwidth

Bandwidth is a measure, in megahertz, that indicates the total amount of data that the monitor can handle per second. The manufacturer provides this specification. To take full advantage of the graphics adapter, match this value with the graphics adapter's clock frequency, also provided by the manufacturer (and sometimes referred to as the pixel rate). The clock frequency indicates the total amount of data that the graphics adapter can handle per second.

Refresh Rate

As noted earlier, the refresh rate refers to the maximum number of frames that can be displayed at a given resolution. The refresh rate depends primarily on the horizontal scan rate (the number of lines of pixels that can be displayed per second) and the resolution. For example, the monitor may have an 85-Hz refresh rate at 640×480 resolution, but at a higher resolution such as 800×600, it may be capable of a refresh rate of only 72 Hz. Be sure to match the refresh rate with the video adapter's capabilities.

What is an acceptable refresh rate? Personal preference plays a role in this choice, but you should know that the higher the refresh rate, the higher the quality of the picture; at lower rates, the picture becomes grainy and flickers. For some people, 60 Hz is acceptable, but the higher the resolution and the larger the monitor, the higher the refresh rate needed to produce clear pictures.

Interlaced versus Noninterlaced Monitor

Interlaced monitors scan the display in two passes. On the first pass, they scan every other line, and then they return on a second pass and scan all of the lines they previously skipped. The human eye can barely (or not at all) detect this subtle scanning technique, and it has been widely used to increase resolution and reduce flicker. Noninterlaced monitors, on the other hand, scan every line in a single pass to produce higher-quality output at a given resolution.

Noninterlaced monitors are best even for servers that do not make heavy use of graphics because of the image quality they offer. Note, though, that some noninterlaced monitors revert to interlaced mode at high resolutions (usually 1,024×768 or higher). For this reason, you should carefully read the monitor's specifications.

Dot Pitch

The dot pitch is the diagonal distance between the center of any two dot triads. A dot triad is a triangular arrangement of three phosphor dots on the screen. Each of these dots is a different color: red, green, or blue. Together they comprise the images that are displayed on the monitor.

As the dot pitch increases, the dots on the screen become more noticeable. Therefore, a low dot-pitch rating gives you a better-quality picture. Aim for monitors that have a dot pitch of .28 or less to ensure that picture quality is not distorted at higher resolutions. Again, your decision here relates more to personal preference than to performance.

Resolution

Resolution is one of the most important attributes to consider when purchasing a monitor. This measurement indicates how fine a detail the monitor can display. The resolution is the maximum number of pixels that can be displayed at once, and it coordinates with the monitor's dot pitch. For instance, an 800×600 resolution means that the screen can display 800 pixels horizontally and 600 pixels vertically. Generally speaking, the higher the resolution, the better the quality of the picture.

Your monitor must be capable of supporting the resolutions you want to use. You need to look at not only the resolution modes that a monitor supports but also the screen size. For instance, a resolution of 1,024×768 viewed on a 14-inch monitor will yield difficult-to-read images even for someone with excellent vision.

PRINTER HARDWARE CONFIGURATIONS AND CONSIDERATIONS

Optimizing the printing process begins with choosing the most efficient hardware that also meets the functional needs of the environment. There are a large number of printing devices to choose from, such as dot-matrix, ink jet, laser, and thermal printers and plotters, as well as many other print devices, depending on your printing needs. It is important to choose the appropriate print device for the functions it will perform in the environment.

Despite the different functionality associated with these various print device types, you can judge their performance by measuring certain common characteristics, including the quality and type of output, speed of printing (typically measured in pages per minute, or ppm), and connection type. Each of these factors can greatly influence the printing process.

Quality and Type of Output

Your first consideration when purchasing a print device should be the quality and type of output that the device produces. Some environments need dot-matrix print devices for impact printing, while others need nonimpact print devices such as plotters, for instance, to produce architectural designs from CAD applications. Other environments, where space and money are factors, may opt for all-in-one print devices that include printing, faxing, and copying capabilities. Once you know what type of printing is needed, you can determine the type of output you require.

Resolution

The type of output you need also determines the output quality you require. No matter whether you are printing text or graphics, or both, the resolution determines the quality of the printed results. Resolution is typically measured in dots per inch (dpi). The higher the dpi value, the better the output quality.

It's not uncommon for print devices to support 1,200 dpi or higher resolution. However, a word of caution is needed here, because higher resolutions usually take longer to print. For example, a print job set at 600 dpi will print faster than the same print job set at 1,200 dpi on the same print device.

Printing Speed

Printing speed is measured either in characters per second (cps) or pages per minute (ppm). The cps rating is typically used only with dot-matrix print devices. The pages per minute attribute of a print device is the maximum number of pages that the print device can output in one minute. This characteristic also depends on resolution: the higher the resolution, the more time it takes to complete a print job. The rating also depends heavily on whether you are printing graphics or plain text. Get the highest ppm rating possible to ensure that print jobs complete as quickly as possible.

Printer Connection

How the print device is connected to Windows 2000 is as important as any of the characteristics discussed so far. Whether the print device is local or remote, it attaches to Windows 2000 through an interface specification. This interface can either expand or limit the amount of data that can be transmitted to the print device for output.

The primary types of interface connections can be divided into two categories: local and network. The two categories can be further broken down by individual print connection specifications. Each specification is defined by its special features and transfer rates.

It is important to note that there is a print connection interface that does not fit into any of these categories: the infrared connection interface. This type of interface provides extremely slow transfer rates that are unacceptable for environments concerned with performance. Local interfaces generally provide transfer rates at least twice as fast as infrared.

NOTE: The serial (RS-232) connection type falls into the local category, but it shares the same performance considerations as the infrared interface. There is not much growth potential for the serial specification, but it is anticipated that infrared technology will eventually overcome its limitations to provide acceptable transfer rates, not only for print devices but for network connectivity as well.

Local Interfaces

Parallel interfaces are for print devices connected locally to the Windows 2000 print server or workstation. They also define the way that the print device is physically attached to the machine.

The first commonly used local interface relied on a unidirectional Centronics type of connection, pictured here:

There have since been many improvements on the local connection specifications to allow greater printing speeds and higher-quality output.

ECP   The Extended Capabilities Port (ECP) specification is a parallel-port standard that supports bidirectional communication between the print device and the rest of the system. ECP is roughly 10 times faster than the older Centronics standard. It is an intelligent parallel interface specification built from the IEEE 1284 specification.

With ECP, the printer port can operate at speeds of 500,000 to 3 million cps. This is a tremendous improvement over the Centronics standard, which has a maximum transfer rate of 125,000 characters per second.

EPP   The Enhanced Parallel Port (EPP) is another intelligent parallel port standard that supports bidirectional communication. Its features and performance are similar to those of the ECP specification. For example, its transfer speed is between 500,000 and 3 million cps.

USB   The universal serial bus (USB) is a peripheral device bus architecture that supports a variety of devices including printers. Although connection speeds are far superior to those of the parallel interface (up to 12 cps), USB's biggest advantage lies in the fact that devices can be dynamically added and removed from the system.

Network Interface

Many print devices are becoming *network aware*, meaning that the device itself can be attached to the network instead of being physically connected to the Windows 2000 print server or workstation. This allows greater flexibility, especially in heterogeneous environments where more than one type of operating system platform uses a single print device.

Connecting the print device directly to the network also increases the transfer rate between the client requesting the print job and the actual print device. In fact, the printing device is more likely to cause a bottleneck than the network interface connection because there is more data coming into the print device than it can use efficiently.

NOTE: For more information on tuning printing, refer to Chapter 13.

CHAPTER 4

Sizing and Designing a Windows 2000 Environment

In Windows NT4, since domain design was chosen based on limited domain administration and management structures, we implemented the design that fit our administration needs and then used performance and tuning procedures to make it work as efficiently as possible. With Windows 2000, because Active Directory provides delegation of administration and management functionality in all design options, an Active Directory design can be chosen with better performance optimization in mind.

If you can plan your Active Directory design with performance optimization characteristics, you can make trade-offs when planning and implementing your Active Directory. However, if you have already implemented your Windows 2000 Active Directory, you will be limited in making major modifications to your AD design based on the tools available to make modifications, so tuning and optimizing what you have already put in place is the sole focus in those scenarios.

This chapter highlights the most prevalent Windows 2000 Active Directory designs and details the pros and cons of each relative to network performance optimization and administration and management concerns.

ACTIVE DIRECTORY DESIGN BACKGROUND

Active Directory designs are influenced by a handful of technical characteristics of Windows 2000, such as how users are authenticated to domain controllers, the impact of replication of domain information across the enterprise, and how information lookup occurs in the Active Directory itself. As with many design decisions, choices need to be made among the trade-offs of various performance components when selecting one design configuration over another.

User Authentication by a Domain Controller

When a user logs onto the network, the first thing that occurs across the LAN or WAN is that an authentication request is sent from the user to a domain controller on the network. This process is similar to what occurred in a Windows NT4 environment. It has always been suggested that a domain controller (in Windows NT4, typically a backup domain controller, or BDC) be established close to the users on the network. In Windows 2000, a network should have at least one domain controller on every segment or collision domain in a LAN environment; in a WAN environment with slower network connections, a domain controller should be placed at every site or on every segment where bandwidth between the client and the domain is less than 256 Kbps frame-relay speed. Having a local domain controller will improve the logon response to the domain and decrease the traffic between the client and the domain controller.

With Windows 2000, if a domain controller that used to be local to the users is in a fault state and not working properly, the workstations will send out a broadcast to look for the domain controller nearest to the station. This may be several hops from the client. Organizations that have a high desire to ensure that logon authentication is not affected by a server failure should place a secondary domain controller on the network on or near the same network segment as the domain controller being backed up. To keep the domain controllers operational, a synchronization process is automatically run that makes sure that all domain controllers connected to the network have the same information.

User Access to a Global Catalog

Those familiar with the way backup domain controllers in Windows NT4 worked will find that the placement of the domain controllers described in the previous section is very similar in the Windows 2000 Active Directory environment. However, one major difference when logging onto an Active Directory domain is an additional step where the client workstation has to contact a global catalog (GC) on the domain to complete the logon process. In addition to just authenticating to the domain, the client workstation needs to have domain-level policies and universal group security policies applied to fully get authenticated to the domain. By definition, these policies are stored in the global catalog of the forest.

Early Windows 2000 domain design guidelines, and many Windows 2000 Active Directory training courses, recommend the practice of having a centralized global catalog, as shown on the left in Figure 4-1, with domain controllers distributed to remote locations. The reasoning behind this early global catalog recommendation was a concern that having too many global catalogs on a domain would saturate bandwidth as the global catalogs all synchronized with each other to keep information between the controllers up-to-date.

After organizations began implementing Windows 2000 in global enterprise environments, it was found that it was taking a significant amount of time, as well as creating significant global-catalog-to-remote-site WAN bandwidth traffic, to have the global catalog so far away from the users. When Exchange 2000 messaging began to be implemented, this problem was exacerbated as e-mail users constantly contacted the centralized global catalog over the WAN connection whenever they wanted to see distribution lists or lists of universal security groups.

The current recommendation for optimized global catalog placement is to make your key site and segment domain controllers also global catalog servers, as shown on the right in Figure 4-1. If you place a domain controller on the other end of a 128 Kbps frame-relay connection of a remote site to improve user logon authentication, it

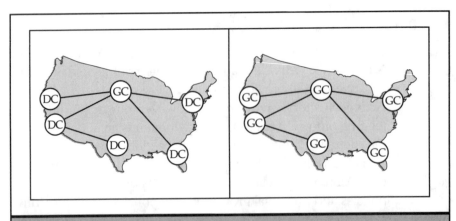

Figure 4-1.   Global catalog placement recommendation

follows from the same logic that those remote users should also be able to access the global catalog with the same level of efficiency.

NOTE: There is a registry hack (posted on Microsoft Technet) for Windows 2000 client workstations that allows bypassing of the global catalog lookup process so that when a user authenticates to a domain controller, a global catalog is not contacted for domain-level or universal security-level policy validation. When the registry modification is implemented, global catalog information that existed before the registry hack will be the information that the workstation uses. If domain or universal group information is relatively static and nothing has significantly changed, the cached global catalog information is fine. However, if the last time the client workstation logged onto the domain was when network security was loose, and then a more restrictive security policy is applied, the workstation will know about only the looser security policy, thus preventing the administrators of the domain from applying the restrictive policy they desire and expect to be applied. It is highly recommended that you not use this registry modification unless you fully review the potential consequences.

While this global catalog placement strategy improves the response time of users to the global catalog information, it does create increased traffic between the remote global catalogs and the root of the forest. Any change to global catalog information must replicate to each and every global catalog on the network. If 50 new users are added along with 20 universal security groups and distribution lists, that information must propagate to all global catalogs on the WAN. Unlike the user lookup and authentication process that is sporadic throughout the day that we improved by placing the domain controllers and global catalogs closer to the users, global catalog replication can be planned or scheduled throughout a day or even scheduled to be completed every several days or once a week. This throttled replication of global catalog information can help restrict the demands of domain replication to nonpeak hours, thus decreasing the impact on the WAN during the middle of the day.

NOTE: Microsoft is expected to make a modification in the next release of Windows 2000 (Windows XP) that will cache the global catalog information on all distributed domain controllers. With this modification, the first time a user accesses the global catalog, a query will go across the WAN, grab the information from the global catalog, and then populate the information on the remote domain controller. An expiration value will be applied to the information. If someone else on the remote domain queries the same global catalog information, as long as the response value hasn't reached the expiration time value, the domain controller will use the cached information, thus increasing the response time of information to the remote user and also eliminating the additional WAN lookup traffic.

Extending the Active Directory Schema

Another best practice that has come out of implementing hundreds of Windows 2000 Active Directory environments is the recommendation that if you plan to extend the Active Directory schema, do so before you get too many servers and distribute too many users and clients in the field. Changes to the Active Directory schema can take several minutes to implement when the directory holds a limited number of objects. However, once you extend the Active Directory to support hundreds or thousands of objects, an AD schema modification can take several hours or even a couple of days to complete to replicate the directory changes throughout the enterprise.

One of the most common directory schema modifications is invoked when Microsoft Exchange 2000 is installed. Microsoft Exchange 2000 adds over 1,000 additional schema objects to the directory, including messaging-specific information such as mailbox attributes, mail routing table attributes, mail storage group attributes, and the like. Before Exchange 2000 can be installed, the schema needs to undergo a major modification to include all of these new attributes, and the changes must be propagated throughout the enterprise. Also, any user, contact, group, or domain object that has already been added to the Active Directory gets significantly modified with the major schema changes to support the new attributes in Exchange 2000. With Microsoft Exchange 2000, the installation command SETUP / FORESTPREP needs to be run from the Exchange 2000 installation media on the root domain of the forest. This process can take 20 to 30 minutes to complete when the forest has a single server in a single location with nothing more than the default users of the domain in the Active Directory.

As an example of how long the process takes in a fully deployed global enterprise, a similar FORESTPREP process was run in a global enterprise with 150 sites where a domain controller and global catalog resided at every site. Some of the most remote sites were connected though a series of daisy-chain regional connections back to the main corporate office with as minimal as 56 Kbps frame-relay connections to the final end destination. When FORESTPREP was run on this enterprise, it took almost two full days to get the Active Directory schema modifications to propagate to all domain controllers and global catalogs of this 3,300-user organization.

If you plan to modify the schema, particularly if you plan to implement Microsoft Exchange 2000 in the future in the organization, it is recommended that you extend the schema early on in the deployment cycle of Windows 2000 domain controllers and global catalogs in the enterprise.

Replication at the Attribute Level

Although the previous sections have described extensive Active Directory global catalog and domain database replication processes, the ongoing replication and synchronization of domain information throughout the enterprise is actually very efficient. Unlike with Windows NT4, where any change to a user record forced the replication of all user information (name, password, group memberships, and so on), with Windows 2000 Active Directory, replication is done at the attribute level. This means that if you change only the last name of a user account, only the last-name information is sent to other replicas of the directory. Since domain object and supporting attribute information is text based, the amount of information replicated throughout the domain is also minimal. A simple resetting of all passwords in a global enterprise that might have taken several hours to propagate throughout a Windows NT4 environment now can be scheduled in the middle of the night and can be completed in under an hour. Windows 2000 Active Directory attribute-level replication greatly reduces the impact of replication of information throughout the organization.

Replication of Group Membership Not at the Attribute Level

User, computer, and printer objects replicate at the attribute level, as described in the previous section, but one major technical characteristic of Windows 2000 Active Directory replication is that members of groups are replicated as a whole instead of by user. In other words, if you add a single member to a group that already has 150 members, all 151 member names get replicated across the domain. This causes two common problems for an organization.

First, for most organizations that use groups as distribution lists for identifying users that should have common security, access, or communication requirements, a new user on the network may be added to several groups in the organization. If these groups are universal groups, the groups and the group membership information for the entire group must propagate to all domain controllers and global catalogs throughout the enterprise. Especially when a product like Microsoft Exchange 2000 is added to an environment where universal groups are the distribution lists for e-mail users, the modification of groups occurs quite frequently. If a new user is a member of a 500-person departmental group, a 1,500-user site group, a 2,500-user division group, and a 5,000-user organization group, and an individual is added to each of these four groups, over 9,500 usernames would need to be propagated across the entire enterprise to make this simple modification.

Second, since Windows 2000 Active Directory delegates administration to multiple administrators with different capacities throughout an enterprise, a single regional, divisional, or companywide group may have several administrators adding, deleting, or modifying objects (such as users) in the groups. If large group membership information takes several minutes to propagate throughout an enterprise, it is very possible that multiple administrators will be making changes to the same large group(s) at the same time. And since the domain controllers in Windows 2000 Active Directory (in native mode) are all read/write repositories of directory information, a successful local domain controller write event could easily be overwritten by a successful local domain controller write event invoked by another administrator in another location. What this means is that if multiple administrators each successfully add a dozen new local users to an organizationwide group, if the information takes a long time to propagate across the enterprise, only the changes of one of the administrators will be retained. All of the changes made by the other administrators will be disregarded since group membership information is an all or nothing replication event. The other administrators are not even informed that their changes were disregarded. The only way to know whether changes were truly successful (or failed globally) is to have logging enabled for successful and failed group membership modifications and to check the logs after the changes are made.

To overcome this potential disregarding of data as well as the significant replication of group membership objects throughout an enterprise, an organization should nest groups in a hierarchical manner. Rather than having multiple groups with large membership lists throughout the enterprise, the organization should create a global group for a region or division, and then place the global group within an organizationwide universal group for the entire enterprise. What this does is keep granular local group membership changes from replicating throughout the enterprise. Any changes to membership of the global group will not be replicated across the enterprise, and since the nested global domain group names do not change, no additional replication states need to occur throughout the enterprise.

The drawback of this process is that while group member information is not replicated throughout the enterprise, the group membership information is also not made readily available throughout the enterprise. If you use something like Microsoft Exchange 2000 as your electronic messaging system and you use security groups as distribution lists for e-mailing groups of users and members of the enterprise in different domains, users of the messaging system will see the name of the nested groups, but they will then have to double-click the nested group to expand the group membership list. If the nested group is a domain local group, and if a user from a different domain wants to view the group membership of the nested domain local group in a different domain, the actual membership information would not be available for a member of a different domain to even view, by definition of domain local groups. In many organizations, knowing exactly who is in a sales or accounting department group at a different site or location may not be important. However, if the actual membership information needs to be visible to other domains, the users should be added to universal groups, where the member information of universal groups by definition is replicated throughout an enterprise.

One more note on optimizing WAN replication and performance enhancements in an Active Directory environment: while an organization may set site replication of domain controllers to occur in the middle of the night or possibly even just once a week to conserve WAN bandwidth overhead, thought must go into making a WAN performance and optimization decision that may drastically affect things like group membership replication synchronization.

NOTE: An change expected to occur in the next release of Windows 2000 (Windows XP) is that group membership itself will be set on an attribute level. This will mean that if user 101 is added to a group that already has 100 members, only the single user that was added to the group will be propagated throughout the enterprise. This will be a significant change that will enhance the performance and administrative integrity of groups and of group membership.

CREATING AN AD DESIGN BASED ON A SINGLE DOMAIN WITH A SIMPLE OU STRUCTURE

The domain design structure an organization chooses can have a dramatic effect on the overall performance of the domain, and that, in turn, affects the end-user experience of logon time and access to information. You no longer need to create multiple domains just to have distributed or delegated administrative control. A single domain in a Windows 2000 Active Directory environment can have the same administrative, management, and security control that forced organizations to create multiple domains in a Windows NT4 environment in the past. Because of this flexibility to create structured administration in a single domain in Windows 2000, one of the domain structures an organization can choose is the creation of a single domain.

No doubt a single domain is most common for a small organization that does not need nor would want to manage and administer a complex multidomain environmental structure. However, even medium-sized organizations with a relatively flat organizational structure find that a single domain can provide the granularity in administration, management, and security to meet the needs of the organization.

Design Description

A single domain with a simple OU structure is an Active Directory design that has a single forest and a single domain tree, as shown in Figure 4-2. In this design structure, the organization could run with just a single domain controller for the entire organization; however, for redundancy and distribution of authentication purposes, the organization would typically have at least a second domain controller on the network. In the event that the first domain controller fails, the second domain controller will be able to continue to authenticate users to the domain. There will need to be at least one global catalog in the network environment, and in the particular domain structure case where the organization is small or has a very flat organizational structure, all of the domain controllers would typically be configured as global catalogs for the organization as well. Having each domain controller also be a global catalog will minimize the number of different servers a user needs to connect to in order to log onto the single domain. Since there is only a single domain, the information stored and replicated as global catalog information is the exact same information as the domain controller information; therefore, there is no decrease in replication data by making a domain controller just a domain controller.

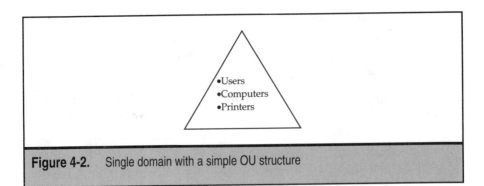

Figure 4-2. Single domain with a simple OU structure

At a small single-site organization with a flat organizational hierarchy, the first domain controller would typically hold the first single master operations (FSMO) roles for the forest and the domain (see the sidebar for more information on FSMO roles). As with any network with multiple physical network segments, putting a domain controller and global catalog server on each segment will improve logon authentication time compared to having a user make multiple hops across routers or complex network connections to reach a distant domain controller and global catalog.

First Single Master Operations (FSMO; pronounced "fizz-moe") Roles

In a Windows 2000 Active Directory environment, not all domain controllers are identical. There is at least one domain controller (for a small single-domain structure), if not two or more domain controllers (for a multidomain structure), that holds master copies of key Active Directory information. There are five key masters. At the forest level:

▼ **Schema Master** The schema master holds the master copy of the Active Directory schema. The schema is what defines all of the attributes of the objects in Active Directory such as First Name, Last Name, Group Membership, and the like. The schema master also defines whether an object is required or optional. For example, First Name is a required schema object attribute for a user account, whereas the user's Street Address attribute is optional. Without the schema master, you cannot modify the schema, such as extending it to include new objects to support functions such as Exchange 2000 messaging.

▲ **Domain Naming Master** The domain naming master controls the addition and removal of domains in the forest. To add a subdomain to the forest root or to add a whole new domain tree requires access to the domain naming master to insert the new domain information into the forest. Without the domain naming master or even administrator access to the domain naming master at the time of adding a new domain, the forest modification would not proceed.

At the domain level:

▼ **Relative ID (RID) Master** For each domain, there is a relative ID (RID) master that controls object identification. Every Active Directory object (user, printer, computer, and so on) has a unique ID. Those unique IDs are used to identify and correlate security, administrative function, and management control. The RID master is unique to each domain in a forest, so a multidomain environment would have a RID master for each domain in the forest.

■ **Primary Domain Controller (PDC) Emulator** For backward compatibility to support non–Active Directory workstation clients and servers, Windows 2000 Active Directory supports a mixed-mode environment. In mixed mode, there is a domain controller in each domain that emulates a Windows NT4 primary domain controller (PDC). The PDC emulator allows these non–Active Directory devices to think that the domain is still a Windows NT4 domain so that an organization does not need to completely upgrade to Windows 2000 on both the servers and desktops all at once. Each domain has a PDC emulator, and trusts can be created between the domains to provide multidomain models common in a Windows NT4 environment such as single-master, multimaster, and fully trusted domain models.

▲ **Infrastructure Master**   The infrastructure master controls the extension of a domain from the perspective of sites, site links, and site link bridges. The infrastructure master maintains a copy of replication partners within a domain and keeps track of synchronization events and propagation information that controls the integrity of domain controller information.

The FSMO roles are accessed only when specific events occur in the domain, such as when a new domain is added to the forest, or when the schema is modified. There can only be one copy of each FSMO role master in a forest (for the forest-level masters) and only one copy of each FSMO role master in a domain (for each domain-level master). Since FSMO roles cannot be duplicated or replicated in a domain, procedures must be taken to back up the FSMO role information so that if the domain controller holding the FSMO roles fails, a restore procedure can be run to replace the failed server and master operations. FSMO roles can be moved to other domain controllers.

In a forest with several domain controllers, there is no easy way to use the standard Active Directory domains and trusts, Active Directory sites and services, or Active Directory users and computers administrative tools to see which domain controller holds which FSMO role master. The best tool that comes with Windows 2000 is the replication monitor (replmon.exe) utility, which can be accessed by installing the Windows 2000 Support Tools on the Windows 2000 CD (\support\tools\setup.exe). The replication monitor can be focused to view the forest root or an individual domain and will note which domain controller in the forest or the individual domains hold the FSMO roles.

Design Impact on Performance

For an organization with a single site, the flat directory design is the simplest design structure, with the least performance impact from the perspective of server and site replication. All users on a network of this type typically are connected to a 10 Mbps or 100 Mbps high-speed network connection. When additional domain controllers are added to the network, they typically are connected to the same high-speed network and can use the extensive bandwidth available on the network to perform any necessary directory replication processes. However, in Active Directory design, since replication is independent of the administration and management designs and roles in the organization, the flat, single Active Directory structure does not directly imply that a complex site replication scheme does not exist. It is possible to have a small organization with multiple sites connected by slow or unreliable connections, where site-to-site replication throttling would need to be implemented. In those cases, site links and site link bridges need to be considered to optimize communication throughout the organization. See Chapters 9 and 10, which address Active Directory and replication performance tuning and optimization.

Design Impact on Ease of Management

With a single flat Active Directory structure, the time and effort needed to manage this structure should be minimal. There is no difference in replication or management of domain local groups, global groups, or universal groups since the single-domain structure functionally treats all of the different group types the same. The administrator of the domain may consider creating a first-level organizational unit container to better organize users, computers, or other domain resources; however, unless security or administration dictates this approach, the organization should just use the default directory structure created when Active Directory was installed. Since organizational units (OUs) can be easily added at any time, and resource objects can be moved to the OUs just by selecting the objects and right-clicking, the domain structure should be modified only when a compelling reason forces the change. Until then, keep the directory structure as simple as possible to keep the management of the directory minimal.

Design Impact on Administration

Most single-domain flat directory environments have centralized administration of users and network resources. These simplified and centralized administration models make a relatively flat Active Directory design easy to manage as well. Unlike in Windows NT4, where you could not delegate administration tasks, Windows 2000 Active Directory does allow you to make a single-domain configuration more versatile for administration by delegating rights and roles to others. Just as a simple directory structure can be modified in the future with multiple organizational units as necessary, a simple administration structure should be implemented and then delegation added in the future if the need arises.

Design Summary

Overall, a flat, single-domain structure for Active Directory is not only simple in concept, but it also provides the basis for fast performance, ease of management, and flexibility in administration delegation. The structure can always be expanded in the future to provide a higher level of granularity based on the needs of the organization; however, the plan should be to keep it simple in the beginning and make the structure more complex only when a specific need arises.

CREATING AN AD DESIGN BASED ON A SINGLE DOMAIN WITH COMPLEX OUs

Another domain structure an organization can choose is one in which a single domain is created just like the single-domain structure summarized in the last section; however, this single domain-structure uses a series of organizational units (OUs) to create distinct segmentation of the organization, typically for administration purposes. This domain structure is frequently used for medium-sized organizations that have fairly good cooperation among the IT administrators, who can delegate administration based on organizational units, not based on a more complex multidomain structure.

Design Description

A single domain with a complex OU structure is an Active Directory design that has a single forest and a single domain tree, as shown in Figure 4-3. Just as in the simple single-domain structure, the domain controller and global catalog information are one in the same since there is only one domain. Multiple global catalogs (GCs) and domain controllers (DCs) are added for redundancy and distribution of authentication only, since the single-domain directory structure could technically run with just a single GC and DC. Most organizations, however, will still choose to have at least two domain controllers to retain redundancy in authentication and domain information in case the primary domain controller fails.

Many organizations with thousands of users and dozens of sites around the world are choosing this design since it offers simplicity in administration and management, yet Active Directory provides the

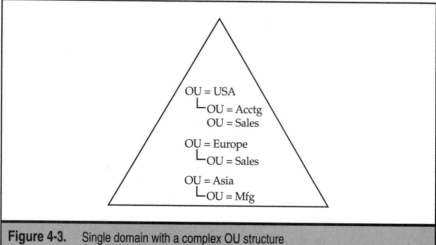

Figure 4-3.   Single domain with a complex OU structure

flexibility to organize information using OUs and delegate administration to multiple administrators. For organizations migrating from Windows NT4 that have single-master and multimaster domain models, the decision is being made to consolidate the resource domains and collapse the domains into organizational units in the Windows 2000 Active Directory. Most organizations installed resource domains in Windows NT4 since that was the only way to distribute administration as well as control replication patterns between remote sites.

In many complex single-domain structures, the organization has several sites around the globe that are connected through a variety of different WAN bandwidth connections. For remote sites with slow WAN connections, global catalog and domain controller placement is critical since there is only one domain and the replication of domain information will occur throughout the domain regardless of remote-site bandwidth. In cases where a remote site is connected to the main corporate office over a relatively high-speed WAN connection (512 Kbps or faster), replication between domain controllers is typically not a problem or concern. In these cases, having the remote-site domain controller also be a global catalog gives the end users a faster experience logging on and accessing global catalog–level information because they do not have to traverse the WAN backbone to acquire the information.

However, for remote sites that are connected over relatively slow WAN connections (128 Kbps or slower), the decision to make a domain controller also a global catalog needs to be evaluated. Administrators need to decide whether the user experience of relatively fast or relatively slow logon times or the time delay entailed in synchronizing global catalogs across the entire enterprise is more important for the organization. A remote site with a limited number of users who typically access information only on their local file server would be a candidate for a site that does not use a local global catalog; the users would have to traverse the WAN connection to access global catalog information. However, if a remote site has dozens of users who share information or even e-mail users throughout the enterprise, those users will be best served by a global catalog local to the site, so that the user experience is optimized.

Another reason to use organizational units in a medium-sized or large domain is the limitation of 10,000 objects per Windows 2000

Active Directory organizational unit. The tools and the performance of Active Directory management and administration are greatly enhanced by breaking the organization into smaller organizational units. However, when adding OUs to the Active Directory structure, having too many OUs and nesting them multiple layers deep creates a whole different problem for logon authentication time. At each organizational unit level, a series of group policies is applied. When the OU depth exceeds four or five levels, the time required to process all of the layers of policies can create a noticeable delay in user logon and authentication time. Therefore, adding organizational units can create levels of granularity that improve administration, but too many organizational units affect logon authentication time.

Design Impact on Performance

For a single domain with complex organizational units, the choice is between centralizing the global catalogs and domain controllers to decrease the replication time between GCs and DCs and not burdening the WAN with replication traffic, or placing the GCs and DCs closer to the users to improve user logon authentication and GC lookup performance. Most organizations choose to improve the user experience and place DCs and GCs closer to the users, meaning that the domain controllers are placed at the remote locations where the users reside. Since all domain controllers in a single domain hierarchy share the same information, if you add 100 users to the main corporate office site, that information must be replicated to servers at all other sites. You may think that a small office with 10 users needs only a 56 Kbps leased line because the users rarely need to access data on the other side of the leased line. However, because you have a single-domain structure, any and all information added or modified at your main connected site still will need to be replicated to the small remote site over the slow leased-line connection, drastically diminishing replication performance regardless of user-to-main-office requirements to access data.

Chapters 9 and 10 provide more detailed information on configuring and optimizing the Active Directory and replication between sites to help you decide whether to centralize or distribute domain controllers.

Design Impact on Ease of Management

As with the single flat Active Directory structure described in the previous section, the time and effort needed to manage this single-domain structure, even with nested organizational units, is minimal. There is still no difference in replication or management of domain local groups, global groups, or universal groups since the single-domain structure functionally treats all of the different group types the same. The organizational unit structure actually helps the administrator manage the domain objects since the grouping of objects provides a better method of viewing the objects and applying security. Since organizational units can be easily added or modified at any time, and resource objects can be moved to the OUs just by highlighting the objects and right-clicking, the domain structure can be easily modified at any time in the future. No fancy utilities are needed to reorganize the domain structure since there is only a single domain to administer and manage.

Design Impact on Administration

For organizations of any size, the ability to break the domain into multiple organizational units provides the means for easier administration and management of the resources of the organization. Particularly for organizations that have relatively centralized IT administration, the single-domain model provides a central depository for all domain objects. As stated several times already in this chapter, the big advantage of Active Directory is that resource administration can be delegated to an organizational unit level. Unlike with Windows NT4, where you could not move a user from a resource domain to another domain on the network, when you put resource objects into an organizational unit of a single Windows 2000 Active Directory, you can simply right-click the object and select to move the object to any other OU in the domain. If you need to move multiple objects, just hold down the SHIFT or CTRL key when selecting the objects you want to move in bulk, and then right-click to move all of the objects to another organizational unit. This level of flexibility provides great improvements in the administration of users, computers, groups, and objects when organizing information in a networking environment.

For example, if an employee changes departments or moves to a different location or facility, with a single-domain model broken into organizational units, the administrator can easily move the user to the organizational unit that represents the new department or facility where the employee now works. This level of flexibility greatly benefits organizations that want to balance replication and authentication time performance optimization with ease of administration and management.

Design Summary

Overall, a single-domain structure with complex organizational units provides flexibility in administration, the ease of single-domain management, and control of domain controller propagation and synchronization. The structure can always be expanded in the future to provide a higher level of granularity based on the needs of the organization, or the organizational unit design can be completely restructured to meet the changing needs of the organization.

CREATING AN AD DESIGN BASED ON MULTIPLE DOMAINS BY ORGANIZATIONAL STRUCTURE

Another domain structure an organization can choose is one where multiple domains are created in a domain tree of a forest. In this design structure, the subdomains designate different organizational departments, divisions, or business units. An example of a subdomain would be a Sales domain, an R&D domain, or a Human Resources domain. This approach is common for organizations that require more granular administration or management functions that cannot be achieved through the easier managed and administered single-domain, multiple-OU structure.

Design Description

A Windows 2000 Active Directory design can have multiple domains connected in a single forest and a single domain tree, as shown in

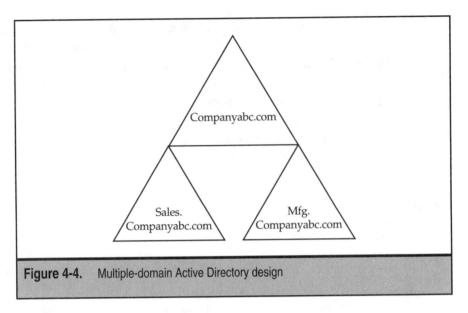

Figure 4-4.   Multiple-domain Active Directory design

Figure 4-4; however, the domain tree is extended with connected subdomains to provide the granular domain structure. The typical goal of creating a forest with multiple domains is to create better distributed security and administration. This is not as necessary as it was in Windows NT4 because delegation in Windows 2000 Active Directory can be done at the organizational level; however, an organization that requires very distinct administration or management of different sets of information may choose to create a multidomain structure. Creating multiple domains just for the sake of creating administrative granularity is costly in hardware and performance since each domain needs at least one domain controller (if not two for redundancy and fault tolerance), so a forest with two domains needs two to four domain controllers, whereas a forest with just a single domain needs just one or two.

In the multiple-domain structure, domain controllers hold information specific to the domain, and global catalogs hold information rolled up from all of the domains in the organization. Therefore, a global catalog contains a larger set of information than just an individual domain controller's set of information. This dictates more thought and planning on the placement of domain controllers and the enabling of the global catalog function on each and every domain controller, as was done in the single-domain models.

Design Impact on Performance

In general, the more domains you have, the larger directory size the organization will have, which equates to longer domain replication time. If an organization has 3 sites with 10 users at each site, and each site needs 2 domain controllers, there will already be 6 servers to support 30 users, and this doesn't even include the file and print and application servers required by the organization. All of these domain controllers need to have their information synchronized and rolled up into the global catalog, so the impact on LAN and WAN performance increases in a multidomain structure.

The size of the Active Directory database can be estimated by the ADSizer utility highlighted in the upcoming sidebar. Armed with the input from several fields of information such as the number of users, the number of sites, the number of domains, and the like, the ADSizer tool will estimate the size of the domain controller and global catalog databases as well as provide information on how long it will take to replicate domain information throughout the forest.

In complex multidomain structures, rather than walking the directory tree to go up one branch of the domain tree and down another branch of the domain tree to share information across users in multiple domains, an administrator can create a shortcut trust between the domains to speed up lookups across the forest.

Active Directory Sizer (ADSizer.exe) Utility

The ADSizer utility can be downloaded from the Microsoft Web site (http://www.microsoft.com/windows2000/downloads/) and is used to determine the size of the databases for a domain as well as the global catalog. The tool is nonintrusive to the domain, meaning that it actually does no direct reading or writing of information on a live Windows 2000 domain. In fact, the tool can be installed on just a stand-alone Windows 2000 Professional desktop system and not even be attached to the domain.

When the ADSizer tool is run, several questions are asked about the number of users, number of groups the users belong to, number of domains, number of sites, and the like. When all of the questions are answered, a report is generated that estimates the size of the Active Directory global catalog as well as the size of the domain databases. Obviously, since the report is generated based on the information entered into the tool, the information created is only as good as the information supplied.

Key to understanding what the database size really means is understanding how the Microsoft Jet database technology works. Even through the ADSizer utility says, for example, that the global catalog should be 83 megabytes in size, the actual data in the database will be considerably less than 83 megabytes. The database includes substantial free space so that when users and other objects are added to the directory, the database is large enough to handle the additions without constantly and dynamically having to increase the database size. Typically, the size described by the ADSizer utility is three times the actual storage space taken up by raw data within the database. Therefore, when estimating the time needed to replicate a database across a WAN connection, the ADSizer information should be divided by three to determine the actual amount of data that will be replicated if the entire database has to be synchronized. Furthermore, while the actual data in this example may be about 30 megabytes in size, since Active Directory object information is text information, this information is greatly compressed when it is finally replicated across the WAN. In independent studies on replication times and data replication amounts, a database estimated to be 83 megabytes in size would have less than approximately 4 megabytes of compressed information sent over the WAN. Of course, this information is based on a single example; however, key to note is that the size of the actual compressed data replicated across the WAN is nowhere near the estimated size of the database.

Design Impact on Ease of Management

Depending on the perspective of the individual making the decision about ease and complexity, a forest with multiple domains will be both easier and more difficult to manage than a single-domain structure. The multidomain structure is easier to manage if you want to administer just a portion of the forest, since the forest is broken into smaller domain units. For example, administrators in Europe who manage 100 users would have an easier time managing their own subdomain just for Europe than administrators managing just a single organizational unit of a 10,000-person global enterprise configured as a single domain. However, the multidomain structure would be harder to manage when the administrators try to administer the entire forest since the entire forest will be broken into multiple domains.

The biggest impact on management occurs when a user changes departments or divisions and crosses a Windows 2000 Active Directory domain boundary in the process. There is no simple way to just move the user from one domain in a forest to another. There are several tools available that provide the ability to perform the cross-domain migration; however, the tools add a level of complexity, unlike the simplicity of just right-clicking a user in a single-domain model and then moving the user to another organizational unit.

Design Impact on Administration

Assuming the perspective that domain administrators want complete control over their domains, having multiple domains provides that level of administrative granularity desired by individual administrators. However, if the organization shares information throughout the entire enterprise and there's a significant need to conduct centralized administration for key processes or tasks, the organization with multiple domains in a forest will have to spend significantly more time and effort administering the domain than would be required if the organization had a single domain broken into organizational units.

Design Summary

Overall, a multidomain structure can provide high performance since subdomain information does not necessarily need to be replicated throughout the entire forest, thus keeping the replication of data limited to a domain. There is significant flexibility in the administration of the multidomain model since each domain has its own domain administrator. And last, a multidomain model provides easy management of objects in the forest because each subdomain can be a department or division with distribution controls, security, and management functions. The biggest drawbacks of the multidomain model are the difficulty in moving users and objects from one domain and the cost of hardware to maintain multiple domain controllers and replica domain controllers throughout the enterprise to keep the forest operational.

CREATING AN AD DESIGN BASED ON MULTIPLE DOMAINS BY GEOPOLITICAL STRUCTURE

When selecting a Windows 2000 Active Directory structure, an organization can choose its design based on a variation of the multiple-domain structure outlined in the previous section. In this variation, multiple domains are created, and the subdomains designate geopolitical structure boundaries. This is a good domain structure for a medium-sized or large organization where the administration and management of the domain is distributed across multiple geographically disbursed locations with different administrative and security needs.

Design Description

This multidomain Windows 2000 Active Directory structure has multiple domains connected in a single forest and a single domain tree, as shown in Figure 4-5, where the subdomains are created to designate the geopolitical framework. Structurally, this is identical to the Active Directory structure with multiple domains noted in the previous section; however, by definition, this design structure is distributed by geopolitical structure, with the infrastructure distributed across multiple sites.

Unlike with Windows NT4, where the geopolitical structure automatically implied that there was slow bandwidth connections

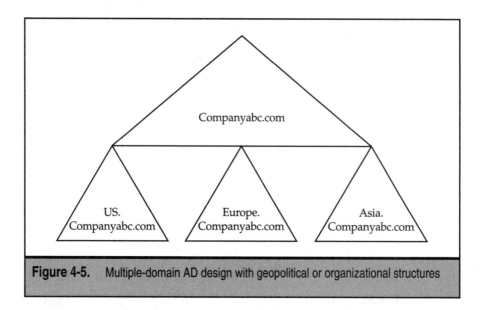

Figure 4-5.   Multiple-domain AD design with geopolitical or organizational structures

between the major regions, Windows 2000 Active Directory designs
do not need to correlate administrative boundaries with site
replication performance. Since sites and site connection performance
is completely independent of the namespace and administration
boundaries, the designer of the domain must evaluate both the
administrative structure and the infrastructure performance
independently.

When evaluating the geopolitical boundaries of a design of this
type, consider whether the sites are connected with relatively high
bandwidth availability, as might be the case with sites in Tokyo,
New York, and London. More commonly, though, sites will be
geographically dispersed, with some sites that have relatively high
bandwidth availability, and other sites with relatively poor
site-to-site bandwidth connectivity. The domain controllers in either
of these configurations will hold information specific to the localized
domain, and the global catalog servers will hold information rolled
up from all of the domains in the enterprise. Each domain will
typically have at least two domain controllers to retain redundancy
in authentication and domain information in the event that the
primary domain controller in the environment fails.

Design Impact on Performance

Using the assumption that the multidomain structure with geopolitical domain boundaries has a mix of relatively high-speed and low-speed connections, the replication design will vary based on the differences in bandwidth connectivity. For the sites with relatively high-speed connections (512 Kbps or faster), you will need to choose between centralizing the global catalogs and domain controllers to decrease the replication time between GCs and DCs and not burden the WAN with replication traffic, or placing the GCs and DCs closer to the users to improve user logon authentication and GC lookup performance. Most organizations choose to improve the user experience and place DCs and GCs closer to the users, meaning that the domain controllers are placed in the remote locations where the users reside. With relatively high-speed connections, either option will work fine since the bandwidth will be able to handle either the replication traffic or the logon authentication traffic demands.

However, for the sites with relatively low-speed connections (128 Kbps or slower), since any and all information added or modified in the main connected site will need to be replicated to the remote site over a slow line connection, replication performance will be drastically diminished regardless of user-to-main-office requirements to access data. In these cases, replication processes should be modified so that propagation occurs during off-peak hours. Chapters 9 and 10 provide more detailed information on configuring and optimizing the Active Directory and replication between sites to help you decide whether to centralize or distribute domain controllers.

Design Impact on Ease of Management

Beyond the management of replication across the distributed sites, administrators must manage domain controllers that are distributed to multiple globally disbursed sites. Many of the secondary remote sites will have slow bandwidth links back to the main office, and secondary sites may be connected to a regional site that then connects back to the main office, creating a nested configuration that adds complexity to the management of the domain controllers and the replication throughout the enterprise. Key to remember when designing bandwidth replication across a geographically disbursed environment is that changes in a remote site may take a very long time to propagate to a remote site connected to a different domain on the other side of the world. For most organizations where users do not travel between remote sites in multiple major regions frequently, the replication of information is not critical; however, its impact on logon authentication and the application of security throughout the enterprise must be taken into consideration.

Design Impact on Administration

The biggest benefit of having multiple domains with geopolitical boundaries is in the area of administration. By creating very distinct domains such as Europe, North America, and Asia, regional administrators can manage and administer the entire domain for the region. Each domain within the forest can have its own logon policy, password length and complexity policy, and domain root administrators. When creating organizational units, domain administrators will have control of the root of their own domains and can create the OU hierarchy that best fits the structure of the region.

While multiple domains is one of the biggest benefits of granular administration, it is also one of the most complex challenges because of the distribution of administration and management of the entire enterprise. For example, since each domain administrator can create his or her own OU structure and group structure, there does not need to be any consistency throughout the enterprise. One domain administrator may create OUs based on the individual countries within the region, another administrator may create OUs based on the individual city names within the region, and yet another administrator may create OUs based on the line of business names within the region. Additionally, Microsoft does not provide a tool that allows the centralized viewing of an entire subdomain-connected forest. Each domain needs to be viewed independently, so an enterprise administrator needs to drill down into a domain and view the contents and properties, and then drill up and down into another domain to view the contents and properties of another domain.

Design Summary

The multidomain structure distributed by geopolitical boundaries provides detailed granularity in administration while at the same time creating a very complex and difficult-to-administer enterprise administration process. For an organization that is structurally administered and managed by region with little enterprise-level sharing of information or combined management, the disbursed domain structure provides domain administrators with full control over their individual domains to make the domain fit the needs of the region. For an organization that is structured with significant enterprise sharing of information and cooperative administration of resources throughout the organization, the multidomain structure does not provide the tools to easily administer the entire enterprise from a single view.

From a performance optimization perspective, this domain design provides a structure that can keep local replication information from having to be replicated to other locations or sites, since domain information does not have to be propagated throughout the enterprise. This, along with the ability to throttle replication based on site links and site link bridge configurations, provides administrators of the organization with flexibility in optimizing the synchronization demands of the organization.

CREATING AN AD DESIGN BASED ON A DEDICATED FOREST ROOT STRUCTURE

Another variation of an Active Directory design is one where the root of the forest is created and secured, and all other administration and management functions are placed at the subdomain level in the domain tree. This design is commonly called the dedicated forest root structure, and it provides better security and control over forest-level resources. When creating an enterprise networking environment, every administrator wants to be the superadministrator, controlling anything and everything in the organization. However, medium-sized and large organizations often want to limit some administrators to one set of information and other administrators to another set of information. Additionally, as noted earlier in this chapter, FSMO roles cannot be replicated, and if they become corrupt, the masters must be restored from a recent backup. All of these challenges facing high-level control in the enterprise dictate the need for a domain design structure that can facilitate better administration and management control.

Design Description

In the dedicated forest root domain structure, a root domain is created with only a limited number of administrators having access to this domain, as shown in Figure 4-6. Off of this root domain is a subdomain (or multiple subdomains), where all common Active Directory objects such as users, computers, printers, and the like are created. Since there is tight administrative object control at the forest

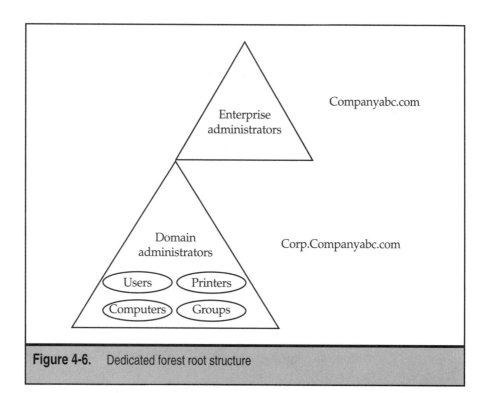

Figure 4-6.   Dedicated forest root structure

root, any changes to the schema or other forest-level FSMO role modifications must be implemented by one of the enterprise administrators. However, the domain-level administrators have complete control over the design structure and management of the entire subdomain for which they have full administrative rights.

Design Impact on Performance

The dedicated forest design structure affects global catalog replication and server distribution since a minimum of two domains are required. However, if all you are doing is protecting the FSMO roles, and all user accounts and OU structures reside in a single subdomain, then you can minimize performance impact by effectively having a single subdomain, with the users and resources of the domain sitting at this subdomain level. The replication of information between domain controllers and the propagation of the global catalog would be no different than if the organization truly

Enterprise Administrators vs. Domain Administrators

In Windows 2000, there are two types of administrators: enterprise administrators and domain administrators. In a single-domain model, the enterprise administrator and domain administrator have the exact same control since the enterprise consists of only one domain. However, in a multidomain structure, domain administrators may have full control over a single subdomain in the forest, or they may be limited to the administration and management of only that single subdomain. An enterprise administrator in a multidomain structure can administer and manage all domains in the forest.

The dedicated forest root structure leverages this enterprise-versus-domain-administration function by providing full domain administration rights to the subdomain administrator, yet eliminating the domain administrator from the enterprise administrators group, which has full control of the parent forest root domain.

used a single-domain model, especially if the forest root domain information changes only on major forest-level events.

Design Impact on Ease of Management

In a dedicated forest root design, since the forest root will have at least two domains, the global catalog will include the information from two or more domains. Although the administrators are distributed for better control of the enterprise, additional management is needed to configure and control the replication of domain controllers throughout the forest. The replication of global catalog information needs to be planned so that changes at the subdomain level are successfully replicated to the forest root.

Design Impact on Administration

The dedicated forest root design provides better security for all objects in the forest root. For organizations that distribute security across multiple administrators, the dedicated forest root design will provide better granular control over root-level objects versus domain-level objects. In highly secured environments, the root-level objects are made available to a limited number of administrators, and all other administrative functions are then delegated to the subdomain level. The big advantage of this domain model is the ability to provide full domain administration functionality to others while protecting the root. The root will undoubtedly contain the root level FSMO roles (see the discussion earlier in this chapter of the importance of the FSMO roles), and the root domain could contain specific enterprise administration accounts or even forest-level servers for which higher management security is desired.

Design Summary

Overall, a dedicated forest root structure can provide high performance if the subdomain structure is limited to a single domain, with organizational units used to distribute users, computers, and other objects within the single subdomain. But most important, the dedicated forest root provides the ability for an organization to control the forest root and limit access to only certain administrators. This can minimize any accidental changes to the FSMO that may affect the reliability of the network, while providing the domain administrators full control over the entire structure of their domains.

CREATING AN AD DESIGN BASED ON A PLACEHOLDER DOMAIN STRUCTURE

Another variation of an Active Directory design is the placeholder domain structure, where the root of the forest is created for the sole purpose of being a placeholder for a domain structure that will be implemented (or is anticipated to be implemented) in the future. As the name of the structure implies, the root simply holds a starting domain structure, for which the namespace can be different and which can be changed in the future.

Design Description

The placeholder domain model challenges the perception that once you install your Windows 2000 Active Directory, you can never change the domain name. By taking advantage of the ability of having multiple domain trees within a forest, a namespace can be installed along with other domain tree namespaces. An example of this implementation is the creation of an Active Directory forest with the name Win2k.local, as shown in Figure 4-7. This domain will be the placeholder domain. A server is then installed with Windows 2000 as a new domain tree of the existing forest. Say for example that this domain is called Cco.com. An administrator can add a new domain tree to this existing forest again and call this domain Companyabc.com. These two completely different namespaces both exist off the root domain Win2k.local, and through the use of migration tools and utilities, objects can be migrated from one domain to another domain within a single forest. Therefore, users created in the Cco.com domain can be moved to the Companyabc.com domain while retaining all security principals for the user object.

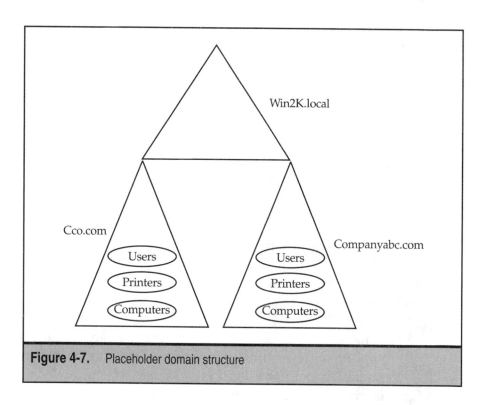

Figure 4-7.   Placeholder domain structure

Organizations can choose to create a fake root domain with the real domain configured as a domain tree off the fake root, or the organization can choose to install the real domain as the root and add a new subdomain with a completely different namespace at any time.

Design Impact on Performance

As with any multidomain forest, a placeholder domain structure has an impact on performance because multiple domain controllers need to be replicated throughout the forest. Since the placeholder root domain will remain static, very little forest-level replication will need to take place on a regular basis. Thus, the impact on performance of a domain structure of this type really depends on what the domain tree structure looks like. If the domain tree is just a single subdomain holding all Active Directory objects, the replication will be localized to just the single subdomain for the namespace. However, if the domain tree structure

Tools Available to Migrate Active Directory Objects

Several tools are available to assist an organization in its migration of Active Directory objects from one domain to another. The moving of objects is necessary in a multidomain structure when a user who belongs to one domain changes positions or moves to a different site and the job change crosses domain boundaries. In Windows NT4, an administrator typically just deleted the user from one domain and created the user again from scratch in the new domain. The problem with this practice is that any security objects applied to that user (such as file access permissions, mailbox profiles, security account access, and the like) have to be re-created after the user migration. When several users are migrated from one domain to another in this fashion, the process of re-creating the users, setting up the security profiles, and then propagating the information can be long and tedious. Certain security policies may be forgotten and not applied, and a security hole or breach may -occur. With the migration tools for Windows 2000, users can be moved between domains with security profiles remaining intact.

The tools available include three that are freely available to all Windows 2000 administrators plus third-party tools (for purchase). The tools vary in ease of use, features and functions, and cost.

▼ **MoveTree** The movetree.exe utility comes on the Windows 2000 media and can be installed by running \support\tools\setup.exe. By default, the tool is stored in the \program files\windows 2000 toolkit\ directory. A readme file in that directory explains how to use the tool. Essentially, movetree is a command-line utility that migrates objects such as user accounts, computers, printers, and the like from one domain to another. It is a complicated tool since the command-line switches necessary to successfully move objects are quite extensive. The destination domain must be in native mode for the tool to properly migrate objects; however, the tool does come free on the Windows 2000 media and can provide a method for migrating objects between domains.

■ **Active Directory Migration Tool** The Active Directory Migration Tool (ADMT) is a graphical user interface (GUI) utility that gives the administrator the ability to select objects from a source domain and choose a destination domain where the objects should be copied. ADMT can be downloaded from the Microsoft Web site (http://www.microsoft.com/windows2000/downloads/). Just like the movetree utility, the destination domain must be in native mode. ADMT not only copies the Active Directory object, but it also migrates security principals between domains. This gives the administrator the ability to move objects without losing the security profile information for the objects.

■ **Clone Principal** Clone Principal, like movetree, is installed by running the setup program in the \support\tools\ directory of the Windows CD media; the program and its supporting files are stored in \program files\windows 2000 support tools\. Clone Principal provides the ability to migrate security profile information between domains, just like the ADMT utility, and it provides a command-line interface to initiate the migration process.

▲ **Third-Party Migration Tools** There are several third-party migration tools available to assist organizations in their migration from Windows NT4 to Windows 2000, or even to consolidate multiple Windows 2000 structures. The NetIQ Domain Migration Administrator (DMA) third-party tool is the basis for Microsoft's ADMT tool. ADMT has very specific functions that it does very well, but NetIQ Domain Migration Administrator provides several more functions and capabilities. One of the major benefits of the third-party version is the ability to place a destination domain in mixed mode. Other feature enhancements of the for-purchase version of the product include the ability to create projects that can be used to prototype a migration in a lab, validate the migration, and then run the migration process from a script created when the test process was invoked.

These tools help the organization migrate objects between domains. They can help administrators create domain structures for moving users between domains or completely migrating all users from one domain to another during a major domain migration modification.

has several subdomains below it in a multidomain structure, the replication between domains will be more extensive.

Design Impact on Ease of Management

If the placeholder domain structure is configured as a single domain tree, the management requirements of the structure will be similar to those for any other multidomain model. With the placeholder domain structure configured with multiple domain trees, providing flexibility in the domain naming structure, the management of the forest will be much more complex as there will be multiple subdomains that will each require its own domain controller for the namespace information. At a minimum, the placeholder domain structure will need a domain controller in the placeholder domain as well as a domain controller in the root of the namespace. For redundancy, the organization may choose to have a second domain controller for each domain.

Design Impact on Administration

The administration of a placeholder domain is no different than the administration of any other single-domain, single-domain with complex OUs, or multidomain model. If the namespace has just a single subdomain for the organization, then it is administered just like a single-domain model. If the namespace has multiple subdomains, then it is administered just like any other multidomain model. All of the performance, management, and administration functions are similar to the more pure domain structures detailed in the previous sections of this book.

Windows 2000 provides several options for optimizing the performance of directory information replication, user logon authentication, and information access. Unlike previous versions of Windows, where the domain design dictated the end result of administration and management characteristics, with Windows 2000 Active Directory, the administration and management functions are somewhat independent of the replication and authentication components. There are, however, several choices that can be made when designing the Active Directory that can minimize the impact on performance and greatly simplify administration and management in the organization. Through a combination of logical design and the tuning and optimization of the design chosen, Windows 2000 can provide the basis for a well-tuned infrastructure environment.

CHAPTER 5

Fault Tolerance and Disaster Recovery Planning

Even though components, computers, and systems have become increasingly reliable, they still can fail. Disk subsystems can and will crash, natural disasters occur, power outages happen. Fault tolerance and disaster recovery planning allow an organization to respond effectively to these events.

Windows 2000 offers a number of underlying technical improvements that make it more fault tolerant and continuously available than previous operating systems, including:

▼ Windows File Protection service

■ Driver signing

▲ Reduced maintenance downtime

Even with these improvements, planning is needed to maximize the capabilities of the operating system. Windows 2000 includes a number of technology features such as clustering and network load balancing that give designers tools with which to implement their fault tolerance and disaster recovery plans.

Fault tolerance and disaster recovery are the prevention of and recovery from failure events. The central concern of fault tolerance and disaster recovery planning is the availability of services and data.

RISK MANAGEMENT

Each organization needs to identify the risks that it faces, prioritize the risks, and determine what it needs to do to address the possibility of those risks materializing. The process of identifying, prioritizing, and addressing risks is called risk management. Here are the steps:

▼ **Identify Risks**   List potential risks to the organization.

■ **Prioritize Risks**   Prioritize risks by assessing their impact and probability of occurrence.

▲ **Address Risks**   Develop mitigation and contingency plans.

Going through the risk management process will ensure that all likely threats are planned for and that effort is not misdirected toward less probable threats.

Identify Risks

The first step in risk management is to develop a comprehensive list of potential risks. It is important not only to look back at what failure events have occurred in the past, but also to look forward to anticipate potential failures.

Organizations face risks from different sources. A risk is any threat that can disrupt the organization's access to services or data. These risks can be internal or external to the organization, either preventing access or simply delaying access.

Some of the more common risks include:

- ▼ Fire
- ■ Earthquake
- ■ Equipment failure
- ■ Virus attack
- ■ Operator error
- ■ Software failure
- ▲ Data corruption

Risks to an organization vary by the type of organization, geographic location, history, and other factors. For example, earthquakes are considered an important risk on the West Coast of the United States. In contrast, cyclones are considered to be an important risk on the coast of East Pakistan, and earthquakes are not. For a large online retailer, loss of Internet connectivity means the loss of revenue on a minute-by-minute basis; for this type of business, this is a critical risk requiring extensive planning. On the other hand, a large brick-and-mortar retailer would not be affected as significantly; for such a company, loss of Internet connectivity is a medium-level risk.

The type of organization also affects the nature of the risks that the organization faces. For example, some large Web hosting organizations need to be concerned about the potential for terrorist attacks on their data centers and thus line their data center walls with Kevlar to prevent bomb shrapnel from damaging their systems.

Sources for developing a list of risks include reference books, historical records, local organizations, business organizations, brainstorming sessions, and so on. The initial list should include as many risks as possible, as the list will be reduced in the priority-setting phase of the risk management process.

Determine Impact

Ultimately, the impact of a risk on users or on the organization is what is critical. Different risks have different impacts on an organization. Likewise, the same risk will have different impacts on different organizations. While it could be argued that all risks are bad, not all are equally bad. For example, the loss of a user's workstation will affect mainly a single user and is probably not equal to the loss a file server, which will affect a large number of users.

Assigning an impact rating to a risk will help quantify the impact that the risk could have on the organization. The rating scale could be based on the financial impact—that is, what is the potential impact of the risk in dollars (how much will it cost the organization if the risk event occurs). Another scale could be simply a 0 to 5 numeric rating, with the high end of the scale indicating high impact. The rating scale should be the same for all the risks being evaluated, to make comparing and prioritizing risks simpler.

Determine Probability

There are many types of risks that an organization may face, but there is a smaller group of risks that the organization is likely to face. For example, an organization in San Francisco, California, would not be well served by a disaster recovery plan that gives equal weight to the possibility of a tornado and the possibility of an earthquake. However, the risk of a power outage is an almost universal risk, which could be faced by any organization anywhere.

Even with a universal risk such as a power outage, the probability of that risk varies from location to location. In most metropolitan areas of the United States, power outages are rare occurrences. In some rural areas, brief power outages are weekly events. In some foreign countries, power outages are regular events and may last for hours or days. For example, in Colombia, South America, the power company routinely shuts down power for one day on weekends to conserve power.

Each risk should be assigned a probability of occurrence. The process of assigning probabilities can be quite extensive and expensive, such as the process that insurance carriers use to evaluate risks. In the case of risk management for fault tolerance and disaster recovery planning, we can afford to be less rigorous. This likelihood of risk can be indicated as a percentage chance of occurrence or even a rating on a scale of 0 to 5. This allows risks to be ranked.

Determine Priority

The priority of a risk can be computed by multiplying the impact of the risk by the probability of the risk:

Priority = Impact × Probability

This ensures that risks that would have high impact but that are not very probable don't influence the fault tolerance and disaster recovery planning process. An example of a high-impact risk is a meteor strike near the site, which would undoubtedly result in a loss of service. However, the likelihood of this occurring is so small as to be almost zero, so the resulting priority will be correspondingly low, and planners can safely ignore it. Another example is a disk failure, where the impact is high and the probability is relatively high. This combination results in a high-priority risk that planners should definitely consider in the plan.

Develop Mitigation Plans

Mitigation planning reduces or eliminates the impact of the risk event should it occur. For example, by using a RAID disk subsystem, the risk of disk failure is mitigated; in the event of a disk failure, the RAID disk subsystem will continue to operate. It is important to note that mitigation does not prevent the risk event from occurring, but rather reduces its impact. In the preceding example, the drive would still fail, but users would still have complete access to their data with only a slight decrease in performance in spite of the loss of the drive.

Fault tolerance is the ability of a system to withstand failure and is the primary method of mitigating risks in the computing world. With fault tolerance, even if a component fails, the computing services that it supports will still be available. There are many technologies that help create fault-tolerant systems, including RAID disk subsystems, ECC memory, and clustering.

For each risk that is identified, one or more mitigation plans should be developed. The resources invested in the mitigation plans should reflect the priority of the risks—that is, high-priority risks should have the most effort and resources devoted to them.

Develop Contingency Plans

Contingency plans enable you to recover from a failure event if it occurs and mitigation was unsuccessful. When a contingency plan is activated, users are affected, but the contingency plan seeks to reduce the impact as much as possible. For example, if two drives fail in a RAID disk subsystem, then the subsystem will fail. The contingency plan might be to replace the server with a hot spare server and restore the system from backup. Users will be affected, but the duration of the impact is reduced by having a hot spare server available to implement the restore process immediately.

Disaster recovery is the process of recovering from a failure event and seeks to reduce the duration and magnitude of the impact to the user. Most disaster recovery processes are manual, such as restoring from tape, switching to a backup site, or starting a power generator.

For each risk that is identified, one or more contingency plans should be developed. As with mitigation planning, the resources invested in contingency plans should reflect the priority of the risks.

Create a Risk Matrix

A risk matrix table summarizes the information generated in the risk management process. The table is typically sorted so that the highest priority risks are at the top. The sample risk matrix shown in Table 5-1 includes some common (and uncommon) risks.

Risk	Impact	Probability	Priority	Mitigation	Contingency
Disk failure	5	4	20		
Mail storm	3	4	12		
Power outage	5	2	10		
CPU failure	5	1	5		
CD failure	1	2	2		
Meteor strike	5	0	0		

Table 5-1. Sample Risk Matrix: Risks Identified and Prioritized

Both the probability and the impact are rated on a scale of 0 to 5, with the higher number indicating a high impact or probability. As the matrix shows, the highest-priority risk is disk failure. The lowest-priority risk is a meteor strike, with an effective probability of zero. Normally risks with a probability of zero are not listed in the risk matrix; this risk was placed in the sample risk matrix for illustration purposes only.

Once risks have been identified and prioritized, the fault tolerance and disaster recovery plans can be created. The mitigation and contingency columns of the risk matrix should be filled in as the fault tolerance and disaster recovery plans are completed.

SCOPE

After you have prioritized the risks, you need to create plans to address them. A threat or risk that materializes is considered an event or an incident. To plan effectively, understanding the likely scope of an incident is critical. An event affecting a small portion of the organization will most likely have a smaller impact on the organization than an event affecting the entire organization. The impact on the organization will in turn guide the level of effort and resources directed toward fault tolerance and disaster recovery planning.

Impact of an Event

To evaluate the impact of an event, you need to classify the computing service it affects as to its importance to the organization. You need to know the cost of downtime in financial terms or in terms of the mission of the organization in order to develop effective plans to prevent downtime of the right services.

Magnitude of Failure

The potential magnitude of the failure event determines the impact of the event and directs fault tolerance and disaster recovery planning. If the failure is local, then recovery efforts are likely to be local. If the failure spans an entire geographic region, then recovery efforts are more likely to be organizationwide, and the failure will have a broader impact and require more effort to resolve.

The magnitude of a failure event can be categorized according to the range of its effects:

▼ **System Level**   These failure events affect a single computer system. Such events include component failures, local database corruption, and operator errors.

■ **Application Level**   These failure events affect an application service, which may span one or more computer systems. For instance, a corrupted Web site might be replicated within several host computers.

▲ **Site Level**   These failure events affect the entire site over a geographic region. Examples of such events include power outages, Internet link failures, and natural disasters.

Service Classification

Computing services such as e-mail, Web, and database access can be classified with respect to their importance to the organization. One way of classifying computing services is to designate them as mission critical, essential, necessary, or desirable.

Mission-Critical Services   Mission-critical services are those needed by the organization to accomplish its mission, the loss of which will result in immediate and ongoing loss of revenue. This designation can be based on business needs, regulatory or legislative requirements, life-threatening conditions, and so on. Examples of mission-critical services include Internet access for an online retailer and access to online medical statistics at a hospital.

Essential Services   Essential services are services necessary for communication within the organization, the loss of which will degrade the organization's performance and result in a loss of revenue over time. Examples of essential services include access to technical support databases for a support call center and access to inventory information for sales staff.

Necessary Services   Necessary services help the organization perform optimally and reduce effort for the organization. Alternative manual methods exist, but are more tedious or time consuming. Examples of necessary services include online medical records for a hospital where hard-copy records exist and online product information for sales staff.

Desirable Services   Desirable services improve the quality of work and the work experience, but are not needed in the normal performance of duties. Examples of desirable services include online corporate policies and procedures, online news services, and online 401k information for employees.

Service Levels

Service levels vary by organization and service classification. Service levels are typically specified by the computing service and include both availability and recovery. Availability times are typically expressed as a percentage of time available, as in the example in Table 5-2.

This scale of availability indicates that a service with 99.9 % availability will be down for a maximum of 8 hours and 44 minutes each year. This scale is sometimes referred to as the *nines of availability* and is expressed by the number of nines in the percentage, which in this example is three nines. This figure normally excludes scheduled maintenance windows or planned downtime.

Availability	Downtime per Year
99%	3 days, 15 hours, 21 minutes
99.9%	8 hours, 44 minutes
99.99%	52 minutes
99.999%	5 minutes

Table 5-2.   Sample Service Availability Table

In addition to availability, service levels need to take into account recovery. This is a combination of both the recovery time and the recovery point. The recovery time reflects the time needed to restore the service back to its operational state and is typically expressed in hours. The recovery point is the point to which data is restored. For a service that is backed up nightly at 11 P.M., this recovery point is the point at which the last backup was made—that is, data up to 11 P.M. the previous evening. This results in a recovery point of 24 hours maximum, assuming the worst-case scenario, in which the failure event occurs just before the nightly backup. For a transactional database with logs, the recovery point might include all data up to the time of the failure—that is, a recovery point of several minutes.

Service levels need to be established by each organization and for each service. Table 5-3 shows a sample service level table.

Service Classification	Availability	Recovery Time
Mission Critical	99.99%	5 minutes
Essential	99.9%	1 hour
Necessary	99%	4 hours
Desirable	99%	24 hours

Table 5-3.   Sample Service Level Table

Once service levels are established, plans can be developed to ensure that the levels of service are maintained. Understanding the service classification and what the service means to the organization in quantifiable terms helps designers and planners to put in place the fault tolerance and disaster recovery plans needed. In addition, service level agreements can be arranged with business units and management.

Service Level Agreements

It is important that service levels be established in cooperation with business units and management, not just within the IT organization. Once service levels are determined, service level agreements can be negotiated and documented with the business units and management to ensure that the appropriate funding is allocated and expectations are set.

Service level agreement discussions provide an excellent opportunity for communication about the capabilities and limitations of computing services, ensuring that realistic goals are set. If the service levels are not appropriate for the business unit's needs, then solutions to elevate the service levels can be discussed, and additional funding secured.

Documented service level agreements are invaluable for guiding IT organization practices and for resolving potential conflicts during failure events.

FAULT TOLERANCE PLANNING

Now that the risks have been classified and the service levels determined, the mitigation or fault tolerance plan can be developed. In essence, fault tolerance is about preventing the failure event from affecting the users or the organization.

Definition

Mitigation planning tries to limit the affect of a failure event on the organization, which is accomplished by making the systems fault tolerant. Fault tolerance is the ability of a system to withstand failures. Mitigation and fault tolerance planning in the computer world hinge on two factors: reliability and redundancy.

Reliability

One way to reduce the impact of failure events on users is to make the systems less likely to fail—that is, more reliable. By preventing failure events through development, design, or implementation, the overall system is made more reliable.

Examples of ways to improve reliability include using the Windows 2000 File Protection service, which prevents operating system files from being overwritten; purchasing brand-name computer systems with good components, to reduce component failures; and ensuring that disks are correctly partitioned, to prevent user data files from filling up the system drives.

These methods will improve reliability, but will not ultimately prevent system failures.

Redundancy

Since system and component failures are inevitable, the way to provide system-level fault tolerance is to plan for redundancy. Redundancy essentially allows services to fail over to a secondary, or redundant, system. This is similar to the buddy system, where team members rely on each other. Redundancy can take many forms: at the component level, the system level, and even the site level.

Component-level redundancy includes RAID disk subsystems and redundant power supplies. With RAID systems, if a single drive fails, the system continues to function with only minimal performance impact. With hardware RAID systems, the faulty drive can be replaced and will rebuild itself without the need to bring the computer system down. With redundant power supplies, a single power supply can fail, and there will be no impact on a computer system. Again, the power supply can be replaced online without bringing the computer system down.

System-level redundancy can be implemented using a variety of features provided by Windows 2000, including network load balancing and clustering. Network load balancing and clustering allow designers to create clusters of application servers that work together to provide application services, with load balancing and failover capabilities. When a single system fails in a cluster, the other application servers work together to take over the load. These features are discussed in the "Technologies" section that follows.

Automatic Processes

Given the need to reduce the impact on users, the planned fault tolerance to failure events should be automatic where possible. Manual fault tolerance solutions will likely affect users and are more appropriate for disaster recovery.

Technologies

Microsoft Windows 2000 includes a number of features and technologies that enhance reliability and provide tools for creating fault-tolerant systems.

Reduced Maintenance Downtime

To reduce the need for both unplanned and planned downtime, Windows 2000 has greatly reduced the number of operations that require a system reboot. An administrator can perform file system maintenance, hardware installation and maintenance, networking and communications, memory management, software installation, and performance tuning, all without needing to restart the system. Windows NT required reboots for many of these common administrative tasks, which caused excessive downtime.

This enhancement results in reduced impact on users due to planned downtime. It allows routine maintenance to be performed on a regular basis without shutting down the system, which results in a more stable platform and less unplanned downtime.

Recoverable File System

The Windows 2000 file system is transactional and highly tolerant of disk failures. The operating system logs all disk I/O operations as transactions, similar to a SQL database. In the event of a system failure, the file system can quickly roll back or roll forward transactions as appropriate when the system is brought back up. This makes the file system extremely fault tolerant.

Automatic Reboot

If a system failure occurs, the Windows 2000 operating system can be set to automatically reboot the system, as shown in Figure 5-1. This reduces the amount of time the system is down, as would occur if a system failure happened during off hours. Rather than wait for a system administrator to respond, the system automatically reinitializes and logs the failure.

Windows File Protection

Windows 2000 protects the operating system files by not allowing third-party applications to overwrite them. The Windows File Protection service verifies the origin of a system file before it is

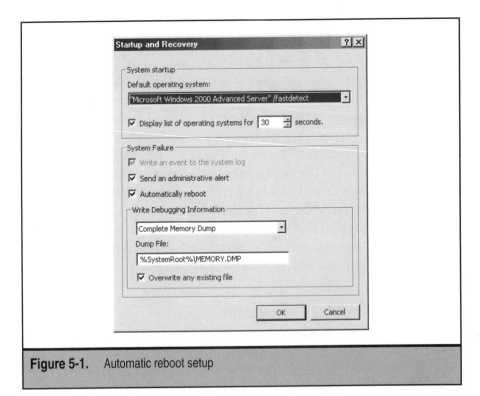

Figure 5-1.   Automatic reboot setup

installed. This ensures that system files are authorized system files. It also prevents the replacement of system files with extensions of .sys, .dll, .ocx, .ttf, .fon, and .exe. The Windows File Protection service runs in the background at all times and protects all files installed by the Windows 2000 Setup program. It detects and prevents any attempts by other programs to replace or move a protected system file. Windows File Protection also checks the digital signature of any new files to determine whether the new file is the correct Microsoft version. This service prevents incorrect versions of operating system files from overwriting the correct ones and destabilizing the system.

Driver Signing

Windows 2000 incorporates a new technology called driver signing. This feature notifies users if a driver they are installing is not a Microsoft-certified driver. Driver signing attaches an encrypted digital signature to a driver file that has passed the Windows Hardware Quality Lab (WHQL) tests.

Microsoft digitally signs manufacturer drivers that pass the WHQL testing process. The digital signature is valid only for that specific driver, and the test will fail if any changes are made to the driver. This signature proves to users that the drivers they are installing are the same ones that Microsoft has tested.

This process improves the reliability of Windows 2000 systems by ensuring that any code installed on the system has passed Microsoft's rigorous testing process.

Faster CHKDSK

The Check Disk (CHKDSK) utility is used to check the hard disk for errors. CHKDSK performance in Windows 2000 has been enhanced by a factor of more than 10; that is, performance is 10 times better than under Windows NT 4.0. After a failure event, CHKDSK will run automatically on restart.

RAID

Disk subsystems can be configured as Redundant Arrays of Inexpensive Disks (RAID), allowing them to achieve higher performance and fault tolerance. This can be done directly with the Windows 2000 operating system or through hardware, using specialized hard drive controllers. Table 5-4 illustrates some of the common RAID configurations.

The most commonly found RAID configurations are RAID 5 and RAID 1 (mirroring). Normally, RAID subsystems are configured using specialized hardware controllers, which perform better and allow advanced features such as hot swapping of failed drives.

Network Load Balancing

The Network Load Balancing (NLB) service allows services to provide fault tolerance to Web servers, streaming media servers,

RAID Level	Configuration	Fault Tolerance	Pros/Cons
RAID 0	Data is striped across two or more drives	None	High performance
RAID 1	Data is mirrored across two drives	One drive	High performance; 50 percent loss of capacity
RAID 0+1	Portions of data are on different disks	One drive	Expensive to implement
RAID 3	Data elements are striped across disks, with parity on one drive	One drive	High bandwidth for large data blocks; loss of one drive in array
RAID 4	Data is interleaved in large stripes	One drive	Higher performance on reads than writes; loss of one drive in the array
RAID 5	Data and parity are striped across all drives	One drive	High performance for small blocks; loss of one drive in the array to parity
RAID 6	Data and two sections for parity are striped across all drives	Two drives	High performance for small blocks; loss of two drives in the array to parity

Table 5-4. Common RAID Configurations

virtual private network (VPN) servers, terminal servers, and other applications. NLB provides this capability by using a group of two or more Windows 2000 Advanced Servers working together. NLB joins this group of computers systems by using the Windows 2000 advanced TCP/IP networking protocol. Organizations can create server groups containing up to 32 servers. NLB is entirely software based and does not require any specialized hardware. Figure 5-2 shows an example of a load-balanced Web service.

NLB provides service fault tolerance, but it does not provide session fault tolerance. In the event that an NLB server in a group fails, any client sessions that the server is hosting will fail as well. The client could restart the connection and establish a new session with another server in the group, but any information being worked on in the failed session would be lost. For session fault tolerance, clustering is the answer.

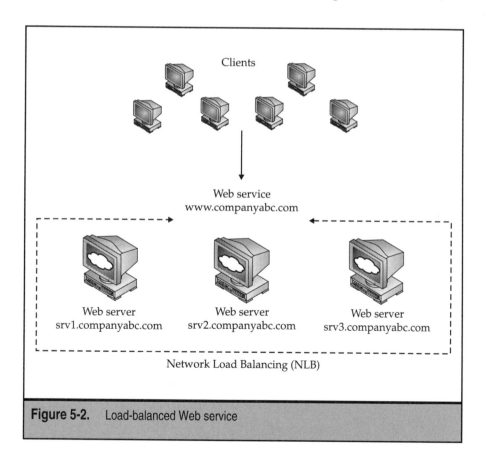

Figure 5-2. Load-balanced Web service

Clustering

Windows 2000 Advanced Server provides server clustering. A server cluster is a set of servers linked together by hardware and managed together by software. The objective of clustering is to provide very high levels of application and data availability. The servers within a cluster perform as a single integrated unit. Should any one server stop functioning, its workload is automatically transferred to the other server, to provide continuous service. This provides seamless system failure protection for users, who do not see any service impact during the transfer. An example of a clustered database service is shown in Figure 5-3.

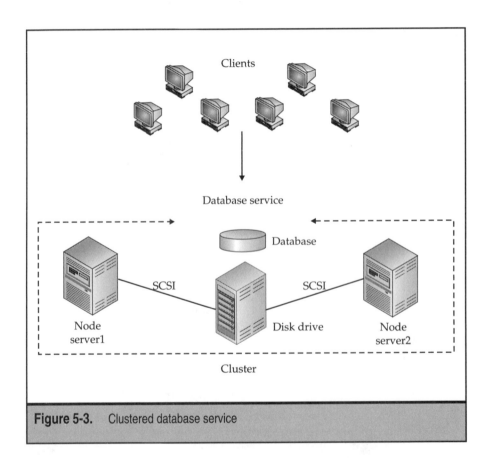

Figure 5-3. Clustered database service

This capability can also be used to perform rolling upgrades, whereby systems are upgraded with no downtime for users. The system to be upgraded is simply brought down and upgraded, with users gracefully failing over to the online cluster node.

Clustering requires no additional software other than Windows 2000 Advanced Server, but it does require specialized hardware configuration.

Improved Storage Management

One of the major causes of failure in existing computer systems is running out of disk space. To prevent this problem, Windows 2000 provides improved storage management capabilities to help maintain free disk space with minimal effort. Online administrative tasks can be performed with no disruption to services, including creating, extending, or mirroring a volume. This allows administrators to add drive space on the fly without bringing down the computer system.

To prevent accidental or intentional overallocation of disk resources, Windows 2000 Server supports disk quotas to monitor and limit disk space use on a user or group basis. The operating system continuously tracks disk space use for users based on the files and folders that they own and will warn or prevent users from using more than their quota of space on a disk.

Techniques

There are important techniques to ensure system fault tolerance, above and beyond the technology options. Many network services have built-in redundancy failover capabilities that should be incorporated into your fault tolerance planning.

Many TCP/IP-based services have built-in redundancy mechanisms, as they were designed to function over the very unreliable Internet. These typically include dual entries for servers; the protocol stacks will automatically try the second entry if the first fails. Some examples of such services include Domain Name System (DNS), Dynamic Host Configuration Protocol (DHCP), and now Active Directory.

DNS Redundancy

Workstations can enter more than one DNS server to perform host name lookups. To provide fault tolerance to workstations, create two or more DNS servers, configure the servers to replicate zones between them, and populate the workstations DNS entries with the server addresses. If one of the DNS servers should fail, the workstations TCP/IP protocol stack will automatically fail over to the second DNS entry. The failover server could even be in a different geographic region. Chapter 10 discusses how to configure DNS replication for maximum performance and fault tolerance.

DHCP Redundancy

A workstation using the DHCP protocol uses a broadcast to initially contact a DHCP server and acquire an IP address lease. After that initial broadcast, it then communicates using directed packets to that original DHCP to renew its IP address lease. If it fails to renew its lease with the original DHCP server, then it will release the lease and send out a broadcast for a new lease. This would be the case if the original DHCP server had failed.

To build in redundancy for DHCP services, create separate DHCP servers and configure them with scopes of address that don't conflict, as in Figure 5-4. If one or the other server fails, the redundant server will continue to issue IP address leases and will pick up workstations that loose the leases that were issued by the failed server.

Active Directory Redundancy

Active Directory also provides fully redundant capabilities. The failover capability is created automatically as new Active Directory domain controllers are created, so administrators don't even need to change the default behavior to get the fault tolerance feature. As new Active Directory domain controllers are created, they register themselves with the DNS server and also register server resource records advertising their address. If a Windows 2000 system tries to access a failed domain controller and does not get a response, it will automatically request an alternative domain controller address from the DNS.

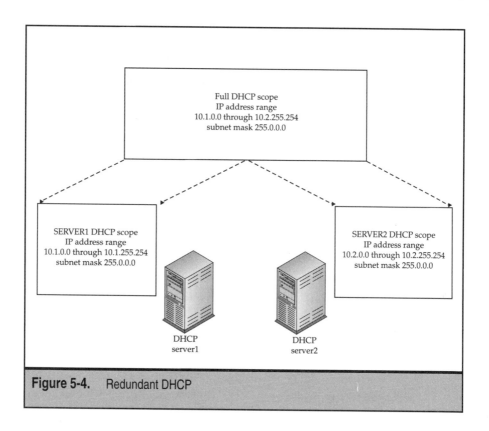

Figure 5-4.   Redundant DHCP

Making sure that Active Directory is always available and performs well is a key factor in a Windows 2000 network. In Chapter 10, we discuss Active Directory redundancy, replication, and performance optimization.

Risk Matrix

After you complete the test plan, the mitigation column of the risk matrix should be complete. Table 5-5 shows the sample risk matrix updated with the mitigation information.

In this example, the mitigation plan for the disk failure risk is to install a RAID subsystem. For the CD failure risk and the meteor strike risk, the priorities were considered too low to warrant mitigation plans.

Risk	Impact	Probability	Priority	Mitigation	Contingency
Disk failure	5	4	20	RAID	
Mail storm	3	4	12	Dual gateways	
Power outage	5	2	10	UPS	
CPU failure	5	1	5	Clustering	
CD failure	1	2	2	N/A	
Meteor strike	5	0	0	N/A	

Table 5-5.   Sample Risk Matrix: Mitigation Planned

Elements of the Fault Tolerance Plan

The fault tolerance plan documentation should be detailed enough for future designers and administrators to understand and adapt the plan. The following paragraphs describe sections you may want to include in your fault tolerance plan. Depending on the size of the organization and the number of systems being planned for, the actual plan may contain fewer or more sections.

Purpose

This section should present a high-level overview of the plan and its goals. A nontechnical manger or layperson should be able to understand this section.

Assumptions

Major assumptions of the plan should be listed in this section. It is important to list requirements such as availability of failover sites and routine updates to the plan.

Scope

The scope of the plan should detail the systems, services, and sites that the plan covers. It is important to be detailed and specific in this section, as well as to list any systems, services, or sites that are specifically not covered by the plan.

Fault Tolerance Plans

Document the specific mitigation measure designed for each service. Include any conditions and requirements that need to be met to implement the design. This section should include diagrams and flow charts wherever possible.

Administration and Maintenance Procedures

List the specific administration and maintenance procedures needed to ensure that the mitigation or fault tolerance systems continue to function properly.

Include monitoring requirements to detect fault tolerance events. There should be a set of routine administrative procedures to test that the mitigation and fault tolerance systems are fully functioning, so that you don't have to wait for a failure event to find out. In addition, include systematic administrative procedures for failing back after a fault tolerance event has occurred and the failed system has been restored.

Service Level Agreements

The specific service level agreements reached and planned for should be documented in this section. This will allow the implemented mitigation plan's actual performance to be measured against the service level agreements and adjustments to be made in the future.

DISASTER RECOVERY PLANNING

In spite of the best-designed fault tolerance system, there is always the possibility that a failure event will occur and affect users. In a contingency situation, the users are affected, and the focus is on how to minimize the duration of the impact. Administrators need to have contingency plans to recover from failure events and restore services.

Definition

Disaster recovery follows either of two courses, assuming that the data is intact: the system can be either repaired or restored.

Repair

If a component or system fails, one of the avenues for recovering services is to repair the failed component or system. For the failure of a component such as a motherboard or network card, this option is viable and attractive. It allows the system to be restored to service quickly, assuming that no other component of the system was adversely affected.

For failures related to data corruption or where a component failure leads to data corruption, the situation is less clear. For example, if a messaging system experiences database corruption due to a system crash resulting from a bad motherboard or network card, then recovery may not be as simple as just replacing the failed component. Restoring services may require repairing the database, a potentially time-consuming task that may not be successful in the end.

If service level agreements are in place requiring a four-hour recovery and a database repair will take two hours with no guarantee of success, a better option might be to immediately initiate a restore operation.

Last, the failure of a disk subsystem may preclude the repair-only option, because data may have been lost. This scenario requires a restore operation.

Restore

Restoring involves replacing either lost or corrupt data from a backup location, normally a tape subsystem. Rather than being an exclusive option, restoring will usually involve repairing the failed system prior to the restore process.

For stand-alone systems such as Web sites and file services, this is a straightforward process of restoring the tape to the repaired system. For complex applications such as the Active Directory service, the Exchange messaging service, or a SQL service, there are many application-specific concerns that need to be addressed. These include replicated data, transaction logs, version restrictions, and naming conflicts.

For these application-specific concerns, you need to create application-specific step-by-step guides to the disaster recovery process. During crises, it is easy to miss what under other circumstances would be obvious steps in a process. In addition, in crisis, it is not always true that the most qualified personnel are dealing with the problem, but rather the most available personnel. The disaster recovery guides should be as straightforward and deterministic as possible, to prevent errors.

Automatic Processes

With mitigation plans, the goal was to have all processes as automated as possible to minimize user impact. Therefore, mitigation planning made use of fault tolerance and redundancy technologies with automatic failover, such as clustering.

In contrast, with contingency plans, the goal is to have qualified personnel determine the specific course of action needed. This is partially due to the extreme nature of a disaster event, where it may be difficult to know in advance what the circumstances are. Given that uncertainty, the preference is for manual processes.

Manual Processes

Manual processes allow considerably more flexibility and human judgment to be brought to bear on the solution than do automatic processes. Processes can be adapted to accommodate unforeseen situations and conditions and to take advantage of opportunities to reduce the duration of the outage.

In addition, disaster events frequently cause failure to a recovery point, which means that there may be data loss. The decision to trigger recovery and thus accept the loss of data beyond the recovery point is typically a decision best made by senior management or executives of the organization.

Technologies

Windows 2000 has numerous built-in technologies and features that assist in the recovery process. Many of these, such as the recoverable file system and automatic restart, were discussed in the "Fault Tolerance Planning" section of this chapter. These features are, for the most part, automatic, and so are appropriate for fault tolerance as well as for disaster recovery planning.

For disaster recovery and repair in particular, safe mode and the Recovery Console are useful tools.

Safe Mode

Similar to Windows 9x, the Windows 2000 operating system can be started using safe mode. Safe mode allows the diagnosis and troubleshooting of system startup problems. In safe mode, Windows 2000 uses basic default hardware settings (mouse, monitor, keyboard, storage, video, system services, and no network) to reduce the chance of conflicts and problems. Booting in safe mode allows administrators to change settings or remove newly installed drivers that may be causing boot problems.

This feature enables quick recovery from failed hardware components and from errant configuration changes.

Recovery Console

The Windows 2000 Recovery Console is a command-line console boot option that allows basic file operations from a safe mode boot. The utility can be installed from the Windows 2000 Setup program. The Recovery Console is used for repairing a system by copying files from a floppy disk or CD to the hard drive, or for repairing a service that is preventing the system from starting. Using the console, administrators can start and stop services, format drives, read and write data on a local disk, and perform other tasks. The console provides a way for administrators to access and recover a Windows 2000 installation while preserving Windows 2000 security. Administrators must still authenticate to the Windows 2000 system, thereby preserving security.

Techniques

There are some techniques that help ensure that disaster recovery is possible. Unlike techniques for fault tolerance, which rely on technology, the techniques for disaster recovery rely on administrative policies. Some of those policies include making full backups, storing tapes offsite, and stocking spare parts.

Full Backups

Tape backup systems can be configured to perform full backups, incremental backups, or differential backups, to name a few of the more common configurations. Incremental and differential backups are used mainly to reduce the amount of time and tape space needed for backups.

The problem with using either or those techniques, rather than performing a full backup every time, is that they increase the time needed for recovery and also increase the risk that a tape failure will affect the recovery process. During a crisis, time is usually at a premium. Both differential and incremental backup techniques require multiple tapes to conduct a restore operation, thus potentially causing the restore process to take longer as each tape is restored. In addition, if a backup spans multiple tapes, there is a greater risk that any one tape will fail and thereby cause the entire restore operation to fail.

Given these concerns, it is recommended that every backup session entail a full backup. This will reduce the amount of time needed for a restore operation and reduce the risk that a tape failure will affect the restore operation.

Offsite Tape Storage

Backup tapes should routinely be taken to an offsite storage location to prevent a site-level disaster from destroying both the original data on the computer system and the backup tapes. Even tapes that are not taken offsite should be placed in a fire-proof safe or cabinet under lock and key for security and fire protection.

Hot Spare Servers and Parts

The typical turnaround time for a server part is at best the next business day with a high-quality manufacturer and a strong repair partner. This means that the spare part needed to bring up a potentially critical server will not arrive until 10 A.M. the day following the failure; it will then need to be installed and tested, and only then can restore procedures be initiated. This could translate to a 48-hour service level. Some manufacturers offer extended server coverage that guarantees that spare parts arrive in 4 hours, but that would still translate to a minimum of 8 hours downtime once restore procedures are factored in.

A useful technique for reducing service-level downtime is to purchase hot spare servers and spare parts. This allows servers to be replaced and repaired without waiting for parts to arrive from the manufacturer or supplier. Hot spare servers can be preinstalled with applications, ready for a restore procedure to be initiated. This will reduce the service-level loss to the minimum time needed to restore the data.

Spare-parts stocking enables the quick replacement of key components. For example, consider a RAID disk subsystem, where the array will continue to operate even if a disk fails. However, if a second disk fails while the manufacturer is shipping the replacement disk, the system will fail. Rather than run the risk of this failure, many organizations stock spare disks. As soon as a disk fails, they replace it immediately from the spares stock.

Risk Matrix

After contingency options have been evaluated, your risk matrix can be completed. Table 5-6 shows the sample risk matrix. It includes several contingency options for some risks, such as either switching to a backup site or using a generator for a power outage disaster.

Elements of the Disaster Recovery Plan

The disaster recovery plan documentation should be detailed enough for future designers and administrators to understand and adapt the

Risk	Impact	Probability	Priority	Mitigation	Contingency
Disk failure	5	4	20	RAID	Tape backup Hot spare server
Mail storm	3	4	12	Dual gateways	Queue mail
Power outage	5	2	10	UPS	Backup site Generator
CPU failure	5	1	5	Clustering	Hot spare server Spares stocking
CD failure	1	2	2	N/A	Spares stocking
Meteor strike	5	0	0	N/A	N/A

Table 5-6.   Sample Risk Matrix: Completed

plan. The following paragraphs describe sections you may want to include in your fault tolerance plan. Depending on the size of the organization and the number of systems being planned for, the actual plan may contain fewer or more sections.

Purpose

This section should provide a high-level overview of the plan and its goals. A nontechnical manager or layperson should be able to understand this section.

Assumptions

Major assumptions of the plan should be listed in this section. It is important to list requirements such as availability of failover sites and routine updates to the plan.

Scope

The scope of the plan should detail the systems, services, and sites that the plan covers. It is important to be detailed and specific in this section, as well as to list any systems, services, or sites that are specifically not covered by the plan.

Disaster Recovery Plans

Document the specific mitigation measures designed for each service. Include any conditions and requirements that need to be met to implement the design. This section should include diagrams and flow charts wherever possible.

Teams

Unlike the fault tolerance plan, which relies on automated systems, the disaster recovery plan requires extensive decision making, manual effort, and teamwork. The disaster recovery teams should be selected well in advance of any disaster. A list of teams may include the following:

▼ **Management**   This team consists of members of upper-level management who are empowered to make any required decisions.

■ **Damage Assessment**   This team consists of senior technical staff responsible for evaluating the disaster and implementing the overall disaster recovery plan.

■ **Information Technology**   This team consists of technical staff responsible for implementing disaster recovery plan tasks related to the IT infrastructure.

▲ **Telecommunications**   This team consists of technical staff responsible for implementing disaster recovery plan tasks related to the network infrastructure.

These teams could be multiperson teams, single-person teams, or even have members with overlapping roles, depending on the size of the organization. There should also be special contacts and teams for specific events that require specialized responses. An example of such a situation is an industrial espionage event, which would require activating a security team and perhaps a legal team.

Administration and Maintenance Procedures

List the specific administration and maintenance procedures needed to ensure that the contingency and disaster recovery systems continue to function properly and will work properly in the event of a disaster.

Include monitoring requirements to detect fault tolerance events. There should be a set of routine administrative procedures to test that the contingency and disaster recovery systems are fully functioning, so that you don't have to wait for a failure event to find out. There should be a lab environment where the disaster recovery procedures can be tested and updated.

A step-by-step disaster recovery guide for each service is very important. In the midst of a disaster, it is easy to make mistakes. The disaster recovery guides should be as simple and deterministic as possible, to prevent any errors during execution. The guides could include assessment criteria for determining the extent of the failure, flow charts for instructions, and clear steps for recovery.

The guides should be tested during the development stages of the plan to ensure that they work in the real world on the organization's existing equipment.

Communication

The communication section is critical for the smooth implementation of the disaster recovery plan. It should contain a list of specific corporate managers and executives who should be notified of the disaster and specify the frequency of updates. The communication section should also contain emergency contact numbers for key vendors and support personnel, with alternatives. The disaster recovery team members and their contact information should also be included in this section.

Given the volatile nature of phone numbers and roles, this section will need to be maintained on a regular basis to be useful.

Service Level Agreements

The specific service level agreements reached and planned for should be documented in this section. This will allow the implemented contingency plan's actual performance to be measured against the service levels agreements and adjustments to be made in the future. This will also allow disaster recovery team members to make informed decisions during the recovery process to remain within service levels.

KEEPING PLANS UP-TO-DATE

As soon as the fault tolerance or disaster recovery plan is printed, it will be outdated. As organizational priorities change, the information technology environment changes, and industry technology moves forward, you need to review, refresh, and update the plans.

Updating

The plans will require updating to ensure that they remain valid and effective in the organization. Updating should be done on a periodic basis even if there are no apparent changes; updating should also be done after any information technology change. This process of updating the fault tolerance and disaster recovery plans is normally included as part of any IT project, so that the process of updating is integrated into the overall processes of the organization.

Plan Review

A review of the plans should be conducted quarterly or semiannually. At the very least, team members' names and contact phone numbers should be updated. The plan should also be verified against the current environment to make sure that it is still accurate. This includes incorporating new sites and additional servers for existing services.

The review should not require significant time or effort and could be accomplished within a single day. However, any major discrepancies should trigger a plan update.

Plan Update

An update requires reviewing the fault tolerance and disaster recovery plans to determine any updates and changes that may be needed. This includes testing the disaster recovery guides to ensure that they are still effective. New procedures may need to be developed for new systems and then the disaster recovery plan updated. The fault tolerance plan should also be reviewed and the failover systems tested and updated.

A plan update requires the involvement of more staff, and requires significantly more effort, than a plan review.

Even though extensive effort is required to develop, implement, and maintain fault tolerance and disaster recovery plans, these plans are critical to the long-term stability of an organization's information technology infrastructure. Components and services will eventually fail; a plan is needed to prevent and recover from disruptions to computing services.

The Windows 2000 platform offers many built-in technologies and features that not only improve the reliability of systems, but also support a wide range of options for fault tolerance and recovery.

PART II

Tuning the Subsystems

CHAPTER 6

Boosting Memory Performance

Running out of memory is one of the most common problems in Windows 2000 Server systems. Basically, when a system runs out of memory, the combined memory requirements of all processes exceed the amount of physical memory on the system. Windows 2000 must then resort to its virtual memory to keep the system and processes running. Running out of memory creates serious problems in response times and in the running of mission-critical applications. It is especially disastrous if the system is also low on disk space. Windows 2000's virtual memory mechanism is a vital component of the operating system, but it is not nearly as fast as physical memory. A depletion of physical memory resources should be avoided at all costs, because it will cause extreme performance degradation.

When it comes to memory, Windows 2000 is a hungry beast; it requires even more memory than its predecessor, Windows NT. Once you give it more memory, it can—and more than likely will—immediately devour it. A viable solution to the problem of insufficient memory is simply to add more memory. In fact, doing nothing else but adding more memory will usually take care of many of your memory-related performance problems. Unfortunately, adding more memory isn't always possible because of budget constraints or the physical limitations of the hardware. Adding more memory may just be postponing the real problem and may lead to greater problems down the road. This fact alone should convince you that it's crucial that you optimize the memory you have even if you are soon getting more memory.

There are many ways to gauge and maintain Windows 2000 memory performance. The key is to know what to look at and when. This chapter provides real steps for successfully boosting memory performance. You will first develop your understanding of how Windows 2000 manages its memory resources, and then you'll examine tried-and-true methods for squeezing the highest level of performance out of your physical resources so you can effectively use the available resources to fine-tune the server's memory configuration. You should also turn to Chapter 3 for information on the hardware aspects of memory. Knowing the hardware aspects in addition to what is discussed here will help you make your purchasing decisions by helping you understand which types of memory provide the best level of performance.

MEMORY FUNDAMENTALS

Many of the operating systems and applications available today are resource intensive, especially when it comes to memory requirements. They require large amounts of memory to run effectively and efficiently. Windows 2000 is no exception. It requires a lot of memory, but it is designed to accommodate its own memory requirements as well as those of even the most resource-intensive applications.

Windows 2000 uses two different memory schemes, physical and virtual, to satisfy potentially large memory requirements. Physical memory is the amount of RAM that is installed on the system. Virtual memory is a logical extension of physical memory that frees up physical memory on the system and allows more processes to execute. In other words, if Windows 2000 did not use virtual memory, the system could afford to execute only processes within the capacity of the amount of physical memory available. Since virtual memory is logical and not physical, it can be related either to unused address space or, more important, to the space on the hard disk that it treats as physical memory. When Windows 2000 resorts to the hard disk for virtual memory, the process is called *paging*. Paging is described in more detail later in this chapter. Virtual memory is completely different from physical memory, but applications are not aware of this. Applications view physical and virtual memory as a single entity and do not even know that Windows 2000 uses two memory schemes. Windows 2000 fools applications into thinking that there is more memory on the system than there actually is. Only the operating system knows how much physical memory is actually on the system; applications cannot differentiate between physical and virtual memory.

Most applications use a linear 32-bit offset to specify the memory addresses they want to reference. Windows 2000's use of a 32-bit logical binary addressing scheme lets applications think they can reference up to 4GB of virtual memory (2^{32} = 4,294,967,296 = 4GB).

The amount of memory on the system may be as little as 16MB, but each application will still think that it has 4GB available for its own use. Applications think they have so much memory available because they view memory as linear; an application just specifies a memory location and does not care or need to know if the code or data is actually in virtual or physical memory.

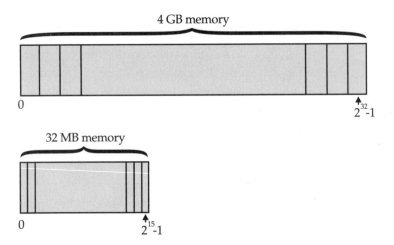

4 GB memory

0

$2^{32}-1$

32 MB memory

0

$2^{15}-1$

NOTE: Although not yet mainstream, more and more applications are being written to accommodate 64-bit addressing. This type of addressing overcomes the limitations of 32-bit addressing to support a greater amount of memory (up to 8GB in Advanced Server and 64GB in Datacenter!). Windows 2000 Advanced Server and Datacenter are the only two versions at this time that are equipped with 64-bit extension support.

When an application requests code or data from a memory address, the address is a virtual address, not a physical one. It is then Windows 2000's responsibility to translate the virtual address into a physical memory address to retrieve the requested code or data. Would it not be simpler to just let the application keep up with its own memory use and locations? Surprisingly, the overhead from making virtual references to information stored in memory is minimal. More important, the virtual addressing scheme gives the operating system control over memory management operations and extends the perceivable amount of available memory. The component responsible for loading data into main memory and assigning it a virtual address is the Virtual Memory (VM) Manager, located within the Windows 2000 Executive, as shown in Figure 6-1. The VM Manager is also responsible for behind-the-scenes translation from virtual to physical addresses. The VM Manager provides a level of control over memory resources and shields the applications from having to know where code or data actually resides.

The Paging Process

As mentioned earlier, applications do not have to worry about memory management. For all they know, every time they refer a particular memory address, it resides in main memory—but this is not always the case. If the information is not contained in main memory, where is it? Code or data that has not been used for a while is swapped out to the hard disk to free main memory. This allows more efficient use of main memory.

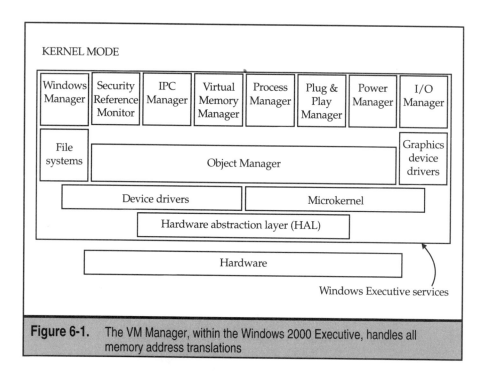

Figure 6-1.   The VM Manager, within the Windows 2000 Executive, handles all memory address translations

Paging, the process of moving information from main memory to a hard disk for temporary storage, is illustrated in Figure 6-2. The information is moved to a paging repository called pagefile.sys. If the information is referenced later, it can be returned to main memory. The next time the applications need code or data, the VM Manager translates the address and checks to see if it is in main or virtual (pagefile.sys) memory. Information located in virtual memory must then be swapped back into main memory so the processor can use it. Only the information in main memory is of any use to the processor. The VM Manager automatically locates or, in some cases, creates a block of main memory that this information can be loaded into. It then updates the addressing tables and informs the processor of the physical address where the code or data resides.

Memory Sharing

Often applications need to communicate with each other and share information. To provide this capability, Windows 2000 must allow access to certain memory space without jeopardizing its security and integrity or that of other applications. Therefore, the VM Manager divides the 4GB virtual memory equally and assigns privilege levels to control access. The upper 2GB of address space is dedicated to kernel mode (privileged) operations to protect the operating system and

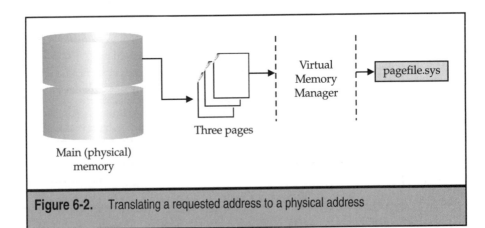

Figure 6-2.   Translating a requested address to a physical address

ensure stability. The lower 2GB of address space allows both privileged and unprivileged code, such as user applications, to access it.

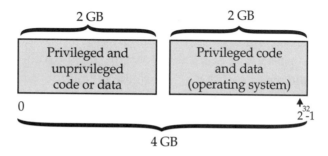

The VM Manager keeps track of each process's memory space with separate translation tables. However, it can dynamically adjust the translation tables so that certain addresses translate to the same pages of main memory for more than one process. This controls the level of access that processes have to another process's memory space. This does not mean, however, that a process can access any memory address defined within the upper 2GB of virtual memory.

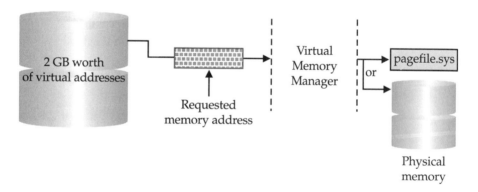

From a performance standpoint, the ability to share memory greatly reduces the amount of memory used by an application. When more than one copy of an application is running, each instance can use the same code and data. This means that it is not necessary to maintain separate copies of the application's code loaded and using memory resources. No matter how many instances of the application are running, the amount of memory needed to adequately support the application's code remains relatively the same. There may be a slight increase in memory requirements, but this is due mainly to new data having to be maintained by the application. For example, if an instance of an application requires 4MB of memory, the next instance will not require that the system provide an additional 4MB to support it. A quick way to verify this is to check the Task Manager's Process tab. To see the memory requirements of an application with more than one instance, do the following:

1. Start the application you want to monitor.

2. Start the Task Manager by right-clicking the taskbar.

3. In the Windows 2000 Task Manager dialog box, select the Processes tab.

4. Scroll down the list of processes running on the system and find the application you want to monitor.

5. Note the amount of memory the application is using with one instance. This is located in the Mem Usage column.

6. Start another instance of the application and watch its memory requirements. You will notice that the second instance uses much less memory than the first.

Paging Is Inevitable

At first thought, you might think that buying a ton of additional memory would prevent Windows 2000 from using its paging scheme, thus increasing performance. Paging is the process of temporarily transferring some of the contents of a system's physical memory to the hard disk until the system needs the contents of that memory again. However, this is not the case; Windows 2000 is designed to use paging no matter how much physical memory is available. Simply put, paging is inevitable. Even if you have 100MB of available memory, Windows 2000 will still use its paging scheme. The more memory you have, however, the less the system will have to rely on paging—although added memory will not altogether eliminate the need to page. The good news, however, is that there are more ways to increase paging performance than just adding more memory.

Windows 2000 is extremely stingy with its memory resources. When you give it more memory, it keeps as much as possible for itself. In fact, Windows 2000 tries to minimize the amount of available memory on reserve. Most of the additional memory is used for caching. This is one of the reasons why paging exists on Windows 2000 systems. There is no way to remove the Windows 2000 paging scheme (for example, you can't delete it through the Registry), but there are ways you can minimize paging. Techniques for boosting paging performance will be discussed shortly.

NONPAGED POOLED VS. PAGED POOLED MEMORY

Windows 2000 determines which system memory components can and cannot be paged out to disk. Obviously, some code, such as the kernel, should not be swapped out of main memory. Therefore, Windows 2000 further differentiates memory used by the system as either nonpaged pooled or paged pooled. These sections of main memory play active roles in determining how the VM Manager handles the paging process.

Nonpaged pooled memory contains occupied code or data that must stay resident in memory. This structure is similar to that used by old MS-DOS programs, where relatively small terminate and stay resident (TSR) programs were loaded into memory at startup. These programs stayed in a certain portion of memory until the system either restarted or shut down. For example, an antivirus program would be loaded as a TSR program to protect against possible virus attacks.

Paged pooled memory is the portion of memory that holds pageable code or data that may be needed sooner rather than later. Any system process that is in paged pooled memory can be paged out to disk, but it is held temporarily in this section of main memory in case the system needs it immediately. Windows 2000 pages other processes before paging system processes out to disk.

Nonpaged Pooled Memory

Processes contained within nonpaged pooled memory stay in main memory and cannot be paged out to disk. This portion of physical memory is used for kernel mode operations (for example, drivers) and other processes that must stay in main memory to operate efficiently. Without this section of main memory, kernel components would be pageable, and the system itself would risk becoming unstable.

The amount of main memory allocated to the nonpaged memory pool depends on the amount of physical memory the server has and the demands that processes place on the system for memory pool space. However, Windows 2000 does limit nonpaged pooled memory to 256MB. This is actually an increase from the 128MB limit in Windows NT 4. Complex algorithms dynamically determine the maximum amount of nonpaged pooled memory on a Windows 2000 system at startup, based on the amount of physical memory in the system. This self-tuning mechanism within Windows 2000 automatically adjusts the size according to the current memory configuration. For example, if you increase or decrease the amount of RAM in the system, Windows 2000 automatically adjusts the size of nonpaged pooled memory to reflect that change.

If the NonPagedPoolSize key entry in the Registry, located in HKEY_LOCAL_MACHINE\System\CurrentControlSet\Control\Session Manager\Memory Management, is set to anything other than zero, Windows 2000 may not correctly allocate the amount of nonpaged pooled memory needed by the system (see Figure 6-3).

You can approximate the size of the nonpaged pooled memory by using the following formulas:

NonPagedPoolSize = MinimumNonPagedPoolSize + ([Physical MB − 4] × MinAdditionNonPagedPoolPerMB)

MaximumNonPagedPoolSize = DefaultMaximumNonPagedPoolSize + ([Physical MB − 4] × MaxAdditionNonPagedPoolPerMB)

where

MinimumNonPagedPoolSize = 256K
MinAdditionNonPagedPoolPerMB = 32K
DefaultMaximumNonPagedPoolSize = 1,024K (1MB)
MaxAdditionNonPagedPoolPerMB = 400K

For example, if a system has 64MB of RAM, it will have approximately NonPagedPoolSize = 256K + ((64-4) × 32K) = 2,176 K (or roughly 2.2MB) allocated to the nonpaged memory pool. NonPagedPoolSize can reach a maximum size of 32MB.

There are also easier ways to approximate the size of nonpaged pooled memory. For starters, there are counters that can be

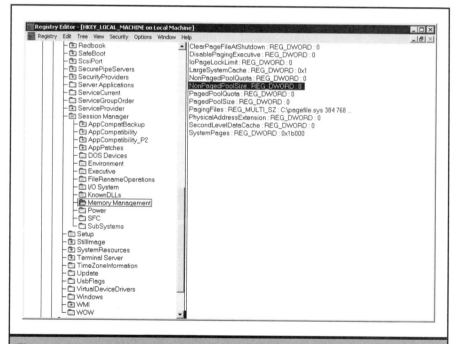

Figure 6-3. NonPagedPoolSize entry within the Registry

monitored using the System Monitor (for information on using the System Monitor, see Appendix A). You can monitor the following:

▼ Memory: Pool Nonpaged Bytes

■ Memory: Pool Nonpaged Allocations

▲ Process: Pool Nonpaged Bytes

The Memory object counters are nonpaged pooled memory approximations for the entire system; the Process counter reflects the size allocated to each process.

The easiest way to approximate the size of nonpaged pooled memory, however, is to use the Task Manager. The estimated size of the nonpaged pooled memory is shown in the Kernel Memory section of the Task Manager's Performance tab. You can also use the Task Manager to view the amount of nonpaged pooled and paged pooled memory an individual process is using. Simply follow these steps:

1. Start the Task Manager by right-clicking the taskbar or pressing CTRL-ALT-DEL and selecting Task Manager.

2. Select the Processes tab and then, from the View menu, choose Select Columns to display the available viewing options for the Processes tab.

3. In the Select Columns dialog box, check the boxes beside the Paged Pool and Non-paged Pool options and click OK.

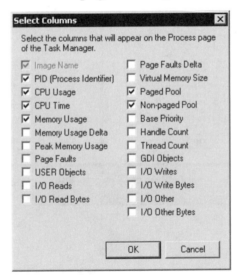

When you return to the Windows 2000 Task Manager Processes window, you will see the amount of space in the paged pooled and nonpaged pooled memory that is occupied by individual processes.

From a performance standpoint, the larger the size of nonpaged pooled memory, the more data can be fit into this space. Since this is physical memory space, information can be written and read much faster than it can on a hard disk. The recommendation for nonpaged pooled memory is simple: give the system enough physical memory so that the nonpaged pooled memory is at least 2MB in size. The more physical memory you have, the larger the nonpaged pooled memory can be. Thus, to increase the amount of nonpaged pooled memory, you must increase the amount of physical memory on the system. However, remember that nonpaged pooled memory is limited to 256MB, so adding memory beyond this point has no effect on the nonpaged pooled memory.

Page Pooled Memory

Any code or data in privileged mode processes that does not always need to be in main memory is considered pageable and can reside in paged pooled memory. This pool typically contains pages of memory that are frequently referenced by the system for processing by the CPU. If the frequency with which pages are referenced decreases or the paged pool approaches capacity, pages can be swapped out to the paging file (pagefile.sys) on the hard disk.

Like nonpaged pooled memory, the paged pooled memory configuration parameters are located in the same Registry hive mentioned earlier in the "Nonpaged Pooled Memory" section.

When the PagedPoolSize parameter is set to zero, the system calculates the amount of physical memory allocated to this pool. This approximation is based on the system's memory configuration. Generally, the size ranges from a few megabytes to a maximum of 340MB of RAM. Obviously, your system is going to need a large amount of RAM before the paged pooled memory size reaches its maximum capacity of 340MB.

NOTE: The maximum value for paged pooled memory size is almost double that of Windows NT 4.

You can also determine the size of the paged pooled memory by hand. The following formulas require you to know the value of the variable MaximumNonPagedPoolSize. Thus, before you begin calculating the size of paged pooled memory, use the formulas presented earlier to calculate the maximum size of nonpaged pooled memory. Then use the following formulas to find out how much physical memory can be used for paged pooled memory.

Temp_Size = (2 × MaximumNonPagedPoolSize [in MB]) ÷ PAGE_SIZE

Size = (Temp_Size + [PTE_PER_PAGE − 1]) ÷ PTE_PER_PAGE

PagedPoolSize = Size × PAGE_SIZE × PTE_PER_PAGE

where

PTE_PER_PAGE = 1,024 bytes
PAGE_SIZE = 4,096 bytes

NOTE: Even if your calculations result in a number greater than 340MB for the size of paged pooled memory, the system will allocate only 340MB.

If this area of physical memory begins to reach capacity or becomes completely full, the system tries to compensate for the lack of paged pooled address space by swapping out those pages of memory that have been least requested to the paging file on the hard disk. As a result, it is very important that the system's memory configuration be sufficient for the tasks that it performs. The more the system has to rely on paging to and from the hard disk, the greater the likelihood that performance will degrade.

FILE SYSTEM CACHE AND THE WINDOWS 2000 CACHE MANAGER

The file system cache is actually the third type of cache used by Windows 2000. For information on the other two types of cache that Windows 2000 uses, refer to Chapter 3. It is different from the other caches because it uses a portion of main memory instead of any of the different varieties of SRAM. As you may suspect, the file system cache is not nearly as fast as the other types, but it does help boost performance.

The Windows 2000 Cache Manager is responsible for adjusting the size of the file system cache. It determines the size of the file system cache based on whether the system is a workstation or server, the amount of physical memory the system has, and the functional configuration of the system. For instance, a Windows 2000 file server with ample physical memory will typically have a larger file system cache than a machine being used as a print server or firewall. Windows 2000 Server systems use a large system cache model, in which any available memory not used by applications or the system is allocated to the file system cache. The Windows 2000 Cache Manager dynamically controls the actual size of the file system cache since memory requirements continually fluctuate.

Does your system have enough memory to support an effective file system cache? The most effective way to find out is to use the System Monitor to watch the cache counters. Your primary concern when monitoring cache counters is the percentage of *hits* and *misses*. A hit occurs when the requested data is found in the file system cache, and a miss occurs when the system has to search elsewhere to find the data. A high percentage of hits and a low percentage of misses means that the system is configured with enough memory to support a large enough file system cache.

When browsing the list of counters within the Cache object, you'll notice four different counters relating to the cache hit ratio:

▼ Copy Read Hits %

■ Data Map Hits %

■ MDL Read Hits %

▲ Pin Read Hits %

Here are some other System Monitor counters that are useful for gauging cache performance:

Object	Counters
Cache	Copy Reads/sec
	Data Flushes/sec
	Lazy Write Flushes/sec
	Lazy Write Pages/sec
	Read Aheads/sec
Memory	Cache Bytes
	Cache Faults/sec
	Pages Input/sec

Why are there four System Monitor counters gauging the cache hit ratio? Because Windows 2000, and applications running under Windows 2000, can read data from the cache in four different ways:

▼ **Copy Read**   When a process requests to read a file, the file system copies the data from the cache into the application's buffer (within main memory).

■ **Fast Read**   Fast reads are similar to copy reads, with one major exception: Instead of communicating with the file system to retrieve the data from the cache, the process retrieves the data directly from the cache. Fast reads typically occur after the initial read request.

■ **Pin Read**   A pin read occurs when data is mapped into the cache so that it can be modified and then written back to the disk. The unusual name stems from the idea that the data is *pinned* in the cache, meaning that it stays in the same memory location and cannot be paged out to disk. This method reduces the number of page faults that may occur when data is requested.

▲ **Read Ahead**   Cache read aheads occur when the VM Manager identifies a process reading a file sequentially. The VM Manager then expects that future read requests will be sequential as well, so it begins mapping larger blocks of data than what the process is asking for. Generally speaking, read aheads offer better performance than the other cache read methods, but performance also depends on the process's read patterns.

One of the most common types of read operations used by Windows 2000, especially on a server running Internet Information Server (IIS), to retrieve pages containing data from the file system cache is measured by the Memory Descriptor List (MDL) counter. Therefore, on Windows 2000 Servers running IIS, the MDL Read Hits % counter is the primary counter to watch to find out whether Windows 2000 has enough memory to supply a large enough file system cache. As stated earlier, a high cache hit ratio shows that there is plenty of memory for the file system cache, and this ratio also indicates how effectively Windows 2000 uses this cache. A realistic goal for this counter, as well as the other cache hit ratio counters, is a ratio of 70 percent or higher; ratios higher than 80 percent indicate exceptional performance. A system experiencing a cache hit percentage below 70 percent may be experiencing a memory shortage. It is advised that you increase the amount of physical memory on such a system.

To figure out the percentage of cache misses, simply subtract the percentage of cache hits from 100 percent. For example, if MDL Read Hits % equals 85 percent, then the cache miss rate is 15 percent.

No matter what the functionality of the server, the Copy Reads Hits % counter gives a good overall picture of a server's cache hit ratio for file read operations. When a process requests data from a file that it has not previously accessed, it is usually a copy read. Moreover, this type of read is more prevalent with small transfers. For this reason, you should always monitor this counter when analyzing the file system cache performance.

BOOSTING PAGING PERFORMANCE

As stated earlier, Windows 2000 is designed to use paging no matter how much physical memory is available on the system. There are many benefits stemming from Windows 2000's use of a paging scheme, but they come with a price. Paging frees up physical memory on the system and allows more processes to execute. When a process needs code or data that has been swapped to the hard disk, the system puts the data back into physical memory and transfers other information to the hard disk if necessary. The difference in performance between a hard disk and physical memory is astounding. For example, a hard disk typically has an access time of approximately 4 to 10 ms, whereas physical memory has an access time of 60 ns or faster. Memory is several orders of magnitude faster than disk speed! This fact alone should make you rush out and buy more memory.

How can you minimize the effects of paging on the system? Adding more memory is the first choice for many to reduce paging activity, because the additional memory reduces the likelihood that the system has to constantly rely on the hard disk. However, there is more to increasing paging performance than simply adding more memory. You can also maximize performance for those times when the system must resort to paging by proactively monitoring the changing memory requirements and properly configuring the paging file (pagefile.sys).

Paging File Location Considerations

During Windows 2000's installation process, the paging file (pagefile.sys) is automatically created using contiguous disk space. The file is always placed in the root directory of the system partition, but this is not always the optimal placement for the file. To get the best performance from paging, you should first look at the system's disk subsystem configuration to find out whether your system has more than one physical hard disk drive. You can use the Disk Management snap-in by choosing Start | Programs | Administrative Tools | Computer Management to view the system's disk configuration, as shown in Figure 6-4. (Refer to Chapter 7 for more information on the Disk Management snap-in.) If your system has only one hard disk, it is highly recommended that you configure the system with an extra drive if at all possible. The reason for this recommendation is simple: Windows 2000 supports up to 16 separate paging files that can be distributed across multiple drives. Configuring the system with multiple paging files allows simultaneous I/O requests to the various disks, greatly boosting pagefile performance for I/O requests.

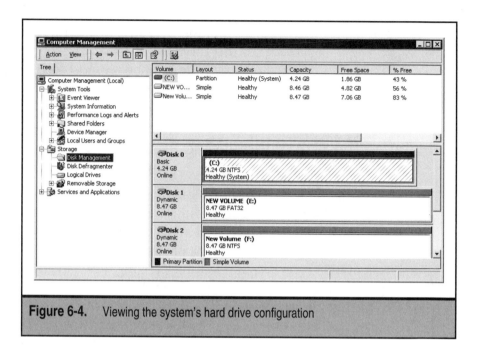

Figure 6-4. Viewing the system's hard drive configuration

A system with only one physical hard drive limits your ability to optimize paging performance. The drive must take care of system and application requests as well as accessing the paging file. The physical drive may have multiple partitions, but you would be ill advised to disperse the paging file among the partitions. Paging files spread across multiple partitions do not increase the hard drive's ability to read or write any faster to pagefile.sys. In fact, this will hamper system performance, because the drive must handle paging requests for more than one paging file. Only when a partition does not have enough space to contain the entire paging file should you place paging files on multiple partitions on the same disk.

Servers with multiple physical drives can use multiple paging files to increase paging performance. The key is to spread the load from paging requests to more than one physical disk. Essentially, the system can handle more than one paging request at a time with paging files on separate physical drives. Each physical drive can access and write information to its paging file simultaneously, which increases the amount of information that can be transferred. The optimal configuration for multiple paging files is to place each paging file on a separate drive that has its own drive controller. However, this may not be a viable solution for most server-based configurations because of the additional expense and the limited number of interrupts available on a system.

Calculating the Size of the Paging File

The most important configuration parameter for paging files is size. No matter how many paging files your system has, if they are not properly sized, the system may have performance problems. If the initial size is too small, the system may have to enlarge the paging file to compensate for the additional paging activity. When the system has to increase the size of the paging file on the fly, it has to create new space for it along with handling paging requests. The system will experience a large number of page faults, and may even start thrashing. A *page fault* occurs when the system must find information outside the process's working set, either elsewhere in physical memory or in the pagefile. *Thrashing* occurs when the system lacks the memory resources (both physical and virtual) to satisfy usage requirements and thus experiences excessive paging. The system will spend more time paging than executing applications. When the system is thrashing, the Memory: Pages/sec counter is consistently above 100 pages per second. Thrashing severely decreases system performance. In addition, dynamically expanding the paging file causes fragmentation. The paging file could be scattered throughout the disk rather than created in contiguous space at boot time, adding overhead to the system and causing severe performance degradation. You should, at all costs, avoid having the system increase the size of the paging file.

NOTE: On NTFS drives, always keep at least 25 percent of the drive's capacity free to ensure that the paging file can be created in contiguous space.

What should the minimum and maximum paging file size be? Microsoft has rescinded its Windows NT 4.0 recommendation of using the sum of the amount of physical RAM plus 11 as the minimum size for a paging file. Now Windows 2000 uses 1.5 times the amount of RAM for the minimum and twice the minimum value for the maximum. This greatly improves stability because it reduces the likelihood that the system will crash because of an incorrectly configured pagefile.

NOTE: For the system to be able to write memory dumps to disk after a system crash, the system partition must have a pagefile size equal to at least the amount of physical memory plus one.

Despite the improvement in the default pagefile configuration, it's still extremely important that you should first approximate the paging requirements under normal or typical use. Compare your approximation with Microsoft's recommendation and use the higher value as the minimum.

NOTE: For systems configured with multiple paging files, the minimum recommended size should be spread across each of the paging files. In other words, it is not necessary to set the minimum requirement as the minimum size for each paging file. If you do so, you'll be wasting precious disk space among other things.

For example, suppose your system's typical paging activity requires at most 386MB from a paging file, and your system has 256MB of RAM. Following Microsoft's recommendation for the minimum paging file size gives you 384MB (256MB RAM × 1.5). Under certain circumstances, your system will have to grow the paging file by at least 2MB to compensate for the inadequately sized paging file. Therefore, it's in your best interest to set the paging file size higher than Microsoft's recommended default value.

So what size should you set the minimum paging file to be? If you set the paging file's minimum value to 386MB, you're still taking a chance on reaching and exceeding the virtual memory minimum. Therefore, it's best to set the minimum to the discovered minimum value plus at least 10 percent (386 + 38.6 ≈ 425) to ensure that even in the busiest of times, the system shouldn't have to expand the paging file.

The important thing to remember here is that you should avoid having the system expand the paging file, because this will have negative effects on performance.

To change the paging file location or size configuration parameters, do the following:

1. Right-click the My Computer icon located on the desktop and select Properties.

2. On the Advanced tab (shown in Figure 6-5), click the Performance Options button.

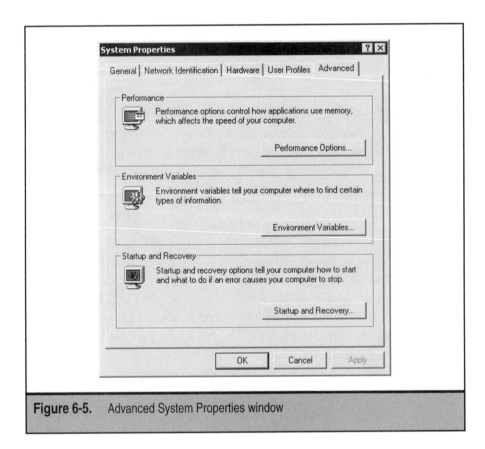

Figure 6-5.   Advanced System Properties window

3. Click the Change button within the Virtual Memory area of the dialog box.

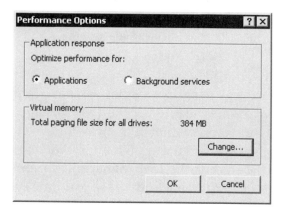

4. To add another paging file to the existing configuration, select a drive in the Virtual Memory window that does not already have a paging file. Then specify the initial size and maximum size of the paging file (in megabytes), click Set, and click OK.

> *NOTE:*   Make sure that you reconfigure the other paging files so that the sum of their minimum sizes reflects the minimum required size for the entire system.

5. To change the minimum and maximum size of an existing paging file, select the drive where the paging file resides. Then specify the initial size and maximum size of the paging file (in megabytes), click Set, and click OK.

6. Click OK in the Performance Options dialog box.

7. Click OK to close the System Properties window.

There are several methods you can use to determine the system's paging requirements so you can set the right minimum paging file size. You can use the Task Manager, Windows 2000 System Information (WINMSD), or System Monitor to find the proper size so the paging file does not have to expand during normal operation.

NOTE: Believe it or not, the absolute minimum size of the paging file is only 2MB. Obviously, however, performance will suffer if you set the size this low, because the system will be forced to expand the paging file until paging requests can be handled adequately.

Task Manager

An easy way to check whether you have configured the correct size for the paging file is to use the Task Manager. This gives you an accurate representation of the way the system is using the paging file along with other vital system information in real time.

After starting the Task Manager (by right-clicking the taskbar), select the Performance tab to see real-time system statistics, as shown in Figure 6-6. The information that is most pertinent for paging file size is located in the Commit Charge section. This section shows whether the Commit Peak approaches or exceeds the Commit Limit, and whether it exceeds the amount of physical memory on the system.

NOTE: Commit Peak refers to the highest amount of physical and virtual memory a system has allocated to processes thus far.

As the system experiences increases in paging activity, the amount of committed memory (Commit Total) increases. Once it approaches the Commit Limit value, the system needs to expand the paging file. The Commit Limit indicates the amount of virtual memory that can be committed to memory without having to expand the paging file. Since the goal is to keep the paging file from expanding, it is imperative that you keep the Commit Total and Commit Limit values far apart. If these values meet, the system must dynamically increase the size of the pagefile. The worst-case scenario, however, is when the Commit Total approaches the sum of RAM plus the maximum pagefile size because the paging file can no longer grow to meet expectations. (This may cause system instability, prevent applications from starting, and result in other anomalies.)

The information presented by the Task Manager's Commit Charge section also shows you whether the system's main memory is sufficient to accommodate the tasks the system performs. If the Commit Total value regularly exceeds the amount of RAM in the

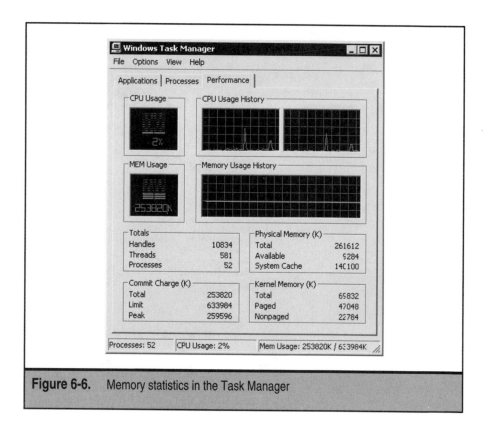

Figure 6-6. Memory statistics in the Task Manager

system, the system may not have enough physical memory. For example, if a system with 64MB (64,948K) of RAM has a Commit Total value of approximately the same amount (64,948K), it is time to increase the amount of physical memory on the system.

Windows 2000 System Information

The System Information snap-in is similar to the Task Manager in that it displays system statistics such as the state of services and memory, but it does not present information in real time. You must manually refresh the display to get current information. For this reason, it is recommended that you do not rely heavily on this tool to calculate the minimum size of the paging file. However, this utility does provide you with a way to quickly approximate the minimum paging file size by looking at the information in the System Summary folder, shown in Figure 6-7.

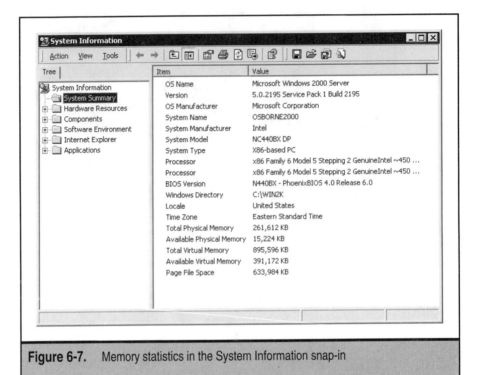

Figure 6-7.   Memory statistics in the System Information snap-in

The System Information snap-in was called Windows NT Diagnostics in Windows NT 4, and it could be started by typing **WINMSD** at the command prompt or in the Run dialog box. In Windows 2000, you can still start the System Information snap-in by typing **WINMSD**, or you can execute it by choosing Start | Programs | Accessories | System Tools | System Information.

System Monitor

The best and most reliable method for determining the minimum paging file size is to use the System Monitor to monitor counters that pertain to virtual memory. Before you start monitoring the counters, be sure that you are at least using the default values for the minimum and maximum paging file size. Anything less than Microsoft's recommendation may cause instability. Now you are ready to monitor memory use for typical operations.

You should start by using four counters to monitor virtual memory: Memory: Committed Bytes and Commit Limit, and Paging File: % Usage and % Usage Peak. Other memory counters are useful to monitor, but you should hold off using them until later in the monitoring process, because the ones you use immediately are the best for discovering the minimum paging file requirements. The four counters you should monitor first are described here.

▼ **Memory: Committed Bytes**   This counter indicates the amount of virtual memory currently used by all processes. It is the amount of virtual memory actually committed, not merely reserved.

■ **Memory: Commit Limit**   The Commit Limit is the maximum amount of virtual memory that can be committed without running the risk of expanding the paging file. This value is just below the sum of the physical memory and the current paging file size. This value does not quite equal the sum of the physical memory and the paging file size, because it subtracts the amount of memory reserved for the operating system.

■ **Paging File: % Usage**   This is the percentage of the paging file that is currently in use by all processes.

▲ **Paging File: % Usage Peak**   This counter indicates the highest percentage of space used in the paging file.

The Commit Limit and Committed Bytes counters work together; if you monitor the counters separately, you will not get the information you need to properly set the paging file's minimum size. Only by monitoring both counters can you correctly determine whether the paging file is approaching or has already reached full capacity. When the size of the Committed Bytes counter approaches the Commit Limit, the system is running out of virtual memory. In fact, the system will warn you if these two values are equal or if the Committed Bytes counter exceeds the limit. It displays a warning advising that you manually need to increase the paging file and restart the system. You must then close some applications, manually increase the paging file, and restart the system.

During normal system use, the Committed Bytes counter should never exceed the amount of physical RAM on the system, especially with a properly configured minimum paging file size. You can provide yourself with some extra reassurance that this situation will not occur during normal operation by adding an alerting mechanism. As an additional precaution, you can use the System Monitor's Performance Logs and Alerts snap-in to alert you when the Committed Bytes value comes within 20 percent of the Commit Limit value.

If the Committed Bytes counter does equal or exceed the Commit Limit value, it is very important to check the number of hard page faults the system is experiencing. Hard page faults introduce significant performance delays because they indicate pages that have had to be retrieved from disk instead of main memory. The counter that shows the number of hard page faults is Memory: Pages/sec. Check this counter for consistently abnormal activity (above 20 pages per second) to further verify that the system is running out of virtual memory and must expand the paging file to compensate.

The two other counters that you should immediately monitor to help determine the minimum paging file size are the Paging File: % Usage and % Usage Peak counters. You can use these two counters together or monitor them separately to get an accurate picture of the percentage of the paging file that is being used. You should keep the % Usage counter equal to or below 40 percent, and the % Usage Peak should stay below 75 percent. Keeping paging activity within these acceptable ranges protects against having to increase the paging file. You can also use these counters to get a rough estimate of how much more physical memory the system needs to keep reliance on the paging file to a minimum. For example, suppose the minimum paging file size is set to 80MB, and the % Usage counter averages around 20 percent. In this case, the 20 percent use rate for the paging file is essentially telling you that if you add memory equal to 20 percent of the paging file, you will accommodate the majority of server functions with main memory instead of the paging file. You can reduce the usage percent to a bare minimum by configuring the system with an additional 16MB or more of RAM.

A little less important than the minimum paging file size but still important to boosting paging performance is the maximum size of the paging file. The maximum value is the largest size to which you ever expect the paging file to grow in the worst-case scenario. Of course, you must have enough free disk space to accommodate this limit. A general rule of thumb is that you should set the maximum value to at least the minimum value plus 50 percent. Microsoft recommends doubling the minimum value to set the maximum value. This is also appropriate if you have enough disk space. In most cases, if you have properly configured the minimum paging file and have set the maximum paging file size to the recommended amount, this value should never be approached.

Windows 2000's reliance on paging provides many benefits to the system as well as to user applications. However, paging can also negatively affect performance. Adding more memory to the system is not always feasible, and it does not always correct the performance problems associated with paging activity. Fortunately, there is more than one way to increase the system's paging performance. Proactive monitoring and proper paging file configuration and location all play key roles in boosting paging performance. Keep in mind that if you properly configure the minimum and maximum paging file sizes, you drastically reduce the risk of compromising performance even during periods of peak memory use.

Reducing Paging File Fragmentation

Many people ask why they shouldn't set the minimum and maximum paging file sizes to the same value to reduce or prevent paging file defragmentation. Although this technique will reduce or prevent paging file defragmentation, it is not advisable. The reason is simple. If you improperly set the paging file size values or don't set them high enough, you run the risk of a system failure or crash. This risk is a far greater concern than the performance hit you may take when the system expands the paging file.

Suppose you set the minimum and maximum sizes to the same value believing that your system won't ever need that much virtual memory. Are you then wasting precious disk space? Now suppose that your system temporarily needs more virtual memory resources than you have allocated. How is Windows 2000 going to compensate?

Windows 2000 tries to expand the paging file, but it can't expand it beyond the maximum paging file size. Here's when the real problem arises: applications or, even worse, Windows 2000, may crash.

Manually Defragmenting the Paging File

There's no doubt that a fragmented paging file causes performance degradation. However, there are better ways of tackling this problem than setting the minimum and maximum paging file sizes to the same value. First, and most important, you can reduce paging file fragmentation when you set the minimum and maximum values appropriately. You can also use a third-party product such as Executive Software's Diskeeper to defragment the paging file, or you can schedule maintenance time to defragment manually.

NOTE: It's important to plan ahead for the manual defragmentation process because it requires downtime.

To defragment the paging file manually, do the following:

1. On the Control Panel, double-click the System applet.

2. On the Advanced tab, click the Performance Options button to display the Performance Options window and then click the Change button.

3. Within the Virtual Memory dialog box, create another paging file on a separate drive and then click the Set button to apply the change. Keep the new paging file the same size as the one you're going to defragment.

4. Reduce the minimum and maximum sizes to 0MB for the paging file that you want to defragment and then click the Set button to apply the change. A warning message will pop up, and you'll need to click Yes to continue.

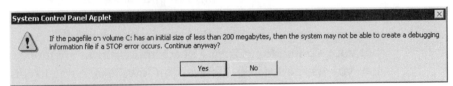

5. Click OK four times (the last window will be the System
    Properties page) and then click Yes to restart the computer.
    Once the system restarts, it will begin using the new
    paging file.

6. After the system has rebooted, run the Disk Defragmenter
    utility from the Start | Programs | Accessories | System
    Tools menu to defragment the drive that originally contained
    the paging file.

7. Re-create the paging file on the original drive after the drive
    has been defragmented.

8. Reduce the minimum and maximum sizes to 0MB for the
    temporary paging file.

9. Click OK four times as you did earlier and then click Yes to
    restart the computer.

MEMORY AND APPLICATION PERFORMANCE

Memory and application performance are interrelated. Applications
depend on memory and Windows 2000's memory management to
perform duties and tasks effectively and efficiently. Windows 2000's
Virtual Memory Manager is responsible not only for the efficiency of
the operating system's memory use, but also for maintaining the
optimal memory configuration for applications.

Memory requirements are dynamic because system components
and user applications do not always use the same code or data every
time they run. Consequently, it is to your advantage to develop a
mechanism to monitor memory requirements so you can act and not
react to increases in memory use. If you haven't done so already,
read Chapter 2 on capacity planning procedures. Increases in
memory use often can lead to memory shortages. There are several
counters that help you monitor the overall effects of memory as well
as the relationship between the Virtual Memory Manager and
applications on the system. There are also other steps you can take to
ensure optimal performance.

Monitoring Counters

The wealth of information you get from the available memory counters enables you to make informed decisions regarding how to maximize memory performance. In addition to the counters that have already been mentioned in previous sections (Paging File: % Usage and % Usage Peak, and Memory: Commit Limit and Committed Bytes), you can use the following counters to help determine whether the system is configured for maximum memory efficiency:

Memory	Available Bytes
	Page Faults/sec
	Pages/sec
Process	Page Faults/sec
	Working Set

Page Faults/sec and Pages/sec

The most important memory counters for you to monitor are Page Faults/sec and Pages/sec. These two counters accurately indicate the amount of paging activity that the system is experiencing.

Paging activity can result from two types of faults: hard and soft. Paging activity occurs when a process, needing code or data, references a virtual address where it thinks the code or data resides. However, only Windows 2000 knows the actual location. If the information being sought does not reside in the process's working set, the process looks for it elsewhere in memory or in the paging file. Soft faults occur when the needed information is found outside of the process's working set but still in main memory. The code or data could be in a number of places within main memory. It may be in the file system cache, in the transition to disk, or in the working set of another process. Soft faults can occur frequently without reducing system performance, because usually the processor is only briefly interrupted.

Hard faults have much more of an effect on system performance. A hard fault occurs when the code or data that the process requested is located within the paging file. The Virtual Memory Manager then must search the paging file for the requested information and pull it back into main memory so the process can use it. The Virtual

Memory Manager must contend with slow disk speed as well as possibly the need to swap enough code or data from main memory to the disk to make room for the process's request. Hard faults can drastically reduce overall system performance and should therefore be kept to a minimum.

To maximize memory efficiency, it is imperative to keep paging to a minimum. Windows 2000 is designed to page code and data no matter how much memory is available. However, if it constantly has to swap data to disk, performance and memory efficiency will begin to decline, because the disk is several orders of magnitude slower than RAM. Using the Page Faults/sec and Pages/sec counters to check the amount of paging will also tell you whether the system needs more physical memory, since Windows 2000's dependency on the disk subsystem for paging rapidly increases only when the amount of physical memory is low.

The Page Faults/sec counter reflects both hard and soft faults, and the Pages/sec counter indicates the number of pages read from or written to disk to resolve hard page faults. The Pages/sec counter is essentially tucked away in the Page Faults/sec counter. You can expect the Page Faults/sec counter to be much higher than Pages/sec, because a Windows 2000 system can tolerate large numbers of soft faults without significantly compromising performance. For most Pentium class or higher machines, acceptable values for the Page Faults/sec counter can be as high as 500 page faults per second, depending on the number of hard page faults the system experiences at this rate.

A key to minimizing paging is keeping the Pages/sec counter consistently lower than 10 pages per second. The counter may occasionally reach 60 pages per second or more, but this value should be reached only for a brief time. For instance, when an application is first executed, you can expect to see the counter sharply peak for a moment while the application is being loaded into memory. The Pages/sec counter also tells you whether the system is excessively paging, or thrashing. The system is thrashing when the Pages/sec value consistently exceeds 100 pages per second. Thrashing should be avoided at all costs because it drags down server performance to intolerable levels. It puts so much stress on the system that you will hear the disk drive constantly churning.

Available Bytes and Working Set

The Virtual Memory Manager is responsible for keeping track of the system's memory resources. One critical responsibility is maintaining a minimum amount of available memory for the operating system and for active processes. On a Windows 2000 Server, the Virtual Memory Manager tries to keep at least 4MB available so the system can handle any sudden increases in memory requirements resulting from the loading of applications into memory, the allocation of more memory to a process, and so on. The Virtual Memory Manager maintains this minimum level of available bytes by dynamically adjusting the space used in physical memory and the paging file.

The Memory: Available Bytes counter measures the amount of free memory dynamically controlled by the Virtual Memory Manager. The goal of monitoring this counter is to make sure that this value does not dip below 4MB. In fact, you should strive to keep this counter value well above 4MB to minimize paging activity. The number of available bytes fluctuates by default because of this value's close relationship to paging activity and the size of a process's working set.

The working set for a process contains code and data that has been recently used by the process, and its size is the amount of physical memory allocated to that process. The size does not include process code or data that exists in the paging file. The Virtual Memory Manager manages the working set dynamically according to the amount of available memory. The maximum size of the working set is determined by the amount of physical memory installed on the machine. There are three categories of working set size:

▼ **Small**   16MB of RAM or less

■ **Medium**   16 to 20MB of RAM

▲ **Large**   More than 20MB of RAM

The size of the working set is finite, and its minimum and maximum values are hard coded within the operating system. As a result, the minimum and maximum sizes cannot be changed or tuned. You can, however, force Windows 2000 to let applications use as large a working set as possible by setting the Applications option for the Server service. Right-click the My Computer desktop icon and select Properties, select the Advanced tab, and then click the Performance Options button to configure this setting in the dialog box that appears.

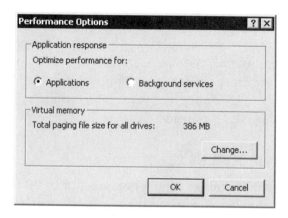

When a process requests a piece of code or data, it assumes that it will be located in its working set. The process continues uninterrupted if the code or data is found within the working set. Otherwise, either a hard or soft fault occurs. You can use the Process: Page Faults/sec counter to examine the page faults for a specific process. This counter is similar to the one in the Memory object except that it shows the paging activity only for the process, not for the entire system. An increase in a process's paging activity indicates that the working set is not large enough to handle the process and signals the Virtual Memory Manager to increase the size of the working set for the process. If the amount of available bytes is above the minimum required by the system (4MB), the size of the working set is increased. Otherwise, the Virtual Memory Manager will temporarily increase the working set so that the page faults caused by the process decrease.

In general, when the amount of available bytes approaches the system's minimum toleration level, the Virtual Memory Manager attempts to recover lost bytes by trimming the working sets of active processes. Of course, this only continues the cycle. The chance that requested code or data can be found in the working set of a process is reduced as the working sets are trimmed. The page fault rate increases because more code and data has to be retrieved from disk instead of from the working set of the process. The system finds itself once again trying to compensate for the increase in page faults.

There is no recommended size for working sets because their size varies with each process and system configuration. Keep in mind that performance is at its best when page faults are kept to a minimum and the number of available bytes is well above the minimum required by the system. Since there are limited tuning parameters for working sets, the most viable way to optimize the working set of a process is simply to configure the system with enough physical memory so that working sets can be increased to their maximum capacity.

Plugging Memory Leaks

There may come a time when you notice that system responsiveness is gradually decreasing to a crawl, when even a simple mouse movement takes what seems like hours to complete. Gradual degradation in performance usually means that a process is leaking memory. Memory leaks are a result of poorly written code. A memory leak occurs when a process robs the system of its memory resources. All processes at one point or another ask the system to allocate more memory for their use. Then when the process is done with that particular memory segment, it releases the memory. A leaky process keeps the memory allocation instead of releasing it to the system for other processes to use. This process repeats itself until memory resources are depleted. At this point, the only way to stop the drain is either to stop the process or reboot the system.

Core Improvements to Combat Memory Leaks

Memory leaks often compromised the reliability and stability of Windows NT. As a result, Microsoft incorporated enhancements into Windows 2000 designed specifically to thwart erratic applications and drivers from draining system resources.

Pool Tagging   Pool tagging, in its simplest form, segments device drivers by dedicating a special memory pool for memory allocation. This is in contrast to the shared memory pool model that Windows NT uses. Although pool tagging is slightly less efficient than the shared memory pool approach, the return is greater reliability and stability. In addition, pool tagging allows vendors to write more concise, cleaner code for device drivers. Many, if not all, of the problems inherent in shared memory pools are nonexistent in Windows 2000.

Device Driver Verifier   The Driver Verifier is a Windows 2000 kernel component that can be used to expose problem device drivers. It tests for memory corruption (including pool corruption), detects device drivers that inappropriately access pageable data, and monitors the way device drivers weather adverse situations such as memory allocation errors. This is an extremely useful troubleshooting tool when you suspect a memory leak or corrupt device driver. The downside to using this tool is that it can cause a slowdown in system performance, so Microsoft recommends that you don't enable it unless you're troubleshooting.

Device Driver Signing   Hardware vendors are constantly revising their hardware products and their associated device drivers. If you install device driver updates without considering or testing the effects they may have on the system, you may be in for a few surprises. In fact, a huge percentage of memory leaks and blue screens of death are caused by faulty or corrupted device drivers. Also, although the hardware may be on Microsoft's Hardware Compatibility List, this doesn't necessarily mean that the device driver update is.

Microsoft has taken a proactive approach to ensure that the device drivers you are installing have been certified by their own testing processes to work correctly with Windows 2000. Through digital driver signing, a process of attaching an encrypted signature to a device driver code, Windows 2000 notifies you regarding whether the device driver may compromise system reliability and stability.

Identifying Memory Leaks

Despite the new features and enhancements included in Windows 2000, there's still a possibility that an application or device driver will cause a memory leak. If you experience a gradual decline in performance or abnormal unresponsiveness, you should immediately assume that the system may have a memory leak. You have won half the battle once you identify a memory leak as a possible cause of the system's performance degradation. Memory leaks are difficult to detect before they degrade performance, because to locate them, you need constantly to watch every process and possibly every thread for abnormal trends. Moreover, you may have to watch for as long as a few weeks before you begin to notice that a process is not releasing memory back to the system.

To conclude correctly that a memory leak is causing sluggish system behavior, you should verify that the system is allocating memory and that the memory resource is continuously being depleted before you begin searching for the source of the problem. Use the System Monitor to watch every counter in the Memory object. Pay close attention particularly to the Pool Nonpaged Allocs, Pool Nonpaged Bytes, Pool Paged Allocs, Pool Paged Bytes, System Code Total Bytes, and System Driver Total Bytes counters, since they provide the best indications of whether a certain memory resource is being depleted. Under normal circumstances, these counters may fluctuate between high and low values. However, if a memory leak exists, one or more of these counters will only rise in value because the memory is not being returned. You can also monitor the Objects: Threads and Objects: Sections counters to see if memory leaks exist. The Threads counter indicates the number of active threads in the system at that given instant, and the Sections counter reports the number of sections created by processes. A section is an area of virtual memory that a process creates to store data for itself or other processes. Both of these counters will increase continually during a memory leak. You should use the Chart view to monitor activity in real time so you can reach a conclusion about the problem as soon as possible.

NOTE: Your chances of discovering memory leaks before they have disastrous effects are greatly increased if proper capacity planning methodologies are used, as outlined in Chapter 2. You may notice, through trends or patterns, that memory is gradually being depleted and is never properly returned to the system.

When you are charting the memory activity, you will see only increases in memory allocation, though you may also periodically see plateaus, where the process has temporarily stopped requesting more memory. It is important to understand that during this period of inactivity, the process has only reached a level where it is not requesting more memory. After a short time, it will once again request more memory resources and continue to hold onto what it already has.

At this point, you have verified that a memory leak exists in the system. Next you need to find out which process is responsible for slowly devouring memory resources and reducing server performance. A good way to simplify your search is to run a second instance of the System Monitor and place both System Monitor windows side by side. Then one window can display the counters relating to total system memory (Memory: Available Bytes, Memory: Committed Bytes, and so on), and the other can display the memory used by each process. Now you can more easily track the times at which memory allocations increase against the memory usage of individual processes.

Start by monitoring the counters within the Process object. Before you get overwhelmed by the sheer number of counters available for the object, be assured that you do not need to monitor every single one. You should single out those counters that will supply you with enough information to accurately pinpoint the source of the memory leak. Each counter has a separate instance for each process (or program) currently running on the system as well as a Total instance for the combined processes. Figure 6-8 shows the Thread Count counter with all possible instances. The following is a list of recommended Process counters to include when monitoring to find the cause of a memory leak:

▼ **Page File Bytes**   This counter indicates the number of bytes that a process has used in the paging file.

■ **Private Bytes**   Private bytes are the number of bytes that a process has allocated to itself that it cannot share with other processes.

■ **Pool Nonpaged Bytes**   This counter includes the number of bytes in nonpaged pooled memory. Nonpaged pooled memory is a limited amount of memory dedicated solely to

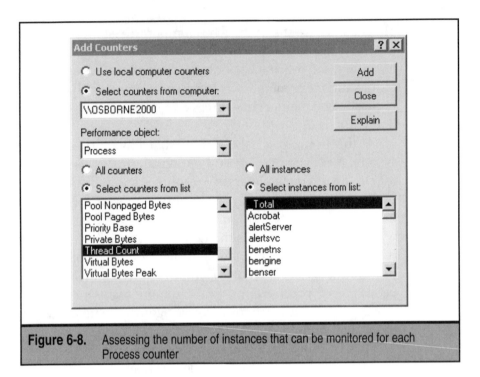

Figure 6-8. Assessing the number of instances that can be monitored for each Process counter

privileged-mode components within the operating system. If a memory leak affects this pool, the amount of memory can be quickly depleted and cause vital system services to fail. If the nonpaged pooled area is affected by a memory leak, the leak could be related to a service that is running.

- **Pool Paged Bytes** This counter is similar to the Pool Nonpaged Bytes counter in that the resource it monitors has limited capacity and is dedicated to system components. Also, as the resource is depleted and not replenished, system services are likely to fail. The difference between this area of memory and nonpaged pooled memory is that pages contained within the pool paged memory can be swapped out to disk.

- **Thread Count** The thread count is the number of active threads for each process. By definition, at least one thread executes instructions for a process. A process can be multithreaded, meaning that more than one thread can simultaneously execute instructions. The process that is leaking memory may spawn many threads, which will increase the counter value.

- ■ **Virtual Bytes** This counter indicates the amount of virtual address space an active process is using. This value does not necessarily mean that disk or main memory pages are being used or committed by the process.

- ▲ **Working Set** This counter indicates the size of a process's working set in bytes. The working set consists of the amount of physical memory that the process is using. It includes pages of memory that have been used by the process's threads. When the process needs more memory resources, it attempts to pull pages from main memory to satisfy the request. If memory resources are low, or if the page resides in virtual memory (pagefile.sys), the VM Manager will not allow the process to add to its working set. Under normal circumstances, Windows 2000 can trim the working set of a process when memory resources are low. However, if the process is leaking memory, the system will not be able to reduce the size of the process's working set.

Since the goal of using these counters is to discover which process is causing problems, you should observe every instance of each counter, with the possible exception of the Total instance, since it does not reflect a specific process running on the system. Once you have added all of the recommended counters and their respective instances, you can begin to watch for places where an increase in memory allocation coincides with a process's use of memory resources. For example, if you notice that Memory: Pool Paged Bytes and the SPOOLSV process always simultaneously increase in value, this process may be the cause of the memory leak.

Once the guilty process has been discovered, you should either replace or correct the process so that it no longer leaks or uses memory inefficiently. Usually you can apply patches or upgrades to alleviate the problems caused by a process. Check with Microsoft or with the company that developed the application to obtain a fix. Remove the process altogether if a remedy does not exist and it causes intolerable system behavior.

Identifying Memory Leaks with Pool Monitor   Obviously, the process of identifying that you have a memory leak and then analyzing which process is the culprit takes a lot of patience and hard work. As a bit of consolation, Microsoft provides a tool that allows you to more easily find the cause of a memory leak. This utility, called Pool Monitor, is located on the Windows 2000 CD in the \Support\Tools folder. Before you begin using this utility, you have to prepare the system by installing the support tools and then using the Global Flags utility (provided in the support tools installation).

Pool Monitor keeps track of nonpaged and paged pool memory usage. More specifically, if a process is allocated memory from either of these pools, the exact memory allocation is recorded. Then when the process is finished using the allocated memory, the amount of memory that it frees up, if any, is also recorded. Pool Monitor calculates the difference between these two values and associates this result with the function tag (enabled by the Global Flags utility) so that you can more easily pinpoint the responsible process.

NOTE: The Global Flags utility allows you to set edit the NtGlobalFlag settings. You need to use this utility because Windows 2000 doesn't enable memory pool tagging information by default.

After you have installed the support tools from the Windows 2000 CD, you can begin configuration with the Global Flags utility. To begin configuring the Global Flags utility and prepare your system to use Pool Monitor, do the following:

1. From the Start | Programs | Windows 2000 Support Tools | Tools menu, run the Global Flags utility as illustrated in Figure 6-9.

2. Check Enable Pool Tagging and click OK.

3. Although you won't be prompted to restart the machine, you'll need to do so to start using Pool Monitor.

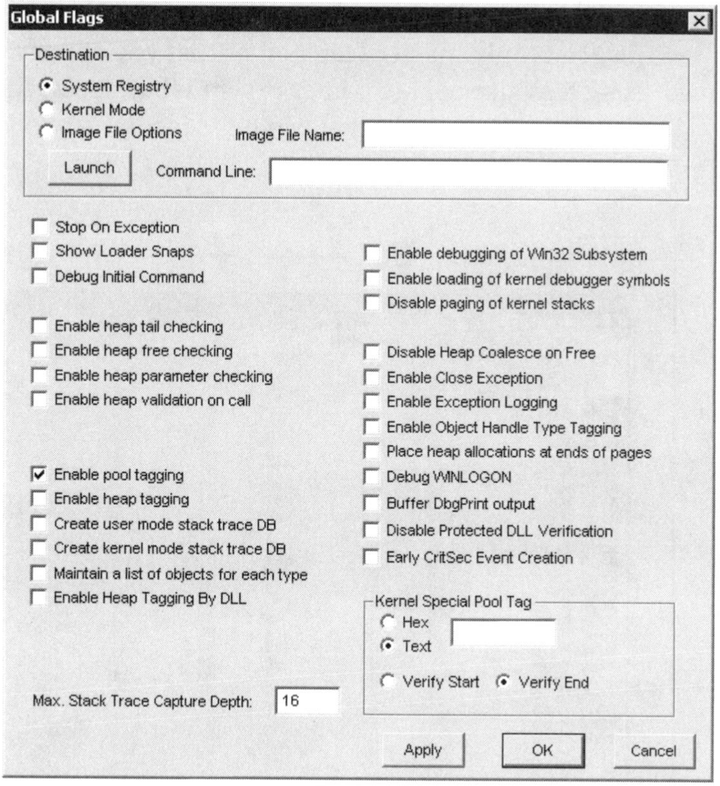

Figure 6-9. Running the Global Flags utility to prepare for Pool Monitor use

At this point, you're ready to use Pool Monitor. Run Pool Monitor at a command prompt by typing **POOLMON.EXE** to display memory allocation information similar to what is shown in Figure 6-10.

As with other command-line utilities, you can specify parameters with the executable file name. The syntax for Pool Monitor is

Poolmon [i*tag*] [x*tag*] [*switch*]

where

itag lists only the pool tag names that you specify
xtag lists all pool tag names except what you specify
switch is a parameter that can massage the screen output (see Table 6-1).

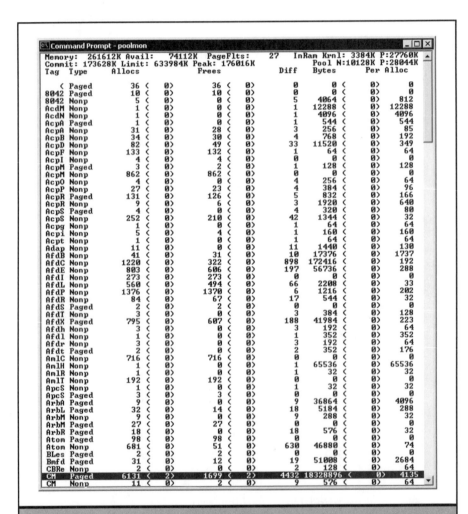

Figure 6-10. Sample display of memory allocation information from Pool Monitor

Switch Parameter	Description
t	Tag name. Use this switch to sort tags alphabetically by name.
p	Pool type. Use this switch to toggle between sorting the tag list by nonpaged and paged.
a	Allocation. Use this switch to sort tags by allocation size.
f	Frees. Use this switch to sort tags by the frees size.
d	Use this switch to sort tags by size the difference between allocs and frees.
b	Max byte usage. Use this switch to sort tags by maximum byte usage.
m	Max byte allocation. Use this switch to sort tags by maximum byte allocation.
e	Toggles end pool totals at the bottom of the data on and off. The default setting is off.
L	Lines. Toggles line highlighting of tags that have changed on and off. The default setting is on.

Table 6-1.   Switch Parameters for Pool Monitor

Be sure to keep this utility running until you can identify the source of the memory leak. Note that the switch parameters are also available to you while the utility is running. You can copy the output information to another application for analysis.

Preventing Memory Leaks

Memory leaks can cause severe performance degradation if they are not caught in time. In most cases, they also cause unnecessary downtime that affects every aspect of the business that relies on the server. Fortunately, there are preventative measures that you can take to help avoid performance reductions caused by memory leaks.

First, it is imperative to keep Windows 2000 current with the latest service packs and hotfixes from Microsoft. Service packs and hotfixes contain operating system enhancements as well as bug fixes. If you do not keep up with these upgrades, you increase your chances of running into memory leak problems. Refer to Chapter 1 for more information on service packs and hotfixes.

Even with the latest service packs and hotfixes, you still run the risk of a greedy process that continually takes memory without returning it to the system. To reduce this risk, establish a burn-in period where you test any new software, including service packs and hotfixes, on a server before you apply the software to Windows 2000 servers in a production environment. The burn-in period should last at least a few days to ensure that the new software does not leak memory or have other negative side effects. This may not always be feasible because of the cost of having another machine available solely for testing, and it may be difficult to mimic a server in the production environment. Allotting the time and equipment will be to your advantage in the long run, however, because you will greatly reduce the chance of downtime associated with memory leaks as well as other problems that might arise from a new installation.

Using RAM Disks

Disk access is clearly the bottleneck in Windows 2000's virtual memory mechanism. Physical memory access times are several orders of magnitude faster than those of the best drives on the market. Despite this overwhelming difference in speed, Windows 2000 still relies heavily on disk drives for many tasks such as storage and paging.

Are there any ways, other than disk caching, to lessen Windows 2000's reliance on the disk subsystem? One possible solution is to create a RAM disk. A RAM disk device driver segments a portion of the system's physical memory during startup to emulate a disk drive. Windows 2000 recognizes this part of memory as another disk drive on the system. You can specify the size of the RAM disk, but the size is ultimately determined by the amount of physical memory on your system. The RAM disk serves the same purpose as other drives on your system: as a storage medium for code and data. It is essentially a hard disk that operates at RAM speeds.

Windows 2000 does not natively support RAM disks. However, there are shareware RAM disk device drivers as well as commercial software packages that allow you to create and manage this type of storage medium.

The advantage of using a RAM disk is the speed at which you can launch processes. Depending on the amount of code and data the RAM disk can hold, load times for processes can be greatly reduced. The information primarily resides in main memory, which consequently reduces the number of times it must be retrieved from a disk drive.

The disadvantages of RAM disks are not so obvious, but you should consider them. First, a procedure must be in place to copy code and data from a storage medium to the RAM disk before a process can take advantage of the RAM disk's speed. The time spent copying information to the RAM disk will more than likely be greater than the time needed to load the information from disk. You can automate the copy procedure through batch or logon script processing, but in the time spent copying, the process could have already been loaded and running.

The other disadvantage of using a RAM disk is more of a fault tolerance than a performance issue. Since RAM disks are volatile, anything contained on the RAM disk is lost when the system loses power or is shut down. Some commercial applications offer a degree of fault tolerance by mirroring the RAM disk to a partition on a disk drive, but usually you have to configure both the RAM disk and the partition so they are of equal size. For example, if your RAM disk is 20MB, you will need to create a 20MB partition for the application to automatically mirror the RAM disk to the partition. For this reason, you should not use a RAM disk for mission-critical processes or data that is dynamic. Although some may argue that the advantages outweigh the disadvantages, one indisputable fact remains: RAM disks expose the system to additional risks.

Reducing Pesky "Out of Memory" Errors

Have you ever tried to run an application and couldn't because you received an "Out of Memory" error message? This is more of an annoyance than a performance problem, but you nevertheless should be aware of this error. The first time I ran into this problem I immediately checked to see what physical and virtual memory resources I had on the system. Ironically, it looked as though I had plenty of room to run more applications. The problem occurs because the size of the application heap is not large enough to run all the applications that you want. The application heap is directly related to the Win32 subsystem (see Chapter 1).

You are more likely to get "Out of Memory" errors on client machines than on servers simply because you're more likely to be running more applications on the desktop. The problem is more common on the older predecessors of Windows 2000. Some older versions default to an application heap size of 512K. Windows 2000 uses 1024K for the initial size.

If you run into this error message frequently, consider increasing the default application heap size under the HKEY_LOCAL_MACHINE\System\CurrentControlSet\Control\ Session Manager\SubSystems subtree. Locate the Windows key and modify the SharedSection parameter. The recommended approach is to incrementally increase the initial value by 512K each time until the error stops. For more information on the "Out of Memory" error, see article Q126962 on Microsoft's Knowledge Base Web site (http://support.microsoft.com/).

NOTE: Be sure to back up the Registry before making any modifications with the Registry editor.

Trimming Server Fat

An easy way to create more available memory for Windows 2000 and applications is to remove anything that the server is not using. This may mean removing or disabling services and processes that are not being used as well as minimizing the number of protocol stacks that the server is using. What you decide to trim depends on the server's configuration, which obviously varies from system to system. Be careful not to remove anything that the server requires to function. For instance, if the system is configured as a RRAS server, you probably shouldn't disable the IPSEC Policy Agent service, but you may want to turn off other services that aren't required by the server.

The amount of memory you conserve or gain also depends on how much memory the process uses. The more memory that you can free, the more memory that becomes available to the resources and system components that need it. Table 6-2 lists a few common services that you may want to disable or set to manual to save memory resources.

Service	Description	Recommendation
Alerter	Lets you send administrative alert messages to other users and computers on the Windows 2000 network.	Keep this service active unless your machine is a stand-alone server, not participating in a Windows 2000 network.
Clipbook	Allows your machine to share data with other machines through the clipboard.	Disable this service unless you plan to share clipboard data.

Table 6-2. Services that Might Be Disabled to Conserve Memory

Service	Description	Recommendation
Messenger	Lets you send and receive pop-up messages, such as administrative alerts.	Keep this service active to receive pop-up messages. These messages may prove very useful in remote communications and may also alert you to important system information.
NetLogon	Required for participation in a Windows 2000 domain. This service is used for authentication purposes.	Keep this service active unless your machine is a stand-alone server, not participating in a Windows 2000 network.
RunAs Service	Allows you to run processes using alternative credentials.	Disable this service unless you need to run certain processes under different credentials.
Server	Allows your machine to share resources with other computers.	Keep this service active unless the machine is a non-networked, stand-alone machine.
TCP/IP NetBIOS Helper Service	Runs the NetBIOS API on top of the TCP/IP protocol.	Remove this service once you've committed to removal of NetBIOS in the Windows 2000 environment.

Table 6-2. Services that Might Be Disabled to Conserve Memory *(continued)*

The following sections discuss a few other features that you may want to disable to free additional memory for the system. They are simply examples; there may be many other ways to reduce resource use on your system.

Disabling the Print Spooler Service

If you do not have a printer connected to the machine either locally or over a network, then there is no reason to keep the print spooler service running. Removing this service will reduce the amount of committed memory by approximately 750K (including paged and nonpaged pool memory). To disable the Windows 2000 Print Spooler service, do the following:

1. In the Computer Management window, expand the Services and Applications snap-in and then select Services.

2. Scroll down the alphabetical list that appears in the right pane until you find the Print Spooler service (see Figure 6-11).

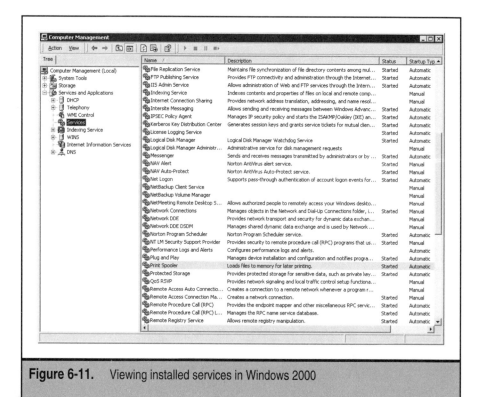

Figure 6-11.   Viewing installed services in Windows 2000

3. Double-click the Print Spooler service to display its properties.

4. On the General tab, open the Startup Type drop-down menu and select Disabled, as illustrated in Figure 6-12. This prevents the service from starting when the machine boots.

5. To begin saving memory resources, click the Stop button to immediately stop the service. Then click OK.

Removing Protocols

Remove any protocols that the network is not using to communicate. Since TCP/IP is the default protocol installed on Windows 2000 and is so widely adopted, there should be limited use of other protocols. Removing other protocols not only frees memory resources, but it also optimizes your server's network I/O performance. For instance, you may not need (or want) IPX/SPX bound to every adapter or service. The gain in memory resources may be minute, but every little bit improves performance. More important, you'll considerably reduce the amount of traffic on the network.

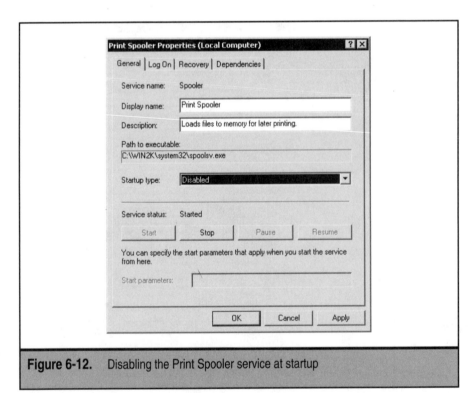

Figure 6-12. Disabling the Print Spooler service at startup

CHAPTER 7

Optimizing the Disk Subsystem

S torage devices are vital components of Windows 2000 Server systems. They not only house the operating system and application code, but they also store the valuable data that your company depends on. How reliable the information is, and how quickly it can be retrieved, are also key factors in Windows 2000 systems. The importance of the disk subsystem should be reflected in the configuration; by no means should you try to cut costs by purchasing lower-quality products.

Equally important to system reliability, availability, and operability is how well the disk subsystem performs under every imaginable condition the server may face. You should—and can—expect high-quality performance from the components that comprise the disk subsystem, even when server use is at its highest. To realistically obtain the best performance, you must look at the many factors that affect it. You must look at who manufactures the component, the type of drive, the type of controller, transfer rates, seek times, configurations, and much more. Get the best equipment that you can afford, and you have won half the battle. For more information on disk subsystem hardware, refer to Chapter 3.

While this chapter focuses on optimizing performance, it also sheds some light on the issue of fault tolerance. It also discusses the importance of striking a balance between fault tolerance and performance optimization. Unfortunately, it is extremely difficult to optimize performance and still maintain the most reliable configuration to protect against disaster. In reading this chapter, however, you will learn many ways to compromise without losing sight of either need.

CHOOSING A FILE SYSTEM

A disk, or volume, is formatted with a file system. This file system determines what the operating system can do with that disk. Windows 2000 presently supports the following file systems:

- ▼ **FAT16** File Allocation Table 16 (16 bits for number of clusters on a disk) is one of the older file systems, used to format small hard disks and floppy disks. It offers few features and is fast due to its simplicity.

■ **FAT32** File Allocation Table 32 (32 bits for number of clusters on a disk) is a newer version of FAT, used to format larger hard disks. It still offers few features.

■ **NTFS 5.0** New Technology File System is used to format medium to extremely large disks. It offers many features and also performance with larger disks.

■ **CDFS** Compact Disc File System is used with CD-ROM.

▲ **UDF** Universal Disk Format is used with DVD.

In this discussion of performance issues, only the FAT16 and FAT32 file systems and NTFS will be examined. These three file systems affect the performance of the disk subsystem the most and are fully supported by Windows 2000. These file systems are examined to highlight their strengths and weaknesses before recommendations are made as to which one you should use on your Windows 2000 system.

FAT16

Since the early MS-DOS era, the file allocation table (FAT) has served as a useful file system for storing code and data. It is one of the simplest file systems that Windows 2000 supports. Of course, FAT was designed without concern for true preemptive multitasking environments like Windows 2000—but can it nevertheless be useful within a Windows 2000 Server environment?

Windows 2000 supports FAT primarily to provide backward compatibility. This allows older applications that were created for MS-DOS to run under Windows 2000. Of course, some DOS-based applications are not capable of running under Windows 2000 due to incompatibilities, such as a DOS-based application trying to write directly to the hardware.

FAT uses a table stored at the root of a volume; the size of the volume dictates the size of the table. When files are created or deleted, FAT is updated to reflect the change. The FAT file system is most efficient for use with volumes of less than 200MB. Volumes greater than 200MB present challenges to the FAT file system because of the size of the table, and performance begins to suffer with volumes greater than 200MB.

Figure 7-1 shows the organization of the FAT file system. Each partition of the FAT file system contains a section for BIOS parameters and two copies of the file allocation table in addition to any files and directories.

FAT has many more disadvantages than advantages in a Windows 2000 environment. The disadvantages include the following:

▼   It provides no means to ensure security.

■   It cannot ensure file integrity. FAT does not keep track of file system transactions like NTFS does, which guards against single-sector failures. Also, NTFS keeps multiple copies of the master file table. The actual number of copies it keeps depends on the size of the volume.

■   It does not support long file names. However, Windows 2000 does provide a workaround. You can use the bits for the file attributes to support up to 256 characters in a name without affecting MS-DOS. In addition, if a file created on a FAT partition exceeds the 8.3 format, Windows 2000 creates a conventional directory entry to support the 8.3 format and also creates one or more secondary directory entries, depending on the number of characters in the file name. A secondary directory entry is created for every 13 characters in the file name.

■   File size is limited. Although it could be argued that the maximum FAT file size of 4GB is large enough to support

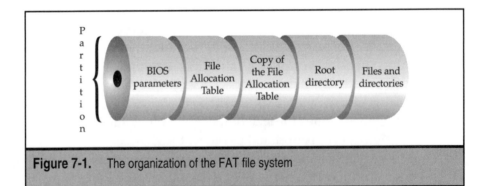

Figure 7-1.   The organization of the FAT file system

most system needs, the more important consideration is how efficiently FAT works with such a large file size, which is unwieldy at best.

▲ The unorganized structure of the FAT file system hinders volume management. The size of the volume is inversely proportional to the efficiency of the FAT file system; as the volume size increases, the efficiency of the file system drops dramatically. Table 7-1 shows how the cluster size increases as the volume size increases. Because the cluster size increases rapidly, there is potential for a lot of wasted space. For example, on a 2GB partition, the cluster size is 32K. If a file is only 10K in size, then there will be 22K of space that is not utilized. If the partition is larger than 2GB, then there will be 54K worth of wasted space. To see the repercussions of using FAT, multiply this wasted amount by the hundreds or even thousands of files that are smaller than the cluster size. The amount of underutilized space quickly adds up.

With all these limitations, it is strongly recommended that you not use the FAT file system on your disk subsystem.

Volume (Partition) Size (MB)	Cluster Size (K)
0 to 32	<1
33 to 64	1
65 to 128	2
129 to 255	4
256 to 511	8
512 to 1,023	16
1,024 to 2,047	32
2,048 to 4,095	64

Table 7-1. Relationship Between Volume (Partition) Size and Cluster Size

FAT32

FAT32 is an enhanced version of the FAT file system that can be used on drives from 512MB to 2TB in size. FAT16 and FAT32 offer compatibility with operating systems other than Windows 2000. If you're setting up a dual-boot configuration, you should probably use FAT16 or FAT32.

If you're dual booting Windows 2000 and another operating system, choose a file system based on the other operating system, using the following criteria:

▼ Format the partition as FAT if the installation partition is smaller than 2GB, or if you're dual booting Windows 2000 with MS-DOS, Windows 3.1, Windows 95, Windows 98, or Windows NT.

▲ Use FAT32 for use on partitions that are 2GB or larger. If you choose to format using FAT during Windows 2000 setup and your partition is greater than 2GB, the Setup program automatically formats it as FAT32.

Even though FAT32 can theoretically support volume sizes up to 2TB, Windows 2000 limits the ability of the operating system to create volumes larger than 32GB. This is by design to force you to use NTFS for larger volume sizes.

NTFS 5.0

Microsoft designed the Windows NT File System (NTFS) to overcome the limitations of FAT. When Microsoft released Windows 2000, they also redesigned NTFS to add many features and to enhance performance. The newly redesigned file system was very imaginatively named NTFS 5.0. It was also designed to accommodate future demands for efficiency in large-scale (multigigabyte and multiterabyte) disk subsystems. In fact, Windows 2000 can handle sizes that probably will not be implemented until a few years from now. For example, Windows 2000 currently supports up to a 64K sector size, which could potentially support a partition of up to 256 terabytes!

Note that NTFS is efficient only with partitions greater than 400MB because Windows 2000 requires some overhead to maintain security (NTFS uses Windows 2000's security model, which includes discretionary and system access control lists), transactional logging (which adds fault tolerance), and other disk management information. This is why some people use FAT instead of NTFS; FAT is more efficient than NTFS on small partitions because it does not require as much overhead. However, there is little, if any, reason why Windows 2000 should have a partition of that size or smaller, especially on a server.

NOTE: The overhead NTFS requires is the reason that you cannot format a floppy with NTFS: there is simply not enough room for both NTFS and data.

Table 7-2 summarizes some of the advantages of the NTFS 5.0 file system.

Advantages	Description
Performance	Fewer accesses to disk required to find files, and faster access.
High-performance content indexing	The Indexing Service provides a fast, easy, and secure way for users to search for information locally or on the network.
Large Disk Sizes	Supports partition sizes of up to 2 terabytes.
Large File Sizes	Supports file sizes of up to 2 terabytes.
Reliability	Adds fault tolerance at the file level, with transaction logging and recovery techniques. Even the boot sector is backed up on the volume.
Security	Both file- and directory-level security, by user and/or group.

Table 7-2. Advantages of NTFS 5.0

Advantages	Description
Encryption	Both file- and directory-level encryption of file to improve security.
Compression	Files can be compressed to save space on the volume.
Name Space	Supports both 8.3 and long file name formats with up to 255-character file names.
Supports Disk Quotas	Allows administrators to track and limit disk usage by user or group.
Change Journal	Keeps a log of all changes made to files on a volume.
Multiple Data Streams	Files can be associated with multiple applications at once.
Reparse Points	Allows the operating system to extend the volume to other devices.

Table 7-2.   Advantages of NTFS 5.0 *(continued)*

As can be seen from the long list of NTFS advantages, NTFS is clearly the file system of choice for Windows 2000. It succeeds in overcoming the limitations of the other file systems that Windows 2000 supports. Moreover, its design promotes efficiency when used with partitions of greater than 400MB.

The maximum drive size for NTFS is much greater than that for FAT, and as drive size increases, performance with NTFS doesn't degrade as it does with FAT. Windows 2000 supports volume sizes up to 2 terabytes and still achieves good performance as the volume size grows, a quality also known as *scaling well*.

NOTE: Although NTFS 5.0 can theoretically support NTFS volumes as large as 16 exabytes, the practical limit is really 2 terabytes. Hard drive manufacturers currently use a standard sector size of 512 bytes. While sector sizes might increase in the future, the current sector size puts a limit on a single volume of 2 terabytes (2^{32} * 512 bytes). For now, 2 terabytes is considered the practical limit for both physical and logical volumes using NTFS.

Although Windows 2000 does not support the older version of NTFS used in Windows NT, it compensates for this by upgrading from the older version to the newer version automatically. When Windows 2000 mounts a volume formatted in the older NTFS file system, it performs an automatic upgrade to NTFS 5.0. This process is very quick and is not proportional to the volume size, meaning that the upgrade will take the same amount of time on a 1GB volume as it would on a 1TB volume.

Windows 2000 also supports the upgrading of FAT16 and FAT32 volumes to NTFS, though not automatically. The FAT volumes can be converted to NTFS 5.0 volumes using the CONVERT.EXE utility.

TIP: Volumes that have been upgraded from FAT to NTFS will not perform as quickly as volumes that were formatted originally as NTFS. To get the most performance, don't upgrade volumes from FAT to NTFS. Rather, backup the data on the FAT volume, reformat as NTFS, and restore the data.

To summarize, NTFS is the recommended file system for Windows 2000 computers because it provides

▼ Better performance

■ Better file security

■ More features

▲ Support for larger hard disks

To help in comparing the relative scalability of the various file systems, Table 7-3 lists the maximum volume size, maximum file size, and the maximum number of files possible on each file system.

Category	FAT16	FAT32	NTFS 5.0
Maximum volume size	4GB	32GB	2TB
Maximum file size	4GB	4GB	2TB
Maximum number of files	65,000	4 million	4 billion

Table 7-3. Comparison of Files System Maximums

Interestingly, these are really the practical maximums for each of the files systems. For example, FAT32 can support volumes larger than 32GB, but Windows 2000 prevents you from formatting a larger volume. Another is that NTFS can support up to 16 exabyte-sized volumes, but current disk technology limits this maximum to 2TB. This then effectively limits the file size from a theoretical 17TB to a practical 2TB, since you would not have a file size larger than the volume size!

TIP: Increase the NTFS log file size to 64MB for large volumes (use the Check Disk command **chkdsk /L:65536**, which will sometime require a reboot to take effect). The default is 20MB and is not usually sufficient for large volumes.

Choosing a File System

Based on the previous discussions, there are really only two reasons to choose anything other than NTFS. Those two reasons are

▼ Dual boot system

▲ Volumes less than 400MB

If the system does not meet those two conditions, then NTFS is the file system of choice. It will provide better performance, reliability, and security.

EFS

The Encrypting File System (EFS) provides the core file encryption technology used to store encrypted files on NTFS file system volumes. Once you encrypt a file or folder, you work with the encrypted file or folder just as you do with any other files and folders. Encryption is transparent to the user that encrypted the file. This means that you do not have to decrypt the encrypted file before you can use it. You can open and change the file as you normally do. However, an intruder who tries to access your encrypted files or folders will be prevented from doing so. An intruder receives an access-denied message if the intruder tries to open, copy, move, or rename your encrypted file or folder.

> **NOTE:**   The Encrypting File System is somewhat inappropriately named, as it is not really a file system in the same sense that FAT, NTFS, and CDFS are. It is more a feature of NTFS, much like compression.

You encrypt or decrypt a folder or file by setting the encryption property for folders and files just as you set any other attribute such as read-only, compressed, or hidden. If you encrypt a folder, all files and subfolders created in the encrypted folder are automatically encrypted. It is recommended that you encrypt at the folder level.

Use EFS to keep your documents safe from intruders who might gain unauthorized physical access to your sensitive stored data (by stealing your laptop or Zip disk, for example).

As it has been stated elsewhere in the book, there is no free lunch. The additional security that EFS brings comes at a performance price. The file transfer incurs an incremental delay as the encrypted file that is being accessed is either encrypted or decrypted by the operating system. The impact is specifically on the processor of the system on which the encrypted file resides, which would be the server in a network share, or the workstation if the file were stored on a local drive.

The degree of performance impact will depend specifically on the processing power of the system doing the encryption or decryption. This is typically negligible on a modern workstation with files encrypted on local drives, as these systems are not typically processor-bound. The impact would be under 1 percent additional load on the processor. For older workstations with processors at the lower end of the scale, this additional load could be as much as 10 percent of the processor time.

For servers, the load can be significant. On a server, there could be many different file accesses occurring simultaneously. If many of these files are protected with EFS, the load on the processor could be 10–25 percent of the total processor load. For file servers on which there will be a large amount of files encrypted (or very large files encrypted), the load should be tested in a lab. If the server would be over burdened by the additional processing overhead, processors should be added or the existing processors upgraded.

To encrypt a file or folder:

1. In Windows Explorer, right-click the file or folder that you want to encrypt and then click Properties.

2. On the General tab, click Advanced.

3. Select the Encrypt Contents to Secure Data check box.

Compression

Windows 2000 supports compression on files and directories for NTFS volumes. Files compressed on an NTFS volume can be read and written by any application without first being decompressed by another program, so the compression is completely transparent to the user and application. Decompression occurs automatically when the file is read and the file is compressed again when it is closed or saved.

Only the Windows 2000 NTFS driver can read the compressed form of the data. When an application or an operating system command requests access to the file, NTFS decompresses the file before making it available. Compression can cause performance degradation when a file decompressed, copied, and then recompressed as a new file, even when the file is copied in the same computer. On network transfers, files are transmitted decompressed and at full size, which affects bandwidth and speed.

Compression is less efficient than decompression, as Microsoft assumed that most data would be compressed once and decompressed many times. Heavily loaded servers with a high percentage of write traffic are not good targets for data compression. Servers with a high percentage of read traffic or with a light workload will not experience significant performance degradation.

Programs that use transaction logging and that constantly write to a database or log should not store their files on a compressed volume or directory. If a program is modifying data through mapped sections in a compressed file, it can produce disk changes faster than the driver can write them. In addition, it is not recommend that user home folders and roaming profiles be compressed because of the large number of reads and writes performed.

BASIC AND DYNAMIC DISKS

Windows 2000 introduces a new type of disk volume and recategorizes an old one. Understanding these changes to the Windows 2000 disk structure is important for creating the initial disk structure, as well as for modifying the disk structure later.

Basic Disks

A basic disk is a physical disk that contains primary partitions, extended partitions, or logical drives. Basic disks may also contain spanned, mirrored, striped, and RAID 5 volumes created using Windows NT 4.0 or earlier. Clients that use MS-DOS can access basic disks, assuming that an appropriate file system is used.

Dynamic Disks

A dynamic disk is a physical disk that is managed by Disk Management. Dynamic disks can contain only dynamic volumes (that is, volumes created with Disk Management). Dynamic disks cannot contain partitions or logical drives, nor can MS-DOS access them. Dynamic disks are also not supported on portable computers.

With dynamic disks, you are no longer restricted to four volumes per disk. There are five types of dynamic volumes: simple, spanned, mirrored, striped, and RAID 5. Only computers running Windows 2000 can access dynamic volumes. You should create basic volumes, such as partitions or logical drives, on basic disks if you want computers running Windows NT 4.0 or earlier, Windows 98 or earlier, or MS-DOS to access these volumes.

A simple volume is made up of disk space on a single physical disk. It can consist of a single region on a disk or multiple regions on the same disk that are linked together. You can extend a simple volume within the same disk or onto additional disks. If you extend a simple volume across multiple disks, it becomes a spanned volume.

A spanned volume is made up of disk space on more than one physical disk. You can add more space to a spanned volume by extending it at any time. In Windows NT 4.0 and earlier, a spanned volume was known as a volume set.

A striped volume stores data in stripes on two or more physical disks. Data in a striped volume is allocated alternately and evenly (in stripes) to the disks of the striped volume. Striped volumes substantially improve the speed of access to your hard disk. In Windows NT 4.0 and earlier, a striped volume was known as a stripe set.

A mirrored volume is a fault-tolerant volume that duplicates your data on two physical disks. It provides data redundancy by using a copy (mirror) of the volume to duplicate the information contained in the volume. The mirror is located on a different disk. If one of the physical disks fails, the data on the failed disk becomes unavailable, but the system continues to operate using the unaffected disk. A mirrored volume is slower than a RAID 5 volume in read operations but faster in write operations. In Windows NT 4.0 and earlier, a mirrored volume was known as a mirror set.

A RAID 5 volume is a fault-tolerant volume with data and parity striped intermittently across three or more physical disks. If a portion of a physical disk fails, you can re-create the data that was on the failed portion from the remaining data and parity. RAID 5 volumes are a good solution for data redundancy in a computer environment in which most activity consists of reading data. In Windows NT 4.0 and earlier, a RAID 5 volume was known as a stripe set with parity.

NOTE: When you format a disk with a Microsoft Windows 2000-based computer, you may observe an increase in the time it takes the computer to format a disk as a dynamic disk (depending on what hardware is installed on the computer). This behavior may occur because the Microsoft Windows 2000 Disk Manager I/O driver (the Dmio.sys file) translates an IOCTL_DISK_VERIFY call as an IRP_MJ_READ call, which can cause some controllers to perform extensive verification when this call is issued. To work around this behavior, you must use the Quick Format option to quickly format your disks to dynamic. This option bypasses the file system verification process, such as, bad-sector detection for non-NTFS file system drives.

Performance: Basic vs. Dynamic Disks

Other than the performance issue in the previous note regarding formatting dynamic disks, there is no real performance advantage in choosing basic or dynamic disks. The decision should be made based on the features needed for a particular server or application.

RAID

RAID—or Redundant Array of Independent Disks—technology has been incorporated into Windows servers since the birth of NT and this continues in Windows 2000. RAID offers many advantages, including a safe means of storing data, easy addition of disk capacity, and enhanced disk drive performance. Simply put, RAID brings improved performance and reliability to a system's disk subsystem.

There are five levels of RAID that are commonly implemented, RAID 0 through RAID 5. Generally, only one is used at a time on a given system, but as you will see later in this section, some of these levels can be combined. The RAID level will dramatically impact the performance of the system, so a good understanding of what the RAID levels mean is very important.

NOTE: Windows 2000 offers software support for RAID levels 0 (striping), 1 (mirroring), and 5 (RAID 5) only.

Although it is important to know what the RAID levels are, it is critical to know how to integrate RAID with your system's functionality. In other words, depending on the server's role in your Windows 2000 environment, you may be better off using a level of RAID that promotes speed and throughput more than reliability, or vice versa.

If performance were the only goal when configuring RAID on the disk subsystem, the recommended choice would be RAID level 0. There would be little need to examine the other levels. However, disk subsystem performance entails much more than just speed. You must also consider data integrity and fault tolerance issues as well, because an unreliable or failed system does not yield high performance. A dead system is the ultimate in performance degradation! Although this book focuses on tuning and optimizing Windows 2000 performance, this section provides an overview of the various types of RAID and how to use them effectively to gain both performance and reliability.

Hardware vs. Software RAID

There are two types of RAID (not to be confused with the levels of RAID): hardware based and software based. Hardware RAID uses on-board processors on the drive controller to perform all of the RAID functions instead of using the CPU and operating system. Most hardware RAID solutions support all levels of RAID and typically allow you to combine levels as well. This type also offers an enhanced level of fault tolerance and controller diagnostic utilities that are not included with software RAID solutions.

Software RAID relies on the operating system, and consequently the CPU, to perform RAID-related I/O operations such as calculating parity information. Software RAID thus places more strain on Windows 2000 and can potentially degrade server performance. However, there is one irrefutable advantage to software RAID, and that is cost. RAID levels 0, 1, and 5 can be implemented through Disk Management, Windows 2000's built-in disk management utility.

As a general rule, hardware solutions perform substantially better than software solutions. Consequently, hardware-based RAID is strongly advised. It not only is the faster option, it is also more reliable than software-based solutions. Note, too, that some hardware-based RAID arrays offer hot-swappable drives and expansion capabilities. Hot-swappable drives provide an added layer of reliability because if a drive fails, it can easily be swapped out and replaced without powering down the system. The expansion capabilities allow you to add drives without having to reconfigure your existing setup.

Hardware-based RAID arrays do not come with a small price tag, but vendor support is abundant. Vendors such as Compaq, Dell, Hewlett Packard, and IBM provide complete hardware-based RAID solutions (drive controller, array chassis, and monitoring software) for Windows 2000. Even though hardware-based RAID is more expensive than software-based RAID, you should consider using it if your budget permits because it offers the best overall performance.

If finances are tight but you need relatively high performance and reliability (most configurations do), then software-based RAID will suffice. You cannot complain about the price because it is built into Windows 2000 without any extra charge. By definition, software-based RAID can cause sluggish server performance because the operating system is used for all RAID functions. You also face serious fault tolerance issues with software RAID level 5. For instance, software RAID level 5 does not allow a damaged or nonfunctional drive to be hot-swapped; the system must be shut down to replace a failed drive.

The following sections describe the RAID levels. You will notice that some offer excellent performance while others are better for increasing fault tolerance, for example, by eliminating downtime or reducing the risk of data loss. The level most appropriate for you will depend on your server's individual characteristics. RAID offers you the ability to strike a balance between performance and reliability.

RAID Level 0: Disk Striping

RAID 0 requires two or more disks so that data can be striped (or split) across multiple disks simultaneously. The group of disks actively striping data is called the stripe set. The more disks that you have in the stripe set, the faster the performance of the disk subsystem. Figure 7-2 shows a RAID 0 stripe set.

Performance increases as the number of disks in the stripe set increases because there are more drives working in parallel, allowing each disk to take a smaller portion of the workload. Because all of the drives can perform I/O simultaneously, the work is completed more quickly. With each additional disk, throughput increases at a rate slightly less than twice the previous throughput rate. However, as the number of drives increases, so does the amount of traffic on the bus, and the rated throughput of the controller may be exceeded.

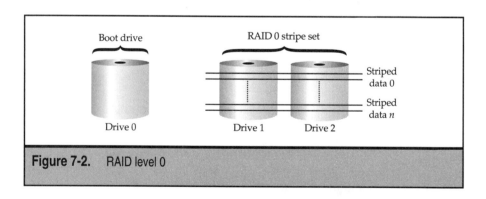

Figure 7-2.   RAID level 0

Before deciding to implement RAID 0, consider a few points. First, hardware-based RAID 0 is preferred over software-based RAID 0 because striping does require some overhead. If software-based RAID 0 is used, Windows 2000 must calculate the striping instead of just letting the controller handle it. The slower the processor, the greater the impact of striping on overall system performance.

Second, to gain the full benefit of RAID 0's performance capabilities, the disks should be of equal capacity because only one I/O operation occurs at a time since the system perceives the stripe set as one disk.

Third, RAID 0 does not offer any redundancy or parity control and so offers no fault tolerance. If speed is all you are after, or if you need high performance and maximum disk capacity, then RAID 0 is an excellent choice. However, if your data is extremely important, you should consider other RAID levels or implement a well-planned backup strategy.

The disk subsystem is, by definition, slower than the CPU and memory. When compared to these two components, it will always be the bottleneck. However, RAID 0 provides the highest level of performance for systems that require extremely fast read and write operations. Moreover, it provides maximum capacity for the disk subsystem.

NOTE: You will see large performance gains if the system's paging file is placed on a RAID 0 stripe set.

Creating a Striped (RAID 0) Array

Using Disk Management, Windows 2000's built-in disk management tool, you can configure and manage the hard disk drives within the system. To build a software-based RAID 0 stripe set, do the following:

NOTE: The system partition (the partition containing %systemroot%, typically the \WINNT directory) cannot be a part of the RAID 0 stripe set.

1. Click the first partition to be included in the stripe set to select it. This partition should be considered free space.

2. While pressing the CTRL key, click at least one more drive to be included in the stripe set. Each drive that you select will be highlighted as shown in Figure 7-3. Each partition to be included in the stripe set should be free space and on a separate physical disk.

3. Once you have selected all of the drives to be used in the stripe set (you can select up to 32 partitions, but each must be on a separate physical drive), choose Create Stripe Set from the Partition menu. Then select Commit Changes Now.

4. Format the drives by choosing Format from the Tools menu.

5. From the Partition | Configuration menu, select Save. This last step saves the RAID 0 configuration information.

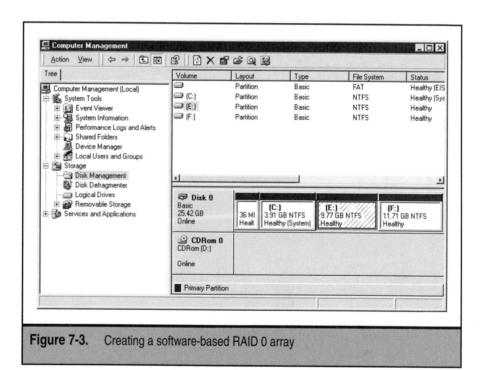

Figure 7-3. Creating a software-based RAID 0 array

RAID Level 1: Disk Mirroring

RAID 1, also known as disk duplexing, mirrors disks. Each disk mirrors, or clones, itself onto another drive of equal size. When data is written to one drive, it is simultaneously written to the other, as illustrated in Figure 7-4. Performance is slightly better than that of a system using no RAID at all. In fact, read performance is almost always better, but write performance is not because a write must occur on two disks instead of one. However, you can slightly increase this performance by placing the drives on their own separate controller.

RAID 1 offers moderate performance with exceptional fault tolerance. If the drive being mirrored develops a problem or even fails, the second drive can immediately take over, though usually only if you are using hardware-based RAID 1. The controller takes the mirrored disk offline and, depending on the controller, may even attempt to alleviate the problem by reformatting the drive and copying the data back to the original disk. Another advantage of hardware-based RAID 1 is that the boot drive can be mirrored (something software-based RAID can't do).

The drawback of RAID 1 is that you immediately lose 50 percent of disk capacity. For example, if you have two 1GB hard disks, the maximum capacity is 1GB, not 2GB, because the second disk is mirroring the other and cannot be used for anything else. Figure 7-5 shows the drop in capacity when using RAID 1 with the Disk Management.

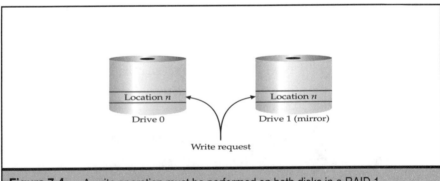

Figure 7-4.   A write operation must be performed on both disks in a RAID 1 configuration

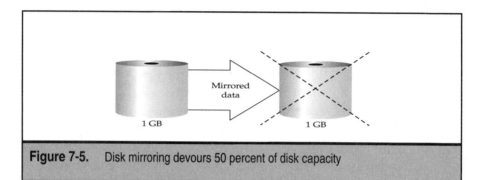

Figure 7-5.   Disk mirroring devours 50 percent of disk capacity

Creating a Mirrored (RAID 1) Array

Hardware-based RAID 1 is highly recommended over software-based RAID with Windows 2000's Disk Management, though the performance drop does not affect the system as much as with other forms of software-based RAID.

> **NOTE:**   Software-based RAID 1 does not limit your ability to include the system partition.

To establish a software-based RAID 1 configuration (mirroring between two drives), do the following:

1. Click the first drive to be included in the RAID array to select it.

2. While pressing the CTRL key, click the second drive to be included. This selects the second drive.

3. Select Establish Mirror from the Partition menu to create the mirror. Then select Commit Changes Now.

4. From the Tools menu, select Format to format the second drive.

5. From the Partition | Configuration menu, select Save. This last step saves the RAID 1 configuration information.

At this point, the system begins writing the information from the first disk to the second disk to establish the mirror.

RAID Level 2: Disk Striping with Parity

Windows 2000 does not implement software RAID 2, and its implementation is expensive. RAID 2 uses a form of striping that requires a parity bit for every byte of code or data. This puts a substantial amount of overhead strain even on high-end controllers, but read and write operations can be performed slightly faster than with RAID 1 implementations. However, to achieve this slightly faster throughput, many drives need to be included in the array.

Due to the high cost, this is recommended only for the most demanding applications. In Chapter 17 on optimizing Exchange 2000, a variation on this version of RAID is recommended for very high-performance messaging servers.

RAID Level 3: Disk Striping with Parity

RAID 3 should be used with caution, if it is used at all. Windows 2000 does not provide software RAID 3, so the only option is to implement it in hardware. The RAID 3 specification does stripe data, like RAID 0, and it contains parity information, like RAID 5, but instead of striping the parity information, it places it all on a single drive. For example, if a RAID 3 configuration contains four disks, three disks will stripe data and the fourth will contain all of the parity information. Moreover, for this level of RAID to operate efficiently, all drive spindles must be synchronized. For these reasons, RAID 3 is not a popular RAID implementation and is not recommended for your Windows 2000 Server environment.

RAID Level 4: Disk Striping with Parity

RAID 4 overcomes some of the limitations of RAID 2 and RAID 3 by sequentially striping data in blocks instead of bit by bit. The way in which this level reads data also differs from RAID 2 and RAID 3 because the read operation is multithreaded. Multiple I/O requests can be handled simultaneously because not every drive is used for the operation. For instance, consider a system with four disk drives using RAID 4. If a chunk of data occupies two data words (a data word is 16 bits long), then one word is read (or written) to the first disk, and the second data word is read (or written) to the second disk. The request is completed without involving the third disk at all. The last disk is used only for parity information, as with RAID 3.

Despite its improvements over levels 2 and 3, RAID 4 is typically not a practical solution for performance or reliability. It can be implemented with hardware-based RAID solutions, but Windows 2000 does not support a software-based solution for this RAID level. RAID 4 should not be considered for enhancing performance or for ensuring reliability.

RAID Level 5: Disk Striping with Parity

Hardware-based RAID 5 implementations are by far the most popular RAID implementations, largely because RAID 5 achieves a balance among performance, reliability, and cost. Software-based RAID 5 can also be implemented through Windows 2000's Disk Management, but this approach is strongly discouraged because of the overhead involved in calculating parity information. If software-based RAID 5 is used, the CPU must calculate the parity information and then send it to the SCSI bus.

As shown in Figure 7-6, RAID 5 does not use a single dedicated drive for parity information. Instead, it spreads the parity information across all disks in the array. In this regard, RAID 5 offers true disk striping with parity, with each drive containing both parity information and data. The advantage to this implementation is that if any single drive in the array fails, the parity information can be used to regenerate the lost data. In addition, some hardware-based RAID 5

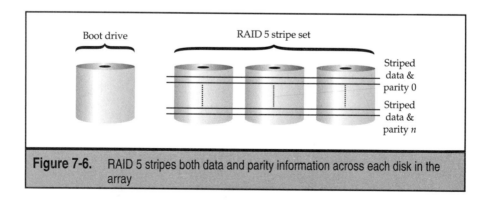

Figure 7-6. RAID 5 stripes both data and parity information across each disk in the array

solutions provide hot-swap capability, as mentioned earlier. In this case, however, simply replacing the drive will initiate the regeneration process without bringing the system down. You can even use a hot spare drive so that if a drive does fail, the controller can automatically detect the failure and begin regeneration without any human intervention.

NOTE: The regeneration process will increase the server's workload and slow performance until the process is complete.

The amount of parity information needed with RAID 5 decreases as the number of drives in the array increases. The overhead accrued with parity information is equal to $1/n$, where n equals the number of drives in the array. For example, a RAID 5 drive array consisting of four 1GB disks will have approximately 25 percent of disk capacity dedicated to parity information. That leaves roughly 3GB for code and data. Table 7-4 shows some sample calculations regarding parity and total storage capacities for RAID 5.

As you can see, if the disks all have the same capacity, calculating the amount of space needed for parity information is easy. It essentially equals the space of one of the drives. Also, adding more drives to the array reducing the parity overhead.

NOTE: Using the same disk capacity for every drive in the array is highly recommended. In addition, every drive in the array should come from the same vendor.

Number of 1GB Drives in the Array (*n*)	Parity Overhead Percentage	Usable Capacity (GB)
6	17%	5
7	14%	6
8	13%	7

Table 7-4. Calculating the Parity Overhead and Total Disk Space in RAID 5

One of the primary reasons why RAID 5 offers better read and write performance than other RAID levels with parity checking is that these operations are multithreaded. Multiple requests can be handled on multiple drives simultaneously. Read performance is only slightly less than that for striping without parity (RAID 0), but write performance is no more than 60 percent that of RAID 1. However, the cost of implementing RAID 5 is much less than the cost of implementing RAID 1.

RAID 5 is clearly the best choice for overall disk subsystem performance, reliability, scalability, and cost. Remember, though, that hardware-based, not software-based, RAID 5 should be used on a Windows 2000 Server to reduce processor load.

RAID Level 6: Disk Striping with Parity

RAID 6 is RAID 5 on steroids. It incorporates an enhanced level of fault tolerance by backing up the striped parity information with additional parity information. In short, there are two sets of parity information: one for data (as in RAID 5) and one for the parity information calculated from the data. RAID 6 can be thought of as a form of redundant redundancy because it adds fault tolerance to the parity information used in RAID 5. The result is that if two drives were to fail at approximately the same time, both drives could be regenerated to recover the lost data.

RAID 6 is a new addition to the various levels of RAID and is currently not supported by Windows 2000. It is clearly geared toward guarding against disk failures and other related disk catastrophes, but it places an additional performance burden on the system, particularly when writes are made to the stripe set. From a performance standpoint, the additional parity information does not justify the degradation in performance that occurs even in high-end hardware-based solutions.

As hardware-based solutions become faster, this new implementation may prove to be a viable solution for both performance and reliability. However, it is unlikely that Windows 2000 will incorporate software-based RAID 6 because of the drastic reduction in performance caused by the parity information overhead.

Combining Levels of RAID

Another benefit of using RAID is that you can combine two levels and reap the benefits of what those levels offer together. This way, you can increase both performance and fault tolerance. You can choose from many combinations of RAID levels, but there are only two viable ways to configure your system for any of these combinations. Both require a hardware RAID controller.

Some RAID controllers support two levels of RAID. When you are evaluating controllers and the likelihood is great that you will incorporate a combination of RAID levels, make sure that the controller supports RAID combinations. The recommended route is to let the controller take responsibility for performing I/O functions for the RAID combination. This approach is recommended for the same reason that a hardware controller is recommended for a single level of RAID: it increases performance.

As you might expect, hardware RAID controllers that support RAID combinations are more expensive than those that do not. If this is discouraging news, you have another option: you can combine hardware RAID with Windows 2000's software RAID. In this case, the hardware controller will be dedicated to providing one level of RAID, and Windows 2000 will handle the other level. This option does not yield the same performance gains as a completely hardware-based solution, but it still provides noticeably increased performance and enhanced fault tolerance.

Many variations of combined RAID levels exist, including RAID 0+1 (RAID 01), RAID 1+0 (RAID 10), RAID 3+0 (RAID 30), and so on. The most popular and, not surprisingly, the best performers are RAID 01 and RAID 10. Both combine mirroring (RAID 1) and striping without parity (RAID 0) to gain the advantages of each level. RAID 01, which mirrors the stripe set, offers impressive read and write performance regardless of whether the I/O transactions are random or sequential. When compared to all other RAID levels and combinations, RAID 01 delivers the best overall performance and fault tolerance. The primary disadvantage of RAID 01 is that your drive capacity drops by 50 percent, as it does with RAID 1. Therefore, you will lose capacity equal to half of the number of drives that are striped. Figure 7-7 illustrates a RAID 01 configuration in which six striped 1GB disk drives are mirrored, thus reducing drive capacity by 50 percent, or 3GB—but still leaving a 3GB capacity.

RAID 01's sidekick, RAID 10, is essentially the inverse of RAID 01. In this case, mirrored drives are striped. The performance and fault tolerance of RAID 10 configurations, such as the one in Figure 7-8, are comparable to those of RAID 01.

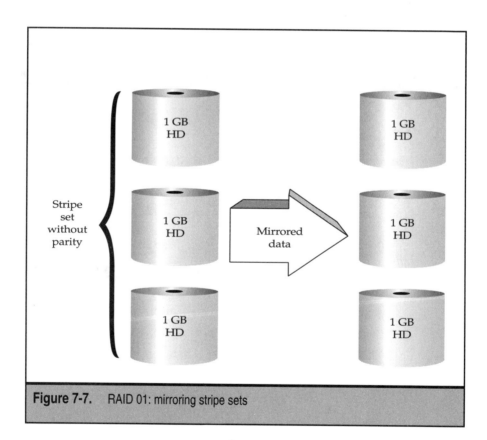

Figure 7-7.   RAID 01: mirroring stripe sets

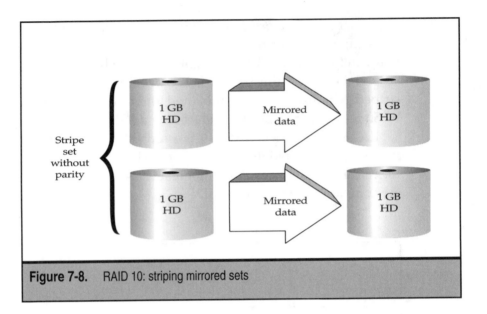

Figure 7-8. RAID 10: striping mirrored sets

RAID Vendors

Table 7-5 lists vendors that manufacture RAID supplies. Some vendors, such as Compaq, Dell, Hewlett Packard, and IBM, supply

Company Name	Web Site
Adaptec	http://www.adaptec.com
Adjile Systems	http://www.adjile.com
Amdahl Corporation	http://www.amdahl.com
Box Hill Systems	http://www.boxhill.com
CMD Technology	http://www.cmd.com
Cybernetics	http://www.cybernetics.com
nStor	http://www.nstor.com
Raidtec	http://www.raidtec.com
Winchester Systems	http://www.winsys.com

Table 7-5. RAID Vendors

complete RAID systems preconfigured, while others focus their attention primarily on RAID controllers or array chasses.

NAS VS. SAN

The need to consolidate Enterprise storage is on the rise because it increases efficiency, decreases redundancy, and simplifies management of data. Two hot storage technologies, Network Attached Storage (NAS) and Storage Area Network (SAN), go a long way in providing the solution.

NAS devices are storage appliances. They are huge, single-purpose servers that you plug into your network and that serve files very fast. The capacity of large NAS appliances is in the terabyte range.

SANs are multiserver, multistorage networks and can grow larger than 400TB. A SAN acts as a secondary network to a LAN. Every server that needs access to the SAN has a fibre channel connection to the SAN. This secondary network relieves the main network of massive data transfer loads because backup traffic occurs between storage devices inside the SAN.

Key Differences

The way NAS and SAN function sounds very similar but there is a subtle difference. Understanding the difference will help you determine which storage method is right for you, should your organization decide that consolidating data is critical to implement.

A NAS appliance uses IP to fulfill the client's request for files, and a SAN uses a SCSI protocol to serve data to network servers. A NAS appliance looks like a large server; a SAN looks like an expansion cabinet that provides additional storage for an existing server. NAS appliances send files when they are requested; SANs grant access to its storage disks.

Which One to Use?

If data consolidation and centralized administration of data is a technology that is key to your business's operation, you should consider a NAS or SAN. Both can provide benefits beyond normal data storage and delivery. The main differences that could help you determine which technology to implement is the cost and performance. A NAS is a device that attaches to your existing network, and a SAN is a separate network; therefore, it's easy to understand that a NAS is much more cost effective than a SAN.

The NAS device is limited by the network connection speed, such as 100BaseT or even Gigabit Ethernet. The SAN uses a SCSI interface, typically fiber channel, which gives it an enormous performance advantage.

▼ **Server-based applications**   The SAN will give the highest bandwidth to the application servers, such as Microsoft SQL or Microsoft Exchange. There is, however, a limited distance that the connection to the SAN can run, typically measured in meters and very expensive fiber runs.

▲ **Client stations**   For network clients, NAS will give the best performance. The single-purpose NAS device has both the optimized embedded code to service many requests simultaneously, and network connectivity to all stations through the network. The limitation is in the bandwidth of any given connection, which will not rival the SAN connection bandwidth.

There are several vendors on the market that produce NAS and SAN solutions. Review the products available from the vendors in the following list.

▼ **NAS**   Compaq, LSI Logic Storage Systems, Network Appliance, Procom Technology, and Raid-tec

▲ **SAN**   IBM, Dell, and Datacore

SECONDARY STORAGE

Windows 2000 gives you plenty of options for primary storage of your data, but it also provides for additional storage through several secondary components.

Removable Storage Management

Removable Storage Management (RSM) is a service for managing removable media (such as tapes and discs) and storage devices (libraries). RSM allows applications to access and share the same media resources. RSM makes it easy for you to track your removable storage media (such as tapes and optical discs) and to manage the libraries that contain them (such as changers and jukeboxes). To access the RSM service, open the local Computer Management MMC in Administrative Tools and double-click Removable Storage in the console tree, as shown in Figure 7-9.

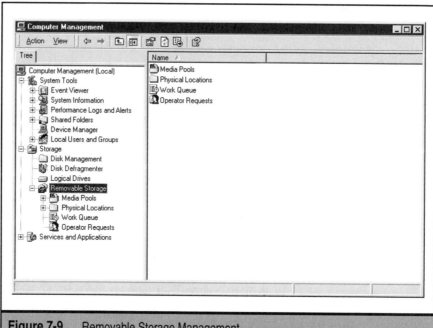

Figure 7-9. Removable Storage Management

Remote Storage

Remote Storage is an application for automatically moving infrequently accessed files from local storage to remote storage. Remote files are recalled automatically upon user request when the file is opened. Any media device attached to the Windows 2000 system, such as a tape drive or Zip or Jaz drive, can be used to store and retrieve the offloaded files.

STRUCTURING YOUR STORAGE

Windows 2000 includes some new technologies for storage management that can make the overall data housing experience better for both the administrator and end user. By using some proactive disk management principles available to Windows 2000, you can keep the amount of data stored on network volumes organized.

Volume Mount Points

If you're a member of the Administrators group, you can use Disk Management to connect, or mount, a local drive in any empty folder on a local NTFS volume. You can format a mounted drive with any file system supported by Windows 2000.

When you mount a local drive in an empty NTFS folder, Windows 2000 assigns a path to the drive rather than a drive letter. Mounted drives are not subject to the 26-drive limit imposed by drive letters, so you can use mounted drives to access more than 26 drives on your computer. Windows 2000 ensures that drive paths retain their association with the drive, so you can add or rearrange storage devices without causing the drive path to fail.

For example, if you have a CD-ROM drive with the drive letter D and an NTFS-formatted volume with the drive letter C, you can mount the CD-ROM drive in the empty folder C:\CD-ROM and then access the CD-ROM drive directly through the path C:\CD-ROM. If desired, you can remove the drive letter D and continue to access the CD-ROM through the mounted drive path.

Mounted drives make data more accessible and give you the flexibility to manage data storage based on your work environment and system usage. For example, you can:

▼ Make the C:\Users folder a mounted drive with NTFS disk quotas and fault tolerance enabled, so you can track or constrain disk usage and protect user data on the mounted drive, without doing the same on the C drive.

■ Make the C:\Temp folder a mounted drive to provide additional disk space for temporary files.

▲ Move program files to another, larger drive when space is low on the C drive, and mount it as C:\Program Files.

Quotas

Disk Quotas track and control disk space usage for volumes. Severe disk and server performance problems result when the network disks reach capacity. Unless disk restrictions have been placed on end users, your server disks could fill up quickly when users decide to dump all of their hard drive data to a directory, or when they decide that the network is the best place to store their downloaded Napster files. Using Windows 2000 Disk Quotas System, administrators can configure Windows to:

▼ Prevent further disk space use and log an event when a user exceeds a specified disk space limit.

▲ Log an event when a user exceeds a specified disk space warning level.

When you enable disk quotas, you can set two values: the disk quota limit and the disk quota warning level. The limit specifies the amount of disk space a user is allowed to use, and the warning level specifies the point at which a user is nearing his or her quota limit. For example, you can set a user's disk quota limit to 50MB and the disk quota warning level to 45MB. In this case, the user can store no more than 50MB of files on the volume. If the user stores more than

45MB of files on the volume, you can have the disk quota system log a system event.

Assigning Disk Quotas

To assign disk quotas:

1. Open My Computer.

2. Right-click the volume for which you want to assign default quota values and then click Properties.

3. In the Properties dialog box, select the Quota tab to display the information similar to that in Figure 7-10.

4. On the Quota Properties page, select Enable Quota Management.

5. Select the Limit Disk Space To option. This activates fields for disk space limit and warning levels.

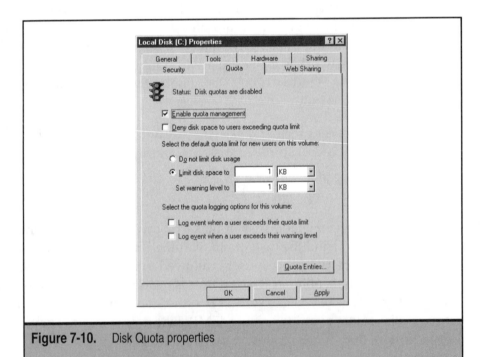

Figure 7-10.   Disk Quota properties

6. Type numeric values in the text fields, select a disk space limit unit from the drop-down list, and then click OK. You can use decimal values (for example, 20.5MB).

Adding New Disk Quota Entries

When you enable disk quotas for a volume, volume usage is automatically tracked for new users from that point on. However, existing volume users have no disk quotas applied to them. You can apply disk quotas to existing volume users by adding new quota entries in the Quota Entries window.

To add new disk quota entries:

1. Open My Computer.

2. Right-click the volume for which you want to add new disk quota entries and then click Properties.

3. In the Properties dialog box, select the Quota tab.

4. On the Quota properties page, click Quota Entries.

5. In the Quota Entries window, on the Quota menu, click New Quota Entry.

6. In the Select Users dialog box, in the Look In list box, select the name of the domain or workgroup from which you want to select user names. Click Add and then click OK.

7. In the Add New Quota Entry dialog box, specify one of the following options and then click OK:

   - **Do Not Limit Disk Usage**   Tracks disk space usage without limiting disk space.

   - **Limit Disk Space To**   Activates fields for limiting disk space and setting warning levels. Type a numeric value in the text field and then select a disk space limit unit from the drop-down list. You can use decimal values (for example, 20.5MB). The value you enter cannot exceed the maximum capacity of the volume.

You can assign disk quotas only on a disk volume that is formatted with the NTFS used in Windows 2000. If you want to administer quotas, you must be a member of the Administrators group on the computer where the drive exists.

Performance Impact of Quotas

Enabling disk quotas will affect the performance and throughput of the operating system, as there are additional disk operations to track disk usage. For a modern server hardware platform, disk quotas will not add excessive overhead. For older or processor-constrained servers, enabling quotas could have a considerable impact on file access.

TIP: Enabling quotas periodically and then disabling them allows you to take advantage of the auditing capabilities provided by Windows 2000 disk quotas without suffering the server performance consequences on a day-to-day basis.

Offline Access to Data

Using Windows 2000's Offline Files feature, you can continue to work with network files and programs even when you are not connected to the network.

If you lose your connection to the network or undock your portable computer, your view of shared network items that have been made available offline remains just as it was when you were connected. You can continue to work with them as you normally do. You have the same access permissions to those files and folders as you would have if you were connected to the network. When the status of your connection changes, an Offline Files icon appears in the status area, and an informational balloon is displayed over the status area to notify you of the change.

When your network connection is restored or when you dock your portable computer, any changes that you made while working offline are updated to the network. If you and someone else on the network have made changes to the same file, you have the option of saving your version of the file to the network, keeping the other version, or saving both.

Your computer must be set up to use Offline Files before you can make files or folders available offline. To set up your computer to use Offline Files, follow these steps:

1. Open My Computer.

2. On the Tools menu, click Folder Options.

3. On the Offline Files tab, make sure that the Enable Offline Files check box is selected.

4. Select Synchronize All Offline Files before Logging Off to get full synchronization. Leave this option unselected for quick synchronization.

MAINTENANCE AND REPAIR

Common sense tells us that a healthy disk subsystem performs much better than one with problems such as corrupted files, damaged sectors, corrupt boot records, poor device driver performance, and fragmentation.

What can be done when a problem does occur? What preventative measures can be taken to reduce the likelihood that the disk subsystem will experience these problems? This section discusses ways to remedy problems that may occur and offers some preventative medicine to head off problems before they affect your system. This section is not intended as a guide to disaster recovery. This section will outline component critical to continued operation of the hard disk system. For more detailed information on fault tolerance and disaster recovery, review Chapter 5.

Some of the procedures, such as backing up and creating the emergency repair disk, are exactly the ones you want to run before making any changes to improve performance. This applies for any Registry changes that you undertake, or even adding components to the operating system. Always have a backup of the system and the Registry prior to any optimization!

In Case of an Emergency

In a perfect world, the preventative measures that you take to ensure reliability and good performance would keep the system operational. Unfortunately, mechanical parts have limited lifetimes and are prone to failure. This is why it is critical to take as many precautions as possible to ensure that you are prepared for the worst.

Creating an Emergency Repair Disk (ERD)

The ERD contains a backup of the system's Registry files so you can restore damaged Windows 2000 system files. Although you cannot reboot the system with the ERD alone, the ERD can help get Windows 2000 to boot on its own by correcting damaged system files. Creating an ERD takes only a few minutes, yet the potential returns are tremendous. It can drastically reduce the amount of downtime if a boot failure occurs.

To create an emergency repair disk, do the following:

1. Run the Backup utility by navigating to Start | Programs | Accessories | System Tools | Backup.

2. On the Welcome screen, click the Emergency Repair Disk button, (shown in Figure 7-11) or go to the Tools menu and choose Create an Emergency Repair Disk.

3. Insert a formatted 1.44MB floppy disk.

4. Check the Also Back Up the Registry check box as shown in Figure 7-12.

5. Click OK.

In Windows NT, an ERD could be used to repair the Registry. In Windows 2000, Inspect Registry File is not available during a repair process. The Microsoft Knowledge Base article Q216337 explains that the Windows 2000 Registry is too large to fit on one disk. To back up the Registry, you must back up the full system, including the system state.

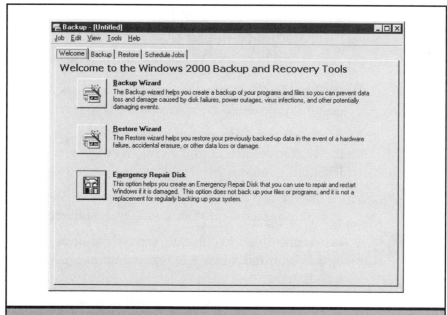

Figure 7-11.   Backup Program welcome menu

NOTE: The Update Repair Info option automatically updates the repair information on the hard disk drive, not the ERD. The information is stored in the %systemroot%/repair directory. *Do not* delete or change this folder, or you will not be able to repair system problems.

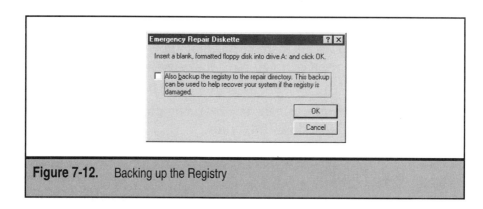

Figure 7-12.   Backing up the Registry

Restoring Windows 2000 Settings Using the Emergency Repair Disk

Follow these steps to restore Windows 2000 settings using the ERD:

1. For Intel-based computers, use the Windows 2000 Setup disks or the Windows 2000 Professional CD to start your computer.

2. After Setup finishes copying files from the Setup disks, the system restarts, and the system enters text-based installation mode.

3. At the Welcome to Setup screen, press R to select the option to repair or recover a Windows 2000 installation.

4. When prompted to enter the type of repair or recovery option required, press R to repair a damaged Windows 2000 installation.

5. Click either Fast Repair or Manual Repair.

NOTE: Pressing M for Manual Repair causes Setup to selectively repair system files, the partition boot sector, or the startup environment. Manual Repair does not repair the Registry. If you press F for the Fast Repair option, Setup automatically attempts to repair system files, the partition boot sector, and the startup environment. The Registry copy that Setup restores is the one created when you first installed Windows 2000. Fast Repair runs automatically and does not require any additional interaction after you press the F key.

6. Follow the instructions that appear and insert the ERD when prompted. If you have the original Windows 2000 CD, you can have Setup verify your disk for possible corruption.

7. When the repair process is complete, the computer restarts, and Windows 2000 runs.

Boot Floppies

The idea of using a boot floppy to gain access to the system is not new, but the usefulness of this approach with Windows 2000 is limited, especially if you are using only NTFS. Nevertheless, boot floppies have their benefits. You may need to create two types of boot floppy: a DOS boot disk and a Windows 2000 boot disk. This section examines the use of these boot floppies to access and possibly repair the system.

Using a DOS Boot Disk A DOS boot disk can be used only on systems using FAT or FAT32, because DOS cannot recognize NTFS partitions. Some system configurations use FAT or FAT32 and NTFS, with FAT or FAT32 being used on the boot partition. If that is the case in your system, then it is highly recommended that you create a DOS boot disk. Here's how:

1. At a DOS-based machine or a machine running Windows 95, Windows 98, or Windows Millennium, open a DOS session and type **FORMAT A: /S** at the command prompt to create the boot floppy.

2. Copy the FDISK utility (FDISK.EXE) to the boot disk. (The FDISK utility is useful for repairing damaged boot sectors.)

Now if you ever experience a problem with booting into the system and the boot partition uses FAT or FAT32, you can use the DOS boot disk to gain access to the system. Once you have gained access, use the FDISK utility to attempt to rectify the problem. More specifically, run FDISK with the undocumented /MBR parameter. This replaces the boot sector. If the problem was caused by a damaged boot sector, the problem will be resolved, and you will be able to access the system with Windows 2000.

NOTE: If your system uses FAT or FAT32 for the boot partition but NTFS for all other partitions, it may be to your advantage to include a shareware utility, NTFSDOS, which allows you to access NTFS volumes from DOS. Otherwise, you will not be able to access NTFS after booting to DOS with the DOS boot disk. NTFSDOS is a product developed by Winternals Software. A trial version can be downloaded from http://www.winternals.com/products/repairandrecovery/ntfsdospro.shtml.

Using a Windows 2000 Boot Disk   Do you need to create a Windows 2000 boot disk? The question can be argued both ways. You should already have a boot disk from the three installation floppies provided by Microsoft, and these can be used to access and repair system files. In one particular case, however, a Windows 2000 boot disk can save you a lot of time and worry. If your system mirrors the boot partition, you should create a Windows 2000 boot disk so that if the system fails to start, you can boot to the mirrored (working) drive.

In any case, a Windows 2000 boot disk will allow you to gain access to the system, and it is easy to create:

1. Format a floppy disk.

2. Copy the NT startup files (BOOT.INI, NTDETECT.COM, and NTLDR) located on the root of the boot partition to the newly formatted floppy disk.

NOTE: BOOT.INI, NTDETECT.COM, and NTLDR are all system files that are hidden in the root directory.

3. If you are mirroring the boot partition, remove the Read-Only attribute from BOOT.INI on the Windows 2000 book disk. Then add the mirrored boot partition to the list of choices. For example, add the following line:

```
multi(0)disk(0)rdisk(1)partition(1)\WINNT="Boot From NT Mirrored Partition"
```

NOTE: The general procedure for creating a Windows 2000 boot disk stops after step 2. Use step 3 only if you are mirroring the boot partition.

Creating the Entire Setup Diskette Set   Besides creating a single boot disk for Windows 2000, you can create the entire Setup diskette set by following these instructions:

1. You need four blank, 1.44MB, formatted 3.5-inch disks. Label them "Setup Disk 1," "Setup Disk 2," and so on.

2. Insert a blank, formatted disk into the floppy disk drive and insert the Windows 2000 Professional CD into the CD-ROM drive.

3. Click Start and then click Run.

4. At the prompt, type the following command, replacing *d* with the letter of your CD-ROM drive and *a* with the letter of your floppy disk drive:

```
d:\bootdisk\Makeboot.exe a:
```

5. Follow the instructions that appear.

Disk Cleanup

Disk Cleanup helps free up space on your hard drive. Disk Cleanup searches your drive and then shows you temporary files, Internet cache files, and unnecessary program files that you can safely delete. You can direct Disk Cleanup to delete some or all of those files. To open Disk Cleanup, click the Start button and then navigate to Programs | Accessories | System Tools | Disk Cleanup.

Disk Cleanup, shown in Figure 7-13, searches the designated drive for specific files that gather on the hard disk over time. As files are opened and closed, or an Internet connection is utilized, temporary files are created that will, sometimes, remain on the hard disk. As time progresses and the hard disks begin filling with files, it becomes critical for optimum performance that the disk has enough free disk space to operate. Microsoft developed the Disk Cleanup feature to understand what form these files take and where they exist on the disk so they can be safely removed to make needed space available.

This Disk Cleanup process is mainly a client activity, rather than a server activity.

Backup

In the event the disaster happens, Windows 2000 now includes a full-featured Backup program that works with several standard backup devices, as well as Iomega Zip and Jaz drives and rewritable CD-ROM drives. The Backup product is a slimmed-down version of Veritas Backup Exec (http://www.veritas.com), distributed specifically for Windows 2000. Clicking the Start button and then going to Programs | Accessories | System Tools | Backup executes the utility.

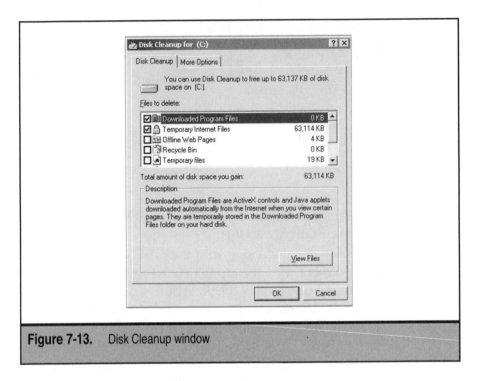

Figure 7-13.   Disk Cleanup window

When the program starts, you are immediately presented with three wizards on the Welcome tab: Backup Wizard, Restore Wizard, and a utility to create the Emergency Repair Disk. These Wizards simplify the tasks of backing up and restoring critical data stored on the Windows 2000 server. Once you are comfortable with the wizards, or if you prefer to delve straight into the workings of a program, you can quickly access the manual version of the Backup and Restore programs on their respective tabs. The wizards may simplify the process, but the Backup and Restore tabs themselves are pretty simple to use.

Backing Up Data

To select the data for backup, you need only click check boxes (shown in Figure 7-14) next to the files or directories to be backed up through the Windows Explorer–like interface. You then choose a backup destination, name the backup media, and click the Start Backup button.

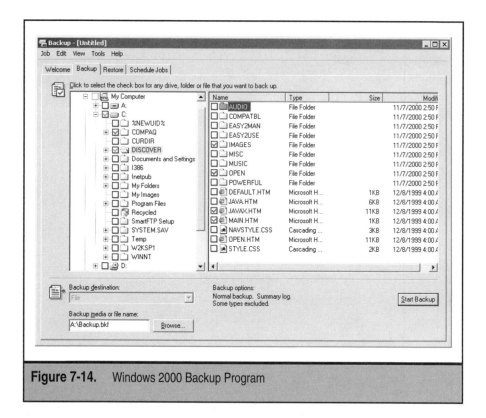

Figure 7-14.   Windows 2000 Backup Program

Restoring Data

Restoring data is just as simple as backing it up using the Restore tab, shown in Figure 7-15. You select the files and folders you want to restore, select where to restore your backed-up files and folders, set the restore options, and start the restore operation

Scheduling Jobs

In Windows NT, the backup utility was limited in function. It could only back up and restore, and it could perform these functions only to certain devices. In addition to backing up and restoring data, the Windows 2000 Backup program allows you to schedule backup jobs to run unattended. This gives Windows 2000 built-in functions that are normally found only in third-party backup programs.

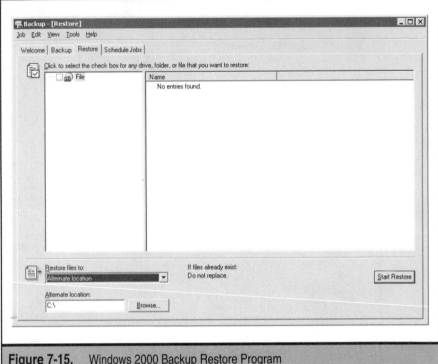

Figure 7-15.   Windows 2000 Backup Restore Program

To schedule a backup, step through the following instructions:

1. Open the Backup utility.

2. Click the Backup tab; then from the Job menu, choose New.

3. Click to select the check box for any drive, folder, or file that you want to back up.

4. Select a file or a tape device as the backup destination and then save the file and folder selections by choosing the Job menu and selecting Save Selections.

5. In the Backup Media or File Name field, type a path and file name for the backup file, or select a tape.

6. Select any backup options you want, such as the backup type and the log file type, by choosing the Tools menu and

selecting Options. When you have finished selecting backup options, click OK.

7. Click Start Backup and make any changes you want in the Backup Job Information dialog box.

8. If you want to set advanced backup options such as data verification or hardware compression, click Advanced. When you have finished selecting advanced backup options, click OK.

9. Click Schedule in the Backup Job Information dialog box.

10. In the Set Account Information dialog box, enter the user name and password that you want the scheduled backup to run under.

11. In the Scheduled Job Options dialog box, in the Job Name field, type a name for the scheduled backup job; then click Properties as shown in Figure 7-16 to set the date, time, and frequency parameters for the scheduled backup. When you have finished, click OK; then click OK again.

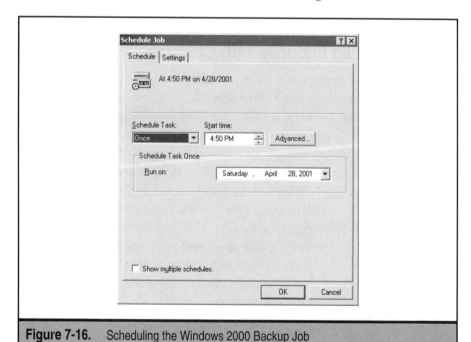

Figure 7-16.   Scheduling the Windows 2000 Backup Job

Windows 2000 Recovery Console

Windows 2000 includes an optionally installed feature called the Recovery Console. The Recovery Console allows a computer with Windows 2000 Professional, Server, or Advanced Server installed to boot to the command line should problems arise that keep the computer from booting. Using the Recovery Console, the computer can generally be repaired using MS-DOS–type commands. While the primary use of the Recovery Console is to repair a down server or workstation, it can also be used to disable services or drivers that are keeping the computer from starting.

The Recovery Console is not part of the default installation of Windows 2000. It must be installed by invoking the following command line, run from the original Windows 2000 CD:

```
I386\winnt32.exe /cmdcons
```

Although Recovery Console is not installed by default, it is a critical piece in bringing servers or workstations back online, and you should seriously consider making this component part of your Windows 2000 installation.

Maintaining File Integrity with CHKDSK

You are probably already familiar with the CHKDSK utility used in DOS-based systems. Windows 2000's CHKDSK, however, is more advanced because it scans for file system integrity on FAT, FAT32, and NTFS partitions. It checks for lost clusters, cross-linked files, and more, and it attempts to correct any errors it finds. It also gives you lots of other file system information, as shown in Figure 7-17.

Windows 2000 automatically runs CHKDSK at startup if it senses file system corruption. You can also manually start the utility. CHKDSK runs in five modes. The first doesn't have any parameters. This is a read-only mode used just to check for any errors in the file system. CHKDSK reports but does not attempt to repair any errors in this mode, so the process is completed quickly. The four other options use the following parameters:

▼ **/FILENAME**   Checks for fragmentation on the specified file.

■ **/F**   Attempts to fix any errors in the file system.

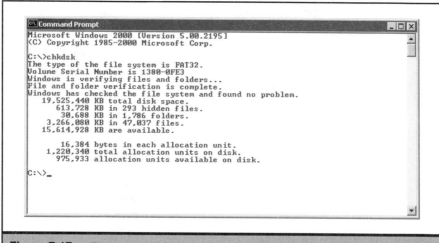

Figure 7-17. File system information reported by CHKDSK

■ **/V** Provides the name and full path of every located on the partition.

▲ **/R** Locates bad sectors on the partition and attempts to recover readable information.

To run CHKDSK, do the following:

1. From the command prompt, go to the partition in question. For example, type **C:**.

2. Type **CHKDSK** without any parameters simply to check for file system errors. If any errors are found, proceed to step 3.

3. Run the CHKDSK utility with the /F parameter to attempt to fix errors found in the file system.

Windows 2000 does a very good job determining if a CHKDSK session is needed and will initiate the process automatically. Only use this utility if you are concerned that there are disk issues that Windows 2000 may not be aware of. In Windows NT 4.0, CHKDSK was an invaluable utility, allowing you to fix disk errors that you may not have known existed otherwise. If Windows 2000 determines that CHKDSK is necessary, you may want to identify if the server has rebooted on its own at some point. You can verify if this is indeed happening by sifting through the System Log. If the system is not rebooting on its own, and CHKDSK is running automatically, consider running vendor-specific hardware diagnostics on the server's hard disks. The disk or the disk controller could be malfunctioning or even worse, could be ready to fail.

Avoiding Cabling and Termination Problems

Many of the problems you are likely to encounter with SCSI-based disk subsystems stem from faulty cabling or improper termination. For example, cables may come loose, lightly shielded cables may not filter electrical noise, or shoddy terminators may not cancel signals. These are simple problems, but they can have serious consequences and can have a large impact on disk subsystem performance. To minimize problems and maintain optimal performance, it is extremely important that you buy high-quality cabling and terminators. Here are some guidelines that you should follow:

▼ Cables should have an impedance rating of at least 90 ohms.

■ SCSI devices must be terminated at both ends.

■ Match termination ends (use active termination whenever possible).

▲ Avoid using external SCSI devices whenever possible.

Using the highest-quality cabling and terminators does not guarantee that you will never encounter problems caused by faulty equipment, but it does shift the odds in your favor. Also, these components are the least expensive in your disk subsystem, so it is easier to squeeze top quality into tight budgets. One source of high-quality SCSI cables and terminators is Granite Digital (http://www.scsipro.com/). Generally, higher-quality products cost more than less-reliable products, but in this case, the price is well justified.

Keeping Your Disk Defragmented

Whether disk defragmentation needs to be performed at all on a NTFS file system has become a topic of hot debate over the past few years, even though defragmentation utilities have been around for ages on DOS- and Windows-based platforms. Microsoft once claimed that using an efficient file system such as NTFS alleviates the need for defragmentation, but this is only partially true. The FAT file system is more susceptible to fragmentation problems than NTFS, but the NTFS file system is not immune to fragmentation either. Up until Windows NT version 4.0, Microsoft did not provide any internal coding that would support third-party disk defragmentation tools. Needless to say, Microsoft now has included a Disk Defragmenter utility with Windows 2000. This utility is actually technology that is licensed from Executive Software (http://www.diskeeper.com), the maker of a popular Windows 2000 defragmentation program called Diskeeper.

NOTE: The version of Diskeeper included with Windows 2000 provides limited functionality for maintaining disk performance by defragmenting volumes that use the FAT, FAT32, or NTFS file system.
This version has the following limitations:
Can defragment only local volumes
Can defragment only one volume at a time
Cannot defragment one volume while scanning another
Cannot be scripted
Cannot be scheduled
Can run only one Microsoft Management Console (MMC) snap-in at a time

What is disk fragmentation and how does it occur? The FAT, FAT32, and NTFS file systems allocate disk sectors into logical units called clusters. Whenever you create or modify a file, Windows 2000 assigns a group of clusters to the file based on the file size. Most files are dynamic, meaning that their sizes can increase or decrease over time, changing the size requirements for the file. Also, when files are deleted, they release free clusters. Over time, the disk becomes fragmented with free clusters and bits of files scattered across the disk, as shown in Figure 7-18.

For example, suppose you create a text file, and Windows 2000 allocates four clusters. You then create many more files on the disk.

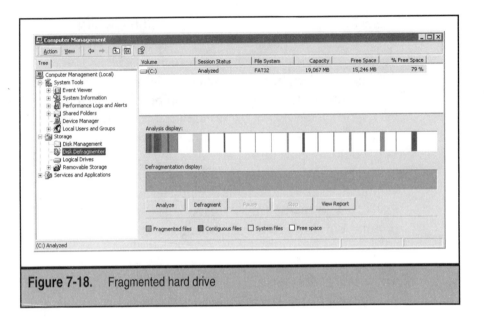

Figure 7-18. Fragmented hard drive

Some time later, you add text to the first file you created, and an additional four clusters are needed to accommodate this additional text. Where do these additional clusters go? They do not fit contiguously with the original clusters and must be placed elsewhere on the disk. Now the file is fragmented.

Although the benefits of hard drive defragmentation are well-known for the FAT file system, the benefits for NTFS have been surrounded in controversy, with different vendors providing different opinions. Even different groups within Microsoft have made conflicting statements about the benefits (or lack thereof) of performing disk defragmentation on NTFS drives. The National Software Testing Lab (NSTL), in conjunction with Executive Software (the maker of the Diskeeper software), at one time released tests showing the benefits of defragmentation for NTFS drives.

All tested system configurations showed significant performance improvements from NTFS defragmentation. Contrary to what you might expect, the faster system configurations benefited more from disk defragmentation than the lower-powered systems.

You can find more information about the NSTL testing methodology and results in the white paper published by NSTL and Executive

Software, at either NSTL's Web site (http://www.nstl.com), or
Executive Software's (http://www.diskeeper.com).

NOTE: Fragmentation can also occur when the paging file is forced to increase beyond its minimum size. This is yet another reason why it is critical to properly size the paging file. Refer to Chapter 6 for more information on configuring the paging file.

Fragmentation negatively affects system performance by significantly reducing the rate at which data can be read from the disk. To read a fragmented file, the disk drive head has to move to various locations to read each fragment. The more a single file is fragmented and the more fragmented files there are on the disk, the more the head has to move from fragment to fragment. This increases the amount of work that must be done to read a file and can drastically reduce the disk's throughput speed. To keep the disk subsystem running at optimal capacity, you should always keep disk fragmentation to less than 10 percent.

MEASURING DISK PERFORMANCE

Many factors play important roles in disk subsystem performance. If you have chosen to configure your system with SCSI, NTFS, and RAID, you are well on your way to optimizing server I/O performance.

Once you have a configuration in place, you need to monitor the disk subsystem to ensure that it can handle your resource requirements now and in the future as they change.

How do you begin monitoring disk subsystem performance? If you try to use the disk counters to monitor performance, chances are good that they will all report zeros, because some of the drivers necessary to gather data from the disk subsystem are not enabled by default. These drivers can cause a slight performance degradation for I/O operations, though their actual effects depend on the system. For instance, performance degradation is greater on low-end Pentiums than on more powerful machines.

In Windows NT 4.0, all disk counters for Performance Monitor were turned off by default. In Windows 2000, the Physical Disk object is turned on by default, and the Logical Disk object is turned off by default. To obtain performance counter data for logical drives or storage volumes, you must type **diskperf -yv** at the command prompt and then press ENTER. This causes the disk performance statistics driver used for collecting disk performance data to report data for logical drives or storage volumes. By default, the operating system uses the diskperf -yd command to obtain physical drive data.

The syntax for Diskperf is as follows:

```
DISKPERF [-Y[D|V] | -N[D|V]] [\\computername]
```

▼ **-Y**   Sets the system to start all disk performance counters when you restart the computer.

■ **-YD**   Enables the disk performance counters for physical drives when you restart the computer.

■ **-YV**   Enables the disk performance counters for logical drives or storage volumes when you restart the computer.

■ **-N**   Sets the system to disable all disk performance counters when you restart the computer.

■ **-ND**   Disables the disk performance counters for physical drives.

■ **-NV**   Disables the disk performance counters for logical drives.

▲ **\\computername**   Is the name of the computer you want to see or set disk performance counters to use.

Disk Subsystem Performance Characteristics

Performance characteristics for the disk subsystem vary from system to system. In addition to the disk components themselves, many variables, such as memory, workloads placed on the system, and the machine's processing power, also affect disk subsystem performance. The capacity planning procedures described in detail in Chapter 2 provide an excellent means for gauging the performance of other system components and how they affect the disk subsystem. Capacity planning also helps you calculate the minimum and maximum values that your system needs for optimal performance so that you can compare the results you obtain from monitoring your disk subsystem.

Keep in mind that the monitoring results may not necessarily represent the performance of the disk subsystem. The results may reveal a symptom of another problem rather than a cause. For example, the disk subsystem may be doing an unusual amount of work because the system is trying to compensate for a lack of memory. (The system relies on the hard disk drives for virtual memory.) If you know that the system is not paging excessively, then you can assume that a component in the disk subsystem is causing the bottleneck. Otherwise, you may just keep blaming the disk subsystem and never uncover the real problem. This is one of the many reasons why it is important to understand and monitor the other factors that affect disk subsystem performance as well.

There are many factors that can affect the disk subsystem, but the more critical factors are the types of applications that the server is running. For example, you can expect a lot more disk activity on a server that runs a large, frequently accessed SQL server database than on a server that only stores user files. Knowing what is affecting the disks on a Windows 2000 server is critical to providing optimum operation and eliminating downtime. The only way to successfully determine how well the disks are performing is to regularly monitor key aspects of the disk subsystem using the Windows 2000 System Monitor described in the next section.

Important Disk Counters to Monitor

All of the available counters for the disk subsystem are contained in the LogicalDisk and PhysicalDisk objects. The LogicalDisk object contains counters pertaining to logical drives or partitions. For example, if a single physical drive has three partitions—C, D, and E—each counter would have these three instances. The PhysicalDisk object holds the counters that measure the characteristics of each physical disk in the system.

> **NOTE:** For information on using the System Monitor, refer to Appendix A.

What counters within these two objects provide the best performance measurements for the disk subsystem? While it could be argued that every counter provides a wealth of information that could prove useful in analyzing performance and capacity, there are a few that are strongly recommended. The counters described here can be found in both objects, and it is important to monitor these counters in both of the objects because they analyze components differently. For instance, the % Disk Time counter in the LogicalDisk object analyzes the time spent servicing requests for a partition, while the PhysicalDisk: % Disk Time looks at the disk as a whole.

% Disk Time

The % Disk Time counter, shown in Figure 7-19, is helpful in determining the amount of activity that the disk is experiencing. Its

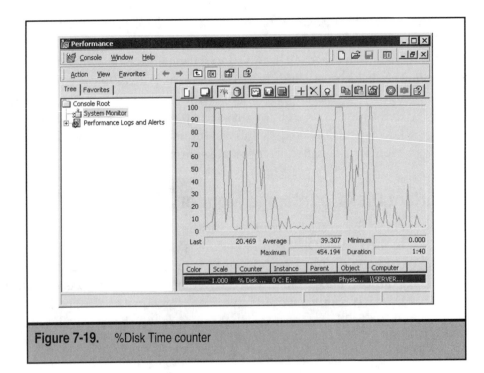

Figure 7-19.   %Disk Time counter

value is the percentage of time that the disk spends servicing read and write requests.

Depending on the server's functions, this counter may reach levels as high as 100 percent consistently. The goal, however, is to keep its value below 55 percent. You'll note in Figure 7-19 that the average utilization is just over 39%, even though the counter swings wildly. As % Disk Time exceeds 55 percent, the reduction in performance will become more and more noticeable. If this counter is consistently averaging above the recommended level, you should seriously consider either upgrading the disk subsystem or offloading some of the server's responsibilities to another server.

Current Disk Queue Length

Current Disk Queue Length indicates whether the disk subsystem can service requests in a timely manner. When a read or write request is sent to the disk subsystem, the request is either serviced immediately or put into a queue. It is put into a queue if the disk subsystem is busy and cannot handle the request right away.

Since the disk subsystem is slower than the CPU and memory, you can expect to see requests frequently placed into the queue. This is not abnormal and does not mean that the disk subsystem is improperly configured. However, if Current Disk Queue Length is always greater than 2, the disk cannot keep up with the rest of the system, creating a traffic jam in which a request cannot be serviced until another has been completed. Using SCSI disk drives in a hardware-based RAID configuration will greatly reduce the likelihood that this type of congestion will occur.

Avg. Disk Bytes/Transfer

The Avg. Disk Bytes/Transfer counter displays the average number of bytes that are transferred to or from the disk. It includes both read and write requests.

There is not a magic number for this counter that tells you that disk subsystem performance is optimal. The appropriate counter value depends on the server's functions and the types of workloads placed on the disk. Generally, though, the larger the value, the better.

If a large number of bytes are being transferred, this simply means that the system can handle a large capacity.

Even though your goal is as large a value as possible for this counter, there will come a point when the disk reaches its maximum transfer capability. Checking Current Disk Queue Length in conjunction with this counter can help you determine the point at which requests start piling up in the queue. This will help you better understand the disk subsystem's saturation point so that you can consider balancing loads between disks or even between servers.

Data Map Hits %

Under the Cache object, the Data Map Hits % shows the percentage of requests in the file system cache that could be resolved without having to retrieve a page from the disk, because the page was already in physical memory. This is a measure of how well the file system cache is doing at servicing file requests from memory cache instead of going to disk for them.

If this value is low (consistently below 80), then add memory to the server to increase the cache size. Alternatively, reduce the memory usage of the server by shutting down used services or by reducing the overall load on the server.

MEMORY USE AND CACHING

Memory tuning and the file system cache (explained in detail in Chapter 6) are keys to ensuring that the disk subsystem performs at optimal capacity. Improper memory and file system cache configurations can have disastrous effects on disk subsystem performance. For example, a system configured with memory that is insufficient to support applications and services relies heavily on the disk subsystem for virtual memory, placing an added (and unnecessary) strain on the disk drives. The disks will constantly be accessed and used as backup for memory, limiting the disk subsystem's ability to service its normal responsibilities.

Onboard Disk Cache

Several caching techniques are designed specifically to improve disk subsystem performance. More advanced drives, such as Seagate's Barracuda family of drives (http://www.seagate.com), incorporate caches on the drives themselves. Most drives available today ship with a minimum of 2MB and a maximum of 16MB of onboard disk cache. The goal of caching is to anticipate requests for code or data and retrieve the requested object before the system asks for it. When the disk drive has a caching mechanism of its own, the amount of processing the system needs to perform can be reduced significantly.

Is a bigger cache size better? The answer depends on how the cache is managed. Some advanced drives segment large caches and include enhanced caching algorithms to increase the cache hit rate and thus improve the effectiveness of the cache. Suppose, for example, that a drive with 1MB of its own cache space does not use any of these enhancements. It fills the entire cache with anticipated code or data. Then another request comes in, and it tries to anticipate future requests by reading in this data (because the anticipated requests are not currently allocated in the cache). However, it must find room in the cache to handle the additional requests. The only choice now is to purge the entire cache memory to service the new request. All of the work performed earlier is essentially wasted because it can no longer be used.

If this large amount of cache space is segmented, however, the drive will essentially have two or more caches at its disposal. Some drives, such as the ones from Seagate, can have as many as four cache segments to divide the cache load. When a cache segment becomes saturated, only that segment is purged. The other segments can still keep their contents and maintain a potentially high cache hit:miss ratio.

What happens when all of the cache segments are full? This is where the advanced caching algorithms make their mark. The drive must decide which cache to purge. It does not want to purge a segment that is about to be used; the drive purges the segment with the least amount of data likely to be used next.

It should be clear that disk read performance can be more efficient with an onboard disk cache. You should be sure to include this feature in your purchase if at all possible.

Turning on Disk Write Caching

Some third-party programs require disk write caching to be enabled or disabled. In addition, enabling disk write caching may increase operating system performance.

To enable or disable disk write caching:

1. Right-click My Computer and then select Properties.

2. Select the Hardware tab.

3. Select Device Manager.

4. Click the plus sign next to Disk Drives to expand this item.

5. Right-click the drive on which you want to enable or disable disk write caching and then select Properties.

6. Select the Disk Properties tab.

7. Click to select or clear the Write Cache Enabled check box, as appropriate.

8. Click OK.

NOTE: Enabling write caching generates the following warning: "By enabling write caching, file system corruption and/or data loss could occur if the machine experiences a power, device, or system failure and cannot be shut down properly." This is normal, and you should disregard it.

CHAPTER 8

Maximizing Network Subsystem Performance

More and more users are sharing resources and applications and accessing information stored either on local servers or on servers located great distances across electronic networks. Sometimes remote resources are so transparent that users do not realize how great a distance their requested information has traveled, or that a reply has likely been returned in a fraction of a second.

Users become acutely aware of network use, however, when a response takes longer than a fraction of a second. The fastest, most optimized system can appear to crawl because of insufferable delays introduced by a slow network. Tweaking and optimizing the network may seem like an insurmountable task, with the numerous pieces of hardware from myriad different vendors (each commanding its own configuration language), servers of all types, a variety of network topologies, and countless applications that comprise your network.

In Windows 2000, Microsoft has completely rewritten the network protocol stack to make it more efficient and to add many features that help optimize performance. Some of these improvements include making TCP/IP the native protocol, increasing the window size, providing support for advanced lower-level transport features, enabling network load balancing, and allowing CPU-intensive tasks to be offloaded to hardware.

Even with the newly written protocol stack that Windows 2000 brings to the table, how can you optimize both the Windows 2000 operating system and the amalgamation of technologies? The key is to divide and conquer. This chapter examines how to break down the network into more easily manageable components and then to optimize each part. Then you will put everything back together so that you can see the big picture again to optimize for future network demands.

NETWORK ARCHITECTURE

A network can be divided into two systems. First, hardware forms the network topology; this includes the wires, routers, servers, and usage protocols and the configuration of all of these components.

The second system consists of the amount and timing of the network traffic over each link. Together these systems make up a unique and always changing environment. You must first acquaint yourself with the terminology and characteristics of the network components before you can jump in and start tweaking these two seemingly disparate systems. This section outlines some basic principles of networking; if you are well versed in this area, you can skip ahead to the "Finding and Removing Network Bottlenecks" section.

The OSI Reference Model

The International Standards Organization (ISO), founded in 1946, published the Open Systems Interconnect (OSI) reference model in 1978 to define standards enabling vendors of different devices and systems to communicate with each other on a network. This seven-layer model has become the standard for designing communication methods among network devices. It is not important to memorize all the responsibilities of each layer, but it is helpful to know the basic function of each, because many hardware devices and configurations reference them.

Each layer of the OSI reference model, illustrated in Figure 8-1, defines a function or a set of functions performed when data is transferred between applications across the network. Any number of protocols, rules that control how a process or function works, may control this function.

Each protocol communicates with other protocols above and below it on the same computer and with a peer at the same layer on a remote system. Information is passed down through the layers until it is transmitted across the network, where it is passed back up the stack to the application at the remote end. Although each layer needs to know only how to pass information up or down from one layer to the next, the layers rely on the fact that each will perform its respective function. This means that you can use a high-level protocol, such as TCP, layer 4, with a variety of layer-1 and layer-2 protocols, such as Ethernet over coaxial cable or Token Ring over twisted-pair cable.

Each protocol layer is concerned only with communication to a peer at the other end of a link and thus creates a *virtual link* to the

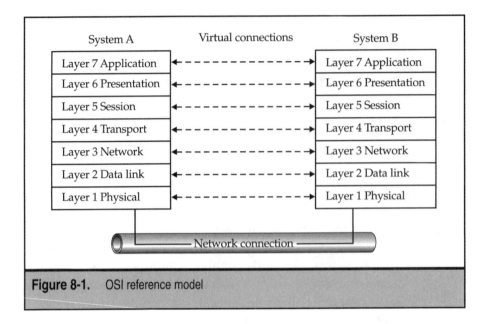

Figure 8-1. OSI reference model

other system at the equivalent level. For example, File Transfer Protocol (FTP) is an application-layer protocol that communicates with peer FTP applications on remote systems. FTP applications are concerned only with FTP functions and do not care whether the physical layer is a serial modem line or a twisted-pair Ethernet connection.

Starting from the bottom, the layers are numbered 1 to 7 and have the following basic functions in network operations:

▼ **Layer 1** The *physical layer* deals with the actual transport medium being used and is sometimes referred to as the wire. It defines the electrical and mechanical characteristics of the medium carrying the data signal, such as coaxial cable, fiber optics, twisted-pair cable, and serial lines.

■ **Layer 2** The *data link layer* controls access to the network and is one of many layers that ensures the reliable transfer of packets across the network. Token passing (Token Ring and FDDI) and Carrier Sense Multiple Access with Collision Detection (Ethernet) are techniques included in layer 2 of the OSI model.

- **Layer 3**   The *network layer* is concerned with moving data between different networks. Protocols at this layer, such as IP and IPX, are responsible for finding the data's destination device.

- **Layer 4**   The primary responsibility of the *transport layer* is to ensure that data reaches its destination intact and in the proper order. The Transmission Control Protocol (TCP) and User Datagram Protocol (UDP) operate at this level.

- **Layer 5**   The *session layer* establishes and terminates connections and arranges sessions between two computers. The Lightweight Directory Access Protocol (LDAP) and Remote Procedure Call (RPC) provide some functions at this level.

- **Layer 6**   The *presentation layer* formats data for display or for printing. Examples of presentation layer protocols are NetBIOS and the Lightweight Presentation Protocol (LPP).

- **Layer 7**   The *application layer* defines the protocols to be used between the application and the lower layers. Examples of protocols at this level include electronic mail (Simple Mail Transfer Protocol), file transfers (File Transfer Protocol), and remote login.

Transport Protocols

The transport or media protocols fall into two main categories: token-passing protocols and collision-based protocols. These differ primarily in how they gain access to the physical medium (the wire or fiber).

Collision-Based Protocols

Ethernet, Fast Ethernet, and Gigabit Ethernet all use a collision-based method to access the wire. Before attempting to transmit a message, a computer listens to the wire to determine whether another computer is already transmitting a message. If it does not hear a carrier for the standard Ethernet span of 9.6 microseconds, the computer will attempt to transmit the message. It must continue to listen while transmitting, because if two computers transmit at the same time, a collision occurs, resulting in incomplete frames, called *runt frames*. Both computers must back off from their transmissions and then retry after a random period of time.

Token-Passing Protocols

Fiber Distributed Data Interface (FDDI) and Token Ring are two types of token-passing protocols that use a completely different method than collision-based protocols for accessing the media. Instead of a computer generating a message for the media whenever that computer has one queued, it must wait to receive the token that is quickly and continuously passed around the ring of computers. A computer can place a message on the media only when it has the token, and it only has the token for a limited time before it must relinquish it to its neighbor, giving all participants an equal opportunity to send messages.

Optimizing Ethernet

LAN protocols operate at speeds in excess of 100 Mbps. However, the achievable data rate, or *throughput*, which is a measure in bits per second, is never as high as the protocol's specification. In the case of the collision-based protocols, it is easy to see that collisions cause a decrease in throughput because each computer must stop transmitting and restart after a short break, resulting in lost time and productivity.

Collisions are such a big problem with collision-based protocols that you can rarely expect to get better than 40 percent of the promised throughput. A 10-Mbps Ethernet segment usually provides a transfer rate of 4 Mbps. Divide this number by 8 to get bytes, subtract another 5 percent for protocol overhead, and you will be lucky to see a 400-Kbps transfer rate.

Not to worry; there are several things you can do to increase throughput on Ethernet:

▼ **Reduce the Number of Users per Segment** For starters, reduce the number of computers sharing the same Ethernet segment. This will reduce the potential for collisions and increase the rate at which completed frames are successfully transmitted to the media.

- **Decrease the Length of Your Segment**   Shortening the length of the physical media will decrease the detection and recovery time for a collision and increase throughput. When a computer at one end of the media wants to send a message, it places bits onto the wire one at a time until the entire frame is on the wire. If the media is long, it will take longer for the bits to travel the length of the wire, and longer for the collision to be detected, than if the wire were very short.

- ▲ **Use Duplexing and Switches**   Traditionally, Ethernet used what is called *half-duplexing*, meaning that a computer could not receive and send data at the same time. Now some network devices use full-duplex Ethernet, allowing simultaneous sending and receiving of data, thus providing faster throughput. Also, Ethernet switching helps to limit the chances of a collision by reducing the number of stations on a particular Ethernet segment. Many computers are connected to the same switch and communicate with each other. Instead of everybody receiving everybody else's messages, which can cause collisions, the switch keeps the messages separate for each member of the switch unless the message is intended for one of the other members.

Optimizing Token-Passing Protocols

Both token-passing protocols and collision-based protocols benefit from having a small physical length. Surprisingly, increasing the number of active stations in token-passing networks has a different result than in Ethernet networks.

- ▼ **Reduce the Physical Length of the Ring**   Token-passing protocols, like collision-based protocols, can be improved by reducing the physical size of the network (a ring in this case). The time a token spends traveling through the empty spaces between stations is time lost for transmitting useful data. By reducing the physical length between stations, you cut down on the travel time between stations and thus improve utilization of the ring. In addition to improving utilization, the ring will appear to be faster because data will travel around the ring in less time.

▲ **Increase the Number of Active Stations**   As odd as it sounds (since the same is not true with Ethernet), you can increase throughput in a token-passing network by increasing the number of active stations. Here is how it works: The time a token takes to travel to the next station is downtime for the ring, which decreases throughput. Valuable time is further lost when the token travels to a station that has nothing to say. Even though the station doesn't add data to the ring, it still takes some of the token's time before it sends the token on its way around the ring. Therefore, to get the most use (that is, to increase the amount of time during which useful data is being transmitted) from your available bandwidth, every station should transmit data when it has the token. This way, you can begin to approach the advertised throughput for your ring (usually 4 or 16 Mbps).

Network Protocols

In an enterprise, Windows 2000 has to be able to communicate effectively with all sorts of computer systems, including legacy systems, the Internet, and even competitors' products that use proprietary protocols. Much of Windows 2000's acceptance in an enterprise will depend on how easily it can be integrated with existing hardware and network protocols.

As we saw in the previous section, physical layer protocols define communication across the physical media. Network protocols help one computer deliver a message to its intended recipient. This section gives an overview of the primary network layer protocols used in the Windows 2000 networking environment, paying particular attention to TCP/IP, which is quickly becoming the protocol of choice for all networking.

TCP/IP

The Internet Protocol (IP) is the workhorse of what is now commonly called the TCP/IP Suite. All of the upper-layer protocols in the upcoming list work through this IP layer of the stack. IP works at the network layer (layer 3), allowing lower-layer protocols (the physical network layers) to communicate with higher-layer protocols. IP provides the method for controlling the transmission of packets from one computer to another. However, it does not provide the guaranteed delivery, flow control, or error recovery usually handled by the higher layers.

Because IP works at the network layer and up, it can work with Ethernet, Token Ring, or FDDI networks or WANs, or all of these. TCP/IP has become the protocol of choice because of its efficiency and widespread acceptance among the PC and UNIX communities. A few of the many protocols included in the TCP/IP suite are listed here:

- ▼ **ARP**   Address Resolution Protocol
- ■ **FTP**   File Transfer Protocol
- ■ **HTTP**   Hypertext Transfer Protocol
- ■ **ICMP**   Internet Control Message Protocol
- ■ **IP**   Internet Protocol
- ■ **NFS**   Network File System
- ■ **RPC**   Remote Procedure Call
- ■ **SMTP**   Simple Mail Transfer Protocol
- ■ **SNMP**   Simple Network Management Protocol
- ■ **TCP**   Transmission Control Protocol
- ■ **Telnet**   Character-oriented terminal emulation
- ■ **TFTP**   Trivial File Transfer Protocol
- ▲ **UDP**   User Datagram Protocol

Typically, there is little to change about IP that will increase network performance. Most variables, such as frame size, are set by default to very reasonable values and do not need to be changed.

Most TCP/IP optimization occurs at the level of the application or with Windows 2000 services using IP over the network (see "Optimizing Network Applications" later in this chapter).

Microsoft has made TCP/IP the core protocol of the Windows 2000 operating system and redesigned it from the ground up. Windows 2000 includes support for all the standard TCP/IP features, as well as many of the new security and performance-enhancing features such as IP Security and Quality of Service. There are also new performance enhancements, including the following:

▼   **Large Default Window Sizes**   The TCP/IP window size is the amount of data that the protocol stack will buffer or receive on a single connection. The larger the value, the less percentage of overhead per connection because more of the bandwidth is dedicated to data bits and less to overhead bits. Windows 2000 uses a default window size (16K) that is twice the size of Windows NT, thus improving performance.

■   **Scalable TCP Window Sizes**   After setting the initial window size, the protocol stack negotiates a larger window size to improve performance by up to one gigabyte. This true window size is the initial window size scaled by a certain factor. The calculation for the true window size is Window-size * 2 ^ Scale. For example, if the initial window size is 65,535 bytes and the scale is 2, then the true window size is 65,535 * 2 ^ 2, or 262,140 bytes. This can result in very low-overhead data transmissions.

■   **Selective Acknowledgments (SACK)**   SACK allows the TCP/IP stack to acknowledge exactly which packets it has received in a series, thus requesting retransmission only of packets lost. Before SACK, the protocol stack would have had to request retransmission of the entire sequence of packets, thus wasting valuable bandwidth on resending packets that had already made it through.

■   **TCP Fast Retransmit**   In standard TCP/IP, a retransmission timer is started after a segment is sent. If the timer expires before an acknowledgment is received, the entire segment is re-sent. This can result in delays in noisy transmissions, as the timer needs to count all the way down. With Fast Retransmit, if the receiver gets a packet with a sequence number that is very far past a previous one in a session, it will send an acknowledgment with the lowest missing sequence number back to the sender and will do this for each packet it gets. If the sender receives three acknowledgments with the same sequence number, then it will abort the retransmission timer and resend the entire sequence of packets immediately. This saves valuable time that would be wasted waiting for the retransmission timer to count down when both sender and receiver know that the transmission was bad.

■ **Round-Trip Time (RTT) and Retransmission Timeout**
With standard window sizes, only one sampling was done per window of data to determine the RTT. This was done on one segment per window, which in an Ethernet network would be 1 out of 44 packets in a 65-kilobyte window size. The RTT is used to determine the retransmission timeout value. For very large window sizes, especially with scaling, the RTT should be recalculated more frequently. In the earlier example using a window size of 262,140 bytes, approximately one packet out of 180 would be sampled. To improve this, the Windows 2000 protocol stack implements a timestamp option that is sent with every data packet and with every acknowledgment. The RTT can be computed with each packet, improving RTT accuracy and thus ensuring accurate retransmission timeout.

▲ **Task Offload**   Task offloading allows tasks normally performed by the protocol to be handed off to the network adapter. This reduces the overhead required by the operating system. A network card that supports this function is required. Functions that Windows 2000 supports for offloading include computing of TCP/IP checksums, TCP/IP segmentation, fast-packet forwarding, and IPSec offloading. For example, offloading the IPSec tasks allows the network card to handle the CPU-intensive encryption and decryption of packets.

NetBEUI

NetBEUI is the extended user interface for NetBIOS, which is an older LAN protocol developed by IBM in the mid-1980s. NetBEUI provides a standard frame format for locating and communicating with other devices on the LAN by using NetBIOS machine names. Each device on the LAN is given a NetBIOS name consisting of no more than 15 characters that NT uses to identify a computer. When a computer has data it needs to send to another device on the LAN, it broadcasts the specific NetBIOS name on the LAN. Every computer on the LAN reads the broadcast packet, but only the device with the matching name responds. In this process, called *NetBIOS name resolution*, the receiving device sends its hardware name to the source device so the two computers can communicate directly.

Although the protocol works very quickly on a small network, as the size of the network increases and more devices attempt NetBIOS name resolution, this broadcast methodology can quickly consume the available bandwidth. This is especially harmful when networks are connected over slower wide area network (WAN) links.

Since NetBEUI uses broadcasts to resolve names, networks with more than a few users can easily clog the system with broadcasts, in a *broadcast storm*. This type of clog is common in large networks that use protocols to broadcast messages to all their users. Although NetBEUI is easy to set up with Windows, it is so chatty that only the smallest of networks should use it.

Fortunately, NetBEUI is not routable, so the broadcasts stop when they encounter a router producing the undesirable condition of isolating all the computers on that segment from the rest of the network. To enable routing of NetBIOS, you can wrap TCP/IP or IPX around the NetBEUI packets before placing them on the network. Even more fortunately, Windows 2000 has switched to TCP/IP as its main protocol and supports NetBEUI only for backward compatibility.

NetBIOS over TCP/IP

Since NetBIOS uses common names for addressing, and IP uses numbers, there needs to be a way to map the two so they are

compatible. The NetBIOS over TCP/IP service is used to resolve
NetBIOS names to IP addresses, and vice versa.

Name Mapping   Windows Internet Naming System (WINS) is one
of several means of associating an IP address with a NetBIOS name.
When you configure TCP/IP on Windows 2000 systems, you can
enter the IP addresses of WINS servers so your system knows how to
reach them even if they are on different subnets. The WINS database
is then populated by the clients.

Another way to associate an IP address with a NetBIOS
name is through the LMHOSTS or HOSTS file (located in the
%SYSTEMROOT%\system32\drivers\etc directory). These files must
be updated manually as the IP address mappings change, and the chore
can become quite tedious as more computers are added to the system,
even if you use automatic scripting routines. Windows 2000
automatically creates the HOSTS file on installation, but the
LMHOSTS file must be created manually.

Windows 2000 can use NetBIOS names and WINS for backward
compatibility with Windows NT and Window 9*x* systems, but the
default is to use Active Directory, LDAP, and DNS to locate
resources. These protocols are much more efficient.

IPX/SPX

Novell's IPX/SPX is another popularly used protocol. The
Internetwork Packet Exchange/Sequenced Packet Exchange
(IPX/SPX) is used within NetWare for file and print sharing.

SPX operates on the transport layer (layer 4) of the OSI model
and ensures the reliability of the end-to-end communication link.
Although SPX guarantees packet delivery and sequencing, it does not
play a direct role in packet routing. IPX operates at the network layer
(layer 3) of the OSI model and handles the addressing of network
devices, keeps track of the routes within the IPX network, and
identifies and locates all the services available on the IPX network.

Unlike NetBEUI, IPX is a routable network protocol. Routing
protocols help to keep track of other IPX network locations and provide
the best route for data to travel between two network devices.

The Service Advertising Protocol (SAP, at layer 5) enables networked devices, such as network servers and routers, to exchange information about available services in an IPX network. Like NetBEUI, SAP messages (SAPs) advertise their services and network addresses to workstations that need access to particular addresses and services.

Since SAPs are broadcast over the network every 60 seconds, they can become a problem as the network grows. In larger networks, it is advantageous to filter SAPs at the routers so their broadcasts do not bog down the network.

SNMP and MIBs

The Simple Network Management Protocol (SNMP) runs at the application layer (layer 6) of the OSI model and is used to manage TCP/IP-based networks and gather statistics on how the network is being used. Usually, an application queries SNMP agents for information from other SNMP-enabled network devices. The most common SNMP commands are listed in Table 8-1.

A management information base (MIB) is used to keep statistics on how SNMP agents are being used. The MIB provides a standard representation of the information available to the SNMP agent and

SNMP Query	Description
Get Request	Retrieves the values of specific MIB variables from an SNMP agent.
Get-Next Request	Retrieves the next instance of information for a particular variable or device.
Set Request	Alters the value of objects that can be written to the MIB.
Get Response	Contains the values of the requested variables.
Trap	Contains information about an event that caused an unsolicited message from an SNMP agent.

Table 8-1. Common SNMP Commands

the location where it is stored. For easy analysis and reporting, the SNMP application keeps a database of all its managed SNMP agents and the information extracted from the MIBs.

Polling Intervals   SNMP agents help you manage your network, but they can become part of the problem if their numbers grow too large. As the number of SNMP agents being managed in a network increases, the amount of overhead for network management may become excessive. To reduce the amount of information transferred from the SNMP agents to the centralized database, increase the *polling interval* between each SNMP request. You can further reduce network traffic generated by SNMP agents by directing them to report only when an unusual event has occurred. You might, for example, use frequent reporting at first to generate your baseline and then set traps on the SNMP agents to report only when a specific threshold, such as a utilization percentage, has been exceeded.

SNMP with Windows 2000   Windows 2000 has built-in support enabling it to act as an SNMP agent, supporting versions 1 and 2C. In this case, the SNMP service accesses the Registry on the local machine and converts this information to a MIB that can be queried by standard SNMP managers.

To load the Windows 2000 SNMP service, follow these steps:

1. Choose Start | Settings | Control Panel.
2. Choose Add/Remove Programs.
3. Choose Add/Remove Windows Components and select Management and Monitoring Tools. Click OK.
4. Select Simple Network Management Protocol. Then click Next.
5. Click Next again. If prompted, insert the CD.
6. Click Finish.

Table 8-2 lists some examples of the MIBs you can use. They may contain extensive amounts of information.

In addition to being configured in the Registry of the SNMP agent, new MIB objects must also be registered in the SNMP

MIB	Description	Installed With
ACS.MIB	The MIB for the Quality of Service Admission Control Service objects.	Base OS
ACCSERV.MIB	RADIUS-ACC-Server-MIB; contains object types for monitoring accounting information between a network access server and a shared accounting server.	IAS
AUTHSERV.MIB	RADIUS-AUTH-Server-MIB; contains object types for monitoring authentication, authorization, and configuration information of a network access server.	IAS
DHCP.MIB	Defines statistics and information about DHCP services.	DHCP
FTP.MIB	Defines statistics and information about FTP services.	IIS
HOSTMIB.MIB	Contains object types for monitoring and managing host resources.	Base OS
HTTP.MIB	Defines statistics and information about HTTP services.	IIS
IGMPV2.MIB	Collects information on what groups are joined on the subnet.	RRAS
IPFORWD.MIB	Defines objects for managing routes on the IP Internet.	Base OS
LMMIB2.MIB	Defines objects used for user and logon information.	Base OS
MCASTMIB.MIB	MIB module for managing IP multicast routing.	RRAS
MIB_II.MIB	Defines objects used for fault analysis as defined in RFC 1213.	Base OS

Table 8-2.   Windows 2000 MIBs

MIB	Description	Installed With
MRIPSAP.MIB	Microsoft-defined MIB for the Routing Information Protocol (RIP).	RRAS
MSIPRIP2.MIB	Routing Information Protocol (RIP2) statistics and information.	RRAS
SMI.MIB	Provides the common definitions for the structure and identification of management information for TCP/IP-based networks.	Base OS
WINS.MIB	Defines statistics and database information about the use of the WINS server.	WINS

Table 8-2. Windows 2000 MIBs *(continued)*

management software application on the management system. For more information about registering new MIB objects in the manager, see the documentation included with your management software application.

When the SNMP service is installed, the base Windows 2000 MIBs are installed in the %SYSTEM_ROOT%\system32 directory. As additional services that have associated MIBs are installed, the system will automatically install the appropriate MIB files. The Windows 2000 Server Resource Kit CD contains two applications that you can use to make a Windows 2000 system to act as a rudimentary SNMP manager: SNMPutil.exe and SNMPmon.exe.

NOTE: For more information about SNMP, see the Internet Engineering Task Force (IETF) Request for Comments (RFCs) 1155, 1157, and 1213. The full text of the RFCs can be found on the IETF homepage at http://www.ietf.org.

Windows Management Instrumentation

Web-Based Enterprise Management (WBEM) is an industry initiative that establishes management infrastructure standards. The WBEM initiative specifies standards for an architecture that provides access to data from different platforms with a consistent look and feel. System management applications can then use this information to create solutions. WBEM is based on the Common Information Model (CIM) schema, which is an industry standard developed by the Distributed Management Task Force (DMTF). Figure 8-2 shows the WEBM architecture.

Microsoft Windows Management Instrumentation (WMI) is Microsoft's WBEM-compliant management interface. It provides a detailed view of the configuration, status, and performance of the Microsoft Windows 2000 system. Anything exposed to WMI becomes automatically scriptable through a common interface. Sources include

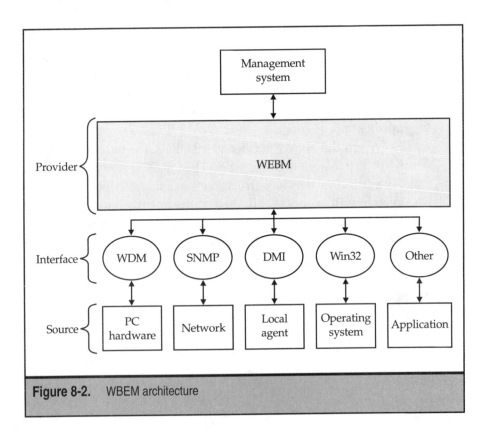

Figure 8-2.   WBEM architecture

a large amount of operating system information as well as the Registry,
System Monitor objects, event logs, and SNMP. Figure 8-3 shows the
WMI architecture. As can be seen in the figure, there is even a WMI
SNMP provider that allows SNMP commands to be translated into
WMI events.

What all this means is that WMI makes the Windows 2000
operating system very manageable through a single, consistent,
standards-based, extensible and object-oriented interface. In addition,
any application or script running on the Windows 2000 system can
access WMI data on the local machine or remotely, provided it has
proper authorization. WMI provides scripting support for the
following scripting languages:

▼   Microsoft Visual Basic

■   Visual Basic for Applications

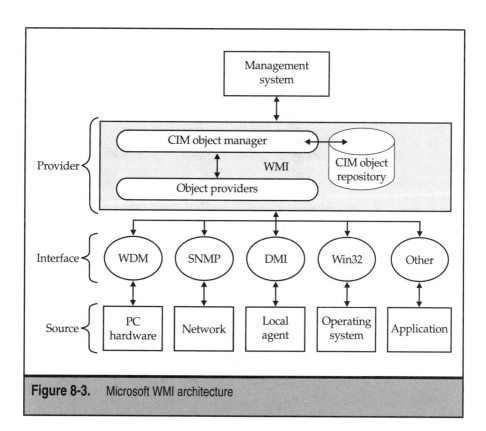

Figure 8-3.   Microsoft WMI architecture

- Microsoft Visual Basic Script
- Microsoft JScript
▲ Perl

FINDING AND REMOVING NETWORK BOTTLENECKS

Every network connection has a bottleneck, a piece of hardware
or software that limits the flow of information being sent from one
computer to another. It is the goal of the network administrator
to find and eliminate the most pervasive bottlenecks. Sometimes
time and money prevent the network engineer from eliminating
bottlenecks, but usually the problem is a lack of knowledge and the
inability to locate bottlenecks. This section outlines some basic steps
you can follow to prevent bottlenecks in your network and how to
identify and eliminate bottlenecks.

Network Design Considerations

The network design should be reviewed for any possible bottlenecks
even before the first packet travels across a network. More often than
not, a basic understanding of the hardware components—and a dose
of common sense—will guide you to the proper network design.
Nonetheless, here are a few points to remember when evaluating
a network design.

▼ **Put Similar Pipes Together**   Do not, for instance, force a
100-Mbps Ethernet segment into a 10-Mbps port on a router.
This example illustrates the importance of being familiar with
your hardware's capabilities and can save you time and
money by helping you eliminate mismatched pieces.

■ **LANs Are Rarely the Bottleneck**   Even though 80 percent of
network traffic is usually local and 20 percent is destined for
remote sites, most often the bottleneck in your network will
be your wide area network (WAN) links. Focus your attention
on optimizing the WAN, because WAN speeds are often

much lower than typical LAN speeds, and purchasing a WAN link with LAN speeds is prohibitive.

■ **Familiarize Yourself with Your Network's Traffic Patterns** Knowing how much information is being moved around your network and knowing the source and destination of the traffic will be of tremendous help in finding future bottlenecks. For example, a server farm located on a 10-Mbps segment might normally be a flag for an upgrade—unless you know that those servers are rarely used, and that 10 Mbps easily meets their demands.

▲ **Monitor, Monitor, Monitor** To successfully optimize any network, you must constantly watch the traffic patterns, hardware usage, and application response times. The next section describes how to use tools to monitor some of the more crucial statistics.

Performance Monitor Counters

In Windows 2000 network environments, network bottlenecks usually reside in the network hardware or in the servers. You can use the System Monitor to help locate the bottlenecks and take corrective measures. Refer to Appendix A for more information about using the System Monitor.

Network Performance

Client-server programs use a request-and-response paradigm. The client computer sends a request to a server, and the server provides a response to the client. Most Windows 2000 functions operate in this way, although any Windows 2000 system can act as either the server or the client. The Workstation and Server services are the two services providing this functionality to Windows 2000 systems, and monitoring these services can be quite useful.

▼ **Workstation Service (Redirector)** The redirector transmits requests destined for servers to the physical network. The

Workstation, or Redirector, service is the client portion of the client-server paradigm.

▲ **Server Service**   The Server service receives the incoming requests and passes them to the Windows 2000 system. Incoming requests can be file, print, or remote process requests. Basically, the server service responds to requests made by clients.

The Redirector Service

Typically, a bottleneck will not be at the client, although this is not always the case. The Redirector service helps connect clients to servers and has several counters that you can monitor to gauge its use (see Table 8-3). One of the more useful counters is Redirector: Bytes Total/sec, which reports the total bytes processed by the

Counter	Description
Redirector: Bytes Total/sec	The rate at which the redirector is processing data bytes. This includes all application and file data in addition to protocol information such as packet headers.
Redirector: Current Commands	The number of requests to the redirector that are currently queued for service. The default value is 5. If this number is much larger than the number of network adapters installed in the computer, you may want to increase the maximum allowance for pending net commands in the MaxCmds Registry in HKEY_LOCAL_MACHINE\SYSTEM\CurrentControlSet\Services\LanmanServer\Parameters.

Table 8-3.   Redirector Service Counters

Counter	Description
Redirector: Network Errors/sec	Serious unexpected errors that generally indicate that the redirector and one or more servers are having serious communication difficulties. For example, a Server Message Block (SMB) Protocol error may generate a network error. Look in the system event log. The default is 45 seconds; values can range from 10 to 65535. You may need to increase the value of the SessTimeout Registry entry in HKEY_LOCAL_MACHINE\ SYSTEM\CurrentControlSet\Services\ LanmanWorkstation\Parameters.
Redirector: Reads Denied/sec	The rate at which the server is unable to accommodate requests for raw reads. When a read is more than twice the negotiated buffer size of the server, the redirector requests a raw read, which, if granted, would permit the transfer of the data without a lot of protocol overhead on each packet. To accomplish this, the server must lock out other requests, so requests are denied if the server is very busy.
Redirector: Server Sessions Hung	The number of active sessions that have timed out and are unable to proceed due to a lack of response from the remote server.

Table 8-3.   Redirector Service Counters *(continued)*

Counter	Description
Redirector: Writes Denied/sec	The rate at which the server is unable to accommodate requests for raw writes. When a write is much larger than the negotiated buffer size of the server, the redirector requests a raw write, which, if granted, would permit the transfer of the data without a lot of protocol overhead on each packet. To accomplish this, the server must lock out other requests, so requests are denied if the server is very busy.

Table 8-3. Redirector Service Counters *(continued)*

redirector for the client. To get a more global picture of network use, you can use the Network Monitor tool included with Windows 2000 Server and SMS, as discussed in more detail in the next section. The Network Monitor will tell you the current utilization percentage and the types of packets being sent over the wire. Remember that on collision-based networks, the utilization percentage should not exceed 40 percent.

NOTE: The Redirector service is called the Workstation service in the Services tool, but is called the Redirector object in the System Monitor tool.

Another counter to watch is the Redirector: Current Commands counter. This counter reports the length of the queue for frames waiting to get on the network segment. The value increases when there is a delay in placing frames on the network, which may indicate a bottleneck inside the computer. This value should not get much larger than the number of NICs installed in the computer.

The Server Service

The Server service is most likely to be affected by memory, CPU, and network bandwidth resource constraints. There are usually many clients requesting services from a single server, and servers usually fulfill several different functions. The Server service receives requests for work, and you can monitor its ability to keep up with the requests with the Server: Work Item Shortages counter. This counter advances when the Server service denies work requests because it is too busy. If this counter continues to increase above a value of 1, you have a serious resource shortage at that computer. Review the use of disk resources as well as CPU utilization to further pinpoint the bottleneck.

The number of instances of failed memory allocation, from either physical memory or paged memory, is recorded by the Server: Pool Nonpaged Failures and Server: Pool Paged Failures counters. Normally, these values should hover around zero. If you see excessive errors, the server is running low on resources, especially memory. To resolve this bottleneck, you can add more physical RAM.

Table 8-4 lists the counters for monitoring the Server service.

Capacity Planning with the System Monitor

To get ahead of your network problems, it is useful to monitor network resources for potential shortages or future bottlenecks, and the System Monitor can help with this task. The key counters listed in Table 8-5 cover the essential bases, including the network segments, memory, hard drive space, and processor utilization on servers. You may find it most useful to watch only a few counters at a time, as the amount of data to be observed and stored can be quite large when many counters are active.

The Performance Logs and Alerts counters can be set to alert you if an event occurs, thereby reducing the amount of unnecessary

Counter	Description
Server: Work Item Shortages	The number of times that no work item was available or could be allocated to service the incoming request. A work item is the location where the server stores an SMB. The number available fluctuates between a minimum and maximum value that is configured based on how the server is configured and the amount of memory on the computer. If work item shortages are occurring, the server may be overloaded. The value can range from 1 to 512. If the Work Item Shortages counter value increases, consider changing the Maxworkitems Registry entry in HKEY_LOCAL_MACHINE\ SYSTEM\CurrentControlSet\Services\ LanmanServer\Parameters. If the actual number of work items consistently matches the maximum set in the Registry, the system consistently initiates flow control, which degrades performance.
Server: Blocking Requests Rejected	The number of times the server rejected blocking SMBs due to insufficient free work items. This counter indicates whether the MaxWorkItem or MinFreeWorkItems server entry may need tuning.

Table 8-4. Server Service Counters

information that you receive. For example, you could have the Performance Logs and Alerts counters send you an alert if the Server: Work Item Shortages value exceeds a specific threshold for a crucial

Counter	Description
Server: Bytes Total/sec	The number of bytes the server sent to and received from the network. This counter provides an overall indication of how busy the server is.
Server: Context Blocks Queued/sec	The rate at which work context blocks had to be placed in the server file system processing queue to await server action. If this counter consistently averages higher than 50 milliseconds, the Server service is a bottleneck for all tasks on remote computers that are issuing remote I/O requests to the server.
Server: Errors System	The number of times that an internal server error was detected. Unexpected errors usually indicate a problem with the server.
Server: Pool Nonpaged Failures	The number of times allocations from the nonpaged pool failed. This counter indicates whether the computer's physical memory is too small.
Server: Pool Nonpaged Peak	The maximum number of bytes of nonpaged pool that the server has had in use at any one point. Indicates how much physical memory the computer should have. If this number consistently increases, the server is running out of the paged or nonpaged pool it originally allocated. If this occurs, you may want to increase the size of the resource.

Table 8-4. Server Service Counters *(continued)*

Counter	Description
Server: Pool Paged Failures	The number of times that allocations from the paged pool failed. This counter indicates whether the computer's physical memory or page file is too small.
Server: Pool Paged Peak	The maximum number of bytes of the nonpaged pool that the server has had in use at any one point. This counter indicates how much physical memory the computer should have.
Server: Sessions Errored Out	Report of autodisconnects and errored-out sessions. To get a more accurate value for errored-out sessions, obtain the value for Server: Sessions Timed Out and reduce the Server: Sessions Errored Out value by that amount.

Table 8-4. Server Service Counters *(continued)*

server. For more information on sending alerts using the Performance Logs and Alerts tool, refer to Appendix A.

Network Monitoring Utilities

Collecting network traffic is not as mysterious as most people believe. You do not need special hardware other than a computer and a network interface card (NIC) that operates in *promiscuous mode*, meaning that the card does not discard traffic messages destined for

Counter	Description
LogicalDisk: % Free Space	% Free Space is the ratio of the free space available on the logical disk unit to the total usable space provided by the selected logical disk drive.
Memory: Pages/sec	Pages/sec is the number of pages read from or written to disk to resolve hard page faults. This counter was designed as a primary indicator of the kinds of faults that cause systemwide delays. It is the sum of Memory: Pages Input/sec and Memory: Pages Output/sec.
Paging File: % Usage Peak	The peak usage of the Page File instance in percent.
PhysicalDisk: % Disk Time	% Disk Time is the percentage of elapsed time that the selected disk drive is busy servicing read or write requests.
PhysicalDisk: Avg. Disk Queue Length	Avg. Disk Queue Length is the average number of both read and write requests that were queued for the selected disk during the sample interval.
Processor: % Processor Time	% Processor Time is the percentage of time that the processor is executing a nonidle thread. This counter was designed as a primary indicator of processor activity. It can be viewed as the percentage of the sample interval spent doing useful work. This counter displays the average percentage of busy time observed during the sample interval.

Table 8-5.   Network Capacity Planning Counters

other computers. To receive data from SNMP agents, you will need special software to coordinate the communication process for you.

Tools

For the sake of simplicity, we are going to divide network-monitoring devices into two overlapping groups: network analyzers and network probes. For basic network utilization measurements, you will need to use only network analyzers, but both types of tools will be covered here.

Network Analyzers   Network analyzers are primarily used for troubleshooting because they work at the lower two layers of the OSI model, the physical and data link layers, and they sometimes contain SNMP support for remote management. Analyzers allow you to capture detailed statistics about the number and types of frames that are currently coursing through the network. In troubleshooting, you can use them to look for collisions, beaconing Token Ring stations (indicating a problem with a neighbor), and percent utilization. Analyzers can also peer into each frame on the network and read its contents, a procedure that occasionally yields nuggets of useful information about a user or an application to help you resolve a problem. Obviously, this ability poses a security risk, because protocols that send information in clear text format such as FTP are considered unsecured. You can easily use an analyzer to capture an FTP session and read the username and password from inside the frame.

Analyzers have uses other than just snooping around frames, such as to record network traffic and play it back to the network at a later time. This can be quite useful when you want to test the way other systems react to a specific request, and you want control over the request. Additionally, you can play back a high-volume traffic capture to stress-test your system and determine the exact level where traffic breaks down.

Because they can filter traffic based on host or destination addresses, analyzers can be used to capture a single traffic conversation between two machines. We will use this feature later to test an application's performance on the network.

Network Probes   Network probes provide added functionality by gathering information about higher layers in the OSI model, and they are usually more permanent fixtures than analyzers. Probes are often PCs with probe software installed on them, or they can be separate hardware devices that are smaller than PCs and have no monitor or keyboard attached to them. Either way, they sit quietly attached to the network gathering network statistics. Administration is performed remotely, via a serial port connected to the back of the probe or on the probe console, if one is available. Although they are not used to read the contents of packets, they can give you information about network layer protocols such as how much of your traffic is IP versus IPX. Table 8-6 lists some vendors for network analyzers and probes.

Microsoft Network Monitor

As mentioned earlier, you do not need a special system to monitor network traffic, and you may already have what it takes right on your computer. Windows 2000 Server comes with a network monitoring tool, called the Network Monitor. The version of

Company and Product	Solution Format	Type	Contact
Network Associates: Distributed Sniffer System	Software and hardware	Analyzer	http://www.sniffer.com
Nortel Networks: Optivity StackProbe	Software and hardware	Probe	http://www.nortelnetworks.com
Compuware: EcoScope	Software	Analyzer	http://www.compuware.com
HP: Network Node Manager for NT	Software	Probe	http://www.hp.com/openview
NetScout Systems: nGenius	Software and hardware	Probe	http://www.netscout.com
Digitech Industries: WAN900	Software and hardware	Analyzer	http://www.digitechinc.com
RadCom: RC-155-c ATM Traffic Generator/Analyzer	Software and hardware	Analyzer	http://www.radcom-inc.com
Xyratex: Gigabit Ethernet Protocol Analyzer	Software and hardware	Analyzer	http://www.xyratex.com

Table 8-6. Network Probes and Analyzers

Network Monitor bundled with Windows 2000 allows you to capture traffic coming from or destined to the machine on which you are running it. However, the version that ships with the Systems Management Server (SMS) can monitor all stations using that segment as well as traffic from other systems with the Network Monitor driver installed.

The component to be installed is called the Network Monitor; it is available with all server versions of Windows 2000. Once installed, it allows a Windows 2000 server to monitor the traffic originating from or destined for the system.

To load the Windows 2000 Network Monitor tool, follow these steps:

1. Click the Start button and choose the Settings option.

2. Choose the Control Panel menu and select the Add/Remove Programs applet.

3. Click Add/Remove Windows Components and select Management and Monitoring Tools.

4. Click the Details button and select Network Monitor.

5. Click Next. Then click Next again.

6. If prompted, insert the CD.

7. Click Finish to complete the installation.

The Microsoft Network Monitor is a powerful tool that you can use to optimize your network. It can track packets up to the network layer, perform filtering on stations or protocols, and conduct packet analysis. To start the Network Monitor, select Network Monitor from the Administrative Tools menu.

NOTE: Unfortunately, with the release of Windows 2000, Microsoft has removed the ability to view network segment information from the System Monitor tool. Previous versions had a Network Segment object, which allowed the System Monitor tool to track the percentage of network segment utilization, percentage of broadcasts on the segment, and other useful information. If you still need that information, you'll need to use the Microsoft Platform Software Development Kit (SDK) for Windows 2000 to access the APIs. See the SDK documentation for specific details on how to access the information. You'll also need to install the Network Monitor Protocol to gain access to the APIs.

To monitor systems other than the one on which the Network Monitor tool is installed, you will need the version of Network Monitor that ships with SMS. To connect to an agent running on another system, choose Capture | Networks and then select the computer running the monitoring agent. Note that you will need to have administrative rights on both machines to do this.

Once the Network Monitor has connected to an active agent, you will see the main Capture window. Click the Capture button, and statistics will start to accumulate, as shown in Figure 8-4.

This window contains information on the utilization of the network. Network Monitor continuously captures traffic until the

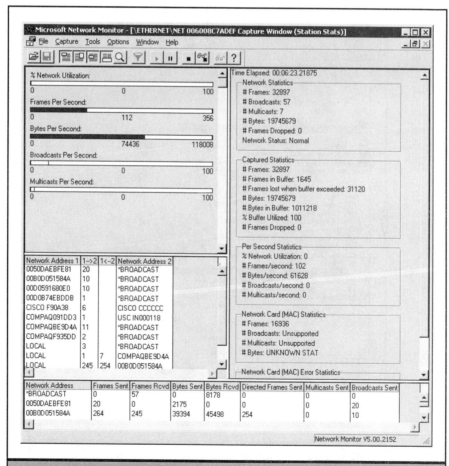

Figure 8-4.   Network Monitor capturing frames

user-defined buffer is filled. Subsequently, newly arrived packets overwrite older packets. You can watch the statistics change over time or stop the capture to view individual packets.

From the Capture menu, click Stop and View. This will end the capture and bring up the packet analysis window, shown in Figure 8-5. Double-clicking a particular frame will open it so you can see its contents.

A tremendous amount of information can be gleaned from analysis of the Network Monitor at the general statistics level and

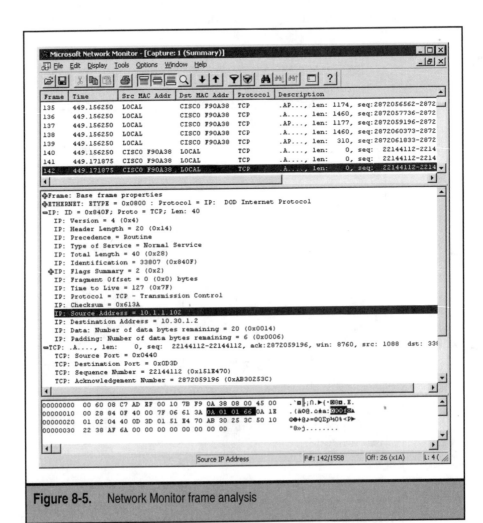

Figure 8-5. Network Monitor frame analysis

at the individual packet level. Monitoring the general use of the network segment is most useful for overall network optimization. Some statistics reported by Network Monitor that you should keep an eye on include the following:

▼ % Network Utilization

■ Broadcast per Second

■ Multicasts per Second

▲ Number of Dropped Frames

TCP/IP Optimization

To tune your TCP/IP network, you will need to familiarize yourself with some of the Windows 2000 built-in TCP/IP commands. The more useful commands are listed in Table 8-7.

Tool	Command	Description
Address Resolution Protocol tool	arp	Displays and modifies the IP-to-MAC translation tables.
Hostname tool	hostname	Displays the host name of the computer.
IP Configuration tool	ipconfig	Displays TCP/IP configuration values.
Line Printer Queue tool	lpq	Displays the status of LPD printers.
NBT Status tool	nbstat	Displays NetBIOS over TCP/IP (NBT) statistics and connections.
Packet Internetwork Groping tool	ping	Tests connectivity between TCP/IP systems.
Router Table tool	route	Displays and modifies the TCP/IP routing table.

Table 8-7. TCP/IP Command-Line Tools

Tool	Command	Description
Name Server Lookup tool	nslookup	Displays information about DNS servers.
Trace Route tool	tracert	Displays information on the route between TCP/IP systems.
Path Ping tool	pathping	Combines ping and trace route functions, testing connectivity between TCP/IP systems and the route between them.

Table 8-7. TCP/IP Command-Line Tools *(continued)*

More information can be found for each of these commands by typing the command followed by **/?** at the command prompt. For example, to learn more about the NBTStat command, you would type

```
nbtstat /?
```

You would then see the following description of how to use nbtstat:

```
Displays protocol statistics and current TCP/IP connections using
NBT (NetBIOS over TCP/IP).
NBTSTAT [ [-a RemoteName] [-A IP address] [-c] [-n] [-r] [-R]
        [-RR] [-s] [-S] [interval] ]
-a (adapter status)    Lists the remote machine's name table given
                       its name
-A (Adapter status)    Lists the remote machine's name table given
                       its IP address
-c (cache)             Lists NBT's cache of remote [machine] names
                       and their IP addresses
-n (names)             Lists local NetBIOS names
-r (resolved)          Lists names resolved by broadcast and via WINS
-R (Reload)            Purges and reloads the remote cache name table
-S (Sessions)          Lists sessions table with the destination
                       IP addresses
```

-s (sessions)	Lists sessions table converting destination IP addresses to computer NETBIOS names
-RR (ReleaseRefresh)	Sends Name Release packets to WINs and then, starts Refresh
RemoteName	Remote host machine name
IP address	Dotted decimal representation of the IP address
interval	Redisplays selected statistics, pausing interval seconds between each display. Press Ctrl+C to stop redisplaying statistics

OPTIMIZING NETWORK APPLICATIONS

To get the most out of your network, it is only natural that you optimize application traffic, which usually makes up the majority of network traffic. Whether you are testing a prepackaged application (such as Microsoft Word) before deploying it on your network or evaluating an in-house application, the basic question you want to answer is the same: How will the application behave in a networked environment? To answer this question, it would be wise to build a laboratory network away from the production network to analyze applications that may one day flow through your network. If you do not have the budget to build a laboratory network, you will have to test applications on the production network. Unfortunately, the production network environment is not as controlled as a lab, and testing could disrupt your production services.

Setting Up a Test Network

Figure 8-6 shows a simple design for a test network. The cloud shape represents a WAN link, a router connection, or perhaps other devices that emulate the production network. If you are testing on your production network, just replace the cloud with all devices in your network between the client and server computers. At one end of the test network is a server computer, and at the other end is a client computer. Network analyzers are placed at each end of the network, one on each network segment, and will be used to monitor the conversation and record precisely when packets leave and arrive at the two computers.

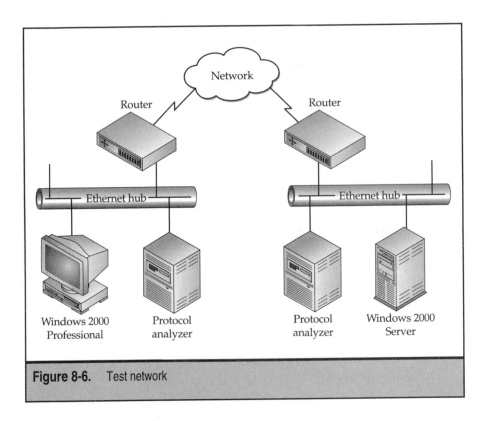

Figure 8-6. Test network

Running a Test

The object of testing an application for the network is to record a conversation and track the number and timing of packets that are sent between two computers, usually a server and a client, during a typical application function. For example, if you are going to test a database application, you might run several tests, one for each of the main types of application function, such as a database query, a record save, or an edit of a previous record.

Follow these steps when running a test:

1. Configure the analyzers to capture packets from only the client and server computers by filtering out all other stations.

2. Coordinate the analyzers to start capturing packets at the same time.

3. Use the client to perform an application function, thereby requesting information from the server.

4. Stop capturing when the function is complete.

5. Repeat these steps for each different type of function.

When you are finished, you will have a collection of analyzer trace files holding the packets used for each function in each direction. Using a simple spreadsheet, you can organize the data to highlight the number of packets traveling in each direction, as well as the number of delays at each computer and on the network. Obviously, it is essential to keep track of each analyzer and its respective files and transactions. Currently, there are no commercial programs available to run analyses automatically, so you will have to do most of this organization by hand. Therefore, it makes sense to keep the analysis as simple as possible.

Analyzing the Results

To keep track of the different types of results, use the following variables:

▼ *Pkt*   The size of the packet (bits, b)

■ *BW*   The bandwidth of the network connection (bits per second, bps)

■ *RT*   The round-trip network delay (seconds, sec)

■ P_c The processing time of the client (sec)

▲ P_s The processing time of the server (sec)

Figure 8-7 illustrates the traffic flow from the server to the client and back again during a simple conversation. In this figure, the client initiates the conversation by sending a request packet to the server, which will arrive after a short network delay. The server does some internal processing for a length of time (P_s) and returns a reply to arrive at the client after a second network delay, producing a total round-trip (RT) delay. The client then performs a processing task for a given length of time (P_c), and the process begins again. This set of simple numbers can be used to describe the application properties.

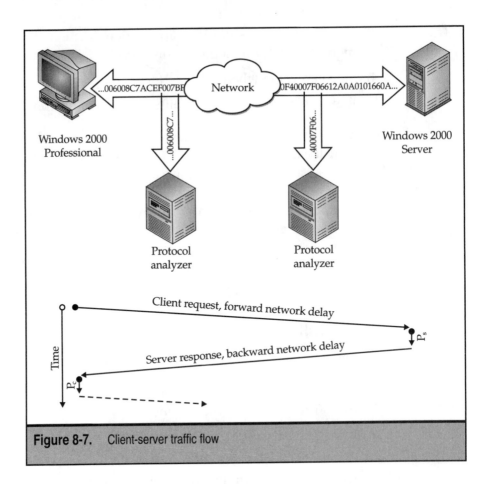

Figure 8-7. Client-server traffic flow

All of these numbers are available to you because you recorded the conversation between the two computers with two analyzers. Unless the analyzers are time-synchronized, however, you can use this method only to determine the one-way network delay. The analyzer clocks are offset by some unknown period of time and tell you when packets arrive using an absolute internal time. Because the internal clocks are probably off by some unknown value, you cannot be certain that the delay between one packet leaving at three seconds and arriving at five seconds is actually two seconds.

Recording the *total* round-trip delay from the client analyzer is the first step toward determining the round-trip delay of the network.

This is the amount of time from when the packet was sent out to when the reply was sent back. Next, subtract the processing time of the server from the total round-trip delay to determine the round-trip *network* delay. The server processing time is the time elapsed from when the analyzer saw the request enter the server to when the analyzer saw the reply leave the server.

How can you use these numbers to optimize applications? First, to be a little more precise, you should better define the processing times of the client and server, P_c and P_s. The processing time is measured by analyzers that are already on the wire or network and includes the time needed for the computer to place and read the packet on the wire. The time used to place a packet on the wire and pull it off the wire is $2 \times Pkt/BW$. Therefore, to get the correct client and server processing times, you must subtract the delays as follows:

$$P_c = P_c \text{(measured)} - (2 \times Pkt/BW_c)$$

$$P_s = P_s \text{(measured)} - (2 \times Pkt/BW_s)$$

Now for the really useful part. You can put all these variables together in a single variable that describes the rate at which the application is running on the network. This variable is called the *application rate (AppRate)*, and it is measured in bits per second:

$$AppRate = \frac{Pkt}{RT + P_c + \dfrac{2Pkt}{BW_c} + P_s + \dfrac{2Pkt}{BW_s}}$$

Although this equation is illustrated for use on a single transaction, it is easy to imagine how the equation could be extrapolated or generalized for a whole application. The basic goal is to maximize the AppRate value for every network application so that it has low latency and appears faster to your users. The following are some general rules to help increase AppRate.

For the application designer:

▼ Decrease the client and server processing time (P_c, P_s).

■ Reduce the number of packets used.

▲ Make the packet (*Pkt*) larger instead of having several small packets.

For the network designer:

▼ Increase the bandwidth (*BW*) to reduce the time it takes to place and read data from the wire.

▲ Reduce the network delay (*RT*) as much as possible.

The AppRate equation will help you pinpoint the bottleneck, usually found in the network delay (*RT*), that prevents your applications from running faster. This variable is very complicated because it involves every piece of hardware that transports the conversation and all the other traffic that was present at the time of the conversation. Nonetheless, narrowing your search for the bottleneck to the physical network has eliminated the application, client computer, and server computer, and their immediate network connections, as the sources of delays. To further delve into the delays found on the network, run the simulations described in the upcoming section, "Proactive Planning."

BOOSTING APPLICATION PERFORMANCE

Tweaking performance will go only so far toward letting you get the most out of applications. To get a larger performance boost, you need to turn to other methods. To boost performance across the network, you can use Quality of Service (QoS). To boost performance on servers, you can use the Network Load Balancing (NLB) service.

In the Fast Lane with Quality of Service

In a standard network infrastructure, all traffic is treated equally. In practical terms, this means that the clerical worker who is browsing music sites on company time and the CEO who is reviewing the financial data from a SQL-based application are given equal access to network services. The Windows 2000 Quality of Service (QoS) is a set of components and technologies that enables the network administrator to treat some traffic differently than other traffic. With QoS, you can put the CEO's SQL-based traffic in the fast lane and relegate the clerk's browsing traffic to the slow lane.

Windows 2000 QoS is but a piece of the total picture; QoS must also be implemented on the other network devices (routers and switches) within the network infrastructure. Windows 2000 QoS interoperates with other QoS participants to ensure that the CEO's fast lane runs all the way through the network infrastructure.

What Is QoS?

Quality of Service (QoS) is the result of implementing a set of QoS mechanisms, such as switches and routers, across both servers and networking components. At the core of QoS is the Resource Reservation Protocol (RSVP), which is an IETF signaling protocol that communicates QoS requests for priority bandwidth through the disparate network devices. RSVP is the communications glue that binds the application, the operating system, and the network devices so they can deliver the services needed by the application. RSVP is media independent, allowing QoS to function over networks that combine different types of low-layer network devices and high-layer applications. Windows 2000 includes a number of mechanisms that support Quality of Service, including the following:

▼ **Generic QoS API**   Windows 2000 QoS has a generic QoS API (GQoS), which programmers can use to specify Quality of Service.

■ **RSVP SP**   The Resource Reservation Protocol service provider (RSVP SP) is the service provider used by the GQoS when an application requests quality of service. RSVP SP interfaces with the platform-independent RSVP specification to communicate with devices along the network path the bandwidth requirements of the application.

■ **RSVP Service**   This service interprets the RSVP protocol for the Windows 2000 OS.

■ **Traffic Control**   Traffic control manages the various data flows requested by QoS-aware applications, acting as a traffic cop to direct the network traffic to the proper traffic lanes within the system.

■ **Generic Packet Classifier**   The Generic Packet Classifier manages the queues to which Traffic Control directs flows.

■ **QoS Packet Scheduler**   The QoS Packet Scheduler enforces QoS parameters for individual data flows.

■ **QoS Admission Control Service**   The QoS Admission Control Service (QoS ACS) takes a subnetwide view and ensures that bandwidth is managed between all devices. This service is not required on all segments, but it should be on those that are congested.

▲ **Local Policy Module**   The Local Policy Module (LPM) integrates the QoS ACS with Active Directory. This allows you to place user QoS permissions in Active Directory.

These Windows 2000 components, when integrated within a larger QoS system, provide a far more detailed level of control over congested networks than was possible before. Applications with lower tolerances for delays can request the proper bandwidth and reasonably expect to get it. For the QoS system to deliver on this, the application must be QoS aware, the hosts need to be QoS participants, and all the devices in between must be QoS participants. Otherwise, the virtual fast lane created for high-priority traffic may come to a screeching halt when it hits a non-QoS part of the path.

While you can speed up and prioritize traffic for particular applications, there is still a finite amount of bandwidth available in any given network infrastructure. Implementing Quality of Service will not create additional bandwidth; it only enables more efficient use of the existing bandwidth.

Specifying the Quality

When specifying Quality of Service, applications need to request the Quality of Service values they require. The parameters include the rate of the flow (TokenRate) and the latency (Latency) and are described in Table 8-8.

Parameter	Description
TokenRate	Similar to the committed information rate (CIR) in frame relay; this is the rate at which the flow can expect to transmit and is expressed in bytes per second.
TokenBucketSize	The largest average frame size.
PeakBandwidth	Similar to the port speed in frame relay; this is the absolute maximum rate at which a flow can transmit and is expressed in bytes per second.
Latency	Maximum acceptable delay between transmission of a data bit by the sender and its arrival at the intended receiver; expressed in microseconds.
DelayVariation	Difference between the maximum and minimum delays a packet can experience; expressed in microseconds.
ServiceType	Specifies the level of service for the flow, which can be: *NoTraffic* (unidirectional connections) *BestEffort* (no guarantees on delivery) *ControlledLoad* (approximates a light traffic network) *Guaranteed* (TokenRate and Latency are guaranteed) *Qualitative* (best possible flow, without knowing the minimum)

Table 8-8.   QoS Flow Parameters

These flow parameters are requested at the application level, rather than by users or you as the administrator. If the network infrastructure is unable to deliver the Quality of Service that the application requests, the infrastructure will deny the request. The application may then fail, request a lower level of service, or choose another option programmatically. However, if the bandwidth is available and the application has the proper authority, these QoS requests can streamline the travel of priority application traffic.

Sharing the Load with Network Load Balancing

Frequently, the performance of an application is not dependent on the network infrastructure but instead is limited by the server itself. Individual servers can be beefed up to handle more clients or to process faster, but often a better solution is to have more than one server handling those incoming clients. Windows 2000 Network Load Balancing (NLB) provides a cost-effective method for doing just that, without extensive and expensive investments in hardware or major modifications to applications.

What Is Network Load Balancing?

The Network Load Balancing service allows up to 32 Windows 2000 Advanced Servers to share a virtual IP address and service client requests coming to that address. It provides scalability and high availability of TCP/IP-based applications and services by combining the servers into a load-balanced cluster. Windows 2000 NLB can be used to distribute incoming HTTP requests among an NLB cluster of Internet Information Services applications.

In addition to each server's own IP address, each server in the cluster shares a common virtual IP address that is used to distribute client requests. Figure 8-8 shows a simple Network Load Balancing cluster of seven HTTP servers.

Network Load Balancing improves the scalability of groups of HTTP servers, File Transfer Protocol (FTP) servers, streaming media servers, virtual private network (VPN) servers, Terminal Service servers, and other key application services.

Previously, techniques such as DNS round robin were used to accomplish similar goals. However, these techniques did not fare well when servers in the cluster were unavailable due to maintenance or system failures. Network Load Balancing is a much more robust and scalable solution.

Network Load Balancing Requirements

For an application to function under Network Load Balancing, it should have the following characteristics:

▼ The client communication must be via TCP/IP.

■ The application must use TCP or UDP ports.

▲ The server application must be able to run concurrently on separate servers.

For best results, install a second network adapter in each Network Load Balancing host for packets addressed to the server. The first network adapter configured for Network Load Balancing handles the client-to-cluster network traffic addressed to the server as part of a

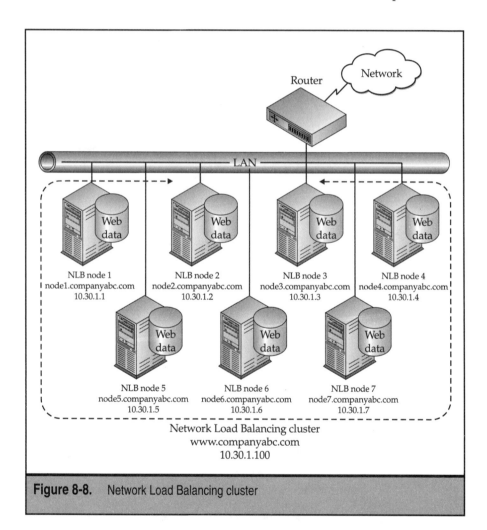

Figure 8-8.   Network Load Balancing cluster

cluster. This configuration with two network cards improves overall performance.

Boosting Performance with Network Load Balancing

Each server is configured to be part of the NLB cluster, as shown in Figure 8-9. The Network Load Balancing service is installed by default, but not enabled. After it is enabled, the parameters can be changed.

To enable performance, each server runs separate copies of the desired server programs, such as IIS server, and has its own copies of the data files. Each server is configured with the shared cluster parameters, which are the same for all computers in the cluster. The virtual IP address shared by the cluster is configured in the cluster parameters. Each server is also configured with its own unique host parameters, which are different across all nodes in the cluster. In

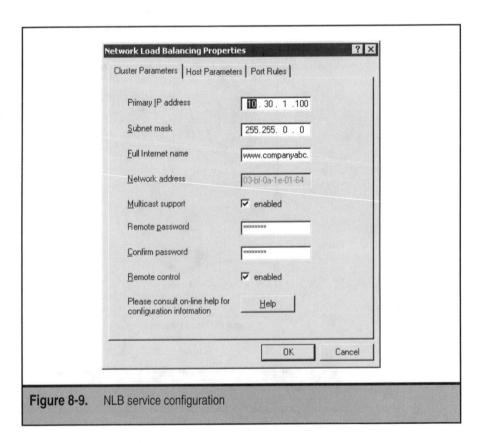

Figure 8-9. NLB service configuration

addition, specific restrictions and loading for the server node are specified.

To boost application performance, Network Load Balancing balances the load of incoming TCP/IP requests across all servers in the cluster. You can configure the load size for each host as necessary, to adjust for individual server capabilities. You can also add hosts to the cluster on the fly, to add capacity to the cluster, simply by configuring the host's protocol stack to support Network Load Balancing.

PROACTIVE PLANNING

The best way to optimize your network is not to tweak existing, ill-conceived network designs, but rather to design a network topology that will perform to its fullest from the start.

Planning for Success

A successful network design must start with a goal, such as to provide server access for 5,000 users or dial-up access for 300 remote users. You will probably have budgetary constraints to work with, but even if you have unlimited funds, you should follow these guidelines when planning to upgrade a site:

▼ **Baseline Your Network Use**   A baseline gives you a snapshot of network use for certain links or components over a given period of time. A good baseline will watch most links at many different times of the day and throughout the week. Depending on how your organization functions, usage may be affected by the time of the month or even the time of the year. The baseline defines the absolute minimum throughput requirements needed and provides a starting point to help guide the design and optimization of the network.

■ **Trend Your Usage**   If a baseline is a snapshot, think of a trend as a movie. It illustrates how your network is being utilized over time, usually up to the present. Values for trending can be obtained from the System Monitor or from a third-party network monitoring utility. These products generally store values for every day or week and provide a graph showing usage of a link or computer resource during a specified time. Trending is especially important because it allows you to make a prediction about the future needs of your network resources. For example, you may have had a 5 percent increase in network traffic over a specific WAN link over a one-year period, and you are reasonably certain that this increase will continue. You can incorporate this data into your network design and plan for future increases.

▲ **Simulate Your Network**   Although you can predict the need for network resources using trends, you cannot predict what will happen if you add more user segments, change the type of routers, or add a new application to the network. These sorts of questions can be answered in two ways: make the change on the production network and watch what happens, or make the change on a model of your network and watch what happens. The latter solution is cheaper and faster and can help you keep your job.

Using Simulations to Optimize the Network

Simulators are software tools that allow you to test a model of your network using different designs or traffic loads. It becomes impossible to predict with any accuracy how network changes will affect the overall performance once the network grows too large. There are simply too many devices, too many routes, and too many traffic conversations going on simultaneously.

A good model of your network will incorporate many of its details such as router characteristics, frame relay properties, and traffic patterns. Because all models operate under the axiom "garbage in, garbage out," you must ensure that as much detail as possible is included in the network model.

Simulators usually use an *analytical* or a *discrete* approach to modeling network traffic. Discrete-event simulation analyzes each packet to determine its behavior and is usually slower than the analytical approach, which makes more assumptions about the traffic. However, some have argued that the analytical method is just as accurate as the discrete-event method. Because of the long simulation time involved in using the discrete-event method, it is recommended that you use the analytical method of simulation for larger networks of more than 50 routers or switches.

Obviously, a model must include simplifications, but how do you know which aspects can be simplified without compromising the integrity of the model? This section outlines the simulation process and helps you understand where to simplify your model.

Preparing to Simulate

Earlier in this chapter, you saw how to conduct a simple application analysis to determine how much traffic a given application generates on the network. This analysis was conducted in a test environment without all the nuances of a real production network. You need to run a simulation before you deploy your application, both to see how it will behave on your production network and to determine what changes must be made to the network to ensure optimum application performance.

Network Topology

Before you can run a single simulation, you must create a representation of the production network, including the topology and the network traffic.

The *network topology* is the framework of the network and refers to both the physical devices that comprise the network and their logical settings. Later you are going to add network traffic on top of this framework to emulate your production network.

Some physical devices that should be included in the representation of the network are the following:

- ▼ Routers
- ■ Computers
- ■ Switches
- ■ WAN links
- ■ LANs
- ▲ Point-to-point connections

Some logical parameters that must be considered are as follows:

▼ Interface settings on routers

■ LAN speeds

■ WAN speeds

■ Router capabilities (such as backplane speed)

■ Routing protocols

▲ Naming conventions

Fortunately, you do not need to enter all of this information in manually. There are programs that use SNMP to query the devices and that can access information stored in the MIB to discover the physical and logical settings on your network.

Network Traffic

It is essential that you model the network traffic in as much detail as is computationally possible, because the current applications will greatly affect the performance of any new applications. Capturing network traffic can be challenging, but it can be accomplished by strategically placing network probes at locations where traffic either originates or terminates. Placing and managing many probes can be time consuming and expensive, but there is currently no other method available for obtaining a snapshot of packets for your entire network.

The better probes obtain information about the traffic all the way up to the application layer, generating usage statistics based on the applications. Some information you should expect from your probes include the following:

▼ Network protocol

■ Application name

■ Source computer

■ Destination computer

■ Number of packets in each direction

- Number of bytes in each direction
- Latency for application
- ▲ Duration of conversation

Although you are going to use the traffic information to complete your model of the network, this information can also be used for other purposes. For example, you can check the latency for applications to see if they are meeting a minimum quality of service value, check the throughput being used by each application, or investigate Web use.

Increasing Simulation Speed

Running simulations of medium-sized networks, with fewer than 50 routers or switches, is very computationally intensive and can take hours, even using the fastest processors, due to the number of different conversations the probes will record during the sampling period. To increase simulation performance, you can remove or consolidate traffic conversations.

Reducing the Number of Conversations   Removing conversations will artificially reduce the amount of traffic represented in the model and will ultimately prove to be undesirable. However, when you have multiple probes capturing data simultaneously, some conversations will be picked up by more than one probe. The conversations are duplicates, and they must be removed. The management console that controls the probes usually removes the duplicate conversations, but if not, then you should remove them yourself.

Conversations with small byte counts have a very small impact on the network and can be removed without affecting the integrity of the model. You can probably remove 40 percent of the conversations and lose only about 3 percent of the network traffic, because many conversations are very small.

Consolidating Conversations   Another step you can take to reduce the number of total conversations and make the simulator run faster is to consolidate conversations that have the same source and destination and are of the same application type. All packets and bytes are added to this consolidation, so no traffic load is lost. You may want to define a specific time frame that both conversations must reside in before consolidation. A simple utility can be created to perform this function. You will enjoy a 40 to 70 percent decrease in the number of conversations by eliminating small conversations and consolidating those that remain.

Running Simulations

At this point, you have a detailed description of the network traffic and the topological layout of your network incorporated into your model. Moreover, you have taken measures to optimize the performance of the simulation by reducing the number of conversations that will run during the simulation. The next step is to run simulations. To start, you should have a specific question in mind, though most questions will relate to network optimization. Essentially, you want to know how the performance, as measured by application response time, for example, is affected when you make a change to the network. Some modifications you might want to make to the network include the following:

- ▼ Change or add WAN links or LANs
- ■ Change or add routers
- ■ Change routing protocols
- ■ Move servers or add servers
- ■ Move users or add users
- ▲ Add or remove an application

The network is an extremely important component for any environment, including Windows 2000, because it serves as the backbone for communication. Windows 2000 includes many new features that help boost performance, including an improved TCP/IP stack, Quality of Service, and Network Load Balancing.

Outside of Windows 2000, the concepts and considerations of the network appear to be overwhelming, and optimizing the network may even seem impossible. This chapter explained how to demystify the complexity of the network by dividing it into manageable sections. The chapter also examined how to design and tune these sections and then piece them together to optimize the network as a whole.

CHAPTER 9

Boosting Active Directory Performance

A
ctive Directory is used throughout Windows 2000, for processes from authentication to encryption to looking up co-workers' phone numbers. It is accessed by end users, administrators, security systems, and applications. Many Windows 2000 features such as Group Policy and Public Key Infrastructure will not function without Active Directory. With its central role in so many facets of Windows 2000, Active Directory must perform quickly. Boosting the performance of Active Directory is key to the performance of all of the other systems that depend on it and is the focus of this chapter.

This is not a chapter on the logical structure of the Active Directory, which includes objects such as accounts and computers, organizational units, domains, forests, and sites. This is a chapter about the nuts and bolts of Active Directory, which includes database files, transaction logs, buffers, and processes. It is very much a view of Active Directory as a database, with a focus on how to optimize access to that database.

We'll first look at the components of Active Directory and then at how to optimize each of the subsystems that those components affect.

ACTIVE DIRECTORY COMPONENTS

Active Directory functionality is delivered by a complex set of processes, modules, and components that include several logical layers. These layers are implemented on a domain controller within the security subsystem, which itself has a number of modules and components. The security subsystem is implemented within the Windows 2000 operating system, as shown in Figure 9-1.

To boost Active Directory performance, a good understanding of these components and their interactions is critical. Depending on the nature of the performance problem, you may need to look at the database (disk subsystem performance), the processes and modules (memory or processor subsystem performance), or the protocol (network subsystem performance, the subject of Chapter 8). Understanding the underlying structure will make this process easier.

Security Subsystem

The Windows 2000 security subsystem controls access to resources, to prevent unauthorized access. The process that actually controls

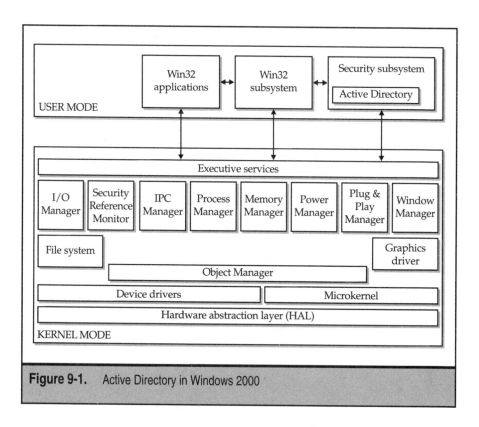

Figure 9-1.   Active Directory in Windows 2000

this access is LSASS.EXE, and all Active Directory components run within its context.

The security subsystem components run under the context of the Local Security Authority security subsystem, which is run as the LSASS.EXE process. You can find this process using the Task Manager, on the Processes tab (Figure 9-2). The components of the process are called modules and are loaded as needed from dynamic link libraries (DLLs).

The components of Local Security Authority are as follows:

▼ **Local Security Authority Server Service**   Enforces security polices and is contained in LSASRV.DLL.

■ **Net Logon Service**   Maintains the computer's secure connection to a domain controller. The code is contained in NETLOGON.DLL.

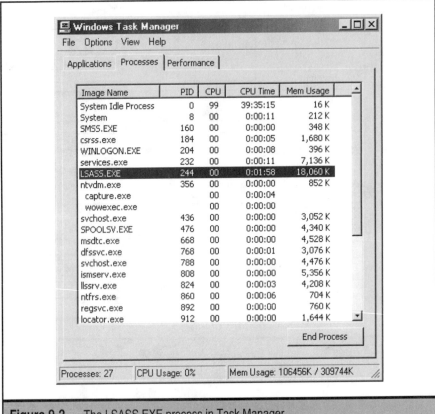

Figure 9-2. The LSASS.EXE process in Task Manager

- **Security Accounts Manager Service** Manages the local security accounts and enforces local policies. The code is contained in SAMSRV.DLL.

- **Kerberos Authentication Protocol** Manages the Kerberos authentication used by Windows 2000 computers and is contained in KERBEROS.DLL.

- **NTLM Authentication Protocol** Manages NTLM authentication, which is used by clients that don't use Kerberos. The code is contained in MSV1.0.DLL.

- **Secure Sockets Layer Authentication Protocol** Manages SSL authentication over an encrypted connection for more secure communications. It is contained in SCHANNEL.DLL.

▲ **Directory Service Module**   Manages the directory replication protocol, LDAP, and manages the directory data. This is really the heart of the Active Directory service and is contained in NTDSA.DLL.

The security subsystem ensures that all access to resources and information is both authenticated and authorized. The subsystem requires all security principals to prove their identity and then verifies that the security principal has permission to access the requested resources.

Active Directory Service

Active Directory runs as a segment of the Local Security Authority (LSA). The LSA presents a logical layering model of Active Directory to clients and applications, as opposed to the code-based view described in the previous section. This logical organization of the services and their interaction makes Active Directory easier to understand and optimize.

The four Active Directory logical layers are described here:

▼ **Extensible Storage Engine Layer**   Manages the physical records.

■ **Database Layer**   Abstracts the physical records to allow applications to issue requests for objects.

■ **Directory System Agent Layer**   Provides a logical integrated view of the directory database and of objects and their functions and their interrelations.

▲ **LDAP, REPL, SAM, and MAPI Interfaces**   Provides client access to the directory database.

The logical connections among the layers are shown in Figure 9-3. The following sections present the technical details of these layers.

Extensible Storage Engine

Active Directory physically lives in a Jet database controlled by an engine called the extensible storage engine (ESE), which is an Indexed

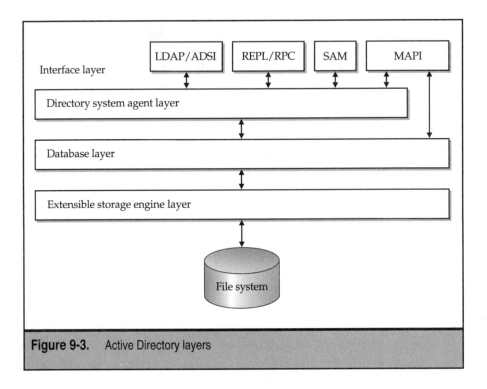

Figure 9-3. Active Directory layers

Sequential Access Method (ISAM) table manager. This is the same database engine used by the Microsoft Exchange messaging system, File Replication Service (FRS), Certificate Services, Windows Internet Naming Service (WINS), and other Windows 2000 systems. The ESE manages the low-level data store and communicates directly with the database file to access individual physical records. The code for this module is contained in the dynamic link library ESENT.DLL.

The ubiquitous extensible storage engine uses a tree structure (B-tree) to store the Active Directory object data. Each page in the database file is a node in the B-tree structure, and a single database can contain over 4 billion pages. Active Directory uses 8-kilobyte pages and thus can hold up to a theoretical maximum of 32 terabytes. This means that the database size is for all practical purposes limited only by disk space and the backup and recovery times.

NOTE: Exchange uses 4-kilobyte pages, as the average size of a message is less than 4 kilobytes. Active Directory uses 8-kilobyte pages because the average size of a database object is larger the average size of a message. If the page size were smaller than the average object, then excessive page faults would occur, and performance would suffer.

The ESE database uses discrete transactions and log files to ensure the integrity of Active Directory. Each request to add, modify, or delete an object or attribute is treated as an atomic transaction. These transactions will succeed only if all operations needed to complete the transaction are successful. If any of the operations needed for a successful transaction fails, then the entire transaction and all operations associated with it will be rolled back.

Database Layer

Whereas the ESE layer manages the physical database and individual records, the database layer abstracts the physical records to allow applications to make requests for objects. No database access calls are made directly to the extensible storage engine; instead, all database access is routed through the database layer. The database layer is implemented in the NTDSA.DLL dynamic link library. The database layer provides an object view of database information by applying logical schema semantics to physical database records, thereby shielding the Active Directory service from the underlying database structure.

NOTE: The database layer is an internal interface that is not accessed by clients, but rather is used by internal Windows 2000 processes such as the directory system agent.

All data that defines an object is stored as attributes, which are stored as columns in the database. An object and its associated attributes are considered a record. The database layer is responsible for adding, deleting, and retrieving individual records; attributes within records; and values within attributes. Here are some examples of objects:

- ▼ Accounts
- ■ Groups
- ■ Group Policy objects
- ▲ Printers

A key long-term advantage of the database layer is that it enables easy future migration of Active Directory to another underlying database engine, such as Microsoft SQL. This migration would require no change to client access methods or to the directory system agent.

Directory System Agent

The directory system agent (DSA) manages access to the database objects in the context of Active Directory. The module containing the DSA is the NTDSA.DLL dynamic link library. The DSA manages the directory and understands what each directory object and attribute is and what function it represents. It knows to check the Active Directory schema to identify the mandatory and optional attributes for particular objects.

For example, when creating an account object, the DSA knows that the user logon attribute must be populated and will not allow objects to be created that violate the database rules. The DSA also manages replication, tracking database actions to determine which will force replication or synchronization.

In a very real sense, the directory system agent is the manifestation of the Active Directory service, and all of the other layers are simply supporting it.

Interfaces

Applications and clients do not directly access the Active Directory service through the directory system agent layer, the database layer, or the extensible storage engine layer. Rather, applications and clients gain access to the directory by using one of the following interfaces supported by the DSA. These interfaces allow a wide range of clients and applications to access the directory data through general-purpose methods.

Lightweight Directory Access Protocol (LDAP)   Clients such as Windows 2000 use the open-standard Lightweight Directory Access Protocol (LDAP) to connect to the DSA. Not only do Windows 2000 clients use LDAP, but Windows 9*x* clients with the Active Directory client components installed also use LDAP to connect to the DSA. Applications that are LDAP aware also use the LDAP interface.

Microsoft also provides a component object model (COM) interface, which is an abstraction of LDAP. This interface is the Active Directory service interface and is widely used by applications and scripting. While presented as a COM interface, the underlying access is still via the LDAP protocol.

Replication Transport (REPL)   Active Directory domain controllers connect to each other to perform replication by using a proprietary RPC implementation. This communication occurs between directory system agents on different domain controllers.

Security Accounts Manager (SAM)   Clients that use Windows 9*x* without the Active Directory client components or Windows NT version 4.0 or earlier connect to the DSA by using the Security Accounts Manager (SAM) interface. In addition, Windows NT 4.0 backup domain controllers (BDCs) in mixed-mode environments use the SAM interface to perform replication.

Messaging Application Programming Interface (MAPI)   Messaging clients, such as Outlook, connect to the DSA by using the Messaging Application Programming Interface (MAPI).

Database Model

The database model that Active Directory uses is a transactional store. There are two sets of files: the database and the transaction logs (Figure 9-4). There are also several other files for administrative purposes.

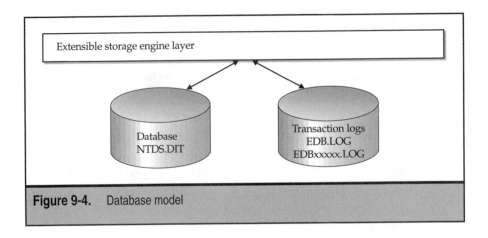

Figure 9-4. Database model

Database

The actual database and its associated partitions reside in a file named NTDS.DIT that is stored by default in %SYSTEMROOT%\ NTDS\NTDS.DIT, which is normally at C:\WINNT\NTDS. The database is divided into three partitions: one for domain data and two for forestwide data. The forestwide partitions are the schema (definition and rules) and the configuration partition (sites, services, and so on). The domain partition contains all objects for the specific domain to which the domain controller belongs. In addition, on Global Catalog domain controllers, the directory partition will contain replicas of key object information from all other domains in the forest.

NOTE: There is also an NTDS.DIT file in %SYSTEMROOT%\SYSTEM32, which is a blank database. This file is initially used to promote a Windows 2000 server to a domain controller. During promotion, the data from the actual domain is replicated to this blank database to populate it.

With all the complex structure of partitions, objects, indexes, and random access to the database, performance for the database file is relatively slow. To boost performance, the extensible storage engine writes to database pages in memory rather than to slow disk and then flushes those pages from memory to disk as it has time.

However, in the event of a system crash, the database could be left in an undetermined state. This could occur if the system were to fail while a user account was being added, if the account had been added but not all attributes set. A system crash would result in the loss of the contents in memory and thus unsaved pages in memory.

The extensible storage engine addresses these two issues of performance and fault tolerance through the transaction logs.

Logs

The transaction logs give the database both speed and fault tolerance. As transactions occur in each domain controller, they are recorded in a series of log files that are associated with each NTDS.DIT file prior to its being written to the actual database file. The data is streamed to the logs as fast as possible and not organized or indexed, allowing the database engine to accept requests at a high rate and giving it time to complete those transactions as needed.

The active log file is named EDB.LOG and is 10 megabytes in size. As transactions are initiated, they are written to the active log file. When the log file fills up, the file is renamed EDBXXXXX.LOG, and a new 10-megabyte EDB.LOG file is created. Old log files are sequentially numbered and are deleted on a regular basis (see "Garbage Collection" later in this chapter). By default, the Active Directory log files are stored in C:\WINNT\NTDS\.

Other Files

There are several other files that are part of the database model, including reserved logs, the checkpoint file, and the temporary database. These files address certain housekeeping, fault tolerance, and accessibility issues and are discussed next.

Reserved Logs   The extensible storage engine writes to transaction logs and will fail if it is unable to do so. To prevent an unexpected crash, the engine creates two reserved 10-megabyte log files (RES1.LOG and RES2.LOG) to use in the event that disk space fills up and the engine is unable to create a new EDB.LOG.

Checkpoint File   The engine writes to transaction logs and attempts to stream transaction records to the logs as quickly as possible. As transactions are added to the logs, the engine keeps track of those transactions that complete. Rather than modify the transaction records in the logs to indicate that a transaction is complete, which would require opening and searching a 10-megabyte flat file, the system merely writes the completed transaction to a checkpoint file called EDB.CHK. This file is updated every time a transaction is successfully and safely written to the database. This file is used in the event of a system recovery to determine which transactions were successfully completed.

Temporary Database File   During normal operation, the Active Directory database file is locked. Thus, it cannot be backed up. To perform a backup, the file must be closed and then backed up. However, this would cause a disruption in access to the Active Directory service. To get around this problem, the extensible storage engine closes the database file (NTDS.DIT) when starting a backup and opens it for read-only access. This allows the file to be backed up and still be accessed in read-only mode by the Active Directory service. If transactions need to be written to the database (which is open in read-only mode), they are instead written to a temporary database call TEMP.EDB. After the backup is complete, the engine opens the main database in read-write mode and copies the changes from the temporary database to the main database.

Processes

Any given Windows 2000 Server may be performing many different functions at any given time. In addition to managing Active Directory, a domain controller may be serving DNS requests with the DNS service, allocating IP addresses with the DHCP service, or managing a public key infrastructure using Certificate Services, to name a few. That being the case, it is important to be able to single out the resource information for the specific application that is being measured, which in this case is Active Directory. To monitor the memory and processor effects of Active Directory, there is really only one process to monitor.

Executables

The entire Active Directory service runs under the Local Security Authority, as was discussed earlier in this chapter. The Local Security Authority process (LSASS.EXE) is the process context under which all the other modules of Active Directory run. This is the only process that needs to be monitored to see all of the resources being assigned specifically to the Active Directory service.

To monitor the resources being allocated to the Active Directory service in LSASS.EXE, use either the built-in Task Manager, the Process Monitor utility from the support tools, or the Windows 2000 Resource Kit utility QuickSlice. See the "Tools" section of this chapter for additional information on both the Process Monitor and QuickSlice.

Dynamic Link Libraries

In addition to the Local Security Authority process, various other modules are loaded on an as-needed basis. The modules are the dynamic link libraries (DLLs) and include the extensible storage engine module (ESENT.DLL), the directory system agent module (NTDSA.DLL), and the various authentication modules. The resources allocated to these modules are all shown under the LSASS.EXE process, so viewing that process is sufficient to track all memory and processor resources being used by the Active Directory service.

DNS

While not the subject of this chapter and not a direct impact on Active Directory database performance, Domain Naming Service performance can affect the perceived performance of Active Directory. Users and applications perform server resource record lookups in the DNS to locate Active Directory domain controllers and services. If users or applications are experiencing difficulty accessing DNS services, they may report delays or problems with Active Directory.

It is important also to ensure that DNS performance is maximized so that server resource lookups do not become a bottleneck.

Modes

A Windows 2000 Active Directory domain is in either mixed mode or native mode. These two modes reflect the level of interoperability with Windows NT 4.0 domains. The mode that an organization chooses will be dictated by the need to maintain backward compatibility with Windows NT 4.0.

Mixed

A mixed-mode domain allows Windows NT 4.0 backup domain controllers (BDCs) to live within the Active Directory domain. To allow this, a Windows 2000 Active Directory domain controller operates in emulated primary domain controller (PDC) mode. When a Windows NT 4.0 BDC is replicated, it sees the emulated PDC as just a standard Windows NT 4.0 PDC. Although all the Windows 2000 domain controllers operate as multimasters, the one specially designated domain controller operating in emulated PDC mode will send updates to all Windows NT 4.0 BDCs.

Native

Native-mode domains do not allow Windows NT 4.0 domain controllers. They also allow certain Windows 2000 specific features, such as universal groups, complete elimination of NetBIOS from the network, and nesting of groups.

Moving from a mixed-mode Active Directory domain to a native-mode Active Directory domain is very easy; however, it is irreversible. In the administrative tool Active Directory Domains and Trusts, select the properties of the domain you want to change. Click the Change Mode button, shown in Figure 9-5. After the change from mixed-mode to native-mode has had time to replicate, simply reboot the domain controllers for the domain.

Table 9-1 summarizes the key differences between mixed and native modes.

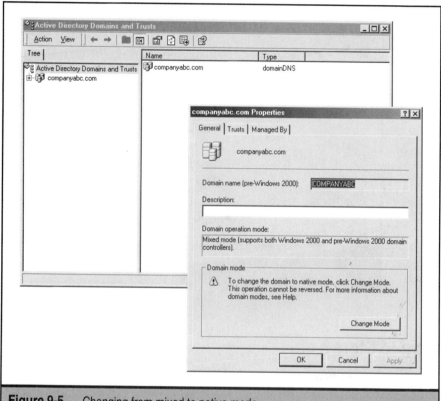

Figure 9-5.   Changing from mixed to native mode

Action	Mixed Mode	Native Mode
Replication	Windows 2000 DCs operate normally, and a single emulated PDC sends updates to all Windows NT 4.0 BDCs.	Only Windows 2000 DCs replicated.

Table 9-1.   Mixed vs. Native Mode

Action	Mixed Mode	Native Mode
Groups	No universal groups, and global groups can't be nested.	Universal groups allowed, and groups can be nested.
Authentication	Kerberos used for Windows 2000 servers, and NTLM used for Windows NT 4.0 servers.	Only Kerberos is used.
NetBIOS	Required for NTLM authentication.	Can be eliminated.

Table 9-1. Mixed vs. Native Mode *(continued)*

What to Store?

Even though the Active Directory database is extensible and very robust, it has certain characteristics as a database that dictates the characteristics of the data that it should be used to store. These include appropriateness of the data, the structured nature of the data, the stability of the data over time, and the size of the data objects.

Appropriate Data

The data in the Active Directory will be replicated and available across the entire enterprise, so it should be data that is worth the effort to replicate. If the data would be better served being locally stored, then Active Directory is probably not the best storage location for it.

For example, it is useful to have employee names and phone numbers available across the organization. It is also worthwhile to have printer definitions available across the organization and published in the Active Directory. In contrast, local phone records are not so useful enterprisewide and are better stored in another system.

Structured Data

The Active Directory database is highly structured and does not lend itself to the storage of unstructured data—that is, the data stored in Active Directory should be fixed-length and data types. Some examples of this are department and address information for employees, which are fixed at a certain size and use a standard format. Word documents (such as resumes) vary greatly in length, structure, and content, and so are not appropriate for storage in the Active Directory system.

Stable Data

The data stored in Active Directory should be stable over time. It should not change more often than the frequency of the replication cycle across the entire organization, and it should preferably change less often than that. In addition, because the data may not be current for at least the length of the replication cycle, clients should be able to tolerate that degree of staleness.

Information such as user names, addresses, departments, and even passwords, while not completely static, do not change frequently. The values are usually stable over much longer than the length of a replication cycle, which may be measured in hours or a day at most. In addition, a delay of a few hours in the posting of a change in a user's department or address will have little or no impact on the organization. Attempting to use the Active Directory system for the storage of information such as stock quotes or real estate listings would be questionable, as the data may change frequently, and the impact of having outdated information may be very high.

Data Size

The database is tuned to replicate relatively small-sized attributes, and performance degrades when the size of attributes gets too large. Attributes are stored in the domain controller memory space during sending and receiving, so a 10-megabyte attribute requires 10 megabytes of buffer space in memory on both the receiving and sending systems. Very large buffers will adversely affect performance.

Keeping the size of the attributes small will improve the overall performance. For example, rather than store a large, full-sized image in the directory for identification purposes, use a smaller thumbnail image to reduce the size of the attribute.

How Much to Store?

Determining what to store is critical; determining how much to store is far less so. The Windows 2000 Active Directory has no reasonable limit on the number of objects that can be stored in the database. The extensible storage engine (ESE) underlying Active Directory can contain up to 32 terabytes of data, which is beyond any reasonable limit.

Given that the technology itself has such a high theoretical limit, what are the practical limits? They depend on how well the database performs as it grows, or its *scalability*.

Scalability

Microsoft has tested logon performance over orders of magnitude differences in the size of the active directory database and found that performance did not vary significantly. This assumes that the appropriate hardware to service the requests is used.

As we saw at the beginning of this chapter, the database engine places no practical limits on the number of objects stored in Active Directory. The Active Directory database has been tested for up to 100 million objects, and performance tests show logon performance for a client to be the same with numbers of objects ranging from one thousand to over a million. As Figure 9-6 shows, this is a scale ranging over four orders of magnitude and is a huge range. With the appropriate hardware, the Active Directory service does not degrade when the size of the database increases.

For example, Active Directory will scale from a small organization of 100 users to a large multinational organization with over 100,000 users. Active Directory has been tested in the lab for up to 100 million objects that resulted in a database of over 260 gigabytes. Even then, searches still were fast, with subsecond response times for finding a single record.

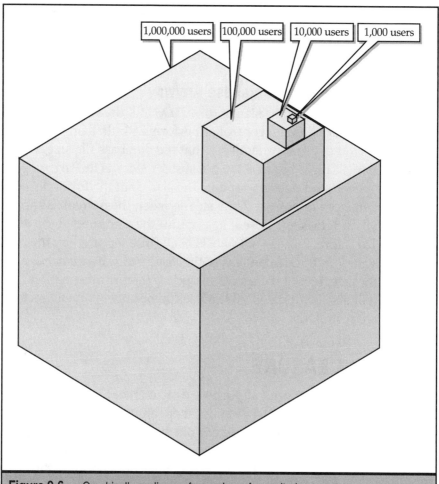

Figure 9-6. Graphically scaling up four orders of magnitude

Mixed Environments

The exception to the size limitation occurs when Active Directory is running in mixed mode with backup domain controllers on Windows NT 4.0. This presents a compatibility problem, as the Windows NT 4.0 SAM database has a recommended maximum of 40,000 objects.

In mixed-mode environments, Active Directory needs to be designed and managed to keep the total number of accounts, computers, and groups to within the 40,000-object limit imposed by the legacy Windows NT 4.0 technology. If this poses a problem, then the recommended solution is to eliminate Windows NT 4.0 backup domain controllers.

How Big Is the Database Anyway?

If you monitor the size of the NTDS.DIT database file while an Active Directory domain controller performs a bulk load operation or over a period of time, you will see that the database file size remains the same. This is because the file system records the size when the file is opened and does not update the size until the file is closed. Active Directory opens the database file when the domain controller boots up and does not close it again until the computer shuts down. Therefore, the size of the NTDS.DIT file reported by the operating system is the size only as of the last restart. If you need to determine the size, reboot the server to update the file information. The file size will also be updated after a backup or after Active Directory services are restarted.

WHAT TO MEASURE

In addition to general-purpose disk, memory, and processor counters, discussed in Chapters 6 and 7, there are Active Directory–specific counters that help you determine the load being placed on a domain controller and how to boost performance. These include the NTDS object for overall Active Directory measurements and the Database object for database-specific statistics.

NTDS Object

The NTDS object contains performance counters that provide statistics about Active Directory performance. The NTDS object provides a good feel for the throughput of the directory system. In addition, it shows replication traffic throughput and load. This is useful for tuning replication performance and is discussed in Chapter 10.

These counters, listed in Table 9-2, are useful for determining the number of clients active at any given time and then relating this value to the load it places on general resources such as the processor or memory.

Counter	Description	Tuning Tips
DS Threads in Use	The number of threads currently in use by the directory service. This counter represents the number of threads currently servicing API calls by clients.	Use to determine whether additional processors are needed.
LDAP Client Sessions	The number of sessions of connected LDAP clients.	Indicates the load being placed on the directory.
LDAP Bind Time	The time (in ms) for the completion of the last successful LDAP binding.	Indicates the load being placed on the directory.
Kerberos Authentications/sec	The number of times per second that clients use a client ticket to authenticate.	Indicates the load being placed on the directory.
NTLM Authentications/sec	The number of NTLM authentications serviced.	Indicates the load being placed on the directory.
LDAP Successful Binds/sec	The number of LDAP bindings (per second) that occurred successfully.	Indicates the load being placed on the directory.
LDAP Searches/sec	The number of search operations per second performed by LDAP clients.	Indicates the load being placed on the directory.

Table 9-2.   Active Directory System Monitor Counters on the NTDS Object

The NTDS object counters are helpful for understanding the load being placed on a server and for deciding whether to add more servers. They indicate whether a server is being overloaded, but they don't give not enough detail for you to determine why the server is overloaded. Active Directory server performance tuning is essentially database tuning, and in the later section, "Database Tuning," you will learn about the tools you need to identify and resolve underlying performance issues.

Database Object

To monitor Active Directory database performance, you use the Database object in System Monitor. The Database object exposes the extensible storage engine (ESE), which is the transacted database system used by many of the Windows 2000 subsystems. In particular, it stores all Active Directory objects. The counters in the Database object can be used to monitor the various database elements, including file, logs, cache, and tables. The Database Performance object must be installed manually, as it is not installed with the base operating system.

Follow these steps to load the Database object in Performance Monitor:

1. Copy the performance DLL (ESENTPRF.DLL) located in %SYSTEMROOT%\SYSTEM32 to any directory (for example, C:\ESENT).

2. Launch the Registry editor REGEDT32.EXE.

3. Create the Registry key HKEY_LOCAL_MACHINE\ SYSTEM\CurrentControlSet\Services\ESENT.

4. Create the Registry key HKEY_LOCAL_MACHINE\ SYSTEM\CurrentControlSet\Services\ESENT\Performance.

5. Select the esent\performance key.

6. Create the value Open of data type REG_SZ and with the string OpenPerformanceData.

7. Create the value Collect of data type REG_SZ and with the string CollectPerformanceData.

8. Create the value Close of data type REG_SZ and with the string ClosePerformanceData.

9. Create the value Library of data type REG_SZ and with the string C:\ESENT\ESENTPRF.DLL.

10. Exit the Registry editor.

11. Open a command prompt.

12. Change to the directory %SYSTEMROOT%\WINNT\SYSTEM32.

13. To load the counter information into the Registry, run the command LODCTR ESENTPRF.INI.

After completing these steps, launch Performance Monitor; there should be a new object called Database. There will be several instances of the Database object, depending on the number of services installed on the server that use the extensible storage engine. The instance to monitor for Active Directory is the LSASS instance.

Cache and Table Counters

During operation, pages of the Active Directory database are loaded from the database file on the disk and placed into memory buffers. They are kept in memory to improve performance—that is, they are cached in memory. The operating system limits the percentage of total memory that the subsystem can use. Cache performance can be monitored using the counters listed in Table 9-3. In general, if there is a problem with cache performance, the solution is to add more memory to the server and thus increase the total memory available for caching.

Counter	Description	Tuning Tips
Cache % Hit	The percentage of page requests for the database file that were fulfilled by the database cache without causing a file operation.	If this percentage is too low, the size of the database cache may be too small. Add RAM.
Cache Page Fault Stalls/sec	The number of page faults (per second) that cannot be serviced because no pages are available for allocation from the database cache.	If this counter is nonzero most of the time, the clean threshold might be too low. Add RAM.
Cache Page Faults/sec	The number of page requests (per second) for the database file that require the Database Cache Manager to allocate a new page from the database cache.	If this number is too high, the size of the database cache may be too small. Add RAM.
Cache Size	The amount of system memory used by the Database Cache Manager to hold commonly used information from the database file or files to prevent file operations.	If system memory is available and the database cache size is not growing, the database cache size may be restricted to an artificially low limit. Add RAM.

Table 9-3. Database Object Cache Counters

Similar to database object cache counters, the table counters shown in Table 9-4 reflect the dependency of the extensible storage engine on memory. If there is not enough memory, then the engine will be forced to cache less of the tables in memory and spend more resources retrieving the tables from the much slower disk subsystem. As with the cache counters, the solution in most cases is to increase the overall memory in the server.

The bottom line is that the cache and table counters are good indicators of the need to increase the memory of a server. For an indicator of the need to review the disk subsystem, see the next section.

Counter	Description	Tuning Tips
Table Open Cache % Hit	The percentage of database tables opened by using cached schema information.	If this number is too low, the size of the table cache may be too small. Add RAM.
Table Open Cache Hits/sec	The number of database tables opened (per second) using cached schema information.	If this number is too low, the size of the table cache may be too small. Add RAM.
Table Open Cache Misses/sec	The number of database tables opened (per second) without using cached schema information.	If this number is too high, the size of the table cache may be too small. Add RAM.
Table Opens/sec	The number of database tables opened per second.	Indicates the load being placed on the database.

Table 9-4.   Database Object Table Counters

File and Log Counters

Ultimately, Active Directory stores its data in a file on a disk drive. That being the case, getting data to or from that file may become a bottleneck if the disk subsystem is too slow, too busy, fragmented, or experiencing hardware problems.

The database object counters for files (Table 9-5) refer to the actual database file NTDS.DIT and monitor performance of that file. If the file counters are high, then either using faster disk subsystems or reconfiguring the subsystems will solve the problem. The solution might include changing the RAID type of a disk subsystem to a higher performance configuration, such as moving from RAID5 to RAID1. It might also include moving other services off the Active Directory subsystem to another disk subsystem or another server. For example, if a Windows server is both an Active Directory domain controller and a SQL server, moving the SQL databases to a separate disk channel might alleviate an Active Directory performance problem.

Counter	Description	Tuning Tips
File Bytes Read/sec	The number of bytes that are read (per second) from the database file(s) into the database cache.	If this rate is too high, the size of the database cache may be too small. Add RAM.
File Bytes Written/sec	The number of bytes that are written (per second) to the database file(s) from the database cache.	If this rate is too high, the size of the database cache may be too small. Add RAM.

Table 9-5. Database Object File Counters

Counter	Description	Tuning Tips
File Operations Pending	The number of reads and writes issued by the Database Cache Manager to the database file(s) that the operating system is currently processing.	A large number of pending operations increases system throughput, but also increases the time required to process individual operations. Typically, a large number means that file operations on the database file or files may be a bottleneck.
File Operations/sec	The number of reads and writes (per second) issued by the Database Cache Manager to the database file(s).	If this number is too high, the database cache size may be too small. Add RAM.

Table 9-6.   Database Object File Counters *(continued)*

The log counters depend on file access and the disk subsystem as well. They are separated from the database file counters so that they can be monitored separately. In high-performance installations, the database file and the logs are stored in separate subsystems. However, the same tuning concepts that apply to database file performance tuning also apply to log performance tuning. Using faster disk subsystems or reconfiguring the subsystems will resolve performance issues. See Table 9-6 for a list of the log counters.

Counter	Description	Tuning Tips
Log Record Stalls/sec	The number of instances (per second) for which a log record cannot be added to the log buffers because the buffers are full.	If this counter is not zero most of the time, the size of the log buffer may be a bottleneck. Add RAM, if memory resources are constrained.
Log Threads Waiting	The number of threads waiting for their data to be written to the log to complete an update of the database.	If this number is too high, the log may be a bottleneck. Consider moving the logs to a less busy disk or channel.
Log Writes/sec	The number of instances (per second) for which the log buffers are written to the log file(s).	If this number approaches the maximum rate at which the medium that is storing the log file(s) can write data, the medium may be a bottleneck. Consider upgrading the medium to a higher performance technology or moving the logs to a separate channel.

Table 9-7.   Database Object Log Counters

TIP: In some cases, the performance of the files and the log counters may mask a problem with the cache, so be sure to verify that the cache counters are not high before taking action on the file counters. If the cache counters are high, solving the cache problem will often resolve the file access problem.

DISK TUNING

The disk subsystem is where the Active Directory data resides, and many of the features of the extensible storage engine are designed to maximize disk performance. It caches database pages in memory buffers for performance, but still must ultimately read and write to disk. To improve that performance, it allows different portions of the database system to be stored on separate drive channels.

Beyond what the database engine can do, there are hardware and software tuning options that can be implemented to boost performance within Windows 2000. This includes configuring the proper drives with the proper RAID class and formatting partitions with the correct file system.

To enhance performance on domain controllers that handle high request rates or to ensure responsiveness in domain controllers with lighter loads, configure the Windows 2000 operating system on one disk channel, the Active Directory database files on a second, and the log files on a third. Figure 9-7 shows the configuration for a high-performance system.

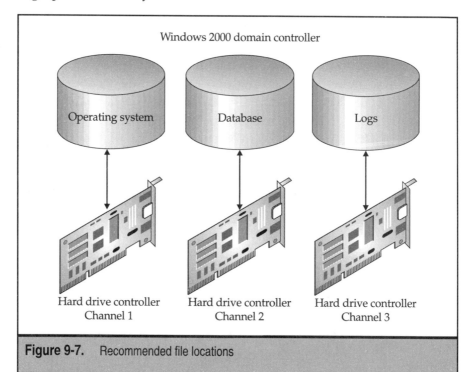

Figure 9-7.   Recommended file locations

This recommended configuration is designed to maximize Active Directory performance. If the anticipated load on the directory will be less than heavy, or if response time will not be an issue, a less robust design can be implemented. After testing and time in production, performance issues and tuning results can be evaluated, perhaps leading to changes in the configuration. This is an effective method of tuning the directory, as it will optimize the configuration to the load actually seen in production.

Database

The NTDS.DIT file should be optimized for performance, but fault tolerance is more important. Active Directory depends on the availability of this file. The system is optimized to preserve the previous information stored in the database, even at the expense of current transactions. Approximately 70 to 90 percent of the operations performed on the database are reads, as most clients are performing lookups in the form of authentications or searches.

Database Profile

The database file will be read from frequently, written to occasionally, and grow quite large, and the data contained in it is sensitive, so you should keep the database on a separate drive channel using RAID5. By default, the database file (NTDS.DIT) and the checkpoint file (EDB.CHK) are installed in the %SYSTEMROOT\NTDS directory.

Hardware-based RAID is preferred for both fault tolerance and performance. The RAID5 configuration provides both single-drive failure protection and good performance on both reads and writes. With RAID5, only one drive is dedicated to fault tolerance, and thus more of the drive space is available for data storage.

Moving the Database Location

Even if the file location was left at the default setting at the initial installation, the location can be changed later. The location of the database can be moved by using the Active Directory Diagnostic Tool and booting the server into Directory Service Recovery mode, following the instructions listed here.

To move the Active Directory database (NTDS.DIT), follow these steps:

1. Boot in directory services restore mode.

2. Log on.

3. At a command prompt, run NTDSUTIL.EXE.

4. At the ntdsutil: prompt, enter **file** to access File Maintenance.

5. At the file maintenance: prompt, enter **move db to e:\database** to move the database file and checkpoint file from the current location to E:\DATABASE. This will also modify the Registry to reflect the new location.

6. Enter **quit** to exit File Maintenance.

7. Enter **quit** to exit ntdsutil.

8. Restart the server.

NOTE: Make sure to back up the database after verifying that Active Directory services are functioning correctly, because restore operations performed from backups made prior to the move will not restore the database correctly.

Logs

Log files preserve the current transactions, relieving the burden from the database. The database can delay writing to the database file, secure in the knowledge that the logs are capturing that information. Given the nature of log files, they are almost exclusively written to and almost never read.

Log Profile

Log files are written very quickly to disk and only read in the event of a problem, so they could be characterized as 100 percent write files. Similar to database files, log files (EDB.LOG, RES1.LOG, and RES2.LOG) are by default stored in %SYSTEMROOT%\NTDS\. For better performance, keep the logs on a drive channel separate from that for the database and use RAID1 for the disk configuration. The RAID1 mirrored configuration will give high performance, albeit at a higher cost, than RAID5 because 50 percent of the disk space is dedicated to fault tolerance. Log files typically are much smaller than database files and are deleted during automatic routine maintenance (which will be covered later in this chapter), so the trade-off is a good one. A single pair of drives is usually sufficient.

Moving the Log Location

Either set up the Active Directory log files when promoting the server, as shown in Figure 9-8, or manually move them later. Moving them manually is the easiest and safest method.

The log files can be moved manually using the Active Directory Diagnostic Utility (NTDSUTIL.EXE), though it must be used in directory services restore mode.

Use the following steps to move the Active Directory logs (EDB.LOG, RES1.LOG, and RES2.LOG):

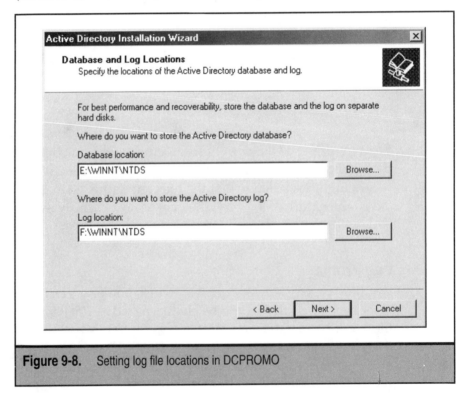

Figure 9-8. Setting log file locations in DCPROMO

1. Restart the domain controller.

2. Press F8 at the "Starting Windows" screen to get into the Windows 2000 Advanced Options Menu.

3. Boot in directory services restore mode.

4. Log on.

5. Open a command prompt and run NTDSUTIL.EXE.

6. At the ntdsutil: prompt, enter **file** to access File Maintenance.

7. At the file maintenance: prompt, enter **move logs to e:\logs** to move the log files from the current location to E:\LOGS. This will also modify the Registry to reflect the new location.

8. Enter **quit** to exit File Maintenance.

9. Enter **quit** to exit ntdsutil.

10. Restart the server.

NOTE: Make sure to check that the log files were created and that Active Directory is functioning correctly after making the change.

Operating System

Because of the load the paging file and system file access place on the disk subsystem, it is important to isolate that load from the server being tuned. Keep the operating system and paging files on separate drive channels from those used for the database and for logs, if possible. If necessary, place the operating system on the same channel as the logs.

DATABASE TUNING

Since Active Directory is fundamentally a database, database tuning is critical to boosting performance. Some processes occur automatically, such as the garbage collection process. Other processes need to be evaluated and implemented manually, including offline defragmentation, specific attribute indexing, and establishment of LDAP policies.

Garbage Collection

Garbage collection is a process that runs on every domain controller every continuous 12 hours of operation, deleting objects and files no longer needed by the directory service. This tidying up helps reduce the administrative overhead needed to maintain the database and keeps the database optimized for performance.

The fact that garbage collection occurs every 12 hours means that if a domain controller is rebooted continuously at intervals of less than 12 hours, the database and log files will continue to grow, and over time, database performance will degrade. Therefore, you should not reboot unnecessarily within a 12-hour period. For example, you should not follow a routine of starting a domain controller at 8:00 every morning and shutting it down at 6:00 every evening.

The garbage collection process performs the following tasks:

▼ Deletes unneeded log files

■ Deletes tombstones

▲ Defragments the database

Log Files

The ESE can create a new log file when the active one fills up (called noncircular logging), or it can overwrite the oldest file when the log reaches a specified number of files (called circular logging). If a system crash prevents the database pages from being flushed from memory to disk, the database engine performs recovery upon restart. The database reads the log files in order and reapplies changes until the database is once again consistent. The log file is no longer needed once all changes have been written to the database file.

In circular logging, the garbage collection process deletes old log files. Noncircular logging consumes disk space until you manually delete old log files after a backup or restart; it saves all database changes and never deletes log files automatically. The Active Directory service default is circular logging.

You can overwrite this default with the following Registry key:

HKEY_LOCAL_MACHINE\CURRENTCONTROLSETSERVICES\
NTDS\PARAMETERS\CIRCULARLOGGING

where

1 = Circular logging (default)

0 = Noncircular logging

While overwriting the default is possible, it is normally recommended that Active Directory logs be set to circular to conserve disk space and reduce the amount of administrative overhead.

> **NOTE:**   In the Microsoft Exchange messaging system, which uses the same extensible storage engine as Active Directory, it is frequently recommended that log files be made noncircular to improve recoverability. The opposite is true of the Active Directory service. Since Active Directory is relatively small and is replicated to sister domain controllers quickly, there is much less need to be able to replay logs in a system recovery situation. More likely, data would be replicated from another domain controller rather than replayed from logs.

Tombstones

Active Directory is a replicated database, which requires that both additions and deletions be propagated between domain controllers. If a domain controller were simply to delete an object from its database, then there would be nothing to propagate to other domain controllers to inform them of the object deletion. To handle this situation, the active directory uses a tombstone flag to indicate the demise of an object.

Rather than physically deleting objects from the database, the directory service removes most attributes and flags the object as being under the tombstone. The garbage collection process removes tombstone objects from the database on each domain controller after 60 days. At that point, the object is actually removed from the database.

The 60-day tombstone lifetime can be changed to reduce the amount of space occupied by deleted objects, even though the space consumed by the tombstone objects is considerably less than that for the full object. Modifying this default should not be done lightly and is not recommended for most installations, as it can lead to inconsistencies between domain controllers during restore processing. In any event, keep the tombstone lifetime longer than the longest expected replication latency in the network, including latency due to intermittent connections.

Defragmentation

As the database file is written to, the extensible storage engine uses the fastest, not always the most efficient, way to fill database pages. To make the database efficient, defragmentation is performed to rearrange the way the data is written in the database file. The garbage collection process performs database defragmentation.

The garbage collection process performs online defragmentation, which is subject to limitations. It chiefly improves the performance of the database; it does not reduce the size of the database. In addition to online defragmentation, offline defragmentation can be performed to reduce the size of the database file. Defragmentation details are discussed in the next section.

Defragmentating the Database

To improve system performance and scalability, the extensible storage engine fills pages in the database as quickly as possible. This is not the most efficient way to fill database pages, as it results in blank spaces in the database file. This occurs because when an object is deleted from one part of the database, that space is not necessarily used immediately; rather than go back and check for all available free pages, the database engine instead allocates new pages. This is a great short-term tactic to increase performance, but a bad long-term strategy as it results in a very large and inefficient database.

Strategically, the garbage collection process performs a defragmentation pass on a 12-hour cycle to make the database efficient once again. This defragmentation rearranges the way the data is written in the database file, putting all the pages together and all the free space at the end of the database file. Figure 9-9 is a before-and-after view of a defragmented database.

Two types of defragmentation can be performed with Active Directory: online and offline.

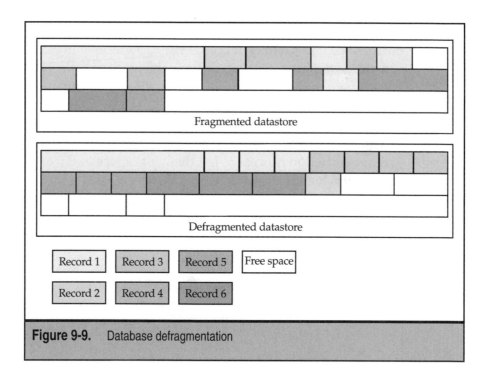

Figure 9-9. Database defragmentation

Online Defragmentation

The extensible storage engine supports online defragmentation, which rearranges the pages within the database file. The database engine runs online defragmentation automatically at 12-hour intervals during garbage collection.

Online defragmentation does not free the empty space in the database file. The empty space in a database file that is not being used to store records is called white space. This space is used by the database file (NTDS.DIT) within the Windows 2000 file system, taking up disk space resources that might otherwise be allocated to other applications. During normal operations, this is not a problem, as the normal ebb and flow of the database will keep the database file size at a reasonable maximum. However, when a large bulk operation occurs, such as the addition of users or a major cleanup of Active Directory, the size of the database file may grow to accommodate additional temporary objects and not shrink back to its normal size. To eliminate the white space, offline defragmentation must be performed.

By default, there is no easy way to check how much white space a database contains, which would serve as a guide to deciding when to run offline defragmentation. To have the garbage collection process log an event in the Directory Service event log, modify the Registry entry Garbage Collection in HKEY_LOCAL_MACHINE\SYSTEM\ CurrentControlSet\Services\NTDS\Diagnostics. The default value is 0, which is to not log the white space. Set the value to 1 to enable the garbage collection process to log the white space in the event log, a sample of which is shown in Figure 9-10.

If the event logs indicate that there is significant white space in the NTDS.DIT file and the amount of disk space that would be

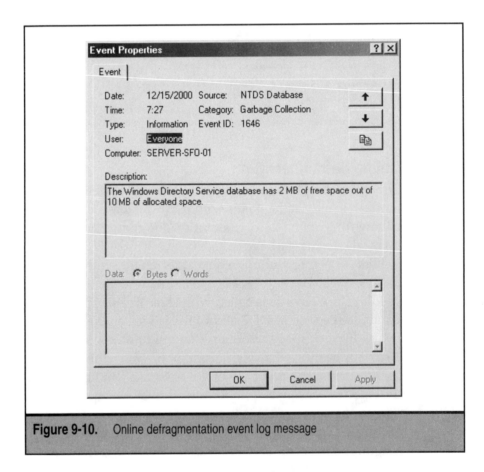

Figure 9-10.   Online defragmentation event log message

recovered is significant to the operation of the server, then the space should be reclaimed. This is done by running offline defragmentation.

Offline Defragmentation

Offline defragmentation performs the same function as online defragmentation: namely, rearranging the pages within the database file to make the database more efficient. In addition, offline defragmentation eliminates white space by reducing, or *compacting*, the size of the database file. The disadvantage of offline defragmentation is that the database must be taken out of service, that is, offline, to perform the defragmentation.

To perform offline defragmentation, take the domain controller offline; then boot in directory services repair mode, using the F8 key at system startup, and run NTDSUTIL.EXE at a command prompt. This creates a second, defragmented version of the database file that should be smaller than the original database file. This file does not automatically replace the original NTDS.DIT file; the new file must be manually copied to the directory, after the original file is archived. Keep the original NTDS.DIT file until the domain controller has been restarted with the defragmented file and been verified as fully functioning.

Attribute Indexing

Another way of boosting the performance of searches within Active Directory is to index key attributes. When an attribute is indexed, directory searches involving that attribute are more efficient than if the attribute had no index. Attributes are indexed when their searchFlags attribute is set to 1, using a tool such as ADSI Edit from the support tools. Changing the value of the bit to 1 builds an index; changing the value to 0 deletes the index for the attribute. The index is built or torn down by a background thread on each domain controller in the forest.

Attributes such as e-mail address (see Figure 9-11) and user principal name are indexed by default. Others, such as the employee ID attribute, are not indexed by default. If an organization were

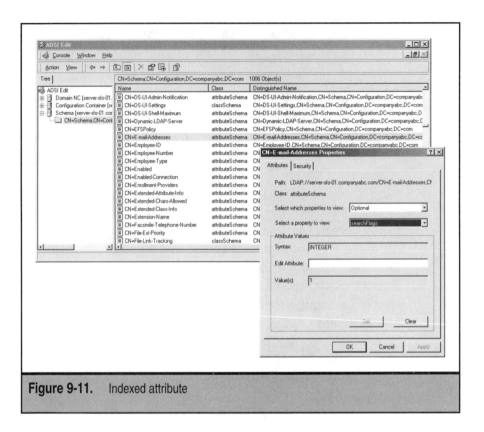

Figure 9-11. Indexed attribute

populating the employee ID field, then it would make sense to change the schema to index that attribute, as shown in Figure 9-12.

After this change takes effect, the domain controller would start building the index on the local domain controller, and the schema change would be replicated to all domain controllers throughout the forest. After the replication process, the employee ID would be indexed on other domain controllers as they receive the schema change.

Indexed attributes should be single valued, with a unique value for each object instance. For example, something like an employee ID would be good to index, because it should be unique for each employee. On the other hand, an attribute such as initials would not be unique across a large organization and would not be a good choice for an index. Even with well-chosen and unique attributes, keep in mind that the more indexed attributes in an object class,

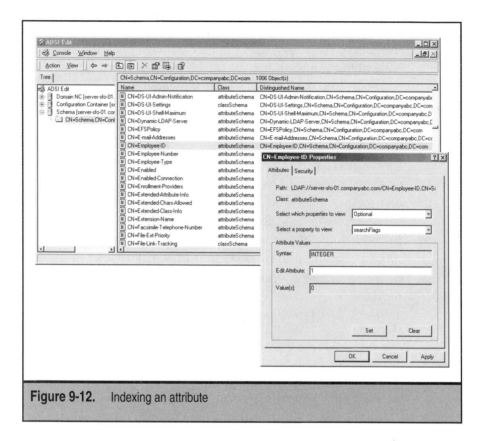

Figure 9-12. Indexing an attribute

the longer the time needed to modify or create instances of the class because of the index-building overhead. For example, if you index a number of attributes in the user account class, it will take longer to create users.

LDAP Policies

Native Windows 2000 clients access Active Directory using LDAP calls. Applications access Active Directory programmatically using ADSI, which uses LDAP to access the directory. Third-party applications that are not COM aware use LDAP calls to access directory information. Version 3 of LDAP has extensions for querying, paging, and sorting that place additional loads on the memory and processor resources, though they reduce network traffic and simplify application development.

All of these methods of access place a load on the system, and the Active Directory LDAP query policies provide a mechanism for controlling the way queries are serviced, allowing performance to be tuned to specific situations and needs.

LDAP Queries

Since the majority of traffic affecting the directory service will be LDAP queries, Active Directory allows administrative limits to be set on those queries. LDAP administrative limits allow administrators to restrict query results, duration, and resource consumption on each server. For example, a bridgehead server might disallow sorting and paged results, allocating more memory and processor resources to site replication. A slow processor server with a lot of memory might be tuned to allow large results to be returned, but to restrict the total requests.

The LDAP query policy applies to a number of query functions. Table 9-7 lists those query functions and their impact on the LDAP server.

Function	Impact on Server
Search	Searches can generate a significant amount of disk activity, take a long time, and return a large data set.
Search with paged results	If a search returns a large data set, the client can have the server return it in increments. The server caches the data until the client releases it.
Search with sorted results	Sorting requires additional disk and processor time on the server.
Search page size	The server can limit the maximum number of values that can be returned from a query.
Change notify	A client can request notification of changes on particular objects in the directory.

Table 9-8.   LDAP Query-Related Functions

Query policy allows limits to be set on the server to restrict resources that are available to clients requesting LDAP queries, paged results, and sorted results. Configuring parameters for query policies can both restrict and make server resources available to clients. In addition, parameters can be set to specify the number of connections allowed for a server and the length of time a connection can be idle.

Default Query Policy Settings

All domain controllers have a default query policy on promotion. If a site policy is assigned, then the domain controller uses this policy. If a specific policy has been assigned to a domain controller, this policy takes precedence over any site policy. The default values are listed in Table 9-8.

LDAP Administrative Limits	Default Values	Description/Search Behavior
InitRecvTimeout	120	Initial Receive Timeout. The maximum time in seconds that the server waits for the initial request before the connection closes.
MaxConnections	5000	Maximum Connections. The maximum number of LDAP connections allowed on the server.
MaxConnIdleTime	900	Maximum Connection Idle Time. The maximum time in seconds that the client is allowed to be idle before the connection is closed.

Table 9-9.   LDAP Query Policy Settings

LDAP Administrative Limits	Default Values	Description/Search Behavior
MaxActiveQueries	20	Maximum Active Queries. The maximum number of search operations allowed on the server.
MaxNotificationPerConn	5	Maximum Notifications per Connection. The maximum number of notification requests allowed per connection on the server.
MaxReceiveBuffer	10485760	Maximum Receive Buffer. The maximum size of LDAP requests, in bytes, that the server will attempt to process.
MaxPageSize	1000	Maximum Page Size. The largest page size allowed by the server.
MaxQueryDuration	120	Maximum Query Duration. The maximum elapsed time (in seconds) allowed for a query to complete.
MaxTempTableSize	10000	Maximum Temporary Table Size. The limit of objects in the temporary table.
MaxResultSetSize	262144	Maximum Result Set Storage. The maximum storage space of the server for all paged result sets.

Table 9-10. LDAP Query Policy Settings *(continued)*

LDAP Administrative Limits	Default Values	Description/Search Behavior
MaxPoolThreads	4	Maximum Pool Threads. The number of threads per processor allocated to answer LDAP requests.
MaxDatagramRecv	1024	Maximum Datagram Receive. The maximum size of datagrams, in bytes, that can be received by the server.

Table 9-11. LDAP Query Policy Settings *(continued)*

The LDAP policies and values can be viewed and changed by using the Active Directory Diagnostic Utility (NTDSUTIL.EXE) in the LDAP Policy menu. While setting the policies does not require the domain controller to be started in directory services restore mode, the domain controller does have to be restarted for the policies to take effect.

TOOLS

The tools covered in this section are designed specifically to boost the performance of Active Directory. These tools have several sources, including the native installation, the support tools on the operating system CD, and the Windows 2000 Resource Kit.

Native Installation

Along with the standard tools such as Performance Monitor, Event Viewer, and Task Manager, the default installation of Windows 2000 Server installs some Active Directory tools.

Active Directory Diagnostic Utility

The Active Directory Diagnostic utility (NTDSUTIL.EXE) is a
command-line tool that provides directory service management. It
maintains the Active Directory store, manages and controls the flexible
single-master operations master, and purges metadata left behind by
abandoned domain controllers (which are removed from the network
without being uninstalled). More important for performance tuning,
this utility performs offline defragmentation and compaction of the
Active Directory database. Offline defragmentation and compaction
is the only way to recover white space in the Active Directory database
file, which is key to optimizing the disk space on a domain controller.
It also allows the LDAP query policies to be viewed and set.

Because of the complexity of the tool, it supports both a
command-line mode and a menu-driven mode. The command-line
mode is somewhat unconventional and simply processes the commands
in sequence, similar to batch file processing. For example, the
command-line shown here will batch-process a series of commands.

```
NTDSUTIL "LDAP POLICIES" CONNECT "CONNECT TO DOMAIN COMPANYABC.COM"
 QUIT "SHOW VALUES"
```

This command line would launch the utility, enter the LDAP
Policies menu, enter the Connect menu, connect to the companyabc.com
domain, quit back to the LDAP Policies menu, and finally show the
current LDAP query policies.

Support Tools

These tools are included on the Windows 2000 media, but are not
installed by default. The support tools include some very useful
utilities, such as the ADSI Edit tool and the Domain Controller
Diagnostic tool. To install these tools, do the following:

1. Insert the Windows 2000 installation media in the
   CD-ROM drive.

2. Select Start | Run.

3. Enter **d:\support\tools\setup.exe**.

4. Accept the defaults.

There should now be a new menu option in the Programs group, Windows 2000 Support Tools.

ADSI Edit

ADSI Edit (ADSIEDIT.MSC) is an MMC snap-in tool that allows low-level editing of Active Directory via the Active Directory Service Interface (ADSI). Objects can be added, deleted, or moved, and the object attributes can be changed or deleted. This tool is useful for browsing the schema and setting object class attributes such as attribute indexing. The tool can also be used to search Active Directory.

Domain Controller Diagnostic Tool

The Domain Controller Diagnostic tool (DCDIAG.EXE) is an executable tool that analyzes the state of a domain controller or controllers, providing a report to indicate any problems. The tool can identify abnormal behavior in a domain controller, behavior that may be degrading performance though not causing the controller to fail.

The tool checks the following:

▼ **Connectivity**   Tests whether domain controllers are DNS registered, are pingable, and have LDAP/RPC connectivity.

■ **Replications**   Checks for timely replication between domain controllers.

■ **Topology Integrity**   Checks that the generated topology is fully connected for all domain controllers.

■ **NC Head Security Descriptors**   Checks that the security descriptors on the naming context heads have appropriate permissions for replication.

■ **Net Logon Rights**   Checks that the appropriate logon privileges allow replication to proceed.

■ **Locator Get Domain Controller** Checks whether each domain controller is advertising itself in the roles it should be capable of.

■ **Intersite Health** Checks for failures that would prevent or temporarily hold up intersite replication.

▲ **Roles** Checks that global role-holders are known, can be located, and are responding.

The tool conducts a series of tests automatically and can be run at the command prompt. A sample output with the default tests is shown here:

```
DC Diagnosis
Performing initial setup:
   Done gathering initial info.
Doing initial non skippable tests

   Testing server: Default-First-Site-Name\SERVER-SFO-01
      Starting test: Connectivity
         ........................ SERVER-SFO-01 passed test Connectivity
Doing primary tests

   Testing server: Default-First-Site-Name\SERVER-SFO-01
      Starting test: Replications
         ........................ SERVER-SFO-01 passed test Replications
      Starting test: NCSecDesc
         ........................ SERVER-SFO-01 passed test NCSecDesc
      Starting test: NetLogons
         ........................ SERVER-SFO-01 passed test NetLogons
      Starting test: Advertising
         ........................ SERVER-SFO-01 passed test Advertising
      Starting test: KnowsOfRoleHolders
         ........................ SERVER-SFO-01 passed test KnowsOfRoleHolders
      Starting test: RidManager
         ........................ SERVER-SFO-01 passed test RidManager
      Starting test: MachineAccount
         ........................ SERVER-SFO-01 passed test MachineAccount
      Starting test: Services
         ........................ SERVER-SFO-01 passed test Services
      Starting test: ObjectsReplicated
         ........................ SERVER-SFO-01 passed test ObjectsReplicated
      Starting test: frssysvol
         ........................ SERVER-SFO-01 passed test frssysvol
```

```
Starting test: kccevent
    ........................ SERVER-SFO-01 passed test kccevent
Starting test: systemlog
    ........................ SERVER-SFO-01 passed test systemlog

Running enterprise tests on : companyabc.com
    Starting test: Intersite
        ........................ companyabc.com passed test Intersite
    Starting test: FsmoCheck
        ........................ companyabc.com passed test FsmoCheck
```

Memory Profiling Tool

The Memory Profiling tool (MEMSNAP.EXE) captures the memory usage of all running processes and saves it to a log file. This is useful for running automatic performance tests and capturing the memory use at key steps. This can be incorporated into a performance testing script or batch file, or even run manually for comparisons between systems.

A partial output is shown here.

Process ID	Proc.Name	Wrkng.Set	Paged Pool	NonPgdPl	Pagefile	Commit	Handles	Threads
00000000	(null)	16384	0	0	0	0	0	1
00000008	System	217088	0	0	24576	24576	204	36
000000A0	SMSS.EXE	356352	5944	1252	1122304	1122304	33	6
000000B8	csrss.exe	1961984	36592	5312	1241088	1241088	445	10
000000CC	WINLOGON.EXE	3072000	38800	50600	6832128	6832128	427	19
000000E8	services.exe	5574656	39208	350124	3096576	3096576	614	35
000000F4	LSASS.EXE	14729216	53516	101616	14020608	14020608	780	41
000001B4	svchost.exe	3166208	26392	34252	1327104	1327104	276	10
000001DC	SPOOLSV.EXE	2904064	27472	15304	2641920	2641920	159	10
0000029C	msdtc.exe	3072000	26160	22424	1708032	1708032	182	20

This log shows that LSASS.EXE was using approximately 14 megabytes of memory and 41 threads.

Process Monitor

The Process Monitor (PMON.EXE) is a command-line tool for monitoring process resource use for each running process. Pmon tracks CPU usage, memory (paged and nonpaged pool) usage, and threads, as well as some global values such as page faults. For Active

Directory purposes, you can use Process Monitor to track the resource use of the Local Security Authority by viewing the LSASS.EXE process.

The Process Monitor tool provides a keyboard interface, so you can use the UP ARROW and DOWN ARROW keys to scroll up and down the list of currently running processes. To exit Process Monitor, press ESC. Use any other key to refresh the PMON.EXE display, or wait for it to refresh automatically. Figure 9-13 shows a sample output of Process Monitor.

Resource Kit Tools

The Windows 2000 Resource Kit has grown since the days of the Windows NT 4.0 Resource Kit. It now includes over 200 tools

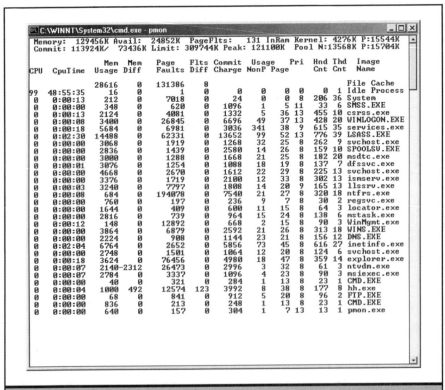

Figure 9-13. Process Monitor sample output

plus 6 books crammed with detailed technical information. While there are many tools, not that many are relevant to Active Directory performance tuning. A few of the more useful tools are mentioned here.

QuickSlice

QuickSlice shows the percentage of total CPU usage for each process in the system. This tool is similar to Process Monitor in the support tools, but it presents the information in a graphical format. A sample screen is shown in Figure 9-14.

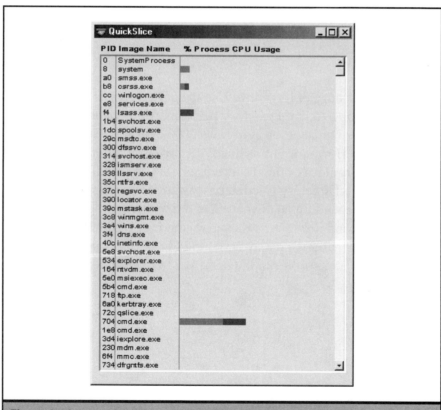

Figure 9-14.   QuickSlice sample output

Active Directory Sizer Tool

The Active Directory Sizer tool (ADSIZER.EXE) lets you estimate the hardware required for deploying Active Directory in an organization based on the organization's profile, domain information, and site topology. The ADSizer tool is discussed in detail in Chapter 4.

This tool is useful for checking existing performance against a well-defined model. If the model predicts significantly better performance than is being attained by the currently deployed server, then additional tuning may be needed.

NOTE: The Active Directory Sizer tool is currently a Web addition to the Resource Kit tools CD, available at http://www.microsoft.com/windows2000/downloads on the Microsoft Corporation Web site. You will also find updates to other Windows 2000 Resource Kit tools, samples, and useful documents at the site.

Because of its central role in so many areas of Windows 2000, boosting Active Directory performance is critical to the overall performance of the Windows 2000 operating system. Boosting the performance of Active Directory is all about boosting the performance of the underlying database. Understanding that the Active Directory is a database is key to tuning its performance.

Depending on the nature of the bottleneck, adding more memory or reconfiguring the disk subsystem may be the key to unlocking performance, or it may be setting LDAP query policies to match the application profile or indexing key frequently searched object attributes.

CHAPTER 10

Boosting Replication Performance

In a multisite organization, Active Directory is the same everywhere. This means that the Active Directory data at the San Francisco office with be the same as the Active Directory data at the Tokyo and New York offices. How does the data get there and how can it be streamlined in getting there? In addition, Active Directory depends on the Domain Naming System (DNS) to work efficiently, or at all in the case of some applications. Thus, DNS also needs to be everywhere that Active Directory is.

Both Active Directory and DNS have built-in default settings that optimize for the lowest common denominator. While the default behavior may be sufficient in some cases, especially in simpler organizations, it is rarely optimal for an organization of even average complexity. There are many opportunities to boost performance of the replication process, as discussed in this chapter.

To boost the replication performance, the first step is to understand the components of the Active Directory and DNS replication systems. The next step is to understand what to measure to get an accurate view of where the system is performing well and, more important, where it is not performing well. This is critical to establishing a baseline of performance. The final step is to boost the performance of the replication systems by adjusting various settings, always measuring and verifying the results against the baseline to ensure that changes made have the desired effect.

COMPONENTS OF REPLICATION

Active Directory and DNS need to be at every site and most likely at more than one domain controller per site. This is accomplished through replication. To understand replication, it is first necessary to know what the components are. The various components, such as connections and zone files, are covered in this section. How they interact and how to boost their performance is covered later in this chapter, in "Active Directory Replication Tuning" and "Domain Name Services Replication Tuning."

Active Directory Components

The Windows 2000 operating system introduced a number of enhancements in its new directory service, Active Directory. The directory service was designed from the ground up to facilitate crucial processes such as replication.

Characteristics of Active Directory Replication

Active Directory has a number of benefits built in that contribute to the effectiveness of the replication process. These characteristics make Active Directory replication very efficient for the task of moving directory information throughout the organization.

Globally Unique Identifier   Objects change over time. For example, users may change their names, addresses, and so on. If a user changes his or her name, administrators still want the same object in Active Directory to represent that user. From a replication standpoint, only the name change should replicate; the entire user object should not need to be deleted and re-created. Active Directory identifies objects internally by identity numbers, not by their names, whatever they may currently be. Objects may be moved or renamed, but their identity numbers never change. This is very similar to social security numbers, which are used to uniquely identify taxpayers in the United States and never change.

An object is identified by its globally unique identifier (GUID), a 16-byte number that is created by the DSA when the object is created. The GUID value is stored in an attribute, objectGUID, which is part of every object and never changes. Objects can be renamed and moved as needed, as the object is tracked by the system using its GUID. This allows the system to replicate only the actual changes made to the object itself, not the entire object.

Attribute-Level Replication   Active Directory supports attribute-level replication. Rather than forcing replication of the entire object or even the entire database, attribute level replication enables only the changes made to an object to be copied between domain controllers, helping to reduce bandwidth. For example, if a user changes a phone number, then only the phone number, with some overhead information, will be transmitted as part of the replication process.

Multimaster Model   Active Directory uses a multimaster model of data storage. This means that the directory can have many copies of the directory, each on different domain controllers, copies that must be kept consistent. Replication is used to maintain data integrity across the domain controllers, to ensure that the information in the database is the same for all copies. Note, though, that the copies of the directory converge over time to a consistent state. This means that at any given point in time, there may be differences in copies of the directory, depending on the changes made to objects and the replication state. However, any given change will replicate in a determined span of time.

Store-and-Forward Replication   Changes made on a domain controller are not sent directly to all other domain controllers. This would result in many connections between domain controllers and excessive traffic on the LAN or WAN. To make replication more efficient, changes are sent to some of the domain controllers, called partners, depending on the replication topology. Those domain controllers store and then forward the changes to their partners, and so on, until the entire set of domain controllers have the change.

Pull Replication   Although changes are often referred to as being "sent," they are in reality requested, or *pulled*, by the destination domain controller. Domain controllers pull updates from their replication partners. This process of requesting updates can be scheduled or can be triggered by a change notification from the originating domain controller.

State-Based Replication   Rather than replicating every change, Active Directory collapses all changes made to an object into a single state. When replication occurs, the object is replicated in the state that exists at the time of the replication. For example, suppose that an administrator updates all the phone numbers for domain users. After doing this, the administrator realizes that the area code needs to be added and so applies that change to the phone numbers. Then the administrator discovers that the phone numbers for some users are incorrect and makes a third change to the phone numbers to fix the errors. When replication occurs, only the final value of the phone number attribute will be replicated rather than the three individual changes that were made. This saves valuable bandwidth and resources.

Flexible Topology   Rather than specify all the different connections between domain controllers, Active Directory allows administrators to use a more general approach to configuring a model of the topology and then configures the detailed connections automatically. The model is based on concepts of sites and site links. Following this model, Active Directory automatically creates replication connections that perform the actual replication. This process is flexible and allows the topology to adapt to changes automatically. Another aspect of this flexibility is that replication is not tied to the Active Directory architecture, allowing replication to flex to geographic constraints.

Update Sequence Numbers

Changes are primarily based on update sequence numbers (USN) rather than timestamps. When an object update conflicts between domain controllers, the AD first looks at the number of times the object has been changed by a domain controller (via the version number of the attribute) and then at the timestamp. If the object was changed an equal number of times by the conflicting domain controllers, then the last writer wins (the update with the latest timestamp). However, if one domain controller has changed the object more times (that is, if its USN has been incremented more times), then that controller's update wins, even if the timestamp of the other controller is later. The concept of the number of changes that have occurred is called volatility and is expressed in the version number of each attribute.

Finally, if two updates have the same version number and occurred in the exact same second, then the originating DSA will break the tie arbitrarily.

Note that you can use the repadmin utility to view the 64-bit USN. The format of the command is REPADMIN /SHOWMETA <OBJECT DN>. See Figure 10-1 for a sample output of the command.

```
Command Prompt                                                                          _ □ ×
C:\>repadmin /showmeta "cn=John Smith,ou=Engineering,dc=companyabc,dc=com"

43 entries.

Loc.USN          Originating DSA  Org.USN   Org.Time/Date       Ver Attribute
=======          ===============  =======   =============       === =========
    9218         SFO\SERVER-SFO-01    9218   2000-12-28 12:35.56   1 objectClass
    9218         SFO\SERVER-SFO-01    9218   2000-12-28 12:35.56   1 cn
    9218         SFO\SERVER-SFO-01    9218   2000-12-28 12:35.56   1 sn
    9242         JFK\SERVER-JFK-01   12098   2000-12-28 12:51.28   1 c
    9242         JFK\SERVER-JFK-01   12098   2000-12-28 12:51.28   1 l
    9242         JFK\SERVER-JFK-01   12098   2000-12-28 12:51.28   1 st
    9219         SFO\SERVER-SFO-01    9219   2000-12-28 12:35.56   1 description
    9242         JFK\SERVER-JFK-01   12098   2000-12-28 12:51.28   1 postalCode
    9218         SFO\SERVER-SFO-01    9218   2000-12-28 12:35.56   1 givenName
    9218         SFO\SERVER-SFO-01    9218   2000-12-28 12:35.56   1 instanceType
    9218         SFO\SERVER-SFO-01    9218   2000-12-28 12:35.56   1 whenCreated
    9219         SFO\SERVER-SFO-01    9219   2000-12-28 12:35.56   1 displayName
    9242         JFK\SERVER-JFK-01   12098   2000-12-28 12:51.28   1 co
    9242         JFK\SERVER-JFK-01   12098   2000-12-28 12:51.28   1 streetAddress
    9242         JFK\SERVER-JFK-01   12100   2000-12-28 12:51.29   2 nTSecurityDescriptor
    9223         SFO\SERVER-SFO-01    9223   2000-12-28 12:40.22   1 wWWHomePage
    9218         SFO\SERVER-SFO-01    9218   2000-12-28 12:35.56   1 name
    9224         SFO\SERVER-SFO-01    9224   2000-12-28 12:40.49   4 userAccountControl
    9219         SFO\SERVER-SFO-01    9219   2000-12-28 12:35.56   1 codePage
    9242         JFK\SERVER-JFK-01   12098   2000-12-28 12:51.28   2 countryCode
    9225         SFO\SERVER-SFO-01    9225   2000-12-28 12:40.49   2 homeDirectory
    9225         SFO\SERVER-SFO-01    9225   2000-12-28 12:40.49   2 homeDrive
    9220         SFO\SERVER-SFO-01    9220   2000-12-28 12:35.57   2 dBCSPwd
    9219         SFO\SERVER-SFO-01    9219   2000-12-28 12:35.56   1 scriptPath
    9219         SFO\SERVER-SFO-01    9219   2000-12-28 12:35.56   1 logonHours
    9219         SFO\SERVER-SFO-01    9219   2000-12-28 12:35.56   1 userWorkstations
    9220         SFO\SERVER-SFO-01    9220   2000-12-28 12:35.57   2 unicodePwd
    9219         SFO\SERVER-SFO-01    9219   2000-12-28 12:35.56   1 ntPwdHistory
    9220         SFO\SERVER-SFO-01    9220   2000-12-28 12:35.57   2 pwdLastSet
    9219         SFO\SERVER-SFO-01    9219   2000-12-28 12:35.56   1 primaryGroupID
    9220         SFO\SERVER-SFO-01    9220   2000-12-28 12:35.57   1 supplementalCredentials
    9242         JFK\SERVER-JFK-01   12101   2000-12-28 12:51.29   2 userParameters
    9219         SFO\SERVER-SFO-01    9219   2000-12-28 12:35.56   1 profilePath
    9218         SFO\SERVER-SFO-01    9218   2000-12-28 12:35.56   1 objectSid
    9219         SFO\SERVER-SFO-01    9219   2000-12-28 12:35.56   1 comment
    9219         SFO\SERVER-SFO-01    9219   2000-12-28 12:35.56   1 accountExpires
    9219         SFO\SERVER-SFO-01    9219   2000-12-28 12:35.56   1 lmPwdHistory
    9218         SFO\SERVER-SFO-01    9218   2000-12-28 12:35.56   1 sAMAccountName
    9218         SFO\SERVER-SFO-01    9218   2000-12-28 12:35.56   1 sAMAccountType
    9218         SFO\SERVER-SFO-01    9218   2000-12-28 12:35.56   1 userPrincipalName
    9218         SFO\SERVER-SFO-01    9218   2000-12-28 12:35.56   1 objectCategory
    9242         JFK\SERVER-JFK-01   12101   2000-12-28 12:51.29   1 msNPAllowDialin
    9223         SFO\SERVER-SFO-01    9223   2000-12-28 12:40.22   1 mail

C:\>
```

Figure 10-1.   Local USN output

The column labeled Loc.USN in the sample shows the current local USN. The Originating DSA and Orig.USN columns show the site and domain controller where the change was last made, as well as the originating USN. You can see from the sample that some attributes were changed on the SERVER-SFO-01 domain controller at the SFO site, and others were changed on the SERVER-JFK-01 domain controller at the JFK site. You can also see the version number of each attribute and the timestamp.

Knowledge Consistency Checker

The Knowledge Consistency Checker (KCC) is an Active Directory process that runs on each domain controller and automatically creates the detailed replication topology. The KCC runs every 15 minutes and creates the replication connections between domain controllers and sites. The Active Directory KCC uses information about the domain controllers, sites, site links, and transports to create and manage the replication topology. Each time the KCC runs, replication partner connections between domain controllers are added, removed, or modified automatically on the basis of what domain controllers are available and where they are in the network.

This automatic process is the key to the flexibility and ease of administration of Active Directory replication. It reduces administrative overhead by allowing administrators to configure only the high-level site topology. The KCC then takes over and creates the optimal connections between all the different servers. As changes occur in the network or in server availability, the KCC automatically reoptimizes and works around any problems.

Connections

Connections are the actual paths that replicate Active Directory information. The KCC creates connections that enable domain controllers to perform replication with each other, both within a site and between sites. Each connection defines a one-way route from a source domain controller to a destination domain controller. For two-way replication between domain controllers, there are two connections.

The connections are stored as objects in Active Directory and are replicated over the same connection, just like any other objects. Even though the KCC creates the connections automatically, administrators can manually create connections if necessary for specific optimizations.

Servers

Each domain controller is represented by a server object in Active Directory. Each server object has a child object, the NTDS Settings object, which stores connection objects for that server. Server objects are associated with sites (that is, they are children of site containers), which allows the KCC to determine the appropriate connections (see Figure 10-2).

When a Windows 2000 server is promoted, it is automatically placed in the appropriate site, and its objects are created.

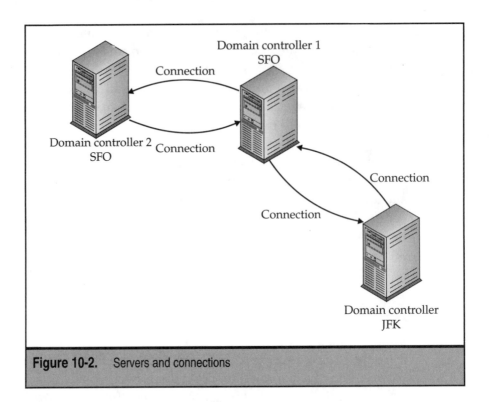

Figure 10-2. Servers and connections

NOTE: If changes are made to the site topology, subnets, or server IP address, the server object does not move automatically and must be moved manually to its new site using the Active Directory Sites and Services tool.

Sites

A site is a group of domain controllers that are well connected in terms of speed and cost; it is usually defined as a LAN. Domain controllers within the same site notify their replication partner domain controllers of changes to the Active Directory database. Then the notified partners request the changes, and the changed data is replicated. This mechanism propagates changes as they occur, which is relatively expensive in terms of bandwidth. This is not usually a problem in well-connected sites, such as LANs.

NOTE: To allow for the possibility of network failure, which might cause one or more notifications to be missed, a default schedule of once per hour is applied to replication within a site, in addition to change notification.

In contrast, replication between these well-connected sites occurs according to a schedule, typically over a WAN. The schedule allows administrators to determine the best time for replication to occur, taking into account WAN usage, network traffic, cost, and other applications. A site is the equivalent of a set of one or more Internet protocol (IP) subnets (see Figure 10-3).

Subnets

Windows 2000 communications is based on the TCP/IP protocol, and the protocol is built into the Active Directory design. Active Directory bases replication on sites, which is defined as groups of IP subnets. Computers are assigned to sites based on their location in a subnet or set of subnets. Subnets group computers in a way that identifies their

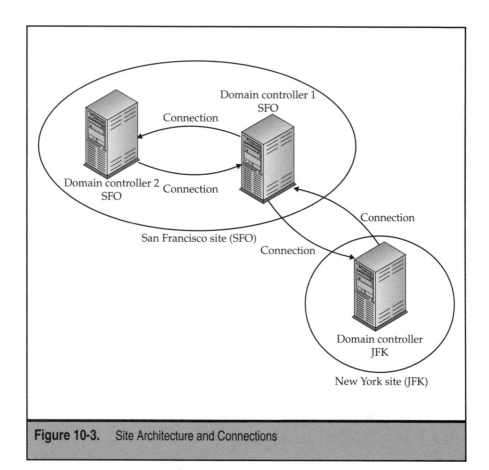

Figure 10-3.   Site Architecture and Connections

physical proximity on the network, as it is assumed that computers within the same subnet will be well connected.

Subnet information is used by workstations during the process of domain controller location to find a domain controller in the same site as the computer that is logging on. This helps ensure that workstations use local resources first, rather than using remote resources and expensive WAN bandwidth. This process is covered in Chapter 12.

More important for replication, the subnet information is used by the KCC during topology generation to determine the best routes between domain controllers. Figure 10-4 shows how subnets group computers. If no subnets are defined, then all servers are automatically placed in the Default-First-Site-Name site: that is, they are all placed in

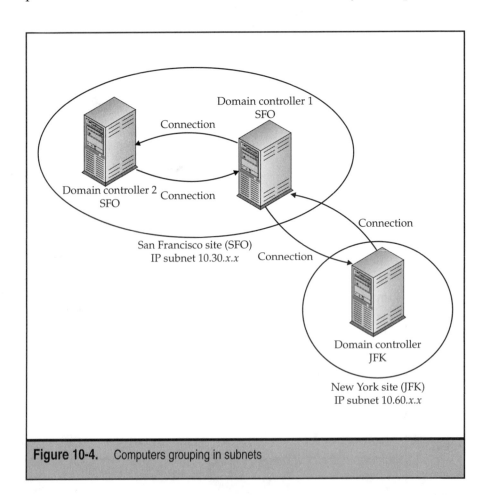

Figure 10-4.   Computers grouping in subnets

a single site, which does not take advantage of intersite replication. This will result in poor performance in large networks. Move servers to the appropriate sites to ensure that Active Directory adjusts replication appropriately.

Site Links

Site links are the links between sites through which the replication connections are established. For Active Directory replication to occur between two sites, a site link must be established between the sites. Site links make up the administrator-specified high-level topology that the KCC uses to generate the detailed topology. The schedule for the site link determines when replication can occur between the sites that it connects. Unless a site link is created, the KCC cannot create connections between computers in the two sites, and thus replication between the sites cannot take place.

Site links are created using the Active Directory Sites and Services tool. The Active Directory Sites and Services tool ensures that every site is placed in at least one site link. A site link can contain more than just two sites, in which case all the sites in the link are connected together. This makes the system simpler to administer, as a single site link can be created for meshed networks.

NOTE: Although site links are not created automatically by the KCC, there is a default site link to which each site is added when it is created. The KCC uses this default site link to automatically create connections. The KCC and replication behavior can be modified by deleting the default site link and manually creating the site links to force connections along specific routes.

Within the site link, the key elements that are specified are the sites that are linked, the replication schedule, and the cost of the link.

The default site link is named DEFAULTIPSITELINK, and all sites are placed in that site link automatically, unless another site link is chosen. This default site bridges all sites, ensuring complete connectivity between all sites. Administrators can change the distribution of sites across site links to modify the replication behavior, as will be discussed later in this chapter.

Bridgehead Servers

When determining the detailed replication topology and creating replication connections between sites across site links, the KCC designates a single server, called the bridgehead server, at each site to perform the replication (see Figure 10-5). This server is typically the oldest available domain controller at the site, based on the GUID of the servers. This bridgehead server receives the changes to Active Directory and then replicates the changes to the remaining domain controllers at the site.

Bridgehead servers can act as bridgeheads only for database partitions that they host: that is, bridgehead servers cannot store and forward information from naming contexts that they do not host in their store. The KCC will create enough bridgeheads to ensure that

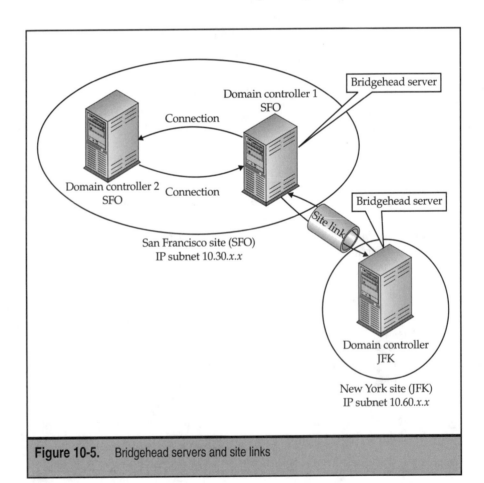

Figure 10-5. Bridgehead servers and site links

all database partitions that are shared between two sites are replicated. In other words, there may be more than one bridgehead server per site.

While the KCC automatically selects bridgehead servers based on the GUID, administrators can also specify which servers they want as the preferred bridgehead server candidates. This forces the KCC to choose the oldest server among the preferred bridgehead servers as the designated bridgehead server for the site.

Site Link Bridges

If sites do not have direct site links between them, then site link bridges can be used to establish the links. In effect, this allows the KCC to establish connection objects between sites as needed, even if there are no explicit site links between two sites. By default, if more than two sites are linked and use the same transport, all of the site links are bridged.

Using site link bridges is very similar to establishing routes within IP networks, where packets can be routed between subnets through network connection on adjacent subnets. Site links with the same IP transport that share sites are bridged by site link bridges, which enables the KCC to treat the set of site links as a single route.

High-Water Marks

The high-water mark is the value of the highest USN that the destination domain controller has received for a specific database partition from each replication partner. The domain controller uses this USN to select the objects that it considers for replication to the destination. The high-water mark ensures that objects within the partition that have already been replicated to the domain controller are not sent again.

The high-water marks for a domain controller can be seen using the Replication Administrator tool, with the command REPADMIN/ SHOWREPS /VERBOSE. Sample output of the command is shown here:

```
C:\>repadmin /showreps /verbose
SFO\SERVER-SFO-01
DSA Options : IS_GC
```

```
objectGuid  : 282bdfc6-d2ed-4d56-84df-5209670f6918
invocationID: 282bdfc6-d2ed-4d56-84df-5209670f6918


==== INBOUND NEIGHBORS =======================================


CN=Schema,CN=Configuration,DC=companyabc,DC=com
    JFK\SERVER-JFK-01 via RPC
        objectGuid: 5769bac7-e786-4b17-899d-af74d2baa047
        Address: 5769bac7-e786-4b17-899d-af74d2baa047.
                    _msdcs.companyabc.com
        ntdsDsa invocationId: 776da351-0e38-4845-b669-332ff2c62a84
        WRITEABLE DO_SCHEDULED_SYNCS COMPRESS_CHANGES
                    NO_CHANGE_NOTIFICATIONS
        USNs: 16057/OU, 16057/PU
        Last attempt @ 2001-01-15 05:46.01 was successful.


CN=Configuration,DC=companyabc,DC=com
    JFK\SERVER-JFK-01 via RPC
        objectGuid: 5769bac7-e786-4b17-899d-af74d2baa047
        Address: 5769bac7-e786-4b17-899d-af74d2baa047.
                    _msdcs.companyabc.com
        ntdsDsa invocationId: 776da351-0e38-4845-b669-332ff2c62a84
        WRITEABLE DO_SCHEDULED_SYNCS COMPRESS_CHANGES
                    NO_CHANGE_NOTIFICATIONS
        USNs: 16069/OU, 16069/PU
        Last attempt @ 2001-01-15 05:46.01 was successful.


DC=companyabc,DC=com
    JFK\SERVER-JFK-01 via RPC
        objectGuid: 5769bac7-e786-4b17-899d-af74d2baa047
        Address: 5769bac7-e786-4b17-899d-af74d2baa047.
                    _msdcs.companyabc.com
        ntdsDsa invocationId: 776da351-0e38-4845-b669-332ff2c62a84
        WRITEABLE DO_SCHEDULED_SYNCS COMPRESS_CHANGES
                    NO_CHANGE_NOTIFICATIONS
        USNs: 16057/OU, 16057/PU
```

```
        Last attempt @ 2001-01-15 05:46.01 was successful.


==== OUTBOUND NEIGHBORS FOR CHANGE NOTIFICATIONS ============


CN=Schema,CN=Configuration,DC=companyabc,DC=com
    JFK\SERVER-JFK-01 via RPC
        objectGuid: 5769bac7-e786-4b17-899d-af74d2baa047
        Address: 5769bac7-e786-4b17-899d-af74d2baa047.
                      _msdcs.companyabc.com
        WRITEABLE
        Added @ 2000-12-29 12:48.53.
```

The high-water marks are the values of the USNs followed by /OU and are shown for each partition and replication partner.

Up-to-Dateness Vector

The up-to-dateness vector is the value of the highest USN that the destination domain controller maintains for updates that it has received from the source domain controller. It is equivalent to a high-water mark for each domain controller, rather than for the database partition. The up-to-dateness vector prevents the domain controller from being sent attribute information that it already has received from an originating domain controller.

The up-to-dateness vectors for a domain controller can be seen using the Replication Administrator tool, with the command REPADMIN /SHOWVECTOR. Sample output of the command is shown here:

```
C:>repadmin /showvector DC=companyabc,DC=com
NRT\SERVER-NRT-01                    @ USN 8658
SFO\SERVER-SFO-01                    @ USN 12586
JFK\SERVER-JFK-01                    @ USN 16075
```

The high-water mark and the up-to-dateness vector help to conserve resources that would be wasted by replicating duplicate or outdated changes. For performance tuning and optimization, these values are very useful for understanding exactly what will be replicated.

Domain Naming System Components

Windows 2000 is based on the TCP/IP protocol, which uses IP addresses to locate computers. The format of IP addresses (dotted decimal notation, such as 10.30.1.2), while perfectly serviceable for computers, leaves much to be desired for humans to use on a regular basis. Friendly names (such as www.companyabc.com) are much preferred. The Domain Naming System provides a service for translating the IP addresses into friendly names. In addition, Active Directory uses the DNS to locate computers and services. It is required for clients to log on and to locate the resources closest to the client.

Servers

Servers in the DNS architecture respond to queries about domains and hosts, a process called resolving. Requests can be issued to resolve host information, to provide domain information, or to provide resource information via resource records. When a DNS server receives requests from clients to resolve host names to IP addresses, the request is known as a forward lookup. Such requests also allow the reverse to be done: that is, IP addresses can be resolved to host names. This is referred to as a reverse lookup. A reverse lookup is generally performed by an application to verify the host name of the system that is requesting services. For example, when a client is downloading software with export restricted 128-bit encryption code from a software vendor, the vendor will frequently perform a reverse lookup of the requesting browser's IP address to ensure that the originating domain is registered in an authorized country.

The DNS server does not necessarily need to actually store the information that it provides to the clients. A DNS server can store information about zero or more domains in its local data store. When a DNS server receives a query from a client, it first looks in its local data store to find the requested information. If it finds the requested information in its store, it responds to the query with the information. If it cannot find the information, then it can initiate a query to another DNS server for the client, respond by referring the client to another DNS server, or simply respond that it has no information related to the request. The specific response will depend on how the server is configured.

The information that a conventional (non–Active Directory–integrated) DNS server stores can be either primary or secondary for any given domain. If a server is primary for a given domain, then the domain is locally updated. The changes are then replicated, or transferred, to secondary DNS servers. These secondary DNS servers hold copies of the primary, or master, domain database. Any given server can be primary for some domains and secondary for other domains. One outcome of this centralized replication architecture is that all changes need to be made on the primary DNS server for a given domain and replicated from there. This is often referred to as master-slave replication.

In contrast to conventional DNS domains, Active Directory–integrated DNS domains allow multimaster replication. This allows domain updates to take place on different DNS servers and be replicated to all other servers. Active Directory–integrated domains are discussed later in this section.

Resource Records

In addition to host-to-IP mappings, the DNS servers data stores contain resource records (RRs) that make up the resource information associated with the DNS domain. For example, some resource records map friendly names to IP addresses, and others map IP addresses to friendly names.

MX and SRV are the most prominent types of resource records, but there are other resource record types as well. Windows 2000 and Active Directory make extensive use of resource records, and of the service resource records in particular. The alternatives would be to manually configure the information in each client, have the clients poll all servers for the information, or have the clients broadcast for servers to respond. The alternatives have high administrative and/or bandwidth requirements, making the service location records very efficient in comparison.

MX Resource Records   Mail exchange (MX) resource records define mail exchange servers for a DNS domain name. A mail exchange server is a server that either processes or forwards mail for the DNS domain name for which the MX record is defined. An example of an

MX record for the companyabc.com domain is shown in Figure 10-6. The MX record is used by the computer using the Simple Mail Transfer Protocol (SMTP) to send electronic mail messages. There can be multiple MX resource records for any given domain, allowing load balancing and fault tolerance.

SRV Records Service location (SRV) resource records specify the location of the servers for a specific service, protocol, and DNS domain. Specifying, or publishing, the information for services allows clients to request information regarding all servers that provide those services within a domain. Rather than just the IP and host name, the DNS is also the repository for the services that the server supports. An example of an Active Directory global catalog SRV record for the forest in which companyabc.com exists is shown in Figure 10-7. This service location record allows clients to locate a global catalog server.

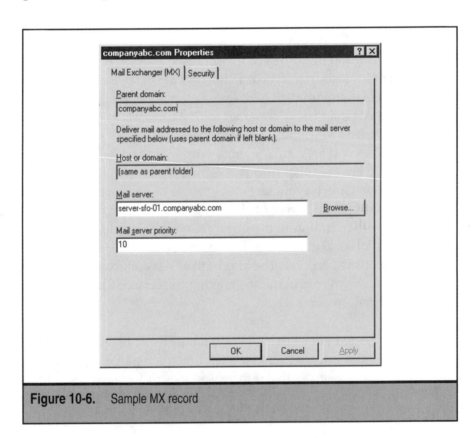

Figure 10-6. Sample MX record

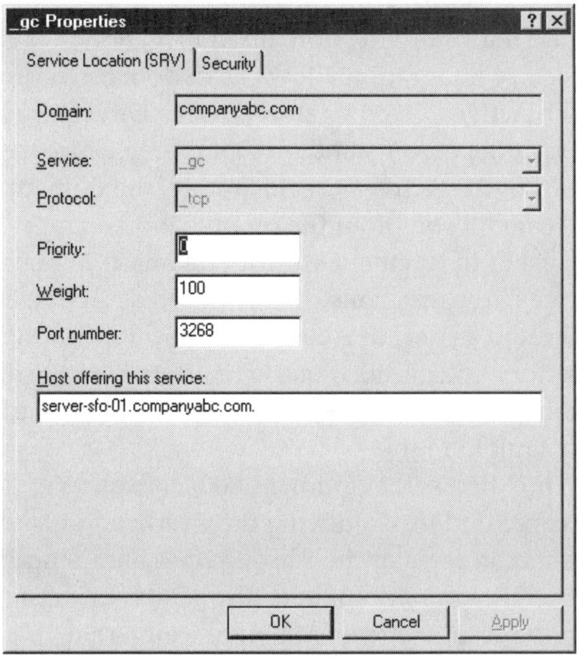

Figure 10-7. Sample SRV record

Zones

A zone is a contiguous portion of the DNS namespace, and each zone is rooted at a specific domain node: for instance, a DNS domain. The zone contains the DNS records of the domain. A zone can contain multiple domains; however, zones usually do not.

The DNS standards do not specify the internal data structure that stores resource records, and various implementations differ. Generally, UNIX servers and the original Windows NT DNS use zones stored on that server in plain text, but this is not required by the specification. With Windows 2000, you can integrate your DNS database with Active Directory, in which case the zones are stored in the Active Directory database.

Active Directory Integration

Rather than store the domain information in zone files, Active Directory integration allows DNS domain information to be stored in the Active Directory store. Active Directory replication provides an advantage over standard DNS alone. Since the domain information is part of the Active Directory store, the domain information is replicated throughout the organization on a per attribute basis with the rest of the Active Directory database. When you store a zone in Active Directory, zone data is stored as Active Directory objects and replicated as part of Active Directory replication. Every Active Directory–integration zone is replicated among all domain controllers within the Active Directory domain. This makes the DNS service very fault tolerant.

The Microsoft Windows 2000 DNS allows DNS clients to make dynamic updates, reducing the overhead of DNS administration. Clients can register their host names and IP addresses automatically. Active Directory domain controllers also register their service location resource records dynamically, relieving the administrator of the task. In addition, updates can be restricted to secure only, forcing clients to authenticate when making updates. This improves security by ensuring that unauthorized records are not added to the domain.

With conventional DNS, only the primary server for a domain can modify the domain. With Active Directory managing the replication process, all domain controllers for the domain can modify the zone and then have the changes replicate to other domain controllers. In effect, all Windows 2000 DNS servers serving Active Directory–integration domains act as primary servers for the zone, accepting updates to the domain. This replication process is called multimaster replication because multiple DNS servers, or masters, can update the zone.

WHAT TO MEASURE

Chapters 6 and 7 discussed general-purpose counters for disk, memory, and processor resources. These counters are good for identifying general resource trends within a system and for tuning the performance of specific subsystems. To effectively tune the performance of replication, you have much more precise counters to examine.

This section looks at the counters needed to monitor performance and load and understand at a very detailed level what the Active Directory and DNS replication systems are doing. These counters can be used by administrators, in conjunction with the general-purpose counters, to monitor and fine-tune the replication systems.

In looking at these counters, the focus will be on the volume and rate of change of that volume. As discussed in previous chapters, it is difficult to evaluate any given value of a performance counter in a vacuum. A value that is normal in one environment may be completely wrong for another environment. For example, for a large organization with lots of changes, a legacy UNIX DNS, and an Active Directory–integrated DNS, a high value for AXFR Request Received might be reasonable, as zone transfers between the different domain name systems would be common. For an organization that is completely Active Directory integrated, that counter should be zero, as all domain information should be replicated via the Active Directory replication mechanisms.

When reviewing these values and using them to tune Active Directory or DNS, it is important to create baselines and have a good understanding of the environment before taking action on the results.

Active Directory Counters

In measuring the performance of Active Directory replication, the process is complicated by the various qualities of the replication. As was discussed in "Active Directory Components" earlier in this chapter, replication differs depending on whether it is performed intrasite or intersite and even on the size of the data being replicated. The system may compress or not compress, based on those factors.

Luckily, there are a multitude of Performance Monitor counters for measuring the various permutations and conditions. The counters are grouped here by the direction of the replication: either inbound or outbound. This chapter also includes a section on the counters used for monitoring the status of the replication overall.

Directory Replication Agent (DRA) is the process that performs the actual replication. All counters involving Active Directory replication within the Performance Monitor have DRA as the suffix to make them easy to select in the NTDS object, as shown in Figure 10-8.

Inbound Replication Performance

Inbound traffic, resulting from the pull nature of Active Directory, reflects the load from requests for updates made by the domain controller to its replication partners. The model thus is many to one, with the many being the replication partners, and the one being the domain controller.

The counters in Table 10-1 show the volume of replication data being received by the domain controller, both within the site and between sites. For traffic between sites, there are counters for both before and after compression. These are useful for determining the efficiency of the compression. A common computation to determine compression efficiency is to divide the after-compression counter by the before-compression counter to determine the compression ratio. Under normal circumstances, the number should be in the 10 to 15 percent range. This applies only to intersite traffic, as intrasite traffic is never compressed.

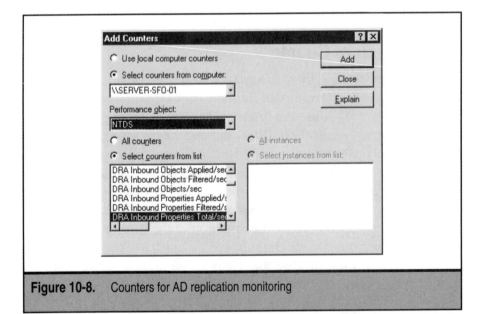

Figure 10-8.   Counters for AD replication monitoring

Counter	Description
DRA Inbound Bytes Compressed (Between Sites, After Compression) Since Boot	Compressed size in bytes of inbound compressed replication data (size after compression, from DSAs at other sites).
DRA Inbound Bytes Compressed (Between Sites, Before Compression) Since Boot	Original size in bytes of inbound compressed replication data (size before compression, from DSAs at other sites).
DRA Inbound Bytes Not Compressed (Within Site) Since Boot	Number of bytes replicated in that were not compressed at the source (that is, from DSAs at the same site).
DRA Inbound Bytes Total Since Boot	Total number of inbound bytes replicated; the sum of the number of uncompressed bytes (never compressed) and the number of compressed bytes (after compression). This is a measure of the actual traffic.
DRA Inbound Bytes Compressed (Between Sites, After Compression)/sec	Compressed size in bytes of inbound compressed replication data (size after compression, from DSAs at other sites).
DRA Inbound Bytes Compressed (Between Sites, Before Compression)/sec	Original size in bytes of inbound compressed replication data (size before compression, from DSAs at other sites).
DRA Inbound Bytes Not Compressed (Within Site)/sec	Number of bytes replicated in that were not compressed at the source (that is, from DSAs at the same site).
DRA Inbound Bytes Total/sec	Total number of inbound bytes replicated; the sum of the number of uncompressed bytes (never compressed) and the number of compressed bytes (after compression). This is a measure of the actual traffic.

Table 10-1.   AD Replication Inbound Byte Counters

The inbound object counters in Table 10-2 show the number of objects that the domain controller is receiving from its replication partners. The Full Sync Objects Remaining counter is very useful in

Counter	Description
DRA Inbound Full Sync Objects Remaining	Number of objects remaining until the full synchronization process is completed. This gives a macro view of what remains to be synchronized in the current cycle, spanning all replication update packets.
DRA Inbound Object Updates Remaining in Packet	Number of object updates received in the current directory replication update packet that have not yet been applied to the local server. This gives a micro view of what remains to be synchronized in just the current update packet.
DRA Inbound Objects/sec	Number of objects received (per second) through inbound replication from replication partners.
DRA Inbound Objects Applied/sec	Number of objects received (per second) from replication partners and applied by the local directory service. This counter indicates how many replication updates are occurring on the server by changes generated on other servers.
DRA Inbound Objects Filtered/sec	Number of objects received (per second) from replication partners that contained no updates that needed to be applied.

Table 10-2.   AD Replication Inbound Object Counters

determining how far along a given cycle of replication is at a macro level, and the Remaining in Packet counter gives the same information at a micro level for the packet last received.

These counters are used to determine whether server processing time is a bottleneck in the replication process, as they indicate that the replication messages have gotten across the replication transport and are being processed by the domain controller. If they take a long time to be processed and applied to the database, then look to other server performance counters to determine the specific resource constraint (such as the processor, memory, or I/O system).

Whereas the object counters reflect new objects, the properties counters shown in Table 10-3 show changes to existing objects. For every object added or changed, the relevant properties are transferred and shown in the counters.

These counters are useful for measuring the rate of change on existing objects, as they vary in direct proportion to the changes to objects. In contrast, values are more difficult to correlate with object changes, as some properties have multiple values. Adding an object

Counter	Description
DRA Inbound Properties Applied/sec	Number of properties that are updated because the incoming property won the reconciliation logic.
DRA Inbound Properties Filtered/sec	Number of property changes that are received during the replication that have already been seen.
DRA Inbound Properties Total/sec	Total number of object properties received from inbound replication partners.

Table 10-3.   AD Replication Inbound Property Counters

will cause all of that object's properties to be replicated, which will tend to skew the numbers.

The inbound value counters measure the rate at which the object attribute values are being changed at or replicated to the domain controller. Each replicated object has at least one property, but each property may have zero or more values.

Distinguished names (DNs), including groups and distribution lists, can have very large value sets. These collections of objects require more effort on the part of the destination domain controller to apply to the Active Directory database than regular values, as they may include significantly larger numbers of values per property and thus a larger number of changes. Hence, there is a specific counter, DRA Inbound Values (DNs only)/sec, to measure this replication traffic.

Table 10-4 shows the inbound value counters.

Outbound Replication Performance

Outbound traffic, resulting from the pull nature of Active Directory, reflects the load from requests for updates made by the replication partners to the domain controller. The model is many to one, with the

Counter	Description
DRA Inbound Values Total/sec	Total number of values of object properties received (per second) from replication partners.
DRA Inbound Values (DNs only)/sec	Number of values of object properties received (per second) from replication partners in which the values are for object properties that belong to distinguished names. This number includes objects that reference other objects. A high number from this counter might explain why inbound changes are slow to be applied to the database.

Table 10-4. AD Replication Inbound Value Counters

many being the replication partners, and the one being the domain controller. This traffic is the data being sent from the domain controller to its replication partners.

The counters in Table 10-5 show the volume of replication data being sent by the domain controller, both within the site and between sites. For traffic between sites, there are counters for both before and after compression. These are useful for determining the efficiency of the compression. As with the inbound counters, divide the after-compression counter by the before-compression counter to obtain the compression ratio.

Counter	Description
DRA Outbound Bytes Compressed (Between Sites, After Compression) Since Boot	Compressed size (in bytes) of outbound compressed replication data (size after compression, from DSAs at other sites).
DRA Outbound Bytes Compressed (Between Sites, Before Compression) Since boot	Uncompressed size (in bytes) of compressed replication data outbound to DSAs at other sites (per second).
DRA Outbound Bytes Total Since Boot	Total number of bytes sent per second; the sum of the number of bytes of uncompressed data (never compressed) and compressed data.
DRA Outbound Bytes Compressed (Between Sites, After Compression)/sec	Compressed size (in bytes) of outbound compressed replication data (size after compression, from DSAs at other sites).
DRA Outbound Bytes Compressed (Between Sites, Before Compression)/sec	Uncompressed size (in bytes) of compressed replication data outbound to DSAs at other sites (per second).

Table 10-5.   AD Replication Outbound Byte Counters

Counter	Description
DRA Outbound Bytes Not Compressed (Within Site)/sec	Uncompressed size (in bytes) of outbound replication data that was not compressed (size per second, outbound to DSAs at the same site).
DRA Outbound Bytes Total/sec	Total number of bytes sent per second; the sum of the number of bytes of uncompressed data (never compressed) and compressed data.

Table 10-5.   AD Replication Outbound Byte Counters *(continued)*

NOTE: If the domain controller is not a bridgehead server, then the number of outbound bytes between sites should be zero.

The outbound object counters in Table 10-6 show the number of objects that the domain controller is sending to its replication partners. Since they are just being sent and not processed, there are not as many counters as for inbound objects.

The counter in Table 10-7 is useful for monitoring what the server is replicating to its partners. If this value drops over a period of time

Counter	Description
DRA Outbound Objects Filtered/sec	Number of objects (per second) acknowledged by outbound replication partners that required no updates. This counter includes objects that the outbound partner did not already have.
DRA Outbound Objects/sec	Number of objects sent (per second) through outbound replication to replication partners.

Table 10-6.   AD Replication Outbound Object Counters

Counter	Description
DRA Outbound Properties/sec	Number of properties per second being sent to replication partners.

Table 10-7.   AD Replication Outbound Property Counter

or remains at zero throughout a replication cycle, it indicates a potential problem.

Similar to the inbound counters, outbound value counters measure the rate at which the object attribute values are being changed or replicated by the domain controller. Each replicated object has at least one property, but each property may have zero or more values.

Distinguished names (DNs), including groups and distribution lists, can have very large values sets. These collections of objects require more effort on the part of the destination domain controller to apply to the Active Directory database than regular values, as they may include significantly larger numbers of values per property and thus a larger number of changes. Hence, there is a specific counter, DRA Outbound Values (DNs only)/sec, to measure this replication traffic.

Table 10-8 lists the outbound value counters.

Counter	Description
DRA Outbound Values Total/sec	Total number of values of object properties sent (per second) to replication partners.
DRA Outbound Values (DNs only)/sec	Number of values of object properties sent (per second) to replication partners in which the values are for object properties that belong to distinguished names.

Table 10-8.   AD Replication Outbound Value Counters

Replication Status

The replication status counters measure requests being made both to and by the domain controller for replication. If the Pending Replication counter is high, the server is not processing requests made by other controllers in a timely manner.

The requests for synchronization, both the total requests made and the total completed successfully, show the number of requests the server has initiated for replication from its partners. The ratio of requests successfully completed to requests made indicates the number of requests being lost, due to either transport failures or server problems on the replication partners.

Table 10-9 lists the replication status counters.

AD Replication Traffic

Another useful way to monitor replication traffic is to use a protocol analyzer such as Network Monitor to capture the packets. This has the advantage of capturing very detailed information, but has the disadvantage of being difficult to decipher because of the level of detail.

Counter	Description
DRA Pending Replication Synchronizations	Number of directory synchronizations queued for this server that are not yet processed.
DRA Sync Requests Made Successful	Number of synchronization requests made to replication partners since the computer was last restarted that were successfully returned.
DRA Sync Requests Made	Number of synchronization requests made to replication partners since the computer was last restarted.

Table 10-9. AD Replication Status Counters

Another problem is that the port used for RPC replication is dynamically assigned at Active Directory startup and is likely to be different for each domain controller. This makes monitoring the traffic difficult. To make monitoring easier, administrators can configure the servers to statically assign the port. The Registry key is HKEY_LOCAL_ MACHINE\SYSTEM\CurrentControlSet\Services\NTDS\Parameters, and the key is TCP/IP Port; the value can be set to any available TCP/IP port value, such as 1349 decimal. Administrators can then configure the protocol analyzer to monitor any traffic to and from the port that was statically assigned. To be effective, this setting needs to be applied to all domain controllers that are to be monitored.

After the port is set to a static value, it is easy to monitor and capture replication traffic between Active Directory domain controllers.

DNS Counters

A number of counters are available for monitoring all aspects of DNS server replication performance, also known as zone transfer performance, to help tune it. Some of the things to look for when tuning include the proportion of zone transfers that are incremental (saving bandwidth) versus full (wasting bandwidth).

The DNS zone transfer, or replication, performance counters really measure legacy DNS replication performance. If the environment is fully Active Directory integrated, then these counters will be zero. If there are legacy DNS servers, such as UNIX or Windows NT DNS, then there will be zone transfer traffic. This could also be the case if one or more of the Windows 2000 DNS servers is configured incorrectly with a secondary or non–Active Directory–integrated zone in what is supposed to be a fully Active Directory–integrated environment.

Full Zone Transfer (AXFR) Counters

The AXFR counters (see Table 10-10) measure full zone transfer activities: both requests and successful transfers. Full transfers occur between older versions of Berkeley Internet Name Domain (BIND) DNS (4.9.3 and lower) and Windows NT DNS. Full transfers also occur on the initial transfer to servers that do support incremental zone transfers but need initially to populate the zone files.

Counter	Description
AXFR Request Received	Total number of full zone transfer requests received by the DNS Server service when operating as a master server for a zone.
AXFR Request Sent	Total number of full zone transfer requests sent by the DNS Server service when operating as a secondary server for a zone.
AXFR Response Received	Total number of full zone transfer requests received by the DNS Server service when operating as a secondary server for a zone.
AXFR Success Received	Total number of full zone transfers received by the DNS Server service when operating as a secondary server for a zone.
AXFR Success Sent	Total number of full zone transfers successfully sent by the DNS Server service when operating as a master server for a zone.

Table 10-10. DNS Full Zone Transfer Counters

These counters are useful to measure for comparison to the incremental zone transfer counters, discussed in the next section.

Incremental Zone Transfer (IXFR) Counters

The IXFR counters (see Table 10-11) measure full zone transfer activities: both requests and successful transfers. Incremental transfers occur between newer versions of BIND DNS (above 4.9.3) and Windows 2000 DNS. Full transfers also occur on the initial transfer to servers that do support incremental zone transfers but

Counter	Description
IXFR Request Received	Total number of incremental zone transfer requests received by the master DNS server.
IXFR Request Sent	Total number of incremental zone transfer requests sent by the secondary DNS server.
IXFR Response Received	Total number of incremental zone transfer responses received by the secondary DNS server.
IXFR Success Received	Total number of successful incremental zone transfers received by the secondary DNS server.
IXFR Success Sent	Total number of successful incremental zone transfers sent by the master DNS server.

Table 10-11. DNS Incremental Zone Transfer Counters

need initially to populate the zone files. After that, the transfers will all be incremental IXFR transfers.

These counters are useful to measure for comparison to the full zone transfers discussed in the preceding section. If there are a high number of AXFR transfers, consider shifting to Windows 2000 DNS or newer BIND versions to improve performance.

Notification Counters

Notifications are sent by master DNS servers when changes are made to the zone files, essentially letting secondary servers know that they need to perform replication. Microsoft Windows 2000 DNS can operate as both a master and a secondary server; notification counters (see Table 10-12) show how many notifications have been sent as a master server and how many have been received as a secondary server.

Counter	Description
Notify Received	Total number of notifications received by the secondary DNS server.
Notify Sent	Total number of notifications sent by the master DNS server.

Table 10-12. DNS Notification Counters

Summary Zone Transfer Counters

The summary zone transfer counters (see Table 10-13) summarize the overall transfers and requests: both those sent and those received by the DNS server. They are helpful in measuring the overall DNS replication traffic.

Counter	Description
Zone Transfer Failure	Total number of failed zone transfers of the master DNS server.
Zone Transfer Request Received	Total number of zone transfer requests received by the master DNS server.
Zone Transfer SOA Request Sent	Total number of zone transfer SOA requests sent by the secondary DNS server.
Zone Transfer Success	Total number of successful zone transfers of the master DNS server.

Table 10-13. Summary Zone Transfer Counters

ACTIVE DIRECTORY REPLICATION TUNING

When looking at how to boost the performance of Active Directory replication, it is important to understand what Active Directory is being tuned to do. Is the directory being tuned to replicate quickly? Is it being tuned to conserve bandwidth? Is it being tuned both to replicate quickly and to conserve bandwidth?

For example, a large centrally managed enterprise might create new user accounts centrally. However, subsidiaries in other sites need to have employees log on as soon as possible after the accounts are created and are complaining that too much time elapses before these new users can log on. This type of environment would be tuning for fast replication.

Or suppose that the links within a corporate WAN are relatively slow and need to be reserved during the day for high-priority mainframe traffic. The Windows 2000 IT management is decentralized, with each location in the organization locally managed and in charge of its local accounts. Mainframe operators are complaining that Active Directory replication is using up the WAN bandwidth and stalling the mainframe operations during the day. This situation would call for tuning for bandwidth conservation, both by scheduling replication time and by reducing the frequency of replication.

When tuning and evaluating tuning techniques, it is important to keep in mind what is needed, where it is needed, and when it is needed. Not all organizations have the same needs, as shown by the preceding examples. In the first example, the view of the corporate directory is enterprisewide, and the timeframe is short. In the second example, the view of the corporate directory is local, and the timeframe is relatively longer.

Replication Process

Active Directory replication differs fundamentally between sites (intersite replication) and within sites (intrasite replication). This difference in replication is designed to optimize the quality of the connectivity and the nature of the access.

Intrasite Replication

Replication within a site is designed to propagate changes quickly. It assumes the high speed and reliability of a LAN infrastructure. This level of connectivity allows immediate data transfers with little cost penalty. When a change is applied to the database of a specific domain controller, the replication process is triggered. The replication process waits a default 5-minute interval and then notifies the first replication partner. After that initial notification, an additional replication partner is notified by default every 30 seconds until all have been notified.

Generation of the topology within a site is achieved by using the minimum number of connections possible, while maintaining a maximum delay within the site. The replication topology in a site is a bi-directional ring, with sufficient additional connections added to keep the number of hops between replication partners to three or less. The maximum propagation delay within a site is the maximum number of hops between a source and destination domain controller times the delay at each domain controller. By default, the maximum number of hops is three and the delay is 5 minutes, for a maximum propagation delay of 15 minutes between any two domain controllers within a site. Figure 10-9 shows an example of a simple ring and of a complex ring. Notice the extra cross-connection in the complex ring, which serves to keep the maximum number of hops within the ring to less than three.

Rather than following scheduled replication intervals, replication between domain controllers within a site is triggered by update messages. This reduces replication latency within a site, allowing changes to be replicated as soon as they are made. Even though replication messages are more frequent within sites, the replication

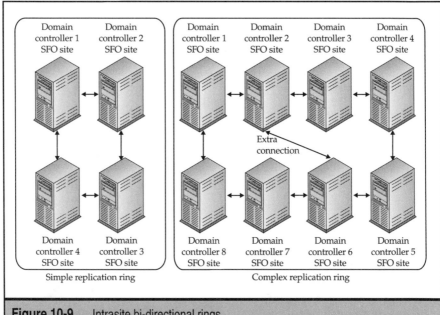

Figure 10-9.   Intrasite bi-directional rings

messages between domain controllers within a site are uncompressed.
While this increases the volume of the traffic, it results in fewer CPU
cycles spent compressing and decompressing the messages. The
trade-off of inexpensive LAN bandwidth resources for domain
controller processing resources works very effectively within sites.

There are certain Active Directory events that trigger notifications.
The notification triggers are as follows:

▼ Add Object

■ Modify Attribute

■ Move Object

▲ Delete Object

The intrasite replication can be tuned by adjusting both the initial
replication delay and the delay between subsequent replications. The

appropriate Registry entries are in HKEY_LOCAL_MACHINE\ SYSTEM\CurrentControlSet\Services\NTDS\Parameters; the keys and default values are listed here.

Registry Key	Description
Replicator notify pause after modify (secs)	This controls the delay in sending an update notification to the first replication partner. Default: 300 seconds (5 minutes).
Replicator notify pause between DSAs (secs)	This controls the delay in sending update notifications to additional replication partners. Default: 30 seconds.

The default values normally are sufficient, but they could be tuned for special circumstances. For example, if Active Directory is supporting an application that needs to have all updates distributed within any given site in less than 15 minutes, then Replicator notify pause after modify (secs) might be set to 60 seconds to force replication to propagate throughout the site in 3 minutes. This setting is based on the maximum three hops between any pair of domain controllers multiplied by the 1-minute delay.

Although not advisable, it is possible to eliminate the creation of the extra optimization connections that keep the maximum number of hops to three or less. To disable the extra connection generation for site SFO in the domain companyabc.com, use the ADSI Edit tool from the support tools and follow these instructions:

1. Launch ADSI Edit.

2. Expand the Configuration container.

3. Expand the CN=Configuration,CN=comapanyabc, CN=com container.

4. Expand the CN=Sites container.

5. Select the CN=SFO container.

6. In the right window pane, select the CN=NTDS Site Settings object.

7. Right-click and select Properties.

8. In the Select a Property to View box, select Options.

9. Enter **4** in the Edit Attribute box to disable intersite KCC topology generation and click the Set button.

10. Click OK.

The attribute is a binary value—for example, 4 decimal is 00100 binary. If the attribute has a value already, then the value should be added to that existing value.

Intersite Replication

Replication between sites is designed to conserve and control expensive WAN bandwidth between sites. To accomplish this, replication between sites is scheduled and balanced to keep costs to a minimum. The cost is determined by several factors, which are covered later in this chapter in "Link Cost." When changes are made in one site, they are stored and forwarded on a scheduled basis along the least-cost route to connected sites. The default schedule for replication between sites is every 180 minutes, or 3 hours.

Replication messages between domain controllers in different sites are compressed, which reduces the load on the WAN. The compression ratio is typically 10:1, in effect reducing the replication message traffic to 10 percent of what it would be uncompressed.

At a high level, the intersite replication can be tuned by adjusting the cost, replication frequency, and schedule using the AD Sites and Services tool. This is shown in Figure 10-10, with the default values for cost, replication interval, and schedule.

However, there are a number of ways to fine-tune the replication behavior and boost performance for intersite replication. The balance of this section explores these.

Tuning Sites, Links, and Bridges

Sites, site links, and bridges are the nuts and bolts of intersite replication tuning. To boost Active Directory replication performance, these components will need to be adjusted.

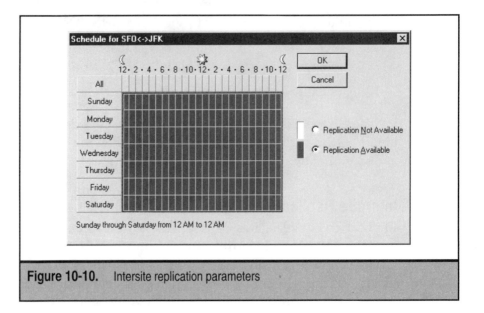

Figure 10-10. Intersite replication parameters

Sites and Tuning

Sites are used to control replication behavior between domain controllers, with the idea that bandwidth is cheap within a site (LAN) and expensive between sites (WAN). The KCC uses sites to determine how to generate connections, creating fewer connections between sites and relying more on bridgehead servers to then replicate the traffic within their respective sites. Replication traffic within sites is uncompressed to reduce the CPU overhead of updates, but it is compressed between sites to reduce the bandwidth requirements on the WAN links. Last, replication is triggered by updates within sites to propagate changes as quickly as possible, but it is scheduled between sites to control WAN bandwidth use.

A site assumes that connectivity within the site is good, which may vary for different organizations. The absolute minimum established by Microsoft is 128K available bandwidth on a 256K physical connection. A better working recommendation would be a T1 physical connection with at least 50 percent availability.

Table 10-14 shows a list of common site connectivity and the possibility of making it a site, which is useful for evaluating site candidates.

Link Type	Speed	Estimated Available Bandwidth	Site Candidate?
Frame Relay	56 Kbps	100%	No
Frame Relay	265 Kbps	50%	Possibly
Frame Relay	512 Kbps	50%	Possibly
Frame Relay	T1 (1.5 Mbps)	50%	Yes
Leased Line	T1 (1.5 Mbps)	50%	Yes
Ethernet 10BaseT	10 Mbps	30%	Yes
ATM	45 Mbps	50%	Yes
Ethernet 100BaseT	100 Mbps	30%	Yes

Table 10-14. Site Connectivity Evaluation

In most environments, determining the link type and speed is a relatively straightforward process. However, it is in almost all cases difficult and time consuming to gather available bandwidth statistics. Frequently the result is that during the design phase of a project, this information is estimated. After deployment, gathering these statistics is an excellent area for performance tuning. Administrators can measure the available bandwidth within sites that are having replication performance problems and, using the preceding table, adjust site boundaries to improve replication performance. The net result would be improved replication within the adjusted sites and better link performance between the sites.

Site Links and Performance

The standard level of performance tuning takes place at the site link level, using the AD Sites and Services tool. This tuning takes place on the site links that connect sites.

If there is more than one site in the Active Directory architecture, then there must be at least one site link connecting each of the sites for replication to occur. A site link specifies a group of sites that can communicate using the same costs, schedule, and replication period, which the KCC uses to create the detailed replication topology for connections. These site links provide the conduit for connections, which perform the actual replication. The site links dictate the replication schedule that their connections use by default.

Adjusting the link cost, replication period, and schedule will affect the performance of all connections that the KCC creates under the link. Adjusting the values in the site link object will propagate those changes to all the connections in the next KCC topology generation, typically every 15 minutes. To help you better understand the effects of changing the cost, replication period, or schedule, each of these parameters is discussed separately in the sections that follow.

Link Cost   Assigning cost values to site links allows administrators to give preference to some network connections over other network connections. The basis for the preference could be monetary costs, bandwidth, speed, latency, politics, or any other factor or set of factors. The Cost setting on a site link provides a relative value for the cost of communication between all sites that are part of the link. This cost is relative to the rest of the topology, rather than to an arbitrary fixed standard. Table 10-15 lists sample costs for some typical network connections.

The KCC uses the site links costs to compute the least-cost path from each site to every other site. The KCC then computes the spanning tree of the least-cost path. The spanning tree is used to create the connection objects.

Network Connection	Cost
T1 to backbone	10
Frame relay 128 Kbps CIR/256 Kbps port	100
56 Kbps AND	500
ISDN 128 Kbps dialup link	1000
Internet VPN	5000

Table 10-15.   Sample WAN Link Costs

One of the methods for fine-tuning Active Directory performance is to ensure that the cost values accurately reflect the actual network connections and their performance characteristics. This will give the KCC the best chance of generating an accurate detailed replication topology. That said, administrators can boost the performance of Active Directory replication where needed by reducing the costs of key links that support high-priority sites that need directory information first. Alternatively, costs for low-priority sites can be raised to allow the rest of the organization to get updates first.

Replication Period   For each site link object, there is a replication period that determines how often replication occurs over the site link during the time that the schedule allows (see the next section, "Schedule"). The default replication period is 180 minutes, or 3 hours. For example, if the link schedule allows replication between 12 A.M. and 6 A.M., and the replication period is set for 60 minutes, replication can occur up to six times during the scheduled time.

This is one of the values most commonly adjusted to tune performance. If left at the default, there could be up to a 3-hour delay in replicating changes between directly connected sites. To put that in perspective, if a user account were created at a central office, that user might not be able to log on at a remote office for 3 hours. Many installations adjust the replication period to 1 hour. To achieve even faster propagation of changes between sites, this can be reduced to its lowest value: 15 minutes.

Intersite replication is scheduled between sites, but administrators can configure a change notification trigger. If the absolute fastest propagation time is needed, see the upcoming "Change Notification" section. It describes a method of tuning intersite replication to achieve the same level of performance as exhibited within sites.

Schedule   Whereas the replication period specifies how often replication occurs, the schedule determines when replication is allowed over a link. This setting is very useful for restricting replication to times when a link is less utilized, such as in the evenings. It can also be used to carve out a space for other traffic.

For example, suppose that an organization has an 11 P.M. payroll batch process that transfers data to the central office, which uses the entire network connection bandwidth for 4 hours and absolutely has to get through. The Active Directory administrator could configure the site link schedule so that replication was not available during the 11 P.M. to 3 A.M. window of time, as is shown in Figure 10-11.

Change Notification   Normally, replication between sites occurs on a scheduled basis. The default frequency is 3 hours, but replication can be scheduled as often as every 15 minutes. This is sufficient in most cases, but for some applications changes need to be propagated immediately. Updates can be replicated immediately using change notification.

Change notification is configured on each site link object using the ADSI Edit tool from the support tools. This gives replication between sites the same immediacy as intrasite replication. It also increases bandwidth utilization, as there will be more frequent updates and additional change notification traffic across WAN network connections. To enable change notification between sites, do the following:

1. Launch ADSI Edit.

2. Expand the Configuration container.

3. Expand the CN=Sites container.

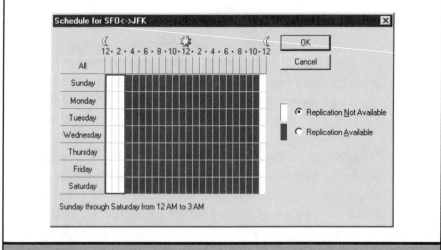

Figure 10-11.   Sample site link schedule

4. Expand the CN=Inter-Site Transports container.

5. Select CN=IP.

6. Highlight the site link object and select Properties.

7. In the Select a Property to View box, select Options.

8. Add 1 to the number in the Value(s) box and enter the result in the Edit Attribute box. This is a binary flag (0001), so verify that the existing value is even prior to changing the value.

9. Click OK.

Site Link Bridges

Site links with the same IP transport that share sites are bridged by site link bridges, which enable the KCC to treat the set of site links as a single route. In a fully routed IP network, this is normally the simplest method of configuration, allowing the KCC to establish connections where needed. The advantage to bridging all site links is that the network description is simpler and easier to maintain, as a site link is not needed to describe every path between pairs of sites.

However, if the network is not fully routed or there are a large number of sites, then the KCC will not be able to optimize the connection, generating excessive slowdowns and possibly even resulting in disconnected sites.

If the default setting to bridge all site links is enabled, the KCC will assume that it can set up connections between all domain controllers in all sites that are bridged: that is, that all sites can be reached directly through the IP transport. This is the most common configuration, in which you can use an ICMP ping to reach any host within the network from any other host within the network. If the network is not fully routed, then deactivate the Bridge All Site Links option on the General tab of the IP transport object property page or SMTP transport object property page. After you do this, you will need to create specific site link bridges to link sites that are not directly connected by site links.

For large networks, even fully routed ones, the default site link bridges may still cause difficulties. When the number of sites and domains reaches a certain number, high CPU utilization will occur whenever the KCC generates the topology (every 15 minutes by default). The default setting creates a single bridge for the entire network, which generates more routes that must be processed than if site link bridges are not used or are applied selectively. As the complexity increases (as the number of sites and domains grow), the processing time increases as well.

Ways to boost performance for large and complex environments is discussed in the upcoming "Tuning for Large Topologies" section.

Topology Generation

The intersite topology (sites and site links) is created by default when sites are created, but it is not generated automatically. The KCC evaluates the replication topology at 15-minute intervals and automatically generates the detailed replication topology (connections).

The KCC runs the first replication topology generation five minutes after the domain controller starts. This gives all of the other services time to start and ensures that full network connectivity is established. This interval can be modified using a Registry editor by changing the REPL TOPOLOGY UPDATE DELAY (SECS) key in HKEY_LOCAL_MACHINE\SYSTEM\CurrentControlSet\Services\ NTDS\Parameters. The time is given in seconds and specifies the wait time before the KCC runs; the default delay is 300 seconds.

After the initial topology generation, the KCC generates the topology every 15 minutes. This interval can be adjusted using a Registry editor by changing the REPL TOPOLOGY UPDATE PERIOD key in HKEY_LOCAL_MACHINE\SYSTEM\CurrentControlSet\Services\ NTDS\Parameters. Again, the time is given in seconds and specifies the time between KCC operations; the default interval is 900 seconds.

Tuning for Large Topologies

The KCC periodically adjusts the replication topology to remain fully connected when domain controllers are added to or removed from the network, when domain controllers are unavailable, and when the replication schedule changes. This process of checking the replication topology can tie up processing and memory resources in large topologies. Large topologies are those containing a combination of many sites, many domains, or many routes betweens sites.

This section examines the techniques for tuning to accommodate these large topologies.

Tuning KCC Processing Time

The KCC processing time is driven largely by the size of the topology. As the size and complexity of the topology increases, so does the number of possible connections. When the KCC is calculating the number of connections and creating the spanning tree, it can consume extensive amounts of processing time. For large organizations, this can slow down the domain controller for minutes or even hours at a time.

Large or complex topologies can be defined approximately by the following formula:

$$(1 + D) * S^2 > 100,000$$

In this formula, D is the number of domains in the forest, and S is the number of sites in the forest. If the 100,000 threshold is exceeded, special steps will almost certainly be required to handle the topology. This formula is graphed for some key values in Figure 10-12.

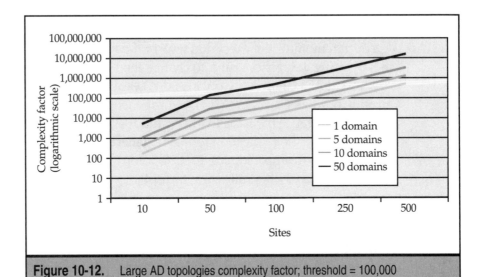

Figure 10-12.   Large AD topologies complexity factor; threshold = 100,000

As can be seen in the figure, even with a single domain, the complexity factor threshold is exceeded when there are over 250 sites. With 10 domains, the threshold is exceeded when there are over 100 sites. Since the processing time is proportional to the complexity factor, the large complexity factors seen in the graph for organizations with more than 250 sites will generate correspondingly long KCC processing times. It is important to note that the complexity factor scale is logarithmic and grows quite rapidly.

Checking the processing time needed by the KCC topology generation process in the current configuration is the first step. A manual check can be conducted by using the Active Directory Sites and Services tool:

1. Determine which domain controller in the site is the current intersite topology generator by viewing the properties of the NTDS Site Settings object in the site container.

2. Select the domain controller indicated.

3. Right-click NTDS Settings for the domain controller.

4. Select All Tasks and click Check Replication Topology.

5. Time the execution of the KCC on that domain controller, which is the time until the pop-up message "Active Directory has checked the replication topology" appears.

You can monitor the execution time of the KCC on an ongoing basis by using a Registry editor to change the 1 KNOWLEDGE CONSISTENCY CHECKER key in HKEY_LOCAL_MACHINE\SYSTEM\ CurrentControlSet\Services\NTDS\Diagnostics. Setting the value to 3 or higher will cause the KCC to log events 1009 and 1013 when starting and completing the replication topology generation process.

Generally, the approximate KCC topology processing time P in minutes is given by the following formula:

$$P = ((1 + D) * S^2) * 0.0000075 \text{ minutes}$$

In the formula, D is the number of domains in the forest, and S is the number of sites in the forest. This assumes a standard hub-and-spoke topology, with a central office and multiple remote offices

configured as separate sites. The measurements were tested by
Microsoft on an Intel Pentium III Xeon at 500 MHz with 1GB of RAM.

The formula is plotted in Figure 10-13 for domains ranging from 1
to 50 and sites ranging from 10 to 500. This is a broad sampling that
most organizations will fall within and reaches the edges of the
performance envelope for KCC processing times.

As can be seen in the figure, the KCC processing times start to
approach 10 minutes for 250 sites even for very few domains. With
large numbers of domains such as 50, the time exceeds 20 minutes
for 250 sites. Since the frequency of KCC topology generation is 15
minutes, the KCC would not have time to complete a full topology
generation before starting a new one. As a rule, the time needed to
perform topology generation processing should be significantly less
than the frequency of the generation.

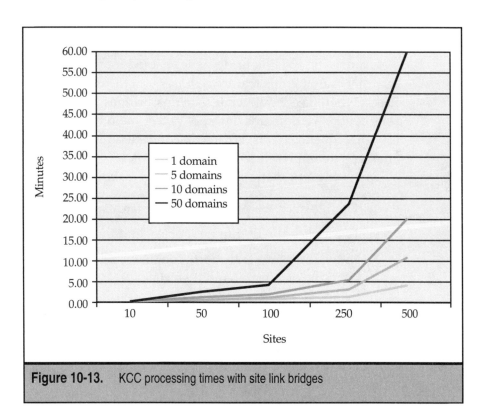

Figure 10-13.   KCC processing times with site link bridges

If the Active Directory topology has a large complexity factor and KCC processing time is high, then administrators have three main options:

▼ Reduce the number of site link bridges

■ Run processing at night

▲ Perform processing manually

Reducing the Number of Site Link Bridges

To reduce the number of site link bridges, disable automatic site link bridging and manually create any required site link bridges. This solution is well suited to hub-and-spoke configurations, as there will be few site link bridges to administer.

Automatic site link bridging indicates that the entire network is fully Internet protocol (IP) routed. In this situation, any computer at a given site can communicate over IP with any computer at any other site. Automatic site link bridging is enabled for all site transports by default. Disabling this feature requires you to add site link bridge objects where needed. Luckily, site link bridges are necessary only if a site contains a domain controller of a domain that is not present in any adjacent site: that is, is directly connected by a site link. Most situations do not require the use of site link bridges.

To disable automatic site link bridging, follow these steps:

1. Double-click the Active Directory Sites and Services snap-in.

2. Right-click the IP transport object and then select Properties.

3. In the Inter-Site Transports container, select the appropriate check box to clear it and then click OK.

If KCC is unable to connect all the sites containing domain controllers of a domain after automatic site link bridging is disabled, the KCC will log event 1311. If this event is logged, verify that the domain controller in question is functioning properly and that the appropriate site bridges are configured.

However, there still may be problems with the automatic generation of the topology even after you have reduced the number of or eliminated site link bridges. As the Active Directory topology complexity increases through the addition of sites or domains, the KCC processing time will continue to increase, albeit more slowly. The next section discusses how to work around this problem.

Running During Off-Peak Hours

Even with site link bridges eliminated, the automatic topology generation process run by the KCC has to perform more processing in direct proportion to the number of domains and sites. While no longer exponential, the processing time still is proportional. Assuming a standard hub-and-spoke topology, with a central office and multiple remote offices configured as separate sites, the amount of time needed depends on the location of the KCC. The processing time for the central office, with more links coming into it, is significantly higher than for remote offices, with fewer links coming into them.

For remote offices, the approximate KCC topology processing time P in minutes is given by the following formula:

$$P = (1 + D) * S * 0.0006$$

In the formula, D is the number of domains in the forest, and S is the number of sites in the forest. The measurements were tested by Microsoft on an Intel Pentium III Xeon at 500 MHz with 1GB of RAM. The formula is plotted in Figure 10-14 for domains ranging from 1 to 50 and sites ranging from 10 to 500.

The processing times shown in the figure clearly indicate that, even for large installations, there is no problem with the KCC processing times. For example, even at the upper end of the range, with 250 sites and 50 domains, the KCC processing time is only about 7.5 minutes. The bottom line is that eliminating the site link bridges is sufficient to reduce the KCC processing time at remote office domain controllers to a manageable level.

For a central office, the picture is a little different. For central offices, the approximate KCC topology processing time P in minutes is given by the following formula:

$$P = (1 + D) * S * 0.0015$$

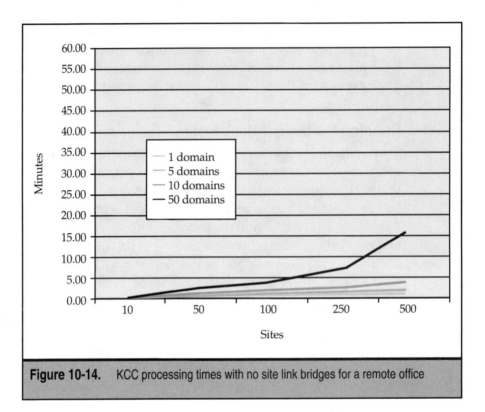

Figure 10-14.   KCC processing times with no site link bridges for a remote office

This formula is plotted in Figure 10-15 for domains ranging from 1 to 50 and sites ranging from 10 to 500.

For small to medium-sized installations, with 10 domains, KCC processing time is less than 5 minutes per topology generation. For larger installations, with 50 domains or more, even 100 sites puts the KCC processing time at 7.5 minutes, and 250 sites puts the KCC processing time at over 20 minutes.

Given the increase, a solution is to run the KCC only during off-peak hours. This is accomplished by disabling automatic intersite topology generation and scheduling a script to run the process during off-peak hours. This assumes that the domain controller will have off-peak windows of time that are larger than the KCC processing time. Use this approach after disabling site link bridging if you find that processing time is still an issue during peak hours.

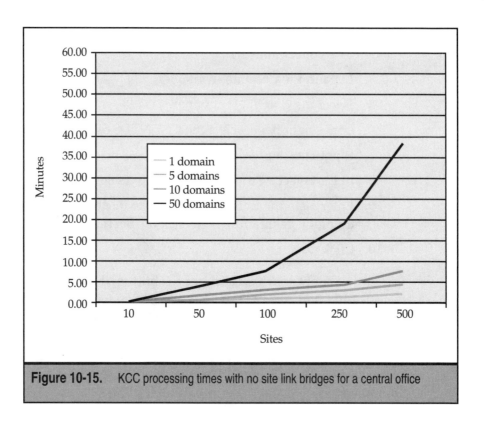

Figure 10-15.   KCC processing times with no site link bridges for a central office

Even though the intersite topology generation process is disabled and run manually, the KCC will continue to perform intrasite topology generation. This is important to note, because while the automatic processing is disabled, the replication topology will not heal itself by automatically regenerating the topology. This lack of self-healing can result in delays or breaks in the replication. The resulting inconsistencies can be tolerated to some degree between sites, but they will cause difficulties within sites.

To disable automatic KCC topology generation for site SFO in domain companyabc.com, use the ADSI Edit tool from the support tools and follow these instructions:

1.   Launch ADSI Edit.

2.   Expand the Configuration container.

3. Expand the CN=Configuration,CN=comapanyabc, CN=com container.

4. Expand the CN=Sites container.

5. Select the CN=SFO container.

6. In the right pane, select the CN=NTDS Site Settings object.

7. Right-click and select Properties.

8. In the Select a Property to View box, select Options.

9. Enter **16** in the Edit Attribute box to disable intersite KCC topology generation; then click the Set button.

10. Click OK.

Immediately after you click the Set button, the change will take effect, and intersite KCC topology generation will be disabled. This setting can be verified by using the AD Replication Monitor tool and generating a report for the site. This will display the site options, in addition to quite a bit of other information. The following listing contains just the information comparing the site options for the modified SFO site and the unmodified NRT site.

```
Site Name:  SFO
----------------------------------------
Site Options          :
NTDSSETTINGS_OPT_IS_INTER_SITE_AUTO_TOPOLOGY_DISABLED
Site Topology Generator: CN=NTDS Settings,CN=SERVER-SFO-
01,CN=Servers,CN=SFO,CN=Sites,CN=Configuration,DC=companyabc,DC=com
Site Topology Renewal  :
Site Topology Failover :


Site Name:  NRT
----------------------------------------
Site Options          :
Site Topology Generator: CN=NTDS Settings,
     CN=SERVER-NRT-01,CN=Servers,CN=NRT,CN=Sites,CN=Configuration,
     DC=companyabc,DC=com
Site Topology Renewal  :
Site Topology Failover :
```

While the KCC could be run manually by changing the value of the NTDS Site Setting attribute to allow the KCC to run and then waiting for the KCC to finish processing, this approach would be tedious to administer on a regular basis. Luckily, Windows 2000 and Active Directory have a much better solution in the ADSI API and Visual Basic scripting. To run the KCC intersite topology generation semiautomatically, use this generate-topology.vbs script:

```
'Manual Inter-Site Topology Generator Script
'     This script runs the Knowledge Consistency Checker (KCC)
'     Inter-Site Topology Generation (ISTG) process manually. It
'     can be scheduled using the Windows 2000 Task Scheduler.
'
'Assumes:
'     1. Script runs on Domain Controller
'     2. Inter-Site Topology Generation is Disabled for Site
'     3. Script runs using proper authority
'     4. Windows 2000 Support Tools Installed

'Setup
Set dll = CreateObject("iadstools.DCFunctions")
dll.enabledebuglogging 1
Set domainController = GetObject("LDAP://localhost/rootdse")
domainControllerName = domainController.Get("dnsHostName")
namingContext = domainController.Get("configurationNamingContext")
DCSite = dll.dsgetsitename
DSAObject = domainController.Get("dsServiceName")
siteContainer = "LDAP://localhost/CN=NTDS Site Settings,CN=" +
    DCSite + ",CN=Sites," + namingContext
Set siteSet = GetObject(siteContainer)
siteSet.Put "interSiteTopologyGenerator", DSAObject
siteSet.SetInfo

'Get Old settings
oldSetting = siteSet.Get("options")
If Hex(Err.Number) = "8000500D" Then
oldSetting = 0
End If

'Enable Inter-site Topology Generation
If oldSetting And 16 Then
```

```
newSetting = oldSetting Xor 16
siteSet.Put "options", newSetting
siteSet.SetInfo
End If

'Run KCC ISTG process
result = dll.TriggerKCC(CStr(domainControllerName))

'Restore Old Settings
SiteSet.Put "options", oldSetting
SiteSet.SetInfo

'End
```

The script executes the following five tasks:

▼ **Perform Setup**   Loads libraries needed and gathers naming context information for the domain controller.

■ **Get Old Settings**   Gathers the existing values of the NTDS options so they can be restored after topology generation.

■ **Enable Intersite Topology Generation**   Sets the hosting domain controller so it is the intersite topology generator and configures the site to allow intersite topology generation.

■ **Run KCC ISTG Process**   Runs the KCC to generate the topology.

▲ **Restore Old Settings**   Restores the old settings following topology generation.

Check the Directory Service event logs for events 1009 and 1013, which indicate the start and end of replication topology checking. For these events to be generated, the diagnostic logging for the KCC must be set to 3 or higher, as discussed earlier in this section. To see detailed events to ensure that intersite topology is being checked, temporarily set the logging value to 4 or higher.

To run this script on a regular basis, such as in the evenings, use the Windows 2000 Task Scheduler. Schedule the process to run during off-peak times when there is a big enough window of processing time to complete the KCC process. When setting up the task, ensure that the task is running with sufficient authority to start the process. For more details on the functions used in the script, see the IADs Tools documentation in the Windows 2000 support tools (iadstools.doc).

Manually Configuring Connections

Given the increasing amount of KCC processing time needed to generate the replication topology, large organizations with high complexity factors may still reach a point where it is not possible to complete the processing of the KCC even during off-peak hours. The solution in those cases is to forego automatic generation and instead configure all connections manually.

At first blush, this might seem to be a very time-consuming endeavor. However, most organizations with very large topologies have a cookie-cutter approach to the establishment of the network topology, most likely using a hub-and-spoke based model. This makes the process of designing and manually creating the replication topology much simpler. The next section, "Connection Tuning," discusses how to tune the connections.

Connection Tuning

By default, the KCC generates all the connections needed to establish replication both within and between sites. Connections do not usually need to be optimized within sites, as KCC does an excellent job of establishing and maintaining the connections needed to form the bi-directional ring. Between sites, if the site link topology has been configured correctly, the automatically generated connections are sufficient for normal situations. One area in which the KCC does not always generate an optimal configuration is in the selection of the bridgehead server for the site. This is an area that you may want to review and adjust.

In addition, fine-tuning can be performed if you have an overall replication goal that works for most sites, but specific goals for applications or sites that have special directory needs.

Connections also will need to be configured if the KCC intersite topology generator has been disabled for performance reasons (see "Tuning for Large Topologies" earlier in this chapter), with all connections created manually. This process requires careful planning and an understanding of exactly where connections are needed.

Bridgehead Servers

Bridgehead servers are subject to heavier replication loads than nonbridgehead domain controllers. In addition, bridgehead servers are the port of entry for replication data between sites, so it is important to know which servers are performing the role when tuning and troubleshooting. Bridgehead servers must be able to accommodate more replication traffic than nonbridgehead servers, and you might want to choose which servers are to carry out this task. Knowing which system is acting as a bridgehead also can be useful for troubleshooting.

Bridgeheads are selected automatically by KCC, but it's useful to specify a bridgehead to control server loads. This can be done in the properties of a server object, using the AD Sites and Services tool. Setting a preferred bridgehead for site transport (see Figure 10-16) forces the KCC to use that server first in its bridgehead selection process. If there is more than one preferred bridgehead server, then the KCC will randomly select among them.

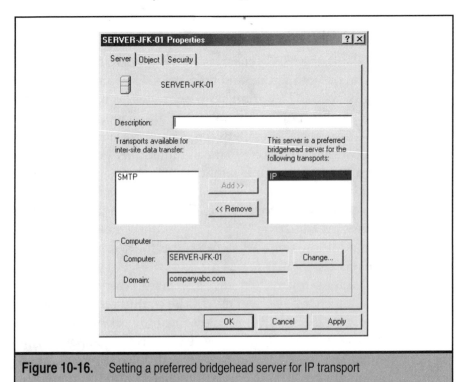

Figure 10-16.   Setting a preferred bridgehead server for IP transport

CAUTION: If none of the preferred bridgehead servers is available, the KCC will not fail over to a nonpreferred server. This behavior can result in a break in the replication topology.

Multiple bridgehead servers may be needed for any given site if a domain controller does not have all of the domain and database partitions to be replicated. These bridgehead servers will share the same site link and the associated properties of the site link, such as cost and schedule.

Connection Schedule

The default schedule for intrasite connections is once per hour, which is not a performance issue because replication is really driven by change notifications within a site. Change notification causes replication to be immediate, so tuning of the connection schedule within sites is not needed.

For intersite connection, there are definite reasons for tuning the default schedule. Each connection has a schedule that is determined by its parent site link. This schedule can be adjusted to meet specific needs. You can set a per-connection schedule that is shorter for specific purposes, such as a server's hosting of a demanding application that needs directory updates quickly. The connection schedule controls how often periodic replication runs, which can be as often as every 15 minutes. The default setting for replication between sites is once every 3 hours, which can be changed in the site link properties.

The schedule for the connections can be set differently than for the parent link. By using the AD Sites and Services tool, administrators can set a schedule of none, once per hour, twice per hour, or four times per hour. The AD Sites and Services tool confines the settings to once every 15 minutes for a specific hour or hours during the week: that is, the granularity level reflects the number of times per hour and not the specific 15-minute intervals in the hour. If a finer level of granularity is needed, it can be achieved with a better understanding of the connection object, schedule attribute, and ADSI Edit tool.

CAUTION: Since the KCC will automatically regenerate the site topology every 15 minutes by default and hence re-create the connection objects, connection schedule tuning should be performed only on manually created connections. Otherwise, schedule changes could be lost at the next intersite topology generation.

Within the connection object schedule attribute, the schedule is specified in octets for each hour of each day of the week. Each octet (four digits in binary format, or *XXXX*, where *X* is zero or one) represents the times that replication can occur within the hour at a granularity level of 15 minutes, indicated by 1 for replication and 0 for no replication. For example, the octet 0x05 represents 0101 binary and indicates that replication will take place twice per hour. More important, it indicates that replication will occur at 15 minutes and 45 minutes past the hour. The octet 0x00 (binary 0000) indicates that no replication will occur during that hour, and the octet 0x0f (binary 1111) indicates that replication will occur four times in the hour.

If needed, the connection object schedule can be edited with the ADSI Edit support tool to select the specific 15-minute intervals that are needed. For example, if the replication needs to occur during the first 30 minutes of the hour and not in the second 30 minutes, then the octet will need to be manually edited to 0x0c (binary 1100). This would have to be done for the entire list of 168 entries, as there are 24 hours in a day and 7 days in a week (24×7 = 168). To edit the entries for the combination of domain companyabc.com, site SFO, server SERVER-SFO-01, and connection SFO-NRT Connection 1, take the following steps:

1. Launch ADSI Edit.

2. Expand the Configuration container.

3. Expand the CN=Configuration,CN=comapanyabc,CN=com container.

4. Expand the CN=Sites container.

5. Expand the CN=SFO container.

6. Expand the CN=Servers container.

7. Expand the CN=SERVER-SFO-01 container.

8. Select the CN=NTDS Settings container.

9. In the right pane, select the connection object CN=SFO-NRT Connection 1.

10. Right-click and select Properties.

11. In the Select a Property to View box, select Schedule.

12. Highlight the entire dimmed Value(s) entry and copy using a right-click.

13. Paste the copied values into the Edit Attributes box.

14. Edit as needed, starting at the twenty-first octet from the left.

15. Click the Set button.

16. Click OK to exit.

NOTE: This particular task is not for the faint of heart. If necessary, copy the string into a text editor and perform a search-and-replace operation there before pasting in.

Manual Connections

While the KCC creates connections automatically, connection objects can also be created manually using the AD Sites and Services tool. Configure manual connections where needed for performance, to fine-tune the replication schedule or if the Active Directory complexity factor is too high for automatic topology generation.

Performance When manually creating connections for the replication topology, one of the most critical factors is performance. Connections should be set up to minimize the overall replication distance and thus the overall replication time. A hub-and-spoke model is one means of reducing the distance across the topology. Where the network topology does not permit this, a regionalized hub-and-spoke model with two or more hubs is also a good solution. There should be a direct connection between the hubs to make this effective. Figure 10-17 shows a regionalized hub-and-spoke design.

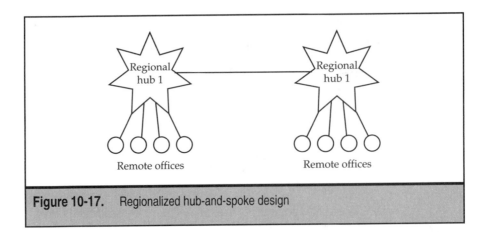

Figure 10-17.   Regionalized hub-and-spoke design

Load Balancing   In topologies with a hub-and-spoke model, it may be necessary to create manual connections to load-balance inbound replication. Bridgehead servers can replicate from only one inbound session at a time, so each spoke would be processed sequentially. In the case of a large number of remote offices, the central office bridgehead server could become a bottleneck. In that case, set up multiple bridgehead servers and configure manual connections to distribute the remote office replication load among the central bridgehead servers. This is also an opportunity to build in fault tolerance, as discussed next.

Fault Tolerance   The KCC provides fault tolerance within sites and between sites under normal circumstances. However, in large topologies, KCC intersite replication topology generation may be disabled due to excessive processing time. Since the KCC will no longer be healing the replication topology through the automatic intersite topology generation process, it is important to build in the fault tolerance capability manually. Build two connections to every site, preferably using separate pairs of domain controllers. To reduce duplicate replication traffic, schedule the connection to execute in alternate cycles. For example, if you are performing replication every 30 minutes, then have the first connection replicate twice in the first hour and then not replicate in the second hour. The second connection would be configured to not replicate in the first hour and then replicate in the second hour. A pair of alternating schedules is shown in Figure 10-18.

While helping boost performance and tune Active Directory efficiency, configuring and maintaining manual connections can result in a significant increase in the administrative overhead needed to maintain the directory services. Microsoft put extensive effort into developing the automatic processes that the KCC conducts for both intersite and intrasite topology generation. Substituting manual administration for these automated processes should be done with care and always with specific measurable performance goals in mind.

NOTE: Rather than set up all the connections from scratch, instead let the KCC run through one topology generation cycle. After that, convert the automatically created connections to manual connections. Then adjust the connections as needed to optimize them.

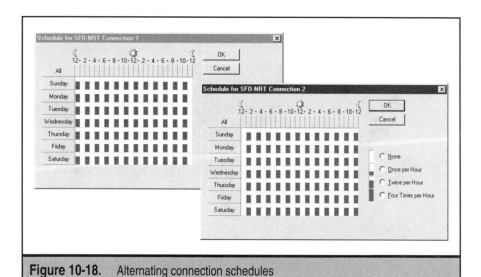

Figure 10-18. Alternating connection schedules

When Do Changes Take Effect?

When changes are made to the replication topology, they need to be replicated to the domain controllers and sites before they can take effect. The following processes occur before replication is performed:

1. Site link created (by administrator).

2. Site link object replicated to intersite topology generator (ISTG) server.

3. KCC runs on ISTG, creating new connection objects for the site.

4. New connection objects replicate to the bridgehead server.

5. KCC runs on the bridgehead server, creating replication partner connections.

6. The bridgehead servers replicates to replication partners.

Until these tasks are complete, the Active Directory infrastructure will continue to replicate using the previous configuration.

Transport Tuning

Most of the techniques for boosting performance covered in this chapter apply to the application layer. This section examines tuning techniques for the replication transport layer.

Replication Transport Protocols

Replication messages need to be encapsulated in a protocol to be sent over the network. These replication transport protocols provide the wire protocols that are required for data transfer. Windows 2000 provides three different types of connectivity for replication of Active Directory information:

RPC   The RPC transport is a high-speed uniform synchronous RPC protocol used exclusively within a site. The RPC transport assumes that there is high-performance connectivity and does not compress the messages sent between domains, which conserves server resources.

IP The IP transport, also known as the intersite RPC transport, is also RPC based, but it is a low-speed point-to-point synchronous RPC protocol used between sites. The IP transport assumes low bandwidth and compresses the replication messages to reduce bandwidth at the expense of server resources.

SMTP The SMTP transport is a low-speed, asynchronous, message-based protocol used between sites with intermittent or no direct TCP/IP connectivity. It has some limitations, which are discussed later in this section.

While the only option for intrasite replication is RCP, when establishing site links the replication transport can be chosen. The connection objects created under the site link inherit the transport of their parent when they are created automatically by the KCC intersite topology generation process. When connections are created manually, the administrator chooses the transport. The default transport for manually created connections is RPC, which, if left as the selection, is corrected on the next pass of the KCC to IP for intersite connections.

Synchronous vs. Asynchronous Communication

With the RPC-based transport protocols, all communication between domain controllers is synchronous. This means that the protocol sends a request and then waits for the response to that request. No other requests are sent until a response is received, unless the request times out. This implies that the request-response cycle must be quick; otherwise, requests will stack up. It also means that there can be only one request outstanding at any given time.

For the SMTP transport protocol, all communication between domain controllers is asynchronous. The transport protocol can have more than one request outstanding at the same time. As a result, multiple inbound SMTP connections to a directory partition replica can be active at the same time, provided that the requests are all for a different source domain controller or directory partition. This allows the connection to have multiple simultaneous requests being processed and to receive the responses whenever they arrive, which maximizes resource utilization and helps prevent bottlenecks.

Asynchronous communication can be very useful in networks with intermittently slow links, such as Internet VPN, where the system can never be sure just which links will be slow or when. The domain controller can send requests to all of its replications partners and receive fast responses where possible, rather than have a few slow links slow down the entire replication process.

Tuning with SMTP Transport

From a performance tuning perspective, there is really only one reason to choose the SMTP transport. This is to allow parallel replication sessions to be established with multiple domain controllers and partitions at the same time. Although SMTP replication usually is slower than RPC replication, the trade-off of having simultaneous sessions can boost replication performance.

While a useful tuning alternative to RPC protocols, the SMTP protocol does have limitations:

▼ The SMTP transport cannot replicate domain partitions, so sites linked via the SMTP transport must contain separate domains within the forest. The reason for this restriction is that some domain components, such as global policy, require the support of the Windows 2000 File Replication Service (FRS), which does not support SMTP for replication.

■ Encryption requires the installation and administrative overhead of an enterprise certificate authority, normally requiring Certificate Services and the purchase of a digital signature from a third party.

■ SMTP replication ignores the Replication Available and Replication Not Available settings on the site link schedule, relying instead on the SMTP gateways to determine availability.

▲ There is no change notification for SMTP-based replication.

Replication Packet Size Tuning

Active Directory sizes packets for each of the transports on the basis of both size and number of objects. The sizes are maximums and are computed by default based on the memory size of the domain controller, except if the domain controller has more than 1GB or less than 100MB of RAM. These default computations can be overridden by setting the appropriate Registry keys.

The Registry keys are not created when servers are initially promoted to domain controllers, so the keys normally will need to be created. All the keys in Table 10-16 are stored in HKEY_LOCAL_MACHINE\System\CurrentControlSet\Services\NTDS\Parameters and are of the REG_DWORD data type.

Since synchronous transport will have only one message, or packet, outstanding at any point in time, then one way to increase the throughput is to make that one message larger.

Transport	Registry Key	Minimum	Default
RPC	Replicator intra site packet size (objects)	1	Default is 1/1,000,000 of RAM, with a minimum of 100 and maximum of 1,000 objects
RPC	Replicator intra site packet size (bytes)	10KB	Default is 1/100 of RAM, with a minimum of 1MB and maximum of 10MB
IP	Replicator inter site packet size (objects)	1	Default is 1/1,000,000 of RAM, with a minimum of 100 and maximum of 1,000 objects

Table 10-16.   Transport Packet Registry Keys

Transport	Registry Key	Minimum	Default
IP	Replicator inter site packet size (bytes)	10KB	Default is 1/100 of RAM, with a minimum of 1MB and maximum of 10MB
SMTP	Replicator async inter site packet size (objects)	1	Default is 1/1,000,000 of RAM, with a minimum of 100 and maximum of 1,000 objects
SMTP	Replicator async inter site packet size (bytes)	10KB	Default 1MB.

Table 10-16. Transport Packet Registry Keys *(continued)*

For example, suppose that during the initial stages of a deployment, a remote office will be creating sites and domain controllers and replicating the large domain database of one million objects. The bridgehead servers are all PIII systems with 256MB of RAM, and network connectivity is high-speed ATM. By default, the intersite transport will have a default objects-per-packet size of 256 objects (256MB of RAM divided by 1,000,000) and will require on the order of 3,900 packets (1,000,000 objects divided by 256 objects per packet) to transmit the domain database. By tuning the Replicator Inter Site Packet Size (Objects) to its maximum value of 1,000, the total number of packets can be reduced to 1,000 (1,000,000 objects divided by 1,000 objects per packet). This would in effect increase the number of available replication slots by a factor of four.

When adjusting the packet sizes, it is important to monitor the impact on the server resources. This is especially true on multirole servers that host application services in addition to performing their duties as domain controllers.

DOMAIN NAME SERVICES REPLICATION TUNING

Active Directory requires DNS to perform properly, so it is important that DNS services be readily available and perform quickly. Windows 2000 DNS offers several benefits to boost DNS performance, including the following:

▼ Active Directory integration

■ Local DNS

▲ Fast incremental zone transfers

DNS Integration into Active Directory

From the perspective of Windows 2000, the most critical decision with regard to tuning DNS replication is whether to make the domains Active Directory integrated. For most organizations and situations, this is the best option. There are numerous benefits, and this setup is very straightforward to configure and maintain.

Benefits

With Active Directory–integrated domains, DNS stores all zone information in the Active Directory store and replicates it using the Active Directory replication system. This replication occurs along with the Active Directory replication, so there is no need to configure and administer a separate replication system for DNS. This gives Active Directory-integrated DNS domains increased fault tolerance and security, easier administration, and better performance.

Reducing the amount of administration time allows administrators to set up DNS servers at every site, which then allows clients to access DNS services locally. This improves the client response times, as well as the load on the WAN links for DNS access. Having DNS set up locally also increases the fault tolerance, as DNS service will remain operational even if WAN links fail.

In addition, Active Directory replicates on an attribute basis, replicating only incremental changes. This improves the performance over conventional DNS, where zone transfers are normally full and transmit the entire zone uncompressed each time replication is performed.

The benefits of Active Directory–integrated DNS domains are summarized in Table 10-17.

Configuration

The easiest method of configuring the load is to configure the DNS server to load the zone data from Active Directory on startup. Choose Properties for the DNS server and select the Advanced tab,

Benefit	Description
Fault tolerance	Active Directory multimaster replication provides greater fault tolerance than using standard zone transfers alone, as it does not rely on a single primary DNS server to update all the secondary servers. There are also full copies of DNS on each Active Directory server, reducing the dependence on the health of a single master server.
Security	Through secure update, all DNS domain updates are fully authorized.
Ease of administration	Servers register themselves automatically through secure dynamic updating, and there is no separate DNS domain replication architecture, as DNS is replicated via Active Directory. DNS servers can be placed at all locations, because of the low administrative overhead.
Performance	DNS replicates on an attribute level with all the benefits of Active Directory replication, rather than using flat-file full-DNS zone transfers. Since DNS servers can be at all locations, client access is local and thus faster, and traffic on WAN links is reduced.

Table 10-17. Benefits of Active Directory Integration

as shown in Figure 10-19. This setting causes the DNS server to look in Active Directory for any DNS domains and creates them on the local server automatically at startup.

The simplicity of this method of configuring the DNS makes it realistic to have a DNS server at every site and possibly on every domain controller. Normally, the barrier to setting up local DNS servers is the overhead required for administrators to manage the replication of the DNS data via zone transfers.

Active Directory–Integrated Zone Transfers

Active Directory–integrated zones fully interoperate with other DNS implementations, supporting all of the standard DNS roles such as primary and secondary servers. This is also a fully modern version of DNS, with performance improvements such as incremental zone transfers and compressed zone transfers.

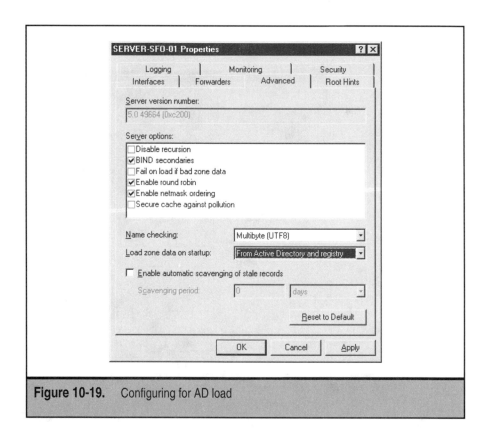

Figure 10-19.   Configuring for AD load

Even if there is an existing DNS infrastructure, converting zones to Active Directory–integrated zones will improve performance with no loss of functionality.

Active Directory–Integrated Zone Transfers

Even if domains are configured as Active Directory integrated, standard zone transfers can still be performed to legacy DNS servers. This allows full integration with existing DNS architectures and zone transfer with BIND and other DNS server implementations.

From the perspective of other secondary DNS servers requesting zone transfers, each of the Active Directory–integrated DNS servers will look like the master for the domain. As shown in Figure 10-20, the Active Directory–integrated domain is a true multimaster implementation of DNS as updates are allowed on all primary domain servers.

As a primary server for the domain, the Active Directory–integrated domain fully supports secondary domain transfers with the

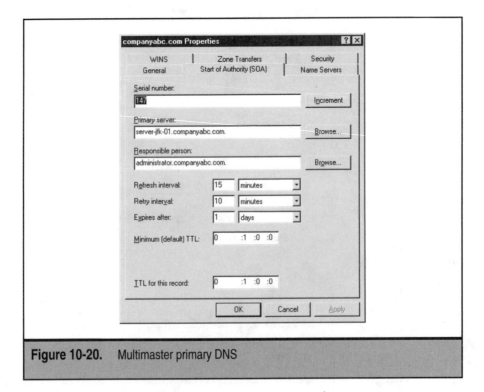

Figure 10-20. Multimaster primary DNS

notification feature. It also supports faster zone transfer features to boost performance, as discussed in the next section.

Fast Transfers

Windows 2000 DNS supports a fast transfer protocol that compresses the zone transfer data to reduce bandwidth consumption and improve performance of the transfer process, with some investment in the CPU cycle for compression. The faster transfer protocol also includes multiple records in a single transfer, which increases the packet size. This reduces the overall number of packets transferred to any given zone, which reduces the overhead usually associated with many small transfers.

Legacy DNS servers running versions of BIND 4.9.3 and below do not support the fast transfer protocol, instead transferring data uncompressed and one record at a time. Servers attempting to communicate using the fast transfer protocol with older DNS servers will receive error messages, and zone transfers will fail. To maintain compatibility with existing DNS systems, the Windows 2000 DNS has the fast zone transfer protocol disabled by default. This is accomplished by checking the BIND Secondaries box on the Advanced tab on the DNS Server Properties screen, as shown in Figure 10-21. To enable fast transfers, uncheck the BIND Secondaries box.

When performing zone transfers with other Windows 2000 DNS servers, the fast transfer protocol is used regardless of the setting.

TOOLS

The tools covered in this section are specifically for boosting the performance of Active Directory and DNS. These tools come from several sources, including the native installation, the support tools on the operating system CD, and the resource kit.

Support Tools

The support tools are included on the Windows 2000 CD, but are not installed by default. The support tools include some very useful

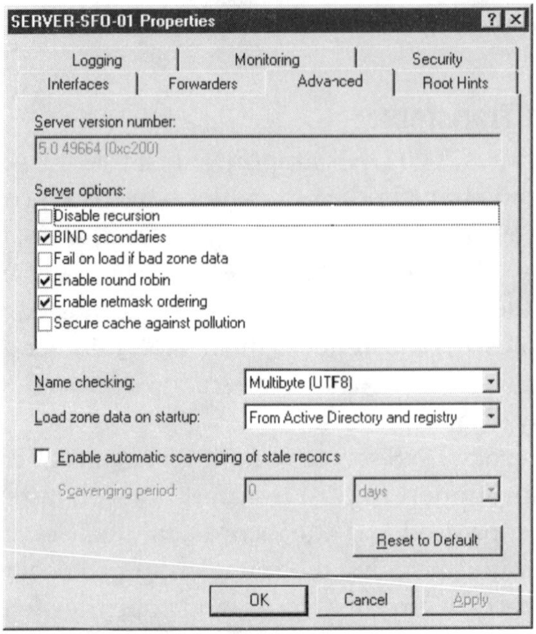

Figure 10-21. Fast transfers disabled (default)

utilities, such as the ADSI Edit tool and the Domain Controller Diagnostic tool. To install these tools, follow these steps:

1. Insert the Windows 2000 installation CD in the CD-ROM.

2. Select Start and then Run.

3. Enter **d:\support\tools\setup.exe**.

4. Accept the defaults.

There should now be a new menu option in the Programs group, Windows 2000 Support Tools.

Active Directory Replication Monitor

Active Directory Replication Monitor is a very useful tool that allows administrators to see the replication topology in a graphical format and influence the replication. The view is from a server perspective, allowing replication to be started manually and replication topology to be checked on a server-by-server basis.

The tool also monitors replication activities and can provide status reports on replication, including reports on the highest USN, the success of the last replication attempt, and the time of the last replication attempt. The tool can be set to monitor manually, or it can be set up to poll on a regular basis, which is, by default, every 60 minutes. Information is displayed for each monitored server, database partition, and connection object. Figure 10-22 shows sample output for three monitored servers.

The tool also can generate a report for a monitored server showing detailed replication information, including the configuration of the KCC, site options, replication status, connections, and other useful information. This report can be very long for complex organizations.

Administrators can also get the properties of a monitored server, to see the inbound replication connections, server flags, FSMO roles, and TCP/IP configuration. The inbound replication connections information is particularly useful, as it shows how the connection

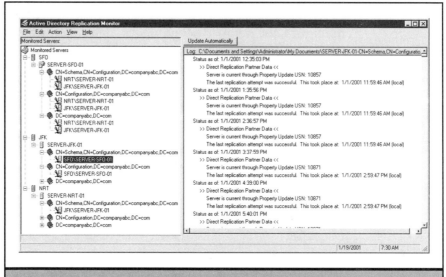

Figure 10-22.   Sample Active Directory Replication Monitor output

was created and why, if it was autogenerated. The server flags summarize the features of the server, including whether the server is a PDC emulator or a global catalog server for the forest and other useful information. The TCP/IP configuration information is helpful when troubleshooting, as the tool may be the only window into the server being used at the time. The TCP/IP configuration tab shows the MAC address, IP address, default route, DNS server, and other information.

Last, the tool can trigger the KCC to perform a knowledge consistency check and also trigger replication on a connection-by-connection basis. Rather than wait for those events to occur automatically (usually at 15-minute intervals at best), administrators can simply right-click the server or connection and initiate the process.

ADSI Edit

The ADSI Edit tool is a low-level editor for the Active Directory database, similar to what the Registry editor is to the Registry. It uses the Active Directory Service Interface (ADSI) to allow the direct modification, addition, deletion, and moving of objects within the directory database. Each attribute of every object can be viewed, changed, and deleted. Figure 10-23 shows a view of the tool.

In the figure, the detailed schedule for an automatically created replication connection on server SERVER-SFO-01 is being examined. The tool allows administrators a far greater degree of granularity for changing objects and settings than provided by the standard interface tools, such as the AD Sites and Services tool or the Active Directory Users and Computers tool. However, the ADSI Edit tool is correspondingly harder to use, and the other tools normally should be used.

CAUTION: The ADSI Edit tool provides no built-in error checking. This means that using the tool requires an understanding of the objects, attributes, and values being changed. Using the tool incorrectly can render the Active Directory inoperable; thus, the tool should be used with extreme caution.

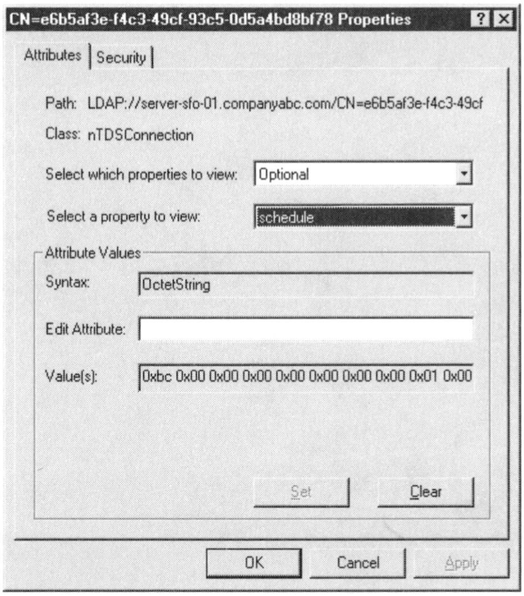

Figure 10-23. ADSI Edit

Windows 2000 Active Directory and DNS provide great built-in capabilities for replicating the directory information throughout the organization. The Active Directory replication system adjusts automatically to many different environments, but it should be tuned to get the most performance out of your system.

The techniques covered in this chapter will help administrators tune the directory for performance, resource conservation, and the demands of large installations, or a combination of the three.

CHAPTER 11

Balancing Security and Performance

Whe system designers and administrators evaluate security strategies, they evaluate them in the context of their impact on performance. It makes no sense to deploy security measures that result in a net loss for an organization when all factors are taken into account. Some of the factors that need to be considered are the value of the data, how the security strategy will affect performance, just what is meant by performance, and what regulatory or legal requirements need to be met.

This chapter examines security and performance on the disk, over the wire, and across the Internet. These three areas are the main target points for security strategies and are, not coincidentally, where performance will be affected.

OVERVIEW

Before looking at the technical aspects of security and its impact on performance, it is important to take a step back and ask what the high-level issues are. The key questions are what is security being balanced against and what should be measured?

Security vs. What?

Security in the abstract is good. However, when balanced against performance, security becomes a series of hard decisions. Should users be affected? Does the data that is being protected justify the ongoing loss of productivity?

In almost all cases, the performance effects of security can be mitigated by additional costs: if the processor cycles are being taxed to encrypt data, buy more processors or faster processors. However, in a time when IT increasingly is being asked to determine return on investment (ROI), the question needs to be asked again: Does the data that is being protected justify the cost?

Value of Data

An important consideration when balancing security and performance is the value of the data. All data has an intrinsic value, though it may be very low in some cases. For example, bank transaction records typically have a very high value, whereas e-mail messages may have less value, and spam messages even less so.

It is essential in balancing security and performance to quantify the value of the data being protected, say by assigning it a dollar value. It would not make sense to spend thousands of dollars to protect data that is worth only tens of dollars, especially if such protection degrades performance.

Performance

The impact of security on performance can be measured in a number of ways. The simplest and most direct measure assesses how the addition of security slows down the access to the data, decreases the overall throughput of the server, or even reduces the maximum load that can be placed on the server. These are very technical and easy to measure.

Cost

Two types of cost can be measured: the cost to implement and the cost to use or operate. The cost to implement can include purchasing licenses, installation, training, and other up-front costs to implement the security measures. This is the cost that most organizations have easy access to, as it will typically have required up-front budgeting.

Surprisingly, the use and operating costs are often the most significant portion of the total cost, yet they are the least well understood. Estimates vary, but over 75 percent of the total cost of security measures comes from use and operating expenses rather than the up-front expenses. These are the costs associated with additional administrative resources required to handle maintenance such as virus definition file updates, solve security-related problems such as lost user passwords, or perform additional steps required for security such as issuing smart cards. For users, these costs typically are the productivity and performance lost as a result of security measures, such as being locked out by password expiration, experiencing slower system performance, or losing a smart card required for access.

Ease of Use

Another type of impact that is vitally important but hard to measure is ease of use. Ease of use refers to the impact on the work of end users and administrators. If a security measure forces users to enter long passwords or carry a physical device with them to gain access to the system, this will affect their performance and productivity. Likewise, if administrators have to spend additional time and effort maintaining security, assisting users as a result of the security measures, or troubleshooting problems, this will degrade the performance of the administrators. This type of impact is difficult to measure and quantify.

Although difficult to quantify, the relationship of security to ease of use is usually easy to understand. As shown in Figure 11-1, as security increases, ease of use decreases.

Windows 2000 does much to alleviate the steepness of the curve through transparent processes such as EFS and IPSec. However, even

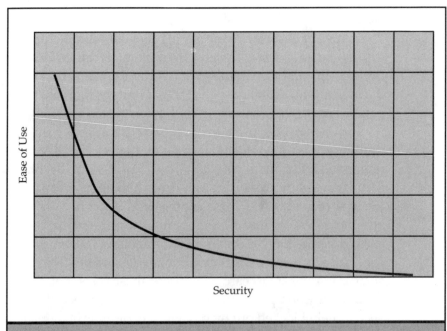

Figure 11-1. Security vs. ease of use

though these are transparent to users, they still require administrative overhead.

Lowest Possible Security Level

The general rule of thumb in balancing security and performance is to use the lowest possible level of security needed to attain the security goals. For example, a two-factor retinal scan system for authenticating users may be more secure than other many other measures, but it is not required nor its cost justified to attain the medium-level security goals of a small business office. For large corporate concerns with highly confidential information or for a military installation, the retinal scan system may be required and its cost easily justified because of the high-level security goals of those environments. Figure 11-2 shows how the cost rises with increased security.

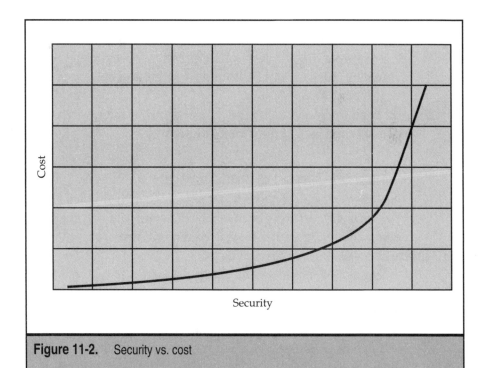

Figure 11-2. Security vs. cost

What to Measure?

The techie answer to the question of what to measure is CPU cycles or processor utilization, or it may be memory utilization or network utilization, or it may even be the throughput of the entire system.

These are important measures, and there are many other technical measurements for evaluating the impact of security on performance. However, there are two other equally important elements to consider: user and administrative performance impact. These factors are often overlooked during testing, resulting in difficult-to-use systems.

Impact on System Performance

First, performance measures needs to quantify the impact of security on the various subsystems. If the security enhancements require additional computations, then what is the impact on the CPU performance? If there is additional disk or network traffic, then what is the impact on those subsystems?

Another area not to overlook is whether enabling security on one element of the system will affect the functions of another element. For example, files stored on NTFS can be encrypted or compressed. However, files cannot be both encrypted and compressed with Windows 2000.

Last, the effect on overall throughput or latency that additional security imposes should be evaluated.

Impact on Users' Performance

An often overlooked factor in balancing performance and security is the impact on users' performance. This impact is sometimes ignored intentionally, leading to the deployment of systems that meet with high levels of user resistance.

Security systems should be as transparent as possible to the users without compromising security. If users have to authenticate every time they click a link while browsing a secure Web site, they are very likely not to use that Web site as a resource. Transparency should not translate to lack of security, but rather to user-friendly security. Many of the security systems that Microsoft has incorporated into Windows 2000 have this quality, such as the Encrypting File System and IP Secure. Users may not even be aware that they are using these security systems and functions, which is exactly as it should be under normal circumstances.

Another impact on user performance is underpowered systems. Network designers frequently design security systems for "average" workstations, only to find that the security measures being used overtax the users' systems. Security overhead can be very high computationally, especially for protocols such as SSL or IP Secure.

Some degradation of user and system performance as a result of security procedures may just be an unfortunate result of business requirements. However, system designers need to make every effort to minimize the collateral damage to users.

Impact on Administrators' Performance

Security measures also affect administrators, and this impact needs to be balanced against the benefits of these measures. Although reduced administrative performance may not cause a security measure to be rejected, it may increase the cost of security if additional administrative resources are required.

File recovery is one area that may be affected by security if measures such as the Encrypting File System are employed. In the event of lost keys, administrators will need to use recovery agent logins to recover files. This could be as simple as logging in as the domain administrator, or the deployment of a certificate of authority infrastructure may be needed to manage recovery agent keys.

If IP Secure is implemented, then the troubleshooting and monitoring of traffic become much more complex. Since IP Secure encrypts packets between the host and destination, as discussed later in this chapter, protocol analysis and content scanning are useless. However, both protocol analysis and content scanning are used by administrators to monitor traffic though the network, for troubleshooting and management of network traffic. Since they require the ability to read the packets, the IP Secure protocol completely prevents these tools from functioning beyond the most rudimentary level.

COMPONENTS OF SECURITY

Understanding some of the key components of security helps balance the competing strategies and technologies. This section discusses the general concepts of authentication, access control, and cryptography as well as the specific Windows 2000 features that facilitate these three general concepts.

Authentication

Everyone is familiar with the scene in war movies where the guard calls out "Halt! Who goes there?" The guard is attempting to verify, or authenticate, the identity of the person. The process is no different for a network operating system. Within a typical network, different levels of access are granted to different entities. If administrators want to assign different access levels to different users, they have to be able to distinguish among those users. This process is referred to as authentication.

Windows 2000 needs to verify the identity of entities requesting access to resources. Windows 2000 uses a variety of methods and technologies to authenticate users. These methods and technologies support different types of access, such as access obtained by a user's typing the account name and password, Web-based access, and keycard access.

Authentication is not just limited to users. Computers and services are also authenticated when they make connections to other servers. For example, a service will authenticate to Active Directory to get proper credentials to access resources or even to start. Computers and services also prove their identity to clients that request mutual authentication, to prevent a hacker from adding another computer as an imposter between the client and the real network server.

Single Sign-On

Users dislike having to authenticate multiple times to separate network servers and applications. A user may have to authenticate when logging onto the desktop computer, then to access a file or print server, then to use a database application, and then again to send e-mail. All of these logons could potentially require different logon names and passwords, and different systems may require users to change their passwords at different intervals. This process is very difficult for the user and jeopardizes security, as users will eventually begin to write down a list of current passwords.

The single sign-on concept requires a user to authenticate only once, to get a set of credentials, which are then used to authenticate to other network applications and services. These subsequent authentication events are transparent to the user and don't require the user to stop and enter authentication information. In Windows 2000, technologies such as Active Directory and Kerberos play crucial roles in delivering single sign-on capability and reducing the impact of security measures.

Interactive Logon

Interactive logon occurs when a user is physically present at the computer while entering credentials. The account being used to log on must have the Log On Locally privilege for that computer, or the logon will fail. An example of interactive logon is pressing CTRL-ALT-DEL at the Windows prompt and then entering a username and password.

Network Logon

Network logon occurs when the user is connecting to a resource across the network. The account logging on must have the Access This Computer from Network privilege on the computer being accessed. An example of network logon is when the user is logged onto a computer and then accesses a file share on a network computer that is running Windows 2000. When the user connects to the network resource, the Windows operating system will transparently attempt a network logon using the current credentials.

Kerberos

The Kerberos authentication protocol is the default Windows 2000 authentication protocol and is a key technology for single sign-on to network resources. The Kerberos protocol was developed at MIT and is used by Windows 2000 to provide fast single sign-on to network resources. The Kerberos protocol verifies the identity of both the user and the network services to ensure mutual authentication.

When a user enters domain credentials, the Kerberos service issues a ticket to the user. This temporary credential identifies the user to network servers. After the first interactive logon, the first Kerberos ticket is used to request other Kerberos tickets to gain access to other network resources.

NTLM

Windows 4.0 used NT LAN Manager (NTLM) as its primary authentication protocol, and Windows 2000 has preserved this protocol so clients can connect to servers running previous versions of Windows NT and to allow older clients to connect to Windows 2000. The NTLM authentication credentials are the familiar domain name, username, and encrypted password. The protocol can be used for interactive or network logon.

To maintain this backward compatibility, the security services on the domain controller maintain a set of NTLM user credentials in the Active Directory. The Windows 2000 client manages the NTLM credentials entered at sign-on on the client side to use for network logon when the client connects to Windows NT 4.0 servers using NTLM authentication. The NTLM security information can be viewed using the Active Directory Users and Computers tool, on the Account tab.

The field is labeled Users Logon Name (Pre-Windows 2000) and is shown in Figure 11-3. Note that the domain name is the NetBIOS name given to the user account's parent Windows 2000 domain, and that there is no separate password field. The NTLM password is the same as the account password.

Smart Cards

Smart cards are an example of two-factor authentication. Two-factor authentication requires users to present a physical object that encodes their identities plus a password. The most common example of

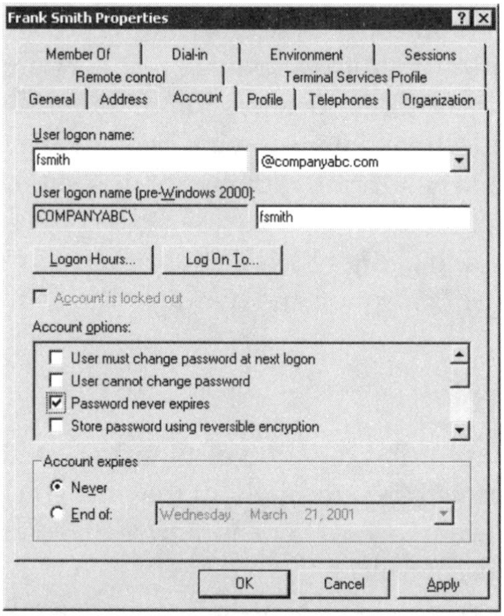

Figure 11-3.   Windows 2000 NTLM authentication

electronic two-factor authentication is the automated teller machine (ATM) card that requires a personal identification number (PIN). The card is the physical object, and the PIN is the password. Smart cards add an extra layer of security onto standard username and password security systems, in that a unique physical object is required to authenticate, which is more difficult to steal then a username. This is particularly important with Windows 2000 and Active Directory, where the username is normally the very publicly available e-mail address.

For businesses, the smart card is becoming a common implementation of two-factor authentication. This card is similar to an ATM card and is physically carried by the user. It contains a chip that stores a digital certificate and the user's private key, which is encrypted for protection. The user enters a password or PIN after inserting the card into a card reader at the client computer to unlock the private key, thus proving the user's identity. Because the private key is carried on a chip in the user's possession, it is very hard for a network intruder to steal. Windows 2000 supports smart card authentication and a variety of readers right out of the box.

Biometric identification is another form of two-factor authentication that is growing in popularity. A special device scans the user's handprint, thumbprint, iris, retina, or voiceprint in place of an access card. Then the user enters the equivalent of a password, usually a four-digit PIN. This approach is expensive, but it makes identity interception and masquerading very difficult.

Access Control

Access control is the equivalent to an armed escort. The escort remains with you throughout the time you are accessing resources and prevents access to unauthorized resources or information. All access is controlled.

The Windows 2000 operating system takes this approach, checking each and every access to ensure that the security principal has appropriate rights.

Granting Access

Windows 2000 implements access control by assigning security descriptors to objects, such as directory objects, files, printers, and services. An object security descriptor includes an access control list (ACL), which defines which security principals (either users or groups) have permission to perform particular actions with that object. The ACL uses the unique security identifier (SID) to identify security principals. An object security descriptor also specifies the level of auditing for the object, as discussed later in this chapter. Administrators and even users can set permissions, assign ownership, and monitor access to objects with the proper permissions.

Permissions don't need to be assigned for every object, but they normally are inherited from the parent of the object. This saves valuable time, allowing Windows 2000 to propagate the security descriptors automatically. Even if security is inherited, administrators or owners can modify the security assignments as needed.

Processing

Using the object ACL, Windows 2000 compares the credentials supplied by the client to the ACL to determine whether the user has the appropriate access rights to the object. The credentials presented by a client contain the SIDs for the account and all group memberships. The access check is done in kernel mode within the security subsystem of Windows 2000 and essentially involves comparing the SIDs presented in the user credentials to the SIDs in the ACL.

Security can be assigned by individual accounts, but this results in administrative overhead and processing overhead. Each security principal that is added to the object ACL incurs an additional incremental performance overhead, to scan the ACL list on each access. Specifying access by groups enables easier management by administrators and reduces the performance overhead needed to process access to objects.

Performance Impact

The logon traffic increases linearly with additional group memberships, as does the size of the Kerberos ticket used as the credential. However, even for an account with memberships of a hundred groups, the size of the Kerberos ticket is only 8K. There may be some additional packets, but not a very large degradation in performance.

When verifying resource access rights, the service providing the resource must check its entire list of SIDs to determine all memberships with which the requesting security principal might be associated. This process increases linearly as the number of groups and entities assigned grows, but again, the overall degradation in performance is negligible.

Physical Access

One element of access control that is outside of Windows 2000 operating system control is physical access. If hackers have physical access to a system, they have the potential for doing almost anything they want with it. A new feature of Windows 2000, the encrypting file system, makes this sort of hacking much harder, but still theoretically possible. This feature is discussed later in this chapter.

Blocking physical access is one of the easiest security concepts to grasp. The next section discusses encryption and other complex, difficult-to-understand concepts. Physical security, however, is well understood by everyone who has a lock on the door at home or who has had to walk past a security guard.

In general, access to server computing resources should be restricted to as few individuals as possible by putting these resources in locked rooms and using sign-in sheets, and auditing these sheets on a regular basis.

Cryptography

Historically, cryptography has been used to pass messages between parties in such a way as to ensure communication secrecy. Cryptography systems use encryption and other processes, techniques, and mechanisms to provide secure communication between those parties while preventing unauthorized hackers from monitoring communications or counterfeiting messages.

Windows 2000 employs cryptography in a number of different ways to ensure the security of the system, including in the Encrypting File System, IP Secure, and even Terminal Services communications via the RDP protocol. However, a performance penalty is exacted for using these techniques.

Scrambled Communications

In its simplest form, cryptography substitutes or transposes letters to create a coded message, traditionally called a cipher, which is used to transform a readable message, called plain text (also called clear text) into an unreadable, scrambled, or hidden message called cipher text. Only someone with a decoding key can convert the cipher text back into its original plain text. The originator of a coded message must share the decoding key in a secure manner with intended recipients who are authorized to know the contents of the coded message. If unauthorized parties can somehow intercept or figure out the decoding key, security is compromised because they can convert the cipher text into plain text and read the contents of the message.

Traditionally, ciphers have used information contained in secret decoding keys to code and decode messages. The process of coding plain text to create cipher text is called encryption, and the process of decoding cipher text to produce the plain text is called decryption. Modern systems of electronic cryptography use digital keys (bit strings) and mathematical algorithms (encryption algorithms) to encrypt and decrypt information.

Windows 2000 uses two types of encryption: private (symmetric) key encryption and public (asymmetric) key encryption. Private key and public key encryption are used in conjunction to provide a variety of security functions for network and information security. One of the reasons for this is that symmetric encryption algorithms are typically hundreds of times faster than asymmetric algorithms. If asymmetric algorithms are used to encrypt large quantities of data (bulk encryption), then performance suffers.

To alleviate this problem, Windows 2000 usually uses public key encryption as part of a technique to exchange symmetric encryption keys, which are then used to bulk-encrypt the data. Examples of this are found in the Encrypting File System and the IP Secure protocol.

Algorithms

The choice of mathematical algorithms used to secure communications or protect data can have a big effect on performance.

For example, Microsoft supports five security algorithms in Windows 2000 IPSec. These algorithms are HMAC MD5 and HMAC SHA for authentication, and DES, DES-CBC, and 3DES for encryption.

Which algorithm is chosen affects not only the security of communication, but also the load that communication places on the systems doing the communicating.

Crypto API

The Crypto application programming interface (API) gives the operating system and developers access to a common suite of cryptographic functions that are handled securely and reliably by the operating system. Windows NT 4.0 provided the low-level cryptography support and modular Cryptographic Service Providers in CryptoAPI. Windows 2000 adds CryptoAPI Certificate Management to support public-key security.

Some of the new features of CryptoAPI include the following:

▼ Support for X.509 version 3 certificates and X.509 version 2.0 CRLs

■ Support for PKCS #10 certificate requests and PKCS #7 for signed and enveloped data

■ Addition and retrieval of certificates and CRLs from certificate stores and location of certificates by attributes and association of private keys

▲ Digital signature, verification, and data encryption support using functions available to applications in HTML, Java, Visual Basic Script, and C/C++

The CryptoAPI features are also used directly by Windows 2000 operating system components, such as the Software Publisher Trust Provider for Authenticode verification, to verify the origin of software being loaded. Other applications and system services use CryptoAPI to provide the common functionality needed to enable public-key security technology.

Completely Safe?

Nothing is completely safe, including encrypted communications. Most of the current cryptographic techniques today rely on large prime numbers that are difficult to factor. RSA Laboratories, one of the leading cryptographic researchers, issued a challenge to crack a 140-bit RSA encryption key. After only one month, that key was successfully cracked. In response, RSA issued a second challenge to crack a 512-bit RSA key, and it was cracked in less than eight months.

The difficulties of code cracking can be surmounted by having numerous computers work in parallel to crack the key. In the future, the computing power needed to crack even today's best codes will reside on desktop or even handheld computers.

ON THE DISK

There are a number of security concerns related to user access to disk resources. These include making sure that users don't access files that they are not supposed to or fill up the disk with files at the expense of other users. Another concern is making sure that users do not compromise the integrity of the system by using resources needed by the operating system, discovering sensitive password information, or corrupting the operating system code.

Windows 2000 has a number of technologies designed to address these security concerns, but each has its own performance penalty when employed. These penalties must be weighed against the security of the system to determine the best balance.

Encrypting File System

Even if file access is controlled, intrepid hackers may be able to get physical access to a system such as a laptop and bypass the access control. Windows 2000 Encrypting File System (EFS) addresses this concern. EFS encrypts files or folders on an NTFS volume on the local computer, so unauthorized individuals cannot read those files even if they gain access.

What Is EFS?

When EFS is enabled for a file or folder on an NTFS file system volume, the operating system encrypts the files using the public key and symmetric encryption algorithms. This feature is available on both Windows 2000 Server versions and Windows 2000 Professional.

Though the underlying cryptography involves complex mathematics, key generation, and protection, administrators and users can take advantage of the feature simply by selecting a check box in the Advanced Attributes dialog box accessed from the File Properties dialog box, shown in Figure 11-4.

Encryption protects files even if a hacker bypasses the Windows 2000 operating system and uses low-level disk utilities to read information

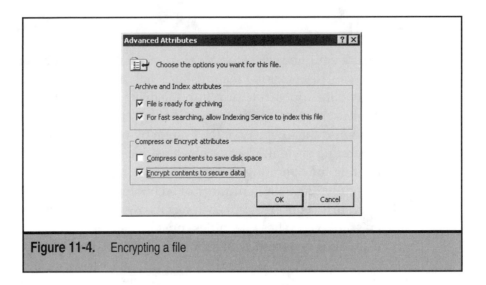

Figure 11-4.   Encrypting a file

directly off the disk. Even if the file bits can be stolen over the network or physically, they cannot be decrypted. This also protects the file from being modified, as it cannot even be read to be modified.

EFS Process

When enabled, EFS automatically encrypts a file when it is saved and decrypts it when the user opens it again. No one can read these files except the user who encrypted the file and an administrator with an EFS file recovery certificate. The encryption technology is coded into the operating system, so its operation is transparent to the user and extremely difficult to attack. Figure 11-5 shows the encryption of the file being saved.

EFS encrypts files using a symmetric encryption key unique to each file. Then it encrypts the encryption key and attaches it to the file, using the public key from the file owner's EFS certificate. Since the file owner is the only person with access to the matching private key, the file owner is the only one who can decrypt the key, and therefore the file. (See Figure 11-6.)

At the same time that the file symmetric encryption key is encrypted with the file owner's public key, the operating system also encrypts the file's symmetric encryption key with the public key of

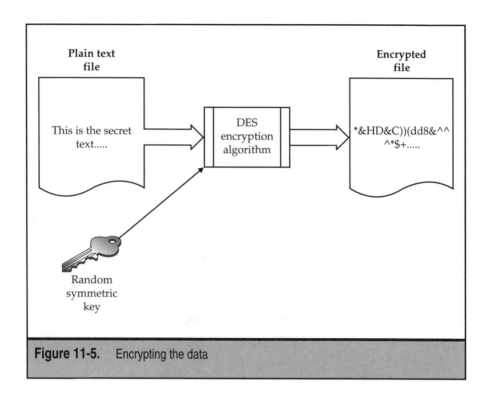

**Plain text
file**

**Encrypted
file**

This is the secret
text.....

DES
encryption
algorithm

*&HD&C))(dd8&^^
^*$+.....

Random
symmetric
key

Figure 11-5.   Encrypting the data

the recovery agent and attaches it to the file. In the event of an
emergency, or should an employee leave the organization, an
authorized administrator can use the private key from that certificate
to recover the file. In fact, multiple recovery agents can be specified,
with the process repeated for each one. (See Figure 11-7.)

Performance Impact

The EFS process is relatively efficient, with the high-performance
symmetric key used to bulk-encrypt the file, and the low-performance
public keys used only to encrypt the symmetric key. Even so, there is a
performance penalty for performing the encryption. This occurs both
when the file is saved and when it is read from the disk by the owner.
It is recommended that the EFS option not be used on files that require
frequent access, at least not without a careful performance analysis.

Another impact on user performance is that files that are
encrypted cannot be shared. This is because the files are encrypted

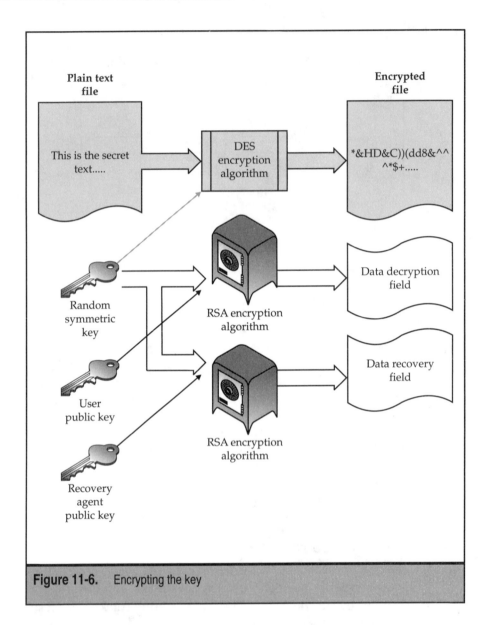

Figure 11-6. Encrypting the key

with the owner's public key, and only the owner has access to the corresponding private key. There is currently no mechanism for granting additional parties access. In the future, Microsoft will be adding this functionality, allowing owners to grant access to other users while retaining the encryption.

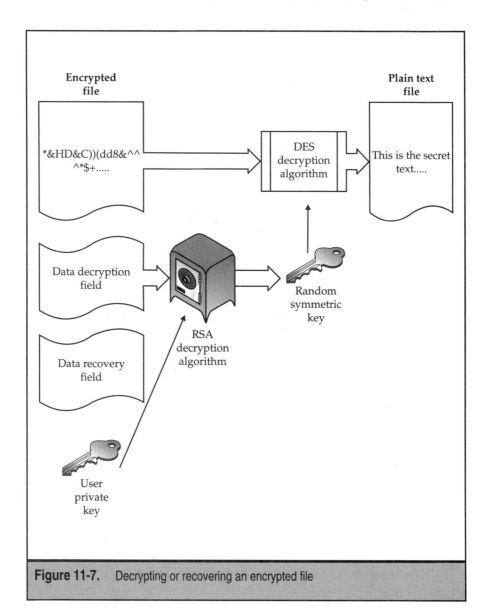

Figure 11-7.   Decrypting or recovering an encrypted file

Partitioning

Partitioning allow barriers to be erected to protect applications and data from being affected, either intentionally or accidentally, by other applications or users. Partitioning forces the operating system, applications, and users each to remain within its own specifically assigned area. For the purposes of this discussion, we will assume that the partitioning is at only the Windows 2000 volume level.

Separate Functions

The idea behind partitioning is that different functions are moved on to different parts of the drive subsystem to reduce the risk of a security breech. For example, if the operating system and the data reside on the same partition, then it is possible through administrative error to assign a user rights to an operating-system-specific area of the partition. A casual user can then inadvertently access operating system data, and a malicious user can use such an error to access and alter the system. Using partitions, functions can be separated into logical groupings, such as applications, operating system, and data (see Figure 11-8).

Putting the operating system onto a separate partition ensures that the components essential to the secure operation of the system, such as the pagefile or dynamic link libraries, are not compromised. Windows 2000 provides a logical barrier by default, the Hide Protected Operating System Files option, but separating the Windows 2000 operating system onto a separate partition affords much better protection.

Creating separate application and data partitions ensures that users' access to data does not give them access to the application code or configuration files. Since application components can frequently run in higher-privilege modes, it is important to ensure that the application code is properly protected. Although it may be tempting to place the application code on the same partition as the operating system, this can present a security risk if users require some level of access to the application code, or if application updates are compromised.

Performance Impact

The performance impact of partitioning the application, operating system, and data is either negligible or even positive. If a single drive or RAID partition of drives is partitioned, then performance will

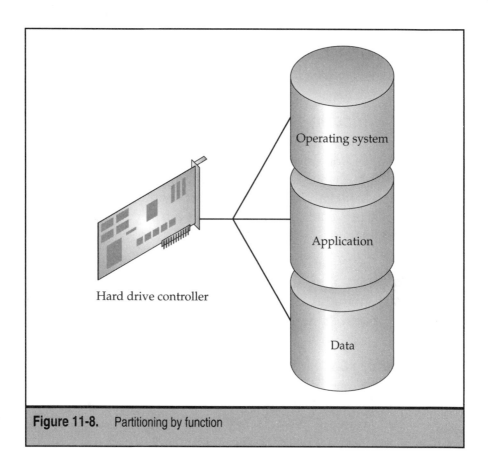

Operating system

Application

Hard drive controller

Data

Figure 11-8.   Partitioning by function

most likely remain the same. If the partitions are placed on different drives and separate controllers, then performance will most likely improve.

An example of an arrangement that improves performance is one in which the pagefile partition and the data partition of an SQL server are moved onto separate drives. Pagefile access would be on a separate spindle from database access, thus allowing simultaneous access and providing much better performance.

Wiping the Pagefile

The Windows 2000 pagefile is used to swap applications in memory to disk, freeing memory resources for other applications. This process allows the system to have a very large virtual memory space. However, the contents of memory is copied directly to disk, and this could potentially compromise the security of a system.

Why Wipe the Pagefile?

The Windows 2000 pagefile is a direct dump of the contents of memory and can contain information such as passwords. Although this information is not easily accessible, a hacker may be able to pull confidential information from the pagefile on the disk.

To prevent this, Windows 2000 can be configured to clear information from the pagefile on the disk.

Wipe on Shutdown

When the system is configured to wipe the pagefile, the system fills the inactive pages in the pagefile with zeros during shutdown.

Performance Impact

During normal operation, pagefile wiping has no impact on performance. The pagefile will still be used as if there were no change. In fact, memory information will still be stored in the pagefile and thus still pose a risk.

A performance impact will, however, occur during shutdown. When the system starts to shut down, it will pause while the inactive pages in the pagefile are overwritten with zeros. This delay can be long, depending on the size of memory, the size of the pagefile, and the performance of the disk subsystem.

The delay will probably not be a significant concern for servers, which are usually shutdown only at infrequent intervals. The delay will be more of a concern for desktop and laptop systems, which likely are shut down daily. Consider implementing this security measure on high-risk systems such as laptops, where the balance tips more to the side of security.

Limitations

Wiping the pagefile zeros out only inactive pages, and some pages being used by the system as it shuts down will not be filled with zeros. Another limitation is that the pagefile will not be wiped for systems that are powered off unexpectedly, crash, or enter a hibernation state.

Setup

The registry change is made under HKEY_LOCAL_MACHINE\ SYSTEM\CurrentControlSet\Control\SessionManager\Memory Management\ to the value ClearPageFileAtShutdown. Set the value to 1 to force the pagefile to be wiped, or to 0 to not wipe the pagefile. By default, the value is set to zero.

Virus Scanning

Computer viruses are being created or modified daily, with well over 10,000 existing today. E-mail is one of the most prevalent applications, and viruses use this route more than any other to infect computers. Infection by a virus can result in loss of data, productivity, and corporate reputation, especially if a company becomes a vector for an infection. The cost of virus infection can be very high on a dollar basis: something like $12 billion worldwide in 1999.

Why Scan?

Virus scanning is one plank in a computer system's defense against viruses. Files are scanned to see if any of the code contained in them matches a pattern found in a virus. Virus definitions are kept in virus definition files (DAT files), which are constantly updated by their manufacturers. If a match is found, then specific actions can be taken, such as deleting the file, cleaning the file to disinfect it, or quarantining the file to allow administrators to examine it.

Scanning Methods

There are several approaches to scanning, including periodic scanning, on-access scanning, and scanning via gateways. Each addresses different concerns and has a different performance impact. On-access scanning scans objects as they are placed on the system, such as when files are saved to a volume or when e-mail messages arrive in a mailbox. This is the best method for ensuring that viruses are detected as quickly as possible.

The limitation to this method is that when new viruses are detected by new revisions of the DAT files, these same viruses in preexisting files will not be detected. To solve this problem, perform periodic rescanning of existing objects against updated DAT files.

Gateways scan all incoming and outgoing traffic for viruses, providing a gatekeeper function to ensure that all incoming and outgoing traffic is checked. Gateways can scan SMTP mail, FTP traffic, and HTTP traffic for malicious code.

Limitations

Virus scanning technology is, by nature, reactive. As new viruses are detected in the wild, antivirus software manufacturers update their DAT files, and customers download them to be protected. By definition, some customers will have to be infected by a new virus or a variation of an old one for it to come to the attention of the antivirus software manufacturers. Antivirus software manufacturers and administrators alike thus play a constant game of catch-up to prevent major outbreaks.

Some applications, such as Outlook with the Outlook security patch, have draconian options to forestall virus infections. In the case of the Outlook security patch, users are essentially prevented from receiving executable attachments via email. While effective, this has a serious impact on user productivity and overall messaging capabilities.

In addition to updating DAT files, users and administrators need to periodically update the antivirus scan engine, adding to the administrative overhead.

Performance Impact

The performance impact of virus scanning on systems can be extensive, consuming 10 to 20 percent of CPU utilization on active systems even when configured properly. The level of CPU utilization depends on the specific nature of the traffic and varies somewhat between manufacturers, but is a good general estimate.

Additionally, scanning decreases the throughput of the subsystems, even when sufficient processor and memory resources are present. Throughput may be reduced by as much as a factor of three—that is, more than three times the amount of time may be needed to transfer messages or files. Under normal circumstances, systems are overengineered and have excess capacity to handle the load. The performance impact becomes more apparent on systems with heavy loads or during peak usage.

OVER THE WIRE

One of the most vulnerable parts of network communication or a client-server session is the traffic over the wire. Any hacker within the organization can capture packets using a protocol analyzer and compromise the data. Fortunately, Windows 2000 includes a number of technologies to make this very difficult to accomplish.

IP Secure

IP Secure is an industry-standard method of ensuring that all over-the-wire communications are secured. This technology is new to Windows 2000 and greatly increases the potential security of the system.

Securing Wire Communications

To secure communications over the wire, Windows 2000 includes IP Security (IPSec). The IPSec protocol uses cryptography-based security to provide access control, connectionless integrity, data origin authentication, protection against replays, and data confidentiality. Because IPSec services are provided at the IP layer of the OSI model (Figure 11-9), its services are available transparently to the upper-layer protocols in the stack and to existing applications without modification: that is, the applications do not need to be aware of the protocol.

If a hacker uses a protocol analyzer to open one of the IP packets sent after a secure session is established, the hacker will see everything

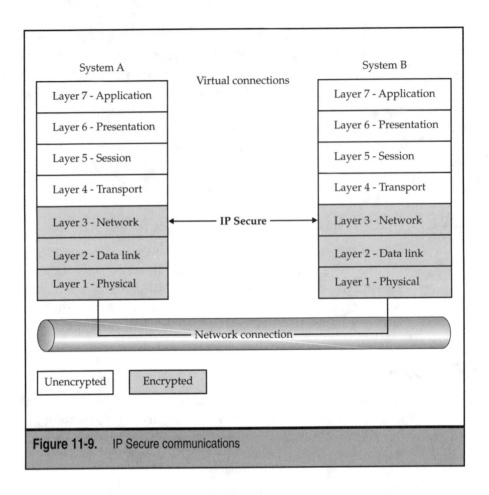

Figure 11-9. IP Secure communications

within the TCP packet scrambled. The only clear parts of the packet are the Ethernet and IP headers, which allow the packet to be routed.

Algorithms

Microsoft supports four main security algorithms for Windows 2000 IP Secure. These algorithms are HMAC MD5 and HMAC SHA for authentication and key exchange, and DES-CBC, and 3DES for encryption of the packets of data.

HMAC MD5   Hash Message Authentication Code (HMAC) is a secret-key algorithm. HMAC provides data integrity and origin authentication through a digital signature produced by a keyed hash function. The Message Digest version 5 (MD5) algorithm is a hash function that can produce a 128-bit value.

HMAC SHA   Secure Hash Algorithm (SHA) is a hash function variation of HMAC that can produce a 160-bit value. By virtue of its increased bit value, HMAC SHA is more secure than HMAC MD5 but requires a slightly longer processing time.

DES   Data Encryption Standard (DES) is an encryption algorithm developed by IBM and approved by the U.S. government as an official standard in 1976. It breaks a plain text message into 64-bit cipher blocks and encrypts each block using a 40-bit or 56-bit key. The U.S. government places restrictions on the export of 56-bit DES, for security reasons. The general cryptographic industry considers even 56-bit DES to be vulnerable to attack with today's computing resources. This specific protocol is not used in Windows 2000 IP Secure, but rather the more secure DES-CBC variation, described next.

DES-CBC   When DES works under the Cipher Block Chaining (CBC) mode (DES-CBC), it applies an exclusive OR operation to each 64-bit plain text block with the previous cipher block before encrypting the block with the DES key. DES-CBC is more secure than pure DES. When the DES option is chosen as the policy, DES-CBC is the true protocol being used.

3DES   In triple DES (3DES), DES encrypts each cipher block three times, making 3DES far more secure than DES. The more secure the algorithm IPSec uses, the more processing time the algorithm requires. Triple DES is by far the most processor intensive of the two encryption protocols.

With the ever-increasing processing power of computers, encryption algorithms have necessarily become more sophisticated to prevent brute-force cracking. To enlist the help of the very hackers who jeopardize their techniques, cryptographic vendors issue frequent challenges to test the limits of their products or technologies. This arms race can be expected to continue for the foreseeable future.

Policy-Based Security

With IP Secure, Windows 2000 system administrators can select
security protocols, select the cryptographic algorithms used for the
services, and maintain the cryptographic keys for each connection
relationship. The services that are available and the types of traffic
for which they are required are configured using IPSec policy. IPSec
policy can be configured locally on a computer or assigned through
Group Policy using the Active Directory services.

The IP Secure policy specifies how computers trust each other.
Administrators can create custom policies that specify IP Secure for
specific protocols, with different levels of security for each. There are
three predefined security policies, as shown in Figure 11-10.

These policies consist of one client policy and two server policies
(see Table 11-1). The predefined policies either have the server
require security or request security. The client policy specifies
whether the client will respond to security requests.

Windows 2000 can use Kerberos (the default), certificates, or a
manually configured shared secret as the authentication method.
The simplest method is to use the Windows 2000 Kerberos-based

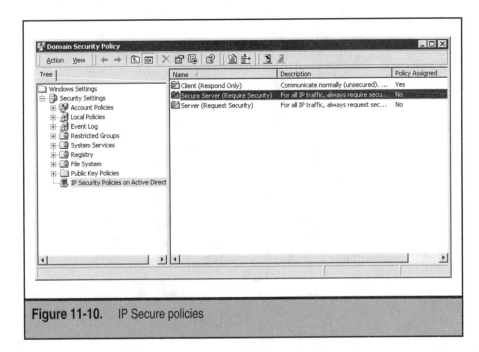

Figure 11-10. IP Secure policies

Policy	Description
Client (Respond Only)	Communicate normally (unsecured). Use the default response rule to negotiate with servers that request security. Only the requested protocol and port traffic with that server are secured.
Server (Request Security)	For all IP traffic, always request security using Kerberos trust. Allow unsecured communication with clients that do not respond to requests.
Secure Server (Require Security)	For all IP traffic, always require security using Kerberos trust. Do not allow unsecured communication with untrusted clients.

Table 11-1. Default IP Secure Policies

authentication, as it requires no configuration. The default setting is shown in Figure 11-11. However, this setting will only work if the two systems are members of the same Windows 2000 Active Directory forest. If the two systems do not meet this condition, then either a certificate or a manually entered shared secret must be used.

Performance Impact

The performance impact of IP Secure can be significant and is proportional to the number of secure connections established. For a single connection, the overhead is approximately 1 percent of the CPU processing time. For 10 simultaneous active connections, this can grow to 10 to 15 percent of the CPU processing time. This becomes a serious performance problem for servers, which need to establish a connection with each of their clients. The processing overhead to secure all those connections can degrade performance, causing problems for latency-sensitive applications such as voice over IP.

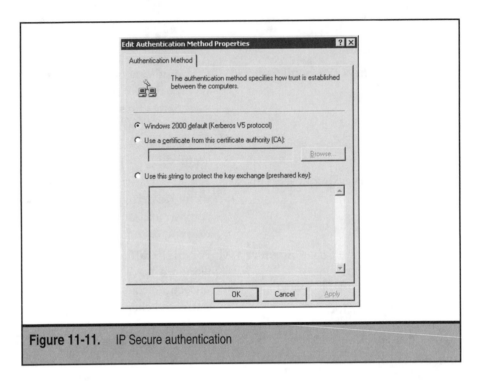

Figure 11-11. IP Secure authentication

In addition to the number of connections, the choice of encryption algorithm can seriously affect the performance. The more secure the algorithm that IPSec uses, the more processing time the algorithm requires. Selecting the triple DES option can increase the processing time by a factor of two, and even a single session may degrade the performance of latency-sensitive traffic, depending on the processing resources of the host system.

The performance problem can be mitigated by limiting the types of traffic that are secured, via policies. Higher-performance systems can be procured with the processing power necessary to handle the load effectively. Alternatively, administrators and designers can take advantage of the offload capabilities of Windows 2000, as discussed in the next section.

Offloading

The Windows 2000 TCP/IP protocol stack supports a feature called offloading, which allows the operating system to hand off the

Manufacturer	Network Card	Purpose
3Com	3CR990-TX-97	Workstation
3Com	3CR990SRV97	Server
Intel	Pro/100 S	Server

Table 11-2. Offload-Capable Network Interface Cards

expensive encryption and decryption operations to specially designed network cards. Both Intel and 3Com have network cards that support this functionality; these are listed in Table 11-2.

When a packet needs to be encrypted, the operating system passes the unencrypted packet along with the encryption requirements to the network interface card. The card contains a special ASIC that will handle the encryption at much faster speeds than the operating system is capable of (the additional or larger ASIC is shown in Figure 11-12). This functionality is completely transparent to the other side of the connection; the result is an encrypted packet that

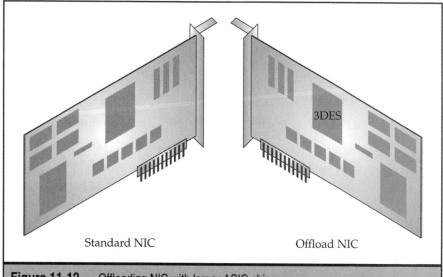

Standard NIC   Offload NIC

Figure 11-12. Offloading NIC with larger ASIC chip

is no different than it would be if the Windows 2000 operating system had encrypted it.

These cards can not only offload the encryption processes from the CPU, they can also offload the TCP segmentation processing overhead. This further improves the performance of systems with the cards installed, even for traffic not secured by IPSec.

Configuring Offloading

After installing the offload-capable network card, ensure that it is configured properly to allow offloading. Verify that the HKEY_ LOCAL_MACHINE\SYSTEM\CurrentControlSet\Services\Tcpip\ Parameters\ key contains the value DisableTaskOffload of type DWORD. The value must be 0 to enable task offloading and 1 to disable task offloading. The default value is 0 to enable task offloading, which will be the value if the key does not exist.

Depending on the type of network adapter and the version of the driver, there may also be customizable options for specifying what to offload. For example, the 3Com network interface card and driver have eight different offloading options (Table 11-3) to accommodate specific configurations. These can be found in the advanced properties of the driver, under the Enable Offloads property. Normally, all options will be enabled, but disabling options is useful for troubleshooting or to test performance.

Parameter	Effect
All Offloads Disabled	No offload functions enabled
cksum	TCP checksum function enabled
cksum-ipsec	TCP checksum and IPSec function enabled
cksum-tcpseg	TCP checksum and TCP segmentation function enabled
cksum-tcpseg-ipsec	TCP Checksum, TCP Segmentation and IPSec function enabled

Table 11-3. Offload Function Options on the Advanced Tab

Parameter	Effect
ipsec	IPSec function enabled
tcpseg	TCP segmentation function enabled
tcpseg-ipsec	TCP segmentation and IPSec function enabled

Table 11-3. Offload Function Options on the Advanced Tab *(continued)*

It is also useful to check the offload capabilities of the card through the Windows 2000 operating system. This ensures that the card has been properly detected by the operating system, and that the offload functions are available. This also allows administrators to verify the algorithms and functions supported, so that the IP Secure policies can be tailored to take advantage of the features of the network card. It will obviously not improve performance to create an IP Secure policy that requires an encryption algorithm that the network card doesn't support, as the operating system will be unable to offload that processing.

The command to show offload capabilities is **netsh int ip show offload**. This will display a list of the offload features that the card offers, as is shown for the 3Com 3CR990SRV97 3XP network card in Figure 11-13.

ACROSS THE INTERNET

Organizations are relying more and more on the Internet as the corporate WAN, both to browse to internal corporate sites and to remotely connect to the internal corporate network. And the Internet is not getting any safer. To ensure data integrity and confidentiality and prevent unauthorized access to resources, Windows 2000 includes a number of security technologies.

In this section, we look at the security elements of the Secure Sockets Layer protocol, the Virtual Private Networking components, and the security features of Terminal Services.

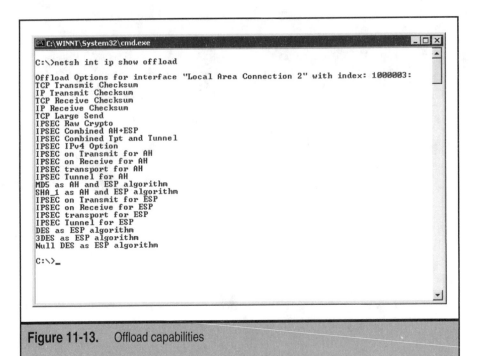

```
C:\WINNT\System32\cmd.exe                                          _ □ ×

C:\>netsh int ip show offload

Offload Options for interface "Local Area Connection 2" with index: 1000003:
TCP Transmit Checksum
IP Transmit Checksum
TCP Receive Checksum
IP Receive Checksum
TCP Large Send
IPSEC Raw Crypto
IPSEC Combined AH+ESP
IPSEC Combined Tpt and Tunnel
IPSEC IPv4 Option
IPSEC on Transmit for AH
IPSEC on Receive for AH
IPSEC transport for AH
IPSEC Tunnel for AH
MD5 as AH and ESP algorithm
SHA_1 as AH and ESP algorithm
IPSEC on Transmit for ESP
IPSEC on Receive for ESP
IPSEC transport for ESP
IPSEC Tunnel for ESP
DES as ESP algorithm
3DES as ESP algorithm
Null DES as ESP algorithm

C:\>_
```

Figure 11-13.   Offload capabilities

Secure Sockets Layer

The Secure Sockets Layer protocol and its close relative the Transport
Layer Security protocol are public-cryptography-based security
protocols. These two security protocols are used by Web browsers
and servers for mutual authentication, message integrity, and
confidentiality across public unsecured networks.

Certificates are at the heart of the SSL and TLS protocols.
Authentication of the Internet server is performed by the Web
browser client (Internet Explorer) when the server presents its
certificate during SSL/TLS secure channel establishment. The client
program accepts the server certificate by verifying the cryptographic
signatures in the certificate against its list of trusted Certificate
Authorities. Fundamentally, the server is proving its identity to the
client browser. Client authentication is also supported by SSL 3.0 and
TLS, meaning that the client can authenticate to the server as well
using a certificate.

What Is SSL?

The Secure Sockets Layer (SSL) protocol uses a combination of public-key and symmetric-key encryption, very similar to the techniques used by IP Secure. As discussed earlier in the chapter, symmetric-key encryption is much faster than public-key encryption, but public-key encryption provides better authentication over unsecured networks. The server uses public-key encryption techniques to authenticate to the client and creates shared symmetric keys by using public-key techniques. These symmetric keys then allow the server and client to conduct rapid encryption, decryption, and tamper detection during the session that follows using symmetric-key encryption techniques.

Performance Impact

Security is achieved at some cost in performance, as the security versus performance graph at the beginning of the chapter showed. The SSL protocol and its attendant encryption algorithms are security features that require significant processing time. They also use additional memory resources to process the encryption and store session keys, which can become important factors for e-commerce Web servers that handle large volumes of traffic and clients. In addition, the SSL protocol uses long keys (up to1024 bits long) to encrypt and decrypt communications.

Network traffic and latency also increases, as the protocols, additional authentication, and key exchanges add to the overall data stream. During a typical SSL session, when a browser requests a page, a delay occurs while the server encrypts the page for transmission. When the server sends the page, the SSL protocol adds more network overhead. To enhance security, SSL also disables proxy and browser caching, which reduces the overall efficiency of the server and client. Finally, once the browser has received the requested files, the pages must be decrypted, making the download time even longer.

The bottom line is that browsing and downloading files from servers using the SSL protocol can be 10 to 100 times slower than from servers that are not using SSL. While this may seem excessive, the alternative of unsecured communication is unacceptable.

Tweaking SSL Performance

To improve the performance of SSL-enabled Web servers, add processors. The primary performance constraint on Windows 2000 and security is processor power. The SSL protocol consumes a significant amount of processor time, mainly for encryption. The Windows 2000 security components are multithreaded, allowing them to run simultaneously on multiple processors. Adding processors improves performance significantly and prevents the processors from becoming bottlenecks. Processors with large secondary (L2) cache space will achieve better performance results, as the processor reads and writes small units of data to the main memory. Secondary cache space improves this access.

Add memory only if security features cause increased paging or shortages in virtual memory; otherwise, adding more memory will not likely help.

NOTE: Adding disk space usually is not going to improve performance of security-related systems. In Windows 2000, security features are very CPU intensive. Unless applications are being swapped to disk, the addition of disk resources is unlikely to improve performance.

SSL vs. IPSec

Both SSL and IP Secure accomplish the same overall goal of protecting communications. They have different advantages, based on their architecture. The SSL protocol works at a higher level in the OSI model, whereas IP Secure works at a lower level. Applications need to be SSL aware to take advantage of SSL features, whereas IP Secure is completely transparent to the applications. IP Secure requires a shared secret to operate, be it a Kerberos ticket, a certificate, or a manually shared secret, and so requires some administrative overhead to set up. The SSL protocol does not require any shared secret to initiate secure communications and is already built into all major browsers. This makes SSL easier to deploy than IP Secure.

Virtual Private Network

A virtual private network (VPN) is an extension of a private network that traverses shared or public networks such as the Internet (Figure 11-14). A VPN enables organizations to share data among computers across a shared or public network while still maintaining the security of an internal network. To emulate a private link, data is encapsulated with a header that provides routing information allowing it to traverse the shared or public network to reach its end point, similar to an envelope used to mail a letter through the postal service. To ensure the privacy of the communications, the data being sent is encrypted. On arrival at the destination, the packet is decrypted and forwarded to the appropriate internal resource.

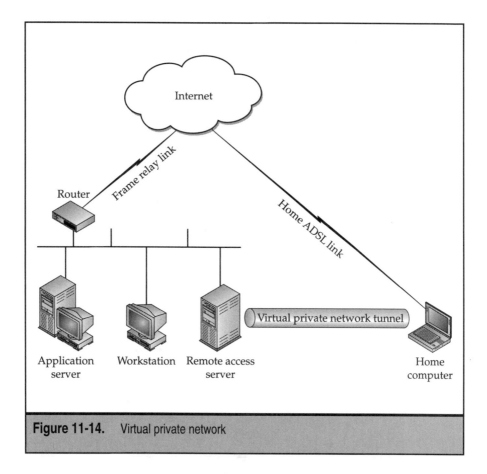

Figure 11-14.   Virtual private network

Point-to-Point Tunneling Protocol

The Point-to-Point Tunneling Protocol (PPTP) encapsulates Point-to-Point Protocol (PPP) frames into IP packets for transmission over the Internet. PPTP uses a TCP connection to create, maintain, and terminate the tunnel. PPTP packets of the PPP frames can be encrypted or compressed, or both.

To authenticate the connection, PPTP uses remote-access-specific authentication protocols, such as the Extensible Authentication Protocol (EAP), Microsoft Challenge-Handshake Authentication Protocol (MS-CHAP), CHAP, Shiva Password Authentication Protocol (SPAP), and Password Authentication Protocol (PAP). For encryption, the VPN must be configured to use MS-CHAP or EAP-Transport Level Security (EAP-TLS). The default authentication is MS-CHAP, as shown in Figure 11-15. This screen can be reached by viewing the properties of the client VPN connection object, selecting the Security tab, selecting Advanced, and clicking the Settings button.

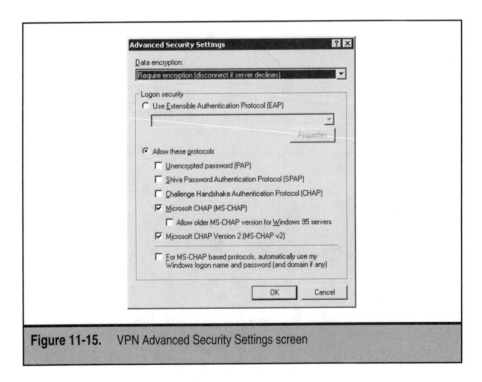

Figure 11-15. VPN Advanced Security Settings screen

Layer 2Tunneling Protocol

Layer 2 Tunneling Protocol (L2TP) is a combination of the PPTP protocol discussed in the previous section and the Layer 2 Forwarding (L2F) protocol. This protocol competes with PPTP. The L2TP protocol incorporates the best features of both PPTP and L2F.

Rather than use expensive connection-oriented TCP, L2TP uses UDP messages over IP networks. This makes the protocol more efficient at transmitting data, as it eliminates the overhead needed to maintain the connection. L2TP does not provide any internal mechanism for encryption (unlike PPTP), instead relying on IP Secure. For secure communication, the end points of the tunnel across the Internet must be configured to support IP Secure.

Performance Impact

The PPTP protocol has a high overhead due to the need to maintain a connection-oriented session and encryption. Unfortunately, PPTP encryption is not offloaded to network cards with that capability.

Terminal Services

Terminal Services is being widely used over the Internet to provide access to remote applications. This technology is very bandwidth efficient, giving end users the look and feel of a local desktop across even slow links such as a dial-up connection to the Internet. However, this technology literally exposes the desktop to the very public Internet. That being the case, it must be very secure.

Terminal Services is also a useful remote administration tool, allowing administrators to remotely access their servers and conduct administrative tasks as if they were at the keyboard of the system. This type of use can help reduce the cost of ownership, but the system must be very secure to prevent security breeches.

What's the Risk?

When an application is run in a Terminal Services session, the server sends only the first screens of the application to the client over the network. The client transmits keystrokes back to the server. Terminal

Services uses the Remote Desktop Protocol (RDP) for all of this data. A hacker could capture each RDP packet and reconstruct the entire session, potentially exposing sensitive information.

To prevent this, Terminal Services can be configured to employ security to protect the communication between the server and the client. In addition, other technologies such as IP Secure or tunneling can be used.

Encryption Levels

The first important security setting is the encryption level you select for the RDP-TCP connection. The RDP protocol uses the RSA Security RC4 cipher, a stream cipher that is very efficient at encrypting small amounts of varying-sized data. RC4 is designed for secure communications over networks and is used in protocols such as SSL. The Terminal Services configuration offers three encryption levels, Low, Medium, and High, as shown in Figure 11-16.

The Low encryption option specifies that only data sent from the client to the server should be encrypted. This one-way encryption is

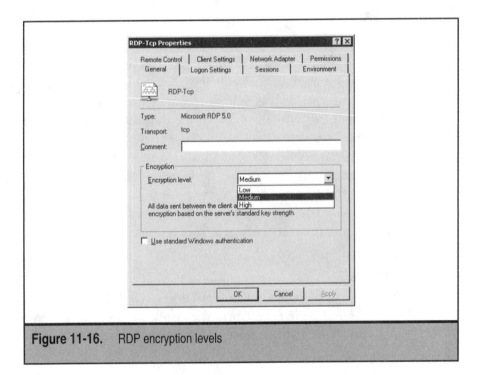

Figure 11-16. RDP encryption levels

useful for protecting the passwords that users enter to gain access to the Terminal Services server. The lack of such protection was and continues to be a major problem with the UNIX telnet protocol, where all passwords are sent unprotected.

The Medium encryption option is the default and encrypts the data sent in both directions. If the client is a Windows 2000 system, then Terminal Services uses a 56-bit key for Low and Medium encryption. If the client is another device such as a WinTerm station, then Terminal Services uses a 40-bit key. Medium encryption offers much greater security, as communications are encrypted in both directions.

With the High encryption option, Terminal Services encrypts data sent in both directions with a 128-bit key. This option requires that the High Encryption Pack be installed on both the client and the server.

Tunneling

Another way to achieve highly secure connections is to run a Remote Desktop Protocol (RDP) session to a Terminal Server within either IP Secure tunnels or VPN tunnels. This gives administrators a single point of configuration, rather than having to monitor security on both the remote access connection and the RDP connection. It also allows administrators to keep the Terminal Servers behind the firewall infrastructure, rather than exposed to the Internet.

Performance Impact

Increasing the encryption level adds computation overhead and latency. This is typically not a problem with lightly loaded servers, but it can be a critical performance factor at higher loads. At minimum, all servers should be configured for Medium encryption to ensure that communications in both directions is encrypted.

With tunneling, the overhead on the Terminal Server will be light, as the overhead for securing the communications will have been transferred to the systems responsible for IP Secure or the VPN. However, the overhead to secure the entire communication link will be correspondingly higher.

Windows 2000 provides many useful tools for protecting information. Information can be protected on the disk, over the network, and across the Internet using the built-in authentication and encryption technologies that ship with Windows 2000.

It is critical when evaluating which specific technology to deploy, such as choosing between the Point-to-Point Tunneling Protocol and the Layer 2 Tunneling Protocol, to understand what the effects on performance will be. The choice of algorithms can make a big difference in the overall performance of the technology, as when using IP Secure and selecting between DES and 3DES as the encryption algorithm. If the security protection of the higher-cost algorithms is needed, however, there are techniques to improve performance, such as using offload-capable network cards.

The choice between security and performance is not just about making the system faster or slower, but it also involves balancing user performance and administrative overhead.

CHAPTER 12

Tweaking Client Performance

Windows 2000 Professional is fundamentally a self-tuning operating system. At startup, it examines the hardware configuration and configures settings to appropriately balance performance. During operation, the operating system constantly monitors conditions and adjusts numerous parameters to meet those conditions.

Even with all of this built-in optimization, the operating system can still benefit from administrator intervention. Sometimes a balanced approach is not what's needed, but rather a tilting of the scales to favor one aspect of performance or another. In this chapter, we examine tuning the client at a high level, then drill down into tweaking the specific subsystems, such as memory and disk.

TUNING CLIENTS

Tuning clients is fundamentally different than tuning servers. In this section, the components that make up a client are looked at from a performance perspective.

To jump-start the process, an outline of a quick results strategy is also presented. This will help quickly identify the source of a performance problem, which is especially useful in situations when there is little information from the end user and lots of pressure from management.

Last, we look at the factors that determine how much a given system can be tuned, so we can know when tuning will be effective and when we should just throw in the towel and buy a new system.

Components of the Client

To tweak the performance of the client, it is important to understand the components that make up the client. While tuning is obviously about making the entire system perform better, it is often making the individual components perform better that results in a greater whole.

Also, knowing what the separate components are and looking at them individually helps you understand their interactions and effects on each other. Performance tuning is much like fixing traffic jams. In looking at a highway system, a traffic engineer might decide to expand a two-lane section of the highway to four lanes to improve traffic flow, not understanding that this will cause a traffic jam farther down the road.

For example, an administrator might double the size of the pagefile because the Windows 2000 Professional system is running low on memory. Good idea, but this then results in substantially increased disk access and contention with a disk-intensive application. The problem is the result of not understanding the relationship between memory and the disk subsystems.

Hardware

The hardware portions of the client that this chapter focuses on are the memory, disk, and the processor subsystems. For today's systems, memory is often the most constrained resource and the most likely source of performance issues. Applications such as Microsoft Office 2000 have very large code bases that use up large quantities of memory, competing with the operating system.

Disk subsystem performance is the next most likely source of performance problems, due in great part to the performance differential between memory and disk. Also, when memory becomes constrained, it places a heavier burden on the disk subsystem, as will be seen later in the chapter.

Last, the processor in most computers shipping today is far less likely to be a performance bottleneck than in previous years. This is very much due to advances in processor technologies and the decreasing price-performance ratio.

One key hardware component not discussed here is the network subsystem. This is also a prime candidate for performance tuning for a Windows 2000 Professional client, but instead of here, it is discussed in great detail in Chapter 8.

Software

The Windows 2000 Professional operating system is the core component in the client software. This is the traffic director and cop in the highway analogy presented earlier. The operating system does an excellent job of automatically balancing resource needs, making the task of tuning much easier. However, Windows 2000 also provides many controls to allow adjustment and tuning, giving administrators the best of both worlds.

Other key components of the client software are drivers, service packs, and hotfixes. These are really extensions of the operating system, adding functionality, bridging the gap between hardware and the operating system, and fixing problems in the operating system.

The last components of the client software, but definitely not the least, are the applications. These are the automobiles that run on the highway, to continue the highway analogy. Arguably, the entire purpose of the Windows 2000 Professional operating system, the processor, the memory, and all of the other components is to serve the application component. This is ultimately the component that the user sees and ultimately the component that needs to be running optimally. The reason for the existence of a highway is to have automobiles travel over it.

Quick Results

This section will help you identify performance problems quickly and find their sources. If the problem is caused by an issue that can be resolved easily, such as by the addition of memory, then this section can help you get quick results.

However, if the problem is more widespread or complex, this section will help you get to the first step in solving it, but may not guide you to quick results. To help you resolve more pervasive and complicated problems, the rest of the chapter will show you how to carefully analyze the entire system and tune all components.

Cast a Wide Net

In a typical scenario, an administrator gets a call from a user complaining that the system is slow—no other information. What is the quickest way to narrow down the problem? The answer is to cast a wide net and see what is caught.

The following counters cast a wide net over the performance of the system, covering all of the key subsystems of a workstation. Open a System Monitor session and add these counters:

▼ **Memory\Available Bytes**   See if this value is low during slow periods.

■ **Memory\Cache Bytes**   See if this value is low during slow periods.

■ **Memory\Pages/sec**   Check whether this value is less than 60 for low-end systems and less than 200 for high-end systems.

■ **LogicalDisk\% Free Space**   Ensure that there is at least 25 percent free space.

■ **PhysicalDisk\Disk Reads/sec**   Check whether this value is high during slow periods.

■ **PhysicalDisk\Disk Writes/sec**   Check whether this value is high during slow periods.

■ **PhysicalDisk\Avg. Disk Queue Length**   Check whether this value is 2 or greater.

■ **Processor(All_Instances)\% Processor Time**   Check whether the total or the value for any one processor is higher than 85 percent.

▲ **System\Processor Queue Length**   Check whether this value is 2 or greater.

After checking these counters, you should have a clear idea of where to take the next steps.

Next Steps

If any one or more of the wide-net counters show problem values, then drill down on those to try to determine what the problem might be. In and of themselves, the counters don't indicate a problem in the subsystem. The values could be normal operating conditions for the workstation or could be problem conditions. Also, a high value in one subsystem may be the result of a constraint in another subsystem. For example, a high PhysicalDisk\ Ave Disk Queue Length may be the result of constrained system memory, resulting in excessive paging and high disk utilization.

The balance of this chapter goes into the details of performance tuning for each of the areas covered by the wide-net counters.

Knowing Your System Profile

Setting expectations is key in any endeavor, performance tuning included. Some systems just lack the overall capacity to perform well, especially with the full-featured applications that users demand today. It is important to let the user, and management, know what is possible for particular systems. Sometimes that means identifying the limits of performance, and at other times it means driving the re-architecture of a system.

Throughout this chapter, a basic system profile classification is developed to help guide the setting of expectations.

Tuning Limitations

A high-performance disk is capable of about 100 random or 300 sequential I/O operations per second. Loading a large application like Microsoft Word requires something like 300 I/O operations. Doing the math for a fragmented disk, it might take 3 seconds to load the application because the files will be distributed over the disk and require random I/O operations.

The system performance could be tuned by defragmenting the disk, as is discussed later in this chapter. After this tuning, the application will load in about one second. That is about a threefold increase in performance as a result of tuning.

However, there is an old saying: "You can't make a silk purse out of a sow's ear." If the system in question is an older low-performance system capable of only 10 random or 30 sequential I/O operations per second, then even after tuning, the best performance that could be hoped for would be an application load time of 10 seconds. That's much better than the 30 seconds it would have taken prior to the defragmenting, but still a long time. Also, there will probably be other constraining factors in the older system (such as memory and processor limitations) that will limit its performance even more.

The bottom line: tuning will help administrators and users get the most out of their systems, but it will not overcome the inherent limitations of systems. Sometimes, as is the case with a sow's ear, bad performance is the best that can be expected.

TIP: In pet stores, you can find dried sows ears sold as dog chews. If you have a system with a 10-I/O-per-second disk subsystem, our considered recommendation is to convert the old system to a dog chew and upgrade to a faster system.

Re-architecting

Sometimes, a given system will need to be re-architected from the ground up to improve performance.

An example of this is a database application in which the client accesses the database over a slow link, such as a remote office workstation that accesses a central office database over the corporate 56-Kbps WAN link. If, after applying the tuning techniques discussed in this chapter, the system performance is still inadequate, then the solution to the performance problem would be to re-architect the database application. In effect, the tuning process has gotten the most out of the system that is possible, and further improvements require changing the application.

MEMORY

Memory has become the limiting component in most Windows 2000 Professional systems. This is not necessarily a bad thing, as it is an easy performance problem to address. In fact, the common response to a performance problem is to throw handfuls of SIMM or DIMM chips at the system, because administrators have had this solution work so often.

This section takes a more analytical approach. Rather than have you waste resources by overengineering the memory, the section shows you how to evaluate memory usage to understand what the operating system needs. This section also shows you how to make do with less memory by reducing the demand—useful knowledge in times of belt tightening.

How Much Is Enough?

The normal response to a performance problem is to throw memory at it and hope that it sticks—that is, solves the problem. This is wasteful from a resource and time perspective, and overengineering the memory may mask the real problem and delay finding it. There are much more effective methods for correctly sizing the memory in a system.

The first step is to verify the amount of memory in the system, which can be done in a variety of ways. The simplest is to look at the Performance tab of the Task Manager, as shown in Figure 12-1. Look at the Physical Memory box, in the Total row. As an added bonus, the available memory is also listed there, in the Available row.

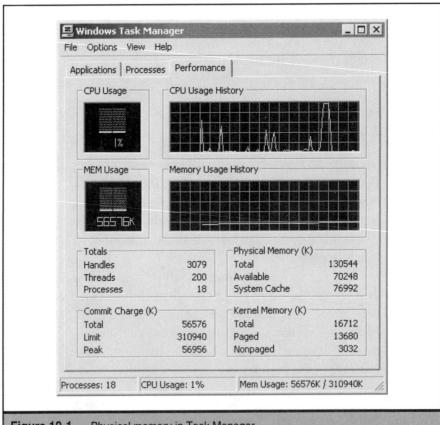

Figure 12-1. Physical memory in Task Manager

Current Usage

To give you a good feel for how memory is being used and whether there is a shortage, Windows 2000 Professional provides a number of Performance Monitor counters. The counters in Table 12-1 are the most important to watch to identify memory shortages.

These counters can indicate current memory shortages, but how can you predict or plan for memory requirements? The next three

Object\Counter	Description
Memory\Available Bytes	Shows the amount of physical memory available to processes running on the computer, in bytes. This counter displays the last observed value only; it is not an average.
Process (All_processes)\Working Set	Shows the current number of bytes in the Working Set of this process. The Working Set is the set of memory pages touched recently by the threads in the process.
Memory\Pages/sec	Shows the number of pages read from or written to disk to resolve hard page faults. This counter displays the difference between the values observed in the last two samples divided by the duration of the sample interval.
Memory\Cache Bytes	Shows the sum of the System Cache Resident Bytes, System Driver Resident Bytes, System Code Resident Bytes, and Pool Paged Resident Bytes counters. This counter displays the last observed value only; it is not an average.

Table 12-1.   Memory Shortage Counters

sections present guidelines for profiling memory usage and classifying it into three general categories. After classifying workstation profiles, it is still important to use the counters in Table 12-1 to check actual performance during testing and during operation.

Low-Memory Profile

A system with a low-memory profile has 32MB of memory. This is the minimum needed to operate according to Microsoft, and the system operates at the minimum level. As a result of swapping and caching issues, discussed later in this chapter, the performance suffers.

A system with this profile is acceptable for light use, for users using a single application such as e-mail.

Medium-Memory Profile

A system with a medium-memory profile has 64MB of memory, and the difference between this type of system and a low-memory profile system is notable. With this quantity of memory, performance increases by as much as a factor of three. In other words, operations that would have taken 30 seconds with a low-memory profile system will be completed in 10 seconds on a medium-memory profile system.

However, if more resource-intensive applications are added and multiple applications are run simultaneously, performance will begin to degrade as swapping increases. Thus, a medium-memory profile system is suitable for medium use, for users using several applications such as e-mail and word processing.

High-Memory Profile

A system with a high-memory profile has 128MB or more of memory. This higher level of memory allows more of the system and applications to stay in memory, avoiding disk swapping. Performance for a single application does not increase significantly (by about 15 percent) over the medium-memory profile system, but performance when using multiple applications concurrently increases dramatically. The increase in performance for a system running three or four applications in the Microsoft Office 2000 suite is about 50 percent over a medium-memory profile system.

Table 12-2 summarizes the three types of memory profiles.

System Profile	Description	Memory (MB)
Low	Light use; single application	32
Medium	Medium use; several concurrent applications	64
High	Heavy use; multiple concurrent applications, including line-of-business applications	128

Table 12-2. System Profiles—Memory

Swapping

Even with advances in memory technology and ever-increasing amounts of memory configured into systems, the operating system's memory use can still outrun the available physical memory. How does the operating system handle this?

Virtual Memory

Although the operating system tries to keep everything in RAM, when everything doesn't fit, the operating system swaps the least recently used memory pages to the hard disk, storing them in the paging file. When a user requires the swapped pages, the operating system loads the swapped pages back into RAM and swaps other pages to disk to make room for the pages that the user needs. This simulation of memory by mapping it to disk is called virtual memory.

To see how much virtual memory your Windows 2000 Professional uses or has used over time, start all of the applications that are normally in use and access the Task Manager to check the Peak Commit Charge value. This value appears in the Commit Charge (K) box on the Performance tab, as shown in Figure 12-2. The commit charge is the number of pages reserved for virtual memory that are backed by the paging file.

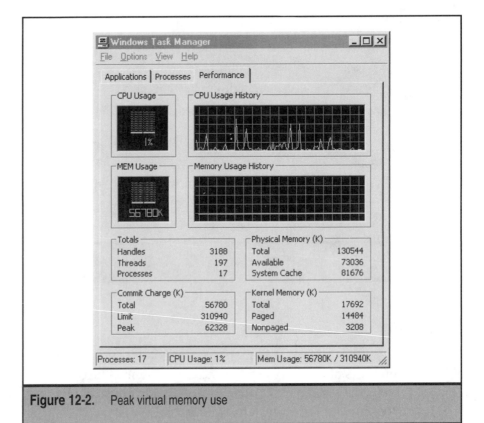

Figure 12-2.   Peak virtual memory use

Impact on Performance

Unfortunately, there is a performance cost to swapping. The disk speed is extremely slow in comparison to physical memory, so the system takes a performance hit by swapping memory to disk. The average computer memory chip today has an access time of 50 nanoseconds, or 5×10^{-8} seconds. Very fast disk access time today is about 6 milliseconds, or 6×10^{-3} seconds. Do a bit of quick math, and it turns out that physical memory is 120,000 times as fast as memory swapped to disk. To put that in human terms, if it takes a minute to get a bit of information from physical memory, then it would take almost 12 weeks to get the same information from disk. Or, the decrease in speed is worse than the difference between sending e-mail to someone and shipping that person a package using Third-Class Book Rate through the U.S. Mail.

So swapping can have a big impact on performance, delaying the launch of applications and the switching between applications. In the case of large line-of-business applications with many dynamic link libraries and loadable modules, the application itself will run slowly as modules are forced to load and unload. Therefore, the placement of the paging file is important and can dramatically affect performance.

To monitor the impact of swapping on the performance of the system, load the counters listed in Table 12-3 into the System Monitor. These counters will give you a good picture of the rate of page faults, which are memory pages being swapped to disk.

For the Memory\Pages/sec counter, the value should be less than 60 per second for older computers and less than 200 per second for newer computers. The value really depends on the disk subsystem, because the page is being written to and read from the disk.

A simple response to a high rate of page faults is to add more physical memory. When this is not possible, try optimizing the pagefile as discussed in the next section.

Pagefile

The pagefile is the source of the most problematic interaction between hardware components. It creates a performance link between memory and disk that is a frequent source of performance problems. This section looks at how to size and place the pagefile for maximum benefit, as well as how to optimize the performance of the pagefile itself.

Sizing

The default size of the pagefile is 1.5 times the physical memory. Expanding the default size of the paging file can increase performance if applications are consuming virtual memory and the full capacity of the existing file is being used. The best way to determine how large the pagefile needs to be is to look at the system workload, which can be done by monitoring the Process (_Total)\Page File Bytes Peak counter. This counter indicates, in bytes, the amount of the paging file used by processes.

Object\Counter	Description
Memory\Pages/sec	Shows the number of pages read from or written to disk to resolve hard page faults. This counter displays the difference between the values observed in the last two samples divided by the duration of the sample interval.
Process (All_processes)\ Working Set	Shows the current number of bytes in the working set of this process. The working set is the set of memory pages touched recently by the threads in the process. If free memory in the computer is above a threshold, pages are left in the working set of a process even though they are not in use. When free memory falls below a threshold, pages are trimmed from working sets. If these pages are needed, they will then be soft-faulted back into the working set before they leave main memory.
Memory\Pages Input/sec	Shows the number of pages read from disk to resolve hard page faults. This counter was designed as a primary indicator of the kinds of faults that cause systemwide delays.
Memory\Pages Output/sec	Shows the number of pages written to disk to free up space in physical memory. Pages are written back to disk only if they are changed in physical memory, so they are likely to hold data, not code. A high rate of pages output may indicate a memory shortage.

Table 12-3.   Page Fault Counters

Consider expanding the pagefile whenever this counter reaches 75 percent of the total size, in bytes, of the pagefile. This will ensure that the pagefile always has headroom. Rather than set a large maximum size, use the same initial and maximum sizes to avoid pagefile fragmentation.

Remember: in the case of the pagefile, bigger is better!

Placement

Windows 2000 Professional puts the pagefile on the same drive as the operating system by default. This means that the operating system's access to loadable modules and settings is in direct contention with the virtual memory system's use of the pagefile. The disk subsystem becomes a bottleneck during periods of high activity in both areas.

Moving the pagefile to a separate drive from the operating system is especially helpful in limited-memory systems, as these systems rely on virtual memory heavily and thus use the pagefile more. For a system with 32MB of memory, the performance improvement can be as much as 30 percent. (See Table 12-4.)

Object\Counter	Description
Memory\Page Reads/sec	Shows the number of times that the disk was read to resolve hard page faults. This counter counts the number of read operations, without regard to the number of pages retrieved by each operation.
Physical Disk\ Avg. Disk Bytes/Read	Shows the average number of bytes transferred from the disk during read operations.

Table 12-4. Paging Disk Bottleneck Counters

Splitting

Putting the pagefile on two separate drives can increase performance in medium-memory profile systems. For example, splitting the pagefile for a low-memory (32MB) configuration only increases the overhead the system has to manage, so the net benefit is less than when you use just one pagefile on a separate drive. In large-memory profile systems (128MB or more), swapping is minimal, and so any net benefits are minimal as well. Where splitting the pagefile is very effective is in medium-memory profile systems (64MB), where workstations will see about a 15 percent improvement in performance over the use of just a single pagefile.

Remember that these benefits require that the drives be actual physically separate drives, not just logical partitions on the same physical drive.

Changing the Pagefile

Changing the pagefile setting requires a reboot, as the system cannot modify its virtual memory profile while in operation.

To change the pagefile setting, follow these steps:

1. On the desktop, right-click My Computer and select Properties.
2. Click the Advanced tab.
3. Click the Performance Options button.
4. In the Virtual Memory box, click the Change button.
5. Modify the setting as appropriate.
6. Click Set to change the settings.
7. Click OK to exit.

Fragmentation

If the current size of the paging file is larger than its initial size, the file probably became fragmented as it grew. Unfortunately, the Windows 2000 native defragmentation tool will not defragment the paging file. Use the counters in Table 12-5 to help identify a fragmented pagefile.

Object\Counter	Description
PhysicalDisk\ Split IO/sec	Reports the rate at which I/O operations to the disk were split into multiple I/O operations. Split I/O operations may result from requesting data in a size that is too large to fit into a single I/O operation, or they may indicate that the disk is fragmented.
PhysicalDisk\ % Disk Read Time	Shows the percentage of elapsed time that the selected disk drive is busy servicing read requests.
PhysicalDisk\ Current Disk Queue Length	Shows the number of requests outstanding on the disk at the time that the performance data is collected. It includes requests in service at the time of the snapshot. This is an instantaneous length, not an average over the time interval. Multi-spindle disk devices can have multiple requests active at one time, but other concurrent requests are awaiting service. This counter may reflect a transitory long or short queue length, but if there is a sustained load on the disk drive, it is likely that this counter will consistently be high. Requests experience delays proportional to the length of this queue minus the number of spindles on the disks. This difference should average less than two for good performance.
Process\ Handle Count	Shows the total number of handles currently opened by this process. This number is the sum of the handles currently opened by each thread in this process.

Table 12-5. Paging File Fragmentation Counters

If the counters indicate that the pagefile is fragmented, see the "Defragmenting the Disk" section later in this chapter for a solution to this problem.

Caching

Administrators do not often look at the Windows 2000 Professional cache, as it takes care of itself for the most part. It has a tremendous effect on performance, however, as it leverages memory to improve disk performance.

Relation to Memory

The Windows 2000 file system cache is an area of memory in which the operating system stores recently used data from the disk. When processes need to read from or write to disk, the operating system first checks to see whether the part of the file requested is in the cache. If the part of the file requested is in the cache, then the operating system can read directly from memory instead of from the slow disk. This gives the operation a 120,000:1 boost in performance, due to the difference in speed between memory and disk I/O. If the data requested is not in the cache, then the operating system reads the information from disk and puts it into the cache in case it is requested again. This technique is called caching.

The size of the cache depends on the amount of physical memory installed and the memory required for applications. Windows 2000 Professional by default allocates 8MB of physical memory for the cache at startup. During operation, the operating system dynamically adjusts the size of the cache as needed, balancing memory requirements among the operating system, applications, and system cache.

Adjusting the Cache Manually

Unfortunately, administrators can't adjust the cache in Windows 2000 Professional through the user interface, though they can do so in Windows 2000 Server and the other server versions. If administrators want to tune the cache manually, they have to do so using the Registry.

Set the value LargeSystemCache in HKLM\SYSTEM\ CurrentControlSet\Control\Session Manager\Memory Management.

This value determines whether the system maintains a standard- or large-size file system cache and influences how often the system writes changed pages to disk. The default is 0 for a standard cache size. Set the value to 1 to increase the cache size.

Increasing the size of the file system cache generally improves workstation disk performance, but it reduces the physical memory space available to applications and services. This is because a larger cache minimizes use of the disk subsystem, but at the expense of memory that might otherwise be used by applications.

Conserving Memory

Sometimes, it is better to conserve memory rather than to add more to the system. This may be the case for older systems, where memory upgrades may be very expensive or simply not available. Laptop systems are a good example of this type of system.

You may also want to conserve memory out of a general sense of fiscal responsibility, to do more with less, a trend that is driving the industry. Rather than spend money to solve a problem, help reduce overhead for the organization by maximizing the use of the existing resources before purchasing more.

This section addresses how to conserve memory resources.

Disk Space

Check the available space on your disks to make sure there is enough for the operating system and pagefile. If you are using a large paging file and space is not available, you may experience the symptoms of a memory bottleneck, as the pagefile will be unable to grow. Better yet, configure the maximum and minimum pagefile sizes so they are the same.

Bells and Whistles

To reduce memory use, avoid using some display and sound features. Features that can drain memory include animated cursors, a large number of desktop icons, large-bitmap wallpaper, and some screensaver programs. Removing or disabling these bells and whistles can reduce the load on a memory-constrained system.

Slimming Down

Interestingly, even though a service that is started may not be using any processor time, it will still be using memory. In many cases, the service will be doing nothing and still reserving megabytes of memory. Use the Task Manager and select the Processes tab to view the memory used by the processes (Figure 12-3). To free memory, turn off services that are not needed. This will save memory and improve system performance. However, it is critical that you understand the ramifications of stopping a service before making any changes.

Also, remove unnecessary network protocols and drivers. Even unused protocols and drivers use memory.

Memory and Applications

Not all applications are created equally. Some applications are designed and written very effectively, using resources wisely. Other applications are less so, demanding more than their fair share of system resources. Unfortunately, the operating system has no way of telling the good from the bad to throttle the resource access, and it really has no business making that decision anyway. Administrators may require certain applications in spite of their performance impact. This is especially true of vertical applications and internally developed applications. In the case of the vertical applications (such as medical, real estate, or legal software), there may not be any viable alternatives. In the case of internally developed applications, there may not be sufficient resources or expertise available to improve the performance.

Use the counters in Table 12-6 to identify specific applications that are using resources heavily.

After you identify resource-intensive applications, you may not be able to do anything about them. However, the information is useful for identifying the profile of the system (medium or large) on which the application may need to be installed or even possibly providing feedback to developers to help them fine-tune the application.

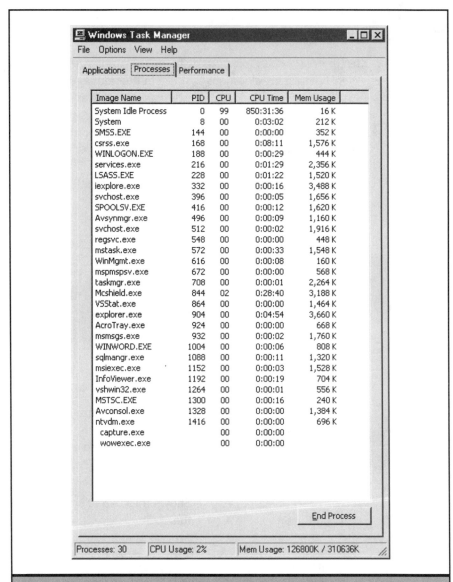

Figure 12-3.   Processes and their memory use

Object\Counter	Description
Memory\ Pool Nonpaged Allocations	Shows the number of calls to allocate space in the nonpaged pool. The nonpaged pool is an area of system memory for objects that cannot be written to disk and must remain in physical memory as long as they are allocated.
Memory\ Pool Nonpaged Bytes	Shows the number of bytes in the nonpaged pool.
Memory\ Pool Paged Bytes	Shows the number of bytes in the paged pool, an area of system memory (physical memory used by the operating system) for objects that can be written to disk when they are not being used.
Process(process_name)\ Pool Nonpaged Bytes	Shows the number of bytes in the nonpaged pool, by process.
Process(process_name)\ Pool Paged Bytes	Shows the number of bytes in the paged pool, by process.
Process(process_name)\ Handle Count	Shows the total number of handles currently opened by this process. This number is the sum of the handles currently opened by each thread in this process.
Process(process_name)\ Virtual Bytes	Shows the current size, in bytes, of the virtual address space that the process is using. Use of virtual address space does not necessarily imply corresponding use of either disk or main memory pages. Virtual space is finite, and by using too much, the process can limit its ability to load libraries.

Table 12-6. Counters for Memory Intensive Applications

Object\Counter	Description
Process(process_name)\ Private Bytes	Shows the current number of bytes that this process has allocated that cannot be shared with other processes.

Table 12-6. Counters for Memory Intensive Applications *(continued)*

DISK AND FILE SYSTEM

After memory, disk performance is usually the workstation bottleneck. The operating system, all applications, and all data eventually resides on disk, so everything must go onto and eventually come off of the disk. This disk is also the safety valve for memory overflows, where the pagefile simulates memory. Compounding this memory overflow problem is the large performance ratio between the memory subsystem and the disk subsystem.

Fortunately, the disk is also a place where a lot of tuning can be done, such as defragmenting a volume, with great effect. This section looks at how to measure the performance of the disk subsystem and how to tweak it to make the disk perform better.

Evaluating the Disk Subsystem

It is important to evaluate the disk subsystem prior to any tuning efforts, to make sure that the tweaks you perform actually help the system, which is not always a foregone conclusion.

Enabling Disk Counters

There are two types of disk counters: physical and logical. Physical disk counters are enabled by default, but logical disk counters are not. Windows 2000 does not enable all disk counters automatically because approximately a 1 percent overhead is required to gather counter statistics.

You can enable counters easily using the DISKPERF command. To enable all counters, do the following:

1. Open a command prompt.

2. Enter the command **DISKPERF –Y**.

3. Close the command prompt.

4. Restart the system.

The PhysicalDisk object counters provide information for each of the physical disks in the system, whereas the LogicalDisk object counters provide information for each of the logical volumes in the system. A number, starting with 0, identifies physical disks, and the appropriate drive letter identifies logical disks (C, D, and so on).

When monitoring logical volumes, remember that they may share physical disks and that your data may reflect contention between those disks. If you have a spanned volume or striped volume with disk controllers that implement hardware-enabled RAID partitions, the counters report physical disk data for all disks in the RAID partition as if they were on a single disk.

Disk Capacity

The capacity of the disk and how much of this capacity is available are important factors in performance and stability. If the drive fills up, then some performance tuning operations can't occur automatically, such as expansion of the pagefile. Another side effect of a disk that is running at capacity is increased fragmentation, and increased difficulty in performing defragmentation, as discussed later in this chapter in "Defragmenting the Disk."

It is difficult to determine exactly what capacity should be available, as the requirements vary by system and by application. Some applications, such as Crystal Reports, require space to write a large number of temporary files. Database queries, especially SQL queries, require local space to store the results they receive.

A good rule of thumb is that at least 25 percent of the disk should be free at any given time. The counters in Table 12-7 monitor the disk space. The counters need to be enabled for the LogicalDisk object to

Object\Counter	Description
LogicalDisk\ % Free Space	Reports the ratio of unallocated disk space to total usable space on the logical volume. There is no % Free Space counter for the PhysicalDisk object.
LogicalDisk\ Free Megabytes	Reports the number of bytes on the disk that are not allocated. There is no Free Megabytes counter for the PhysicalDisk object.

Table 12-7.   Disk Usage Counters

be available. Interestingly, in Windows NT, the counters were visible, but always read 0, when they were not enabled. This led to some confusion, which Microsoft has forestalled in Windows 2000 by not exposing the objects when the counters are disabled.

For workstations, these are counters that are useful to monitor on a routine basis to ensure that the drives don't fill up.

For standard workstation profiles, it is useful to add a minimum disk capacity criterion. Whereas memory requirements are relatively precise, disk capacity is much more flexible. Microsoft requires a minimum of 680MB of disk space to install Windows 2000 Professional, but this is woefully inadequate for normal use. Table 12-8 gives more reasonable capacities that take into account applications and pagefile use.

Disk Performance

In the old days (pre-2000), disk performance was much more of a concern. Most workstation systems were underpowered from a memory perspective, which led to significant paging overhead. This taxed the disk subsystem and made it appear to be the bottleneck; however, this really masked a memory bottleneck.

In today's modern computing environment (post-2000), memory is much more plentiful, and thus there is significantly less paging than before. This reduced paging load has allowed memory to once

System Profile	Description	Memory (MB)	Disk (GB)
Low	Light use; single application	32	2
Medium	Medium use; several concurrent applications	64	6
High	Heavy use; multiple concurrent applications, including line-of-business applications	128	10

Table 12-8.   System Profiles—Disk Capacity

again assume its rightful place as the recognized bottleneck in the average system. In addition, disk subsystem performance has improved dramatically.

Nevertheless, you still need to monitor disk performance on workstations. An example of a common performance issue is application launching, where applications take tens of seconds to load. At this time, the application executables are being read from the disk and placed in the system cache. Once the applications are in cache, access to them should be much faster. If it is not, then the counters listed in Table 12-9 can help you determine whether the disk is the source of the problem.

For each of the counters in Table 12-9, there are specific read and write counters that allow administrators to determine more exactly what or where the performance impact is. If any of the combined read-write counters in the table has a high value, then the administrator should immediately drill down and examine the corresponding read and the write counters separately. The exception to this is the % Idle Time counter, which does not have corresponding read and write counters.

Object\Counter	Description
LogicalDisk\ Avg. Disk Queue Length PhysicalDisk\ Avg. Disk Queue Length	Tracks the number of requests that are queued and waiting for a disk during the sample interval as well as requests in service. As a result, this counter may overstate activity. If more than two requests are continuously waiting on a single-disk system, the disk may be a bottleneck.
LogicalDisk\ Current Disk Queue Length PhysicalDisk\ Current Disk Queue Length	Indicates the number of disk requests that are currently waiting as well as requests currently being serviced. This value is subject to wide variation unless the workload has achieved a steady state and you have collected a sufficient number of samples to establish a pattern.
LogicalDisk\% Disk Time PhysicalDisk\% Disk Time	Reports the percentage of time that the selected disk drive is busy servicing read or write requests. Because this counter's data can span more than one sample and consequently can overstate disk use, compare this value with % Idle Time for a more accurate picture.
LogicalDisk\% Idle Time PhysicalDisk\% Idle Time	Reports the percentage of time that the disk system was not processing requests and no work was queued. Note that this counter, when added to % Disk Time, may not equal 100 percent, because % Disk Time can exaggerate disk use.

Table 12-9. Disk Performance Counters

NOTE: If the workload consists of random bursts of high activity, counters will register high activity rates followed by long periods of idle time. Average counter values can be misleading with these types of workloads, as the disk can appear to be not busy even though it is busy during the bursts of high activity. To determine how well the disk system is handling the bursts, sample at short intervals when the activity occurs.

Queue Length

Even more than the use percentage counters, the queue length counters can reveal true performance bottlenecks. The reason for this is that in a high-throughput system, high utilization should be acceptable. Many systems are overengineered, so that if the system approaches maximum use, there is a problem. In a well-engineered system, this simply means that the system is being used to its maximum potential.

In contrast, according to queuing theory, a queue length that is consistently over 2 will be a bottleneck. This is because as new items arrive in the queue, the queue will either grow continuously or be forced to put backpressure on the new items. Backpressure is a generic term for any feedback mechanism that forces a host or process to slow down the rate at which it submits requests. In practice, Windows 2000 puts backpressure on new disk requests. Although queues are most likely to grow when the system is very busy, they can still grow when use is well below maximum capacity. This can happen if requests arrive at irregular intervals, or if they take a long time to service.

NOTE: A queue is essentially a waiting line, similar to a line for a bank teller. Queuing theory is the mathematical theory of queues, or waiting lines. A. K. Erlang of the Copenhagen Telephone Company initially developed the theory for telephony purposes in the early 1900s. It has since been expanded to include computer science, manufacturing, air traffic control, and many other disciplines. There is quite a bit of math behind it and different models, but for the purposes of performance tuning, queuing theory can be distilled to a simple rule of thumb: on average, keep queue length to less than 2.

The values of the queue counters for disks are related to the number of physical disks the counters represent, also known as spindles for the fact that each separate physical drive has its own spindle. In other words, the queues are really analogues for the disk partitions themselves, and the queue counters sometimes represent more than one physical drive (as in a RAID system). If the value of Avg. Disk Queue Length exceeds twice the number of spindles or drives, then there is probably a bottleneck.

Throughput

Throughput is a measure of how fast a *flow* of information is passed through the system, rather than how fast a *piece* of information is passed through the system. Throughput is a better indicator of performance than just read and write times, because it measures how much real work gets done.

Use the counters in Table 12-10 to measure the throughput of the disk subsystem. Use these counters in conjunction with other counters to determine the causes of low throughput.

As with the disk performance counters, the counters in Table 12-10 give the total for both read and write operations. Should high values be observed, immediately begin monitoring the read and write versions of the counters to understand at a finer level of detail the nature of the high values.

Improving Throughput

To improve throughput, limit the use of file compression and encryption. These features can consume quite a bit of overhead and will degrade throughput. Use them sparingly and only where specifically required.

Another way to improve throughput is to place multiple drives on separate I/O buses, particularly if a disk has an I/O-intensive workload. Many workstations have dual PCI IDE buses, and systems with dual drives can place a separate drive on each one. Of course, there may be ramifications for systems that have other devices such as CD-ROM drives, so testing and a complete understanding of the effects are required.

Object\Counter	Description
LogicalDisk\Disk Bytes/sec PhysicalDisk\Disk Bytes/sec	Indicates the rate at which bytes are transferred and is the primary measure of disk throughput.
LogicalDisk\Avg. Disk Bytes/Transfer PhysicalDisk\Avg. Disk Bytes/Transfer	Measures the size of I/O operations. The disk is efficient if it transfers large amounts of data relatively quickly. Watch this counter when measuring maximum throughput.
LogicalDisk\Disk Transfers/sec PhysicalDisk\Disk Transfers/sec	Indicates the number of read and write operations completed per second, regardless of how much data they involve. Measures disk utilization. If the value exceeds 50 (per physical disk in the case of a striped volume), then a bottleneck may be developing.
LogicalDisk\Avg. Disk sec/Transfer PhysicalDisk\Avg. Disk sec/Transfer	Indicates how quickly, in seconds, data is being moved. The counter measures the average time for each data transfer, regardless of the number of bytes read or written. A high value for this counter may mean that the system is retrying requests due to lengthy queuing or, less commonly, disk failures.

Table 12-10.   Disk Throughput Counters

Disk I/O vs. Memory I/O

The symptoms of a memory shortage are similar to those of a disk bottleneck. When physical memory runs low, the system starts paging. The less memory the system has, the more paging that occurs and the more the disk is used, resulting in a greater load on the disk system. Therefore, monitor memory counters along with disk counters when investigating a performance problem with your disk system, as it may really be a memory problem in disguise.

Defragmenting the Disk

Defragmentation is one of the most effective performance enhancing tweaks that you can perform. Defragmentation usually generates a significant performance increase that spans booting up, launching applications, and saving data, making it visible across a wide spectrum of activities.

File Fragmentation

If a file resides entirely in one location with no breaks on a disk, it is said to be contiguous. A fragmented file is separated into pieces that are stored in one or more places on the disk. File fragmentation is a normal process and affects files stored on both FAT and NTFS file systems. The operating system allows files to become fragmented as a trade-off for being able to write files to disk quickly wherever there is free space. Otherwise, the operating system would have to slow down writing while it moved files around to free up a contiguous stretch of disk space.

While fragmentation allows files to be written to disk quickly, over time it degrades performance. This is because the operating system has to move the disk head to all the different points on the disk to read the fragmented files. Fragmentation also gets worse over time, as more files are added and deleted. Large files stored on a workstation, such as a database file, can be fragmented into thousands and even tens of thousands of individual chunks on the disk. Eventually, fragmentation slows read and write operations to a fraction of their original performance. It also affects rebooting, as it takes longer to read files from disk due to fragmentation. Fragmentation is also a process that does not fix itself over time, but rather gets worse and worse.

Identifying Fragmentation

Administrators can run the defragmentation utility to get a report on the state of disk fragmentation. This is a manual endeavor and is somewhat intrusive. If you are monitoring on a continuous basis, then using the performance counters is easier. Although there are no fragmentation-specific counters, the split I/O counters listed in Table 12-11 can be used as indicators of fragmentation.

If the split I/O counters start reading high, then the administrator can initiate defragmentation.

Defragmentation

Defragmentation is the process of making fragmented files and free space contiguous. As both FAT and NTFS volumes can deteriorate and become badly fragmented over time, defragmentation is a vital system maintenance action. Defragmentation programs shuffle files around to consolidate the file fragments into contiguous files. This is similar to the tile puzzle game, in which there is a single open space to slide the tiles into, and the player has to move the tiles around to complete a pattern.

Object\Counter	Description
LogicalDisk\Split IO/sec PhysicalDisk\Split IO/sec	Report the rate at which the operating system divides I/O requests to the disk into multiple requests. A split I/O request may occur if the program requests data in a size that is too large to fit into a single request, or if the disk is fragmented. Factors that influence the size of an I/O request can include application design, the file system, or drivers. A high rate of split I/O may not, in itself, represent a problem. However, on single-disk systems, a high rate for these counters tends to indicate disk fragmentation.

Table 12-11. Disk Fragmentation Counters

Windows 2000 includes a utility called Disk Defragmenter that will defragment the volumes. Prior to defragmenting, the tool will allow administrators to generate an analysis of the disk to see if defragmentation is necessary. The analysis will recommend that the volume be defragmented based on the fragmentation level of the volume. This saves unnecessary work if the drive will not benefit from defragmentation. The analysis shown in Figure 12-4 indicates a significant number of fragmented files and free space that is also badly fragmented. As can be seen, there are not very many contiguous files. This is an example of a badly fragmented drive with about a 27 percent file fragmentation, and the Disk Defragmenter is recommending that the drive be defragmented.

While defragmenting, the system will use between 30 and 50 percent of CPU time and about 50 to 80 percent of the disk I/O subsystem time, as is shown by the sample System Monitor graph in Figure 12-5. This

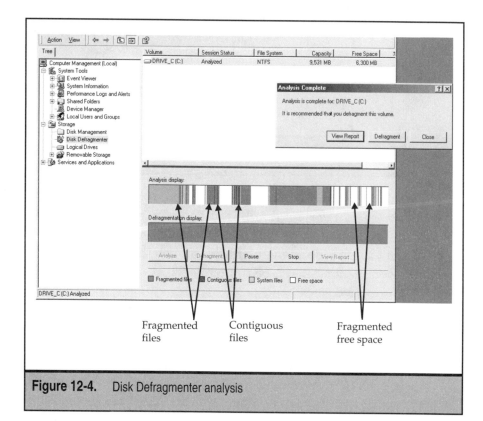

Figure 12-4. Disk Defragmenter analysis

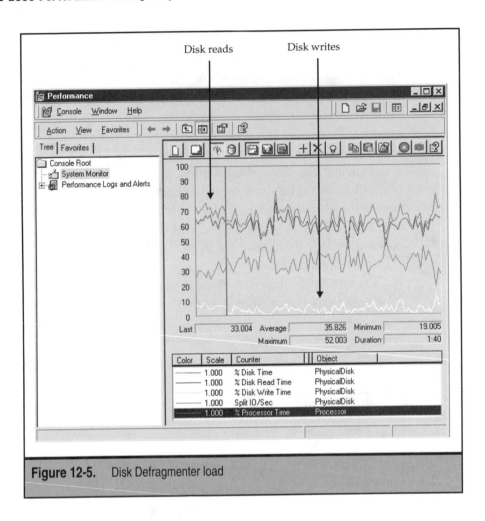

Figure 12-5. Disk Defragmenter load

screen shot was taken while Disk Defragmenter was running. The disk I/O is mostly reads and few writes, as might be expected. Given the load that defragmentation places on the system, it is not usually recommended that it be run while the system is being used for productive work.

To effectively defragment a drive, the Disk Defragmenter needs free space in which to shuffle the files. In NTFS, the master file table (MFT) is an index file that maps everything stored on a volume. There is at least one entry in the MFT for every file on an NTFS volume. Each entry contains such information as the size, time and date stamps, security attributes, and data location. Windows 2000 reserves 12 percent of the space on a volume for the exclusive use of the MFT.

This area is known as the MFT zone and shows up as free space. The Windows 2000 Disk Defragmenter cannot use this reserved area, so it is normally recommended that at least 30 percent of the volume be free to perform defragmentation effectively. If it is not, then the Disk Defragmenter may continue to report that defragmentation is needed even after a defragmentation pass. To eliminate this problem, free up disk space and rerun the defragmenter.

After defragmenting a disk, the Disk Defragmenter will display the results graphically and also generate a report. As can be seen in Figure 12-6, while there are still some file fragments, the majority of the volume is contiguous. The free space is also much more consolidated. In the report, the file fragmentation is at about 3 percent as opposed to 27 percent prior to running the utility.

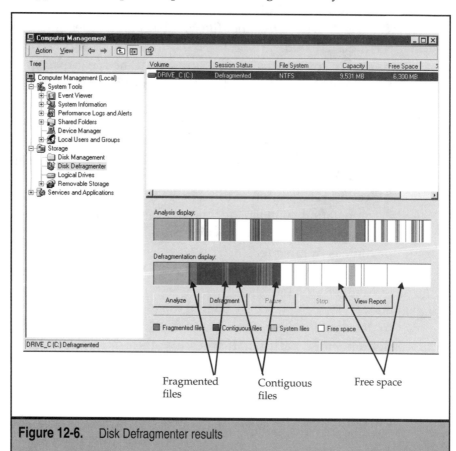

Figure 12-6.   Disk Defragmenter results

When to Defragment

Given the high impact on performance of fragmentation, it is recommended that defragmentation be performed on a regular basis for all workstations to ensure that the hard disk is operating optimally. Once a week is a good rule of thumb, though this schedule can be adjusted for systems with few local files.

New systems, upgraded systems, or systems with recently installed applications also benefit from defragmentation. The action of loading the operating system onto a brand new workstation, upgrading the operating system, or installing software can create both file and free-space fragmentation.

Pagefile Fragmentation

The pagefile, like any other file, is subject to fragmentation. Normally, the file is created early in the life of the system and will thus be created in contiguous space. However, if the file grows after that, then it will most likely add space from noncontiguous areas of the disk and thus become fragmented. If it is fragmented, performance can degrade severely due to increased disk I/O times. This is particularly bad for the paging file, as it compounds the already huge difference between memory and disk I/O times. To verify that the pagefile is fragmented, run the Disk Defragmenter analysis and view the report. The section of the report with the heading "Pagefile Fragmentation" will list the total size of the pagefile and the number of fragments. If this number is higher than 1, then the pagefile is fragmented.

Unfortunately, the Windows 2000 Disk Defragmenter will not defragment the paging file. A workaround is to find a partition with enough space to hold the paging file, use the Disk Defragmenter to defragment the partition, and then move the paging file to the defragmented partition. If necessary, the original partition can then be defragmented, and the pagefile can be moved back to its original partition.

Alternatively, there are third-party defragmentation utilities that can defragment the pagefile.

Tuning the Configuration

This section describes some additional tuning techniques ranging from buying recommendations to Registry tweaks for I/O.

Buy the Best

When obtaining disk systems, use the most intelligent and efficient disk subsystem components available for your system. This includes the controller, I/O bus, cabling, and disk drives. Upgrade to faster-speed or wider-bandwidth components if possible. This will generally decrease transfer time and improve throughput, leading to improved performance. Use intelligent drivers that support interrupt moderation or interrupt avoidance to alleviate the interrupt activity for the processor due to disk I/O.

Disable Short Names

Another performance tip is to disable the creation of short names. By default, the Windows 2000 operating system will generate MS-DOS–compatible file names (eight characters followed by a period and a three-character extension) when creating files on NTFS partitions. This is in addition to the actual file name and is used for compatibility with older clients such as Windows 3.x and 16-bit applications.

If you are not supporting these types of clients or applications, then turn off this setting by changing the default value of the NtfsDisable8dot3NameCreation Registry entry in HKEY_LOCAL_MACHINE\SYSTEM\CurrentControlSet\Control\ Filesystem. The default is 0, which will have the operating system generate the names. Changing it to 1 will stop the generation of names and improve performance.

Disable Last-Access Update

Windows 2000 updates the date and time stamp of the last access on NTFS directories whenever it accesses them, even when it just traverses the directory. Consider disabling the last-access update stamp. For a large NTFS volume, this update process can slow performance. To disable automatic updating, change the value of the NtfsDisableLastAccessUpdate Registry entry in HKEY_LOCAL_MACHINE\SYSTEM\CurrentContolSet\Control\ Filesystem from 0 to 1. If the REG_DWORD type entry is not already present in the Registry, then add it before setting the value.

This change is effective only on systems with a large number of directories.

Bypass I/O Counts

By default, the Task Manager continuously measures data for process I/O operations, even if the Task Manager is not open. This allows administrators to track system performance at any given moment by launching the Task Manager, whereas launching System Monitor would show data only from the time that the monitor started. There are 20 different data points. The performance data can be viewed on the Processes tab in Task Manager (see Figure 12-7). Columns can be added to the Process tab view by choosing Select Columns from the View menu and then checking the data points to view.

However, everything comes at a price. The system is always collecting this information from all processes, regardless of whether it's used. In a multiprocessor environment, the processors on which a process runs share this data. When a process that generates considerable disk and network I/O runs on several processors, updating the shared measurements can slow the system.

You can improve the performance of I/O-intensive operations on systems by configuring the system so that it does not collect data for global I/O counters and Task Manager process I/O counters. To do so, add the entry CountOperations to the Registry as a REG_DWORD type in HKEY_LOCAL_MACHINE\SYSTEM\CurrentControlSet\ Control\Session Manager\I/O System. The I/O System key may need to be created. Set the entry value to 0 to tell Task Manager to no longer provide per-process I/O measurements. The system will need to be restarted for the change to take effect.

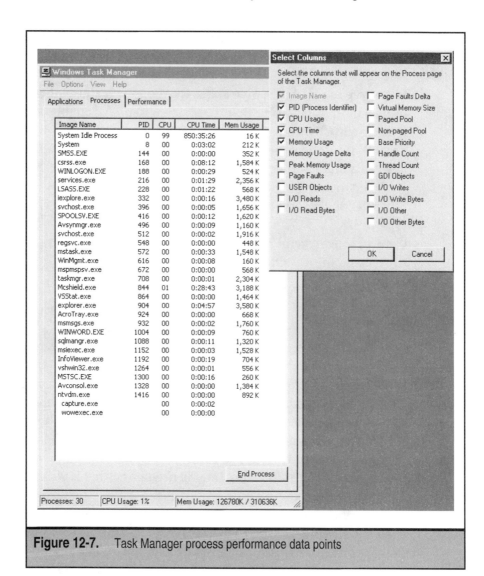

Figure 12-7.   Task Manager process performance data points

Modify Master File Table Reservation

As indicated previously in this chapter, the MFT is an index of all of the files on the drive. For systems with a large number of files, reserve the appropriate space for the master file table. If the NTFS volumes will contain relatively few files that are large, leave the value of this Registry entry at 1 (the default if no Registry entry exists). Use a value of 2 or 3 for moderate numbers of files, and 4 (the maximum) for volumes with a large number of smaller files. Setting the Registry entry to a value greater than 1 causes the system to reserve more of the drive space for the index, allowing it to grow quickly and so ensuring that the space remains available and reducing MFT fragmentation. However, be sure to test any settings greater than 2 because these higher values cause the system to reserve a much larger portion of the disk for the master file table.

To change the MFT space reservation, add the NtfsMftZoneReservation entry to the Registry as a REG_DWORD type in HKEY_LOCAL_MACHINE\SYSTEM\CurrentControlSet\ Control\FileSystem. Then set the value to the appropriate setting for the files on the system.

PROCESSOR

Because of advances in technology, and because Moore's Law is turning out to be true, the power of today's processors is becoming less and less of a performance bottleneck. Moore's Law, stated by Gordon Moore of Intel Corporation in 1975, states that the number of transistors on a chip will double every two years, as shown in Figure 12-8. The number of transistors is a measure of the processing power of a computer chip, so in effect the processing power of chips is doubling every two years. Intel is predicting that it will have 1 billion transistors on a chip by 2012!

With the phenomenal advances in computing power, there have been equally phenomenal advances in the features and functionality of the software that runs on those processors. In the 1990s, operating system and application development for desktop systems often outpaced processor capabilities. With the introduction of Windows 2000 Professional, with its focus on performance, a nice balance of features and performance has been achieved.

In fact, in typical circumstances, the processor on a Windows 2000 Professional system often is more than 90 percent idle while the computer is in use. For a typical configuration running common applications such as Microsoft Office, a Web browser, and other desktop software, performance is affected more by memory, disk, and network constraints than by the speed of the processor.

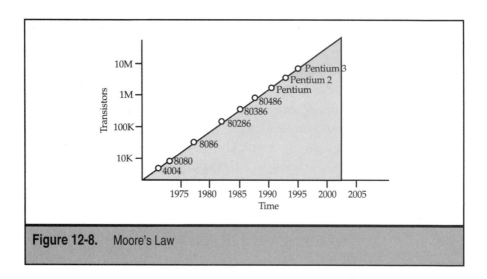

Figure 12-8. Moore's Law

NOTE: This balance is at the desktop level, where processing power is more than sufficient to meet the needs of the average desktop user. This is not necessarily true of server environments, where the client-server model puts a far greater load on server processors.

Although the processor is often idle for a typical user, there are still cases where the processor is a bottleneck and can benefit from performance tuning. For example, vertical applications, the security configuration, and hardware issues may make processor tuning beneficial. This section offers solutions to reduce processor load.

Is There a Problem?

A typical processor in computers sold today executes 100 million instructions or more per second, but often it takes many seconds to download files or Web pages even on a fast network connection. In this case, the user is waiting on the network more than on the processor. A slow system does not necessarily mean that there is a processor bottleneck. On the other hand, if the administrator has enabled IP Secure to protect the network traffic from hackers, then the bottleneck may, in fact, be the processor on the system because of the need to encrypt and decrypt packets.

It is important to systematically identify the source of a problem so you can adjust the system in the appropriate places.

Quick and Dirty

Once again, a user reports that the computer system is running slowly and contacts the administrator. Sure enough, on investigation, the administrator finds high processor utilization. The user needs a quick solution, not a long performance tuning process with baselining and analysis. How can the administrator identify the source of the problem quickly?

To quickly track down the application or process that is causing the high processor utilization, follow these steps:

1. Launch Performance Tool.

2. Click Add to add a counter.

3. Select Process\% Processor Time and select the All Instances radio button.

4. Click the Add button.

5. Click the Close button.

6. Right-click the graph and select Properties.

7. Select the Histogram radio button in the View window.

8. Click the Close button.

9. Click the Highlight button (the light bulb icon on the menu).

With the Performance Monitor now configured, the administrator can see a histogram of all running processes and their individual processor utilization values. There may be quite a few processes, but scrolling through the legend at the bottom of the System Monitor will highlight the corresponding counter in the graph to make it easy to identify. The instance name in the legend identifies the application, such as iexplore for Internet Explorer. The monitor also shows maximum, minimum, and average values for the counters, making performance counters easy to set up and monitor without having to watch the counters constantly.

This technique can help the administrator identify a problem process quickly, so the administrator can perform triage by stopping the application or altering a problem configuration. After the initial crisis is resolved, the administrator can then start a more considered performance analysis to arrive at a longer-term solution.

Utilization and Queues

The counters shown in Table 12-12 can help you determine at a high level whether the processor is impacted. Processor utilization is the common measure of the amount of work that a system is doing, and a good rule of thumb is that a well-tuned system should have a sustained processor utilization value of below 85 to 90 percent.

The queue length counters, however, are better indicators of processor bottlenecks than are the percentage utilization counters. The reason for this is that in a high-throughput system, high utilization rates should be acceptable. Many systems are overengineered, so that if the system approaches maximum utilization, there is a problem. In a well-engineered system, a high utilization rate simply means that the system is being used to its maximum potential.

In contrast, the processor queue length is a good indicator of bottlenecks. According to queuing theory, a queue length that is consistently over 2 very likely indicates a bottleneck. Although queues are most likely to grow when the system is very busy (that is, when the processor utilization rate is high), they can still grow when utilization is well below 85 percent. This can happen if requests arrive at irregular intervals, or if they take a long time to service.

Object/Counter	Description
Processor/ % Processor Time	Shows the percentage of time the processor was busy during the sampling interval. This counter is equivalent to Task Manager's CPU Usage counter. For the total processor utilization rate systemwide in multiprocessor systems, use the Processor(_Total)\ % Processor Time counter.
System/ Processor Queue Length	Performs an instantaneous count of threads that are in the processor queue.

Table 12-12.   Processor Counters

Interrupts

High counts for interrupts, which can be checked using the counter in Table 12-13, can affect processor performance and may signal hardware problems. The Processor\ Interrupts/sec counter reports the number of interrupts that the processor is servicing from applications or hardware devices. Even in a completely idle state, expect interrupts to be higher than 100 per second for a system running Windows 2000 Professional. While a system is running a processor and I/O-intensive operations such as disk defragmentation, interrupts may average more than 250 per second.

The interrupt rate is dependent on the rate of disk I/O operations per second and network packets per second. The range varies from system to system, so a baseline should be established. If the interrupt counter values are out of range, the system may have hardware problems or older hardware such as 16-bit network adapters.

Context Switches

A context switch occurs when the kernel switches the processor from one thread to another—for example, when a thread with a higher priority than the running thread becomes ready. Context switching activity is important and can be measured using the

Object/Counter	Description
Processor\Interrupts/sec	Shows the average rate per second at which the processor handles interrupts from applications or hardware devices. High activity rates can indicate hardware problems.

Table 12-13.   Interrupts Counter

counters in Table 12-14. A typical rate of context switches per second for a Windows 2000 system is 200 to 300 when several applications are running. A rate of 1,000 would be considered very high.

Context switches can be a problem if the rate is either too high or too low, as compared to a baseline established prior to troubleshooting performance problems. An application that dominates the processor lowers the rate of context switches because it does not allow processor time for the other applications. A reasonable rate of context switching usually means that the processor is being shared equally. A high context-switch rate often indicates that too many threads are competing for the processors on the system, forcing the processor to juggle the threads.

System Profiles for Processors

To round out the system profiles for workstation loads, Table 12-15 adds processors to the specification. A typical system today ships with the high-end profile, which is appropriate for applications such as Microsoft Office 2000, the Internet, and multimedia applications.

Object/Counter	Description
System\Context Switches/sec	Shows the average rate per second at which the context switches among threads on the computer. High activity rates can result from inefficient hardware or poorly designed applications. The counter reports systemwide context switches.
Thread(_Total)\ Context Switches/sec	Reports the total number of context switches generated per second by all threads.

Table 12-14. Context Switch Counters

System Profile	Description	Memory (MB)	Disk (GB)	Processor
Low	Light use; single application	32	2	P 133 MHz
Medium	Medium use; several concurrent applications	64	6	PII 300 MHz
High	Heavy use; multiple concurrent applications, including line-of-business applications	128	10	PIII 500 MHz

Table 12-15.   System Profiles—Processor

The processor recommendation for the high-end system profile is targeted at business or home users. For systems running vertical applications such as CAD/CAM, development or engineering applications, the processor and memory requirements will likely be much higher.

It is important to note that for systems with medium and low system profiles, tuning is much more important. With the advances in processor performance, an Intel PIII 500 MHz is essentially overqualified for most desktop applications and coasts most of the time. This is not true for the Intel PII and even less so for the Pentium, which struggles to barely run the operating system. Performance tuning provides the edge that keeps those systems functional.

Point Source

Slow performance can come from a single process, or point source, that is using an excessive amount of processor time. Since Windows 2000 can provide detailed resource utilization and performance data all the way down to the process and thread levels, it is simply a matter of looking for the information. This is usually easy to find, though the problems revealed are not always easy to resolve. Use the counters in Table 12-16 to track down process performance problems.

Resolution of problems related to point sources of processor use, assuming that the application represented by the process has to run on the system, usually comes down to rewriting the application or upgrading the system.

Object/Counter	Description
Process/ % Privileged Time	Shows the percentage of time that a process was running in privileged mode.
Process/ % Processor Time	Shows the percentage of time that the processor was busy servicing a specific process.
Process/ % User Time	Shows the percentage of time that a process was running in user mode.
Process/Priority Base	Shows the base priority level of the process (the possible values, from lowest to highest, are Idle, Normal, High, and Real Time). Windows 2000 schedules the threads of a process to run according to their priority. Threads inherit their base priority from their parent processes.

Table 12-16.   Process Counters

That said, in some cases the problem may be related to the configuration. For example, virus scanning applications can be configured for on-access scans, to scan files for viruses when the files are saved to disk. If the virus scanner is configured to scan all files, then it can create a performance problem when scanning files such as data files, text files, and other types of files that are not susceptible to viruses. The solution is to properly configure the virus scanning application to scan virus-prone files such as executables, dynamic link libraries, and scripts.

Diffuse Source

If slow performance is not traceable to a single process, but rather seems to be the result of many processes, then the system slowdown has a diffuse source. This will usually mean that the system as a whole is overburdened, so tasks and applications will need to be offloaded to improve performance. Alternatively, capacity can be added in the form of processor upgrades or additional processors.

Tuning Performance

With regard to the processor specifically, there is very little tuning that can be done. It is hard wired, encased in ceramic, and buried deep inside the computer system. That being the case, the two options for tuning are to reduce the load on the processor by sliming down or to bulk up the processor by adding another one or replacing it with a bigger one.

Slim Down

If your system is experiencing performance problems, decrease the number of processes and threads that are running on the system. This means reducing the number of applications running on the system.

For systems in which a single process is causing a performance problem, consider not running the process. This may seem a simple-minded solution, but it is worth looking at. If the application in question is a screen saver, the decision should be straightforward; the most obvious answer is sometimes the right answer.

In other cases, a line-of-business application may be consuming a good percentage of the resources. However, this application cannot be removed as it is critical to the business function of the system. However, you can still slim down the system by removing less-critical applications. For example, consider eliminating personal Web servers, instant messaging applications, or fancy screen savers. While not reducing the load that the line-of-business application places on the system, this will reduce the overall load on the system and free up resources for the line-of-business application to use.

Bulk Up

For systems with point source application performance problems, consider adding a second processor or upgrading the existing one to bulk up the capacity. Adding a processor is effective only if the application is multithreaded, as adding a processor will then allow the application to run on multiple processors. A single-threaded application will not benefit from a second processor, as the system cannot distribute thread activity across processors. In that case, run the application on a faster processor or on a computer with extra processing capacity.

Measure the proportion of active threads to verify the likely benefit even for applications purported to be multithreaded. If the threads in a process are inactive most of the time, then simply adding a processor will not help performance. This can be the case if an application has been written to be multithreaded but is not optimized to run on multiple processors. On the other hand, if there are a high proportion of active threads, then the additional processor will likely translate to performance gains.

Under normal circumstances, using a faster processor will usually yield more performance improvement than installing additional processors. This is because additional management overhead is required to juggle the processors, which takes away some of the benefits.

General Tips

This last section offers some general tips for reducing processor load. Some of these offload processing work from the processor, and others reduce the load by decreasing the amount of processing required.

16-Bit vs. 32-Bit Applications

If a problematic application is a 16-bit application, check whether there is a 32-bit replacement. Switching to a 32-bit application will not only improve the performance of the system, but also will increase reliability and reduce memory consumption.

Application Priority

Use the START command. This command has /low, /normal, /high, and /realtime switches to start programs with varying levels of priority. This command is the only means of externally influencing the priority of individual programs.

Virus Scanning

As indicated earlier, virus scanning can be a source of performance problems. Virus scanning can both generate high utilization rates from the scanning process and also slow down throughput while objects wait to be scanned, even though the processor may not be fully utilized.

Obviously, file scanning requires additional overhead and places additional load on the system. However, the load should not be more than 5 to 10 percent of additional processor utilization in the worst case. If the scanning process is using more processor time than that, then there might be a configuration problem. Verify that the scanning application is properly configured to scan virus-prone objects rather than all objects. Improper configuration is typically the cause of performance problems related to virus scanning.

Network Cards

To reduce the load of network traffic on the processor, use fast network cards. A 16-bit network interface card uses more processor time than a 32-bit PCI card. Using PCI-based cards reduces the number of interrupts that the processor gets and thus reduces overhead.

Offload-Capable Network Cards

As discussed in Chapter 11, systems that are running IP Secure will use more CPU processing time as they encrypt and decrypt packets. Using network cards with offload capability allows the operating system to move those CPU-intensive operations to the hardware. They also have the added benefit of also offloading TCP segmentation work, further reducing processing time.

CHAPTER 13

Fine-tuning Printing

When you think of performance, you probably rarely consider printing as a means to increased productivity or efficiency. In fact, printing is the one service that many take for granted on Windows 2000 systems. Users assume quick and easy printing of their documents, letterhead, forms, graphics, and so on, and many IT professionals simply install printers on Windows 2000 and forget about them.

There is nothing wrong with sticking with the simple printing capabilities of your system, especially considering the ease with which Windows 2000 furnishes print services. However, there are many configurable options that help boost printing capabilities and streamline print server resources, though printing is usually the last place people look to improve performance.

Printing can be a major performance factor on Windows 2000 server systems, though it is usually not much of a concern on workstations or client machines, even when a printer is installed locally. Even so, in either case, the principles and recommendations presented in this chapter will help create a more efficient printing environment for both the Windows 2000 Server product line and Windows 2000 Professional.

TERMINOLOGY

To understand the printing process, hardware configuration considerations, and optimization techniques discussed in this chapter, you need to become familiar with a few terms:

▼ **Printer**   Also known as the logical printer. The printer is the interface between Windows 2000 and the hardware (the printing device). This term is often incorrectly used interchangeably with the printing device.

■ **Printing Device**   The actual hardware that produces the output (that is, the physical printer). It is not uncommon for the printing device to be called the printer.

- **Printing Device Driver**   The software driver that is loaded to communicate with the printing device.

- **Printer Pool**   A logical grouping of two or more identical devices. Client machines perceive a printer pool as a single entity. In other words, from the users' standpoint, they appear to be printing to a single printing device.

- **Printer Port**   The port to which the printing device connects to communicate with the system. The printer port can either be a physical port (such as a LPT, COM, or Universal Serial Bus, or USB, port) or a logical port on the network that uses the Universal Naming Convention (UNC) name (for example, *\SERVERNAMEPRINTERNAME*), an HP JetDirect interface, and so on.

- **Spooler**   The component composed of dynamic link libraries (DLLs) responsible for receiving, processing, scheduling, and distributing print jobs.

- **Spooling**   One of several processes performed by the spooler. This process writes the contents of the print job to the spool file for temporary storage.

- **Despooling**   The exact opposite of spooling. This process reads the contents of the spool file and sends the contents to the printing device.

- **Print Job**   The source code, usually in a native print-control language, that results from a printing request.

- **Line Printer Daemon (LPD)**   A TCP/IP print service that receives print jobs from line printer remote (LPR) clients, such as UNIX machines.

- ▲ **Queue**   The sequence in which documents wait to be printed.

WINDOWS 2000 PRINTING ENHANCEMENTS

A multitude of enhancements and features have been added to Windows 2000. While some of the features listed here don't necessarily provide a performance boost, they do increase the scope of Windows 2000's printing and management capabilities. This in turn leads to greater productivity for both end users and administrators.

▼ **Easier TCP/IP Printer Installation**   A new port, called the Standard Port for TCP/IP, takes much of the pain out of installing and configuring a network printer.

■ **Enhanced Printer Drivers**   New driver capabilities have been added to Windows 2000 that can provide faster, more efficient printing. Two in particular, the Universal and PostScript 5.0 drivers, bring exceptional quality and performance to printing under Windows 2000.

■ **Improved Feedback**   With SPM, you can now get more detailed status information than you could using LPRMON in Windows NT.

■ **Integration with Active Directory (AD)**   The integration of Active Directory (AD) with Windows 2000 print services enhances network printing by allowing users to easily locate printers based on attributes or capabilities. For example, a user can search AD for a printer that prints 15 or more pages per minute, prints color, is located in close proximity, and so on.

■ **Internet Printing**   Windows 2000 offers a multitude of new ways to send print jobs. The most notable is Internet printing, which allows you to send print jobs via the Internet.

■ **Remote Port Administration**   Windows 2000 now enables you to administer remote printer ports.

▲ **System Monitor Integration**   You can now monitor printing activity, errors, and so on through the System Monitor. For example, you can monitor Bytes Printed/Second and Job Errors.

Print Spooler Enhancements

Windows 2000 also has improved core printing services. Several key performance improvements have been made in the print spooler, including the following:

▼　The local port monitor and the print processor are now merged into the Localspl.dll file (the local print provider). This decreases the number of DLL files the spooler has to load at startup.

■　The Spoolsv.exe file (the router) has been removed from the spooler startup time, which significantly reduces the number of DLL files loaded and minimizes the load time.

▲　The number of print spooler I/O operations have been greatly reduced.

PRINTING BASICS

Before you can fine-tune any Windows 2000 subsystem or component, you must understand how it operates. Think of Windows 2000 as a sports car. You may be able to drive it, but would you even think about trying to work on the car's engine if you did not know the first thing about mechanics? You would not know where to look for problems much less how to give it a tune-up. Printing under Windows 2000 is no different. This section explores the basic printing process and management concerns to give you a better understanding of what can and should be done to improve printing efficiency and speed.

The Printing Process Under Windows 2000

Contrary to what you may believe, when a user prints a job, it doesn't go directly to the printer. By default, it goes through a series of logical procedures before it finally reaches the printer for output. This section describes the process that occurs when a Windows 2000 client issues a print request to a Windows 2000 print server. The printing process varies depending on the operating system that the client machine is running. These differences are outlined in Table 13-1.

Client Operating System	Client Redirector	Communication Protocol
Windows 95	LAN Manager MS Network Client for Windows	NetBEUI NWLink (IPX/SPX) TCP/IP
Windows 98	LAN Manager MS Network Client for Windows	NetBEUI NWLink (IPX/SPX) TCP/IP
Windows 3.x (16-bit)	LAN Manager MS Network Client for Windows Windows for Workgroups Built-in Redirector	NetBEUI NWLink (IPX/SPX) TCP/IP
MS-DOS (assuming that applications are network aware)	MS Network Client for Windows Windows for Workgroups Built-in Redirector	NetBEUI TCP/IP
UNIX (with RFC 1179 LPR support)	RFC 1179–compliant LPR support to print to Windows 2000's Standard TCP/IP port	TCP/IP
Macintosh	Default Macintosh printing support	AppleTalk TCP/IP
Windows NT	Default NetBIOS support and Workstation service	Any Windows NT–supported protocol (for example, NetBEUI, NWLink, or TCP/IP)
Windows 2000	Default NetBIOS support and Workstation service	Any Windows 2000–supported protocol

Table 13-1.   Communication Structures for Print Clients

Initially, when a user creates a printing job, the application that is being printed from issues a request to the graphics device interface (GDI). The GDI then communicates with the appropriate printer driver before generating the request in a print control language, such as PostScript. If the wrong printer driver has been installed, the print control language may not be compatible with the printing device. Since GDI runs in kernel mode instead of user mode, this initial step reduces the number of calls that need to be made to the Win32 subsystem, therefore promoting faster printing.

NOTE: Most Windows-based clients printing from a Windows application make application calls to the GDI. There are, however, a select few applications that actually load the printer driver when they're started. This is the exception, though, rather than the norm.

The application requesting the printing creates an output file called a device driver interface (DDI) journal file. The GDI is responsible for translating the commands into DDI commands that can be interpreted by the print processors and printer driver.

After the print job request has been generated in a language the printer can understand, the client sends a remote procedure call (RPC) to the Print Spooler service (SPOOLSS.EXE) on the client machine. Then the Print Spooler service tells the spooler's router (SPOOLSS.DLL) to find and establish communication with a print server. The connection to the print server is established through an RPC call, and the print job is sent to the print server. If the printer is attached locally, the print job is sent back to the client spooler, and the client machine is considered the print server.

The spooler's router on the print server receives the print job. The data type of the print job received by the print server varies depending on the type of client that sent the request. The default data type for Windows 2000 clients is enhanced metafile format (EMF). Windows 2000 clients can use other data types as well, such as the commonly used RAW format. (See "Print Job Data Types" later in this chapter for more information.)

NOTE: If the data type is not specified, the print job defaults to the data type set for the print processor on the print server.

Next, the router hands the print job to the spooler's local print provider on the print server, which spools the print job to disk. Then the spooler's local print provider polls the print processors until a suitable data type is found, and that print processor then takes the print job. Depending on the data type, the print processor may need to alter the print job so that it prints correctly.

At this point, the separator page processor gains control over the print job and checks to see whether a separator page has been specified. If no separator page is specified, the print job is despooled to the print monitor. There are two paths the print job can take from here; the decision depends on whether the printing device is bi-directional. If the device is bi-directional, the job goes to the language monitor before heading off to the port monitor. Otherwise, it goes directly to the port monitor, which transmits the print job data to the actual printing device.

Finally, the printing device receives the print job. As it receives the print job, it converts each page into a bitmap image before printing it on paper.

Figure 13-1 presents a simplified illustration of this process.

Creating a Printer

Installing and configuring printing services under Windows 2000 could not be easier. With the Explorer interface shell and the addition of Plug and Play support, this process is simpler and more efficient than it is for most other operating systems, including predecessors of Windows 2000. Although the focus of this chapter is not the set up and management of printers, the administrative tasks for printing services must be well understood before you proceed to more advanced, technical topics.

When you create a printer, you are not configuring the printer hardware but, rather, providing a definition of the hardware to which you are connecting. The printer will appear to be connected directly to the server, regardless of whether the printing device is local to the server or connected to the network via its own network interface. (The various types of interfaces are discussed in Chapter 3.)

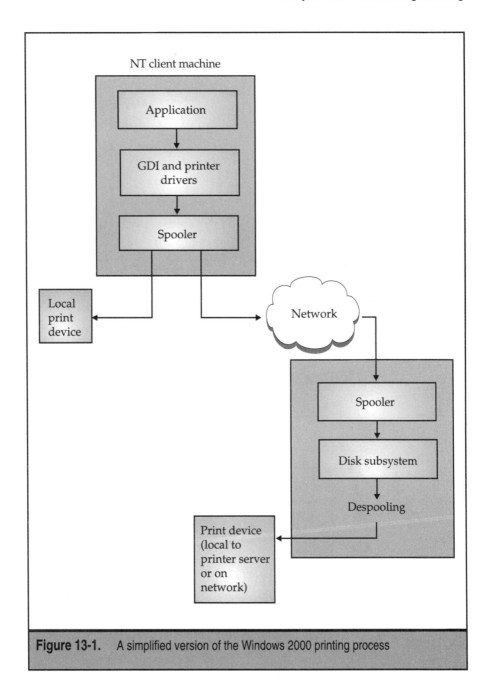

Figure 13-1.   A simplified version of the Windows 2000 printing process

To create a printer definition, you must be a member of one of the following groups:

▼   Administrators

■   Domain administrators

■   Print operators

▲   Server operators

If you are not a member of one of these groups, you must be given specific privileges through an Organizational Unit (OU) or Group Policy Object (GPO).

   If you have the proper permissions, follow these steps to create a printer:

1.   Double-click the Printers folder on the Control Panel or open the Printers folder by choosing Start I Settings I Printers. You'll see this screen:

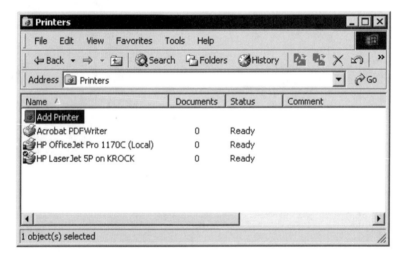

2.   Double-click the Add Printer icon to start the Add Printer Wizard; then click Next to proceed.

3.   The Add Printer Wizard presents two choices: Local Printer or Network Printer (see Figure 13-2). Select Local Printer because it is the only viable option here to create a printer on a print

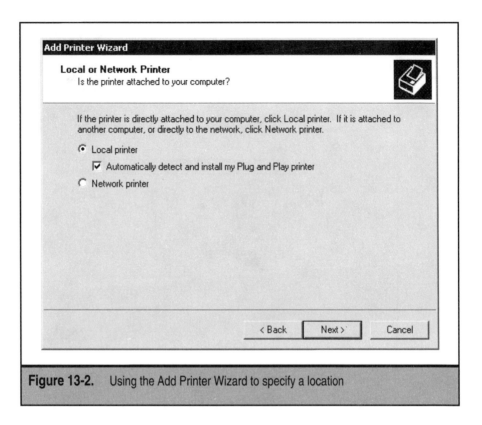

Figure 13-2.   Using the Add Printer Wizard to specify a location

server; the Network Printer option is for client machines wanting to connect to a printer already created on a print server. If the printer is Plug and Play compatible and the printer is attached directly to the server, keep the Automatically Detect and Install My Plug and Play Printer check box selected. Then click Next to continue.

4. If the printer isn't Plug and Play compatible, you'll see the window shown in Figure 13-3. It asks you to specify how the printer is connected to the print server. If it is physically connected to the server, select the appropriate port and then click Next. Otherwise, you can add either a DLC or TCP/IP port connection, as described in the next step.

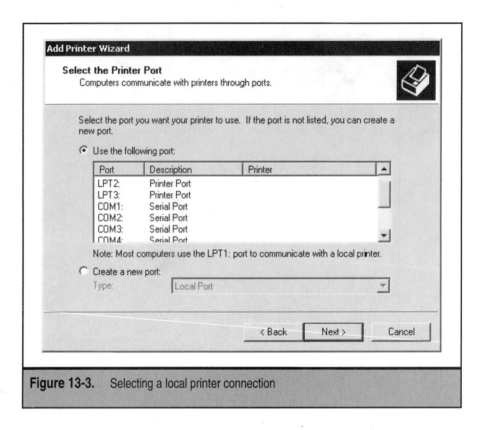

Figure 13-3. Selecting a local printer connection

5. If the printer has its own network connection, such as a DLC or Standard TCP/IP port connection, choose Create a New Port to select the port type. Depending upon what you choose (for example, Local Port or Standard TCP/IP Port), when you click Next you'll see either one of the windows shown next.

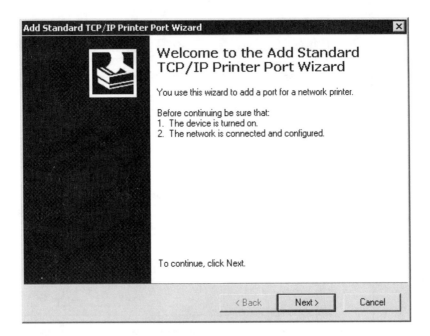

 NOTE: If you chose Standard TCP/IP Port, the Add Standard TCP/IP Printer Port Wizard appears and steps you through the specification of the TCP/IP settings to create the printer port.

6. Select a printer driver. Windows 2000 supplies drivers for a variety of printers for you to choose from, as you can see in Figure 13-4. You can also install a driver from a diskette or other media by choosing Have Disk. To check whether Windows 2000 natively supports the printer, scroll down the Manufacturers list to select the vendor and then choose your printer from the Printers list. When you are done, click Next.

7. Specify a name for the printer. This name identifies the printer on the network browse list.

8. If you are sharing the printer, you need to set it up so others can print to it through the print server, as shown in Figure 13-5. When you are finished with this screen, click Next.

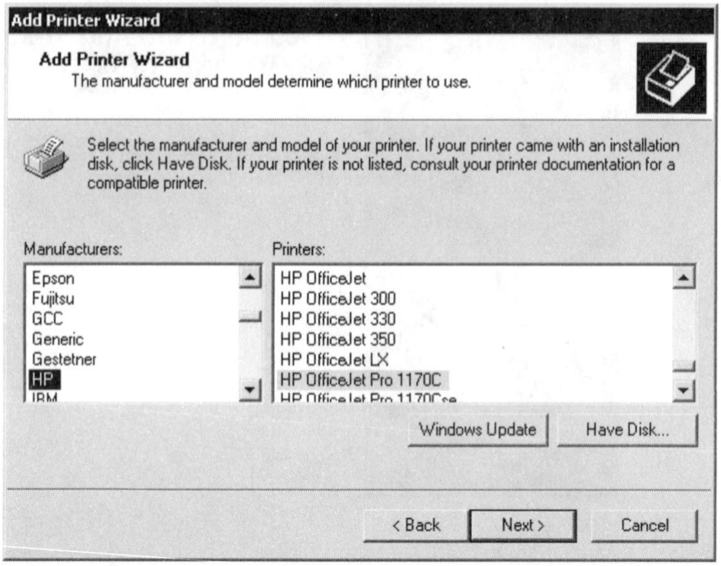

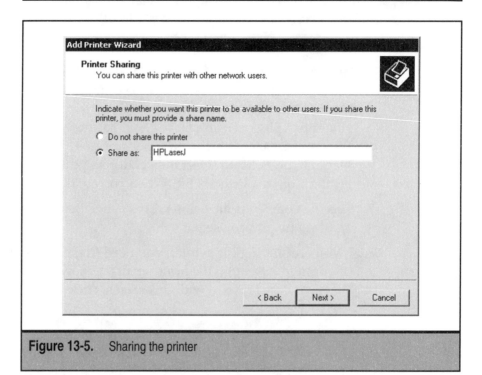

Figure 13-4. Selecting the appropriate printer driver

Figure 13-5. Sharing the printer

9. Optionally, specify a location and comment for the printer definition and then click Next.

10. Specify whether you want to print a test page.

11. Click Finish to complete the installation. If prompted, choose the path for the installation files.

Print Job Data Types

Windows 2000 maximizes interoperability with other operating system environments by defining different print job data types. This is a necessary piece in the printing process because not all environments handle printing in the same way, and different environments may use entirely different formatting and print commands.

The data type tells the print server's spooler what kind of print job this is. The spooler can then determine whether the print job needs to be modified to print correctly. The Print Server service on the client machine is responsible for assigning the print job a data type. If no data type is assigned, then the default data type of the print server is used. For most Windows-based environments, the default data type typically is RAW. However, Windows 2000's default data type is EMF, also known as NT EMF.

EMF

Enhanced metafile format (EMF) is the default data type for Windows NT 4.0 or higher clients printing to a Windows NT 4.0 or higher print server. This data type has many advantages over many of the data types previously used.

NOTE: EMF is not the default data type for PostScript printers. In addition, when adding a printer to a Windows 2000 client, you must choose the Network Printer Server option rather than the My Computer option during installation to establish EMF as the default data type.

The EMF data type boosts printing performance in a variety of ways. First, EMF emulates client-server capabilities with its rendering functions. Only a small portion of the print job's rendering is done on the client machine, freeing the client machine to perform other duties in a more timely fashion. After the EMF information is generated by the GDI, the client regains control, and the information becomes a background process for spooling. The print job is then sent to the print server for completion of the rendering process. The greatest performance gains occur with the largest print jobs.

Another advantage of EMF is its *device independence,* which means that it can be used with any printing device and so is more flexible than other data types. Typically, print jobs with the EMF data type also are easier for devices to manage because they generally are smaller than the same print jobs with the RAW data type. In addition, this reduced size enables EMF print jobs to finish slightly faster than print jobs using the RAW data type.

The EMF data type also preserves print quality. EMF ensures that the fonts used on the client machine are the exact ones that the print server will use, which keeps font substitution to an absolute minimum and results in print jobs that retain the same quality as the original document on the screen.

The only time EMF is not the preferred data type is when you are using a PostScript printer. For PostScript printers, the RAW data type provides better performance, in part because of the different formatting associated with this type of printing, and is the default data type.

RAW

The RAW data type is formatted in the printing device's *native print control language.* This means that no additional alterations are needed, and that the print job is ready to print as is. Because the format uses the printer's native print control language, the RAW data type is device dependent. At first glance, RAW may seem to provide faster printing than EMF because the data type provides a ready-to-print format, and no additional encoding or decoding is necessary for the printer to recognize it. However, this is true only when printing to a PostScript printer, primarily because for other types of printers, the GDI and printer device drivers on the client machine perform all rendering operations. Relying more on the client to perform the operations with the RAW format causes longer foreground printing times and can more easily tie up resources at the client.

RAW [FF Appended]

The RAW [FF Appended] data type is used on those rare occasions where the application being printed from is incapable of properly finishing the print request. In this situation, the application does not append a form-feed character to the end of the job, which prevents the last page from being printed when it is sent to a PCL printing device. This data type tells the print server's spooler to add the form-feed character to the end of the print job. No other changes are made to the print job. Windows 2000 never automatically uses this data type by default. If you want to set it as the default data type, you must manually set it as the default. For instructions on how to override the default data type, see "Checking or Overriding the Default Data Type" later in this chapter.

RAW [FF Auto]

The RAW [FF Auto] data type is similar to the RAW [FF Appended] data type in that it also can tell the spooler to append a form-feed character to the end of a print job. The difference, however, is that this data type actually checks to see whether a form-feed character already exists. This adds to the time needed for a print job to complete, and for performance reasons it should be used only rarely. As with the RAW [FF Appended] data type, Windows 2000 never defaults to this data type; you must set it manually.

Text

The Text data type is used for print jobs that contain ANSI text. The print processor (WinPrint) and the print device driver use this data type to create a new print job to print the text of the original print job. This ensures that ANSI text is printed correctly and conforms to the printing device's default font, form, orientation, and resolution.

Generally, this data type is used only when the printing device cannot properly interpret a print job containing simple text. For example, the character set may be printed if a simple text file does not specify its character-mapping scheme.

PSCRIPT1 (PostScript)

The PSCRIPT1 data type is used only for print jobs from a Macintosh client that contain PostScript code when the printer shared by

Windows 2000 is not PostScript compatible. This data type tells the spooler to interpret the PostScript code to create a bitmap image of the page. The GDI and printing device driver convert the image to the printer's native print control language.

Checking or Overriding the Default Data Type

To check or modify the default data type for a particular printer on the Windows 2000 print server, do the following:

1. Choose Start | Settings | Printers or double-click the Printers folder on the Control Panel and then select the printer for which you want to check or modify the default data type.

2. Choose Properties from the File menu or right-click the printer icon.

3. On the Advanced tab, click the Print Processor button.

4. The Print Processor dialog box that appears lists the type of print processor used and highlights the default data type. To change the default data type, simply select the data type you want, as shown here, and click OK.

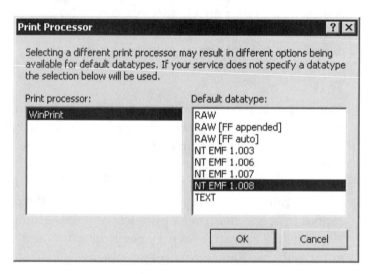

5. On the printer's Properties page, click OK.

OPTIMIZING THE PRINTING PROCESS

Windows 2000 provides excellent printing process optimization. This eliminates the need to tune the system to increase printing performance in environments where only limited printing is performed or on workstations. However, in environments with medium to heavy printing workloads or on a Windows 2000 Server dedicated as a print server, printing optimization is necessary to improve and maintain performance. This process includes choosing the appropriate hardware, as outlined in Chapter 3, as well as fine-tuning the operating system. This section highlights the most important areas that should be considered to increase printing performance.

Maximizing Available Resources

It goes without saying that all machines should be equipped with adequate resources to complete their responsibilities. This is no different for printing, but it's important to note that memory and ample disk space for spooler and shadow files are vital to the printing process. For example, if the disk is full (or it's in serious need of defragmentation), printing could slow to a crawl.

> **NOTE:** Memory and disk resources for printing aren't just for the print server. Ample memory and disk space considerations apply to client machines as well.

Cleaning Up Print Jobs

In Windows NT 4.0 and earlier, shadow files were deleted only during the reboot process. With Windows 2000, you rarely have to reboot the machine so it's important to check the spooler folder to see if Windows 2000 is leaving behind these files. It's also a good idea to check for orphaned spooler files. Any left-behind spooler or shadow files should be deleted periodically.

Font Management

Font management can affect printing performance. The way you perform font management affects disk capacity, server memory requirements, and printing speed. You should pay particular attention to this aspect of printing performance if you are using an international version of Windows 2000 (supporting a large character set), or if Windows 2000 is used in a print shop environment. Print shops tend to use a large number of fonts and character sets, increasing resource requirements for the system.

In performing font management, you need to consider font drivers, the types and number of fonts on the system, and the font cache. Each of these aspects is described next.

Font Drivers

Windows 2000 natively supports many different types of fonts, including bitmap, vector, and TrueType fonts. However, sometimes additional font types are needed that require third-party (external) font drivers. Usually, though, this occurs only in print shops that have specialized printing needs. Although many font vendors do supply relatively reliable font drivers, it is recommended that you use as few additional drivers as possible.

Third-party font driver information is located in the following Registry subkey: HKEY_LOCAL_MACHINE\SOFTWARE\ Microsoft\WindowsNT\CurrentVersion\Font Drivers. You should use the software provided by the font vendor to manipulate any entries in this subkey. The font drivers native to Windows 2000 do not have entries in the Registry.

Font Types and the Number of Installed Fonts

The type and number of fonts used on the system are closely related and can have a large impact on system performance if they are not properly managed. It is best to use the fonts natively supported by Windows 2000, but there are times when this will not suffice. Some systems have relatively few fonts installed, while others may have literally thousands. Keep the number of installed fonts to a minimum because fonts can quickly chew up memory and disk resources. Fonts typically vary in size from just a few kilobytes to several hundred kilobytes. Removing a few will not free up very much disk space, but when you remove a large number of them, you can potentially save vast amounts of disk space.

One way to keep the number of installed fonts to a minimum is to use only TrueType fonts in Windows-based applications. However, you must make sure that none of the Windows-based applications require other font types such as bitmap, vector, or third-party fonts. If this is a viable option, you can disable the use of non-TrueType fonts in Windows-based applications by manipulating the following Registry subkey: HKEY_USERS\.DEFAULT\SOFTWARE\ Microsoft\Windows NT\CurrentVersion\TrueType.

There are two parameters in this Registry subkey: TTEnable and TTonly. To have only TrueType fonts available for Windows-based applications, do the following:

1. Start the Registry Editor by typing **REGEDT32** at the command prompt or in the Start | Run box.

NOTE: It is recommended that you use only the REGEDT32 Registry Editor to make these changes.

2. Open the TrueType Registry key listed earlier, as shown in Figure 13-6.

3. If the TTonly parameter exists, double-click it to display its properties and then change the value to **1**.

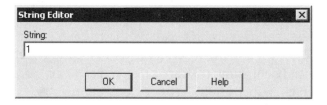

4. Click OK to close the window.

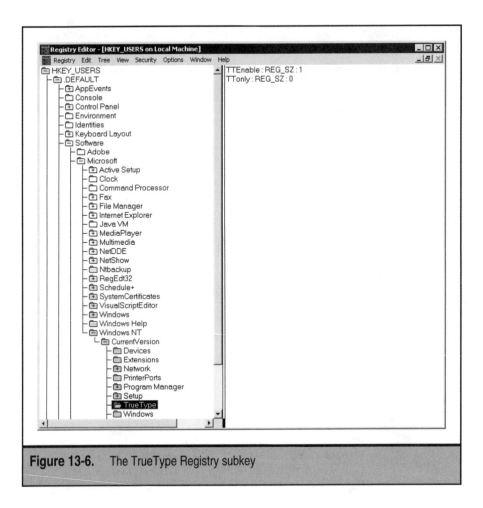

Figure 13-6. The TrueType Registry subkey

Print Logging

Every time a print job is serviced, Windows 2000 logs the event in the Event Viewer's system log. You can imagine that it does not take long for the log to become cluttered with print informational messages. Depending on how the Event Viewer is configured to handle the log file when it grows to a certain size, the log file can quickly consume disk space, or it may even stop logging system events, which could have devastating results.

In addition to taking up disk space, print event logging also momentarily diverts Windows 2000's attention from other more, important tasks. Although print logging's effects on performance are not alarming, you still should minimize its impact on system performance. You can choose among error, warning, or informational event logging. It is recommended that you keep error or error and warning event logging turned on.

There are two ways to modify print event logging: through the Printers folder and through the Registry. The safest and easiest way is through the Printers folder, though both methods are described here.

To modify print event logging through the Printers folder, do the following:

1. Choose Start | Settings | Printers and open the Printers folder.

2. From the File menu, select Server Properties.

3. Select the Advanced tab.

4. Check the print event logging options that you want to use, as shown in Figure 13-7. Then click OK.

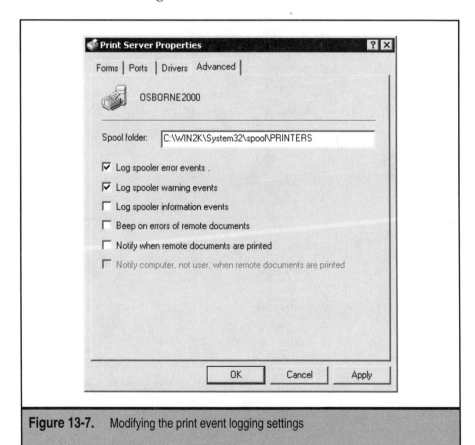

Figure 13-7. Modifying the print event logging settings

To modify print event logging through the Registry, do the following:

1. Start the Registry Editor by typing **REGEDT32** at the command prompt or in the Start | Run box.

2. Open the following subkey (as shown in Figure 13-8): HKEY_LOCAL_MACHINE\SYSTEM\CurrentControlSet\ Control\Print\Providers.

3. Double-click EventLog to display the DWORD Editor used to modify the parameter.

Figure 13-8. Disabling print event logging using the Registry

4. In the DWORD Editor, select Decimal and then type **1** for error event logging only or **3** for error and warning event logging. Then click OK.

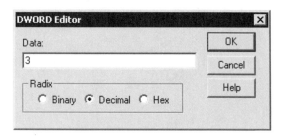

Tweaking the Print Spooler Service

The Windows 2000 Print Spooler service is responsible for almost every aspect of printing. It is actually a collective arrangement of printing components that work together to process print requests. It consists of four separate components that act as a single entity and are responsible for receiving, processing, scheduling, and distributing print jobs. These four components are summarized in Table 13-2.

Spooler Component	Associated Files	Description
Local print provider	Localspl.dll	The local print provider handles many local printing tasks such as writing the print job to a spool file, keeping track of administrative information (user name, document name, data type), and polling installed print processors for recognition purposes.

Table 13-2. Print Spooler Components

Spooler Component	Associated Files	Description
Remote print providers	Win32spl.dll Nwprovau.dll	Remote print providers are used when the printing device is remote (such as a Windows 2000 print server). Windows 2000 supplies two versions: one for Windows Network print servers (Win32spl.dll) and one for Novell NetWare (Nwprovau.dll).
Print processors	Windows: Winprint.dll Macintosh: Sfmpsprt.dll	Print processors work closely with the printer driver to despool print jobs and can alter the print job's data type, if necessary.
Print monitors	Localmon.dll Hpmon.dll Lprmon.dll Sfmmon.dll	There are two types of print monitors: language monitors and port monitors. Language monitors support bi-directional printing devices, and port monitors control the I/O port to which the printing device is connected.

Table 13-2. Print Spooler Components *(continued)*

Even though the Print Spooler service is very important for printing, it does not have a higher priority than most other applications. In fact, it has the default priority, which is typically 7 for Windows 2000 Professional and 9 for Windows 2000 Server and higher, like every other noncritical system process.

To give the printing process a boost, you can modify the various priorities associated with the Print Spooler service. These settings can be changed only through the Registry. The most notable performance boosts from these Registry modifications will be on print servers that service a large number of print jobs or a large number of printing devices. It is not advisable to change the default Print Spooler settings on workstations or servers that are not very busy, primarily because the performance difference may not be noticeable enough to warrant messing with the Registry. Before you start changing Registry parameters, be sure to back up the Registry.

There are three spooler priorities that are worth experimenting with on busy print servers: PortThreadPriority, SpoolerPriority, and SchedulerThreadPriority. Their properties are listed in Table 13-3.

Parameter	Data Type	Data Value	Description and Recommendation
PortThread Priority	REG_DWORD	0 (indicates that the default value is used)	Sets the priority level for each defined printing port's thread. Consider increasing this value to 1 for print servers.

Table 13-3. Maximizing Print Spooler Priority Levels

Parameter	Data Type	Data Value	Description and Recommendation
Spooler Priority	REG_DWORD	0x20 (NORMAL_ PRIORITY_ CLASS) (not listed if default values are used)	Sets the priority class for the print spooler. If the default setting is used, there will not be a visible entry for this parameter. Consider increasing this value to 0x80 (high priority) for print servers.
Scheduler Thread Priority	REG_DWORD	0 (indicates that the default value is used)	Sets the priority of the scheduler thread, which is responsible for assigning print jobs to ports. Consider increasing this value to 1 for print servers.

Table 13-3. Maximizing Print Spooler Priority Levels *(continued)*

These services are located in the following key:
HKEY_LOCAL_ MACHINE\SYSTEM\CurrentControlSet\Control\Print.

As Table 13-3 shows, SpoolerPriority does not appear in the Registry if the default setting is used. To change this priority, you

must add the SpoolerPriority setting manually. To add the
SpoolerPriority value, do the following:

1. Start the Registry Editor by typing **REGEDT32** at the command
   prompt or entering it in the Start | Run box. Go to
   HKEY_LOCAL_ MACHINE\SYSTEM\CurrentControlSet\
   Control\Print.

2. Select Add Value from the Edit menu to display the Add
   Value dialog box.

3. In the Value Name box, type **SpoolerPriority** and then select
   REG_DWORD as the data type.

4. Click OK. This will cause the DWORD Editor dialog box to
   pop up.

5. In the Radix grouping, select Hex and then type **8** to boost the
   priority to HIGH_PRIORITY_CLASS, as shown here:

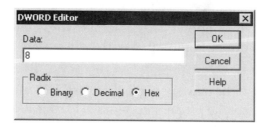

6. Click OK to add the new value.

Optimizing the Spooler File

As long as the print spooling option is enabled, Windows 2000 spools print jobs to disk before actually sending them to the printer. The default location for the spool file (%SYSTEMROOT%spool) is on the same partition as the rest of the system files, and the increased load caused by read and write operations on the drive can severely hamper performance if the server has to support a large number of print requests.

One of the easiest ways to increase printing performance is to move the spooling file to a different location. More specifically, you should change the default location to a new directory on another physical drive. The spooler location change is especially critical to maintaining optimal performance if Windows 2000 is functioning as a print server. As with most system changes, this change can be accomplished through the Registry; however, there is also a simpler way to change the location of the print spool file. Use the following steps to modify the spool file's location:

NOTE: If you change the default spool file location through the user interface (as described here), this change will apply to all printers.

1. Create a new spool file directory, preferably on a separate physical drive. Putting the directory on a separate physical drive ensures that the spool file workload does not interfere with the workload associated with the normal operation of Windows 2000. In other words, the disk subsystem will not be bombarded with both system requests and print spooler requests.

2. If the new spool file directory is located on an NTFS volume, set the proper permissions for this new directory. For example, give the Authenticated Users group Change permission.

3. Choose Start | Settings | Printers and open the Printers folder.

4. From the File menu, select Server Properties.

5. Select the Advanced tab.

6. To modify the spool file location, type the new path for the new spool folder that you created earlier.

You also have the option of modifying the print spool file location through the Registry. The parameter is located in the following Registry subkey: HKEY_LOCAL_ MACHINE\SYSTEM\ CurrentControlSet\Control\ Print.

You must then add (or modify) the following:

▼   Value name: DefaultSpoolDirectory

■   Data type: REG_SZ

■   Value: New path location of the spool file

▲   Default value: %SYSTEMROOT%\System32\spool\PRINTERS

The advantage of using the Registry to modify the print spool file location is that you can change the location for individual printing devices. For instance, if a Windows 2000 print server is home to five different heavily used printing devices, you can direct each printing device to use a separate print spool file directory. To change the print spool file location for individual printing devices, simply go to the printing device's subkey (located under the subkey defined earlier) and modify the SpoolDirectory parameter so it points to another directory. Also, if you have enough physical disks, you can spread the workload of those print spooler files to separate physical disks, which will greatly improve the disk read and write times while spooling because each physical disk has its own heads to perform the spooling functions.

Whether you change the print spool file location through the Printers folder or the Registry, the modifications will not take effect until the system is restarted.

Network Printing

Network printing is a common approach in many environments because of its scalability and flexibility. Instead of configuring each workstation with its own printing device, one or more printers can be shared over the network, and network-aware printing devices can be conveniently located throughout the network instead of being confined to the location of the server or workstation. This section discusses opportunities for boosting printing performance and efficiency and for reducing the effects of printing on the rest of the environment.

Network Protocols

The most common protocols used to print over a Windows 2000 network are TCP/IP and Data Link Control (DLC). The protocol that you choose will depend both on the configuration of your print server and on the protocols that are supported by your printing device. For instance, since the Windows 2000 print server is already running TCP/IP, then it is better to use TCP/IP instead of adding another protocol stack to the server's configuration.

DLC typically is used to connect to mainframe environments, but it can also be used to connect to Hewlett-Packard printing devices that are directly connected to the network. Other manufacturers rarely provide printing device connectivity through DLC. Like TCP/IP, DLC needs to be installed only on the Windows 2000 print server. Clients can print to the DLC-enabled HP printing device without having the DLC protocol stack installed. However, this protocol has many limitations. For instance, DLC is a nonroutable protocol so, depending on the network topology, it may encounter boundaries that it cannot cross. Also, Microsoft's implementation of DLC does not support communication between machines (other than printing devices and mainframes) because it is not designed to work with the Redirector or Server services.

NOTE: The DLC Registry entries are located in this subkey HKEY_LOCAL_ MACHINE\SYSTEM\CurrentControlSet\Services\DLC.

TCP/IP, on the other hand, is widely supported by various printing device manufacturers. This gives you a greater number of choices, which increases scalability and flexibility for printing.

For more information on optimizing network configurations and protocols, refer to Chapter 8.

Minimizing Printing Effects on Active Directory

As mentioned earlier, Windows 2000 allows users to quickly find printers using the AD. When you share a printer, you're more than likely going to publish it in AD.

The most effective way to minimize the effects of publishing printers within AD involves AD's pruning features. Pruning in AD is very similar to pruning a tree. When you prune away the "bad" parts, you end up with a healthier, more efficient directory.

An option that provides the best performance boost is *pruning printers that are not automatically republished* in AD. By default, Windows 2000 doesn't prune printers when the print server or workstation doesn't respond to requests. Essentially, an AD published printer exists but is unavailable. Configuring pruning when a printer isn't automatically republished can be accomplished via the Group Policy Object (GPO) and the Registry. The recommended way is through the GPO so that pruning can be applied to more than one machine at a time (see Figure 13-9).

Reducing Print Browsing Traffic in Mixed-Mode Environments

Any time a printer is shared from a Windows 2000 workstation or print server in a mixed-mode environment, its existence is announced to the rest of the network. The printer is published in AD, and in addition a broadcast message is issued by the Print Spooler service every ten minutes. The broadcast messaging adds to the traffic that already exists on the network and can affect network performance.

Although print broadcast messages can cause network degradation, the good news is that you can choose among several options to reduce the amount of traffic generated by print device sharing on a network. All of these modifications are performed through the Registry in the following subkey:
HKEY_LOCAL_ MACHINE\SYSTEM\CurrentControlSet\ Control\Print.

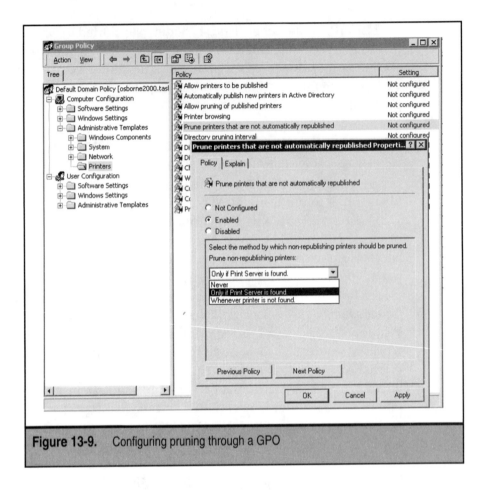

Figure 13-9. Configuring pruning through a GPO

This subkey contains three parameters that you can use to manage the print browsing traffic: DisableServerThread, ServerThread Timeout, and NetPrinterDecayPeriod. These three parameters can dramatically affect network performance.

▼ **DisableServerThread** This parameter completely removes the spooler's ability to broadcast messages notifying other machines of shared printing devices. The default value is 1, which means that notification is enabled. Changing this value to 0 disables notification. It is recommended that you keep this Registry parameter enabled. Otherwise, users will be able to connect to the printing device only manually. For example, a user would have to know the UNC name for the printer (*SERVERNAME*) to connect.

- **ServerThreadTimeout**   This parameter specifies the length of time that passes between print browsing notifications. Modify this value instead of disabling notification altogether. The default value is 360,000 ms (6 minutes). Increasing this value can greatly reduce the amount of print browsing traffic on the network. It is recommended that you at least triple this value (to 1,080,000 ms, or 18 minutes) to reduce the frequency of announcements.

- ▲ **NetPrinterDecayPeriod**   This value represents the amount of time that the machine sharing the printing device caches the shared printing device lists. Depending on how much you increase the ServerThreadTimeout parameter, you should change this value to maintain the print browse list. For example, if you set ServerThreadTimeout to more than one hour, you should increase this parameter to one and a half hours, or at least 1.5 times the ServerThreadTimeout parameter value.

Gaining Efficiency with Printer Pools

In an environment with more than one printing device, sometimes a particular printing device will be used more heavily, and other printing devices may be underutilized. To combat this problem, Windows 2000 can tie printing resources together into a single entity called a *printer pool*.

A printer pool is a logical grouping of two or more identical printing devices. Printer pools are viewed as a single printing device, and all of the printers that participate in the pool are shared under one share name. Any configuration changes made to the printer pool affect every printing device in the pool. Therefore, all printing devices in a pool must use the same printing device driver, and for greater efficiency, the printing devices should be identical. You can, however, mix different print connection types to include more printing devices. For instance, you can include both network and local printers in a pool.

The use of printer pools allows Windows 2000 to use printing resources more effectively and efficiently. When a print job is sent to a printer pool, Windows 2000 hands off the print job to the first available printing device. This way, no one printing device is favored, and print jobs are less likely to experience delays.

Printer pools involve a few inconveniences. First, users do not know which printing device will service a print request. However, if you physically group the printing devices close together, users will be able to find their print jobs. You should also use separator files when implementing printer pools to help users differentiate one print job from another.

Another inconvenience relates to the processing that occurs when one of the printing devices experiences technical problems, such as a print jam or mechanical failure. In this case, any print job that is sent to that printing device may never be printed because no built-in intelligence tells Windows 2000 to redirect the print jobs to another, operational printing device. However, the efficiency gained from printer pools far outweighs the few inconveniences they pose.

Creating a Printer Pool   If you have the proper hardware (that is, several identical printing devices or printing devices that use a common print device driver), the process of creating a printer pool is extremely easy. To configure a printer pool in Windows 2000, do the following:

NOTE: The following steps assume that the printing devices have already been created. If any of the printing devices has not been defined, refer to "Creating a Printer" earlier in this chapter.

1. Choose Start | Settings | Printers and open the Printers folder.

2. Select the printing device by clicking the printing device icon.

3. Go to the printing device's Ports tab on the Properties page by right-clicking the printing device icon, selecting Properties, and then selecting the Ports tab.

4. Select Enable Printer Pooling on the Ports tab to enable printer pooling, as shown in Figure 13-10.

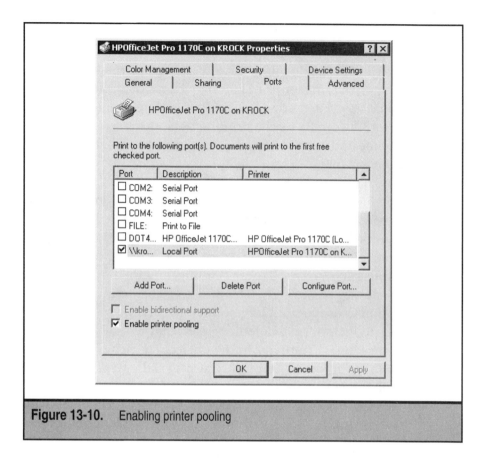

Figure 13-10. Enabling printer pooling

5. Select all of the ports that the printer pool will use. For example, if the printer pool will contain three printing devices, select the port location for each device.

6. Select the Sharing tab and enable sharing.

7. In the Share Name box, type the name for the printer pool that will be displayed on the network. Then click OK.

Scheduling

Scheduling is one of the most underutilized Windows 2000 printing configurations. Many users do not realize its true effectiveness, especially in environments where the printing workloads are vastly disparate in size. For example, your environment may typically print large and small print jobs throughout the day, but the large print jobs may not be needed immediately or even on that day. In other words, though the smaller print jobs may be needed at once, the large jobs could be printed after hours. If scheduling is not used, those large print jobs can tie up the printing devices for considerable amounts of time and keep the smaller, more urgent jobs from printing in a timely fashion.

Printer scheduling is the best solution in this situation. It allows you to define and configure a printer with different names signifying different scheduling priorities. After a printing device is defined, you can configure another instance for printing large print jobs after hours. Give the second instance of the printing device a different name, such as After-Hours Printing, and then change its scheduling properties accordingly. This will give clients another printing device option to use to print large print jobs. Instead of printing large print jobs to their normal default printer, they can send them to the After-Hours Printing printing device. The print job will be queued on the Windows 2000 print server until the time you specified in the scheduling properties for that printing device.

Here's how to configure another instance of a printer and change its scheduling properties on the Windows 2000 print server:

1. Choose Start | Settings | Printers and open the Printers folder.

2. Double-click the Add Printer icon to begin adding another printing device definition for a given printer. Be sure to configure this instance of the printing device in exactly the same way as the original.

3. When the Add Printer Wizard prompts you for the name of the printer, type a name that describes what the printing device is used for, such as **After-Hours Printing**.

4. After the printing device instance has been created, right-click the printing device icon and choose Properties.

5. In the printing device's Properties dialog box, select the Advanced tab as shown in Figure 13-11.

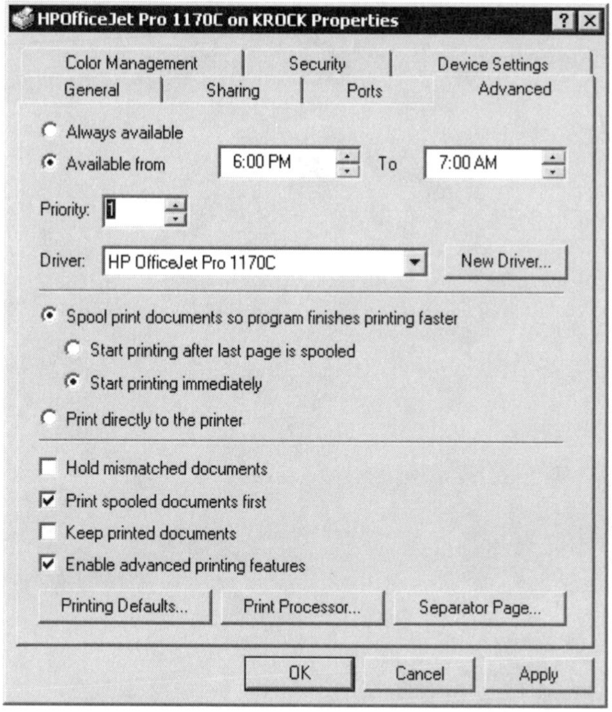

Figure 13-11. Scheduling printing

6. Change the Always Available property to Available From so that the printing device is available only after hours (for example, from 6:00 P.M. to 7:00 A.M.).

As users print to this printing device instance, the print jobs will be spooled and stored in the disk subsystem on the Windows 2000 print server until 6:00 P.M. Since the print jobs are stored on the print server's hard disk until the printing device becomes available, you need to make sure there is ample disk space to hold them. It is also a good idea to configure a separate spooler file, preferably on a separate hard disk drive, to ensure adequate read and write times as well as storage space.

CHAPTER 14

Tuning with the Registry

The Windows 2000 Registry is a repository containing a wealth of information pertaining to the system configuration. It is a database that uniquely describes a system's hardware configuration, security policy, installed system and application software, user-specific settings, file associations, and much more. Unfortunately, users rarely fully understand the Registry's capabilities and uses, in part because of its complexity and because many are intimidated by the potentially disastrous effects that a manual configuration change may have on the overall system. These concerns are justified; the Registry is not a Windows 2000 component that should be taken lightly. Windows 2000 relies heavily on the Registry to operate, and thus it is critical that you understand its approach to system configuration so you can fully grasp and make use of the Registry's capabilities.

Many of Windows 2000's default values provide moderate to good performance. However, the default system and environment variables may not meet the specific demands placed on the system by your organization, so to get the most out of the system, you will need to make some configuration changes. Throughout this book, many system configuration changes are recommended to optimize specific system components or subsystems. Some of these can be accomplished through an application or system interface, but others require direct manipulation of the Windows 2000 Registry. Unfortunately, there is not always an application or system interface that you can use to make configuration changes to boost performance. To truly uncover the performance capabilities of Windows 2000, you will often need to tweak settings particular to your system configuration by changing the Registry.

This chapter gives you the information and survival skills you need to manipulate the Registry so you can boost performance while maintaining system reliability. This chapter focuses on four key topics related to system performance and the Windows 2000 Registry:

▼ The Registry and its role in system performance. Many of the recommendations in this book require you to edit the Registry directly.

■ How to modify the Registry safely.

■ The importance of backing up the Registry to maintain system reliability and stability.

▲ How to keep the Registry operating efficiently so the database itself does not negatively affect system performance.

NEW WINDOWS 2000 REGISTRY FEATURES

With the number of differences between Windows NT and Windows 2000, you'd expect that there would probably be a revolutionary new Registry. On the contrary, there's actually not that much difference between the Windows 2000 Registry and its predecessors. The few differences that do exist are listed here:

▼ **HKEY_DYN_DATA** This infamous missing root key that could be viewed through REGEDIT (not REGEDT32) in Windows NT no longer exists in Windows 2000.

■ **Registry and Group Policy Interaction** Group Policy inherits the System Policy's ability to make modifications to the Registry. In addition, Group Policy can also change keys that are in binary data format. This extends Group Policy functionality by enabling Group Policy to modify more Registry keys than its predecessor.

■ **Per-User Class Registration** The HKEY_CLASSES_ROOT key in Windows 2000's predecessors served as an alias to HKEY_LOCAL_MACHINE\Software\Classes. Now it's an alias to two subkeys: HKEY_LOCAL_MACHINE\ Software\ Classes and HKEY_CURRENT_USER\Software\Classes.

▲ **HKEY_CURRENT_USER\Software\Classes** This subkey is new to Windows 2000. It pertains to application associations defined by the user.

HOW THE WINDOWS 2000 REGISTRY CAN BOOST PERFORMANCE

How is familiarizing yourself with the Registry going to help you boost performance? For starters, Windows 2000's default settings in many cases simply cannot give you the level of performance that you expect and need. Although there are a limited number of ways to optimize server performance through the UI, not all configuration parameters can be tweaked. Those configuration parameters that you can't tweak through the UI, you'll have to modify through the Registry. By familiarizing yourself with the Registry's organization, you will learn where to find those configuration parameters and what settings to use for each parameter. Figure 14-1 presents a simplified version of the Registry organization.

As an IT professional responsible for the well being of your Windows 2000 environment, you must know where various types of system configuration information are located in the Registry and how to change these settings to get the best performance from Windows 2000. To effectively optimize Windows 2000, you need to be well informed about the Registry.

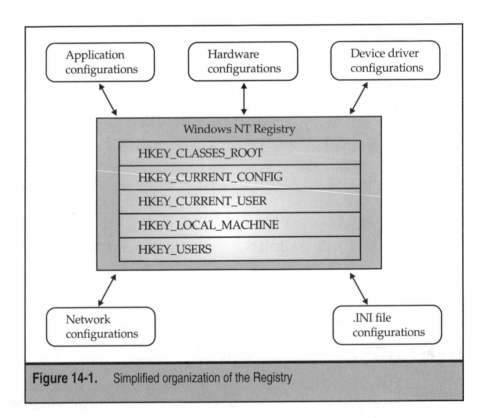

Figure 14-1. Simplified organization of the Registry

Beyond .INI Files

Older versions of Windows operating systems relied on .INI files for configuration parameters. However, .INI files offered only primitive organization, lacked security, did not provide user-specific settings, and suffered from other limitations as well.

NOTE: For backward compatibility, Windows 2000 allows applications to use .INI files, and Windows 2000 also keeps many .INI files so that older programs can write to and reference these files.

The Registry consists of keys and subkeys, which may or may not contain value entries. The Registry keys are analogous to the bracketed headings in .INI files, and the Registry value entries correspond to the information located below the headings in the .INI files. This is the extent to which .INI file structure is similar to Registry organization. Unlike .INI files, the Registry permits multiple configuration levels with subkeys and allows multiple types of values.

All information pertaining to .INI files can be found in the following key: HKEY_LOCAL_MACHINE\SOFTWARE\Microsoft\ Windows NT\CurrentVersion\IniFileMapping. The subkeys under this location contain a string value, which essentially serves as a pointer to the Registry location that contains the information located within the .INI file section. Each string begins with either SYS or USR, corresponding to HKEY_LOCAL_MACHINE\SOFTWARE or HKEY_CURRENT_USER, respectively.

WINDOWS 2000 REGISTRY ARCHITECTURE

The Registry is an organized conglomeration of hardware-, software-, and user-related information. It includes information regarding the devices present on the system, operating system and application configuration parameters, user profiles, and much more. The basic structure of the Registry, shown in Figure 14-2, looks much like a tree with its roots, branches, and leaves turned upside down. The Registry's structure is hierarchical, with multiple configuration levels

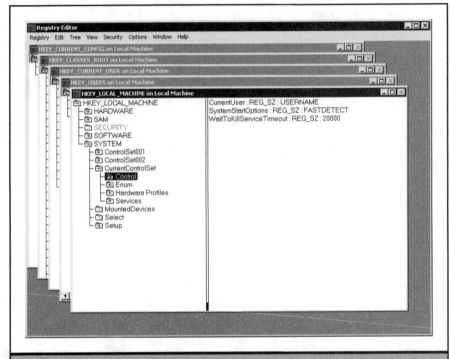

Figure 14-2. Registry structure with keys, subkeys, value entries, and values

specified by keys, subkeys, value entries, and values. A *value entry* is a parameter within the key or subkey, and a *value* is the specific value for the parameter.

Keys and Subkeys

A *key* is a top level of organization in the Registry. Each key can have subkeys branching off of it and can also contain value entries or values. Each subkey can, in turn, be considered the key for the information branching off of it.

There are five keys in the Registry that are called *root keys* or *hives*. These are permanent keys within the Registry, and they represent the highest level of organizational structure. Notice that in Figure 14-2, each window within the Registry represents a root key. The five root keys are described in Table 14-1.

Registry Root Key	Contents
HKEY_CURRENT_CONFIG HKEY_CLASSES_ROOT	Hardware configuration information. File associations and OLE information.
HKEY_CURRENT_USER	Information about the user currently logged on, such as desktop settings and network connections.
HKEY_USERS HKEY_LOCAL_MACHINE	Local user account information. Information on each user is stored in a separate subkey. System configuration information and parameters, such as hardware, software, and security settings.

Table 14-1.   Registry Root Keys (or Hives)

The Registry information is divided into categories under the root keys. Root keys are hard-coded within the Windows 2000 operating system; you cannot delete them, nor can you add another root key to the Registry.

Interestingly, some of the root keys are subkeys of other root keys. The root keys that are also subkeys of other root keys are linked to one another. Table 14-2 lists the root keys and their respective links.

Storing the Registry

Where is the Registry information stored? By default, all Registry information is stored in the %SYSTEMROOT%\System32\Config directory. This includes SYSTEM.ALT and .LOG files, which serve as backup files. Table 14-3 lists the files you will find in the %SYSTEMROOT%\System32\Config directory and their Registry root keys and paths.

Root Key	Corresponding Root Key and Link (Path)
HKEY_CLASSES_ROOT	HKEY_LOCAL_MACHINE\ SOFTWARE\Classes
HKEY_CURRENT_CONFIG	HKEY_LOCAL_MACHINE\ SYSTEM\CurrentControlSet\ Hardware Profiles\Current
HKEY_CURRENT_USER	HKEY_USERS (current user logged on)

Table 14-2.   Registry Root Key Links

HKEY_LOCAL_MACHINE

The HKEY_LOCAL_MACHINE root key contains information pertaining to hardware devices and software installed on the system, including bus types, system memory, device drivers, and startup parameters. The first level below HKEY_LOCAL_MACHINE has five subkeys—HARDWARE, SAM, SECURITY, SOFTWARE, and SYSTEM—as shown in Figure 14-3.

Registy Root Key	File Path
HKEY_CURRENT_CONFIG	%SYSTEMROOT%\ System32\Config\System
HKEY_LOCAL_MACHINE\SAM	%SYSTEMROOT%\ System32\Config\SAM
HKEY_LOCAL_MACHINE\Security	%SYSTEMROOT%\ System32\Config\Security
HKEY_LOCAL_MACHINE\Software	%SYSTEMROOT%\System 32\Config\Software
HKEY_LOCAL_MACHINE\System	%SYSTEMROOT%\System 32\Config\System

Table 14-3.   Root Key and File Paths

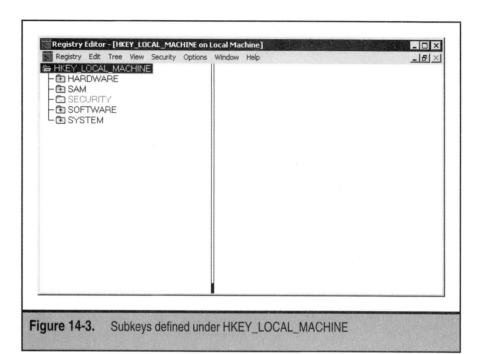

Figure 14-3.   Subkeys defined under HKEY_LOCAL_MACHINE

HKEY_LOCAL_MACHINE\HARDWARE   This subkey contains all the hardware information for the root key. It is a volatile subkey because its information is discarded when the system shuts down and then rebuilt when the machine restarts. NTDETECT.COM is responsible for gathering hardware characteristics and passing this information to this subkey. NTDETECT.COM detects hardware components such as the following:

▼ Bus type

■ Adapter type

■ Communication ports

■ Keyboard

■ Mouse

■ Video

▲ Floppy disks

The information then is passed down to the subkeys under HKEY_LOCAL_MACHINE\HARDWARE, as listed here:

▼ **HARDWARE\DESCRIPTION** Receives hardware descriptions collected by NTDETECT.COM.

■ **HARDWARE\DEVICEMAP** Contains the mappings of devices to device drivers.

▲ **HARDWARE\RESOURCEMAP** Contains resource mappings that the devices use, such as physical memory ranges and interrupts.

HKEY_LOCAL_MACHINE\SAM As shown in Figure 14-4, this subkey is dimmed; the information contained in this subkey is unreadable by default. This subkey contains sensitive account information such as user passwords and domain associations. This subkey is directly linked to the HKEY_LOCAL_MACHINE\SECURITY subkey.

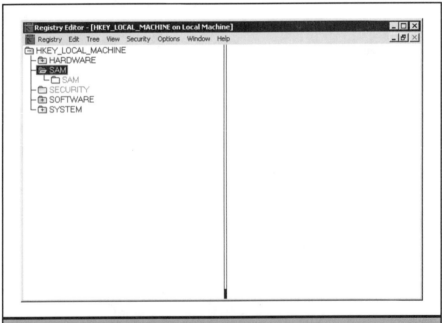

Figure 14-4. The HKEY_LOCAL_MACHINE\SAM subkey

HKEY_LOCAL_MACHINE\SECURITY As with the HKEY_LOCAL_ MACHINE\SAM subkey, the information in this subkey cannot be accessed by default because of security concerns. This subkey defines user and group permissions and includes information regarding whether to install device drivers, add printers, install applications, and so on.

HKEY_LOCAL_MACHINE\SOFTWARE This subkey stores application-specific information such as paths to executables and licensing information. The application settings in this subkey are applied globally because HKEY_LOCAL_MACHINE is the same for every user who logs onto the machine. This is unlike HKEY_CURRENT _USER\Software settings, because those settings are tailored for individual user accounts; for example, one user may execute completely different applications than another, so application settings are not applied systemwide.

You can also find information pertaining to the Windows 2000 operating system in this key. HKEY_LOCAL_MACHINE\ SOFTWARE\Microsoft\Windows NT\CurrentVersion contains Windows 2000 operating system information such as the build number and the actual %SYSTEMROOT% directory path.

HKEY_LOCAL_MACHINE\SYSTEM This subkey is of major importance to Windows 2000 because it contains detailed information on previous control sets, the current control set, Windows 2000 setup, and disks for the Disk Management snap-in. When the Disk Management snap-in prompts you to write disk signatures, the information, such as drive letters and RAID settings, is stored in the HKEY_LOCAL_MACHINE\SYSTEM subkey.

The current control set is important to the operation of Windows 2000; it defines the profile used by the system. Subkeys under CurrentControlSet provide detailed information on services running on the machine, the computer name, instructions for Windows 2000 in case the system crashes (for example, whether to reboot, produce a crash dump, and so on), and directory paths to the Registry information files. The previous control sets are used for additional hardware profiles and the Last Known Good Configuration profile.

HKEY_CLASSES_ROOT

HKEY_CLASSES_ROOT is an alias for the HKEY_LOCAL_MACHINE\ SOFTWARE\Classes and HKEY_CURRENT_USER\Software\ Classes subkeys, which house information regarding file associations, shortcuts, OLE, and so on. Every registered file name extension has its own key with a REG_SZ value that essentially points to the application that will be launched to work with the specified file name extension. For example, when you double-click a file name with the .TXT extension from Windows Explorer, Notepad's association with this type of extension launches Notepad to read the file. Most systems have a large number of registered applications such as the ones shown in Figure 14-5.

NOTE: The HKEY_CURRENT_USER\Software\Classes alias is a new feature in Windows 2000.

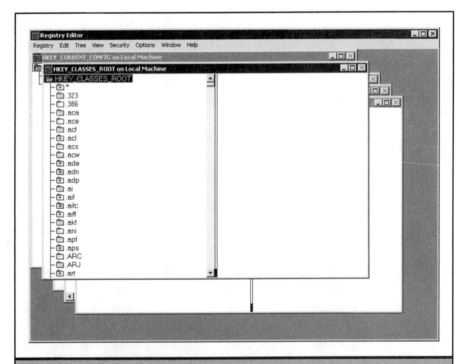

Figure 14-5.   Information such as file associations located in HKEY_CLASSES_ROOT

HKEY_CURRENT_CONFIG

The HKEY_CURRENT_CONFIG root key was introduced in
Windows NT 4.0 for compatibility reasons for users running
applications on both the Windows 95/98 platform and Windows
2000. This key is actually an alias of the HKEY_LOCAL_MACHINE\
SYSTEM\CurrentControlSet\Hardware Profiles\Current subkey.
Figure 14-6 shows that these two keys are the same.

HKEY_CURRENT_USER

The HKEY_CURRENT_USER root key is a pointer to HKEY_USERS\
<SecurityID>, which pertains to the user currently logged on. The
information that it points to includes user preferences such as
desktop preferences, keyboard layout schemes, network drive
mappings, and software preferences. The HKEY_CURRENT_USER
key is created each time a user logs on using the specific profile of
that user. If the user is logging on for the first time, a default profile
is used.

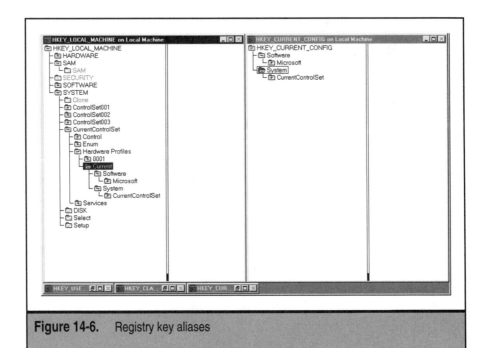

Figure 14-6.   Registry key aliases

Common subkeys contained within the HKEY_CURRENT_USER root key are the following:

▼ AppEvents

■ Console

■ Control Panel

■ Environment

■ Identities

■ Keyboard Layout

■ Network

■ Printers

■ RemoteAccess

■ Software

■ SYSTEM

■ UNICODE Program Groups

▲ Volatile Environment

NOTE: When a user is not logged on, the system uses the key.

HKEY_USERS

HKEY_USERS contains a subkey for each user account. However, only two subkeys for the user currently logged onto the system and the default profile appear. It's also important to note that profiles for user accounts accessing the system remotely are not loaded into this key but are loaded into the Registry of the local machine.

The subkeys, like the ones shown in Figure 14-7, are explained here:

▼ .DEFAULT   This is the default profile used during startup. If no user is logged onto the system, this is the profile being used.

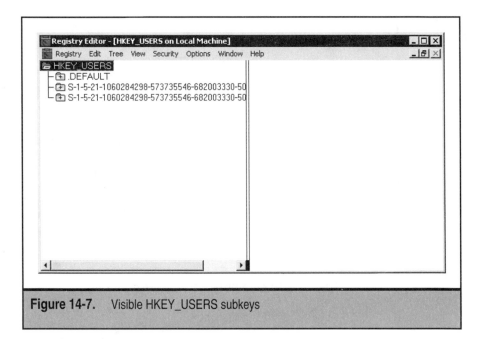

Figure 14-7.   Visible HKEY_USERS subkeys

■   *<SecurityID>*   The SecurityID, also known as the SID,
    identifies the user currently logged onto the system.

▲   *<SecurityID_Classes>*   This subkey holds all of the class
    information for the user currently logged onto the system. The
    information in this subkey is also in HKEY_CLASSES_ROOT.

Value Entries and Values

The information contained within the Registry is maintained by
value entries. A value entry has three components: the value's name,
the value's data type (listed in Table 14-4), and the actual value. The
most common data types are REG_BINARY, REG_DWORD, and
REG_SZ. You will likely use these common data types more than
any other data types to modify settings.

Value Data Type	Description
REG_BINARY	Raw binary data that can also be displayed in hexadecimal (hex) format. Most of the system's hardware components use this data type, and their settings can be viewed in Windows 2000's System Information.
REG_DWORD	A 32-bit number (4 bytes) that can be displayed in binary, hex, or decimal format. This value type is usually used for device drivers and services.
REG_DWORD_BIG_ENDIAN	A 32-bit number.
REG_EXPAND_SZ	An expandable data string that represents environment variables. The variables, such as %SYSTEMROOT% and %USERNAME%, are replaced by the actual values.
REG_LINK	A Unicode symbolic link. This type typically links to another Registry key or subkey. For example, the HKEY_CURRENT_USER root key aliases the HKEY_USERS subkey.
REG_MULTI_SZ	An array of strings. Each string is separated by a NULL character.
REG_SZ	A string that usually represents a description. This description is readable (that is, not cryptic).

Table 14-4. Registry Value Data Types

BUILT-IN REGISTRY EDITORS

Windows 2000 supplies two versions of the Registry Editor: REGEDIT.EXE and REGEDT32.EXE. Both allow you to directly modify the Registry on the local machine as well as on remote machines. However, there are some subtle differences between the two versions that you should be aware of. These differences determine whether you should use one or the other.

REGEDIT

REGEDIT, shown in Figure 14-8, is the Registry Editor that is also included with previous versions of Windows. On Windows 2000 systems, REGEDIT is installed by default in the %SYSTEMROOT% directory. Although you can use REGEDIT to view hives, keys, subkeys, and so on, it does not include all the functionality or data types that its counterpart, REGEDT32, does.

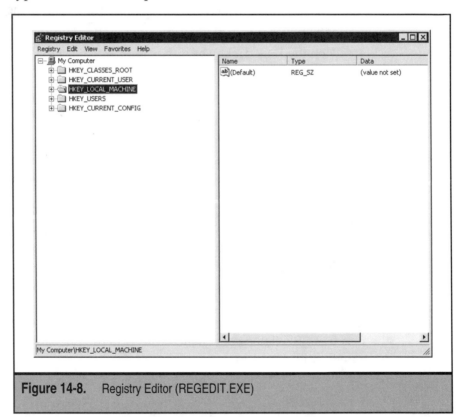

Figure 14-8.   Registry Editor (REGEDIT.EXE)

Although REGEDIT hasn't really changed much, two new, useful features are included with Windows 2000. First, you can now bookmark locations that you frequently use within the Registry, using the Favorites menu. Second, REGEDIT opens to the last key or subkey that you previously opened.

Having REGEDIT start with the last key or subkey that you had open is a Catch-22. Although it can save you time searching through the Registry for the last key you worked with, it may pose a security risk by exposing a modification you made. If this concerns you, you can easily stop the Registry from displaying the last key or subkey. To do so, do the following:

1. Open REGEDT32.

2. Open HKEY_CURRENT_USER\Software\Microsoft\ Windows\CurrentVersion\Applets\Regedit.

3. Double-click the LastKey value, remove the entry in the String box, and then click OK. This removes the value of the last key opened, but it doesn't stop the REGEDIT feature.

4. Click the Regedit key and then click Permissions on the Security menu.

5. Remove Full Control permissions for any user for which you don't want REGEDIT to display the last key opened. When you're done, click OK.

6. For those users for which you can't remove the Full Control permission, click the check box next to Deny to deny them full control.

REGEDIT's functionality is somewhat limited because it does not let you set Registry key security or view or edit some value data types. The data types that you cannot modify are REG_EXPAND_SZ and REG_MULTI_SZ. For instance, if you try to view REG_EXPAND_SZ, the editor displays a binary data type rather than a string data type. Moreover, if you attempt to modify these data types, REGEDIT saves them as REG_SZ data types, which prevents the relevant parameter from performing its duties.

REGEDIT's biggest advantage over its counterpart is its extensive search capabilities. You can use REGEDIT's Find dialog box, shown here, to search for keys, values, and data within the Registry structure. REGEDIT's search capabilities far exceed those of REGEDT32.EXE.

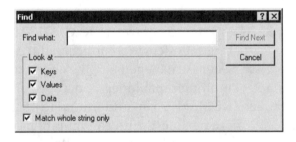

Because REGEDIT combines rather limited functionality with robust search capabilities, you should use it only to search for Registry information. This approach helps ensure that the Registry does not lose security-related information—or worse, become corrupt.

Searching the Registry

To search for a key, a value, or data using REGEDIT, do the following:

1. Open REGEDIT either from the Start | Run menu or by typing **REGEDIT** at the command prompt.

2. In the left pane of the REGEDIT window, select My Computer. This allows the search algorithm to search the entire Registry. If you want to search a specific key or subkey, just select the appropriate key.

3. From the Edit menu, choose Find to display the Find dialog box.

4. In the Find What box, type the key name, value name, or data value that you are searching for.

5. Click Find Next to start the search.

REGEDT32

REGEDT32, shown in Figure 14-9, is the Registry Editor commonly used for Windows 2000 and is located in the %SYSTEMROOT%\ System32 directory. It does not have the clean, intuitive user interface of REGEDIT, but instead looks and feels like the old File Manager. Despite its appearance, however, REGEDT32 is the Registry Editor of choice because it offers more functionality than REGEDIT, such as Registry security management, the ability to modify any Registry parameter, auditing capabilities, and a special read-only mode.

Because REGEDT32 can perform more operations than REGEDIT, you have more flexibility with configuration settings. One important option that you should always use is Read-Only Mode. This option will not allow any changes to be saved to the Registry, so you can safely peruse the Registry. It is recommended that you use this option until you are ready to make a specific configuration change.

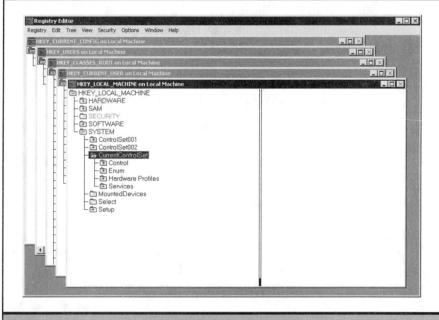

Figure 14-9.   The preferred Registry Editor

Creating a Key

As you are preparing your server for blazingly fast performance, you are bound to come across a situation where you will need to add a key to the Registry. You may also, in rare cases, sometimes need to install a driver or service that does not have its own installation program to guide you through setup procedures and make Registry changes on its own; this, too, may require adding a key to the Registry.

To create or add a Registry key, do the following:

1. Select the key or subkey under which you want the new key to appear.

2. Choose Add Key from the Edit menu to display the Add Key dialog box.

NOTE: The Add Key option will not appear if you are in read-only mode. To disable read-only mode, uncheck Read-Only Mode on the Options menu. You will also need appropriate access rights to add a key.

3. In the Key Name box, shown here, type the name of the key you want to add.

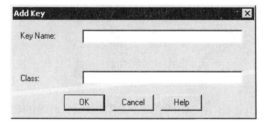

4. If you already know the class to which this key belongs, you can specify it in the Class box, or you can leave this box blank for now. It is recommended that you keep the Class box blank.

Adding a Value

Adding a value means adding a parameter to an existing key or to a key that you have just created. When you add a value, you must also assign it an appropriate data type.

To add a value to the Registry, do the following:

1. Select the key or subkey under which this value will exist.

2. Choose Add Value from the Edit menu to display the Add Value dialog box, shown here.

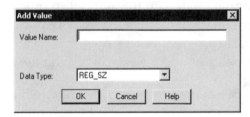

3. In the Value Name box, type the name of the value to be added.

4. In the Data Type pull-down menu, select the appropriate data type for the value to be added.

5. Click OK. A dialog box appropriate for the data value selected now appears. For example, if the data type is REG_SZ, the String Editor dialog box appears, as shown here.

6. Type the value corresponding to the data type.

Viewing or Modifying Remote Registries

When you start REGEDT32, by default it opens the Registry of the local machine. However, you can also view or modify the Registry on a remote Windows NT or Windows 2000 machine, if you have the appropriate permissions. To view or modify the Registry on a remote Windows NT or Windows 2000 machine, choose Select Computer from the Registry menu. You can either browse a list of machines to choose from, or you can type the machine name in the Computer box. Once the remote Registry hives are loaded, you can work with the remote Registry just as you would the local Registry.

NOTE: The Auto Refresh feature isn't available when working with a remote Registry.

Removing Registry Information

The ability to delete Registry keys or value entries is necessary to maintain the Registry, but it is also one of the most dangerous options you have. To delete a key or value entry, either select Delete from the Edit menu or press the DELETE key.

CAUTION: If you accidentally delete a key or value, there is little you can do to restore it. To ensure the Registry's integrity, it's recommended that you at least write down the key, subkey, or value information before deleting it. The best safeguard is to make sure you have a recent backup of the Registry.

BACKING UP THE REGISTRY

No backup methodology would be complete without including the Registry. It's extremely important that you keep an up-to-date backup copy of the Registry for emergencies, such as the inadvertent deletion of a key or value. There are several methods that you can use to back up the Registry and safeguard your machine's data.

Backing up the Registry on a regular basis is crucial to the stability of the system. If the Registry becomes corrupted either by a system process or direct modification, the entire machine can be rendered useless unless you have properly prepared for such a disaster.

The following sections explore some common, but important, ways to back up the Registry.

Using the Windows 2000 Backup Utility

You can use either Windows 2000's built-in backup program (NTBACKUP.EXE) or a third-party backup program to back up the Registry. If you use a third-party solution, make sure that it can back up the Registry.

Windows 2000's backup utility, shown in Figure 14-10, is a new and improved backup utility compared with the previous versions for Windows NT. It's found on the Start | Programs | Accessories | System Tools menu. The most notable improvements are the following:

▼ **Media Types** NTBACKUP allows you to back up data to more than just tape. You now have many options for the placement of your backup data.

▲ **System State Data** This option, illustrated in Figure 14-11, allows you to back up the machine's System State, which includes the Registry, boot files, system files, COM+ Class Registration, Active Directory, SYSVOL, and cluster service information.

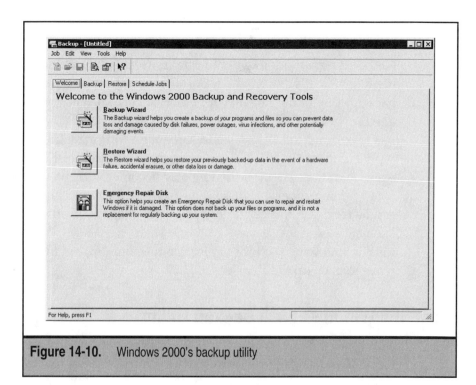

Figure 14-10. Windows 2000's backup utility

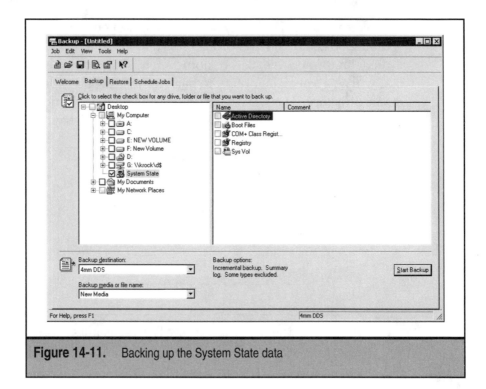

Figure 14-11.   Backing up the System State data

When you want to back up the Registry, simply select the System State option. When you back up the System State data, a copy of the Registry files are automatically saved in %SYSTEMROOT%\ Repair\Regback.

Creating an Emergency Repair Disk (ERD)

Another simple yet very effective way to back up the Registry is to create an ERD. The creation of an ERD is a different process in Windows 2000 than you may expect. You used the RDISK or RDISK /s command in Windows NT, but you now use the Windows 2000 backup utility (RDISK has been completely replaced). If you look back at Figure 14-10, you'll notice the Emergency Repair Disk option on NTBACKUP's Welcome tab.

To create an ERD, simply select this option on the Welcome tab. A dialog box, shown here, prompts you to insert a blank, formatted diskette in the A drive. Before doing so, it is highly recommended that you also select the option to back up the Registry files to the repair directory. The reason for doing so is that this option may make it easier to recover from a corrupt or damaged Registry.

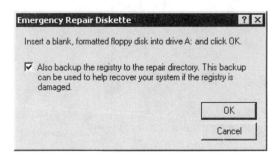

NOTE: Any time you make a change to the system, it's advised that you create a new ERD.

Backing Up the Registry with REGEDT32

REGEDT32 offers an alternative option for backing up the Registry. You can also use this approach to view a remote machine's Registry. By using the Save Key option on the Registry menu, you can save copies of Registry keys and subkeys in data files. These files can later be used to restore or replace a key or even rebuild the entire Registry. There is one exception, however. You cannot use the Save Key option to save volatile keys. In other words, you cannot save keys that are created at startup and deleted when the system is shut down. Some volatile keys, such as HKEY_LOCAL_MACHINE, have some nonvolatile subkeys that can be saved.

Saving a Key or Subkey

To save a key or subkey using REGEDT32, do the following:

1. Select the key or subkey that you want to save.

2. Select Save Key from the Registry menu to display the Save Key dialog box, shown here.

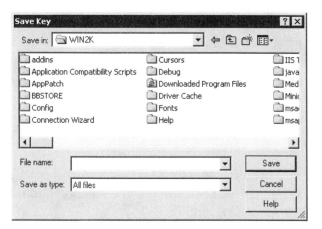

3. Type the name of the file. It is recommended that you use the name of the key as the name of the file.

Restoring a Previously Saved Key or Subkey

To restore a previously saved key using REGEDT32, follow these steps:

1. Select the key that you want to restore from a data file.

2. Select Restore from the Registry menu to display the Restore Key dialog box, shown here.

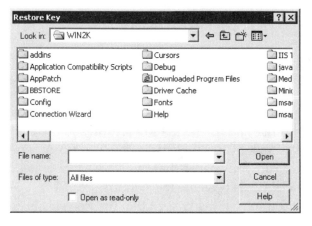

3. Browse for the location of the data file or type the full path and file name.

4. Click Open. You will be warned that you are about to overwrite the key and all of its subkeys.

5. Click Yes to continue.

Fast Exports and Restores

Since performance is also about being as efficient as possible, there is a quicker and easier way to export the Registry. You can export the entire Registry or a specific key with the following command:

```
"regedit /e c:\output.reg"
```

Type the command at the command prompt or run line, where c:\output.reg is the location and file name you want to use for the export.

You can export a specific key by entering the following:

```
"regedit /e c:\output.reg HKEY_LOCAL_MACHINE\System\CurrentControlSet\Control\Idconfigdb"
```

When you specify a key, such as the one given here, REGEDIT exports that specific key.

When it comes time to restore the key or entire Registry, all you have to do is double-click the output file.

TWEAKING THE REGISTRY FOR OPTIMAL PERFORMANCE

Clearly, Windows 2000 relies heavily on the Registry for system configuration information. Users often think of the Registry as the place to go to tune the system for optimal performance, especially if the UI—for instance, the Control Panel—does not have the instrumentation needed to perform such tweaks. Rarely, however, do users look at the Registry itself as a component to be optimized. How can you ensure that the Registry operates as effectively and efficiently as possible for Windows 2000?

You have already seen that the Registry is an excellent place for fine-tuning system components since it contains hardware, software, and user configuration settings. You will now see that the Registry presents an opportunity to boost Windows 2000 performance, not by adding or modifying a Registry configuration parameter, but by modifying the database itself.

A Lean, Mean, Configuration Machine

The Registry is a massive organizational structure containing almost everything you could ever want to know about a Windows 2000 system. For instance, when you add, modify, or remove hardware and software components, most, if not all, of the changes are reflected in the Registry. However, sometimes when hardware or software components are removed, they leave behind remnants of their existence. It is not uncommon to find Registry entries for a component that used to be a part of the system but was long ago deleted.

Don't hastily assume that Windows 2000 is at fault for leaving defunct or invalid information in the Registry. Most often, it is the hardware component or application's uninstall program, or lack thereof, that doesn't completely remove its entries from the Registry. In fact, application entries are usually the ones left behind in the Registry, since the Registry's hardware inventory procedures are volatile, meaning that Windows 2000 always builds its hardware inventory at startup.

The Registry can quite easily accumulate fatty deposits left over from the installation, uninstallation, and removal of software components, but to get the best possible performance from Windows 2000, the Registry must be kept lean and mean. All those fragments left behind from applications and system components need to be cleaned out from the Registry so that invalid data is not referenced or the Registry database does not grow large with unneeded information.

Cleaning the Registry

If you have ever tried to remove all references to an application by hand, you know how agonizing this process can be. Many of today's applications try to help by including an uninstall utility, which attempts to remove all of the application's code, data, and Registry entries. Uninstall utilities not only save you considerable time; they also reduce the risk that you will damage or corrupt the Registry with manual Registry edits.

Although many developers are building in uninstall utilities, there still are a large number of applications without one. Moreover, available uninstall utilities vary in how well they perform their duties. Consequently, Microsoft has developed its own utility, called RegClean (see "RegClean" just ahead for information on how to obtain this utility), to help reduce the clutter in the Registry. There are also a growing number of third-party utilities that are not application specific that are designed to remove invalid Registry entries.

Add/Remove Programs   Windows 2000 provides its own means of removing applications and invalid Registry entries through the Add/Remove Programs applet available from the Control Panel (see Figure 14-12). Most applications can be installed through this applet, and most applications can be removed through it as well.

Although the Add/Remove Programs applet may appear to be the perfect solution for uninstalling applications and removing their associated entries from the Registry, in most cases, the applet simply kicks off an application's uninstall utility. If the application does not

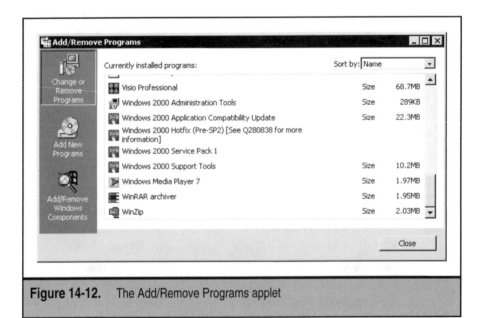

Figure 14-12.   The Add/Remove Programs applet

have an uninstall utility, or if it has been deleted or corrupted, you are out of luck. Even if the system is able to start the application's uninstall utility, you still have to rely on the application to remove itself completely, including any Registry entries it may have added.

RegClean The RegClean utility searches the Registry for invalid entries and then removes them. RegClean 4.1a or higher isn't officially compatible with Windows 2000, but there does not appear to be any incompatibility issues. The latest version of this utility can be located at Microsoft's FTP site (ftp://ftp.microsoft.com/Softlib/ mslfiles/regclean.exe).

CAUTION: As with any program or utility that can modify the Registry, it is critical that you back up the Registry before you execute RegClean.

When you run RegClean, as shown in Figure 14-13, it scans the Registry to find any erroneous values or invalid entries. If it finds any errors, it writes them to a file called UNDO.REG before removing

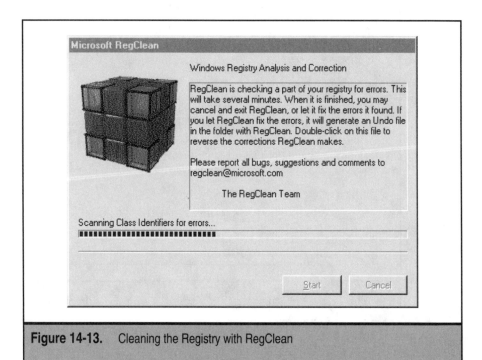

Figure 14-13. Cleaning the Registry with RegClean

them from the Registry. It is recommended that you review UNDO.REG with a text editor, such as Notepad, to see what changes have been made to the Registry. The UNDO.REG file is also created as a safeguard against the accidental removal of entries or values that are still needed. Figure 14-14 shows an example of the contents of the UNDO.REG file after running RegClean.

NOTE: RegClean is not designed to fix a corrupted Registry.

Figure 14-14.   Sample UNDO.REG file

To install RegClean, do the following:

1. Double-click the RegClean executable that you downloaded from Microsoft's FTP site to extract the files needed to run RegClean.

2. Go to the directory that you specified in step 1 and double-click the RegClean executable to start the program.

You can optionally create a shortcut to RegClean or add it to the Programs folder for easier accessibility.

Windows Installer Cleanup Utility (MSICUU.EXE)   You won't have to go far for this useful utility. The Windows Installer Cleanup Utility is located in the \Support\Tools directory on the Windows 2000 CD. MSICCU, shown in Figure 14-15, is designed specifically to remove Registry entries from an application installation that used the Windows Installer.

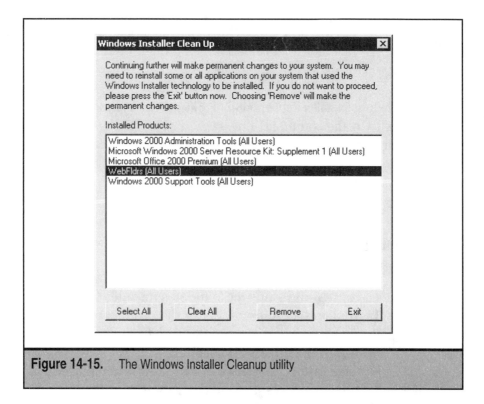

Figure 14-15.   The Windows Installer Cleanup utility

If you ever abruptly terminate an installation or, worse, experience a failed installation using the Windows Installer, the Registry will more than likely contain remnants of the application. Even if you don't experience any installation problems thereafter, there are still unwanted Registry entries left behind. To keep the Registry as clean as possible so that it runs as efficiently as possible, use the MSICCU utility to clean up.

NOTE: MSICCU doesn't remove files from an application; it removes only associated Registry entries.

To use MSICCU, do the following:

1. At the command prompt or in the Run box, enter **MSICCU**.

2. In the Windows Installer Clean Up window, select the program for which you want to remove the Registry entries and click Remove. Do not choose Select All, because if you're having problems with all applications using Windows Installer, you're probably having more problems than you think.

Windows Installer Zapper (MSIZAP.EXE)   The Windows Installer Zapper utility is the command-line version of MSICCU. Surprisingly, this command-line version has slightly more functionality that the GUI tool. Typing **MSIZAP** at the command prompt gives you the syntax for using the utility. The syntax is

MSIZAP [*] [A] [P] [T {product code] [!]

where

* removes all folders and Registry entries, adjusts shared DLL counts, and stops the Windows Installer service.
T removes all information for the product code specified.
P removes the In-Progress subkey from the Registry.
S removes rollback information.
A changes ACLs (permissions) to Admin Full Control.
! forces a Yes response to any prompt for the user.

PART III

Optimizing Connectivity and MS BackOffice

CHAPTER 15

Internet Information Server

With the Internet's popularity still exploding and the possible uses of the Internet expanding, keeping a Web presence reliable, stable, and available is essential. Whether you're hosting your own Web site for internal or external purposes, you're an Internet service provider (ISP), you're an application service provider (ASP), or you're a management systems provider (MSP), you're responsible for supplying a wealth of information and functionality that doesn't come without a price.

The price you pay, of course, depends first of all on how available and reliable you make Internet Information Server (IIS). Availability means keeping the service operational and able to handle requests. Reliability, on the other hand, stretches the definition of availability to include the handling of requests without failure. These two terms are frequently intermingled and even misused. The bottom line is that you have to design for an appropriate level of redundancy and acceptable number of failures. The higher the levels of availability and reliability you provide to IIS, the higher the price tag because of the additional hardware, increased bandwidth, multiple Internet pipes, greater amount of administration and maintenance, and other resources you will need. Once you've planned and designed the availability and reliability levels, you can incorporate appropriate levels of performance to match.

As you may already know, a successful implementation of an Internet/intranet Web site can be a very complex and exhausting task, but the payback makes it worth the effort. Windows 2000 and the bundled IIS help facilitate the process of designing, building, and maintaining a Web site.

NOTE: With any service or application that you're fine-tuning in Windows 2000, you must first ensure that Windows 2000 is performing as effectively and efficiently as possible. If you haven't already done so, examine the performance considerations and recommendations in the other chapters of this book related to Windows 2000.

NEW IIS 5.0 FEATURES

Each new version of IIS brings a wealth of new and improved features that provide a robust and scalable architecture for Web, FTP, and other related Internet technologies, and Windows 2000's built-in IIS 5.0 is no exception. The features mentioned here are not all the new features of IIS, but they're the ones that will have the most impact on performance. Keep in mind that IIS performance isn't just about speed; it's also about improved manageability and security, among other things.

Microsoft has organized these new features into several categories: security, administration, programmability, and Internet standards.

Security

▼   **Digest Authentication**   In addition to the previously supported authentication mechanisms, Windows 2000 has added this secure and robust authentication mechanism that is especially designed for authenticating users across proxy servers and firewalls.

■   **Server-Gated Cryptography (SGC)**   SGC is an extension of the Secure Sockets Layer (SSL) technology that allows companies with export versions of IIS to use strong 128-bit encryption.

■   **Security Wizards**   To simplify administration tasks, IIS provides wizards to help configure security settings on the server. They include the Web server certificate, permissions, and certificate trust lists (CTL) wizards.

■   **Kerberos Version 5 Compliance**   The integration of Kerberos with IIS allows you to pass authentication credentials among connected Windows 2000 computers. Kerberos far outperforms the LAN Manager authentication method.

■   **Certificate Storage**   IIS certificate storage takes full advantage of the certificate services that are provided with

Windows 2000's Certificate Server. It is now integrated with the Windows CryptoAPI storage. The Windows Certificate Manager provides a single point of entry that allows you to store, back up, and configure server certificates.

▲ **Fortessa** Fortessa is a United States government security standard for the Defense Message System. IIS now complies with this standard to provide bulletproof Web-based messaging.

Administration

▼ **Reliable Restart** In previous versions, you often had to restart the server to restart IIS services, incurring costly downtime. To avoid this, Windows 2000 includes IIS Reliable Restart, which is a faster, easier, more flexible one-step restart process. The administrator can restart IIS through the Computer Management or Services Microsoft Management Console (MMC) snap-ins as well as by using the command line. Windows 2000 will also attempt to restart the IIS services automatically if the INETINFO process terminates unexpectedly. This promotes higher reliability and stability.

■ **Process Accounting** When a server is hosting more than one Web site, it's often useful to know how each Web site affects the system's CPU utilization. Process accounting does just that; it provides information about how individual Web sites use the server's CPU resources.

■ **Process Throttling** Process throttling allows you to limit the percentage of CPU utilization for individual Web sites. When you use this in conjunction with process accounting, it becomes particularly useful because you can give more processing power to your more critical Web sites.

▲ **Less Dependence on the Registry** IIS 5.0 no longer relies heavily on the Registry. Instead, it depends on the IIS metabase. This promotes a higher degree of reliability because it essentially places a partition between IIS and the rest of the system. You'll still find Registry keys for IIS, but this is for backward compatibility with earlier versions of IIS as well as older applications. Moreover, the IIS metabase supports object inheritance, providing a more efficient way of managing IIS configuration settings.

Programmability

▼ **New Active Server Pages (ASP) Features**   ASP is a server-side scripting language that has been supported by previous versions of IIS. Improvements have been made to streamline performance and IIS scripts. These improvements include reduced interprocess communication, reduced lock contention, improved SMP scaling, and much more.

■ **Application Protection**   IIS increases reliability for your Web applications by either *pooling* processes or isolating them from other processes. Pooled processes run in a common memory space that is separate from memory areas where core IIS services are running. This protects core IIS services and other applications from erratic processes.

▲ **Active Directory (AD) Support**   IIS fully supports AD through ADSI 2.0. This gives you greater flexibility in configuring Web sites because you can create your own custom AD objects using ADSI.

Internet Standards

▼ **Web Distributed Authoring and Versioning (WebDAV)**   WebDAV allows you to manage the file- and directory-related properties of a Web site through a standard HTTP connection. The added convenience can save you a lot on administration efforts.

■ **FTP Restart**   If you've ever had to stop a download (or had a download get interrupted) when using FTP and then later tried to resume downloading, you're probably well aware that you often had to start the download from scratch. Now you can resume the download from where you left off.

▲ **HTTP Compression** HTTP compression combines compacting of Web pages with caching of static files to enable users to see Web pages more quickly. Clients and servers that are compression enabled can use this feature.

DESIGNING AND PLANNING IIS PERFORMANCE

One of the most frequently asked questions when sizing a Web server is "How many users can IIS support with a particular hardware configuration?" Unfortunately, there aren't recipes or simple answers to this question. Identifying the hardware requirements for a Web server is a complex, dynamic process. The number of users connecting simultaneously, as well as their usage patterns, will almost always vary significantly each time users request information from IIS services. Plus there are so many other variables related to other services such as the back-end database and message transfer that contribute to the overall performance of the Web site.

You cannot determine hardware requirements based on just a few parameters. In fact, even if you do define the variety of factors that affect IIS performance, they still constantly change. However, by using the capacity planning procedures described in Chapter 2, you can begin to determine the basic hardware requirements of the Web server and scale accordingly. These procedures will also help you proactively identify system bottlenecks and changing hardware requirements.

Determining Web Site Capacity

Web server capacity planning is by far the most effective means of determining workloads placed on the system. You can begin sizing the Web server by identifying parameters, such as whether or not the Web pages are static or dynamic, what type of database is used, what type of server scripting is used, and so on. This is assuming, of course, that Windows 2000 will be used only as a Web server. If other functionality is built into the server, there will be additional hardware requirements. Ensuring the overall efficiency and performance of the server consideration for all hardware components is key. For more information on hardware, refer to Chapter 3.

Memory

IIS and its related services (World Wide Web and FTP) must reside in memory. When determining how much memory is enough for the Web server, take into account the additional resources needed for IIS and its services, the memory to be used by Windows 2000 and other services on the machine, and the memory requirements for generating dynamic content.

The more memory IIS has available to use, the faster it can process user requests. To provide substantial performance, the absolute minimum amount of physical memory recommended for an IIS system is 128MB. This recommendation is only a starting point for determining the amount of memory you should use. For more information on memory, refer to Chapter 6.

Increasing the Amount of L2 Cache   A large amount of L2 cache on any system can significantly improve performance. This is especially true for IIS systems because their instruction paths involve many different components that take advantage of the L2 cache. Most important, however, is the fact that today's processor speeds far exceed memory speeds. The faster L2 cache is used as a buffer and frees up the processor sooner, so that it can move on and process more requests.

For even relatively small sites, you should configure the IIS system with at least 1MB of L2 cache. For more information on L2 and other forms of cache, refer to Chapter 3.

Processor

Overall, the processing power required by basic IIS services is minimal. However, additional workloads placed on the server by dynamic content can significantly increase processing power requirements. Avoid configuring the Web server with anything less than a Pentium II processor, even if you're providing only static HTML pages. If you anticipate supporting several hundred or more simultaneous connections with static content, a Pentium III class processor or higher is the recommended minimum processor. However, if the same scenario includes dynamic content, it is highly recommended that you either incorporate a Pentium III or higher SMP machine or architect the load balance on two or more machines.

You'll notice a significant improvement in the speed at which IIS handles requests with fast processors. In fact, increasing the processor speed (as well as the L2 cache size) will give you the most boost for your money. In addition, IIS directly benefits from Windows 2000's increased efficiency with multiple processors. Adding more processors to a server or even adding servers in a cluster or network load balancing (NLB) arrangement will not only pump up performance; it will also allow you to scale to meet ever-changing needs.

Network Subsystem

Providing high-speed network access to client machines is critical to IIS performance. If clients are unable to obtain information from IIS in a timely manner, the results could be damaging to your business. Consider these factors when estimating the network hardware requirements for IIS:

▼ Simultaneous user support

■ Data transfers between the client and the IIS system

■ Connection types between IIS and the Internet

▲ Bandwidth usage limitations when IIS is configured with the Internet Services Manager (ISM)

There are many choices, such as the ones outlined in Table 15-1, for the connection between IIS and the Internet. Of course, the higher the bandwidth, the more users you can adequately support. However, cost also is a major influence in determining the connection type.

Perform a rough calculation of the expected network traffic between IIS and the Internet before you make any hardware purchases. You can use a simple formula, such as

Required bandwidth =
Number of users connecting per second × Total number of bytes transferred × 8 (for bps)

to get a general idea of anticipated network requirements. For example, if 120 users connect each minute (2 users per second) and

Connection Type	Bandwidth	Recommended Maximum Number of Supported Clients
56K	56 Kbps	50
ISDN	64–128 Kbps	100
Frame Relay	56 Kbps–1.544 Mbps	50–1,000
Dedicated 256K	256 Kbps	200
Fractional T1	128 Kbps–1.544 Mbps	100–1,000
T1	1.544 Mbps	1,000
T3	45 Mbps	1,000 or more

Table 15-1.   Common WAN Connection Types

10K of data is transferred to and from the client machine, then the connection type needs to support 20K per second (160 Kbps). In this example, a 56 Kbps connection would not satisfy those requirements.

NOTE: Most ISPs, ASPs, and MSPs have redundant network connections, but many companies hosting their own Web sites do not. Determine how much it would cost you if the Web site network connectivity went down for an hour or more. If the price is high or intolerable, seriously consider adding a second network connection.

The bandwidth of the NIC is also critical, especially if a connection is made to a database on the internal network, or if IIS serves as an intranet server. A 10-Mbps Ethernet adapter or a Token Ring adapter running at 16 Mbps is suitable for many environments. However, if IIS provides dynamic content to lots of users, these connection types can quickly become saturated. Consequently, if a 100-Mbps or greater network segment is present, it is recommended that you use an adapter capable of supporting a minimum of 100 Mbps. For more information on optimizing the network subsystem, refer to Chapter 8.

Hardware Redundancy

In Chapter 5, we examined fault tolerance and disaster recovery considerations for Windows 2000 systems. When you're building a Web site, these considerations are no different. You have to take into account some protection against component or system failures. How much would it cost the company if the Web site became temporarily out of commission? Even a small or mid-size company could lose thousands, if not hundreds of thousands, of dollars per hour that the Web site is down.

Once you have an understanding of how much downtime would cost the company, you can work with your budget to design the most reliable site possible. Who knows; you may even be able to increase the budget for the Web site to match the reliability requirements. The bottom line is that the more it costs the company to be down, the more redundancy you should provide.

Planning and designing hardware redundancy for the Web site doesn't just include the internal hardware components (memory, disks, controllers, processors, power supplies, and so on). It also includes networking hardware (routers, switches, hubs, cables, NICs, and so on) and even entire systems.

Creating a Scaleable, High-Performance Web Site

Now that we've examined some hardware considerations, you should begin analyzing two other key ingredients for a scaleable, high-performance Web site: system architecture interactions and scalability. These two considerations are equally important for properly sizing a Web site. They're related to the hardware considerations mentioned earlier, but they also involve software aspects of the system. The complexity of these considerations will vary for each Web site, but again your decisions will depend on the type of Web site you're planning to offer, the number of expected simultaneous hits, the expected response times for end users, and much more. By keeping these considerations in mind when you're planning and designing your Web site, you'll be better prepared to manage any volume of traffic your site may experience.

System architecture interaction refers to the way in which all of the service components (for example, back-end support mechanisms such as Microsoft SQL Server) communicate. Scalability refers to the ability to expand hardware and software requirements to meet the ever-changing requirements of a system. There are various ways to scale your Web site, but they can be segmented into two categories: scaling in and scaling out.

System Architecture Interactions

Web sites are becoming more and more complex. Many rely on various back-end systems to support the front-end services (that is, what the end user sees). The types of back-end systems you employ and the interactions among them can significantly affect performance. This holds true whether you're running everything on a single server or your Web site has a multitude of servers.

The first set of decisions that you'll need to make involve choosing the type of back-end systems needed to support what you'll offer on the Web site. This can include choosing messaging, database, transaction, and customer relationship management (CRM) systems. As you add back-end systems, the decision process can become increasingly involved. For instance, suppose you're planning to use a database system. Do you need to provide connectivity to the company's CRM database or to a legacy system? Can you or should you run the database on the Web server? What other services or systems will interact with the database? What's the anticipated amount of communication between the database and other services and how will it affect performance? These are just a few of the questions that you should be asking yourself, and, of course, the answers will vary from environment to environment.

You also need to consider the resource requirements for each back-end system. Some may be memory-intensive applications; others may be processor or network intensive. Each system, with its own resource requirements, may also be interacting with the other Web site systems, so it's important to properly size each system so that they don't negatively affect the overall Web site. Chapter 16 gives you insight on how to tune MS SQL Server 2000, and Chapter 17 discusses how to optimize MS Exchange 2000. If you're using or planning to use either of these systems, be sure to check out these chapters.

> **NOTE:** MS Application Center 2000 promises to help you simplify Web application management, scale Web software components to meet changing needs, and provide the highest level of application availability for your Web site. For more information on Application Center 2000, visit http://www.microsoft.com/ applicationcenter/.

Scaling In

Scaling in means that you're expanding the internal components (processors, memory, disk subsystem, and so on) of a server to handle increasing workloads. A simple example is adding another processor to your system when you have a single-processor server and need to boost it's processing power up by 100 percent. This is by far the easiest way to scale your Web site, especially from cost and manageability standpoints. Right out of the box, Windows 2000 supports more processors and memory than its predecessor. Table 15-2 lists the various flavors of Windows 2000 and the number of processors and amount of memory each supports.

Scaling Out

Scaling out means using multiple servers that are identical in functionality to handle the same workloads. As you might expect, this form of scalability can boost performance well beyond that provided by scaling in. For example, if you need to scale beyond a Windows 2000 Datacenter Server with 32 processors, you can scale out with additional Windows 2000 Datacenter 32-way systems. Scaling out also provides an additional level of redundancy that you wouldn't be able to achieve with a single server. Its biggest

Windows 2000 Version	Maximum Number of Processors	Maximum Amount of Physical Memory (GB)
Server	4	4
Advanced Server	8	8
Datacenter Server	32	64

Table 15-2.   Windows 2000 Scalability Capabilities

disadvantage, however, is that it can introduce a significant amount of complexity into design, installation, and administration.

DNS Round Robin Probably the oldest way to scale out your Web site using multiple servers is by using DNS Round Robin. This method uses DNS to associate multiple IP addresses (that is, multiple servers) with a single domain name entry, such as www.perpetuitysys.com. When the client machine requests information from http://www.perpetuitysys.com, the request can be handled by any of the IP addresses defined in DNS for that domain name.

The workload can actually be distributed across multiple, identical Web servers. Clients connecting to a particular Web site are unaware of which server is processing their request. Figure 15-1 illustrates a client system connecting to a Web site a total of three times. Each time the client connects, a different server seamlessly handles the request.

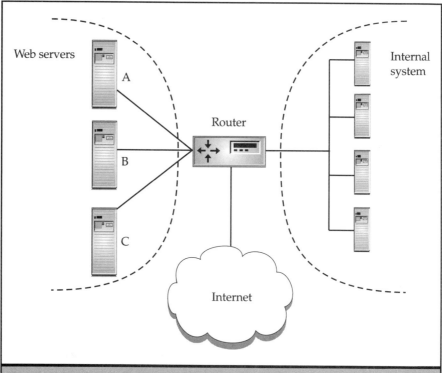

Figure 15-1. Distributing the load using DNS Round Robin

Network Load Balancing (NLB)   NLB is a clustering-based technology that provides application or service scalability by balancing client requests across multiple servers (also known as nodes). It has some similarities to DNS Round Robin, but there are many differences; for instance, port rules determine which node handles the next incoming request rather than requests going to each server in succession, NLB runs as a network driver on Windows 2000, NLB can be used with server-based clustering technology, NLB can more easily recover from node failure, and much more. Grouping similar servers into an NLB cluster not only promotes scalability, but it also provides higher performance and availability. You can group as many as 32 servers in an NLB cluster.

NOTE: NLB is available only with Windows 2000 Advanced Server and Windows 2000 Datacenter Server.

NLB runs as a network driver in conjunction with the TCP/IP protocol stack, as shown in Figure 15-2. Each node has its own unique IP address, but client requests are distributed throughout the

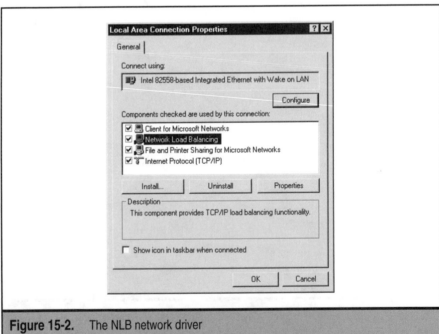

Figure 15-2.   The NLB network driver

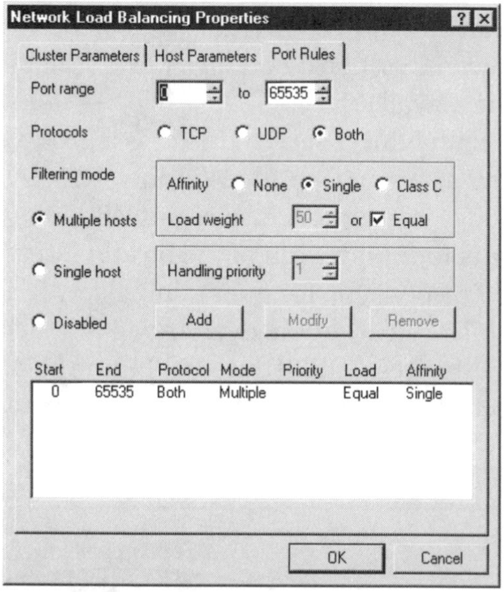

Figure 15-3. The Port Rules tab

NLB cluster through the cluster IP address. Depending on how you configure the port rules (see Figure 15-3), you can have client requests distributed equally among the nodes, you can specify a client affinity (that is, you can link a particular client to a specific node), you can specify a handling priority (where the highest priority gets the request for a defined port rule), or you can assign load-weight percentages. The latter option is useful when nodes in the NLB cluster have different processing capabilities.

NLB cluster nodes communicate with each other through either multicast or broadcast messages. This significantly boosts availability because if a node fails or goes temporarily offline, the NLB cluster automatically detects the failure and redistributes the load to other nodes. This messaging is also useful when nodes are added to the NLB cluster.

Clustering   The second clustering technology available in Windows 2000 Advanced Server and Windows 2000 Datacenter Server is *server clusters*. The goal of server clusters differs slightly from that of NLB.

Server cluster functionality focuses on providing high availability and scalability to your Windows 2000 network environment, whereas NLB focuses primarily on providing scalability, higher performance, and some availability.

As with NLB, a server cluster is a group of computers that work together as a single entity. Windows 2000 Advanced Server supports two nodes in a server cluster, and Windows 2000 Datacenter Server supports four nodes out of the box. In a server cluster, each node is equally responsible for maintaining server and application availability. In addition, every node is attached to one or more storage devices, as illustrated in Figure 15-4. These storage devices are used to share data and applications between two or more nodes.

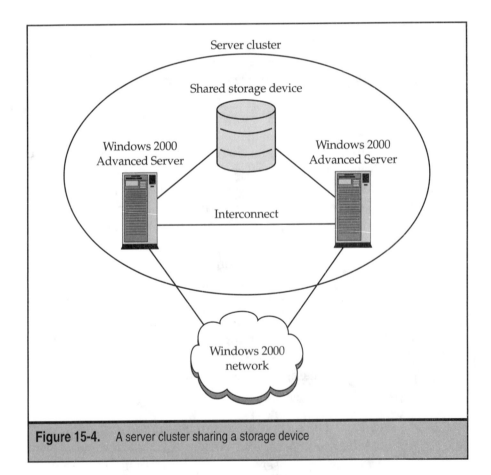

Figure 15-4.　A server cluster sharing a storage device

The two basic operation modes for Windows 2000 server clusters are the following:

▼ **Active/Active Clustering**   *Active/active clustering* is the most productive and efficient operational mode that you can use. In this mode, all nodes are operating under workloads (they're services clients), and they can provide recovery services for any application or node that goes offline. The benefit is that hardware resources are used more efficiently. In other words, resources aren't wasted by sitting idle while waiting for an application or node to go offline.

▲ **Active/Passive Clustering**   *Active/passive clustering* provides the highest level of availability, stability, and performance. In this mode, one node is actively providing services while the other is sitting idle waiting for the active application or node to go offline. Although this mode provides the highest level of security for your Windows 2000 server cluster, the downside is that you are wasting valuable resources.

Although server clusters offer numerous benefits to your Web site, clustering is one of the more expensive options (there are heavy resource requirements such as a shared storage medium and interconnects), and you introduce a new level of complexity. Depending on your budget and the determined cost to the company of having the Web site unexpectedly go down, server clustering may be well worth the investment.

Combining Server Cluster and NLB Technologies   You can have the best of both worlds by combining server cluster and NLB technologies. The combination essentially takes the active/active cluster approach and enables NLB to increase reliability and performance. The advantage is that you're truly providing a highly available, reliable, scaleable, and high-performance Web site.

Third-Party Scalability Solutions   There are several third-party solutions for creating scaleable, high-performance Web sites. The solutions vary from vendor to vendor; Table 15-3 provides a list of vendors that offer either hardware- or software-based solutions for Windows 2000.

Product	Company	Web Site
Big IP Controller	F5	http://www.f5.com/
EnView	Amdahl	http://www.amdahl.com/
ftServer	Stratus	http://www.stratus.com/
Legato eCluster for Web Servers	Legato	http://www.legato.com/
Local Director	Cisco	http://www.cisco.com/

Table 15-3.   Scalability Solutions for Windows 2000 Environments

Tweaking the Physical Architecture

So far, we've discussed numerous Web site planning and designing performance considerations, ranging from individual server hardware components to the ways that various Web site services may interact. Now we're on the homestretch; it's time to look at the physical architecture of the Web site. Whether you already have a Web site in place and you're looking at ways to improve performance, scalability, and so on, or you're starting from scratch, the best way to analyze the physical architecture is by using a logical diagram of the Web site. A logical diagram, like the one shown in Figure 15-5, gives you a high-level perspective on your entire site and should, at a minimum, include all of the physical entities and connections that constitute the Web site.

Essentially, you can group a Web site's physical architecture into two categories: flat and tiered. A flat physical architecture (see Figure 15-5) has all of the components laid out in the logical diagram on a single network. A tiered physical architecture uses two or more networks to segment the different tiers or functionalities of a Web site.

As you'd expect, a flat physical layout is simpler and easier to manage when compared to a tiered layout. From a performance point of view, however, a flat architecture is susceptible to congestion, which can lead to slower overall performance. The slowdown that's actually experienced clearly depends upon how busy your Web site becomes,

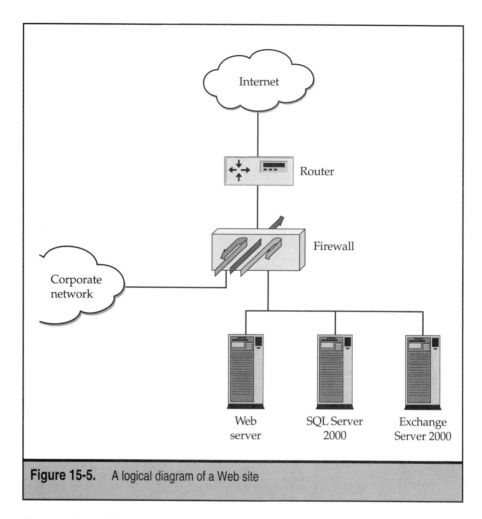

Figure 15-5.   A logical diagram of a Web site

the number of services supporting the Web site, and the amount of traffic generated from the interaction of the back-end services.

A tiered physical layout, shown in Figure 15-6, definitely has advantages from a performance point of view, but they don't come without cost. The cost isn't always necessarily from the additional hardware needed to segment the network (routers, switches, and so on) or from the need for additional servers. The real cost comes from the extra complexity of managing the system. However, generally speaking, if the Web site has several different system interactions and experiences high volumes of traffic (or is expected to), the performance benefits outweigh the costs of segmenting the Web site's physical architecture.

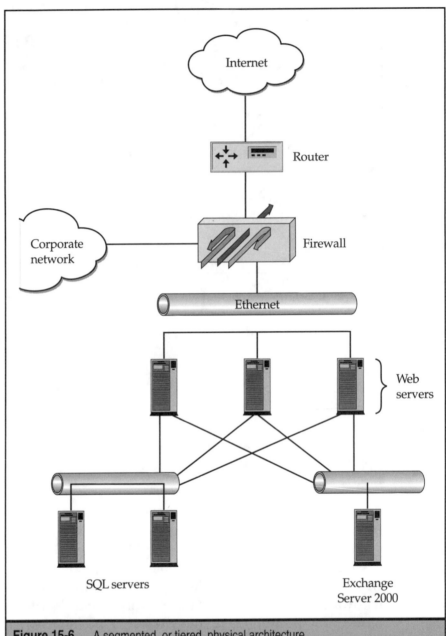

Figure 15-6. A segmented, or tiered, physical architecture

PUMPING UP IIS SERVICES

IIS is a stable and mature Web server platform, and many of the default settings may be suitable for your Web site. However, it's important to know the parameters that will most likely affect IIS and your Web site's performance. Most of the performance-related parameters can be tweaked directly through the ISM snap-in. Through ISM, shown in Figure 15-7, you can manage all IIS services. Microsoft also provides a browser-based interface similar to ISM, but for simplicity we'll focus on the ISM snap-in.

WWW (Web) Services

The WWW service, also known as the Web service, is the most commonly used IIS service. As you can see in Figure 15-8, this service manages Web browser-related traffic, virtual servers, Web browsing authentication, and much more. This service also allows you to tweak some Web-related network settings such as bandwidth throttling.

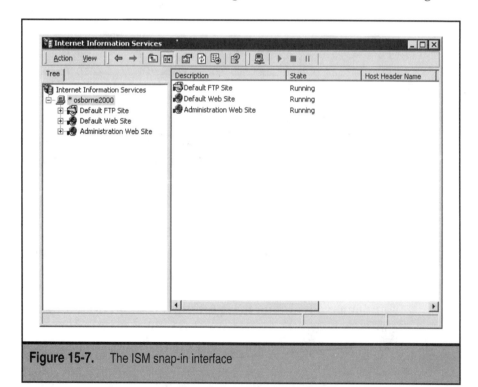

Figure 15-7.   The ISM snap-in interface

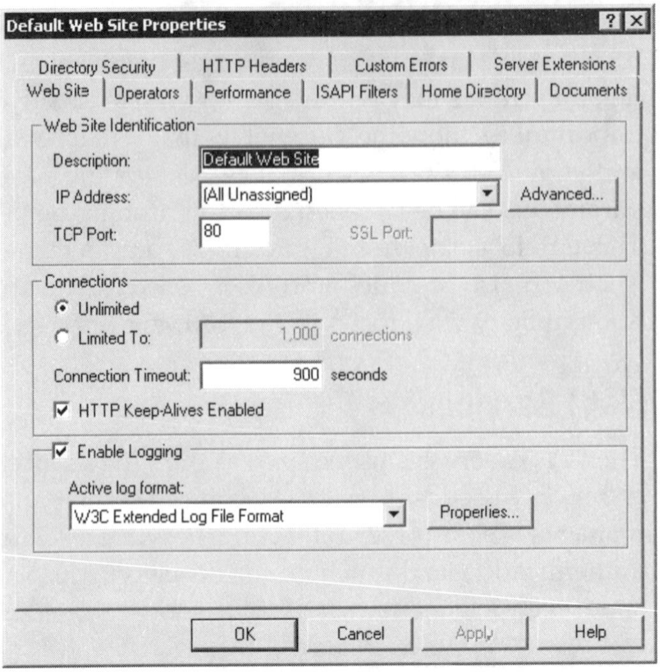

Figure 15-8. Web Site Properties screen

Web Site Properties

Figure 15-8 shows the Web Site tab. This tab lets you specify two types of configuration settings relating to performance: connections and logging. You can limit the number of simultaneous connections to this site as well as specify a connection timeout value. By default, IIS allows an unlimited number of simultaneous connections and a connection timeout of 15 minutes (900 seconds). You can use these two settings to keep response times within acceptable ranges. For example, after doing some testing, suppose that you discover that the Web site's performance degrades after 500 users connect simultaneously. Using these settings, you can limit the number of connections to 500, or you can also reduce the connection timeout value and allow slightly more users to connect simultaneously.

Before enabling this option, determine the ratio between server performance and the number of simultaneous connections the server is supporting. For instance, if the Web server's performance begins to decline while supporting 850 connections, then limit the number of simultaneous connections to a value below 850 (for example, to 800 connections). To determine an accurate ratio, monitor the counters listed in Table 15-4.

Object	Counter	Recommended Value
Memory	Page Faults/sec	< 250
	Pages/sec	< 20
	Available Memory	> 4MB
Processor	% Processor Time	< 50
Physical Disk	% Disk Time	< 55
	Avg. Disk Queue Length	< 2
Web Service	Current Anonymous Users	The number of anonymous users connected simultaneously
	Current Non-Anonymous Users	The number of nonanonymous users connected simultaneously
	Maximum Connections	The maximum number of established connections associated with the Web service

Table 15-4.   Counters for Determining the Ratio Between Server Performance and the Number of Simultaneous Connections

The final configuration setting on the Web Site tab specifies logging of IIS events for this Web site. By default, IIS uses W3C Extended Log File Format and stores the log files in the %SYSTEMROOT%\System32\LogFiles directory. By clicking the Properties button, you can customize log settings such as location and much more, as illustrated in Figure 15-9. To keep IIS running as efficiently as possible, it's important to move logging away from the system partition. Ideally, you should place logging on an entirely different drive that can sufficiently handle a large number of writes. For more information on the disk subsystem, refer to Chapter 7.

Performance Properties

In addition to limiting the number of connections (as mentioned earlier), you can also configure each Web site's performance characteristics. In particular, you can tune your Web site according to the number of hits you expect per day, limit the network bandwidth available to the site, and set the maximum CPU usage for this site.

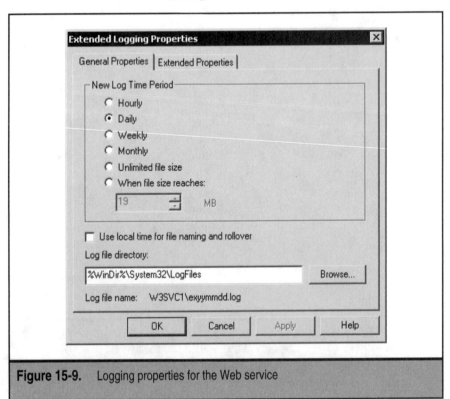

Figure 15-9. Logging properties for the Web service

Balancing Network Connections and Memory IIS makes it easier to improve upon one aspect of performance without compromising another. The sliding scale, shown in Figure 15-10, allows you to tune the server's performance based upon the number of connections you anticipate per day. Adjusting the sliding scale helps IIS decide how much memory it can use for Web services.

NOTE: This option can be applied either globally or to each Web server on your network. Settings configured per server overwrite the default Web site properties.

Microsoft recommends setting the sliding scale to a value higher than the number of anticipated connections. A higher setting will increase the amount of memory the server uses and increase

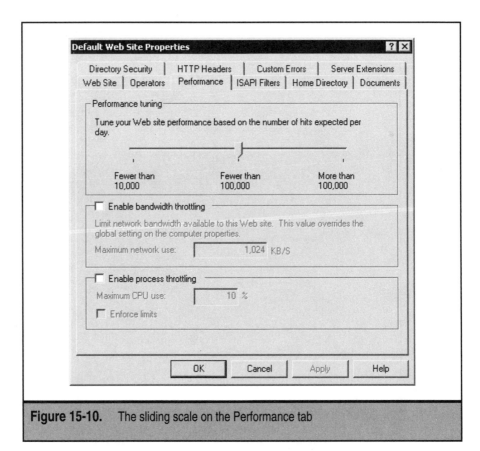

Figure 15-10. The sliding scale on the Performance tab

connection response times. However, there may be more connections than you realize. Web browsers connecting to the Web server typically make more than one connection to help transfer information to the client machine. If the number of hits on the Web server is 1,000, there may be as many as 4,000 actual connections.

Controlling Network Resource Consumption   Increased performance often comes from the ability to control resources rather than just tweak them. Network resource consumption strategies, such as limiting the network bandwidth available to the Web site and limiting the number of connections, epitomize good control of resources and can significantly improve the Web server's performance.

By selecting Enable Bandwidth Throttling in the Default Web Site Properties dialog box (see Figure 15-11), you can specify the exact amount of bandwidth each Web site is able to use. Otherwise, you can enable this setting on a per-site basis.

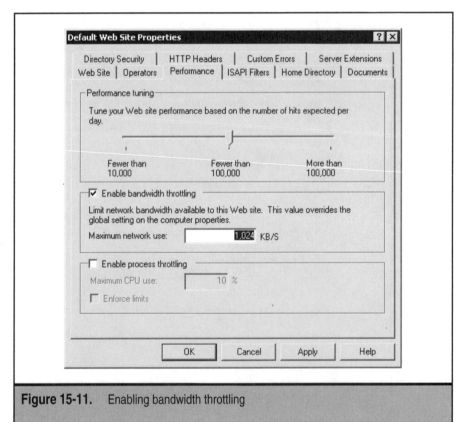

Figure 15-11.   Enabling bandwidth throttling

How much network usage do you want to allow? The answer depends on the bandwidth of the Internet connection as well as how frequently the Web site is being connected to. For example, if the Web server has a dedicated 56K link to the Internet, limiting bandwidth usage, instead of improving IIS performance, may have adverse effects. Users trying to connect may experience unusually slow response times or may frequently receive Server Busy messages. To find the most suitable bandwidth limitation value and determine the Web server's typical bandwidth requirements, analyze the Web Service: Bytes Total/sec counter using the Performance Monitor. It is recommended that you not limit network bandwidth usage to below 50 percent of the link's capacity, because doing so can degrade response times.

Process Throttling   The Enable Process Throttling option, shown in Figure 15-12, allows you to tame processes and prevent them from devouring too much server processing power. This option watches over the processes that are set for High (Isolated) protection (see "Application Protection" later in this chapter for more information). When isolated processes exceed their processing limit, IIS makes note of it by writing to the event log. You can also configure process throttling to enforce the limits you set and prevent processes from exceeding the limit by checking the Enforce Limits box.

Process throttling is primarily useful when you're hosting more than one Web site. Sometimes one or more processes on one Web site may consume too much CPU time and cause significant slowdowns for the other Web sites you're hosting. Process throttling works in conjunction with process accounting, which records a process's CPU use for a specific Web site. Since process throttling and process accounting are generally Web site–specific, there's a limitation to the granularity to which you can monitor processes and control throttling. In other words, if one of the hosted Web sites has more than one application running out-of-process, the throttling is applied to the site and not to an individual process. There is a workaround, however, for monitoring and throttling individual applications running out-of-process on Web sites with multiple out-of-process applications—you can write a script using either of the following

Default Web Site Properties ? ✕

Directory Security | HTTP Headers | Custom Errors | Server Extensions
Web Site | Operators | Performance | ISAPI Filters | Home Directory | Documents

┌─ Performance tuning ──
│ Tune your Web site performance based on the number of hits expected per
│ day.
│
│ ├─────────────────────┘─────────────────────┤
│ │   ╲   │
│ Fewer than   Fewer than   More than
│ 10,000   100,000   100,000
└──

┌─ ☑ Enable bandwidth throttling ─────────────────────────────────
│ Limit network bandwidth available to this Web site. This value overrides the
│ global setting on the computer properties.
│ Maximum network use: [1,024] KB/S
└──

┌─ ☑ Enable process throttling ───────────────────────────────────
│ Maximum CPU use: [10] %
│ ☑ Enforce limits
└──

[OK] [Cancel] [Apply] [Help]

Figure 15-12. Enabling process throttling

variables to monitor and throttle a specific application running
out-of-process:

▼ **CpuAppEnabled**   Enables process accounting and throttling
for an isolated Web Application Manager (WAM) application.

▲ **CpuCgiEnabled**   Enables process accounting and throttling
for a CGI application.

NOTE: You can't target individual, out-of-process applications even with the
scripting variables if they're running in the IIS out-of-process pool.

Activating Process Accounting   The default percentage to throttle a
process is 10 percent, and in most cases this isn't adequate. In fact,
if you're not careful, you can seriously put a strain on resources for

isolated applications (and consequently the entire Web site) by enabling process throttling and enforcing those limits without first monitoring the processes' CPU consumption.

So before you start using process throttling, you'll want to enable process accounting for each Web site to get a good idea of usage patterns. To enable process accounting, do the following:

1. In the Web Site properties window for each site (or the default Web site), select Enable Logging and then select W3C Extended Log File Format.

2. Click the Properties button located next to the active log format.

3. In the Extended Logging Properties window, select the Extended Properties tab.

4. Scroll down until you see Process Accounting. Select Process Accounting, as shown in Figure 15-13, and then click OK.

5. Click OK again to close the Web Site Properties window.

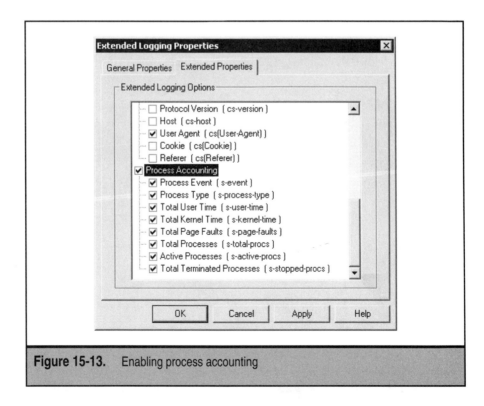

Figure 15-13. Enabling process accounting

At this point, you're logging the appropriate information about the processes. You can later review the CPU consumption and apply the appropriate limits.

Home Directory Properties

A home directory is the topmost (root) directory for the Web site. A home directory is created by default for the default Web site, and it's required for all other sites that you create. It's also important to note that this directory is mapped to the Web site's domain name. For example, if your site's domain name is www.mydomain.com and its home directory is C:\INETPUB\WWWROOT\MYDOMAIN, then when you connect to http://www.mydomain.com/, you're accessing files located in the home directory.

As you can see in Figure 15-14, you can choose the location of your home directory; you can specify the hard disk of the IIS server,

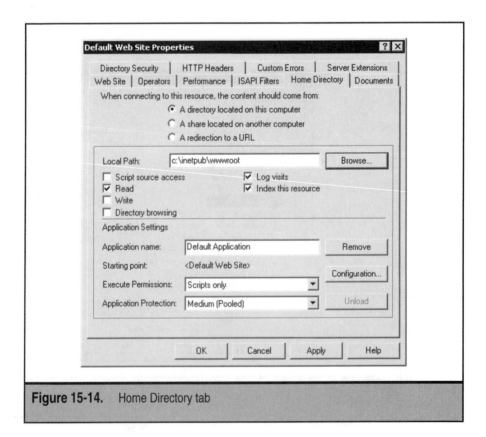

Figure 15-14.   Home Directory tab

a shared directory on a remote computer, or redirection to another uniform resource locator (URL). Considering the amount of use that a site may experience, it's best to move the Web site's home directory away from the system partition so that you don't create additional disk subsystem overhead.

Application Protection   From the Home Directory tab, you can also configure access privileges for the home directory and provide application settings. The path's access privileges include read, write, directory browsing, and other options. Application settings include the directory's execute permissions (None, Scripts Only, or Scripts and Executables) and the following application protection levels:

- ▼ **Low (IIS Process)**   The process runs as a part of the IIS processes and in the same memory space. This setting isn't recommended because it significantly reduces reliability and stability.

- ■ **Medium (Pooled)**   By default, processes such as applications or scripts that are run from the Web site are pooled. This means that they run in a memory space that is separate from the rest of IIS (ensuring reliability of IIS), but at the same time they run in the same space as other processes specific to the Web site. Although this is the default setting, it's a compromise between a site's reliability and resource consumption. It provides some application protection without consuming an exorbitant amount of memory.

- ▲ **High (Isolated)**   An isolated process runs in its own separate memory space. This setting provides the highest degree of reliability because the process is separated from IIS and other processes. It gives the highest level of protection to the applications, but it also requires a lot more memory than the other settings. This setting is also good to use when you're running a mix of applications.

NOTE: Performance for isolated ASP applications is the same, if not better, than in-process application performance on Windows NT 4.

Application Configuration   ASP applications can create and track session information for each user accessing them when Enable Session State is selected. This information follows the user until the session ends or the user stops using the application. Session states are enabled by default with a timeout value of 20 minutes. Thus, if a user doesn't formally exit the application and the session becomes idle, the session won't close until after the 20-minute timeout has expired.

Instead of holding onto session state information for that period of time, you can free up resources sooner by reducing the session timeout value. Those freed resources can be used to service other requests. For more information on tuning ASP session states, refer to "Minimizing Resources Used by ASP Applications" later in this chapter.

NOTE: Reducing the session timeout value is also a good security precaution to prevent SYN attacks on the Web server.

FTP Services

FTP is the File Transfer Protocol of the Internet and can affect how well the system performs. It provides file transfer services for users connecting through the Web browser, the command prompt, or a third-party FTP utility.

Limiting the Number of FTP Connections

A large number of users trying to access the FTP service on IIS can cause overall server performance to quickly and significantly decline. It is highly recommended that you place the FTP service on a separate server if you expect high numbers of simultaneous hits. This allows the Web-servicing capabilities of the server not to be compromised by the high volume of FTP requests and provides positive security measures.

Limiting the number of simultaneous connections to the FTP service will help prevent a decline in system performance and give you more control over the service. A customized message can be displayed to those users who have been temporarily denied access to the FTP service. To limit the number of FTP connections to the server, do the following:

1. In the Internet Information Services Manager window, right-click the FTP site (or default FTP site) and select Properties.

2. On the FTP Site tab, illustrated in Figure 15-15, select Limited To and then specify the number of concurrent connections for the site.

3. Change the connection timeout value from its default of 900 seconds (15 minutes) to a lower value. The value to use depends on the server's available resources and the amount of idle time you want to permit.

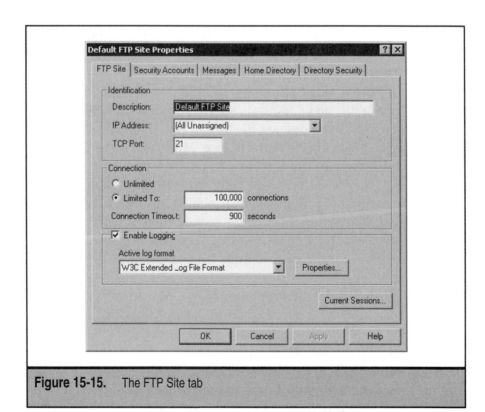

Figure 15-15. The FTP Site tab

NOTE: Use the FTP Service: Maximum Connections counter to find the maximum number of simultaneous connections in a given time period before limiting the number of FTP connections.

Controlling FTP Logging

IIS gives you the option of enabling logging, or tracking, of FTP-related information. For instance, you can keep track of who is accessing your FTP server, the types of transactions they are performing, and much more.

By default, IIS logs FTP-related information, though not all organizations are required to or are interested in tracking FTP server activity. It is generally recommended that you keep logs for troubleshooting and informational purposes. The benefits of retaining these logs outweigh any negative effects that logging may have on IIS performance. Performance effects will vary from site to site, depending on the amount of information being processed and written to disk. The more information being logged (which is affected by the number of connections, usage patterns, and so on), the greater the effect on performance.

You can log FTP-related information to a Microsoft IIS log file format file, an ODBC data source such as a SQL Server database, or a W3C extended log file format file. Using the standard logging mechanism affects performance significantly less than logging connection information to a SQL database. (For more information on SQL Server performance, refer to Chapter 16.) However, the benefits of logging to a SQL database include immediate and up-to-date information and the ability to create custom reports with tools such as Access and Crystal Reports. The preferred and default method of logging is using the extended log file format because of its simplicity and flexibility.

By clicking the Properties button next to W3C Extended Log File Format in the Active Log Format drop-down box, you can configure the log settings, such as new log time periods (when to start a new log file), the log file location, naming conventions, and the information to catalog (see Figure 15-16). Although FTP logging may not generate a significant amount of log file activity, it's best to move logging away from the system partition to a drive that's less busy. It's also important to keep the information you log to a minimum.

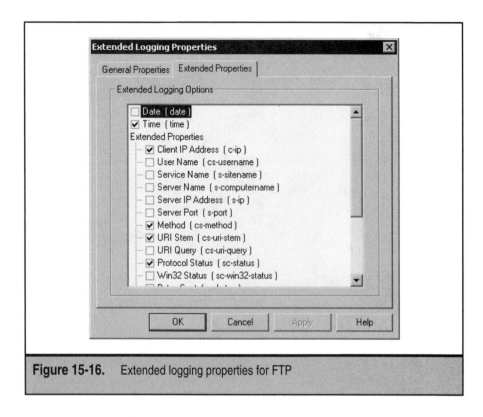

Figure 15-16.   Extended logging properties for FTP

USING THE SYSTEM MONITOR TO OPTIMIZE IIS

The System Monitor uses many of the objects and counters normally employed to gauge overall system health as well as specific IIS objects and counters. These are the objects specifically related to IIS:

- ▼ Active Server Pages
- ■ FTP Service
- ■ HTTP Indexing Service
- ■ Internet Information Services Global
- ▲ Web Service

We've already discusses some of the counters in these objects; however, there are several other counters that are just as important. Some of these are listed in Table 15-5, and others are explained in the sections that follow.

Object	Counter	Description
Active Server Pages	Memory Allocated	The total amount of memory, in bytes, currently allocated by Active Server Pages.
	Request Execution Time	The number of milliseconds that the system took to execute the most recent request.
	Request Wait Time	The number of milliseconds that the most recent request spent waiting in the queue.
	Requests Executing	The number of requests currently executing.
	Requests/Sec	The number of requests executed per second.
	Transactions Total	The total number of transactions since the service was started.
	Transactions/Sec	The number of transactions started per second.
HTTP Indexing Service	Active queries	Current number of running queries.

Table 15-5. Counters Used for Monitoring IIS Performance

Object	Counter	Description
	Current requests queued	Current number of query requests queued. Compare this number to the number of active queries to determine query response times. Keep this number as low as possible.

Table 15-5. Counters Used for Monitoring IIS Performance *(continued)*

Analyzing IIS Caching

File system cache is a critical component of IIS system performance optimization. Because IIS is memory intensive, it relies heavily on the file system cache. Use the System Monitor to analyze the effectiveness of the cache, but do not attempt to change any cache configurations directly. Analyzing the cache will tell you whether IIS is supplied with ample cache space and physical memory. For a more detailed analysis of the file system cache and memory, refer to Chapter 6.

Cache Efficiency

Monitoring the percentage of cache hits is extremely important. The goal is to achieve a cache hit rate of 70 percent or more. High percentages translate to exceptional performance.

The most common type of cache read on an IIS system is the memory descriptor list (MDL) read, because MDL reads often retrieve cached Web pages and FTP files. This may vary, however, with each IIS configuration as well as with the content being provided.

Use the System Monitor to verify that the MDL read is the primary cache read on your server. You can do this by monitoring the cache object every few hours during a 24-hour period. Various types of reads can occur on a IIS system, including the following:

▼ **MDL Read**   MDL reads retrieve pages containing data from the file system cache.

■ **Copy Read**   When a process issues a request to read a file, the file system copies the data from the cache into the application's buffer (within main memory).

■ **Fast Read**   Fast reads retrieve data directly from the cache. Fast reads typically occur after the initial read request.

▲ **Pin Read**   A pin read occurs when data is mapped to the cache so it can be modified and written back to the disk. Data is *pinned* in the cache, meaning that it stays in the same memory location and cannot be paged out to disk. This method reduces the number of page faults that may occur when data is requested.

Once you have identified the primary cache read method your system uses, the System Monitor can analyze the cache hits ratio for that particular type of cache read. For example, if you determine that the MDL read is the most common type of cache read, examine the Cache: MDL Read Hits % counter to check its efficiency. The counter should have a value of at least 70 percent for optimal performance.

What can you do if the cache read counter is less than 70 percent? When the value is less than 70 percent, this usually signifies that the system does not have enough physical memory. First, check the Memory: Cache Faults/sec, Memory: Page Faults/sec, and Memory: Pages/sec counters. Their values should be very small if the system has an adequate amount of physical memory. To improve the cache hit ratio, add more physical memory to the system. Windows 2000 uses a portion of the additional physical memory to add to the file system cache and improve the cache hit ratio, as well as overall system performance. Therefore, the more memory, the greater the chance you have of a cache hit.

NOTE: If you're using the HTTP Indexing Service, it's also important to monitor the HTTP Indexing Service's % Cache hits counter. Use the preceding guidelines to determine whether the indexing cache is performing to expectations.

Cache Size

How much file system cache is enough to manage cache read requests? Keep the cache size as large as possible to maintain system performance and efficiency; however, there is no specific cache size to use a guideline, because the appropriate size varies with every system configuration.

Monitor the counters listed in Table 15-6 to determine whether the cache size is large enough to hold a sufficient amount of IIS-related data. Closely analyze the times when the cache size is at its lowest value to determine whether the cache hit ratio is low (70 percent or lower). If the smallest cache size is coupled with a low cache hit ratio, check the available memory on the system. Typically, the available system memory will be low as well. The combination of these factors will cause a decrease in performance and signify that the system needs more physical memory to accommodate IIS caching requirements.

Object	Counter
Memory	Available Bytes
	Cache Bytes
	Cache Faults/sec
	Page Faults/sec
Cache	MDL Read Hits %

Table 15-6. Counters for Monitoring Cache Size and Efficiency

OPTIMIZING SERVER-BASED SCRIPTING

The Web has become a popular and efficient means of conducting business in a global marketplace. Many companies use the Web to dynamically present product, company, service, and other types of information to otherwise unreachable audiences. Shopping at online stores, making airline reservations, and checking bank account information are just a few of the things you can do directly on the Web, regardless of your physical location.

Behind the scenes, server-based scripting on an IIS system allows companies to create and manage dynamic content on their Web sites. Server-based scripting includes, but is not limited to, the Common Gateway Interface (CGI), the Internet Server API (ISAPI), Java, Active Server Pages (ASP), audio, and video. The type of server-based scripting you choose to implement is important because each script can significantly affect the performance of IIS and, consequently, affect the way your company does business over the Internet. This section identifies the server-based scripting types that have the most profound effect on resource requirements and IIS performance and describes ways of optimizing the scripts to minimize negative performance.

The Common Gateway Interface

CGI has been the most common means of communicating from a Web site to an external data source. As the name implies, CGI acts as a gateway between a Web server and other resources, such as a database or an e-mail program. Moreover, CGI is portable across many different operating system platforms, including UNIX, Windows 9x, Windows NT, and Windows 2000, and can be written either as executables or as scripts to be read by an interpreter. The scripts themselves can be written in many different languages, including PERL (Practical Extraction and Reporting Language) and Sun Microsystems' Java.

Despite its popularity and portability among other operating systems, CGI requires more server resources (memory and processing power) than other server-based scripts, such as ISAPI or ASP. CGI usually has slower response times because applications or scripts run a separate process each time a client request is received. As the number of requests increases, the resource requirements to support those requests also increase. This can cause a severe slowdown in performance and decrease client response times. ISAPI and ASP applications, on the other hand, are loaded into memory only once, no matter how many times the application is used. CGI applications can take as much as five times the resources to run as ISAPI or ASP applications. As a result, it is recommended that you use ISAPI or ASP applications in place of CGI-based applications to prevent poor performance when providing dynamic content on an IIS system.

NOTE: FastCGI is a successor to CGI that incorporates improvements that enhance performance. Although it reduces some of the overhead associated with CGI, FastCGI scripts and executables still run in separate memory spaces, thus requiring more resources than ISAPI or ASP.

Active Server Pages

ASP is at the forefront of dynamic content creation, enabling you to run ActiveX scripts and ActiveX Server components on the client or the server. By executing ActiveX scripts and ActiveX Server components on the server rather than the client, you achieve client-side operating system independence without compromising the dynamic content. Moreover, the time it takes for data to be transferred to and from the client and server is drastically reduced because all processing is done on the server. Only the resulting HTML code is transferred back to the client.

ASP supports both JScript and VBScript natively, and ActiveX scripting plug-ins are available for REXX, PERL, and other scripting interpreters. ActiveX Server components can be created in Java, Visual Basic, Visual C++, and other languages. ASP also extends its compatibility by easily integrating with any ODBC-compliant database, such as Microsoft SQL Server, Oracle, and Sybase databases.

ASP is loaded only once and runs as a multithreaded service. Moreover, it is optimized to manage a large number of user-initiated requests and can significantly reduce the amount of network traffic generally associated with dynamic content. As mentioned earlier, ASP passes only the resulting HTML code to the client, which is significantly less of a load than transferring ActiveX components or executables.

Improving ASP Performance

Although you benefit immediately by using ASP, there are ways to improve its performance. In addition to following the recommendations presented here, you should refer to Microsoft's article on boosting ASP performance, "25+ ASP Tips to Improve Performance and Style," which can be found at http://www.microsoft.com/technet/iis/tips/asptips.asp.

Buffering ASP Applications   Typically, IIS transfers ASP-requested data to the client as it is generated. However, this can result in diminished performance for transfers across the network or Internet connection. By buffering the ASP application's response to the client, you can deliver the content in its entirety and, consequently, improve the client response time. The additional memory needed is minimal, and the benefits of buffering far exceed the cost of supplying additional memory resources to the ASP application.

Buffering for ASP applications is enabled by default. To verify that buffering is enabled, do the following:

1. Open the ISM from the Start | Programs | Administrative Tools menu.

2. Right-click the Web site and select Properties to display the site properties.

3. On the Home Directory tab, click the Configuration button, located in the Application Settings section. The Enable Buffering setting is located on the App Options tab, as shown in Figure 15-17.

Minimizing Resources Used by ASP Applications   Each time a client initiates a request to an ASP application, IIS maintains a session state

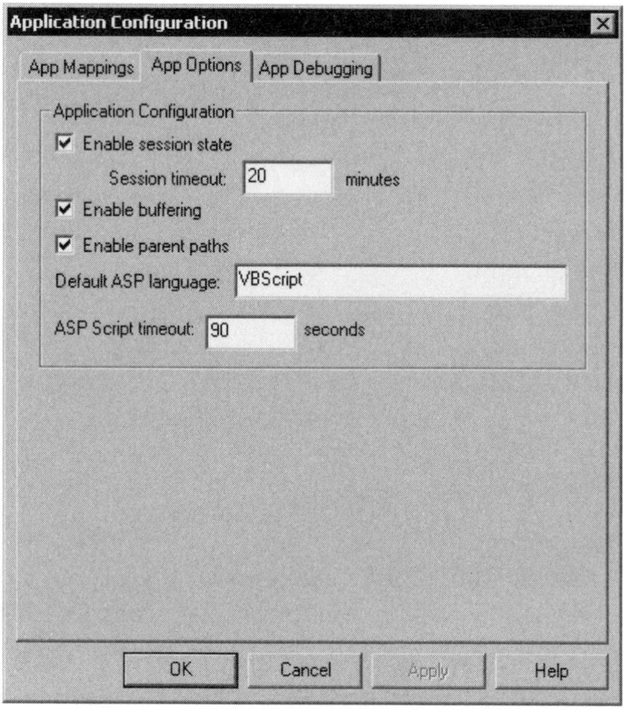

Figure 15-17. Verifying that ASP buffering is enabled

for the client. Maintaining session state information requires memory, processor, and other resources on the server. As more users connect to the Web site, the number of session states also increases. Session state information is kept by IIS unless the client disconnects or the session timeout value expires.

In previous versions of IIS, you could disable session state information only for the entire server, not on a per-application basis. In the current version of IIS, disabling session state information entirely could affect system functionality and is not recommended. If you need to keep session information, minimize the duration of sessions to gain more control over system resources. Minimizing session duration is especially beneficial for sites with large numbers of user connections.

Java

Java has been widely accepted in the industry for its functionality and flexibility in providing dynamic content. Its popularity really took off because it's a platform-independent programming language. Developers can write a Java application once, and then it can be run on any UNIX variant, Windows 9*x*, Windows NT, Windows 2000, and other systems.

The ability to run on different platforms is made possible by a client-side interpreter or Java Virtual Machine (VM). After downloading the Java code, the VM takes into account any platform-specific considerations before displaying the application to the client.

From a performance point of view, Java has typically been really slow, but improvements both in how the code can be written and in the interpretation at the client end have made Java applications run faster. Version 1.2 and above has numerous enhancements, including speed, and Java components are weighing less with more functionality. Microsoft, too, has improved its version of the VM with increased load-time performance, heightened security, and much more. Despite Java's simplistic approach to developing dynamic, Web-based applications, speed isn't always on a par with ASP-based applications.

PERFORMANCE-ENHANCING UTILITIES FOR IIS

There are many tools at your disposal to help you keep IIS fit and running at peak performance levels. Some of these tools are explored here.

The HTTP Monitoring Tool

The HTTP Monitoring Tool is a browser-based Windows 2000 Server Resource Kit utility that collects vital statistics about IIS performance in real time. One of the biggest advantages to using this tool is that it's capable of monitoring several IIS machines in a cluster.

Even though you may have installed the Windows 2000 Server Resource Kit, the HTTP Monitoring Tool must be installed separately. It's located in the \Apps\Httpmon folder on the CD. Before you install this utility, you must install SQL Server version 6.5 or higher for data collection and storage on the same machine or at least have access to the SQL server from the machine on which you've installed the HTTP Monitoring Tool.

After you've installed SQL and the HTTP Monitoring Tool, use the HTTPMon Configuration Manager, shown in Figure 15-18, to configure the utility before you proceed to monitor your IIS server or cluster.

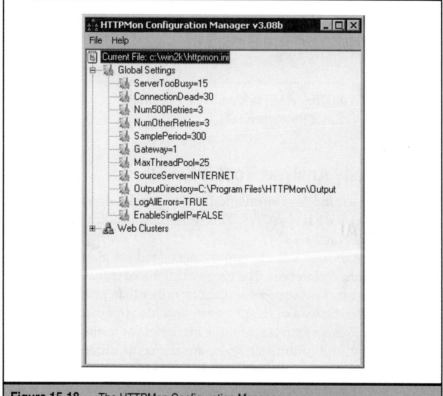

Figure 15-18.   The HTTPMon Configuration Manager

Web Application Stress Tool (WAST)

WAST is one of a couple of load simulation tools provided in the Windows 2000 Resource Kit. It stresses the IIS system with a variety of activity that closely represents activity that your Web site may experience. Some of the load simulation parameters that you can customize are the number of users that connect to the Web site, the size and type of data being transferred to and from the client and server, the frequency of requests, and the performance counters watched. The beauty of this utility is that you can customize simulation parameters and increase or decrease the amount of stress on the system.

After you run the load simulation, WAST reports back to you so that you can analyze the results. Some of the details that you'll receive in the report are the total number of hits and requests and any performance counter data.

NOTE: WAST is found in the \Apps\Webstress folder on the Windows 2000 Server Resource Kit CD.

Web Capacity Analysis Tool (WCAT)

The second load simulation utility provided in the Windows 2000 Resource Kit is WCAT. This utility can be found in the \Apps\wcat folder on the CD.

Although this utility provides a load simulation like WAST, it has several differences. The biggest difference is that it is a capacity-sizing tool for client-server simulations rather than just a test for the IIS server. Instead of requiring one machine (for example, the IIS server), it requires a minimum of three machines for testing purposes (server, client, and controller). There are also some differences in what it can simulate, such as cookies and HTTP keep-alives.

For your convenience, Microsoft includes predefined test suites so you can start testing immediately with little configuration. These predefined tests include the following:

▼   ASP tests

■   Basic tests

■   HTTP keep-alive tests

▲   SSL tests

After running the predefined or customized load simulation, you can review its comma-delimited log file in a spreadsheet or database for analysis.

XTune

Xcache Technologies offers a utility called XTune that's designed to analyze IIS configuration settings and then recommend any changes to increase the server's performance. This relatively simple tool provides a powerful way to tweak your IIS settings.

XTune is a free utility that can be downloaded from the company's Web site at http://www.postpointsoft.com/. It's also an MMC snap-in so it can be integrated into the ISM.

As with any configuration changes to IIS, before installing the product be sure to back up the IIS metabase because XTune makes modifications (see "Maintaining the IIS Metabase," next). After following the installation procedure and registering the product, you can begin using XTune to tweak IIS settings. You'll notice another tab called XTune in the properties window for the Web site and the server, as illustrated in Figure 15-19. Clicking the Recommended button on the XTune tab automatically changes the current settings to more appropriate levels. Review these changes before applying them to IIS.

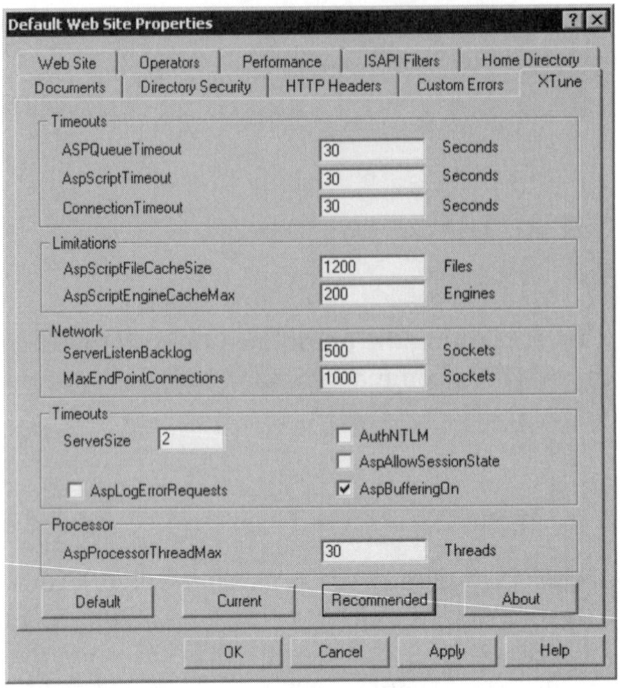

Figure 15-19. Tweaking IIS with XTune

MAINTAINING THE IIS METABASE

IIS doesn't require a lot of maintenance, but because IIS relies on the metabase, it's important that you back up the metabase. Creating a separate backup for the metabase in addition to your disaster recovery mechanisms can speed up recovery of IIS in case a configuration change or third-party installation corrupts the metabase.

To back up the IIS metabase, do the following:

1. Open the ISM from the Start | Programs | Administrative Tools menu.

2. Right-click the IIS server you want to back up and select Backup/Restore Configuration.

Configuration Backup/Restore

Previous backups

Backups:

Location	#	Date/Time

Create backup...   Restore   Delete

Close   Help

Figure 15-20. The Configuration Backup/Restore window

3. In the Configuration Backup/Restore window, shown in Figure 15-20, click the Create Backup button.

4. Specify the name of the backup in the Configuration Backup window and click OK.

5. Click the Close button to close the Backup/Restore Configuration window.

Restoring the IIS metabase is just as simple. In the Backup/ Restore Configuration window, choose the backup that you want to use and then click the Restore button. A message will appear, as shown here, warning you that the restoration may take a considerable amount of time, it will replace all configuration settings, and it will temporarily take IIS offline. Click Yes to continue the restore procedure.

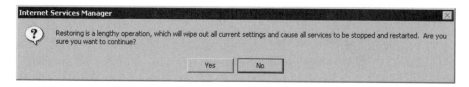

Internet Services Manager

? Restoring is a lengthy operation, which will wipe out all current settings and cause all services to be stopped and restarted. Are you sure you want to continue?

Yes   No

CHAPTER 16

SQL Optimization

As a network administrator or system engineer, you may find yourself in a situation in which you have to buy, configure, monitor, and manage a server with a database. Ideally, the organization that you are working for should have a specialist—a database administrator (DBA)—to handle such events. Unfortunately, because of various constraints (usually financial in nature), such is not always the case. You should be able to perform basic tasks and know when to ask for specific help when issues require specific knowledge and experience that you do not have in your arsenal.

To help you make the appropriate decisions with regard to these matters, we will define the issues surrounding the following activities:

▼ Selecting a server to run SQL Server and satisfy the requirements of your database

■ Configuring SQL Server, monitoring, identifying bottlenecks, and improving performance

▲ Designing databases and applications

You may not be able to perform all of these activities effectively yourself, but you need to know the difference between what you can and cannot do, and when to hire the appropriate expert to achieve optimal results.

SYSTEM SELECTION AND CONFIGURATION

As with other Windows systems, every component plays an important role in how well the server performs. For instance, a system with a powerful processor, an ample amount of RAM, and a slow disk drive will more than likely fail to meet the needs of the environment simply because the disk subsystem is inadequate. However, the relative importance of each component varies depending on the functional configuration of the server. The hardware components with the most influence on SQL Server performance are the processor, the memory, and the disk subsystem. When you design a SQL Server implementation, it is important that you make sure that the hardware components complement one another so that one inadequate component does not destroy the performance capabilities of an otherwise awesome server.

If possible, get a specification from the vendor of the database application. But remember: you should not follow that specification blindly. You need to see the vendor's performance test scenario in the context of your own environment. For example, although the vendor may cite the number of concurrent users as a critical parameter, the nature of the work performed by those concurrent users is also important. One possible scenario is that all such users are performing small transactions (insert, update, and delete) on the same tables. Such users often do not create problems for each other. SQL Server uses a locking mechanism to prevent access to a record while it is being changed. Typically, problems occur when a couple of users run reports on those same tables at the same time. They block updates to the tables and vice versa. Overall performance of the system will seem diminished.

Ask your vendor for contacts in other organizations that are already using the database application. The experience and tips provided by those organizations can save you a substantial amount of time and money.

If an internal team is developing the database, you should insist on doing regular performance testing right from the early days of development. If performance is established as a benchmark during development, developers will focus on it. It is possible to write an application that will run quickly on slow systems and an application that will run slowly on even the fastest systems.

System configuration is an important question, but you cannot solve all problems using brute force (that is, more hardware) or a silver bullet (for example, by configuring some server or database parameter). In some cases, a database or the application that accesses it will have to be redesigned—a group of improperly written queries (or even a single one) can make your system crawl.

Operating System

This is a book about Windows 2000, so it is not very likely that we will recommend any other operating system besides Windows 2000. But this preference is not based merely on personal or commercial bias. At the time of this writing, Microsoft and IBM continue to battle for the leading position on the TPC-C benchmark test. Each has achieved best results several times, only to be overthrown by the other contender mere weeks or months later. Naturally, each company is trying to prove that its own database (DB2 or SQL Server) is the fastest solution. What is interesting in this ongoing battle is that IBM is not using an AS/400 with an AIX or OS/400 platform, or even a mainframe, but a cluster of Intel servers running Windows 2000.

Processors

At one time, it was possible to run Windows NT and SQL Server on processors that are not compatible with the Intel Pentium family (for example, the Alpha processor from Compaq), but such is no longer the case. The 32-bit Windows 2000 runs only on Pentium-compatible processors from Intel, AMD, and others.

Whether to use a single fast processor or multiple processors is the major configuration decision you face when designing a SQL Server implementation. The decision should be based on the types of transactions the database will primarily be handling, even though SQL Server relies heavily on server processing power. There is no one correct answer, but a little knowledge of how SQL Server uses CPU resources will allow you to make a more informed choice.

Older versions of SQL Server were able to run different queries in parallel on multiple processors. SQL Server 2000 and SQL Server 7 can run a single query in parallel on multiple operating system threads on multiple processors. This enables the results of complex parallel queries that access large amounts of data to be obtained more quickly and efficiently. There is a complex algorithm for determining whether it is possible and beneficial to run a query in parallel. SQL Server takes into consideration the presence of multiple processors, the load on the server, the expected duration of the query, the type of the query, and the available memory.

You need to understand the types of transactions (OLTP versus OLAP) you plan to run on the server before you choose between faster processors and more processors. *OLTP* stands for *online transaction processing*. OLTP systems typically have many concurrent users that execute a large number of transactions. For example, airline reservation systems often use OLTP to offer customers quick and efficient reservation services. On the other hand, *OLAP (online analytical processing)* is commonly used to describe queries within a data warehouse or data marts. Relative to OLTP systems, OLAP systems tend to have fewer users and transactions, but each individual query consumes more resources.

Using more processors always provides better optimization for OLTP systems since SQL Server is able to run multiple, simultaneous queries.

OLAP queries are typically more complex, but there are generally not so many of them. If SQL Server is able to split a complex query into parallel queries, its execution will benefit from the presence of multiple processors. Unfortunately, it may not always be able to do so, so in some cases it is better simply to have faster processors. Faster processors were more critical in the past, since older versions of SQL Server could not run a single query on parallel threads.

Investing in an SMP-capable motherboard, even if you're starting with just a single processor, is highly recommended. Regardless of the types of transactions you run, you will then be able to scale the solution for future growth without abandoning your initial system purchase.

As desirable as multiple processors may be, you should not necessarily buy a system with as many processors as possible. There is a point of diminishing returns—a third CPU is more useful than a fourth (which is more useful than a fifth, and so on).

You will not likely have many options when you select the processor speed (and price). Intel and other vendors are producing faster chips (almost every month), and only the newer (faster, but more expensive) processors are available on the market.

Make sure that you buy processors designed for servers (not for multimedia or game desktops). One simple criterion is the amount of processor cache that will be used to speed up access to RAM. Consider the case of the user who bought a server with Pentium II processors and 1GB of RAM and was dismayed to find that the server was very slow. After a week of optimization attempts, the user finally had the top 512MB removed from the processor, and the server started to perform as expected. The better solution at that time would have been to buy older Pentium Pro processors. They were nominally slower, but they would have been able to cache available RAM, and the system would have been faster.

Memory

Windows and SQL Server both tend to devour as much memory as you can feed them. For this reason, and because memory is relatively inexpensive, you should configure the server with as much memory as possible. Although the minimum required amount of memory is 64MB, it is recommended that you initially configure the server with a minimum of 128MB. Moreover, production servers can benefit immensely from initial configurations of 256MB or more. In fact, it is not uncommon to find large-scale SQL Server installations with up to 4GB of RAM.

A standard 32-bit address can access up to 4GB of RAM. By default, 2GB are reserved for the operating system, and 2GB are available for applications such as SQL Server. It is possible to specify the /3GB switch in the Boot.ini file in Windows 2000 Advanced Server (and Windows NT 4.0 Enterprise Edition), and then 1GB will be reserved for the operating system, and 3GB will be available for other applications.

It is possible to use even more memory. The Microsoft Windows 2000 Address Windowing Extensions (AWE) API allows addressing of 8GB on Windows 2000 Advanced Server and almost 64GB on Windows 2000 Data Center. AWE extends standard Win32 memory management functions and dynamically maps nonpaged memory (above 4GB) into the 32-bit address space when required.

We have discussed the minimum requirements and the maximum configuration, but how much physical memory does your system actually need? To help you make this difficult decision during the initial configuration stage, here is some advice: ideally, SQL Server should hold all tables, indexes, queries, and stored procedures cached in memory (RAM is thousands of times faster than any disk). This option may not be available to you if you have a data warehouse with a 500GB database, but if your OLTP database is 200MB, you do not need 1GB of RAM. It won't hurt, but your SQL Server will also work properly with less RAM than that. Use the principles of memory performance monitoring presented in Chapter 6 to monitor the server once the database is in production. Nothing can replace the empirical approach.

> *TIP:* You should also check how your system is using memory, whether for background services such as SQL Server or for front-end applications. You could also configure Windows to give priority to background applications if nobody will physically work on the server (choose Control Panel | System | Advanced | Performance).

Disk Subsystem

You can take one giant tuning step forward if your initial configurations help to speed up your disk subsystem–related I/O, which is always the slowest task a computer performs. Many performance problems stem from ill-configured disk subsystems, so it is important not to exacerbate this bottleneck.

RAID

Properly configuring the disk subsystem by using multiple disks and an intelligent, hardware-based RAID controller can boost many types of database operations. Where budgets allow, steer clear of software RAID solutions on your SQL Server machines. NT's software RAID solutions tend to use up a great deal of valuable processor time. Refer to Chapter 7 for more information on the disk subsystem and on related options such as hardware and software RAIDs.

You have won half the battle when you implement a hardware-based RAID solution, but to win the war you must choose the proper RAID level for SQL Server. RAID 10 is an ideal choice for your data devices, but its high cost may be impractical for many sites. On the other hand, RAID 5 (stripe sets with parity) provides reasonable read/write performance for data devices, but RAID 1 (straight mirroring) is better for much faster, write-intensive operations. RAID 1 ends up being a more efficient choice than RAID 5, because maintaining the transaction log requires basically just a series of sequential writes.

It is important to create the transaction log on a physically separate disk or RAID. It is written serially, and use of a dedicated disk (or array) allows the disk heads to stay in place for the next write operation.

Implement the following real-world solution to combine both performance and fault tolerance economically: Place your data on a RAID 5 array with at least three, and preferably four, physical disks. Then place your log device on a separate RAID 1 array. If you can afford it, put your OS, SQL Server configuration, and page files on a separate RAID 1 array; otherwise, place these items on the array that has the most free space.

Traditionally, administrators have made their biggest mistakes when estimating the capacity of the disk subsystem. Space is needed for the database, transaction logs, backup files, import and export files, growth of existing tables, implementation of new features (and associated tables), and so on. The rule of thumb is that you should buy a disk that is five times larger than your database. This amount may seem excessive, but you will need it.

Using SQL Server with Caching Disk Controllers

Hardware-based disk controllers that support writeback offer great performance benefits. However, the potential for data corruption exists if they cannot guarantee the execution of all log writes in all circumstances. Therefore, it is imperative that you consult the hardware vendor to ensure that its RAID controller is appropriate for writeback use in a SQL Server database system.

Don't Use File Groups to Improve Performance

If you do not have RAID with stripped disks, you can improve the performance of the SQL Server database by placing different parts of the database (for example, critical tables and indexes) physically in files that reside on different hard drives and which are accessed through different controllers. In this way, controllers and hard drives will work effectively in parallel, and the performance of your disk subsystem will be better.

Unfortunately, this strategy requires a precise knowledge of the I/O usage patterns exhibited by your application, as well as a large amount of manual work, planning, and management. Even if you do manage to come up with an efficient solution, your application's I/O patterns may change over time, making your initial solution a potential bottleneck. RAID provides the same benefits without any of these downsides.

FAT vs. NTFS

You can place your SQL Server database files on an NTFS, NTFS5, FAT32, or FAT partition (but not on a compressed drive). There actually is not much difference between running SQL Server on FAT versus running it on NTFS. Writing to a FAT partition may be a little faster (less than 5 percent), but the speed comes with some costs. You cannot take advantage of ACL security on your device files, and unlike NTFS, FAT does not offer dynamic marking of bad disk sectors.

If you do not have some unusual requirement (such as the need to dual-boot with Windows 98), you should always use NTFS partitions.

Backup Storage

On earlier versions of SQL Server, backup procedures decreased the overall performance of the system, so, on 24/7 systems, administrators often backed up to disk instead of to tape. Later, Windows Backup would pick the database backup files and send them to tape.

Backup no longer has much impact on SQL Server performance. SQL Server 7, and especially SQL Server 2000, contain improved backup and restore components. You can perform a database backup under a full load with minimal impact on your users.

The fastest tape backup systems at the time of this writing are DLT tapes. Unfortunately, they are very expensive. If you cannot afford them, you might investigate DAT tapes. There are also other options such as optical disks, magneto-optical disks, and alternative backup networks.

In some environments, network administrators prefer to perform a full (file) backup of the server instead of database backups. Such an approach has many disadvantages. If the database is online, backing up its files is completely useless. For example, while you are creating a backup, the server might execute a transaction that updates something in the area that is already backed up and something in the area that is not yet backed up. File backup would pick up only half of that transaction; it's as if you were transferring money from one account to another, and you lost $200 in the process. It is possible to buy backup software that will stop SQL Server in order to back up database files, but you may consider service outage to be an extreme performance problem. SQL Server usually performs some maintenance jobs at the same time as database backup (for example, the integrity of data and index pages is checked and fixed if needed, index statistics are updated, and the transaction log is cleared). If only a file backup is executed, all of these chores are skipped.

Network

If you are a network administrator, you probably already know a great deal about configuring, monitoring, and improving network performance. Here, though, are two ideas that may help prevent network access from becoming a bottleneck on the server. If a 10/100MB Ethernet NIC is not enough, you can use other technologies such as Gigabit Ethernet or fiber optics. If these solutions are too expensive (or you do not want to change the complete network), you can put more than one NIC in a server and configure the NICs to work in parallel as one.

TIP: You should also set the server's File and Printer Sharing properties to Maximize Data Throughput for Network Applications.

Usually, network performance problems are a result of improper configuration or some problem on the network other than the apparent bottleneck. If there are no configuration problems, network traffic will likely be an issue only in cases where a database is used in a two-tier fat-client or file-database scenario. You will find more information on this topic in "File-Database and Fat-Client Scenario," later in this chapter.

Other Services

You should not run other services on the database server. A typical error is to use a database server as a file server, PDC, BDC, or printer server. All of these services are competing for resources with SQL Server and therefore slowing down database access. There is another reason why you should not run them together. Even if there are problems with database design (such as normalization, blocking, or suboptimal queries), your developers or your vendor may use the fact that you are running other services on the same machine as a shield to cover problems that they have introduced.

Weigh the advantages and disadvantages carefully when considering solutions that place a Web server, a middleware server (an application server such as MTS), and a database server on a single machine. This approach has these advantages:

▼ **The Application Resides on a Single Server**   Access from one component to the other is faster since communications are not mediated through the network (the memory and bus on the motherboard are much faster).

■ **The Implementation Cost (at First Glance) May Be Lower**   One server should be cheaper than three servers (although you do not need the same quality of server for all of these functions).

■ **The Maintenance Cost (at First Glance) May Be Lower**   It should be easier to manage one server than three (but the complexity of management will be increased when you have different components on the same server).

▲ **Single Point of Failure**   If the server is working, then the system works.

This approach also has these serious disadvantages:

▼ **Competition for Resources** The operating system, Web server, middleware server, SQL Server, and the components within them compete for resources and slow each other down.

■ **The Different Subsystems May Require Different Server Configurations** Optimal performance of each subsystem may require mutually exclusive server configurations.

■ **The Complexity of System Management Is Increased** The administrator has to take care of three subsystems that may have contradictory requirements.

■ **Single Point of Failure** If any of the subsystems fail, the whole system will be unavailable.

▲ **Troubleshooting Is More Complex** Problems become more convoluted incrementally with each additional application running on the server.

SERVER AND DATABASE CONFIGURATION, MONITORING, AND OPTIMIZATION

From time to time, you will be forced to dig into the database environment. This section will not make you a DBA expert in database performance, but we would like to point you in the right direction.

Tools of the Trade

Select Start | Programs | Microsoft SQL Server to see the group of client tools for managing SQL Server. If you want, you can use the SQL Server setup disk and install client tools on your workstation for remote monitoring and administration.

Service Manager

SQL Server itself is implemented as a couple of services running under Windows. You can control the way these services start in the usual manner, using a Control Panel applet (Administrative Tools) or

using the Service Manager utility that you will find on the menu or
as an icon in the status line of the server (see Figure 16-1). You can
switch between servers and between services using combo boxes.
You can reference the local server in three ways: by entering the
server name, by typing '(local)', or by entering a period '.' in the
Server combo box.

The *SQL Server* service is the most important service. It is the
actual database server program. It receives queries from users,
executes them, sends responses to calling applications, and manages
data in database files. All other services need this one in order to run.
SQLServerAgent is an automation service that manages the scheduled
execution of tasks and notifies administrators of problems that occur
on the server. *Distributed Transaction Coordinator (DTC)* manages
transactions that span multiple servers; this service ensures that
changes that need to be made to data stored on different servers are

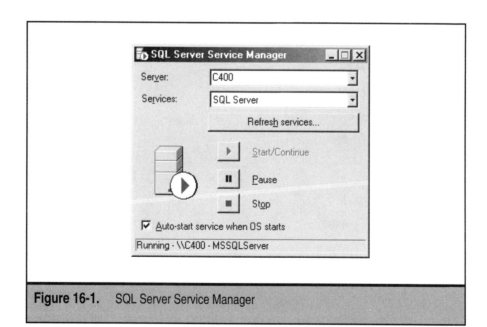

Figure 16-1.   SQL Server Service Manager

completed successfully. *Microsoft Search* is an implementation of Index Server used to manage full-text indexes. *Analysis Services* implements online analytical processing (OLAP) and data mining.

Query Analyzer

The most basic way to work with SQL Server is through the Query Analyzer (see Figure 16-2). This tool allows DBAs to write and execute queries against the server.

SQL Server is released with a list of system stored procedures that DBAs can call to monitor and control the environment. In some cases, their use is required, but unless you know what you are doing, you should not play with them.

However, you will see here how to use Query Analyzer to connect to the server and use it, and how to use the system stored

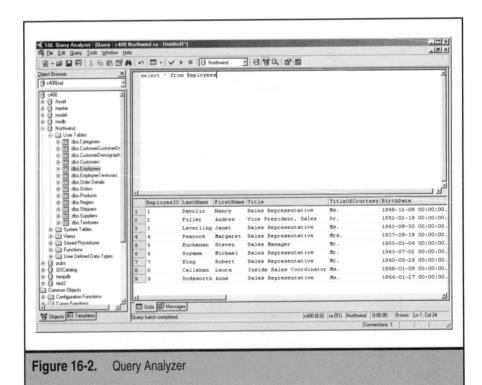

Figure 16-2. Query Analyzer

procedure sp_who, which lists all users and processes connected to
the system.

1. Run Query Analyzer (choose Start | Programs | Microsoft
   SQL Server | Query Analyzer).

2. Query Analyzer prompts you for a server, login name,
   and password. If you have not changed the server since
   installation, you can enter **sa** as the login name and an empty
   string ' ' as the password. The name of your machine is the
   name of the SQL Server. If you are working on the server, you
   can type a period '.' instead of the server name.

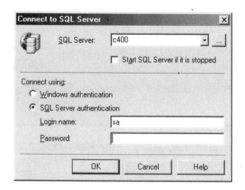

3. You can select Windows Authentication (members of the
   Administrators group for the domain should automatically
   have the System Administrators server role on SQL Server
   and therefore have all the necessary rights), or you can select
   SQL Server Authentication and type username and password.

   If the application is unable to connect to the server, check
   whether the Microsoft SQL Server service is running and
   whether you correctly typed the name of the server and
   your login name and password. If all of these are okay,
   you can use the Server Network Utility and Client Network
   Utility to check protocols or define aliases (for more
   information, consult the SQL Server Books On Line).

4. Once you have logged in successfully, the application opens the Query window that you use to write code. Type the following code:

```
exec sp_who
```

5. To run the stored procedure, you can select Execute from the Query menu, click the green arrow on the toolbar, or press CTRL-E. The application splits the screen to display both the query and the result (see Figure 16-3).

The sp_who stored procedure lists active processes on the current server and the login names of the users who started them.

Another interesting stored procedure is sp_lock. It lists all locks that users have acquired on the database resources. Although the term *lock* may sound negative, locks are necessary for concurrent use of database resources in multiuser relational database systems. Problems occur

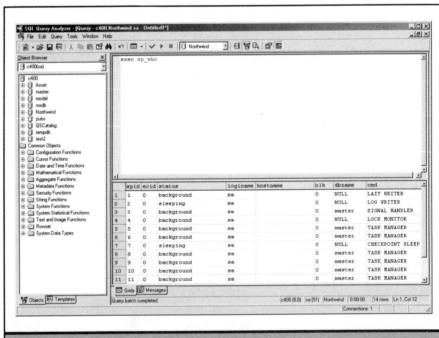

Figure 16-3. Query and results panes of Query Analyzer

when a user or process acquires locks but does not release them. Other users are then blocked from using those resources. (Try to execute the procedure and see the result on your server.)

Enterprise Manager

Many administrative jobs can be accomplished using Enterprise Manager (see Figure 16-4), which visually represents database objects stored on the server and provides tools for accessing and managing them. Like other MMC snap-ins, it contains a console tree (on the left) and a details pane (on the right).

The *console tree* presents database and server objects in a hierarchy designed for easy navigation. The *details pane* shows details of the node (object) selected in the console tree. If the user selects a folder with tables or stored procedures, the details pane lists the tables or stored procedures in the current database.

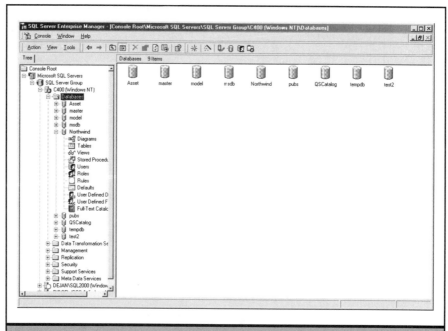

Figure 16-4.   Enterprise Manager

In some cases, the details pane displays the *taskpad*—a complex report showing the state of the database or server that can also be used to manage the database or server (see Figure 16-5). Taskpads are implemented as HTML pages. Activities can be initiated by clicking links or buttons within a taskpad.

Here's an example of Enterprise Manager use:

1. Run Enterprise Manager (choose Start | Programs | Microsoft SQL Server | Enterprise Manager).

2. If necessary (if you have never opened Enterprise Manager before), register the first server with which you will work. Provide the name of the server, your login name, and your password. You can accept default values for Server Group and all other options. When the connection parameters are

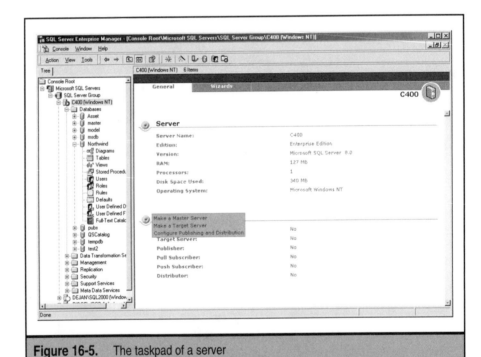

Figure 16-5. The taskpad of a server

correct, Enterprise Manager displays a window for managing
SQL Server.

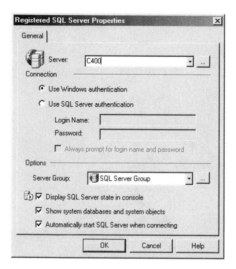

3. Expand the SQL Server Group node, then the server node,
   and finally the databases node.

4. Select the Northwind (or Pubs) sample database; Enterprise
   Manager offers you lists of diagrams, tables, stored procedures,
   views, and other database objects (see Figure 16-6).

5. Right-click a database to see the database Properties window
   (see Figure 16-7). You can use this window to see and change
   database options and files.

You should not play with database properties unless you know
what you are doing. We will discuss some of these in "Setting
Database Parameters," later in the chapter.

SQL Profiler

SQL Profiler is a component of SQL Server designed to monitor
activities on servers and in databases. You can use this utility to
capture queries against a database, the activities of a particular user

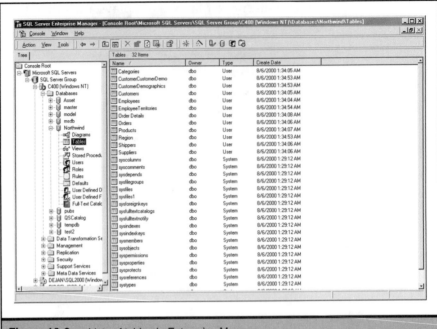

Figure 16-6.   Lists of tables in Enterprise Manager

application, login attempts, failures, errors, and transactions. It is often used to improve the performance of a system, since a DBA can gather information about actual workload (including query duration). To start SQL Profiler, follow these steps:

1. Run the program (choose Start | Programs | Microsoft SQL Server | Profiler).

2. On the File menu, choose New; then choose Trace.

3. From the SQL Server list, select the server to be traced and then enter parameters for the connection, including the login name and password. Profiler opens the Trace Properties dialog box, shown in Figure 16-8.

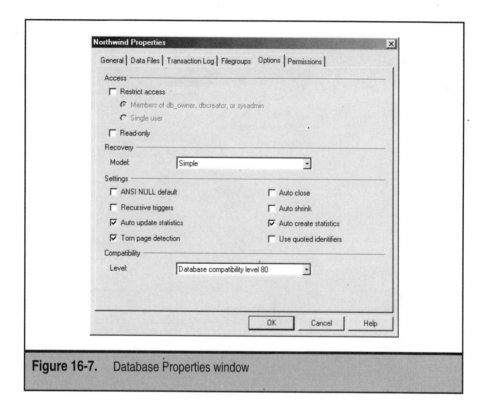

Figure 16-7. Database Properties window

4. If you want, you can change the name of the trace in the Trace Name box, change the server the trace will run on in the Trace SQL Server list, and select a trace template on which the trace will be based in the Template Name list.

TIP: Until you learn more about events that can be traced, use predefined trace templates.

5. Select Save to File to capture the trace to a file or select Save to Table to capture the trace to a database table. You can also leave everything in window (in memory) and save it later.

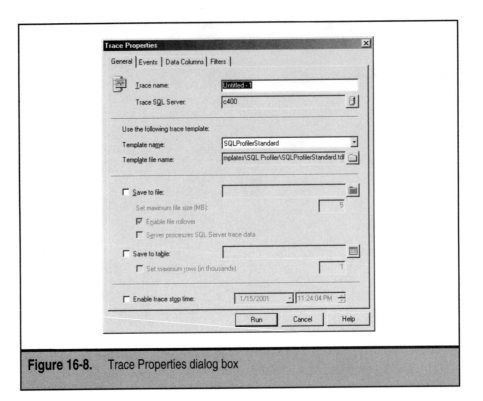

Figure 16-8. Trace Properties dialog box

6. To specify a stop date and time, select the Enable the Trace Stop Time check box.

7. Switch to the Events tab (see Figure 16-9) to select the SQL Server event classes that you want to trace.

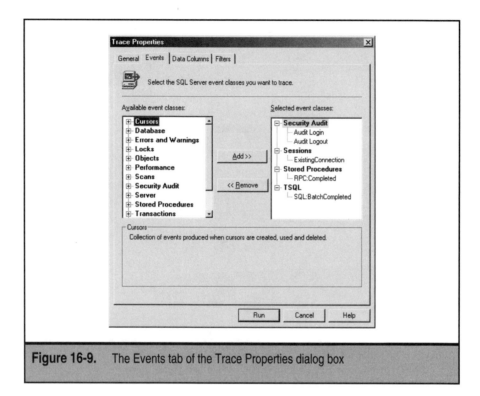

Figure 16-9. The Events tab of the Trace Properties dialog box

8. Switch to the Data Columns tab (see Figure 16-10) to select the columns that you want to appear on the trace.

9. Switch to the Filters tab (see Figure 16-11) to create criteria for capturing events. Initially, SQL Profiler will ignore only events created by itself.

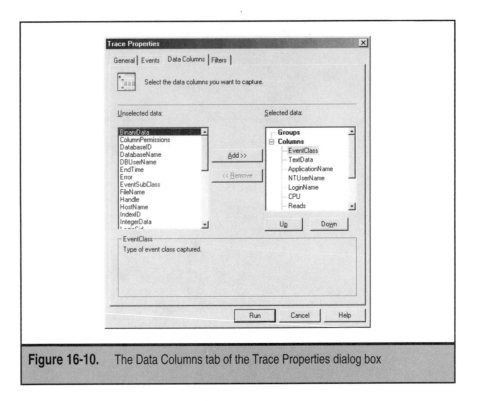

Figure 16-10. The Data Columns tab of the Trace Properties dialog box

10. Click Run when you are ready to start the trace. You will get results like those in Figure 16-12.

Windows System Monitor

We will not go into detail on the use of the Windows System Monitor (or Windows NT Performance Monitor) since it is covered in detail in Appendix A. You should just note that there are SQL Server–specific counters defined to monitor the following:

▼ Memory use

■ I/O processing

■ User connections

■ Locking

▲ Replication activity

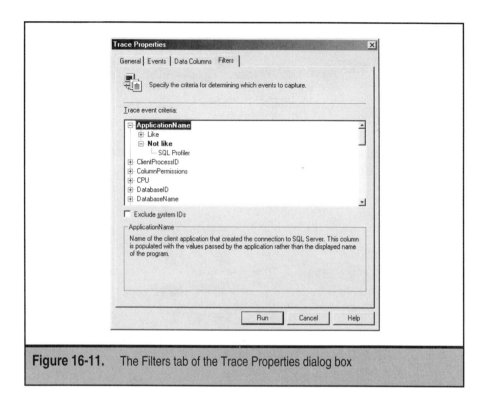

Figure 16-11. The Filters tab of the Trace Properties dialog box

Using Server Configuration Options

SQL Server 7 was the first database server designed to monitor and optimize itself. SQL Server 2000 does an even better job. Both require little or no tuning by the DBA. Although SQL Server has many parameters that can be used to tune its behavior, their use is neither necessary nor recommended. Even if an administrator manages to find a combination of server parameters that gives the best performance under current working conditions, these conditions will change over time, and it is better to leave SQL Server to monitor and configure itself in real time.

Most frequently used server parameters can be configured using Enterprise Manager. If you right-click the server node in Enterprise

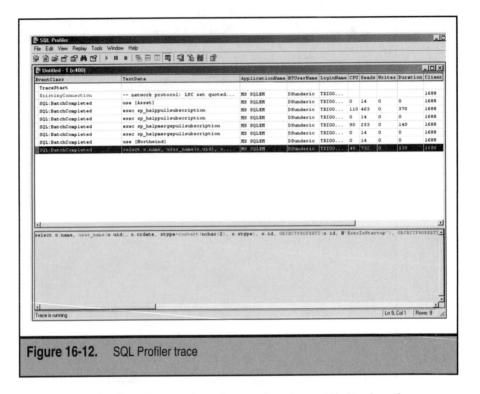

Figure 16-12. SQL Profiler trace

Manager and select Properties, the application will display the
following dialog box:

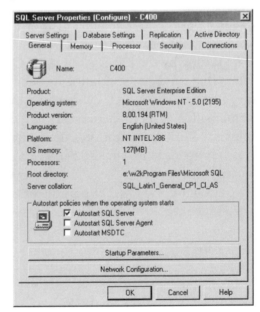

The other tabs are more interesting than the first one. Most of them allow you to set various server options and see existing values. You just need to switch between the Running Values and the Configured Values options, as on the Memory tab shown here:

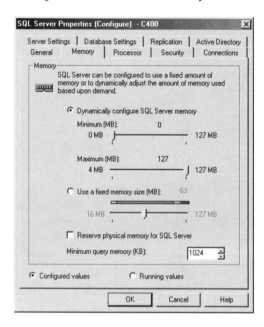

Parameters that are not available from this dialog box must be set using the sp_configure system stored procedure in the Query Analyzer. For example, to list minimum, maximum, new, and current values of configuration parameters, execute the stored procedure without parameters (see Figure 16-13).

In fact, you will not initially be able to see all parameters. SQL Server hides advanced options. To see them, you first must enable them. Execute the following:

```
EXEC sp_configure 'show advanced options', 1
```

SQL Server will report the following:

```
DBCC execution completed. If DBCC printed error messages,
contact your system administrator.
Configuration option 'show advanced options' changed from
0 to 1. Run the RECONFIGURE statement to install.
```

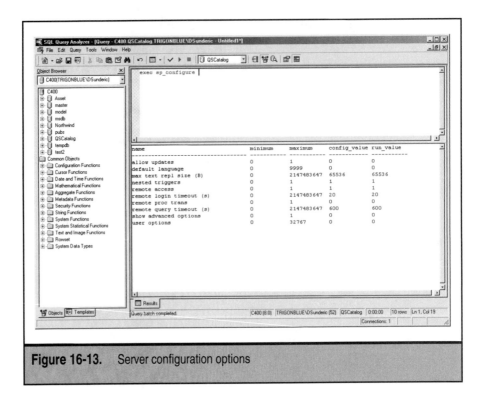

Figure 16-13. Server configuration options

For the configuration option to take effect, you must now execute the RECONFIGURE statement:

```
RECONFIGURE
```

Now you can list all parameters. All of these statements can also be executed together, but they must be separated by GO statements (see Figure 16-14).

Some of SQL Server's parameters are considered to be more critical, so administrators are required to issue the RECONFIGURE WITH OVERRIDE statement. Some configuration options require that SQL Server be restarted before they can take effect.

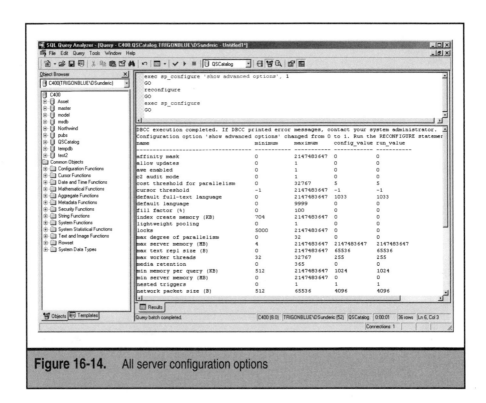

Figure 16-14. All server configuration options

Table 16-1 shows a list of server configuration options.

Configuration Option	Restart Required	Advanced	Self-Configured	Minimum	Maximum	Default
Affinity mask	X	X		0	2147483647	0
Allow updates				0	1	0
AWE enabled	X	X		0	1	0
C2 audit mode	X	X		0	1	0

Table 16-1. Server Configuration Options

Configuration Option	Restart Required	Advanced	Self-Configured	Minimum	Maximum	Default
Cost threshold for parallelism		X		0	32767	5
Cursor threshold		X		−1	2147483647	−1
Default full-text language		X		0	2147483647	1033
Default language				0	9999	0
Fill factor	X	X		0	100	0
Index create memory		X	X	704	2147483647	0
Lightweight pooling	X	X		0	1	0
Locks	X	X	X	5000	2147483647	0
Max degree of parallelism		X		0	32	0
Max server memory		X	X	4	2147483647	2147483647
Max text repl size				0	2147483647	65536
Max worker threads	X	X		32	32767	255
Media retention	X	X		0	365	0
Min memory per query		X		512	2147483647	1024
Min server memory		X	X	0	2147483647	0
Using nested triggers				0	1	1
Network packet size		X		512	65536	4096
Open objects	X	X	X	0	2147483647	0
Priority boost	X	X		0	1	0
Query governor cost limit		X		0	2147483647	0

Table 16-1. Server Configuration Options *(continued)*

Configuration Option	Restart Required	Advanced	Self-Configured	Minimum	Maximum	Default
Query wait		X		−1	2147483647	-1
Recovery interval		X	X	0	32767	0
Remote access	X			0	1	1
Remote login timeout				0	2147483647	20
Remote proc trans				0	1	0
Remote query timeout				0	2147483647	600
Scan for startup procs	X	X		0	1	0
Set working set size	X	X		0	1	0
Show advanced options				0	1	0
Two-digit year cutoff				1753	9999	2049
User connections	X	X	X	0	32767	0
User options				0	32767	0

Table 16-1. Server Configuration Options *(continued)*

The settings discussed in this section are the ones that will have the most impact on system performance, but they do not include all settings available within sp_configure.

Affinity Mask

If the system is configured with more than one processor, you can use the affinity mask to prevent SQL Server from using certain processors. Through Windows 2000, the affinity mask allows you to limit the running of SQL Server threads to specific processors. This is similar to the /NUMPROC parameter placed in the BOOT.INI file limiting the number of processors Windows 2000 can use.

Why would you ever do this? Processor architectures typically assign certain low-level tasks to specific fixed processors. For example, an eight-CPU Intel-based machine runs all I/O handling through the first processor (CPU = 0), and all delayed processor call interrupts for the first network interface are handled by the last processor (CPU = 7). In this case, SQL Server performance, on a busy server with heavy network and I/O loads, may be improved by preventing SQL Server from using the first and last processors. Although using the affinity mask sounds promising for performance, do not change this value unless you have a solid understanding of the affinity mask and have a powerful system.

Locks

You either have enough locks or you don't. Each configured lock takes up 96 bytes, so you don't want to arbitrarily set locks through the roof. However, queries will fail if you run out of locks during processing. The best course of action is to leave the default value (0) and let SQL Server manage the number of locks dynamically.

Max Worker Threads

The Max Worker Threads setting acts like a mini transaction processing (TP) monitor, monitoring the use of physical OS-level threads to manage SQL Server connections. SQL Server asks Windows to assign a separate thread to each new connection until the number of user connections is greater than the max worker threads value. After that point, SQL connections are managed in a round-robin fashion among a pool of OS-level threads. The default value for this parameter is 255, but you can sometimes achieve better results if you reduce it. You will need to experiment with this parameter for optimal performance, but keep in mind that not every SQL user needs to have his or her own NT thread. In fact, this value should be relatively low compared to the number of user connections.

Memory Options

Memory allocation in SQL Server 2000 is controlled by the Min Server Memory and Max Server Memory options. They define the range in which SQL Server can allocate memory dynamically.

SQL Server periodically queries the amount of available physical memory on the system. It will increase or reduce the amount of acquired memory (buffer cache) to keep 4 to 10MB of physical memory free to prevent excessive paging of virtual memory. (Naturally, SQL Server will not increase the amount of allocated memory unless there is a need.)

You should probably manipulate these options only in cases in which SQL Server is not the only server on the system. If the same machine is also running, for example, Microsoft Search, Analysis Server, or another instance of SQL Server, you may need to use memory parameters to prevent these servers from starving each other. When calculating limits, you should take into account the requirements of the operating system and all other services on the machine.

Priority Boost

The Priority Boost option increases SQL Server's Windows scheduling priority. The default value is 0, which corresponds to a priority base of 7. If you set this option to 1, SQL Server will have priority 13 within Windows.

You should change this value only on a server that is dedicated to SQL Server. You should also monitor the server closely after the change. Sometimes the server is not able to shut down, leading to communication problems because Windows is not able to perform other tasks.

Query Governor Cost Limit

The Query Governor Cost Limit is an advanced option that limits the time in which a query can run on the server. Running time can be an issue, especially on data warehouse systems. The default value is 0, which allows all queries to run as long as they need to.

Although you set this value as a number of seconds, this does not mean that a query will be interrupted after that amount of time has elapsed. SQL Server examines each query before executing it and estimates its cost and then executes only queries for which the cost is lower than the specified value.

Open Objects

The Open Objects parameter controls the number of database objects that can be open at any one time, including, but not limited to, tables, indexes, views, and procedures. The structure for each open object does not consume a large amount of memory (about 70 bytes), but performance can be degraded if the value of this parameter is set too low.

Since SQL Server configures this option dynamically itself, it is best to leave the default value (0).

Setting Database Parameters

As discussed earlier in this chapter, there are several configuration parameters that can affect the behavior of the database. You can set them using the database Properties window (see Figure 16-8) or the sp_dboption system stored procedure or by using the SET clause of the ALTER DATABASE statement.

To see a list of all settable options, execute sp_dboption without parameters. To see options set for a specific database, execute sp_dboption with the database name as a parameter. We will now look at options that can affect performance.

Auto Create Statistics

All indexes have distribution statistics that SQL Server uses to navigate through tables and views. SQL Server estimates the best way to access records in the case of a key or range of keys specified in a query. Distribution statistics indicate the selectivity and distribution of these key values. Selectivity defines the number of rows identified when a query specifies a single key. A unique key (column) has high selectivity, and the query will select a single row. If the query identifies

1,000 records, then selectivity is low. To understand the issue of distribution of key values, consider the Country field in a Sales database; if most customers are from the United States, SQL Server should not use that index to access records, but if there are just a few customers from, for example, Australia, that index is perfect for accessing records.

When the Auto Create Statistics database option is set to true, SQL Server automatically creates any missing statistics during optimization. This option should be left set to true.

You can set Auto Create Statistics using sp_dboption:

```
Use master
Exec sp_dboption 'Northwind', 'auto create statistics', 'TRUE'
```

You can also set it using this entry:

```
ALTER DATABASE Northwind
SET AUTO_CREATE_STATISTICS ON
```

The state of this database property can be tested using the DATABASEPROPERTYEX function:

```
SELECT DATABASEPROPERTYEX ('Northwind', 'IsAutoCreateStatistics')
```

Auto Update Statistics

If the Auto Update Statistics option is set to true, SQL Server automatically updates any out-of-date statistics during optimization. This option should be left set to true; otherwise, any statistics could become useless.

AutoClose

When AutoClose is set to true, SQL Server automatically closes the database and frees resources after the last user logs out. The only problem is that the next user has to wait for the database to be opened. You should not set this option to true on a production server. The only scenario in which this setting might be useful is when the development server is on a laptop computer or workstation.

AutoShrink

You can use AutoShrink to have SQL Server periodically check the database and shrink database files if possible. The use of this option on a production server is not recommended. It is better to schedule such work to be performed in off-peak hours.

Torn Page Detection

SQL Server logically records information in 8K data pages. However, all I/O operations in Windows are performed in 512-byte sectors. Therefore, it is possible that, due to a power failure, SQL Server may start to write a page and never complete it. When the Torn Page Detection option is set to true, SQL Server checks pages for such problems. You may improve the performance of the server slightly by skipping this check, but you should skip it only if you have a UPS system on the server.

NOTE: If an incomplete page is detected, SQL Server raises an I/O error and closes the connection. If the page is detected during recovery, the database is marked as suspect (and users will not be able to use it). Because the database has lost data integrity, it should be restored from a backup copy.

Optimizing the tempdb Database

The tempdb system database holds temporary stored procedures and temporary tables. These objects are sometimes created explicitly by a user and sometimes implicitly by SQL Server. You can envision this database as a workspace that SQL Server and users and programs use to store some intermediate result temporarily. Developers sometimes use it as a sandbox to develop and test a solution. Objects are usually deleted as soon as they are not needed, but if something is left longer, it will be flushed when SQL Server is restarted.

In earlier versions of SQL Server, you could move tempdb into RAM instead of storing it on the hard drive. Later versions managed memory better, so it was more beneficial to leave more memory for SQL Server; if something in tempdb was used often, the system would cache it.

There are a few things relating to the tempdb database that you need to take care of to achieve optimal performance:

▼ Set tempdb to expand automatically when it is full. If a query's intermediate result fills tempdb and the system is not allowed to expand tempdb, SQL Server will terminate the query.

■ Set the initial size of tempdb and the file growth increment percentage to reasonable levels. If tempdb has to expand often, that process will add to the time needed to execute queries.

▲ Place tempdb on a fast disk system. To further improve performance, you can stripe tempdb over multiple disks (you can use RAID 0 since preserving the content of tempdb in the case of a failure is not critical) or use file groups to place tempdb on different disks from those used by the data pages of user databases (however, management of this solution may be very complex).

Optimizing the Transaction Log

The transaction log is the part of each database that records each modification of the data (such as each insert, update, or delete operation). Here are some guidelines for optimizing the transaction log:

▼ Create the log on a separate disk or array (RAID 1 is the best option). This way, disk heads stay in place, ready to write the next transaction.

■ Set the initial size and file growth increments of the transaction log file so that SQL Server does not have to expand the log frequently. If the log has to be expanded too often, system performance may suffer.

▲ Do not allow SQL Server to shrink the size of the log file automatically. Shrinking should be performed manually (or scheduled) during off-peak hours. Otherwise, the performance of the system will be affected as the server locks pages and moves them around.

Using Network Libraries

SQL Server Network Libraries, commonly referred to as Net-Libraries (or Net-Libs) in SQL Server lingo, are not the same as network protocols. Net-Libraries are special communication layers that abstract the network so a SQL Server client application developer does not have to write directly to the network. SQL Server supports the following Net-Libraries:

▼ Named Pipes

■ Multiprotocol

■ NWLink IPX/SPX

■ TCP/IP Sockets

■ AppleTalk ADSP

▲ Banyan VINES

For the client and server to communicate, a pair of matching Net-Libraries must be used. In general the Net-Library is selected to match an underlying network protocol, although Named Pipes and Multiprotocol both support TCP/IP, NetBEUI, and NW Link IPX/SPX.

Microsoft testing has shown that the TCP/IP Sockets Net-Lib is slightly faster than the other choices on fast networks, but the difference is negligible, and the network is rarely the bottleneck. Consequently, it is not necessary to make a decision concerning the Net-Lib based on performance considerations. In fact, on fast networks, Named Pipes may be a better option because of its ease of use, many features, and many configuration options. Named Pipes is an even better choice when the client application is running on the server. Local Named Pipes runs in kernel mode and therefore is extremely fast.

On slower networks (such as dial-up connections or WANs), performance may be more critical. Named Pipes is more interactive than other choices—a series of requests and responses are transferred over the wire to control the transport of data. TCP/IP has a lower overhead and is a better choice for slower networks. TCP/IP Sockets features windowing and delayed acknowledgment to improve performance even more.

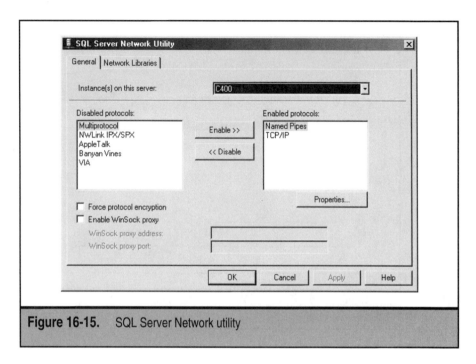

Figure 16-15.   SQL Server Network utility

Multiprotocol is often chosen because it can run over most network protocols, and because it offers some advanced features such as encryption. However, in terms of performance, it is not the best choice.

You can choose which Net-Lib a server supports by using the SQL Server Network utility (see Figure 16-15).

On each client system, you can select the Net-Library to use to access each server by using the SQL Server Client Network utility (see Figure 16-16).

If a client application accesses a server through an ODBC connection, you can select the Net-Lib while you are creating (or editing) DSN. Click the Client Configuration button in the Microsoft SQL Server DSN Configuration Wizard (see Figure16-17).

Optimizing the Backup Process

Backups in SQL Server 2000 can be executed while the server is under load, which is very important in 24/7 production environments. Although performing backups slows down the server, the slowdown is slight, and performance degradation usually goes unnoticed by users.

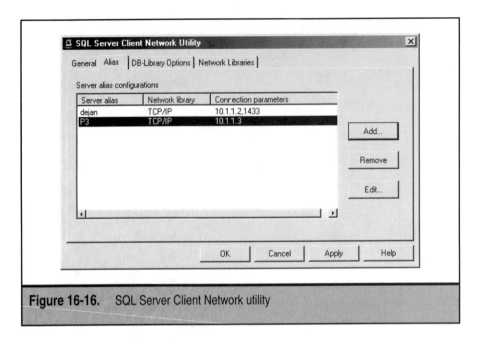

Figure 16-16. SQL Server Client Network utility

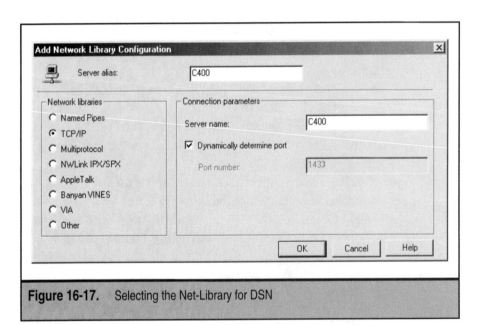

Figure 16-17. Selecting the Net-Library for DSN

However, in the case of very large databases, you can improve backup performance by writing the backup to multiple backup devices in parallel. Naturally, the restore process will also be faster if read from multiple backup devices in parallel.

You can also reduce the time needed to restore the database by using differential backups instead of transaction log backups.

Optimizing the Import Process

DBAs are often required to load information from other data sources into SQL Server databases. Proper configuration depends on all the parameters of the environment. This section won't teach you how to load to SQL Server, but here are a few tips:

▼ Use a nonlogged bulk-copy operation (set the database Select Into/Bulkcopy option to true to enable it).

■ If possible, use the BULK INSERT statement rather than the bcp utility to load text files into SQL Server.

■ It is usually faster to drop indexes from the target table before starting a load and to re-create them after the load is completed.

■ If nobody is using the table during the load (no one should be anyway), lock it using the TABLOCK hint.

■ If possible, specify more than one row in each batch to be processed at a time (the more the better).

■ If a table has a clustered index, try to order source information before loading and then use the ORDER hint when loading.

■ If SQL Server is running on a system with multiple processors, partition data in multiple files and load them in parallel.

▲ When copying data between two clustered tables on two machines running SQL Server, bulk-copy the data to a text file using the SELECT statement with an appropriate ORDER BY clause to create an ordered data file. Then bulk-copy the file, using the ORDER hint, to the target server.

APPLICATION AND DATABASE DESIGN

Sometimes you choose the right hardware, you perform an optimal installation of required software and SQL Server, and you configure and manage the server and database resources ideally, but the system is still slow. An improperly written query or a poorly designed database schema can dramatically degrade the performance of even the fastest platform. It is important for you to be aware of typical problems that can occur and to be able to identify them. Then you can ask your vendor or development team to remedy them.

Query Optimization

SQL Server's ODBC driver allows an administrator to log queries that are taking a long time to execute. This option can be set while creating a new data source (a new DSN), or it can be set later for an existing one. Just enable the Save Long Running Queries to the Log File option on the Configure DSN Wizard screen (see Figure 16-18).

Some queries simply take a long time to execute, and you cannot do anything about it, but a database specialist will often be able to tweak indexes, rewrite the query, or change the database schema to

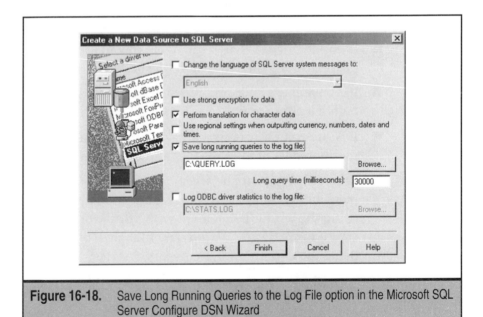

Figure 16-18. Save Long Running Queries to the Log File option in the Microsoft SQL Server Configure DSN Wizard

dramatically reduce execution time. However, it is not enough to know that the "database is slow." A DBA will do a much better job if he or she has a group of problematic queries to review.

Monitoring is great, but you can also control the length of query execution. As mentioned earlier, you can stop queries that will take more than a specified amount of time to execute if you set the Query Governor Cost Limit option using sp_configure, or if you set the query governor option on the Server Settings tab of the SQL Server Properties form, as shown here:

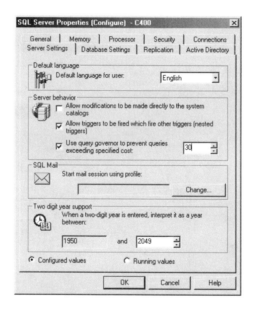

Using Indexes

The most important tool for improving the execution of queries on a table is the *index*. Like the index of a book, which enables a reader to find a piece of information without reading the entire book, the index of a table allows the server to access the required record without scanning the entire table. The index of a book contains words and page numbers, and similarly, the index of a database contains a list of values from the table and pointers to the records that contain them.

The rule of thumb is to create an index for each column (or combination of columns) that is specified frequently as a criterion for a query.

NOTE: You should not just blindly add an index for every column in a table. Although indexes improve the performance of the table by decreasing the amount of time the server needs to find a record, they also reduce the performance of the system because each modification statement (INSERT, UPDATE, or DELETE) potentially changes the indexes defined on the table. Those updates to the index may require substantial time.

To see the indexes of a table, right-click a table in Enterprise Manager and choose All Tasks | Manage Indexes from the pop-up menu. Enterprise Manager displays the following dialog box:

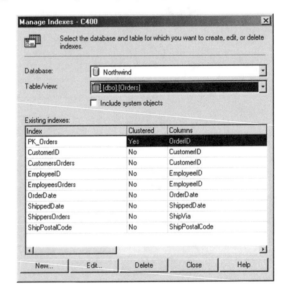

NOTE: Although it is easy to manage indexes this way, there are many parameters that you should take into account when creating an index. For instance, indexes can be clustered or nonclustered, indexes can be created on columns that are more or less selective, an index can be unique, an index can be created on multiple columns, and so on. This is a major topic that goes beyond the scope of this book, and it is best to leave it for the database developer experienced in physical database design.

Index Tuning Wizard

There are several ways to create and manage indexes, but we will
review just one more. The Query Analyzer has a tool called the Index
Tuning Wizard (see Figure 16-19). Its purpose is to analyze a query
(or a set of queries) and recommend index(es) that will improve
performance.

1. On the welcome screen, click Next. In the screen that follows,
   you must select the server, database, and tuning mode before
   analysis can start. Click Next.

2. You now identify the workload to be analyzed. It could be
   a single query, obtained by an ODBC driver that was set to
   record long-running queries, as described earlier. However,
   that query might be so obscure that it would never be
   repeated. It is much better to run the wizard against a typical
   daily workload. You can use SQL Profiler, as described earlier
   in this chapter, to record the workload in a workload file or a
   SQL Server trace table.

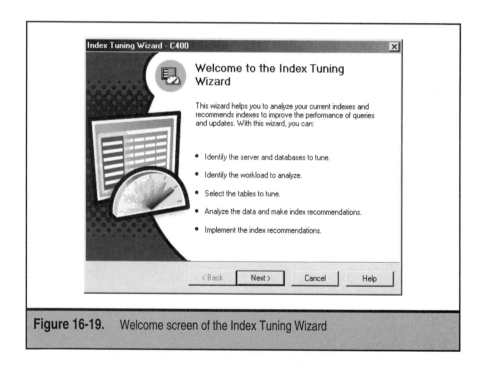

Figure 16-19.   Welcome screen of the Index Tuning Wizard

3. Next you need to specify which tables you want analyzed. You can select all tables or just those that were referenced in the query.

4. At this point, you need to be patient while SQL Server analyses the workload. The result appears on the next screen of the wizard (see Figure 16-20).

5. The next step applies the proposed changes to the database.

File-Database and Fat-Client Scenario

The crucial feature of client-server architecture is an intelligent database server that returns only the required piece of information to the client.

File-databases are database systems in which information is stored in sequential files that contain relational tables (and usually other database objects such as indexes and queries), without a server program. They are sometimes called indexed sequential access method (ISAM) databases. Typical examples are dBase, FoxPro, Clipper, Access, and Paradox. *Fat-client* is a subtype of client-server

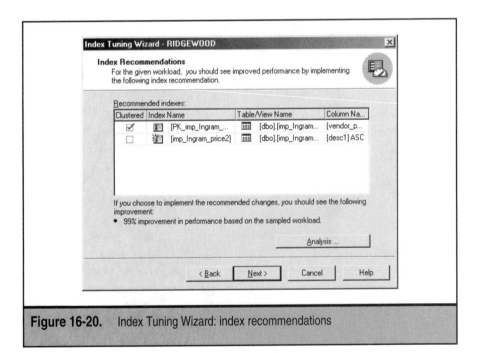

Figure 16-20. Index Tuning Wizard: index recommendations

architecture in which business rules are implemented in the client application, and information is stored in a relational database system. Typical example are client applications written in Visual Basic, C/C++, or Delphi with data storage on SQL Server, IBM DB2, or Oracle databases.

In both cases, most database record processing is performed on the client instead of on the server. Complete tables (fat-client) or, even worse, complete files (file-databases), are transferred to the client and processed there. For example, instead of requesting only the final results of sales for a period of time from a stored procedure or a query, applications may request all sales records and perform a summary on the client. Although the operation is mathematically the same, the result of performing this operation on the client is dramatic degradation of system performance.

The proper solution is to change the architecture of the system, not to implement a bigger pipe. TSQL (and ANSI SQL) are very refined languages, and their features should be used to process information on the server and return only the result to the client.

Using Database Access Libraries

Microsoft offers many different database access libraries that client applications can use to connect to SQL Server (ADO, RDO, JET, DAO, DirectODBC, OLEDB, ODBC, DB-Library, and more). It is very important not to use something that is too slow or too complicated to develop.

Since many client-server developers now working with SQL Server worked initially with Access, you will often be faced with architecture that relies on components written for Access (for a file-database scenario). Since it is possible to use JET or DAO to access SQL Server, developers sometimes decide to work with a familiar object model. Everything works fine in a laboratory or development environment, but when the application is deployed, everything becomes terribly slow. It is wrong to use JET or DAO to access SQL Server. These are written for Access MDB files. If you use SQL Server Profiler, you will see that, for each query, JET asks three pages of additional questions to find out all possible details of target database objects, resultsets, columns, data types, and so on.

Things could be even worse. Sometimes an application is written for Access, and management decides to move it up to SQL Server. It is simple to upload all tables to SQL Server and create links in Access MDB files to reference them. That approach initially reduces development cost, since the client application does not have to be changed, but the performance penalty is severe. Stay away from such systems. They have to be rewritten.

There are performance differences among ADO, RDO, ODBC, OLEDB, and DirectODBC, but they are not so dramatic. It is acceptable to select one of these based on ease of use and the experience of the development team. In theory, ODBC API performs most quickly, but it is difficult to use. It is better to use RDO or ADO, because these are more user friendly. Developers won't have to focus on low-level intricacies of usage, and they will be able to focus on writing proper queries and data access methods.

Using Cursors and Resultsets

Operations in a database are performed on the set of all rows that satisfy the criteria specified. This set is usually called a *resultset* (or sometimes a *recordset* or *rowset*). Unfortunately, it is difficult to design interactive applications that work with an entire resultset. Designers of database systems have therefore invented a new mechanism—*cursors*—for bridging differences between the set-oriented world of relational databases and the need to process records individually in interactive applications.

There are two types of cursors:

▼ TSQL cursors

▲ Database API cursors

TSQL cursors are constructs in TSQL that allow users to process each record individually. Their use slows down an application, since records are processed individually and they occupy resources in the tempdb database. You should specifically request your development team or vendor not to use them. You can detect TSQL cursor usage using SQL Profiler—just add Cursor events to a new trace.

Database API cursors are part of all data access mechanisms (such as ADO, RDO, ODBC, OLEDB, and DB-Library).

Developers can choose the implementation and behavior of the cursor by selecting one of the following types:

▼ *Static cursors* contain complete snapshots of selected records. They occupy a considerable amount of space, but they do not use a large amount of network bandwidth, since they ignore changes that occur in the database after its creation.

■ *Keyset-driven cursors* contain only pointers to member records, so the application and user are aware of changes on records modified by other users. They do not require a large amount of resources, but they increase network traffic significantly.

■ *Dynamic cursors* periodically refresh the content of individual records and the membership of records in the cursor, making the application and user aware of all changes that occur in the database. However, they have the most impact on network traffic and database performance and should be used only in extreme situations.

▲ *Forward-only cursors* have a severe usability limitation: users and applications cannot fetch a record that has already been fetched; they can only move to the next record or close the cursor. Therefore, the internal operations of this cursor are much simpler and require fewer resources.

Modern database APIs such as ADO can work with *disconnected recordsets*. In these, ties between the client (recordset) and server resources (records in the database) can be temporarily broken, thereby reducing network traffic. Disconnected recordsets can later be reconnected, and changes will be saved to the database.

If no cursor is requested, SQL Server returns the complete result to the caller in a form called the default resultset (it used to be called a firehose cursor). This is the fastest method for retuning and processing the result. It does require extra work on the client side, but it is the preferred method.

OLTP vs. DSS

Online transaction processing (OLTP) databases are typically designed to support a large number of concurrent users adding and changing information. Decision support systems (DSS) are typically designed to store historic information and allow business analysts to query (read) it and make decisions based on the results. (There are various ways to implement DSS, such as data warehouses, data marts, and OLAP cubes.)

Ideally, OLTP and DSS systems are different databases on different servers, but sometimes, under resource constraints, organizations take shortcuts that have performance implications. For example, the same database and same tables may be used for both updating and reading. To allow concurrent work by many people, SQL Server uses locks to prevent other users (or programs) from reading information until the change is completed, or to prevent changes until reading is finished. Users who are reading do not (b)lock each other out for long, nor do users who are updating.

A better solution is to put users who are mostly changing information on one server and database, and to put users who are mostly reading on another. A quick and dirty solution would be to just replicate the OLTP database as-is and run reports and queries against a copy. You can call such a solution a reporting database.

NOTE: OLTP systems work faster when a table has fewer indexes. Since DSS systems are designed to be queried, they benefit from a higher number of indexes.

Normalization and Denormalization

To further improve the performance of queries and reports, an organization must change the structure of its decision support system database.

OLTP databases are *normalized* (optimized for quick updating and minimal storage requirements). This chapter isn't the place to cover the details of the formal theory of normal form, so what follows is a quick overview. In a normalized database, information is broken into different entities (and stored in different tables), along with their relationships. For example, a Product table should not contain a Vendor field, but just a VendorId value—the number that references the vendor record (see Figure 16-21). The name of the vendor (along with other vendor information such as phone number and address) should be stored in a record in the Vendor table. That way, if the vendor name (or phone number) needs to be changed (for example, say the vendor is acquired by another company), just one record in the Vendor table needs to be changed; all Product records that reference it keep the old identifier, but it now points to the new name (or phone number).

Unfortunately, this is not an optimal configuration for reading. SQL Server has to first find the Product record and then the associated Vendor record. Queries and reports are processed faster when information resides in a single record in a single table. The design method used to achieve this goal is called *denormalization*. A popular type of DSS system that uses this method is called a *data warehouse*. Tables in such a system form a so called star-join schema.

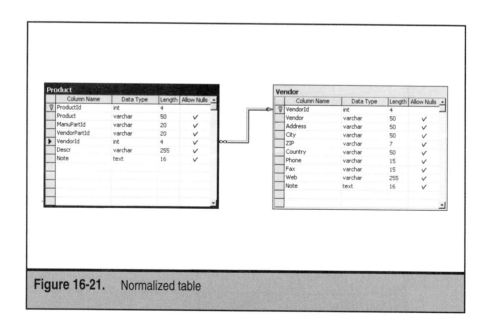

Figure 16-21.   Normalized table

Data in denormalized tables can be stored using less space, but these tables are designed and optimized so that queries and reports executed against them are completed in the shortest possible time. In the preceding example, for instance, the query or report would return information more quickly because the product record contains the vendor name as well (see Figure 16-22).

Neither normalization nor denormalization are tasks that a network administrator should perform. They require significant changes to existing system components. You should be able to identify the problem and request the proper solution.

NOTE: On a few occasions, I have been hired as a consultant by companies experiencing performance problems on their OLTP systems. In these cases, management was planning to replace the existing system with its equivalent from another database vendor. Unfortunately for the sales team of the new vendor, the problem was solved by creating a new database to run reports.

Product

Column Name	Data Type	Length	Allow Nulls
ProductId	int	4	
Product	varchar	50	✓
ManuPartId	varchar	20	✓
VendorPartId	varchar	20	✓
Vendor	varchar	50	✓
Descr	varchar	255	✓
Note	text	16	✓

Figure 16-22.   Denormalized table

Using OLAP

Although tables in a data warehouse are optimized to return results quickly, SQL Server still has to scan a large number of records to provide, for example, a summary of sales results for a company.

OLAP servers (such as Analysis Server in SQL Server 2000) record aggregations of data stored in a data warehouse in special data storage areas called *cubes*. When the sales total, for example, in a particular time period within a particular region is required, a client application requests just that value from the OLAP server. Since the server contains only preaggregated values, only one value will be accessed in data storage and returned to the client. This process is much faster than accessing thousands or millions of records in a SQL Server data warehouse to perform a summary.

Since it is not likely that such history will change, it is a good idea to invest some time in calculating aggregates and providing the space to store them. Users will get results instantly, and overall performance of the system will be impressive.

Using Table Partitioning

Application vendors are supposed to stress-test their systems under full load and with a database containing records equivalent to what might be collected over the course of many years. Systems should have procedures and features to address the fact that tables will grow larger and larger. Unfortunately, this process does not always take place.

If a table contains millions of records, even when proper indexes are present on it, access will be slow. SQL Server will use the index to access records, but the hierarchy inside the index will be very deep, and the time required to access a record will be longer than usual.

Solutions are sometimes very simple and sometimes more involved. Usually, it is not necessary to store the complete history of the company in the OLTP system. Ideally, historic information should be archived to the company's data warehouse (and dropped from the OLTP system). Unfortunately, such a system does not always exist. It is not a trivial effort to develop the data warehouse, the processes needed to load information into it, and client applications for querying and reporting.

The simplest thing that you can do in this case is to create a table with an identical structure. Then you can copy older records into it and drop them from the original table. You can even go a step further: instead of a single table with archived records, you can create a set of tables that will store horizontal subsets of records. Often, records are split based on the time of some event. For example, billing information can be split based on the purchase date in monthly or quarterly tables (see Figure 16-23). This kind of solution is sometimes called *horizontal partitioning*. It is applicable when you can identify one horizontal subset of the table that is used more often than the rest of it.

A different solution is possible when a table is very wide—when each individual record occupies a substantial amount of space. SQL Server stores information on 8K data pages. If a record is larger, fewer records are stored on one 8K page, and more I/O operations are needed to fetch the same number of records. If you can establish that some fields are needed more often than others, you can perform

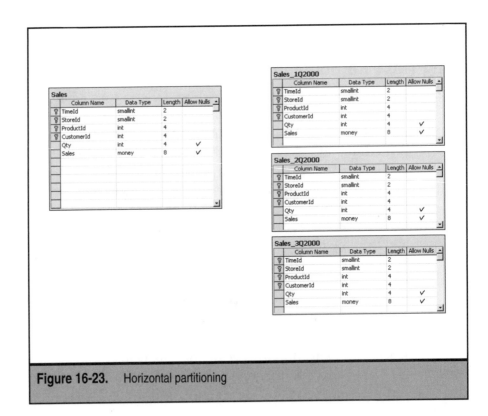

Figure 16-23.   Horizontal partitioning

vertical partitioning of the table. You can create two tables (see Figure 16-24): one will store fields that are often used, and the other will store fields that are seldom used. More records (of the first table) will fit on the single data page, fewer I/O operations are needed, and more records are cached in memory. However, this solution requires changes to the application, and you may not be able to make them yourself, but you can ask the vendor to make them for you.

Using Federated Servers

You can improve the performance of the database server by implementing faster CPUs, more memory, and faster hard drives. This approach is often called *scaling-in* (you can call it brute force as well). Unfortunately, there is a point of diminishing returns. After that point, performance will be the same no matter how much more effort you invest.

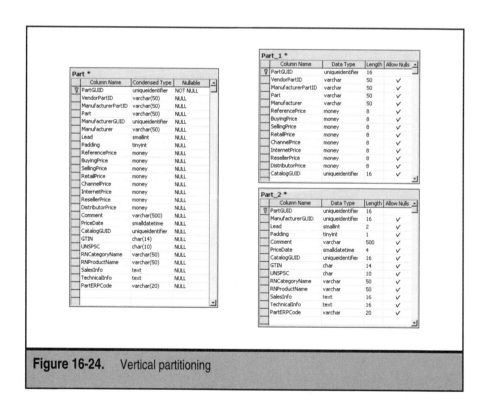

Figure 16-24.   Vertical partitioning

IT managers dream about platforms that have a linear return on hardware investment (a platform that doubles in performance when installed hardware resources are doubled). Updateable, distributed, partitioned views allow SQL Server 2000 to have such an effect. An application developer can partition data horizontally on a set of identical tables across a cluster of two or more servers (see Figure 16-25). Then a view is created that references a union of tables on different servers. The Query Optimizer is intelligent enough to prompt just the appropriate server when a request to read or modify the record is received.

Records of the original table are split among member tables on federated servers. There must be a criterion to determine that a record belongs to a certain server—a *data routing rule*. The rule must be selected so that it splits data requests among member servers as uniformly as possible.

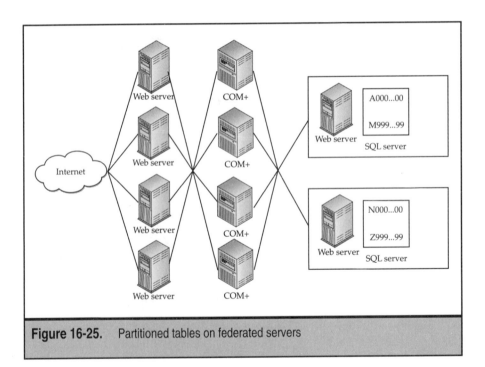

Figure 16-25. Partitioned tables on federated servers

> **NOTE:** Proof of the value of this method lies in the fact that SQL Server and DB2 are dethroning each other every couple of weeks for the number-one position on the TPC-C benchmark. Oracle's database currently does not support this method and is left behind, even though its testing is performed on a much more expensive platform.

Again, this solution is not something that a regular network administrator can implement on his or her own. Although it sounds like a simple solution, it requires an experienced database specialist to implement it. However, once it is accomplished, the database can support the busiest Web site or the largest enterprise.

> **NOTE:** The transaction rate achieved by SQL Server 2000 in one TPC-C benchmark test in 2000 was such that it could handle all e-commerce transactions that Amazon.com and eBay.com processed together in 1999 in just two days.

Federated servers are great, but they are not the holy grail that will solve all the IT department's problems. In fact, linear scalability comes with a price. Although federated servers work as a unit, they are all independent systems that must be monitored and administered separately.

CHAPTER 17

Optimizing Exchange 2000 Server

When considering tuning and optimizing a Microsoft Exchange 2000 environment, those familiar with Exchange version 5.5 will find Exchange 2000 tuning very similar in some ways and very different in others. There are enough differences between versions of Exchange that you should set aside any preconceived ideas of what's best in the configuration and maintenance of Exchange and view the Exchange 2000 environment as a completely different product.

In tuning and optimizing Exchange 2000, there are three themes to keep in mind: design an effective Exchange 2000 environment, implement the effective design, and perform maintenance procedures to keep the Exchange 2000 environment running in its optimum state. Since the design of Exchange 2000 is built on Active Directory, please see Chapters 4 and 9 on designing and tuning an efficient Active Directory for an effective core directory service. This chapter picks up where the other chapters leave off by focusing on the implementation of specific Exchange 2000 components and then addressing the maintenance procedures to keep the Exchange 2000 environment running in an optimal state.

In many networking environments, it will not be necessary to completely reconfigure the servers and organizational structure based on recommendations in this chapter, but suggestions are made to help the reader better understand where performance can be improved. Use the strategies outlined here to determine the current performance of an existing Exchange environment and to tune it, as well as to project and model future demands to proactively manage growth in the use of the messaging application.

MICROSOFT EXCHANGE FUNDAMENTALS

Microsoft Exchange 2000 is a client-server electronic messaging system that splits functions and tasks between the Exchange server and the Exchange client. Functions such as routing of messages between users or transmission and receipt of messages to the Internet are core components of the Exchange server. Functions such as composing messages or sorting messages within a folder in Exchange are core components of the Exchange client. Therefore, performance in an Exchange environment depends on the optimization of the client, the communication link between the client and the server, and the performance of the Exchange server itself. Additionally, the communication link between the Exchange server and any external data source such as the Internet or the WAN connection to another Exchange server also indirectly affects the performance of the Exchange environment. Electronic message communication typically is considered bursty information since messages are created by a user or queued by the messaging server and then sent either on demand or after a specified delay to complete the electronic transaction.

Microsoft Exchange 2000 runs as a Windows 2000 application service, so the server that Microsoft Exchange is running on will be affected by the demands of the Exchange services. Because of this, any of the Windows 2000 management tools such as Event Viewer (to log the status of errors), Performance Monitor (to review server performance), and Task Manager (to review operating server drivers) that have been described earlier in this book all apply in analyzing the operations of an Exchange environment. As described in previous chapters, Windows 2000 provides a variety of built-in tools, and additional third-party add-in tools are available, to assist in the analysis of the environment for Window s 2000 and now Exchange 2000.

For example, the databases used to store electronic messages in Exchange 2000 are based on the Microsoft Jet database technology. Jet is the same database format used in Microsoft Access. Jet is a highly efficient information storage system that does not require a separate database management system such as SQL Server to store and retrieve information; however, like any database, it needs to be configured and tuned properly to make it work as efficiently and effectively as possible.

The Exchange environment relies on Windows 2000 security to authenticate user access to electronic messages stored in the user's personal mailbox as well as access to information stored in public storage locations and shared information of other users (such as calendars and shared message folders). Using Windows 2000 security, users are required to authenticate to Windows 2000 domain controllers. This authentication for user access adds demand requirements that can affect LAN and WAN infrastructure performance.

Microsoft Exchange 2000 uses the concept of public and private folders for user storage of information. A private folder is the user's personal message storage mailbox. When a user receives an electronic message, the message is stored in the user's private folder store. Messages by default are stored on the Exchange server to centralize message storage management; however, a user can store messages in offline folders or separate data files for the purpose of mobile messaging, as will be described later in this chapter, in "Configuring Hardware for Optimal Performance." Public messages are stored in public folders that have security access shared by multiple users. The creator or owner of the public folder controls security access. There are dozens of options available to allow users to read public messages but not modify or delete them, read and write messages but only edit or delete messages that the user created, and the like.

Many organizations use public folders to store, or post, a copy of a message for shared access by multiple users rather than sending the message to multiple users as e-mail. This use of Microsoft Exchange 2000 public folders minimizes the number of messages sent, received, managed, and stored within Exchange, which minimizes traffic on the network, thus improving systemwide performance.

In addition to handling electronic message storage, Microsoft Exchange 2000 also manages external message communications. External message communications include communications to the Internet, communications with other Exchange servers, and message communications to other LAN- or legacy-based message systems such as Lotus Notes, Novell GroupWise, and Microsoft Mail. The connector service provides both inbound communication and outbound communication of messages to these other environments. These services add demands on the server and the LAN and WAN infrastructure.

Other workgroup electronic communications functions include faxing, voicemail communications, document imaging, and document management. Add-ins to Microsoft Exchange typically run as additional Windows 2000 services. These services can be configured and installed on the same Exchange server that manages the users' private folders and the organizational public folders, or the services can be installed on completely separate Windows 2000 servers. The decision to distribute these functions to improve individual server performance is outlined later in this chapter in "Creating Multiserver Configurations."

Unlike previous versions of Microsoft Exchange, which had a completely separate directory database for mailbox names, distribution lists, and address books, Exchange 2000 uses Windows 2000 Active Directory for user security, the user directory, and distribution lists. The management utility for Exchange 2000 is called the Exchange Service Manager and can be used to administer the resources of a single Exchange server or, in a larger environment, all Exchange servers in an organization's site or global design.

Core Components of Exchange

Key to the optimization of Exchange 2000 is understanding which components are dependent on Windows 2000, and which are not, as you will learn throughout this chapter. The core components of Microsoft Exchange 2000 storage system include the information store, storage groups, private and public information store databases, and logs, as shown in Figure 17-1.

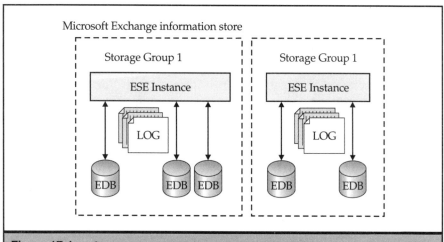

Figure 17-1.   Core components of Microsoft Exchange 2000

Information Store

The information store in Microsoft Exchange 2000 is the Windows 2000 service that manages the databases where messages are stored. Unlike in previous versions of Microsoft Exchange, where the information store designation also included the actual message databases, as a result of several enhancements in data storage functions and physical storage media supported by Exchange 2000, the databases are now separated from the information store function.

Key to the role of the information store is the assignment and tracking of messages throughout the Exchange data structure. Each message has a unique message ID assigned to it. This ID is used for tracking as the message is routed from user to user or from an internal user to an external user. This message ID is also used to ensure that there is only one copy of each message stored on the Exchange server. Instead of storing multiple copies of each message, only one copy of the message is stored in the message database. When multiple users receive the same message, each user has a link between the private inbox message list and the actual message itself. When the user presses ENTER to access the message, the actual message from the information store is then opened and sent to the user. Single-instance storage minimizes disk storage space on the Exchange server. A shared message is finally deleted from the Exchange server only when every user who references it deletes that message from their mailbox.

The Exchange 2000 information store also manages automatic defragmentation and compression of the message stores to keep the message system running as efficiently as possible. This will be discussed in depth in "Optimizing Server Performance Through Ongoing Maintenance" later in the chapter.

When users log on to review any of their electronic messages, they see only a table of contents of their messages that shows who sent the message, when the message was sent, the subject of the message, and any of a few dozen other fields of information, displayed in table format. When the user highlights a message and either presses the ENTER key or double-clicks the message, the message is accessed in the Exchange database and sent to the user. This data request on demand limits server-to-client data traffic to only the information requested by the users. Rather than sending all messages to a user, only information the users require is sent, thus reducing client-to-server message communication traffic.

Storage Groups

New to Exchange 2000 message information management is the concept of the storage group. In previous versions of Microsoft Exchange, a server could have only one private message store database for user mailboxes and one public message store data for shared workgroup or enterprise message information per server. This single-database-per-server concept imposed great limitations since a very large single database is difficult to manage, administer, and maintain, so organizations were forced to either have servers with very large single databases or to add multiple servers at a single site to distribute information stored in databases across multiple servers.

With Exchange 2000, a single server can now have up to 4 storage groups, each containing up to 6 databases, for a total of 24 databases supported on a single server. This level of scalability provides a significant amount of expandability on a single server, with extensive support for several databases on a single system. The section "Configuring Hardware for Optimal Performance" later in this chapter describes how to determine the optimum number of databases within an appropriate number of storage groups for best system performance.

Private Information Store

The private information store is where all of the users' mailboxes and messages for an administrative group or organization are stored. Each message is stored in the private information store and has a message ID assigned to it. An organization can have one private information store for the whole organization, or the organization can distribute the storage of user mailboxes across multiple databases and multiple servers. It is most logical to distribute users based on sites, so that the users in one city access their mailboxes (the private information store) on the Exchange server at their site, and others in another city access their mailboxes (and the corresponding private information store) on the Exchange server at their site. However, for organizations with thousands of users at a single site, the users' mailboxes may be distributed across multiple Exchange servers that reside at the same site.

The information stores are large, single files that are created with more than the storage capacity needed for the existing messages in the database. The purpose of preallocating disk space is to secure additional disk space on the Exchange server to make sure that the server has enough storage space to manage incoming and outgoing messages. The size of an information store database is determined automatically by the Exchange server during installation and changes dynamically to accommodate the storage demands of the server. The users do not have direct access to the message store. Unlike legacy file-based message systems (such as MS-Mail or cc:Mail) that allowed users to access server data directly using a file-system-type access to mail messages, with Exchange 2000, users can access Exchange information only from an access client such as Microsoft Outlook, POP3 mail client, Web client, or any of the Microsoft Office applications.

There are critical performance factors that need to be considered when distributing users across multiple databases and multiple Exchange servers. The advantage of having all users at a site on a single Exchange server is that there is virtually no delay time when sending a message from one user to another user, since a single Exchange server will have only one copy of the mail message, and the sender will be able to reference the message ID and so will the recipient. However, if the two users were at the same site but on different servers, the message would need to be routed from one Exchange server to the other. This will cause traffic on the network due to the requirement of physically routing a copy of the message from one server to another, and it will also entail additional storage demands since a copy of the message will need to reside on each server. In cases where messages are predominantly routed within a site and within a specific workgroup, it is best to keep all users in the workgroup on the same server. This will minimize server-to-server traffic and external traffic between servers.

To optimize a server by moving user mailboxes onto the same server as the other mailboxes in a workgroup, do the following:

1. Launch the Windows 2000 Active Directory Users and Computers administrative tool.

2. Right-click the name of user.

3. Select Exchange Tasks.

4. Select Move Mailbox.

5. Choose the destination server the mailbox should be moved to.

NOTE: The private information store file typically is stored on the Exchange server in the <\program files\exchsrvr\first administrative group\> directory in a file called priv.edb.

Public Information Store

The public information store is the message database for shared folders on the Exchange server. Similar to an individual's mailbox stored in the private information store database, the public information store database holds the folders where shared messages, files, and postings are saved in the Exchange 2000 environment. Through the use of folder-level security, administrators and users on the network can assign security rights to individual users, groups of users, or all users in the organization to access a public folder or series of public folders.

Microsoft Exchange public folders can be used to centrally store information for an organization to provide the services similar to an intranet. Just as an intranet provides the ability to store company templates, marketing documents, policy information, and the like, the Exchange public folders can also be used to store common information. This strategy of using Exchange to store common shared information drastically minimizes the number of messages that get sent to "all users" on the network, which otherwise can create message traffic problems, message routing problems, and message storage problems for the organization. A sample public folder hierarchy is shown in Figure 17-2.

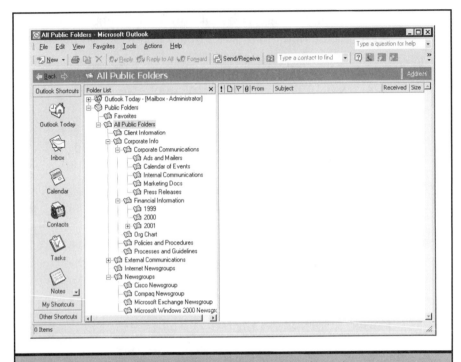

Figure 17-2.   Example of an Exchange 2000 public folder hierarchy

NOTE: The public information store file typically is stored on the Exchange server in the <\program files\exchsrvr\first administrative group\> directory in a file called pub.edb.

Transaction Logs

In addition to having message databases, each Exchange storage group has a transaction log. Instead of having information from a user written directly to a message database, which can cause corruption to the database in the event of a failed database read or write, messages from a user session in a Microsoft Exchange environment are written to a transaction log file on the Exchange server, and the information is then flushed to the database. By default, the Exchange databases and the log files are stored on the same physical hard drive on an Exchange server; however, for performance optimization as well as to distribute the central point of failure, the log files should be stored on a completely separate physical disk platter from the Exchange databases.

Transaction logs play an important part in the processing, tracking, and management of messages in an Exchange environment, and procedures need to be followed for the proper placement of the files, file backup, and restoration and recovery of the files in the event of a system failure. Transaction log management is covered later in this chapter, in "Configuring Hardware for Optimal Performance."

The Exchange 2000 Directory

In previous versions of Microsoft Exchange, the Exchange system directory was stored in a file called DIR.EDB; however, in Exchange 2000, the Active Directory of the network is the master directory for the Exchange organization. The directory in Exchange contains all of the resource information available to users in the Exchange organization such as usernames, distribution lists, and routes to external resources such as the Internet. The top level of the Exchange environment is the organization, which can be split into administrative groups (called sites in Exchange version 5.5), which are grouped by distribution lists made up of individual users. The master catalog of Exchange resources is called the global catalog (GC) (formerly called the global address list (GAL)). This entire directory structure is shown in Figure 17-3.

Organizations that have multiple messaging systems often need to share directories or global address books across the various messaging systems. This function requires swapping user and distribution lists from messaging system to messaging system, or *directory synchronization*. Directory synchronization allows an organization to maintain a single directory of users that may include users across multiple messaging systems. With Microsoft Exchange 2000 and the inclusion of LDAP version 3 directory capabilities, organizations have the option of implementing a directory synchronization process or using an on-demand directory lookup process. While directory synchronization adds a service load on the synchronization server of from 1 to 5 percent of processor utilization,

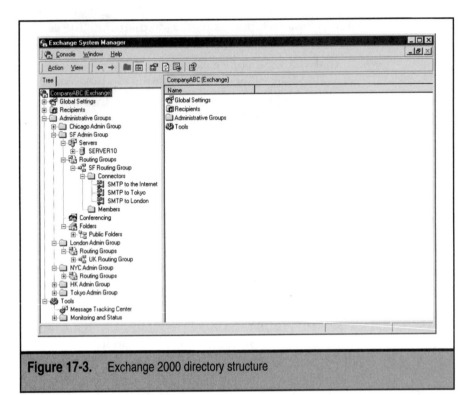

Figure 17-3.   Exchange 2000 directory structure

any user access of the directory is localized and does not put
additional load demands on the server. Through the use of LDAP,
a directory request is made of the host system and displayed on
demand. While this does not put a significant load on the Exchange
server, it does require the client to request a directory view from the
remote system on each directory request.

NOTE: The directory store file is stored on all Windows 2000 global catalog
servers with intra-organizational directory synchronization managed by the
Active Directory.

Connectors

Connectors are Windows 2000 Services running on an Exchange
server that manage inbound and outbound communications to other
messaging systems. The connectors relay messages between servers

so that the message ultimately ends up at its destination. Some connectors also perform directory synchronization with other messaging systems so that the global catalog can include Exchange organization information as well as external organization information.

When linking multiple groups of servers together, there are four methods of interconnecting the groups:

▼ **Intersite Communication (High Speed)**   For communication with a server or group of servers within an organization but at a different physical location, if high bandwidth exists (speeds of greater than 512 Kbps), an organization can choose not to use any connector and rely on the built-in Exchange 2000 SMTP-connector to route messages between servers.

■ **Intersite Communication (Low Speed)**   For communication with a server or group of servers within an organization but at a different physical location where the site-to-site bandwidth is low (less than 256 Kbps), an organization would typically create a routing group consisting of servers in each respective location and connect the two locations together using the Microsoft Exchange routing group connector (RGC). The routing group connector provides a gateway between groups of servers that can be monitored and managed from site to site. Routing group connectors are similar to the site connectors that were used in Exchange version 5.5.

■ **External Internet Communication**   For communication with a server or group of servers outside of the Exchange organization, the SMTP connector (called the Internet Mail Service in Exchange version 5.5) is used. The SMTP connector provides managed communication between the Exchange organization and any SMTP host. Note that an SMTP component is installed at the time that Exchange 2000 is installed; however, this is different from the SMTP connector. The SMTP component is the core service that handles any SMTP server-to-server communication (intersite, intrasite, or external), whereas the SMTP connector is set up to specifically point to a destination server or group of servers for managed SMTP communication.

▲ **Specific Messaging System Support**
Communication   Exchange 2000 comes with a number of
specific connectors for managed communication between
Exchange 2000 and messaging systems such as Lotus Notes,
IBM/Lotus cc:Mail, Novell GroupWise, and Microsoft Mail.

Critical to Exchange 2000 performance are the number of
messages and the processor bandwidth of the Exchange server
managing the inbound, outbound, and synchronization of user lists
in the Exchange environment. Special consideration needs to be taken
when analyzing these processes to determine the quantity and scope
of bandwidth demands on the environment for processing this
information. The performance factors that need to be monitored in
analyzing the Exchange 2000 connectors include outgoing message
volume, incoming message volume, and message queue length. The
message volume for both incoming and outgoing messages should be
less than 60 percent of the total message traffic of the organization. If
the message volume exceeds 60 percent, further analysis should be
performed on the total byte count of connector message
communications. This could be conducted by comparing the total
bytes sent and received with the total throughput capacity of the
connector. If communications throughput exceeds 70 percent of the
total message volume, the connector performance is being affected,
and you should either increase the bandwidth capacity of the
connector (add a faster connection to the Internet or to the external
messaging system) or move the connector to a different server, thus
offloading the performance demands of the system connector.

Event Logging Basics

Microsoft Exchange uses the same event and error logging
mechanism as Microsoft Windows 2000, so every error in Microsoft
Exchange, and potentially every message being sent or received in
an Exchange environment, can be logged and tracked. To activate
message tracking and logging, open the Exchange Administrator
program, choose Routing Group | Connectors, select the connector
option to activate diagnostic logging, select the diagnostics tab, and
turn on diagnostic logging for each of the functions you want to
track, as shown in Figure 17-4.

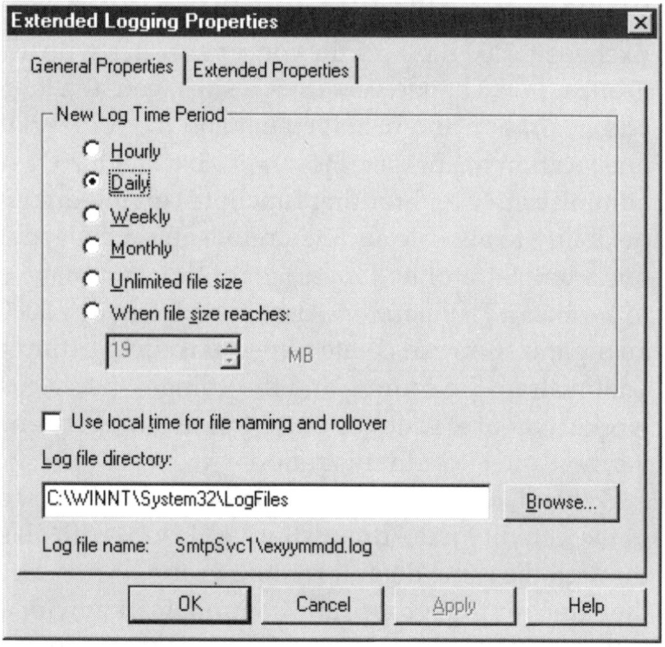

Figure 17-4.   Enabling diagnostic logging in Exchange 2000

Microsoft Exchange uses the Microsoft Windows 2000 Event Viewer utility to store, look up, and manage logged events. This tracking monitors problems with Exchange services (errors in SMTP message routing, errors connecting to the Internet to send SMTP messages, and the like), errors in internal message routing, logon and logoff attempts by Exchange users, and automatic message store compaction.

The important factor to keep in mind about logging is that the more logging options activated, the more frequently the Exchange server will write to the disk logs. This affects disk storage space on the server and takes system processing time. Logs provide valuable, detailed information on the system status that can help a trained administrator find a potential or existing problem in the messaging environment.

Administrative Groups and Routing Groups

Exchange 2000 replaces the concept of sites with administrative groups. In Exchange version 5.5, sites were the targets of both administration and management and the routing of messages from one location to another. However, Exchange 2000 separates the administrative and routing functions, giving organizations the flexibility to allocate administrative and management functions to one administrator and message routing and management functions to another administrator. Also, in an Exchange 2000 environment, an organization can create a special routing group to better administrate the routing and throttling of messages from a priority workgroup of executives or personnel independent of the physical location and site administration.

When Exchange 2000 is initially installed, all servers are installed in the default First Administrative Group, with all servers routed through the same default routing group. When servers are part of the same routing group, any communication with another server is transmitted using SMTP. Exchange 2000 requires the SMTP component to be enabled before the Exchange 2000 software can be installed on the system. Through the SMTP component, all server-to-server communications within a common routing group are transmitted immediately. If there are 30 Exchange 2000 servers in a single site, each server will transmit information to another server in the routing group directly. For servers that are connected on a common LAN or WAN backbone, this immediate transport of messages typically works fine.

When an organization is WAN connected with slow WAN links between sites, typically administrators want better control of when messages are routed and how messages are routed from site to site. For example, if a server in Chicago has a large attachment to send to a user on a server in Tokyo and there are several routes the message can follow, the administrators of the organization will want to route the message using the most efficient and effective route. If the Chicago site is connected to San Francisco with a T1 line and also with a T1 line to a site in Los Angeles, but the Los Angeles site has to route messages to Tokyo through San Francisco, the organization would want a message from Chicago to Tokyo to go through San Francisco since it is only two hops from Chicago to Tokyo through San Francisco, whereas it is three hops through Los Angeles: Chicago to Los Angeles, then Los Angeles to San Francisco, and then San Francisco to Tokyo.

When this level of management of routing of information from one server to another is desired, the enterprise can break the Exchange organization into multiple routing groups and then put routing group connectors between the routing groups. In the preceding example, Chicago would be one routing group, San Francisco would be another, Los Angeles another, and Tokyo another. The link between Chicago and San Francisco can be given priority for any messages destined for Tokyo. This segmentation of an Exchange 2000 organization provides better management of communication from one location to another.

When an Exchange 2000 organization includes Exchange version 5.5 servers, the environment is said to be running in mixed mode. Mixed mode provides full backward compatibility with the Exchange version 5.5 site structure, but while it provides compatibility to older Exchange server configurations, it also constrains the Exchange 2000 environment to an Exchange version 5.5 structure. This means that the administrative groups and routing groups are tied together. After all Exchange version 5.5 servers have been upgraded to Exchange 2000, the organization can switch to Exchange 2000 native mode (choose Exchange Service Manager, right-click the organization name, choose Properties and then Change to Native Mode, and click OK). Once in native mode, the organization can split up administrative groups and routing groups. In many cases, an organization may continue to keep the administration and management down to the physical site level; however, the organization may centralize the routing functions in an IT structure. Restructuring routing groups enables an organization to better manage communication between servers, which is especially important in today's enterprise environments, where the bandwidth between physical sites is significantly greater than in the past and can support high-speed transport protocols with less throttling of information between sites.

NOTE: Once an Exchange 2000 organization has been changed to native mode, it cannot be switched back to mixed mode, so make sure that all Exchange version 5.5 messaging servers, bridgehead servers, Web access servers, and foreign connector and services gateways have been upgraded to Exchange 2000 before changing to native mode. Also, do not confuse native and mixed modes in Exchange 2000 with native and mixed modes in Windows 2000; they are completely different modes. Mixed mode in Windows 2000 is used when the Windows 2000 environment has pre–Windows 2000 servers and workstations (such as Windows 95, Windows 98, and Windows NT). In Windows 2000, when all servers and workstations have been upgraded to Windows 2000, the Windows environment can be upgraded to native mode. An Exchange 2000 native- or mixed-mode environment is completely independent of whether the Windows 2000 environment is in native or mixed mode; therefore, an Exchange 2000 organization can switch to native mode even if Windows 2000 is still running in mixed mode.

Installable File System (IFS), or WebStore

In Exchange 2000, Microsoft introduced the Installable File System (IFS), commonly known as the WebStore. This technology will be implemented in several of the upcoming Microsoft products as a standard method of multiplatform access to stored information and data. The WebStore in Exchange 2000 exposes mail messages, calendar appointments, contacts, and other typical messaging system information right from a file share prompt. This means that a user can read and write information stored in Microsoft Exchange 2000 in four ways:

▼ **32-bit Outlook Client** A user can access information in Exchange using the 32-bit Microsoft Outlook client. The client software can view and format mail messages, calendar appointments, contact information, notes, and to-do lists. Information can also be dragged and dropped into the Outlook client: for example, Microsoft Word documents and Excel spreadsheets.

- **Outlook Web Access** A second common method of accessing Exchange information is from the Outlook Web Access browser-based messaging client. Outlook Web Access can also format mail messages, calendar appointments, and other Outlook information in a structured view.

- **File System Access** The Installable File System (IFS) provides a third method of access to Exchange information through the use of common file share structures. An Exchange folder can be shared and mapped just like any other disk folder in a Windows environment. This allows an administrator, manager, or user to create shares for public folders or personal folders. When another user needs to access the information, for instance, to write information from Microsoft Word to the folder, instead of having to drag and drop the information from within an Outlook client, the user just chooses File | Save As and saves the information to the drive share, as shown in Figure 17-5. To access information, the user can just choose File | Open and access the folder information. Just as with regular file shares, a root folder share can provide access to subfolders, so a hierarchical structure of cascaded folders can be made available to users. Also as with normal file shares, security can be applied to the root folder or any subfolders, providing secured communications (read, write, modify, create, delete) at any level in the folder structure.

- ▲ **Internet Information Server (IIS) HTTP and FTP Access** The Installable File System also enables an organization to publish folder and file information using Microsoft Internet Information Server (IIS) for HTTP and FTP access. This can be a good solution for an organization that wants to share files with clients or vendor partners using standard Web file access and transfer protocols. By publishing information through a Web server, an organization can make select files or folders easily available for download or access external to the organization.

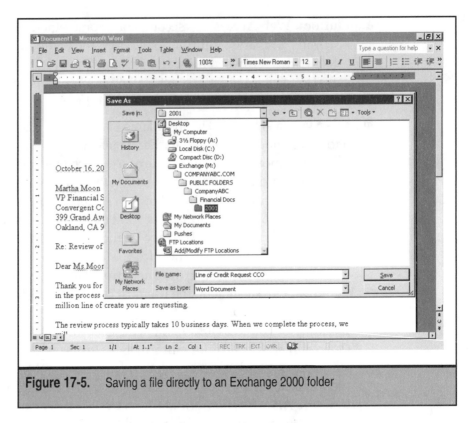

Figure 17-5.   Saving a file directly to an Exchange 2000 folder

IFS in Exchange 2000 greatly enhances the ability for an organization to make information available to internal and external users who were limited in their ability to access the same information in the past. Through the use of secured communications at the file and folder levels, the organization can maintain a high level of security and keep the information accessible to the appropriate people.

CONFIGURING HARDWARE FOR OPTIMAL PERFORMANCE

Since Microsoft Exchange 2000 works under Windows 2000, all of the factors that affect Windows 2000 Server performance described in the first two parts of this book affect the performance of Exchange 2000. The unique demands on the Exchange server such as multiple message databases, services, and logging are what add stress to the Windows 2000 Server in a Microsoft Exchange environment.

RAM and CPU Configuration

Although every operating environment is unique, and configurations differ from organization to organization, there are some relatively simple rules of thumb to use when determining the size of the server and amount of RAM for an Exchange server. Many organizations think that Microsoft Exchange requires a "big" server compared to other messaging systems. Given the same number of e-mail users on Microsoft Exchange, an organization typically can use the same server configuration as other messaging environments. The big difference when using Exchange 2000 occurs when an organization adds functionality or consolidates users in a single Exchange server; then the need for a larger file server becomes apparent. It is the added groupware functionality of Microsoft Exchange, such as WebStore access, intranet document management, network faxing, group and personal scheduling, and remote dialup access functions, that increase demands and require a faster server processor and more memory in an Exchange server.

In a Windows 2000 environment, server RAM plays as important a role as processor speed in determining the capabilities of the server for managing network resources. The more memory in a Windows 2000 Server, the more caching space is available on the server disk, which improves the performance of the network file server. In a network environment in which hundreds of users are accessing the same file server, if the server has more memory, it can potentially service disk read and write requests from RAM rather than having to constantly access the hard disk. When memory is rated in nanoseconds and hard drives are rated in milliseconds, the difference in performance is significant for cached information access.

Also, as more add-in applications such as search engines or document indexing and management utilities are added to Microsoft Exchange servers, the demand on file server RAM by the applications and add-ins increases.

Typically, the rule of thumb for memory in a file server in a highly optimized server configuration is 128 megabytes of base memory plus 16 to 64 megabytes of memory for each add-in application (faxing, search engines, and so on). Thus, a server with 16 gigabytes of disk storage space and Microsoft Exchange installed on top of Windows 2000 should have approximately 128 to 192 megabytes of memory installed. If the same server is also providing WebStore functionality and Web Access services, the same system should have 192 to 256 megabytes of memory.

Table 17-1 shows typical examples of the relationship between the number of users and the common baseline configuration appropriate for an Exchange file server.

Users per File Server	Electronic Mail Only	E-mail/Scheduling/Document Management/Faxing
1 to 100 users	Pentium II processor, 8GB disk space, 128MB RAM	Pentium II processor, 16GB disk space, 192MB RAM
250 users	Pentium III processor, 16GB disk space, 256MB RAM	Pentium III processor, 32GB disk space, 384MB RAM
500 users	Dual-processor Pentium III, 32GB disk space, 384MB RAM	Dual-processor Pentium III, 48GB disk space, 512MB RAM
1,000 users	Split the users across two servers in an administrative group	Split the users across two servers in an administrative group, consider adding a third server for more document and information storage
2,500 users	Split the users across four servers in an administrative group	Split the users across four servers in an administrative group, consider adding fifth and sixth servers for more document and information storage

Table 17-1.   Sample "Per-Server" Configurations for Microsoft Exchange

Although Table 17-1 suggests server configurations, it is advised that you run a capacity analysis utility (described in "Capacity Planning for an Exchange Environment" later in this chapter) to determine the optimal configuration based on the server performance capabilities for your organization.

As noted in Table 17-1, for large and very large workgroups or organizations, the organization may want to consider spreading users or services across multiple servers rather than continuing to add more RAM or more processors. However, for basic e-mail messaging functions, organizations have been able to get 3,500 to 5,000 simultaneous users (over 20,000 overall mailboxes) on a single quad Pentium III server, and for very light Web access use, organizations have been able to store more than 50,000 mailboxes (with more than 5,000 simultaneous connections) on a single quad Pentium III server. Most organizations want not only a high density of users with exceptional performance; they also want very high reliability and quick recovery for the messaging environment. Organizations with fewer users on more systems have a more robust failover and recovery environment.

Hard Drive Configuration

In Microsoft Exchange, the disk storage demands of the file server have a direct relationship to the message storage requirements of the organization. Microsoft Exchange stores user name and folder information in the Active Directory, user mailbox information in the information store databases, and messages in the message database. The administrator of the network does not have to worry about how to manage these storage units. All the administrator needs to do is provide enough disk storage space to handle the storage needs of the organization.

Variations in the type of hard drive hardware (Fast or Wide SCSI, SCSI-2, PCI, cache controller, and so on) can increase the performance of server access based on core hardware improvement specifications. See Chapter 7 for hardware recommendations for the disk subsystem. Obviously, the faster the drive speed, the faster the disk transfer speed, and the better the hardware performance.

Boot Drive

The boot drive is the typical location of the \winnt directory for Windows 2000 executables and DLLs, or Windows executable programs, that are loaded and run as various components are used on the Exchange server. The boot drive is commonly the location for storing the Microsoft Exchange program files as well. Having both the Windows 2000 files and the Microsoft Exchange program files on the boot drive of the server does not drastically affect the server performance. It is common to have a boot drive storage space of 4 gigabytes or more to store all of this information.

The boot drive also is the default location for the Windows 2000 pagefile. You can move your pagefile to a different drive location, but if the drive you put your pagefile on is not accessible on bootup, the system will not boot. The importance of the pagefile is that when the system runs out of RAM, the system will write the overflow information to the system pagefile. As data is read from the server hard drive and then overflows back to the server drive, the drive read/write performance becomes a server bottleneck. Beyond just the performance degradation caused by the server's swapping of memory to disk is the fact that when the initial pagefile size is exceeded, Windows 2000 starts to allocate additional disk space to the pagefile dynamically. When the pagefile is created, disk space is allocated contiguously on the server drive; however, when Windows 2000 is forced to extend the size of the pagefile dynamically, it allocates additional space wherever it is available. This creates a fragmented pagefile on the server. The obvious solution is to have sufficient RAM in the server to prevent the swapping of information to disk in the first place.

Data Drive

The data drive is typically the large storage system for the message databases of the Exchange server. This is the location to direct the placement of Exchange 2000 storage groups. Microsoft Exchange 2000 comes in two versions: Standard Edition and Enterprise Edition. The Standard Edition supports only a single Exchange 2000 storage group for private folder information, with a maximum database size of 16 gigabytes. The Enterprise Edition enables an organization to have up to 4 storage groups, each with up to 6 databases, with a virtually unlimited size for each database.

For performance optimization purposes, it is beneficial for an organization to split the Exchange databases into multiple smaller databases, each stored on a different physical data drive, than to put all of the storage information for an organization in one large database on a single storage subsystem. Each database has a separate index for information, and when the index gets extremely large, it takes a long time to parse it to find the required information. When the database is broken into smaller segments, it is easier to search each of these indexes to find the required information.

Additionally, all databases in a single storage group in an Exchange 2000 environment share a common log file. When very large message attachment files or hundreds of small attachment files are written to multiple databases in a single storage group, the writing of information to the storage group may be delayed as the single log file in the storage group queues the read and write requests. However, if the same amount of information is stored in multiple storage groups, each with its own log file, information can be written in parallel to the multiple databases, multiple storage groups, and multiple transaction logs at the same time.

When creating multiple storage groups and writing to multiple databases within multiple storage groups, you should create multiple physical drive storage units for each set of databases. This countermands a common file system practice of taking several large hard drives and making one large RAID partition out of the drives. Instead, if you take several smaller hard drives and format them individually into separate physical drive partitions, each database and/or each storage group will have its own set of drive platters and read/write mechanisms, increasing the access performance of the Exchange messaging system.

By default, the message databases are stored on the same drive where the Exchange program files are stored. The default location for these files can be moved by opening the Exchange Service Manager administrative tool, under the Server configuration options, within the Storage Group section, and specifying the directories in which the various files should be stored. This is shown in Figure 17-6.

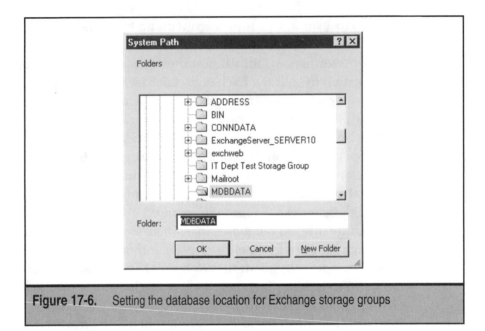

Figure 17-6. Setting the database location for Exchange storage groups

Log Drive

Microsoft Exchange 2000 automatically logs all message transactions in separate message logs to enable recovery of lost messages in the event of a system failure. The log files are typically stored in the same directory as the main message databases. However, because messages are simultaneously stored in both the information store and the log files on the server, extensive disk write sequences are performed.

Exchange 2000 Drive Configuration Recommendation

The optimum configuration for the Exchange server is to have the Windows 2000 system files and pagefile on a dedicated boot drive, the Exchange information store databases on a dedicated data drive configuration, and the log files on a third hard drive subsystem. An Exchange server can run more efficiently if it reads and writes information to multiple drive units instead of bottlenecking on a single drive subsystem.

Disk Fault Tolerance

Disk fault tolerance is critical to minimizing the loss of information caused by system failure. An organization can implement disk fault tolerance through either hardware management or software management. Microsoft Windows 2000 provides software disk fault tolerance for disk mirroring and disk striping, whereas hardware disk fault tolerance requires the purchase of a disk controller that supports hardware fault tolerance.

When possible, an organization should favor hardware fault tolerance over software fault tolerance. The advantages of hardware fault tolerance over software fault tolerance include the following:

▼ **Faster Performance**   Because hardware fault tolerance is managed by a controller card or other hardware device, processing performance is not compromised in providing fault tolerance functionality for the system. Software fault tolerance requires that a certain level of the operating system and system processor be made available to manage the disk fault tolerance of the operating software.

▲ **Error Trapping**   If hard drive subsystem failure occurs, a system that uses software fault tolerance may be affected by the subsystem fault, which potentially can cause the server to halt network operating system functions. A hardware fault tolerance system potentially can isolate the disk failure from the operating system functions and prevent the operating system from halting processing operations.

If the file server hardware vendor provides utilities to create fault-tolerant disk configurations for the server, use the hardware fault tolerance options for disk mirroring, duplexing, or data striping rather than the software options included in the Windows 2000 Computer Management administrative tool.

In an optimized Exchange environment that has a separate boot drive, data drive, and log file drive, follow these fault tolerance suggestions for each of the three separate physical drives:

▼ **Boot Drive**   Drive mirroring is a good solution to ensure protection of system boot processes. A Windows 2000 server cannot boot without a valid boot drive; having mirrored boot drives provides redundancy.

■ **Data Drive**   Data drives on most file storage systems typically involve combining the available storage space on multiple physical drives into a single RAID 5 configuration; however, as described earlier in this section, it is beneficial to the organization to split the databases and storage groups across multiple smaller physical drives, thus improving drive read and write responses. For fault tolerance on these drives, implementing hardware mirroring can ensure data integrity for the information stored in the databases.

▲ **Log Drive**   Since the log drive stores only message logs, the log drive can just be a nonfault-tolerant configuration. By definition, the log drive is a backup of the primary data drive information, so it provides redundant services anyway. Thus, the loss of the log drive has no impact on the integrity of the information stored in the Exchange databases. However, an Exchange 2000 server must be able to write to the log files for all transactions, so if the log drive fails, the Exchange server actually halts operation. Therefore, for data integrity purposes, only a single log drive is needed; however, for server integrity purposes, an organization may choose to implement mirrored log drives.

Server and Storage Group Optimization

As noted in the previous section, multiple servers and multiple storage groups can be used in Exchange 2000 to distribute databases (and thus access load) across multiple drive platters as well as create independent log files and indexes to increase performance. Multiple servers and storage groups can also be used by administrators to specifically distribute load across multiple drive subsystems or servers based on the type and volume of use of the clients in the Exchange environment.

Distributing Load Across User Groups

An organization can specifically create multiple storage groups based on the frequency of access by users of the Exchange environment. Rather than having the frequent users of Exchange all accessing the same server or reading and writing information from the same database, logging can be set so that reports can be generated to identify the users who place the highest demand on the Exchange environment. Once the users have been identified, their mailboxes can be moved to other servers or storage groups, thus distributing the load of the high-demand users across the available resources on the network.

Distributing Load Based on Storage Demands

Another way of determining user demand is by monitoring storage demands. The user or group of users with the highest storage demands can be identified, and their mailboxes can be evenly distributed across the available servers and storage groups in the organization, thus distributing the high read/write load users throughout the Exchange environment.

Distributing Load Based on Information Routing Requirements

The third most frequent method of leveraging multiple servers and storage groups to improve communication performance is monitoring and identifying the information routing demands of the organization. Unlike with the other two options, where you want to identify the users with the highest demands and split them across multiple servers or storage groups, with information routing demands, when communication workgroups or users are identified, you want the users or groups of users that communicate most frequently to be combined on the same server or access information from the same storage group, if possible. As information is routed from user to user, if the users are stored on different servers, a copy of each user's message and transaction needs to flow across the LAN or WAN and be read or written to two different servers, thus increasing transport traffic and read/write requests. However, if users or groups of users with high communication demands share the same server or storage group, then the information does not need to flow across the LAN or WAN, and because Exchange 2000 supports single-instance storage (SIS), attachments sent to multiple users are stored only once per storage group.

For example, if a user sends a 10-megabyte attachment to five different people whose mailboxes are stored on five different servers, over 50 megabytes of information will be transmitted over the LAN/WAN, as the information has to flow to each of the five servers and be stored independently on each of them. However, if the six users are all part of a communication workgroup and are stored in the same storage group on the same server, then when a user sends the same 10-megabyte attachment to those five users, only one copy of the attachment is saved on the server, with links to the common message sent to the five users pointing back to the common attachment. There is no communication traffic across the LAN or WAN, thus drastically improving the overall throughput of information throughout the Exchange environment.

Creating Priority Storage Groups

One technique that is frequently used to improve access and performance by key users is the practice of creating priority storage groups. A priority storage group is nothing more than an Exchange storage group created with a limited number of key Exchange clients sharing the priority storage group. Rather than having 2,000 users stored in a single storage group on a system all sharing the resources of a common storage group, a small storage group can be created on the same server or possibly even on a completely separate server to service the messaging needs of, say, 100 priority executives. Since these users will not have to share the same database, logs, or possibly even the same server as hundreds of other users, their access times and the organization's ability to perform frequent backups, defragmentation, and database compaction of the data for this group are optimized.

While this technique can improve the response time for a server handling an individual's or group of priority individual's requests, this solution does not address any latency in the transfer of messages from the priority server to other servers in the organization, or the time and effort needed perform independent maintenance and service on the priority server. Therefore, the organization should evaluate the performance gains versus the cost of maintenance, support, and server-to-server latency before adopting a multiserver or multistorage group environment for priority user access.

CREATING MULTISERVER CONFIGURATIONS

One way to increase the number of users in an organization without overloading a single server is to distribute the users and the message processing services across multiple servers in the organization. This also provides distributed functions to minimize the central point of failure in the environment. By distributing server functions, large organizations can distribute the management of large sets of users and functions (Internet, fax routing, document management, e-mail, and intranet) to multiple individuals.

Multiserver Configurations

In an organization with hundreds or thousands of users with extensive groupware function demands, although a single server could be upgraded with sufficient memory, processing speed, and disk or network I/O capacity to handle all of the communication demands of the organization, a significant bottleneck is created by placing this much load on a single system. To avoid this bottleneck, organizations can distribute the Exchange server functions to multiple servers.

Private and Public Store Servers

The private information and public information stores can be stored on two separate servers. By making the private information store databases the only messaging databases on a server, mailbox management for individual users is thus moved to a single server.

Private store servers allow an organization to distribute the number of user mailboxes based on the performance capabilities of the Exchange server in the environment. Additionally, if the organization acquires more users and can benefit from distribution of the message mailboxes themselves across multiple servers, the organization can segment the organization into separate Exchange sites.

As with private information stores, public information stores can be moved to a single server that manages only the public information storage needs of an organization. Dedicated public store servers are common in organizations that use Exchange for their organization groupware and intranet needs. The public store is the logical location for an organization to store template documents or publicly accessible messages.

Application Servers

There are many third-party add-in services for Exchange that can provide fax, voicemail, document routing, or other electronic communication services. These add-in services can be added to an existing Exchange server as Windows 2000 services, or depending on the volume of transactions or the capacity of the Exchange server, a dedicated application server may be more appropriate for an organization. Most organizations distribute the add-in application server functions to a dedicated server when more than 70 to 100 users will be using the server for normal messaging and calendaring functions. Therefore, in a small organization or a small workgroup or site of an organization, a single Exchange/add-in application server combination is adequate. There are many cases when distribution of server functions to an additional server is dictated by the add-in software itself, which may limit the number of adapters that can be installed in the server for add-in boards such as fax boards and communications adapters.

Some of the add-in software configuration options are outlined in Table 17-2.

Third-Party Add-in Option	Tunable Configuration Options
Inbound/outbound faxing	Requires fax adapter boards to send and receive faxes. Boards vary in hardware type from ISA to PCI. Boards that offload processing to the fax adapter itself will provide less load to the server processor. Fax software can be installed on a dedicated server to distribute processing load from the Exchange server to the fax server.

Table 17-2. Performance Impact of Add-in Software for Microsoft Exchange

Third-Party Add-in Option	Tunable Configuration Options
Document routing	Document routing puts demands on the server processor and disk subsystem. As a document is routed from user to user, the Exchange server has to determine the intended recipient, the location of the recipient, and the route in which to forward any documents or provide notification. Additionally, document routing stores routed files on the server disk, creating disk read and write demands.
Document management	Document management software gives users the ability to check in and check out documents to the server. This creates a load on the server's processing capabilities and disk subsystem. An index or card file is created for each document as it is accessed. Tracking the status of the document and storing the document create the load on the server.
Pager gateway	Numeric and text pager links require a modem on the server to dial and send pager information. Because most modems use standard serial port communication processes that are interrupt driven, every time the modem is invoked to send a page, the processor is interrupted to communicate with the modem. While this may have a nominal impact on the Exchange server, if many pages are sent throughout the day, it could have a greater impact on the performance of the server.

Table 17-2.   Performance Impact of Add-in Software for Microsoft Exchange *(continued)*

Third-Party Add-in Option	Tunable Configuration Options
Voicemail integration	Voicemail integration in Exchange allows the Exchange server to act as voicemail server. This requires an adapter to link the Exchange server to the phone switch or PBX to accept incoming phone calls. When messages are stored, a data stream is created to ensure that the entire message is received. Voice messages can be very large, and file and disk storage management becomes important in managing Exchange server communications.
Web/POP3/IMAP messaging	There are a number of ways to get access to Exchange 2000 messages over the Internet. Access to these message formats requires that the Microsoft Internet Information Server (IIS) be activated. IIS could be installed on the Exchange server or on a separate server. The decision whether to use a dedicated IIS server depends on the number of mailboxes being used for access with this method and the organization's security controls for external access.

Table 17-2. Performance Impact of Add-in Software for Microsoft Exchange *(continued)*

OPTIMIZING OUTLOOK WEB ACCESS USE

With previous versions of Exchange, most clients in the Exchange environment used the 32-bit Outlook client. However, with the enhanced features and functions of the Outlook Web Access browser, many organizations are using the Outlook Web Access client as their primary or sole client for Exchange information. Therefore, optimizing the implementation and integration of Outlook Web Access in an organization can now be critical.

With the expectation that many organizations will use the Outlook Web Access client as the primary user client for Exchange, Microsoft enables organizations to leverage built-in Windows 2000 and Exchange 2000 technologies to scale and enhance the performance capabilities of Outlook Web Access. The Outlook Web Access load is distributed through the use of front-end and back-end Outlook Web Access servers.

Front-End Outlook Web Access Servers

A front-end Outlook Web Access server is a Windows 2000 server that has the Outlook Web Access components installed on the system. This is the server that Web clients browse to for an Outlook session. The front-end server handles all HTTP, POP3, and IMAP4 protocol sessions. When a user establishes a connection to the front-end server, the first thing that occurs is a validation of the user's credentials for logon authentication. Once the user has been authenticated to the network, the front-end server communicates with the back-end servers to access the user's mailbox information.

A front-end server can be a single server in a networking environment, and in fact the front-end server can also be configured as the back-end server for an Exchange 2000 environment with minimal Outlook Web Access use. Typically, when more than 20 or 30 users are accessing the Exchange Outlook Web Access simultaneously, the organization should consider getting a dedicated front-end server.

NOTE: To optimize the performance of the front-end servers to be focused solely on the protocol communications for Outlook Web Access, as well as to enhance the security of communication of the Outlook Web Access servers, all back-end components installed on the Exchange 2000 Outlook Web Access front-end server should be removed. This includes the Exchange 2000 information store functions, databases, messaging routing, domain management, and replication information not used on the front-end servers.

When the number of client sessions on a single Outlook Web Access system extends beyond 150 or 200 simultaneous connections, the organization should consider adding another front-end server. Through the use of the Windows 2000 Advanced Server network load balancing (NLB) technology, up to 32 front-end servers can be linked together to form an NLB-cluster, thus distributing the logon front-end load across multiple servers, all pointing back to a series of back-end servers in the environment.

NOTE: To be able to use network load balancing, the organization must use Windows 2000 Advanced Server and the Exchange 2000 Enterprise Edition on the Outlook Web Access front-end servers. Because there is no easy way to upgrade from the Windows 2000 Server Edition to the Windows 2000 Advanced Server Edition of networking software, an organization should be certain that it expects to perform network load balancing for its front-end Exchange servers in the near future so that the appropriate version of the Windows 2000 and Exchange 2000 software is installed on the systems during initial installation.

Back-End Outlook Web Access Servers

While the front-end Outlook Web Access servers handle the protocol portion of communications for Web-based messaging clients, back-end servers are implemented to support the hosting of the users' mailboxes for the Exchange environment. The back-end servers are nothing more than the initial Exchange 2000 servers installed on the network. These servers host the Exchange 2000 mailboxes, folders, and message routing functions of Exchange.

An organization does not need to have one front-end server for every back-end server in the environment. All front-end servers point to all back-end servers in the Exchange 2000 administrative group. An organization that has a large number of users accessing Exchange from a Web browser may have several front-end servers network load balanced together, with a single back-end server managing the back-end communications. However, an organization that has just a few users accessing Exchange using a Web browser may find itself with just a single front-end server, with several back-end servers managing the mailboxes for the predominantly 32-bit Outlook client users. And as noted earlier in this section, the front-end services do not necessarily need to reside on a dedicated server, so a single server can be both the front-end and back-end server for an entire administrative group of back-end servers.

CAPACITY PLANNING FOR AN EXCHANGE ENVIRONMENT

Capacity planning in an Exchange environment has three different roles during the life of the server. First, prior to the purchase and installation of the Exchange server software, capacity planning is used to determine the size and capabilities of the new server. Second, after the server has been installed and users are using the system, an analysis is performed to confirm that the server configuration is adequate for the demands of the environment. Third, as the demands of the server change (through addition of users, addition of or changes in add-in applications, increases in inbound and outbound message traffic), incremental capacity analysis is used to ensure that the server can continue to meet the needs of the organization. Capacity planning was addressed in detail in Chapter 2 of this book; this section addresses additional components that are specific to Exchange 2000.

Sizing a New Server Configuration

Before an organization deploys Microsoft Exchange for its messaging environment, tests are usually conducted to determine what size server is appropriate for the organization. The goal of the tests is to determine what server processor, amount of memory, and disk storage capacity is appropriate for the organization. For organizations already using electronic messaging, much of the historical information on message traffic is readily available. Organizations new to electronic messaging or those that will be using some of the advanced groupware capabilities of Exchange will have to estimate their usage and the demands on the server.

There are a few options for determining the size of a new Exchange server. Integrated into Exchange is a free utility called Load Simulator, commonly called loadsim (loadsim.exe). Third-party add-in utilities that provide additional analysis tools for determining the requirements for an Exchange messaging system are also available.

Using Loadsim

The loadsim program can simulate the following:

▼ User-initiated actions (based on user interaction)

- User actions such as sending, receiving, replying to, saving, deleting, and forwarding electronic messages

- User interaction with public folders

- User interaction with Microsoft Scheduler for personal and group scheduling

- Electronic form use, views, and access

▲ Background processes (based on server transactions)

- Transmission and receipt of external messages (Internet messages, MS-Mail messages, site-to-site messages)

- Replication of public folders between multiple sites

- Automatic database compaction and defragmentation

As noted, some of these actions are user initiated and directly affect the interaction between the client and the server, and some of these actions are background processes that affect the performance of the server based on server-invoked transactions. When analyzing the impact of each of these types of processes on the Exchange server, note that the user-initiated actions will typically grow in proportion to the number and activity of the users within the environment. The background processes of the server will grow in proportion to the number of servers, sites, and external connections of the organization.

Loadsim is not a stand-alone modeling simulator, but rather an actual load generating utility. Loadsim will create actual messages and traffic on a network based on the load parameters specified in the configuration of the loadsim utility, so that actual network and server performance can be measured.

Loadsim provides fixed input and output characteristics that are run against an Exchange server in a lab or prototype environment to determine the effects of the load on the server. The four levels for performance testing in loadsim are categorized as very light, light, medium, and heavy. While there are pages of information that describe the various differences in tested characteristics of these levels of users, Table 17-3 summarizes the basic differences.

The value of the results from loadsim depends on accurately determining whether the organization has users that are very light, light, medium, or heavy users of messaging. Most messaging administrators do not know what their users' message traffic patterns are; however, there is a utility that enables existing Exchange 2000 administrators or Outlook client users to analyze historical user traffic. This utility is called storstat.exe, and it is available in the

Parameter	Very Light	Light	Medium	Heavy
# of Nondefault Folders	0	20	40	60
# of Messages per Folder	0	5	5	5
# of Messages in users Inbox	0	1	4	9
# of Messages in Deleted Items	0	1	1	1
Usage (Hrs/Day)	12	8	8	8
# of Messages Sent per Day	4	5	15	30
# of Messages Received per Day	10	23	66	120

Table 17-3. Loadsim Standard Parameters

Microsoft Backoffice Resource Kit; it can also be downloaded from Microsoft. With the storstat utility, a user's mailbox is analyzed, and a single-page report is created noting the average number of messages sent, messages received, number of messages with attachments, size of messages, and the like. All a user needs to do is execute the storstat.exe utility from any Windows 95/98, Windows NT, or Windows 2000 workstation, and the utility will automatically generate a report for the user's message box. The report generated is similar to the one shown here.

```
*********************************************************
Service Provider:  Microsoft Exchange Server
Message Store:  Mailbox - Rand Morimoto
*********************************************************
Total msgs in entire store:  2500
Average messages sent per day is 27.33
Largest number of msgs sent a day is 49
Average number of recipients on a message is 3
Average number of replies per day is 6
Average number of forwards per day is 2
Average number of msgs received per day is 27.33
Maximum number of msgs received in a day is 83
Largest # of messages in any folder is 987
Average folder size is 1847.53K
Number of Inbox rules is 3
```

With the general analysis of average user messaging traffic generated by the storstat utility, an organization can better calculate its messaging use for loadsim reports. Rather than creating a report based solely on averages, loadsim works on the basis of ninety-fifth-percentile statistics. What this means is when the loadsim utility is expected to process a mail message in less than two seconds, it counts only successful transactions that take two seconds or less to complete, not one transaction that takes one second and one transaction that takes three seconds, for an average of two seconds. This provides a more accurate view of events.

The graphs generated by loadsim show the number of users per server based on the relative score of acceptable performance levels.

The score is based on a series of predetermined acceptable response times based on the ninety-fifth percentile for average user demand requests to an Exchange server. The predetermined ninety-fifth percentile for acceptable response to users for read transactions is calculated as Read = 301 ms. Similar response charts calculate ninety-fifth percentile ratings as Send = 1212 ms, Reply = 701 ms, Reply All = 822 ms, Forward = 962 ms, Move = 401 ms, and Delete = 411 ms. Loadsim then uses a predetermined weighting factor as a multiplier of these response times based on the number of times the function is performed during the average day. The results of multiplying the response times by the weighting factor creates the score that is then used to determine the maximum number of users for a specific Exchange server configuration. The greater the processing capacity of the server, the greater the tolerance for the score, and thus the more users that can be added to the server. Loadsim provides a good relative comparison of server configurations based on predetermined transaction numbers. By using the storstat.exe utility to calculate the user transactions for messaging of real-user interactions and fitting those into one of the loadsim models, a messaging administrator can estimate the number of users that can share a server.

Third-Party Performance Analysis Tools

A number of third-party utilities are available for performance and capacity analysis of a Windows 2000 environment. The tools vary as to how and what they measure. Some of the differences to be aware of include the following:

▼   **Real-Time or Simulated Load**   Performance analysis tools vary based on whether they analyze actual read and write information on a production Exchange server, or whether the analysis is conducted merely by simulation. It is better to have a tool that actually tests the read and write requests of a real server so that the load on the organization's LAN, WAN, and actual make and model of hardware is tested as part of the process. Some analysis tools are purely mathematical simulators, so they use a presumed environment and produce reports based on mathematical calculations, with theoretical results. Determine whether the tool you are evaluating reads and writes to a real Exchange server to produce the output results.

- **Intrusive or Nonintrusive Analysis** If you select a tool that actually reads and writes information directly to an Exchange 2000 server, you should determine whether the tool can safely read and write information to an existing production server, or whether a test server should be installed instead. Some intrusive test tools actually overwrite any and all information stored in an Exchange database, populating the database with spurious information that is hard to remove after the test. Typically, these intrusive test tools are intended to be run solely in a test environment on servers that are set up only for test purposes and then reformatted and refreshed after the tests.

- **Simulation of User Interaction** Key to a test of Exchange performance is analysis of real or simulated user interactions, such as message reading and writing, attachment sending, file information access, and the like. The simulation should reflect the types of use of the organization. If all the test tool does is simulate basic sending and receiving of mail messages, yet the organization actually plans to use Exchange for very heavy groupware functions with forms processing, message routing, and large file read/write requests, the tool may not test the appropriate type or level of system communications.

- **Client-Type Access** Because Exchange 2000 supports four uniquely different types of client access methods, it is important to test and simulate the client access (32-bit Outlook, Outlook Web Access, Webstore, or HTTP/FTP) most applicable to the common user access. Web access places a much heavier transaction load on the front-end Outlook Web Access server and little demand on the Exchange server itself, whereas groupware functions from a 32-bit Outlook client place a significantly higher demand directly on the Exchange server.

▲ **Transaction Routing**   One of the major components in validating system demand is the analysis of the routing of information from one Exchange server to another, or if the organization has very high levels of external message communications, then the analysis of routing of information from the Exchange server to an external SMTP, cc:Mail, Lotus Notes, or other messaging system. Message routing performance typically is revealed in the length of time it takes for a message queue to flush. For outbound communications, this is the amount of time messages that are sent from users sit in the Exchange 2000 server until they are finally processed by the Exchange server and sent to other servers. For inbound communications, this is the amount of time it takes for messages to be received by the Exchange 2000 server and then parsed and processed for internal routing to the appropriate user.

Testing Beyond Exchange

During any server capacity analysis, the component being tested (in this case, Microsoft Exchange) should not be the only application environment tested. Just as other applications (for instance, mainframe access, file and print access, data warehouse interactions) affect the performance of Exchange, the implementation and use of Exchange affects these other existing applications. Testing should include other demands on the network to ensure that the implementation of a new messaging system does not negatively affect the performance of the rest of the environment. Capacity analysis testing should also measure file and print access as well as SQL/database access on the network. These measurements can be conducted independently, or the analysis can be conducted as part of the entire testing process of Exchange server.

Using Performance Monitor for Capacity Planning

As organizations extend the services provided by the Exchange environment or add more users to the Exchange organization, they need a way to determine whether an existing server is being overloaded or running as efficiently as it should be. Administrators need to know whether the network is running slowly, why messages take so long to be sent and received, why users complain that their messages never get through to their recipients, and the like. The administrator needs to determine whether there is a bottleneck in the network, and if there is, where the bottleneck resides. Obvious bottlenecks include the server processor, memory, disk capacity, and network adapter, but also can include Internet connections, mail relay servers, WAN connections, third-party add-in applications, and the like.

As described in Chapter 2 of this book, Microsoft provides an administrative tool called Performance (sometimes referred to as perfmon, a legacy name from the tool that shipped with previous versions of the Windows operating system). In addition to the performance testing criteria outlined in Chapter 2 specific to Windows 2000 Server, there are testing components specific to Exchange server that can be analyzed and reviewed.

▼ **Log Byte Writes per Second (under object MSExchangeDB)** This component displays the rate that data is written to the log files on the server, or the linear information processing capabilities of the Exchange environment. When the number of log byte writes per second increases, it means that more information is being processed by the server. This statistic is used to identify times of peak communication with the Exchange server; this statistic can then be used to analyze the Log Sessions Waiting object to determine whether a bottleneck exists during peak transaction periods.

■ **Log Sessions Waiting (under object MSExchangeDB)** This component displays the number of log sessions waiting for a transaction to be completed. Whereas Log Byte Writes per Second showed the log writing capability of the Exchange server, Log Sessions Waiting shows the server capacity. Log Sessions Waiting should be zero for a server that has plenty of bandwidth to handle transaction requests; however, in busy server environments, this number will be greater than zero. When log sessions are waiting, the server does not have enough capacity to manage the transactions being requested. If Log Sessions Waiting is greater than 2 for more than 50 percent of the active operations of the server, server performance is not adequate. If this value occurs frequently, a faster server processor, faster hard disk subsystem, or faster LAN or WAN I/O may be necessary. By reviewing the individual Performance Monitor statistics for server processor, disk I/O, LAN and WAN I/O, and RAM use, the network administrator can determine which of these individual components may be the bottleneck on the server.

■ **SMTP Queue Is Backlogged (under object MSExchangeSMTP)**   Since the SMTP manages messages to other Exchange servers and external message sources such as the Internet, if the SMTP queue is backlogged, external communications resources are overloaded. Like the Log Sessions Waiting object, SMTP Queue is optimal at zero, where no transactions are queued and waiting to be processed, but could realistically be greater than zero. Concern is warranted when the value of this object exceeds zero for more than just a few minutes and never clears to zero for an extended period of time during a day. By looking at additional queue states such as for the MS-Mail Connector, and cc:Mail Connector, performance bottlenecks on external communications resources can be found and tracked to a specific connector or series of connectors in the organization.

▲ **Private Information Store or Public Information Store Are Backlogged (under object MSExchangeIS)**   When the private or public information stores are backlogged, there is an overload of message delivery processing for individual user mailboxes or shared public folders. This can be caused by a large number of users accessing the Exchange private information store, the large size of messages being read or written by users, or the distribution of messages between users for the private information store object. If the organization is using document management or document routing software or is using an Exchange server as an intranet where large datasets are being managed and manipulated, the public information store statistic will be affected. Again, both of these numbers should ideally be zero, and definitely should not remain above zero for an extended period of time during the day. If they remain greater than zero throughout a day, additional analysis of hardware I/O components such as the processor, disk, RAM, or network I/O should be performed to determine what hardware component needs to be upgraded to keep the backlog value for the information stores at zero.

The trick to reviewing and analyzing the Performance tool statistics for Exchange is not to expect the statistics to tell you exactly where the problem resides. The statistics gathered by the Performance tool for the objects listed here can tell you only that a problem exists. You must then use these Performance tool components to identify what object is the source of the problem. In most cases, problems occur because of improperly configured or tuned hardware components (drive configurations, caching, LAN adapter performance, or the like) that affect the components of the Exchange server environment. When properly used, the Performance tool can alert the administrator to impending problems in Exchange server or other related server components.

Planning for Additional Load on an Existing Server

You also need to analyze what an increase in the number of users or server function demands will do to the performance of the environment. The goal is to determine the existing operation of the server, determine the growth requirements of the organization, and then model the growth to determine whether the server will be sufficient.

Baseline

A baseline is a level that the administrator can use as a starting point for comparative analysis of the environment. The best things to baseline in an Exchange server environment are: server processor utilization, server RAM utilization, network LAN and WAN bandwidth utilization, number of messages sent and received by users at the site, and gateway and connector traffic. Start by creating a baseline standard of the working environment at all different times of the day, since demand loads differ at morning, midday, and evening within any communications environment. Then determine the performance of the server for various levels of system capacity during these various times of the day to determine the impact of the various loads and demands in the environment. With baselines during normal and stressed periods of the day, week, or month, if a problem in the network is reported, the administrator can run performance analysis and compare the current performance with the baseline.

Baselines are not something created once, with the results filed in a notebook for any future comparisons. Baselines are dynamic and should be re-created periodically to confirm that they reflect the most current status of the network. If users are added to the network, the baseline for the organization will change, and new statistical information should be collected. Also, if new applications or services, such as Internet connectivity, a new software application, network faxing, remote network access, or enhanced WAN connectivity capabilities, are added to the network, each of these can affect the state of the network to the point where a new baseline should be created.

Modeling Performance Requirements

With a solid, up-to-date baseline in place, before changes are made to the network, an organization can model and even project with relative accuracy any changes in the environment. For example, if the organization has added 20 new users to the network twice before and each time a new baseline was taken, if the organization wants to add 20 more users to the network, a comparison can be made using the historical data. If this data reveals that network performance diminished by 3 percent each time 20 new users were added, then it can be assumed that this new addition of 20 users will also decrease network performance by 3 percent.

To confirm this expectation, actual modeling of performance can be conducted. First, make sure that you have a baseline of the existing system performance. Then determine the expected increase in demand or growth for the network. Set up a performance modeling utility such as loadsim or a third-party analysis tool to model the additional load. The utility will be able to determine the effect of the new load on the capacity and capability of the environment.

USING REPLICATION TO MINIMIZE COMMUNICATION TRAFFIC

In many Exchange environment configurations, you may not need to constantly upgrade servers, LAN connections, or WAN router links to maintain the performance capability of the environment. Instead of tuning and upgrading servers to handle message workload, you can also consider strategies that extend the existing infrastructure to handle the increased demands of the organization. These strategies include implementing replication services from server to server as well as using public folders for centralized message storage.

Fundamentals of Replication Services

As organizations begin to deploy public folder shares, share schedules, and electronically route information throughout the organization, the need to communicate outside of a single Microsoft Exchange server to other Exchange servers in different business units becomes critical. Microsoft Exchange provides the mechanism for replicating selected information from one server to another.

The replication information can be anything from a single folder all the way through the entire public folder structure of the entire organization, depending on whether the users on other Exchange servers or at different sites need to access the shared information. An example of sharing an entire public folder structure is an organization that is storing only corporate policies, marketing documents, and global client information in public folders. This information is valuable to all members of the organization and should be readily available to all employees regardless of their location.

However, an organization that splits its public information storage into global information and regional information may have some folders on its servers that are corporatewide and should be replicated, and some folders that have local business information that does not need to be replicated. In this case, the organization can designate replication of only those folders that have global corporate information and leave the rest of the folders locally accessible with no replication to other sites.

Site-to-Site Replication

Once the organization determines what information it is storing and what information needs to be replicated from site to site, it needs to configure its Microsoft Exchange servers to replicate the information, set up a security system to prevent users from accidentally or purposely deleting or modifying information, and manage the information that is replicated throughout their organization.

On the Microsoft Exchange server, the Exchange administrator can identify which folders should be replicated with other Exchange servers and how often the information should be replicated. During the replication process, the Exchange servers communicate with each other and compare the information to be replicated. The servers then determine which information is not identical and so needs to be copied. The information may be different because something was added to a folder that needs to be replicated, something was deleted from a folder, or the content of a message or object within a folder was modified. The Exchange servers then determine what information needs to be sent and what information needs to be received between the two servers; then they begin the process of updating files, objects, and stored information.

The replication process can be configured to run continuously throughout the day whenever information is found to be out of sync and in need of updating, or Exchange server replication can be updated at a specific time (or at specific times) during the day. There is a distinct trade-off between up-to-date information and server performance. To keep the information up-to-date between sites, the organization needs to implement continuous replication; however, replication can use 10 to 15 percent of the server's available processing bandwidth. Many organizations elect to minimize the frequency with which information is replicated between sites throughout the day based on the organization's need for current information. It is best to run baseline comparisons with and without replication activated to determine the demands that replication makes on the server's capacity.

The frequency of replication depends on the bandwidth capability of the Exchange servers and the need to have updated information on both servers. If an organization requires up-to-date information, but the Exchange server updates information only once a night, the users potentially are using information that is an entire day old and may be of little value. The organization may have a requirement than information be updated hourly; however, if the two Exchange servers rely on very slow 19.2 Kbps data line, during a full replication process, the Exchange servers can potentially tie up the entire bandwidth, leaving no communication link bandwidth available for other business purposes.

Checking Replication Status

Once the information is secured, someone within the organization needs to determine how often the information should be examined and maintained. If the information is relatively static (like company policies or procedures), it may need to be reviewed only once a quarter or once a year. However, if the information needs to be updated weekly or monthly, as company marketing information or company product information may need to be, then the old information needs to be deleted so that it is not accidentally used or accessed (or unnecessarily taking up disk storage space). New information can then be updated on the server.

Global Catalog Replication vs. Message Replication

You should note that replication of the global catalog is a completely different function than replication of message information and public folders in an Exchange environment. As noted throughout this section, message information and public folder replication is administered through the Exchange Service Manager and is specific to communications within Exchange 2000. However, global catalog replication of users, distribution lists, or other message directory information is managed from the Windows 2000 Active Directory Sites and Services administrative tool.

Since Active Directory is the source and repository of all directory information within an Active Directory environment, and the global catalog is the directory catalog, all replication relative to directory information is outside the scope of Exchange 2000. Refer to Chapter 10 for information on managing the replication process of Active Directory.

OPTIMIZING SERVER PERFORMANCE THROUGH ONGOING MAINTENANCE

Everyone knows about defragmenting hard drives and compressing files to improve the performance of information access on a workstation or in a general database environment. The same can be done to improve the performance of Microsoft Exchange since the Exchange server is nothing more than a database system of messages. Exchange 2000 provides automatic compaction and defragmentation of its databases; however, there are different levels of tuning that are worth noting. In the discussions that follow, *IS maintenance* and *compaction* refer to automated server maintenance, and *defragmentation* refers to a manual server maintenance process.

IS Maintenance

IS maintenance is the automatic tuning of the Exchange information store that takes place between the hours of 1 A.M. and 6 A.M. Information store maintenance performs the following tasks:

▼ **Tombstone Compression** Tombstone compression occurs when a message is deleted by all users on the Exchange server and no longer needs to be stored. The message is automatically eliminated from the Exchange server; however, a hole still exists where the message used to reside. During IS maintenance, the hole is filled in with other active messages, leaving the end of the Exchange message store as the area of free message storage space.

- ■ **Index Aging**   Index aging is the maintenance of the indexes created by users when there are different views of information in a message store. There is always a default view that users see when they access a folder; however, different views of the information stored in a folder can be created to simplify the visual display of information on users' screens. An index is created for each view created by users and is stored on the Exchange server. The indexes are maintained on the server as long as the user accesses the different views, but if the indexes are not used, they are deleted from the system to free up disk space on the server.

- ▲ **Message Expiration Management**   The administrator of an Exchange server can set expiration dates or limits on folders. These folder expiration times cause automatic clean up of the message database on a nightly basis.

Compaction

Compaction is the process of online defragmentation and reclamation of unused disk storage space. Exchange 2000 has a garbage collection interval, at which time expired tombstones are permanently deleted. After the expired tombstones are deleted, the database is defragmented for efficiency, with open spaces in the message databases filled in with other messages. However, the size of the Exchange server message database is not changed, and any unused space is marked as available for use. The only way to compact, defragment, and compress the message store database file is to perform an offline compression operation called defragmentation.

Defragmentation

Defragmentation is the offline defragmentation of the Exchange message information stores. Offline defragmentation is more efficient than online defragmentation since the process has full access and full server bandwidth to manage the information store. During offline defragmentation, the Exchange services need to be stopped, and the utilities run from a DOS or command prompt. The defragmentation utility in Exchange 2000 is the ESEUTIL.EXE tool. During offline defragmentation, all expired tombstones are deleted, open spaces within the database are filled with messages compressed within the message store, and excess message database storage space is released, thus decreasing the size of the information store databases.

Staggering Backups by Storage Groups in Exchange 2000

Because Exchange 2000 provides the ability to divide message information into multiple databases as well as into multiple storage groups, the backup process can be optimized to back up information in a logical process. Rather than backing up all of the databases in a single storage group, thus affecting the performance of a single server or the logs of a single storage group, an organization should consider backing up databases across multiple servers and then databases across multiple storage groups, thus minimizing the direct impact on a single storage group.

While this staggering of backups is irrelevant for most organizations that back up their network nightly, when a limited number of users are online on the network anyway, because Exchange 2000 gives organizations the ability to create priority storage groups (as noted earlier in this chapter), a priority storage group can be set for backup several times during the day, thus improving recoverability of an Exchange environment in the event that a server or drive subsystem fails during the middle of the day.

Many backup and maintenance practices need to be reconsidered, since Exchange 2000 decreases the database size and provides a new mechanism that distributes information across multiple servers and multiple storage groups that did not exist in previous versions of Exchange.

OPTIMIZING THE EXCHANGE CLIENT

Now that we have reviewed the optimization capabilities of the server component of the Microsoft Exchange server configuration, we will now look at the client component in this client-server environment. In Microsoft Exchange, the client component of the Exchange environment is just as important as the server component of the system. While the server manages the messages, the transfer of the messages from server to server, or from the server to the Internet, the client component manages electronic forms, filtering of message views, and general rich text display of the Exchange messages.

Latest Release of the Client

Over the life of the Microsoft Exchange product, there have been significant improvements in the client software available to access the Exchange environment. The two major clients are called the Exchange client and the Outlook client. The Exchange client was the first-generation client software for Exchange. It supported DOS, Windows 16-bit, Windows 32-bit, and the Macintosh. The Exchange client is the client found in Windows 95 (and is also known as the Windows Messaging client). The Exchange client has separate programs for scheduling and for the address book. In mid 1997, Microsoft announced that it was focusing future-generation clients on Outlook. The Outlook client integrates messaging, calendaring, contact address book, notes, journaling, and intranet capabilities in a single application. The advantage of the Outlook client is the ability to have one program manage all electronic messaging and groupware functionality. This simplifies the cross-platform support of a single interface for multiple functions across multiple operating environments. Today, the Outlook client supports Windows 16-bit, Windows 32-bit, Macintosh, and Web formats.

It is important to maintain the latest release of the Exchange or Outlook client to ensure the best performance of the client software. Since the client software makes up 50 percent of the client-server functionality of Exchange, the client performance is crucial to the overall user access to the system. The latest release of the clients for Exchange are noted on the Microsoft Exchange Web site (http://www.microsoft.com/exchange) and are frequently downloadable (although, by licensing requirements, some of the client updates require that an existing version reside on the hard drive of the system being upgraded).

Client Hardware Configuration

The client hardware is important in the performance of the client-to-server interaction with Exchange. Although the basic functions of Exchange can be run on very low-performance Web-based terminals, the full groupware capabilities of Exchange typically require a Windows 32-bit workstation with at least 32 megabytes of memory and at least 100 megabytes of available disk space. Most organizations have found that the Outlook client runs best on a system with 64 to 96 megabytes of memory. Most systems are used for more than just messaging, and more RAM is needed to load the desktop operating system, one or two other desktop productivity applications such as a word processing program or an Internet browser, plus the 32-bit Outlook client. The increased performance of the client system is needed since functions such as message sorting, message filtering, and message management occur on the client system, not on the Exchange server.

Client Service Uses the NetBIOS Name

One factor frequently overlooked in performance analysis of an Exchange environment is the effect of the use of the Windows NetBIOS name in resolving client and server names. The Exchange client uses NetBIOS names to find the Exchange server; thus, if the organization is using TCP/IP as its sole communications protocol in a Windows environment, a method to resolve the NetBIOS name with a TCP/IP-compatible lookup process is needed for the Exchange client to find the Exchange server. In a purely Windows 2000 environment, name resolution is handled solely by the Domain Naming System (DNS); however, most organizations still have a mix of non–Windows 2000 systems, so that name resolution depends on the implementation and use of Windows Internet Naming Service (WINS) or the use of a static file on the client called the LMHOST file.

On a congested network, the time needed for a client to resolve a name with a LAN- or WAN-based WINS or DNS server can be significant enough to slow down the process of finding and connecting to the Exchange server. If it takes a long time for a client to authenticate and access the Exchange server, a test should be performed to determine how long it is taking for the client to resolve the NetBIOS name over the network. This can be accomplished through the use of built-in Windows tools such as ping.exe, tracert.exe, and nbtstat.exe.

Using PST Instead of the Information Store

Many organizations that want to minimize the traffic on their networks use local personal store (PST) files to manage messages with minimal impact on the Exchange server itself. A PST file is a separate file, typically stored on a user's local hard drive, where messages are copied from the Exchange server to the PST when the user accesses the Exchange server. The advantage of the PST file is that all messages are transferred once from the Exchange server to the PST file, and thereafter any time the user wants to access the file, the request is managed locally (with no demands placed on the LAN, WAN, or Exchange server).

While this offloads demands external to the client, the PST file method eliminates all administrative benefits that Exchange 2000 provides. A non-PST-configured Exchange client allows the administrator to put limits on the age and storage demands of the Exchange client, forcing Exchange users to perform periodic maintenance of their mailboxes. Exchange also does not normally depend on users to back up their own PST files on a regular basis, but going to a PST-based environment makes it up to the users to maintain backups of their messages (whereas most organizations now place the responsibility of backup and network maintenance in the hands of professional I/S personnel). Further, the PST method does not allow users to roam from station to station or from operating system environment to operating system environment. Messages reside only in the PST file sitting on the user's workstation, and if the user decides to work remotely or from another workstation, the PST does not follow the user.

It is commonly found that although the PST file method offloads a significant amount of bandwidth and storage demands from the Exchange server and infrastructure, it places too many responsibilities on the users and drastically limits the organization's ability to leverage the centralized management and mobile access functions of the product.

Remote Access Exchange

For organizations that have remote and mobile users, Microsoft Exchange provides functionality that improves system performance and offers user-level efficiencies. Microsoft Exchange for remote users is handled by the exact same client software as used by LAN-based users; thus, users need no retraining, and no special software needs to be purchased. The configuration of a remote Exchange user requires one additional step. This additional step creates a file called the Offline Store (OST) that is a replica of the user's message information stored on the Exchange server. When a user dials into Microsoft Exchange, the user can work offline, creating messages that are queued in the OST file. When the user elects to synchronize offline and Exchange server messages, any messages stored in the offline queue are sent to the Exchange server, and any messages waiting for the user on the Exchange server are copied to the user's offline store file. Any modifications or changes the user makes to the offline store file are automatically updated to the Exchange server. Thus, if messages are deleted, moved, or edited, the changes are reflected on the Exchange server after synchronization. If the user logs onto the network over the LAN, because all messages were synchronized offline from the remote system, the LAN-connected user sees the state of all messages just as if the user were working offline. Changes are forwarded, updated, modified, and replicated across all platforms.

A common additional use of Microsoft Exchange's remote access functions is at remote sites that have limited WAN bandwidth connection to a centralized Exchange server. Rather than installing an Exchange server at every single site or trying to have users connected full time over a very slow 19.2 Kbps line, an organization can implement Offline Stores to have users' messages created and queued on their local hard drive. When they synchronize their message boxes, outbound messages are sent to the Exchange server, and inbound messages are retrieved to the client. This enables the use of Exchange in limited-bandwidth environments.

Optimizing a Microsoft Exchange 2000 environment is not that much different than optimizing performance in a standard Microsoft Windows 2000 environment. The tools used to tune and optimize the two environments are similar. For Microsoft Exchange, however, you can apply additional tools and utilities to perform analysis, baselining, tuning, and management functions specific to the electronic messaging components of Exchange.

It is crucial that you perform capacity analysis testing and project performance demands when implementing Microsoft Exchange. Very few products make as many demands on the entire Windows 2000 infrastructure as electronic messaging. From basic electronic mail messages to group appointment calendar management, these tasks are core to many businesses these days. With the use of the new groupware capabilities that Exchange and third-party Exchange add-ins provide, such as voicemail integration, document routing, document imaging, and Internet connectivity, the impact of client-to-server communications, large file transfers and storage, and mobile computing on the Windows 2000 infrastructure is greater than ever before.

CHAPTER 18

Maximizing Terminal Services

Windows 2000 Terminal Services provides a thin-client approach to computing, hearkening back to the days of main frames. All of the computing takes place at a centralized large computer, and all of the data is accessed from that central computer. The clients are basically dumb terminals, though the client software may be running a full-sized desktop. The clients can run in a Web browser, on hand-held devices, or on full-sized desktop computers. The technology allows for local printing and file access (with some extensions).

Terminal Services can lower the total cost of ownership, though initial capital costs may be higher. This increase in capital costs is due to the fact that while the client costs are lower, the server infrastructure cost grows correspondingly and is typically over-engineered to handle the worst-case client load. Where the total cost of ownership is lowered is in the long-term savings on reduced maintenance overhead. This reduction in maintenance overhead is especially true as the number of users supported increases and the size of the Terminal Server infrastructure grows. However, as the Terminal Server infrastructure grows, it needs to be tuned to ensure fast performance and scalability. This chapter describes not how to set up a Windows 2000 Terminal Server, but how to maximize performance of the Terminal Services.

COMPONENTS

From a performance perspective, four components are key to the performance of a Windows 2000 Terminal Services installation: the server, the client, the application, and the network link (see Figure 18-1). These all can be optimized to varying degrees.

Slow performance in any of these components can lead to a bottleneck in the end user experience. Before optimizing the installation, however, you need to understand the components.

Server

The server is the center of the Terminal Services infrastructure, where all the computing takes place. It is also where both user application

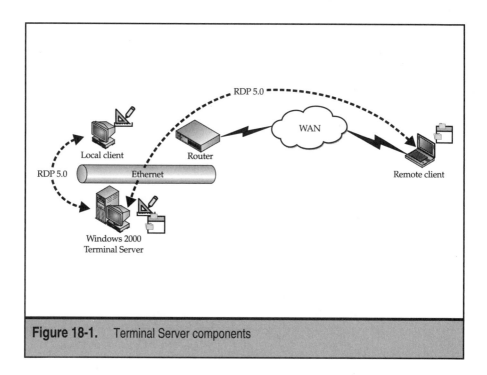

Figure 18-1. Terminal Server components

processing and most of the communications processing (such as compression and encryption of the data to be transmitted) occurs.

Hardware

Sessions share the same hardware platform, as they are running virtually on the server. The processor and memory are usually the key constraining hardware resources, with disk access and network access being secondary.

Each independent session is allocated a portion of memory initially and can request additional memory as needed. Memory is allocated from the central pool of virtual server memory, which is finite and bounded by the combination of physical memory and the pagefile. This is exactly the same as with a Windows 2000 desktop or server, only multiplied by the number of user sessions attached to the Windows 2000 Terminal Server.

Terminal Services sessions share the processor of the server, so overall processor power can make a big difference in performance.

However, as discussed in the "Applications" section later in this chapter, not all applications are created equal with regard to processor load, so the applications you are running can determine just how big a difference overall processor power makes. During operation, processor time is allocated among the operating system and the various sessions. Again, since the sessions all run on the server, they all share the same processor resources.

Disk resources are also shared by the operating system and terminal sessions, but this turns out to be less of a constraining factor than the processor or memory. Most applications are relatively frugal with disk access, though there are exceptions. For example, if physical memory is constrained and sessions request more than is available, the operating system will allocate more than the available physical memory, using the virtual memory capabilities of Windows 2000. In other words, it will swap memory to the pagefile on disk, increasing the utilization of the disk subsystem.

The network interface is used both for local data access, such as access to a database or file share, and for session traffic, such as screen scrapes and mouse movements (the user interface). Database and file access depend on the application being used, as does user interface traffic. The Terminal Services connection protocol is very efficient in transmitting the user interface, so this is less of problem than might be expected.

Operating System Resources

Even though sessions get their own desktop when establishing a session, they really don't get a completely unique operating system. Some of the core operating system and application code is cloned for each user, but still there are many shared software components that users have to contend for.

One of the resources that has the greatest impact is the paging file. The operating system creates a single pagefile or collection of pagefiles that all processes share. A user running an application that requires lots of memory may force a page swap of other process memory to the pagefile. If two users are doing this, they will, in effect, contend for the pagefile, even though the operating system is handling the memory allocation and swapping.

Other operating system resources that will be contended for are the Registry and system services. With few user sessions, this is not too much of a problem. With many users on a single server, this can become a bottleneck. Applications that are requesting access to the Registry or system services will have to wait for those resources to become free, degrading overall performance. To make matters worse, in any organization users on a Terminal Server will tend to use the same applications at the same time. This exacerbates resource contention.

Terminal Services Modes

Windows 2000 Terminal Services can operate in either of two modes: remote administration and application server. The mode used dramatically changes the behavior of the service.

Remote administration mode is new in Windows 2000 and allows a fully graphical view of a Windows 2000 Server for remote administration purposes. Administrators can use any of the tools and access all aspects of the server from any Terminal Services client. Clients are discussed later in this chapter.

Application server mode allows administrators to set up a Windows 2000 Server so that multiple clients can access applications and desktops from a Terminal Services client. The applications are installed, managed, and run on the Windows 2000 Server, with screen images being sent to the clients, and the clients sending mouse and keyboard information to the server. Figure 18-2 shows the server being set for application server mode.

This chapter focuses almost exclusively on Terminal Services in application server mode. There is little need to maximize performance in remote administration mode, whereas there is a great need to maximize performance in application server mode.

Clients

Operating System

Windows 2000 Terminal Services clients support a wide variety of operating systems. There are clients for:

▼ Windows 2000

■ Windows NT

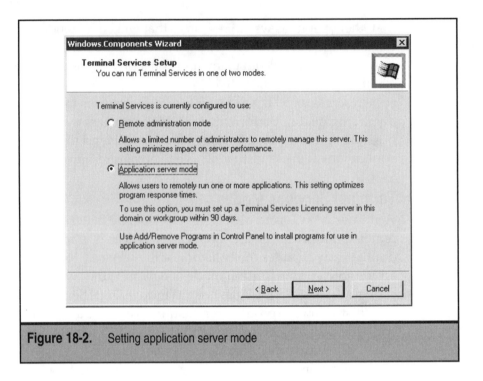

Figure 18-2. Setting application server mode

- Windows 9.*x*
- Windows for Workgroups 3.11
- ▲ Windows CE

Although not directly supported by Microsoft, third-party vendors also provide support for Terminal Service on other operating systems, such as UNIX, Apple Macintosh, and MS-DOS.

Terminal Service Clients

Available Terminal Service clients include the following types:

- ▼ **32-Bit** The 32-bit client is used for Windows 2000, Windows NT, Windows ME, and Windows 9.*x*.

- **Terminal Services Advanced Client (TSAC)** TSAC allows users to access Terminal Services through a browser using an ActiveX Control. TSAC is supported by Windows 2000,

Windows NT, Windows ME, and Windows 9.x running Internet Explorer 4.0 and above.

■ **16-Bit**   The 16-bit client is used for Windows for Workgroups 3.11 with MS TCP/IP-32.

▲ **Windows CE**   The Windows CE client is used for Windows CE-based terminals and hand-held devices. Windows CE is the name of Microsoft's palm-sized PC operating system.

The clients all provide a full virtual Windows 2000 desktop to the device with very few hardware requirements.

Hardware Profile

Terminal Services is designed to be a thin-client solution, which means that it does not require a high level of resources at the client side. As can be seen from the range of client types supported, Terminal Services provides quite a bit of support for older operating systems. Going hand in hand with older operating systems is older hardware, which tends to have dramatically lower performance. Fortunately, Terminal Services was designed to be able to run on clients with a reduced hardware profile.

Each client requires very little resource overhead to run, so if an application can be launched, it will run effectively. Some additional processing power is useful for compression, and some additional disk space is needed for bitmap caching, but these are not required.

Windows Terminal Devices

In addition to standard PC systems, there are now CE-based Windows Terminal devices, commonly called WinTerm devices, after the popular Wyse WinTerm. In these devices, the Remote Desktop Protocol (RDP) client is built into a dedicated box. Some have the monitor built in, and others require an external keyboard, monitor, and mouse.

The Windows Terminal devices typically are small, are easy to configure, and require very little maintenance. They have no moving parts, such as a hard drive, so they have good mean time between failure rates.

The disadvantage is that they are relatively expensive, especially when the additional cost of the back-end infrastructure is taken into account. There are also some cultural barriers to overcome, as most users are accustomed to having a full-fledged system on their desks.

Applications

Applications are both the reason for having Terminal Services and the most likely source of performance problems. In effect, Terminal Services delivers applications to remote desktops. Applications are also the least controllable aspect of the Terminal Services infrastructure, as users may be using well-behaved 32-bit applications on one hand and poorly designed, memory-hogging, processor-hoarding, single-user 16-bit applications on the other.

Application Footprint

When evaluating the performance of a Windows 2000 Terminal Services infrastructure, you need to take into account the resource requirements of the application. This is sometimes referred to as the application footprint. The more resources required to run the application, the bigger the footprint of the application.

A small-footprint application will typically not require very much processing time or memory to run. Examples of small-footprint applications include Notepad and Calculator. Admittedly, in today's office environment, there are few small-footprint applications.

Applications with medium-sized footprints require reasonable amounts of processing time and memory. Examples of these types of applications include the Microsoft Office suite and Internet Explorer. These are some of the most common applications used in office environments.

Large-footprint applications are those that require extensive processing time and memory. Examples of large-footprint applications include Microsoft Visio and many custom line-of-business applications.

Graphics

The amount of graphics that an application generates also affects system performance. The original Windows NT Terminal Server

Edition had serious performance problems when applications used even a moderate level of graphics.

Windows 2000 Terminal Services is markedly better at handling graphics than previous versions, thanks to extensive work by Microsoft to address the problem. The improvement is so great that running a Windows 2000 Terminal Services session and browsing the Web using Internet Explorer is almost the same as when working from a dedicated Windows 2000 desktop.

That said, application graphics do place an additional load on the Windows 2000 Terminal Services infrastructure. This is especially true when many sessions launch graphics-intensive applications simultaneously. The "Application Tuning" section explores ways to reduce the load that graphics place on the system.

Local Resources

Applications also share access to local resources on the Terminal Server, such as directly attached printers, CD-ROM drives, hard disk drives, and the network connection. Fortunately, Windows 2000 is a multiuser operating system and designed to handle resource contention among various processes, and so works well within the multiple-session model of Terminal Services. Unfortunately, this sharing of services does result in degraded performance if too many sessions attempt to use the same resource at the same time.

Network Link

Normally, the network link is a given. It is typically too expensive to modify, and any solution is built around the network link. Servers can be upgraded, clients can be replaced, and software can be improved, but network links are immutable. Even where they are subject to change, it is not within the scope of this book to optimize network infrastructures.

Nevertheless, it is important to understand the effects that the network link has on a Windows 2000 Terminal Services session. This section also discusses the Remote Desktop Protocol (RDP) .

Connection

The connection over which the session is being conducted is important to the performance of the session. The two factors that influence performance are the bandwidth and the latency of the link. Bandwidth, essentially, is how fast data can come through the connection. Latency is how long it takes for any given bit of data to travel from one end of the connection to the other.

Terminal Services has been designed to handle low-bandwidth conditions very well, but it does not tolerate latency quite as well.

Remote Desktop Protocol

The Remote Desktop Protocol (RDP) manages the communication between the server and the client. It is based on and extends the T.120 protocol standards. Version 5.0 introduces a number of features and performance improvements over version 4.0, including:

- ▼ **Improved Algorithms**   The algorithms for sending screen updates have been improved to reduce sensitivity to link latency and low bandwidth. This improvement has reduced overall response time by 50 percent and bandwidth used by 80 percent over the RDP 4.0 client.

- ■ **Improved Client**   The RDP clients have been tuned to reduce local CPU utilization as compared to the RDP 4.0 version.

- ■ **Compression**   While still using the same compression algorithms as in version 4.0, the algorithms have been tuned to reduce the bandwidth needed and also to reduce server overhead.

- ■ **Bitmap Caching**   Bitmaps are cached in memory to avoid having to retransmit the same bitmaps during a session, reducing bandwidth needs.

- ■ **Glyph Caching**   Glyphs are bitmap representations of characters and their font information. Bitmap representations allow clients to display fonts that they might not have installed locally. Caching them reduces the overhead of transmitting the glyphs over the connection.

- ■ **Persistent Bitmap Caching**   In addition to caching the bitmaps during the session, version 5.0 also can cache bitmaps on disk between sessions. This further reduces the bandwidth requirements.

- ▲ **Encryption**   Version 5.0 provides a measure of protection against hackers by encrypting the data using a 56- or 128-bit implementation of RSA Security's RC4 cipher, though at the expense of performance.

Many of these new features are targeted at improving the performance of the connection. The next section looks at the effects of changing the settings for these and other features.

TUNING THE COMPONENTS

Microsoft has done a great job of optimizing Windows 2000 Terminal Services and the Remote Desktop Protocol, making the administrator's job much simpler. Unlike with some parts of Windows 2000, tuning Terminal Services is straightforward and painless.

This section looks at ways to tune the server, client, and applications. It also discusses how to build large server farms to support more users than a single server can.

Server Tuning

The two main constraining factors in a Windows 2000 Terminal Server are the memory and the processor. This section discusses the settings that you can adjust.

Evaluating Performance

Evaluating the performance of a Windows 2000 Terminal Server requires looking for bottlenecks and resolving them. Detecting a bottleneck in a Terminal Services server is similar to detecting bottlenecks in a standard Windows 2000 Server, but the baseline values for the counters may be different. For example, high memory utilization on a Terminal Server may be normal if the server has a large number of concurrent users, whereas the same high value in a Windows 2000 file server may signify a problem.

For general tuning parameters, refer to the following chapters in this book:

▼ Chapter 6, "Boosting Memory Performance"

■ Chapter 7, "Optimizing the Disk Subsystem"

▲ Chapter 8, "Maximizing Network Subsystem Performance"

Follow the guidelines in the appropriate chapter to tune the server. The balance of this chapter discusses tuning details that pertain to Terminal Servers.

Remote Administration vs. Application Server Mode

Although the remote administration and application server modes both use the same basic technology, the remote administration mode is designed to keep the server overhead low, and the application server mode is designed to improve client performance. To accomplish this, the remote administration mode does not load some of the application compatibility code that is used by the application server mode. Also, the remote administration mode leaves the Windows 2000 Server optimized for background services, whereas the application server mode changes the focus of Windows 2000 Server optimization to application performance (see Figure 18-3).

Microsoft recommends that remote administration be enabled on all Windows 2000 Servers, for ease of administration. Running in remote administration mode has minimal impact on the performance of the server, as intended. The number of sessions is also limited to two concurrent sessions, as the main purpose of the remote administration mode is to administer the host server. Given these factors, no tweaking is required.

For a Windows 2000 Server running in application server mode, however, there are definite advantages to tweaking the configuration. With a large number of users, performance does become a concern. Even a relatively small number of users running a poorly configured application on a poorly tuned server can result in performance problems.

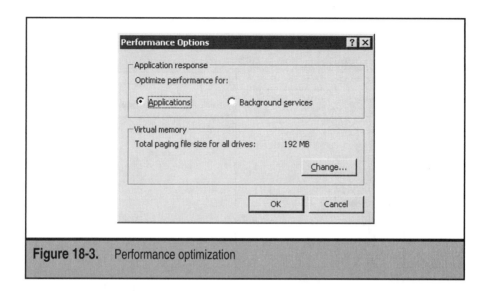

Figure 18-3. Performance optimization

Server Settings to Tweak

The server settings specific to Windows 2000 Terminal Services are not very numerous, as shown in Figure 18-4, and only two are really useful for performance tuning.

The server settings are configured using the Terminal Services Configuration tool, under the Server Settings folder. The settings relevant to performance are as follows:

▼ **Terminal Server Mode** This displays, but does not allow you to change, the terminal server mode. When the server is in application server mode, performance is improved for sessions. To change the mode, go to Add/Remove Programs in the Control Panel.

▲ **Active Desktop** This setting determines whether the sessions are allowed to use Active Desktop, which can be a major performance issue. Active Desktop allows active Web content to be placed on the desktop, which is a very graphics-intensive approach. Active Desktop is enabled by default; it should be disabled to reduce overhead.

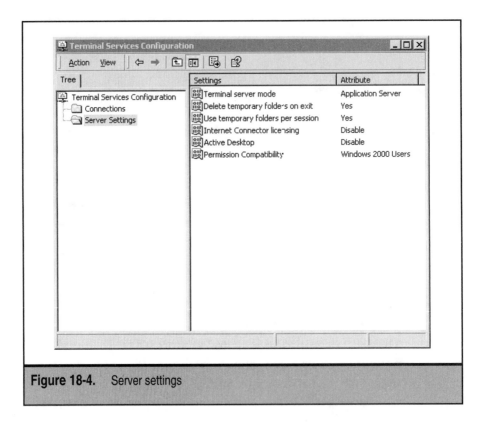

Figure 18-4. Server settings

In the Connections folder, there is really only one performance-specific configuration. This is the encryption setting, which determines the level of encryption that the server and client perform to ensure communication secrecy. By default, encryption is set to medium (see Figure 18-5).

The encryption setting indicates the following:

▼ **Low** With this setting, data sent to the server from the client is encrypted with a 56-bit key, which protects passwords that the user enters. Data sent to the client from the server is not encrypted, so data displayed on the virtual screen is potentially visible. This setting keeps the encryption overhead low on the server, while still providing password protection.

■ **Medium** This is the default setting, which encrypts communications in both directions for security. The key used is a 56-bit key, which provides reasonable security with a reasonable processing overhead.

▲ **High**   This setting is the same as the medium setting but uses a 128-bit key to encrypt communications. This encryption is much more secure, but you incur a performance penalty. It also requires that the Windows 2000 High Encryption Pack be installed on the server, and that the client be using the equivalent.

Windows 2000 Terminal Servers configured for high encryption incur about a 5 percent processor performance penalty for the additional encryption. On the client side, the performance difference is negligible, as the amount of data being sent to the server is very small.

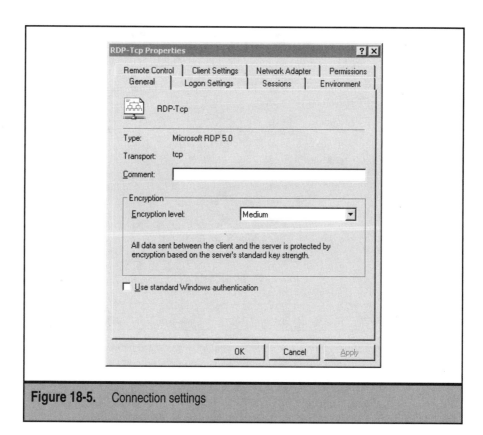

Figure 18-5.   Connection settings

Client Tuning

The client for Windows 2000 Terminal Services is simple—as it should be, since it is the equivalent of a dumb terminal from the mainframe world. Even so, there are some settings that can be adjusted to improve performance.

Client Settings to Tweak

Interestingly, there are very few client settings to configure (see Figure 18-6). Since the client has been optimized to provide high performance over a low-bandwidth connection, there are not many optimization points on the client side. There are really only two client performance options: data compression and bitmap caching to disk.

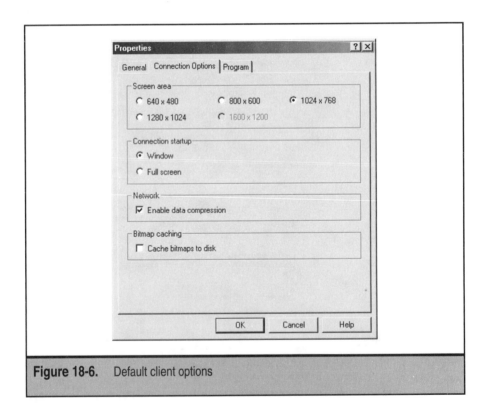

Figure 18-6.   Default client options

Compression

Data compression reduces the size of the data transferred over the connection and is turned on by default. Compression achieves about a 50 percent reduction in the size of data sent, with only a 2 percent increase in processor utilization. This is an excellent return on processor investment.

In environments where Terminal Services is used with high-bandwidth LANs, as a method of reducing application management or for other reasons, the recommendation for Windows NT 4.0 Terminal Services was to disable compression. This was because compression had a significant impact on processor performance on both the server and client, which was not a good trade-off due to the available bandwidth on the LAN.

With the improved efficiency of the Windows 2000 RDP 5.0 protocol compression, it is now recommended that compression remain enabled even in high-bandwidth LAN situations.

Caching

Terminal Services can perform two types of caching, as indicated earlier in the chapter. Memory caching of bitmaps and glyphs during a session is enabled all the time. Persistent bitmap caching, called bitmap caching in Figure 18-6, allows the cache to persist between sessions by storing the cached bitmap on disk. This takes up approximately 10MB of storage space on the local client hard disk. The savings overall is relatively small: only about a 5 percent reduction in data transferred over an extended time.

If there is plenty of local disk space on the client and the user will establish multiple sessions on the same computer over time, then it is recommended that persistent bitmap caching be enabled. However, if local disk space is at a premium (such as on legacy systems) or the user will not establish a session from that system again (as in an Internet kiosk at an airport), then the recommendation is to leave persistent bitmap caching disabled.

Application Tuning

Windows Terminal Services is designed to run well-designed 32-bit applications as is. The definition of "well designed" is that they follow Microsoft's Application Specification for Desktop Applications (available at http://msdn.microsoft.com/certification/appspec.asp).

Unfortunately, there are many applications in use on Windows 2000 systems that are neither 32 bit nor well designed. There are legacy applications, 16-bit applications, and others that require special handling and configuration.

In addition, an application may be well designed and still have potential problems when deployed on a Windows 2000 Terminal Server. This is the case for very processor-intensive applications such as compilers or both graphics- and processor-intensive applications such as computer-aided design (CAD) programs. These applications are simply not suited for deployment on a thin-client model.

Application Development

The time to address most of the problems that may arise in running applications on a Terminal Server is when the application is under development. This is the time to ensure that the client is 32-bit (not usually a problem today), that the application doesn't generate unnecessary graphics, and that the application runs in multiuser mode. Following the Microsoft Application Specification during development ensures that the application will run well on both a stand-alone Windows 2000 desktop and a Windows 2000 Terminal Server virtual desktop.

Here are some pointers to keep in mind in application development:

▼ **Message Boxes**   Pop-up message boxes will appear on the console screen if they are not implemented correctly. Ensure that the guidelines for message pop-up boxes are followed.

■ **Background Tasks**   Many applications initiate background tasks to handle low-priority operations. These tasks compete with foreground tasks for processor time. However, on a heavily loaded Terminal Server, each session is, in effect, a foreground task. Background tasks may get very little processing time and take much longer to complete than expected.

■ **Splash Screens** Splash screens appear while an application is starting, usually displaying the corporate logo and application name. In a Terminal Services environment, they add no value and add to transmission traffic. Don't use them.

▲ **Animation** Many applications today include bells and whistles such as animated graphics, icons, or pop-up characters to make the application fun. One infamous example of this is the Microsoft Office Assistant, "Clippy." On a Windows 2000 Terminal Server, these "features" serve only to bog down the server processor and degrade the performance of the client as it waits for graphics updates from a dancing paperclip. They are not a good use of resources.

Application Type

Some applications are just not good candidates for deployment using Terminal Services. In the Terminal Services deployment model, users share resources, and virtual screen images are transmitted over the wire. This limits the types of applications that can be used effectively on the platform. Some of the key types of applications to avoid are listed here:

▼ **Processor-Intensive Applications** Applications that require significant amounts of processor time are not good applications to deploy using Terminal Services. Since all users share the processing resources, any application that requires most of the processing time will negatively affect the other users on the system.

■ **Graphics-Intensive Applications** Graphics-intensive applications such as CAD or desktop publishing programs are not good candidates for deployment on a thin-client model. The screen images will take some time to get to the client, degrading performance for the rest of the users as well as for the client. The screen images also are constantly updated, exacerbating the problem.

- **MS-DOS/16-Bit Applications**   If an application will not work on a Windows 2000 Server, then it will not work on a Windows 2000 Terminal Server. Some legacy applications also use processing methods that don't function well on a multiuser system, such as polling for device input or allocating excessive amounts of memory.

- **Single-User Applications**   Some applications, even though well behaved, are simply designed to run only one instance on a given system. These include some administration applications.

For applications such as these, alternative deployment models will need to be identified.

Tweaking Applications

Some applications can be adjusted from their default out-of-the-box state to make them suitable for deployment with Windows 2000 or to optimize their performance to allow more users on the server. Here are some settings that you can change:

- **Launch Banners**   Many applications include switch settings that allow applications to launch without banner screens and logos.

- **Adjust Settings**   Some applications have adjustable refresh rates or graphics levels. Adjust these as appropriate to reduce graphics overhead.

- **Eliminate Bells and Whistles**   If possible, eliminate the bells-and-whistles graphics from the user interface. This is a less common option.

For example, Microsoft Office 2000 has various settings to optimize the performance of the product on Windows 2000 Terminal Services. These can be found in the Microsoft Office 2000 Resource Kit (http://www.microsoft.com/Office/ORK) and include a special installation transform for Terminal Services and the Motionless Office Assistant, otherwise known as the Clippy killer. The Motionless

Office Assistant provides the same functionality as the Office Assistant, but with no animation.

Adjusting the Desktop

The Windows 2000 desktop itself can be tweaked to reduce overhead. There are many "way cool" Windows 2000 features that provide animation, smooth transitions, or very colorful backgrounds. These feature improve the stand-alone desktop experience but reduce the performance of Windows 2000 Terminal Servers.

Disable Wallpaper   Set wallpaper to None and enforce it with Group Policy. Group Policy in general provides an effective mechanism for delivering desktop settings to desktops.

Minimize Graphics   Administrators can use Registry keys to control the user desktop to minimize graphics use. Use the following Registry key to eliminate the animation effects used by the Windows 2000 shell: HKEY_CURRENT_USER\ControlPanel\Desktop\WindowMetrics. Create the string value MinAnimate (type REG_SZ) and set the value to 0 to disable animation effects. This setting reduces the graphics overhead for each user. You can also change the value of this entry by double-clicking Display in the Control Panel. Select the Effects tab and unselect Use Transition Effects for Menus and Tooltips in the Visual Effects box to disable the animation effects.

The problem with this setting is that it affects only the current user, and there is no Group Policy setting to make this change easily for other users. To set the values for all users of the system, use the UserOverride Registry hack described next.

Override User Settings   A useful technique is to override the user setting in the Registry. Administrators can use a Terminal Server Registry hive to override user settings, such as wallpaper, animation effects, and screen savers. Create a key named UserOverride in HKEY_LOCAL_MACHINE\System\CurrentControlSet\Control\TerminalServer\WinStations\RDP-tcp. Then re-create the user keys and values that you want to override as they appear in the HKEY_CURRENT_USER\Control Panel\Desktop key.

For example, to override the Windows animation effects for all users, set the following key: HKEY_LOCAL_MACHINE\System\ CurrentControlSet\Control\TerminalServer\WinStations\RDP-tcp\ UserOverride\ControlPanel\Desktop\WindowMetrics\MinAnimate.

Building Large Servers

When designing and optimizing Windows 2000 Terminal Servers to support a large number of concurrent users, there are some additional concerns that need to be addressed. To tune the system, administrators need to be able to predict the load that a given number of users will place on a system.

In addition, as the number of users grows, limitations in the Windows 2000 architecture begin to affect scalability. This is not just a performance issue, where users will experience slower and slower performance as the load increases. There is, in fact, a limit based on the Windows 2000 memory model and processor architecture. This section will explore some alternatives to simply scaling up a given server, to get around the inherent limitations.

Profiling Users

To plan for and build large servers, you must be able to model the target environment. To accomplish this, it helps to create a user profile that generalizes different user types.

Light Users   Users who work on one small or medium-sized application at a time can be characterized as light users. Such a user might be entering data or checking e-mail, printing every so often.

Medium Users   Medium-level users work with several medium-sized applications concurrently, for instance, checking e-mail, working on a Word document, and working on a spreadsheet at the same time. Such a user prints frequently and generates a fair amount of e-mail.

Heavy Users   Heavy users have a large application open, such as Microsoft Project or Visio, as well as several medium-sized applications, such as Microsoft Outlook, Word, and Excel. They generate a fair number of messages with attachments.

Sizing Memory and Processors

The best method of sizing a server is to evaluate and measure the load that typical users present. From there, user counts can be extrapolated and verified through testing. Table 18-1 shows sample memory requirements for the three user profiles.

In addition to the per-user memory requirements, an additional 128MB of memory is needed for the operating system and services.

The other major factor in sizing a Windows 2000 Terminal Server is the processor requirements. It is both difficult and misleading to measure the load that an individual user places on a server, as processor time is allocated on an as-needed basis. A better measure is the number of users that a given processor configuration can support, as it is both more realistic and easier to test. Table 18-2 lists the approximate number of users some standard processor configurations support.

For the tests reported in the table, the systems were configured with Intel Pentium III 500 MHz processors, with 2MB of cache and 4GB of RAM. In testing the processor loads, sufficient memory was allocated to more than support the number of users anticipated. Higher counts could be achieved with eight-processor systems, but the server would begin to experience the memory issues described in the next section.

User Class	Memory per Session (MB)
Light	4
Medium	8
Heavy	10

Table 18-1.   Memory Needed per User

User Class	1 CPU	2 CPU	4 CPU
Light	100	200	350
Medium	30	75	125
Heavy	20	50	75

Table 18-2.   Sessions Supported per Processor

Large Memory Limitations

Windows 2000 is a 32-bit operating system and runs on 32-bit
processors, which means that it uses 32 bits to address memory.
Thus, the address space that Windows 2000 can access directly is
limited to 4GB of memory. The next generation of the system,
Windows XP, will also run on 64-bit processors as a 64-bit
operating system, allowing it to address a lot more memory.

Windows 2000 Advanced Server and Windows 2000 Datacenter
Server can support more than 4GB of RAM by using the Intel
Physical Addressing Extension (PAE) specification. Windows 2000
Advanced Server can support up to 8GB of RAM, and Windows 2000
Datacenter Server can support up to 64GB.

Unfortunately, Windows 2000 Terminal Services uses the 2GB of
address space that is allocated to the kernel. When the PAE switch is
enabled, this address space does not increase, and Terminal Services
does not make use of the Address Windows Extensions (AWE) API
needed to access the additional memory. Thus, there is no performance
benefit to installing more than 4GB of RAM in a Windows 2000
Terminal Server, even if the PAE switch is used.

In effect, the memory requirements of sessions become the
limiting factor for very large Terminal Server installations.

Building Server Farms

Where individual servers are limited by the memory requirements,
farms of Windows 2000 Terminal Servers can be built to handle large

user populations. Whereas increasing the load that an individual
server can support is sometimes referred to as scaling up, adding
servers to a server farm is referred to as scaling out.

There are three main approaches to scaling out: DNS Round
Robin, Network Load Balancing, and third-party solutions.

DNS Round Robin   Implementation of DNS Round Robin is
straightforward. Multiple Windows 2000 Terminal Servers are
created (such as TS01, TS02, and TS03), but a common name is
assigned to the group (such as TS), and host records are created in
DNS. Each host record uses the common name TS, but with the IP
address of the individual server. As clients request the TS service,
DNS routes them round-robin fashion among the host records.

The disadvantage to this approach is that users get the host name
that's next in the round robin, even if that server is busy or offline. Also,
if a user disconnects from a session and then attempts to reconnect, the
user will be unlikely to get the original server and thus not reconnect
to the original session. For DNS Round Robin, disconnects should
be disabled.

Network Load Balancing   Network Load Balancing (NLB) is similar in
effect to DNS Round Robin, but it uses the Windows 2000 Advanced
Server or Data Center Server load balancing feature. A group of servers
participates in an NLB group, which shares information about the load
on each server. Clients connecting get the least-busy server and also do
not get directed to an offline server. However, as with DNS Round
Robin, clients are not guaranteed to be reconnected to a server they
have disconnected from, so disconnects are usually disabled.

Third-Party Solutions   Third-party vendors, such as Citrix, provide
load-balancing solutions that also allow disconnects. The load
balancing is more effective than with either DNS Round Robin or
NLB and allows administrators to direct users to specific servers. The
disadvantage is that there is an additional charge for the third-party
product, as well as additional training and support required.

PART IV

Appendixes

APPENDIX A

A New Look at the Powerful System Monitor

Throughout this book, we've referenced countless system components that you can use to gauge system performance. There are many third-party tools that are available to monitor these individual system components, but Microsoft has provided such a utility with Windows 2000. You can use the System Monitor to measure individual system components or the overall performance of local and remote computers. This Microsoft Management Console (MMC) snap-in is one of the most commonly used monitoring and troubleshooting tools from Microsoft. It allows you to monitor and analyze system performance data in real time and to collect log data for future scrutiny. The System Monitor can also alert administrators when system values exceed or fall below specified values, and it can report on the data that it has collected.

This appendix begins by introducing the System Monitor included with Windows 2000, providing you with a basic understanding of this tool's capabilities. This appendix then explores the ways you can use the System Monitor to monitor your system, describing the various monitoring options available to you so you can more effectively use this utility. You will also learn about other applications that you can use in conjunction with the System Monitor to enhance your monitoring capabilities.

OVERVIEW OF THE SYSTEM MONITOR

The System Monitor is tailored for performance tuning for your Windows 2000 system environment. It provides information that can be used to detect problems and optimize the system. It captures, or takes snapshots of, system performance characteristics at periodic intervals that can be used to see the behavior of the system, measure the load on system components, predict future resource requirements, and alert you to potential failures of system components.

NOTE: The interval between snapshots of system performance data ranges from 1 second to 45 days.

Like any application, the System Monitor uses some of your system's resources. However, the amount of resources it uses depends on the frequency of data collection, the number of objects or counters being measured, and the location of log files. Typically, the System Monitor uses a minimum of 5MB of memory and minimal processor time (1 to 5 percent). Adding the disk and network subsystem components to your monitoring scheme also adds to the resource load. Although the System Monitor's effects on system resources are minimal, you still should be aware of them.

1at Is Monitored

Each Windows 2000 computer has components that the System Monitor can monitor. These components can be hardware or software components that perform tasks or support workloads. Many of these components have indicators that reflect certain aspects of their functionality that can be accurately measured in terms of the rate at which tasks are accomplished. For example, the Network Segment: Total bytes received/second counter shows you the number of bytes placed on the Windows 2000 system by the network subsystem. All collected data comes from the counters that the System Monitor monitors.

Objects

In Windows 2000 systems, many of the components that comprise an entire system are grouped into *objects* based on their characteristics. For example, anything pertaining to the processor is located in the Processor object, and anything pertaining to memory is located in the Memory object. Objects are grouped according to functionality or association within the system. They can represent logical mechanisms, such as processes, or physical entities, such as hard disk drives.

The number of objects isn't limited to what Windows 2000 provides. All Microsoft BackOffice products have objects that can be evaluated and tracked by the System Monitor. Objects can also be created by third-party vendors, so that you, as an IT professional, can use the System Monitor to monitor your own components. Microsoft has purposely chosen to let outside vendors create objects and counters specific to their own applications or devices that the System Monitor can read.

The number of objects present on a system depends on the system configuration. For instance, Internet Information Server (IIS) counters won't be present if the system isn't running that application. However, the following common objects can be found in every system:

▼ Cache

■ Logical disk

■ Memory

■ Paging file

■ Physical disk

■ Process

■ Processor

■ Server

■ System

■ Thread

▲ Network-related objects (Network Interface, TCP, UDP, and so on)

Counters

Each object contains *counters*. Counters typically provide information about use, throughput, queue length, and so on for a particular object. For example, all counters pertaining to the paging file are contained in the Paging File object. The System Monitor uses the counters within an object to collect data. The information gathered from these counters is then displayed in the System Monitor window or dumped into a data file.

Instances

If your system has more than one similar component (two hard drives, four processors, and so on), each one is considered an *instance* of that component. Each instance in the system has an associated counter that measures its individual performance. Counters with multiple instances also have an instance for the combined instances. Shown here is an example of the PhysicalDisk counter with multiple instances:

III A-1

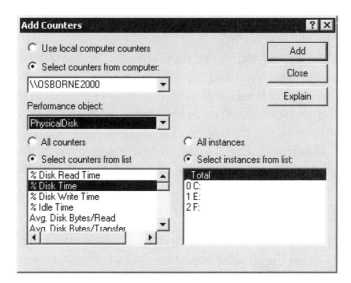

ses of the System Monitor

So far, we have seen that the System Monitor monitors and collects system performance statistics and can be used to notify support staff of impending bottlenecks and failures. Here is a summary of some of the possible uses for the System Monitor:

▼ Monitoring performance in real time or historically

■ Monitoring the effects of system configuration changes

■ Identifying bottlenecks

■ Troubleshooting performance problems

■ Identifying trends and patterns in system performance

■ Creating performance reports

■ Determining resource capacity

■ Monitoring local or remote machines

■ Notifying administrators when specified resources approach thresholds

▲ Exporting data from counters to other products for further analysis

Charting Performance

Counter statistics can be monitored in real time with the System Monitor. This is similar to the Chart view in Windows NT's Performance Monitor, which lets you actively watch the values of selected counters. The results of the collected data appear in a histogram (bar chart) or graph. As you can see in Figure A-1, the graph format produces a chart that looks something like an electrocardiogram used for monitoring a heartbeat. The charting format you choose is determined mainly by personal preference. You may find one format more suitable than others for viewing your system.

To begin viewing counters in real time, follow these steps:

1. Select Performance from the Start | Programs | Administrative Tools menu to open the System Monitor.

2. Select the System Monitor in the left pane.

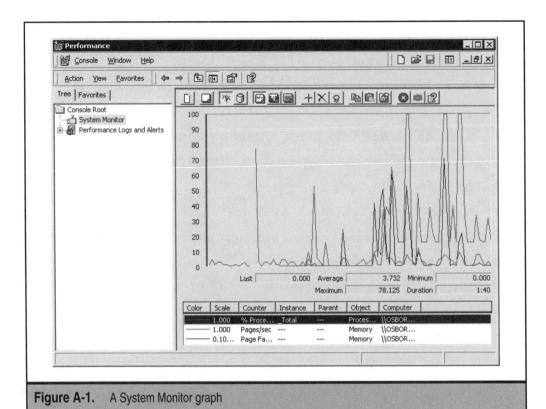

Figure A-1.   A System Monitor graph

3. Click the + button in the right pane to add counters to monitor.

4. If you want to monitor a remote machine, choose Select Counters from Computer and then enter the UNC name of the computer in the box below it as shown here.

A-2

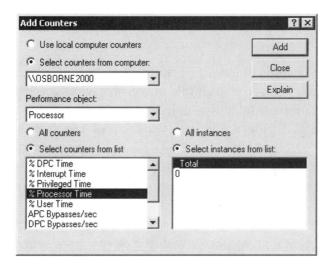

5. Choose the object you want to monitor.

6. Select the desired counters within the object; you can also select the All Counters option to select all the counters for a given object.

NOTE: If you're not sure whether to add a certain counter, click Explain in the Add Counters dialog box to gain a better understanding of the particular counter.

7. Click Add to add the counter to your monitoring scheme.

8. Add more counters if desired.

9. Click Close when you are finished.

NOTE: You can highlight an individual counter by selecting the counter and pressing CTRL-H. There's also an easier way now with System Monitor: just select the counter you want to highlight and click the highlight button in the right pane. This helps you differentiate that counter from the rest.

Toggling Views

The default view for the System Monitor is the graph format. However, you can easily switch to histogram or report viewing. Using the button bar, you can choose among any of these formats. For instance, you can click the View Report button to view the real-time data in a report format, as shown in Figure A-2.

Customizing the System Monitor

There's nothing difficult about customizing the System Monitor, but it's important to realize that you can and should customize what you're viewing. The reason is that certain customizations can help you better understand the data that you're viewing. If, for example, you want to look at specific threshold values, you may find it a bit easier to read the data in the report format. The discussion here describes the options that you have for customizing the System Monitor to suit your personal preferences.

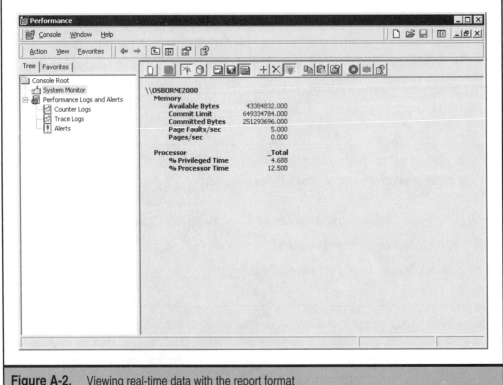

Figure A-2. Viewing real-time data with the report format

Many of the customizations can be accomplished using the button bar that's provided in the right pane of the System Monitor. The buttons are as follows (from left to right):

A-3

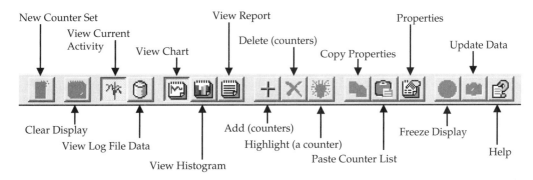

Customizing the System Monitor View

You can perform the greatest level of customization in the System Monitor Properties window, shown in Figure A-3.

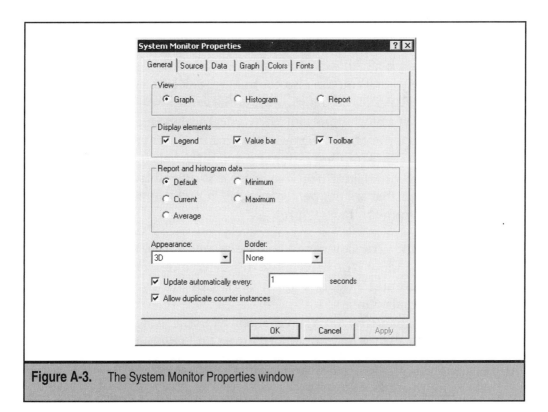

Figure A-3.   The System Monitor Properties window

General Tab   The General tab offers several options for changing the look and feel of the System Monitor. You can do the following:

▼ Change the view to graph, histogram, or report format.

■ Choose the display elements (legend, value bar, and toolbar).

■ Modify the report and histogram data (we recommend keeping the default values).

■ Change the appearance and border.

■ Specify when automatic updates take place, if at all.

▲ Specify whether to allow duplicate counters.

Source Tab   The Source tab allows you to choose between retrieving data from current activity or a log file. If you choose to view data from a log file, you also have the option of specifying the time range.

Data Tab   To add more counters while still keeping the System Monitor Properties window open, switch to the Data tab. You can also specify color, width, style, and scale for each counter displayed, as shown in Figure A-4.

Graph Tab   The Graph tab allows you to specify a name for the title and vertical axis of the graph. You can also control the look and feel of the graph itself by choosing the vertical and horizontal grids, vertical scale numbers (the default selection), and most important, the vertical scale values. The vertical scale values are important because you can set the minimum and maximum values according to the sampling rating. By default, labels 0 to 100 are displayed (for 0 to 100 percent). You may want to change this value when monitoring counters that are not percentages, such as the number of frames sent and received from the TCP/IP protocol.

Colors and Fonts Tabs   The Colors and Fonts tabs can be used to dress up the System Monitor window. You can choose different colors for the time bar, background, foreground, grid, and much more. However, you can't change the color of the actual counters.

The Font tab manages all fonts simultaneously in the System Monitor window. You can't change an individual counter font without changing the rest of the window.

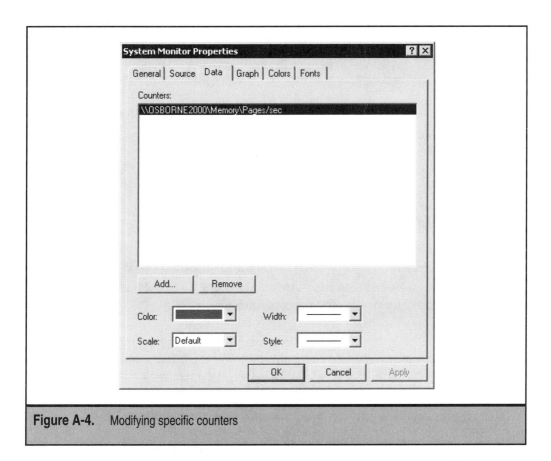

Figure A-4. Modifying specific counters

ERFORMANCE LOGS AND ALERTS

Working in conjunction with the System Monitor is the Performance Logs and Alerts service. It stores the data it collects in a data file, or log. Logged data isn't viewed in real time, so logging provides a historical perspective on system performance. As mentioned in Chapter 2, logging is the preferred approach in capacity planning because it makes it easier to interpret trends or patterns in system performance. It also provides a mechanism for storing data in a convenient format for future scrutiny. You can use the System Monitor to replay the cataloged performance data, or you can easily export it to other applications.

NOTE: Because Performance Logs and Alerts runs as a service, you don't have to be logged on to collect vital system statistics. This is a vast improvement over its predecessor in Windows NT.

Performance Logs and Alerts serves three functions: it monitors counters, collects event traces, and provides an alerting mechanism. These three functions can be found by expanding Performance Logs and Alerts in the Performance window.

Working with Counter Logs

Counter logs allow you to record system activity or usage statistics for local and remote machines. In addition to starting and stopping the Performance Logs and Alerts service manually, you can also configure the service to start and stop automatically or to log data continuously.

NOTE: You can now log data from individual counters (instead of entire objects). This helps keep the amount of data you're logging to a minimum.

To begin logging activity using the counter logs, follow these steps:

1. Start System Monitor by selecting Performance from the Start | Programs | Administrative Tools menu.

2. Expand Performance Logs and Alerts and then select Counter Logs.

3. Choose New Log Settings from the Action menu, or right-click in the right pane and select New Log Settings. You'll be asked to supply a name for the log, as shown here:

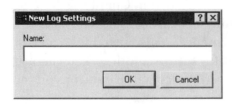

4. After you name the log, click OK; a properties window for the new log file appears, as shown in Figure A-5. On the General tab, click Add to add counters to monitor.

5. In the Add Counters dialog box, add the counters that you want to monitor by clicking the Add button. When you're done adding all of the counters, click Close to return to the counter log's properties window.

6. Specify the snapshot interval (the default is 15 seconds).

7. On the Log Files tab, you can specify the location of the log files; the name of the log file, including how to end log file names; the file format of the log file; and any log file size restrictions. See the "Log Files Tab" section later in this appendix for more information.

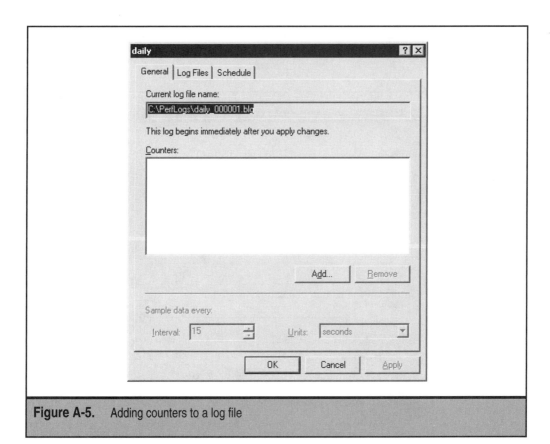

Figure A-5.   Adding counters to a log file

8. The Schedule tab lets you specify more options for starting and stopping the log file. You can also specify the action to take when the log file closes. See the "Schedule Tab" section later in this appendix for more information.

Log Files Tab

As mentioned in step 7 (see Figure A-6), the Log Files tab offers many options. These options are important because they can not only affect your monitoring methodology, but some can also affect your system's performance.

Log File Location By default Performance Logs and Alerts stores all log files in the C:\PerfLogs directory. This should be immediately changed to another disk drive. Assuming that this drive is also your system partition, both Windows 2000 and monitoring are competing against one another for resources by using the same drive. Moving all of the disk I/O associated with Counter

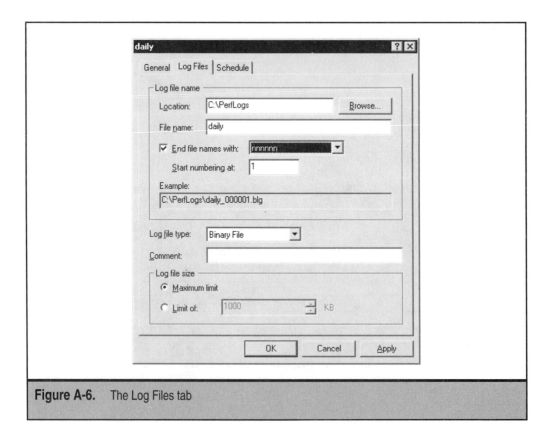

Figure A-6.   The Log Files tab

Log writes to the drive frees valuable resources and enables your system to function more efficiently.

End File Names   A convenient way to keep track of log files is to end the log file name with a number or a date. The default configuration enables this feature, and we highly recommend that you use this naming mechanism, especially if you're considering creating sequential log files.

Log File Type   Log files can now be saved in two types of text format as well as two types of binary format. Table A-1 list these formats and gives a brief description of each.

Log File Size   The log file size setting enables you to control the growth of log files. Here are some of the benefits of using this feature:

▼   Controlling the size of the log files makes them easier to manage.

■   You reduce the chances of running out of disk space.

▲   Limited data collection is easier to analyze.

NOTE: Windows 2000 limits the size of the log file to 1GB.

Log File Format	Description
Text File - CSV	Comma-delimited file. This file format can easily be read by spreadsheets such as Microsoft Excel.
Text File - TSV	Tab-delimited file. This file format is suitable for viewing with spreadsheet and database programs.
Binary File	This format refers to a sequential, binary format that uses the .BLG extension. Use this file format when creating multiple sequential logs.
Binary Circular File	This format refers to a circular, binary format that uses the .BLG extension. After the log file reaches its capacity, it will begin to overwrite data starting from the beginning of the file.

Table A-1.   Log File Formats

Schedule Tab

As mentioned earlier, the Schedule tab (see Figure A-7) has a variety of options that control the starting and stopping of the log file as well as options that become effective when the log file stops.

Of course, you can always manually start and stop a log file using the CD player–like buttons located in the Counter Logs pane, but the real advantage of the Schedule tab comes when you configure automatic start and stops. In the Stop Log section, you can specify when to stop the log in seconds, minutes, hours, or days. You can also opt to stop the log file at a specific time and date, or when it reaches a 1000KB capacity.

Also located in the Stop Log section of the Schedule tab are options to start a new log when a log file closes and to run a command.

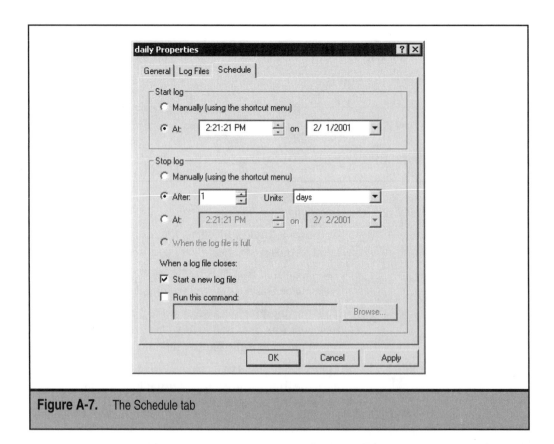

Figure A-7. The Schedule tab

Creating Sequential Logs   You can now more easily manage log files by creating sequential logs. Sequential logs are useful because you can keep separate log files for specified periods of time. For instance, if you want to create a log file for each day of the week, you easily do so by creating sequential logs.

There are a few important points to remember when you configure Performance Logs and Alerts to create sequential logs:

▼   Use the End File Names With check box on the Log Files tab and choose the Numbers format unless you're confident that the maximum capacity you specified won't be reached.

■   Use the binary format.

▲   On the Schedule tab, at the bottom of the Stop Log section, choose Start a New Log File.

orking with Trace Logs

Trace logs record data when an event from the operating system or an application occurs. Events are classified as either system provider or nonsystem provider events. Examples of system provider events include, but aren't limited to, the following:

▼   Hard disk I/O

■   Process creations and deletions

■   Thread creations and deletions

■   TCP/IP errors

▲   Page faults

Trace logs differ from counter logs in the type of data they collect as well as in the frequency of the data collection. Trace logs monitor events continuously instead at intervals.

The process of creating a trace log is very similar to that for creating a counter log, explained earlier. To create a trace log, click Trace Log under Performance Logs and Alerts in the left pane of the Performance window; then right-click in the right pane and select New Log Settings. Name the log file; the trace log properties window appears.

In the trace log properties window, shown in Figure A-8, notice the similarities with the counter log properties window. The General tab is slightly different, and there is an additional tab called Advanced. The Log Files and Schedule tabs are identical to the ones for the counter log.

General Tab

At the top of the General tab, you can see that the log file name ends in .ETL. You then see the available system and nonsystem providers that you can monitor. By selecting Events Logged by System Provider, you can choose events by selecting the check boxes beside them. The Page Faults and File Details events are not checked by default because they tend to produce a tremendous amount of data. If you plan to monitor these events, Microsoft recommends monitoring them for a maximum of two hours at a time.

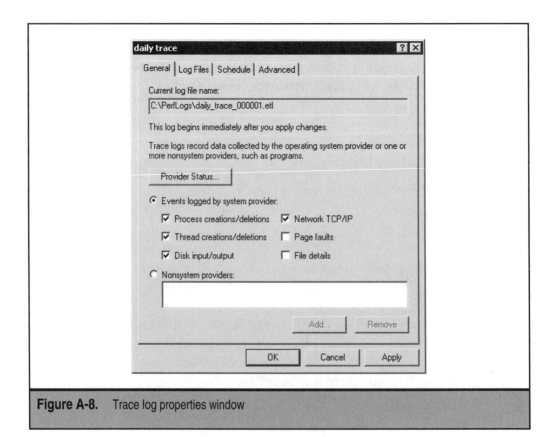

Figure A-8.   Trace log properties window

Click the Provider Status button to display a list of the current providers and their status (enabled and running or stopped), as shown here:

Advanced Tab

The Advanced tab, shown in Figure A-9, lets you configure buffer settings. Data that is being logged is first transferred to memory buffers before the data is written to the trace log. By default, the buffers are filled to capacity before the data is written to the log file. In most scenarios, we recommend keeping the default settings.

wing Log Files with the System Monitor

Once you have a log file containing raw system performance data, you can retrieve and analyze the data that has been collected. For now, we will just explore how to use the System Monitor to open the log file for analysis; later in this appendix we will explore how to use Microsoft Office applications to reduce the size of and analyze log files.

To view a log file, follow these steps:

1. In the left pane of the Performance window, select System Monitor.

2. In the right pane, right-click and select Properties.

3. On the Source tab, click Log File and then click Browse to locate the log file you want to view. Click OK when you've selected the log file.

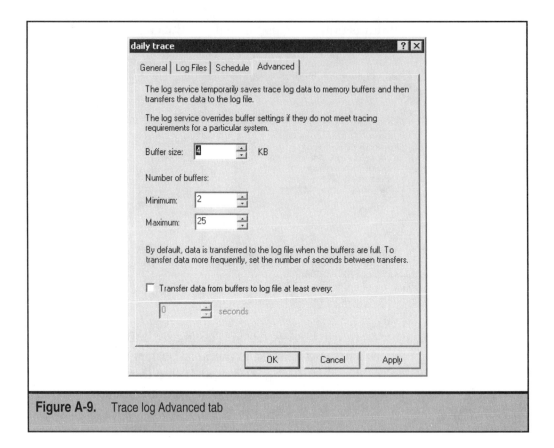

Figure A-9.   Trace log Advanced tab

4. You can either click OK to view the entire log file or click the Time Range button to specify the time you want to view.

5. At this point, you can also switch to the Data tab and select the counters you want to view.

Working with Alerts

Alerts can be set on any available counter to notify the administrator when a specified condition occurs, such as when processor use exceeds 90 percent. If a counter exceeds or falls below the value that you specify, the Performance Logs and Alerts service triggers an alert that logs the event and can also trigger another event, such as sending a notification message, starting a performance data log, or running a program.

NOTE: Make sure that the Alerter service is running before trying to configure an alert log. Also, if you plan to send notifications when an alert is triggered, make sure that the Messenger service is started.

To create an alert, do the following:

1. In the left pane of the Performance window, click Alerts under Performance Logs and Alerts.

2. Right-click in the right pane and select New Alert Settings.

3. Name the alert and click OK.

4. On the General tab, you can optionally add a comment to identify the alert.

5. Click Add to display the Select Counter window and add the counters that you want to monitor. Click Close when you're done.

6. For each counter that you want to monitor, specify the condition that will trigger an alert, as shown in Figure A-10.

7. Set the snapshot interval (the default is every 5 seconds).

8. Select the Action tab and choose the events that will occur when an alert is triggered (see Figure A-11). Note that any action specified here will apply to all counters being monitored in this alert log. If you want to have different actions for different counters, you'll need to create separate alert logs.

9. Select the Schedule tab to modify the start and stop times for alert logging.

CRITICAL RESOURCES TO MONITOR

The System Monitor can monitor several different counters available on Windows 2000 systems, including counters provided by Windows 2000, Microsoft BackOffice, and third parties. It is imperative that you carefully select the counters

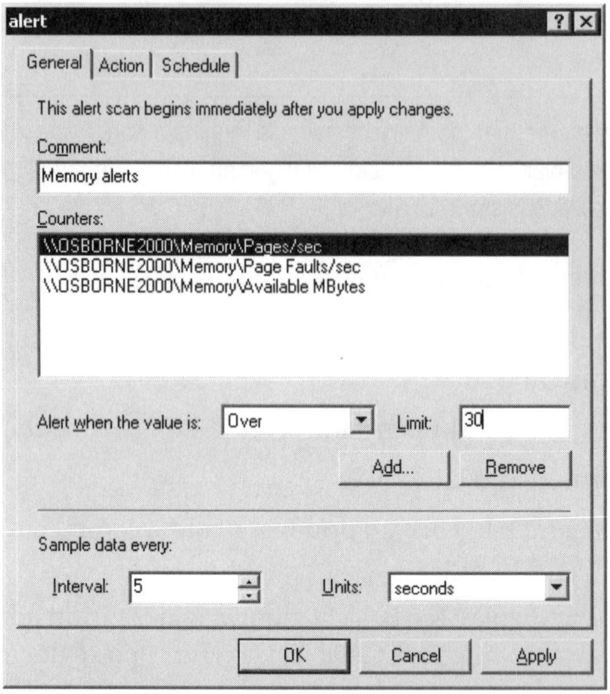

Figure A-10.   Specifying alert conditions

to monitor, because the amount of information collected can quickly become unwieldy and, ultimately, useless. A general rule of thumb is that you should monitor the four common contributors to bottlenecks:

▼ Memory

■ Processor

■ Disk subsystem

▲ Network subsystem

As mentioned in Chapter 2, these critical resources are often the first components to degrade system performance. For example, it is more common for an application server to have slow response times due to slow disk access

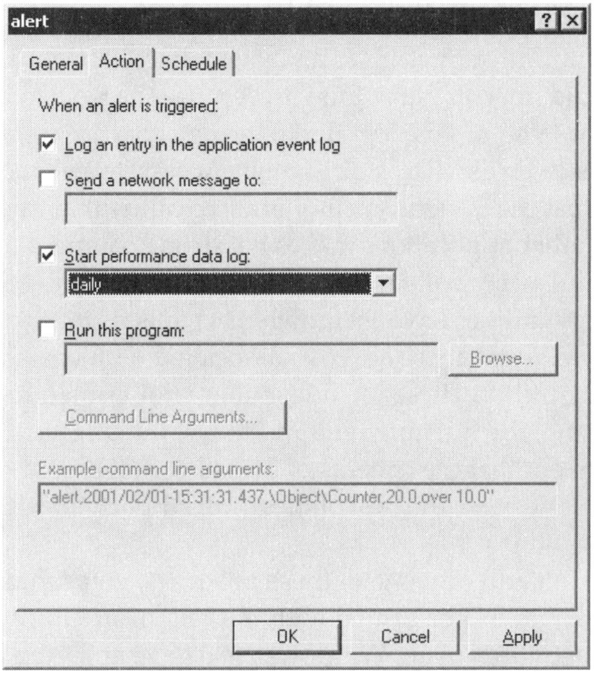

Figure A-11.   Specifying that action that occurs when an alert is triggered

or lack of memory than it is for the server's performance to be degraded due to its remote access service.

In addition to monitoring the four common contributors to bottlenecks, it is also imperative that you closely watch the resources that affect the way the server functions within the Windows 2000 environment. A Windows 2000 Server may be configured to handle file and print sharing, application sharing, domain controller functions, or any combination of these and more. The functions that you use determine which resources you should closely monitor. Devising a monitoring scheme where you include the four common contributors as well as the resources pertaining to the server's functions will greatly increase your ability to boost your system's performance.

ANALYZING DATA WITH MICROSOFT EXCEL

Using the System Monitor by itself to analyze data collections is somewhat limiting. You should not complain, though, because the System Monitor is a free utility. It also allows you to save log files in formats that are suitable for use with other applications, such as Microsoft Excel or Access, to enhance the analysis process. The fact that the System Monitor is a free utility that can easily share its information with other applications makes it a strong competitor against the more powerful third-party system monitoring utilities.

Most third-party utilities have their own mechanisms for analyzing the data that they collect. However, there are costs associated with using any third-party system monitoring utility. These include, but are not limited to, the price of application licensing, the learning required to use the utility, and the need to convince management that the benefits of investing in the third-party product outweigh the costs. Even so, the capabilities of third-party products make them worthy of investigation.

Before you go out and buy one of these products, you should be aware of the analysis that can be performed with the Microsoft Office suite. Most Microsoft-based networks using Windows 2000 have at least a few of the products packaged in this suite. If your environment is one of the many out there that uses Microsoft Office products, you are in luck. The System Monitor integrates extremely well with Microsoft Excel and Access so that you can use these tools to help analyze system performance data. The results you get with Excel can help you more easily interpret the data as well as provide reports to management. If you do not have these products, you can still use another spreadsheet or database application to overcome the System Monitor's limited ability to make sense of collected data.

Charting Performance with Excel

Excel can read both the .TSV and .CSV formats that the System Monitor creates, but the .CSV format is designed specifically for spreadsheets. For this reason, it is better to save the data in the Text File - CSV format.

1. Assuming that you have saved a counter log in the Text File - CSV format, begin by starting Microsoft Excel.

2. From the File menu, choose Open.

3. In the Open dialog box, shown in Figure A-12, select Text Files from the Files of Type drop-down list.

4. Specify the location and file name for the log file by browsing the directory structure in the Open dialog box.

5. Click Open.

The log file is now opened in Excel. You will see a data set that looks similar to the one in Figure A-13. The data set can be used in many different ways. For example, you can use Excel's conditional formatting, PivotTables, to analyze the collected data. You can also chart the data to make it easier to interpret and search for trends or patterns. The rest of this example focuses on how to chart a given set of data.

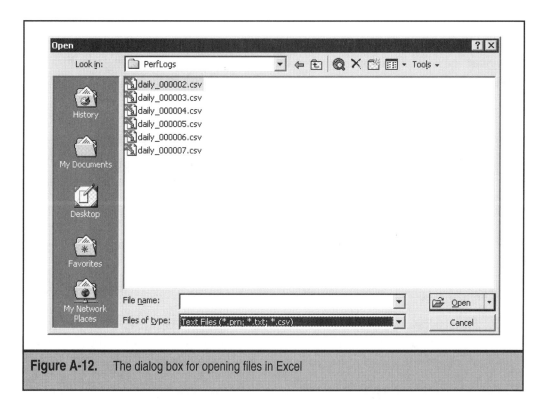

Figure A-12.   The dialog box for opening files in Excel

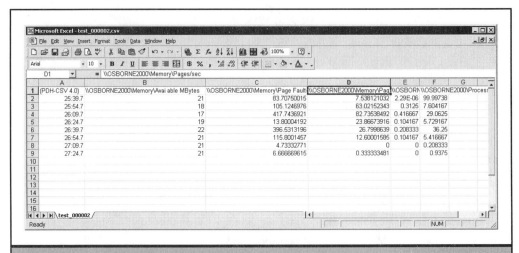

Figure A-13.   A sample data set from a log file opened in Excel

Charting the Data with Excel

Now that the CSV file is open within Excel, you can begin charting the data you select. To create a chart within Excel, do the following:

1. Highlight the cells containing data that you want to chart.

2. Start the Chart Wizard by selecting Chart from the Insert menu.

3. The Chart Wizard steps you through the chart creation process. On the first screen, select the type of chart you want to use, such as the Area Chart type.

NOTE: To view a sample chart for your selection, click and hold the Press and Hold to View Sample button.

4. Click Next.

5. Specify the data ranges to be charted, as shown in Figure A-14. If you highlighted data before starting the Chart Wizard, the Data Range field is automatically filled in for you. You can change this value if it is not correct.

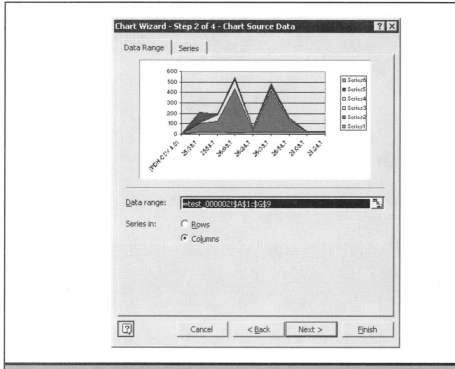

Figure A-14.   Specifying the data range

6. Select the Series tab. A series represents an individual counter that will be displayed in the chart. The series legend is displayed beside the actual chart.

7. Select a series and type a name for the series in the Name box.

8. In the Values box, the values to use should be automatically specified. However, you can change these values if necessary.

9. Repeat steps 7 and 8 for each series-to-counter relationship. If you need to add or remove a series, you can do so by clicking Add or Remove directly under the Series box.

10. Click Next.

11. In the next Chart Wizard dialog box, give the chart a title and optionally provide names for the *x* axis and *y* axis. This dialog box also lets you further customize the chart. For this example, you can use the default custom configurations.

12. Click Next.

13. Specify whether you want to create a new worksheet for the chart or export the chart to an existing worksheet. (It is wise to keep the data and charts on separate sheets. To do this, click the button next to As New Sheet.)

14. Type a name of your choice for the new worksheet that will contain the chart.

15. Click Finish.

APPENDIX B

Sources of Windows 2000 Information

The wealth of information that exists for Windows 2000 (and Windows NT) is astounding, but at the same time it can be overwhelming. It's easy to spend an enormous amount of time researching solutions or technologies, so it's critical that you understand which resources are available to you. It's also important to know which information sources best fit your particular need at the time. This appendix is a compilation of several important resources designed to assist you in finding the right information at the right time.

MICROSOFT'S SOURCES OF INFORMATION

Whether you're trying to quickly solve an immediate problem or simply researching a particular aspect of Windows 2000, Microsoft is probably the most obvious choice for information you need. Microsoft places several types of information media at your disposal.

Microsoft Windows 2000 Resource Kit

The Windows 2000 Resource Kit is a series of books and a CD containing detailed information on Windows 2000. The resource kit also contains an indispensable arsenal of utilities and supplemental help files aimed at simplifying Windows 2000 administration, maintenance, and much more. Once you start using the volumes of information and utilities, you'll find that you don't want to work without them.

The resource kit is available through Microsoft, major software retailers, and most bookstores (both online and traditional).

Microsoft TechNet

Undoubtedly, Microsoft TechNet is one of the best resources to turn to for help in troubleshooting and researching Microsoft products and technologies. TechNet exists in two forms: you can obtain articles and white papers online at http://www.microsoft.com/technet, or you can pay for a yearly subscription to the CD-based version.

There are several advantages to investing in the yearly TechNet subscription. With the CD version, you get all of the information that is online, plus you also receive the resource kit, service packs, and other utilities.

Moreover, you can perform customized querying without having to be connected to the Internet.

crosoft Developer Network (MSDN)

MSDN is similar to TechNet in that it is a subscription service offering volumes of information on all Microsoft products. However, MSDN is specifically tailored for Windows developers and isn't a necessity for system administrators or systems engineers.

MSDN provides development information through software development kits (SDKs), driver development kits (DDKs), white papers, and even operating system and BackOffice software, depending on your membership level. The three subscription levels are Library, Professional, and Universal. For more information on MSDN, visit MSDN Online at http://msdn.microsoft.com/.

NDOWS NT/2000 USER GROUPS

Windows NT/2000 user groups exist in many major cities around the world. These organizations help promote public and professional knowledge of Windows NT and Windows 2000 operating systems. In addition to the local user groups, there is the Worldwide Association of NT User Groups (WANTUG). WANTUG represents Windows NT/2000 user groups around the world and helps promote the local user groups. Its Web site (http://www.ntpro.org/wantug/) has a complete listing of all of the user groups, so check to see if one is in your area. If you visit WANTUG's Web site and can't find a user group close to you, you can consult the Web site for information on how to start one yourself.

Windows 2000 Magazine and *SQL Server Magazine* also promote and assist user groups through the Alliance of Windows IT Professionals (AWITP). AWITP helps user groups with membership, technical education, and much more. For information see http://www.win2000mag.com/AWITP/.

EWSLETTERS AND DISCUSSION GROUPS

An effective way to keep up with the latest news on Windows 2000 with minimal effort is either to subscribe to a newsletter or visit a discussion group.

Site Description	Web Site Address
NTBUGTRAQ	http://ntbugtraq.ntadvice.com/
W2KNews	http://www.sunbeltsoftware.com/
Windows 2000 Magazine's Discussion Forum	http://www.win2000mag.net/Forums/
Windows 2000 Magazine's Update	http://www.win2000mag.net/email/

Table B-1.   Windows NT/2000–Related Newsletters and Discussion Groups

The discussion groups are particularly useful because they allow you both to gain valuable information from other Windows 2000 users and to ask questions and help others. The groups help build community among users. There are a number of sites worth visiting; a few of them are listed in Table B-1.

OTHER WINDOWS NT/2000–RELATED WEB SITES

Although they vary in content, the Web sites in Table B-2 are excellent resources for up-to-date information on various aspects of Windows NT/2000.

Site Description	Web Site Address
2000tutor.com	http://www.2000tutor.com/
32bit.com	http://www.32bit.com/
About.com—Focus on Windows NT/2000	http://windowsnt.about.com/compute/windows2000/
ActiveWin	http://www.activewin.com/
Admin911.com	http://www.admin911.com/
Beverly Hills Software Windows NT/2000 Resource Center	http://www.bhs.com/

Table B-2.   Windows NT/2000–Related Web Sites

Site Description	Web Site Address
Computer Measurement Group	http://www.cmg.org/
Computing.Net (technical support site)	http://computing.net/
Demand Technology (system management software)	http://www.demandtech.com/
Device Driver Development for MS Windows	http://www.chsw.com/ddk/
Essential Windows NT Links	http://www.prineas.com/Links/NT/index.html
Exploring Windows NT (ZD Cobb Group publication)	http://www.zdjournals.com/ewn/index.htm
Frank Condron's World O'Windows	http://www.conitech.com/windows/
Fortel	http://www.fortel.com/
GartnerGroup Interactive	http://gartner5.gartnerweb.com/public/static/home/home.html
Geo's Windows NT Tips	http://www.nthelp.com/
HighGround Systems (storage)	http://www.HighGround.com/
Labmice.net	http://labmice.net/
Microsoft	http://www.microsoft.com/
NeoTech - Windows Tips & Tricks	http://www.geocities.com/SiliconValley/6591/
NT Toolbox	http://www.nttoolbox.com/
NTWare.com	http://www.ntware.com/
Paul Thurrott's SuperSite for Windows	http://www.winsupersite.com/
SearchWin2000.com	http://www.searchwin2000.com/
Sunbelt Software	http://www.sunbelt-software.com/
System Internals	http://www.sysinternals.com/
TechRepublic	http://www.techrepublic.com/
The Thin Net	http://thethin.net/winnt.cfm
Windows IT Library	http://www.windowsitlibrary.com/

Table B-2.   Windows NT/2000–Related Web Sites *(continued)*

Site Description	Web Site Address
Windows NT Adapter Card Help	http://www.wi-inf.uni-essen.de/~schwarze/nt/hard.html
Windows NT and Windows 2000 FAQ (formerly NTFAQ.com)	http://www.ntfaq.com/
Windows NT Interactive Archive	http://www.winntia.com/
Windows NT Resource Site	http://www.interlacken.com/winnt/default.htm

Table B-2.   Windows NT/2000–Related Web Sites *(continued)*

Some report the latest news, performance tips, and bugs and fixes, and some have links to other Windows NT/2000–related Web sites.

USENET NEWSGROUPS

USENET newsgroups are public discussion groups similar to the discussion groups mentioned in the section "Newsletters and Discussion Groups." The primary difference is that newsgroups use the Network News Transport Protocol (NNTP) for the delivery and exchange of messages. You can read and post to the newsgroups listed here (or any other newsgroup) using a newsreader program. The other option is using a Web-based newsgroup service such as DejaNews (http://www.dejanews.com/). Here is a list of some newsgroups to try:

▼ comp.os.ms-windows.nt.admin.misc

■ comp.os.ms-windows.nt.admin.networking

■ comp.os.ms-windows.nt.admin.security

■ comp.os.ms-windows.nt.advocacy

■ comp.os.ms-windows.nt.announce

■ comp.os.ms-windows.nt.misc

■ comp.os.ms-windows.nt.pre-release

- comp.os.ms-windows.nt.setup

- comp.os.ms-windows.nt.setup.hardware

- comp.os.ms-windows.nt.setup.misc

- comp.os.ms-windows.nt.software.backoffice

- comp.os.ms-windows.nt.software.compatibility

▲ comp.os.ms-windows.nt.software.services

AGAZINES

The following table lists several excellent Windows NT/2000–related
magazines—you can visit them online or you can subscribe to their print version.

Magazine	Web Site Address
ENT Magazine	http://www.entmag.com/
Exchange & Outlook Magazine	http://exchange.devx.com/
Microsoft Certified Professional Magazine	http://www.mcpmag.com/
MSDN Magazine	http://msdn.microsoft.com/msdnmag/ default.asp
Network World Fusion	http://www.nwfusion.com/
Performance Computing	http://www.performancecomputing.com/
Windows 2000 Explorer	http://www.explorermag.com/

AINING

Nothing compares to real-world experience, yet professional training is an
excellent way to quickly gain insight into the various technologies surrounding
Windows 2000. Microsoft has a channel called the Microsoft Certified Technical

Education Center (Microsoft CTEC), formerly known as the Microsoft Authorized Technical Education Center (ATEC), that stipulates requirements that training centers must meet to be considered certified to train users on Microsoft products. Despite the certification, it's important to ask for CTEC and instructor credentials before taking a course because quality will vary. For a list of CTECs, visit the Microsoft CTEC Web site at http://www.microsoft.com/ctec/.

If you're interested in pursuing training for Microsoft Certified Professional (MCP), Microsoft Certified Systems Engineer (MCSE), or other individual certification, visit Microsoft's site for training and certification programs at http://www.microsoft.com/train_cert/. This site is full of information pertaining to the various certification programs, certification requirements, training options, and much more.

APPENDIX C

About the CD

ost, if not all, performance optimization can be performed using Windows 2000's built-in features and components. Even though some optimizations don't require third-party utilities, they usually enhance functionality and make life easier. Throughout this book, many third-party utilities have been referenced to help you increase productivity, reduce administration time, maximize performance, and much more for your Windows 2000 environment. For your convenience, four of these utilities are included on the CD and are described here. For any additional information regarding these utilities, visit the companies' web sites, which are listed here.

PATROL

http://www.bmc.com/windows2000/

PATROL, from BMC Software, is a suite of products for capacity planning and resource management. The suite provides a multitude of features, ranging from centralized monitoring of performance statistics to prediction and diagnostic analysis.

SuperSpeed

http://www.superspeed.com

SuperSpeed from SuperSpeed Software boosts performance by placing application data or an entire disk partition into system memory. Applications and services can retrieve data at RAM speeds rather than through slower, constrained disk I/O. This utility has been certified for Windows 2000.

AppManager

http://www.netiq.com/products/Operations/AppManager_Suite/

AppManager, from NetIQ, is a capacity planning and resource management utility that allows you to proactively identify performance problems. In addition to monitoring Windows 2000, it can monitor a variety of applications and hardware components. Another of its strengths is its ability to integrate well with other NetIQ products and several third-party applications such as Computer Associates Unicenter TNG, HP OpenView, and Tivoli Enterprise.

INDEX

Note: Page numbers in *italics* refer to illustrations or charts.

Symbols & Numbers

 A

B

H

P

X

Z

INTERNATIONAL CONTACT INFORMATION

AUSTRALIA
McGraw-Hill Book Company Australia Pty. Ltd.
TEL +61-2-9417-9899
FAX +61-2-9417-5687
http://www.mcgraw-hill.com.au
books-it_sydney@mcgraw-hill.com

CANADA
McGraw-Hill Ryerson Ltd.
TEL +905-430-5000
FAX +905-430-5020
http://www.mcgrawhill.ca

**GREECE, MIDDLE EAST,
NORTHERN AFRICA**
McGraw-Hill Hellas
TEL +30-1-656-0990-3-4
FAX +30-1-654-5525

MEXICO (Also serving Latin America)
McGraw-Hill Interamericana Editores S.A. de C.V.
TEL +525-117-1583
FAX +525-117-1589
http://www.mcgraw-hill.com.mx
fernando_castellanos@mcgraw-hill.com

SINGAPORE (Serving Asia)
McGraw-Hill Book Company
TEL +65-863-1580
FAX +65-862-3354
http://www.mcgraw-hill.com.sg
mghasia@mcgraw-hill.com

SOUTH AFRICA
McGraw-Hill South Africa
TEL +27-11-622-7512
FAX +27-11-622-9045
robyn_swanepoel@mcgraw-hill.com

**UNITED KINGDOM & EUROPE
(Excluding Southern Europe)**
McGraw-Hill Education Europe
TEL +44-1-628-502500
FAX +44-1-628-770224
http://www.mcgraw-hill.co.uk
computing_neurope@mcgraw-hill.com

ALL OTHER INQUIRIES Contact:
Osborne/McGraw-Hill
TEL +1-510-549-6600
FAX +1-510-883-7600
http://www.osborne.com
omg_international@mcgraw-hill.com

LICENSE AGREEMENT

THIS PRODUCT (THE "PRODUCT") CONTAINS PROPRIETARY SOFTWARE, DATA AND INFORMATION (INCLUDING DOCUMENTATION) OWNED BY THE McGRAW-HILL COMPANIES, INC. ("McGRAW-HILL") AND ITS LICENSORS. YOUR RIGHT TO USE THE PRODUCT IS GOVERNED BY THE TERMS AND CONDITIONS OF THIS AGREEMENT.

LICENSE:

Throughout this License Agreement, "you" shall mean either the individual or the entity whose agent opens this package. You are granted a non-exclusive and non-transferable license to use the Product subject to the following terms:

(i) If you have licensed a single user version of the Product, the Product may only be used on a single computer (i.e., a single CPU). If you licensed and paid the fee applicable to a local area network or wide area network version of the Product, you are subject to the terms of the following subparagraph (ii).

(ii) If you have licensed a local area network version, you may use the Product on unlimited workstations located in one single building selected by you that is served by such local area network. If you have licensed a wide area network version, you may use the Product on unlimited workstations located in multiple buildings on the same site selected by you that is served by such wide area network; provided, however, that any building will not be considered located in the same site if it is more than five (5) miles away from any building included in such site. In addition, you may only use a local area or wide area network version of the Product on one single server. If you wish to use the Product on more than one server, you must obtain written authorization from McGraw-Hill and pay additional fees.

(iii) You may make one copy of the Product for back-up purposes only and you must maintain an accurate record as to the location of the back-up at all times.

COPYRIGHT; RESTRICTIONS ON USE AND TRANSFER

All rights (including copyright) in and to the Product are owned by McGraw-Hill and its licensors. You are the owner of the enclosed disc on which the Product is recorded. You may not use, copy, decompile, disassemble, reverse engineer, modify, reproduce, create derivative works, transmit, distribute, sublicense, store in a database or retrieval system of any kind, rent or transfer the Product, or any portion thereof, in any form or by any means (including electronically or otherwise) except as expressly provided for in this License Agreement. You must reproduce the copyright notices, trademark notices, legends and logos of McGraw-Hill and its licensors that appear on the Product on the back-up copy of the Product which you are permitted to make hereunder. All rights in the Product not expressly granted herein are reserved by McGraw-Hill and its licensors.

TERM

This License Agreement is effective until terminated. It will terminate if you fail to comply with any term or condition of this License Agreement. Upon termination, you are obligated to return to McGraw-Hill the Product together with all copies thereof and to purge all copies of the Product included in any and all servers and computer facilities.

DISCLAIMER OF WARRANTY

THE PRODUCT AND THE BACK-UP COPY ARE LICENSED "AS IS." McGRAW-HILL, ITS LICENSORS AND THE AUTHORS MAKE NO WARRANTIES, EXPRESS OR IMPLIED, AS TO THE RESULTS TO BE OBTAINED BY ANY PERSON OR ENTITY FROM USE OF THE PRODUCT, ANY INFORMATION OR DATA INCLUDED THEREIN AND/OR ANY TECHNICAL SUPPORT SERVICES PROVIDED HEREUNDER, IF ANY ("TECHNICAL SUPPORT SERVICES").

McGRAW-HILL, ITS LICENSORS AND THE AUTHORS MAKE NO EXPRESS OR IMPLIED WARRANTIES OF MERCHANTABILITY OR FITNESS FOR A PARTICULAR PURPOSE OR USE WITH RESPECT TO THE PRODUCT. McGRAW-HILL, ITS LICENSORS, AND THE AUTHORS MAKE NO GUARANTEE THAT YOU WILL PASS ANY CERTIFICATION EXAM WHATSOEVER BY USING THIS PRODUCT. NEITHER McGRAW-HILL, ANY OF ITS LICENSORS NOR THE AUTHORS WARRANT THAT THE FUNCTIONS CONTAINED IN THE PRODUCT WILL MEET YOUR REQUIREMENTS OR THAT THE OPERATION OF THE PRODUCT WILL BE UNINTERRUPTED OR ERROR FREE. YOU ASSUME THE ENTIRE RISK WITH RESPECT TO THE QUALITY AND PERFORMANCE OF THE PRODUCT.

LIMITED WARRANTY FOR DISC

To the original licensee only, McGraw-Hill warrants that the enclosed disc on which the Product is recorded is free from defects in materials and workmanship under normal use and service for a period of ninety (90) days from the date of purchase. In the event of a defect in the disc covered by the foregoing warranty, McGraw-Hill will replace the disc.

LIMITATION OF LIABILITY

NEITHER McGRAW-HILL, ITS LICENSORS NOR THE AUTHORS SHALL BE LIABLE FOR ANY INDIRECT, SPECIAL OR CONSEQUENTIAL DAMAGES, SUCH AS BUT NOT LIMITED TO, LOSS OF ANTICIPATED PROFITS OR BENEFITS, RESULTING FROM THE USE OR INABILITY TO USE THE PRODUCT EVEN IF ANY OF THEM HAS BEEN ADVISED OF THE POSSIBILITY OF SUCH DAMAGES. THIS LIMITATION OF LIABILITY SHALL APPLY TO ANY CLAIM OR CAUSE WHATSOEVER WHETHER SUCH CLAIM OR CAUSE ARISES IN CONTRACT, TORT, OR OTHERWISE. Some states do not allow the exclusion or limitation of indirect, special or consequential damages, so the above limitation may not apply to you.

U.S. GOVERNMENT RESTRICTED RIGHTS

Any software included in the Product is provided with restricted rights subject to subparagraphs (c), (1) and (2) of the Commercial Computer Software-Restricted Rights clause at 48 C.F.R. 52.227-19. The terms of this Agreement applicable to the use of the data in the Product are those under which the data are generally made available to the general public by McGraw-Hill. Except as provided herein, no reproduction, use, or disclosure rights are granted with respect to the data included in the Product and no right to modify or create derivative works from any such data is hereby granted.

GENERAL

This License Agreement constitutes the entire agreement between the parties relating to the Product. The terms of any Purchase Order shall have no effect on the terms of this License Agreement. Failure of McGraw-Hill to insist at any time on strict compliance with this License Agreement shall not constitute a waiver of any rights under this License Agreement. This License Agreement shall be construed and governed in accordance with the laws of the State of New York. If any provision of this License Agreement is held to be contrary to law, that provision will be enforced to the maximum extent permissible and the remaining provisions will remain in full force and effect.